Configuring SAP R/3 FI/CO

Configuring SAP™ R/3™ FI/CO

Quentin Hurst
David Nowak

SYBEX®

Associate Publisher: Richard Mills
Contracts and Licensing Manager: Kristine O'Callaghan
Acquisitions & Developmental Editor: Melanie Spiller
Editors: Judy Flynn, Elizabeth Hurley
Production Editors: Shannon Murphy, Elizabeth Campbell
Technical Editor: Mark Driver
Book Designer: Franz Baumhackl
Graphic Illustrator: Tony Jonick
Electronic Publishing Specialist: Adrian Woolhouse
Proofreaders: Dave Nash, Patrick J. Peterson, Molly Glover,
    Jennifer Campbell, Laurie O'Connell, Alison Moncrieff
Indexer: Nancy Guenther
Cover Designer: emdesign
Cover Photographer: emdesign

Library of Congress Card Number: 99-69298

ISBN: 0-7821-2597-2

Manufactured in the United States of America

10 9 8 7 6 5 4 3 2 1

ACKNOWLEDGMENTS

nother special thank-you to my wife, Ilene, and son, Garrhett, for enduring all of the long nights and weekends without me. This book could have never been finished without your support. A very special thank-you to all of my family and especially to my parents, Jeff and Loretta, and brother, Jay, for all of their help and support, which made the completion of the book possible.

I would also like to express gratitude to Bruce Allen and Richard Walling for affording me the opportunity to begin my SAP implementation career.

Quentin

I would like to thank my wife, Shearon, and all my family for the support and guidance they showed over the course of this project.

David

We would like to thank Melanie Spiller, Elizabeth Hurley, Judy Flynn, Shannon Murphy, and all the staff at Sybex for their efforts. Thank you to Amy Dawson for her exceptional design work associated with the Virtuoso, LLC advertising page. And a special thanks is due to One System Group, LLC, for allowing us access to their SAP R/3 system to develop and screen-print the case company solution.

CONTENTS AT A GLANCE

TABLE OF CONTENTS

INTRODUCTION

The purpose of this book is to remove the veil of secrecy surrounding SAP configuration techniques and concepts and provide you with a detailed blueprint for FI/CO development. The FI and CO modules have always been the backbone of all SAP implementations. Regardless of the module scope of a project, you almost always need FI due to its tight integration with the rest of the modules in SAP, and in most cases, you'll want CO to facilitate your managerial reporting. In addition to teaching concepts and theories of FI/CO development, this book covers general configuration methods and tools that can be applied across all SAP functional modules.

To meet your business needs, SAP provides a great deal of flexibility in its software. Because of this, a universal FI/CO configuration solution would be impossible to present in terms of a book or any other type of media. Instead, *Configuring SAP R/3 FI/CO* walks you through the configuration that is required to get SAP FI/CO up and running (as well as delving into very detailed and complex configuration of advanced system components). Configuration theories are supported by the use of a case company model. Extreme Sports Inc. is used to define the business requirements that are configured and presented throughout the book. An explanation of Extreme Sports' business and organizational structure is explained in a later section of the introduction. As the configuration takes place, keep in mind that the screen prints and menu paths that are presented are based on version 3.1h. Note that the functionality covered in this book is the same regardless of version, and most of the tables that are shown have not changed from version to version. We are teaching you how to configure SAP FI/CO regardless of version so that you can configure your company's system based on your unique business requirements.

Is This Book for You?

This book is for anyone who would like to work in SAP's main product, R/3, and its most popular modules, Financial and Controlling (FI/CO). It is primarily intended for project implementation team members, developers, and persons who work in SAP support organizations. In writing this book, we also want to allow and encourage people who may have expertise in another SAP module to learn FI/CO. In addition, this book makes an excellent textbook companion for those colleges and universities whose curricula covers SAP design and development. It will take you from the basic concepts all the way through to some very advanced configuration topics and techniques.

How This Book Is Organized

This book begins with an explanation of the FI module and its configuration. The similar but different CO module is covered in the same fashion. Each chapter is about a specific submodule within FI/CO.

The chapters have been logically ordered so that prerequisite configuration has occurred before you begin configuration on a new submodule. If you are new to configuration, it is a good idea to begin with Chapter 1 and proceed on through the rest of the chapters in order. If you already have configuration experience, you can use the table of contents and chapter headings to skip to the appropriate subject matter.

Conventions Used in This Book

Throughout this book, we have used some basic conventions to help you understand our instructions. We included easily identifiable shortcut boxes for quick references. The menu path for configuration steps is included in the text of each chapter. The menu path and transaction code for each configuration step is also broken out into separate "configuration shortcut boxes." We believe you'll find that these shortcut boxes will be quite useful as a reference tool as you are configuring your project. We also based our project on one business model, Extreme Sports, for ease and continuity.

Reference is made to standard SAP commands and button bars (green arrow, save, create, and so on). In each case, when we refer to a button, we'll provide a screen print that shows the button in question. SAP course material is an excellent source for more information on the standard SAP nomenclature.

Case Company Background

One of SAP's biggest selling points is the software's flexibility in handling multiple industries and organizations regardless of the complexity of the business solutions.

To accommodate this flexibility, it must allow for numerous solutions using the standard platform of tables and structures. And by introducing unique configuration settings for each implementing company, it addresses the need for complex solutions.

It would be an impossible task to document the necessary configuration settings for every industry and every business solution. However, it is not inconceivable to provide insight into how to interpret the options available to you when configuring the various modules in FI and CO.

To assist in this endeavor, we will describe the configuration for a fictitious company, Extreme Sports, as you progress through the book. Although the company's configuration will be documented, the discussion will not be limited to that specific solution. Many options and field settings will be illustrated and discussed. When configuration must occur in a specific order, the proper sequence will be provided.

We will now give you some background information about Extreme Sports and an example of its hierarchy solution.

Extreme Sports (ES) is a U.S.-based manufacturer of sporting equipment and apparel. Founded in 1989, the company has seen its business grow 60 percent a year over the last 3 years. The revenues for 1999 were $750 million.

Extreme Sports' sales organization consists of six regionally based offices located in New York, Chicago, Los Angeles, Atlanta, Seattle, and Kansas City. The sales organization employs approximately 250 sales representatives who sell 6 distinct product lines: ski equipment, ski apparel, mountaineering/hiking equipment, surfing equipment, surfing apparel, and custom boats.

To compensate for the extraordinary growth it has enjoyed, Extreme Sports has expanded its manufacturing base from four to six plants. The last two plants have both been constructed in Mexico, and the company is considering building a third next year.

Extreme Sports has made the decision to convert to SAP because of the fragmented nature of its current financial, profitability, and manufacturing systems. The corporation is made up of four legal entities: ES Ski & Surf, Inc.; ES Mountaineering, Inc.; ES Custom Boats, Inc.; and ES Mexico, S.A. In addition, Extreme Sports has decided to create a shared services organization to support the accounting, human resources, purchasing, accounts payable, and IS functions. The vehicle for this organization will be a fifth company called ES Services, Inc.

The corporation has moved all its legal entities to a calendar fiscal year, removing the 4-5-4 calendar previously held by ES Custom Boats, Inc. Below you will find an illustration of the corporation as it was developed in SAP.

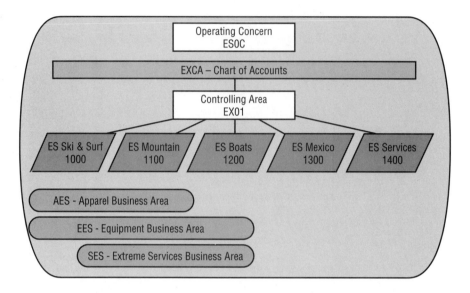

Throughout the book, we will be providing you with the configuration settings to support Extreme Sports' organization.

CHAPTER 1

Configuration Tools

FEATURING:

▶ **INTRODUCTION TO SAP**

▶ **A NEW APPROACH TO SYSTEM CUSTOMIZATION**

▶ **THE IMPLEMENTATION GUIDE**

▶ **THE ONLINE SUPPORT SYSTEM (OSS)**

Before you undertake your first SAP configuration project, it is important to understand the concepts behind table-driven customization as well as some of the tools, tips, and tricks that can be used. The purpose of this chapter is to provide the foundation for successfully carrying out SAP FI/CO configuration.

Although it is a must-read for people new to configuration, we also feel that configuration "old-timers" can pick up a trick or two from this chapter. Before beginning, it is important to note that the terms *customization* and *configuration* are used interchangeably throughout the book.

Specifically, we will cover the following topics in this chapter:

Introduction to SAP

The SAP System Environment

Transports

Other Methods of Table Maintenance

Finding the Table to Customize

The Databrowser

Modifications to Source Code and User-Exits

Introduction to SAP

SAP stands for Systems, Applications, and Products in Data Processing. SAP was founded by five German engineers in 1972. Today, SAP is the world's largest Enterprise Resource Planning (EPR) software company and the fourth largest computer software company overall. SAP is an integrated system, which means that all SAP modules are designed to share information and automatically create transactions based on various business processes.

SAP R/3 is the client/server version of the software. The "3" in R/3 stands for the three-tiered client/server architecture. SAP R/2 is the mainframe version of the software. The "2" in R/2 stands for the two-tiered mainframe architecture. There are several releases of R/3, ranging from 2.*x* to 4.*x*. Throughout this book, we will be using version 3.1h. Although there have been several changes in the 4.*x* releases, much of the functionality covered in this book is unchanged in version 4.*x*. Some of the screens may have changed in later releases, and there may be new functionality available, but the process of configuration remains the same regardless of the release. The goal of this book is not to teach you how to implement one specific solution, but to teach you how to configure. Attempting to cover every possible configuration scenario you might encounter would be an impossible task. After reading the book, you will be able to apply what you learned to configure your system based on your business requirements. Throughout the book, we use the terms *SAP* and *R/3* interchangeably to refer to the SAP R/3 system.

We've listed some common terms that explain different parts of the SAP system; you will see them used throughout the book:

ABAP (ABAP/4)   ABAP/4 stands for Advanced Business Application Programming/4th Generation Language. SAP is coded in ABAP. ABAP is also used for any extensions or extra programs that are written for SAP. ABAP is similar to other fourth-generation languages and is a first cousin of COBOL, without the JCL.

Basis   Generally SAP projects, and the folks who work on them, are lumped into two groups—technical and functional. The technical system includes ABAP, database administration, transport management, security, authorizations, and so on. Basis is a subset of the technical folks; they take care of all technical components of the system except for ABAP. The Basis group, in more common terms, consists of your project Database Administrators (D.B.A.s) plus more.

Variant   A variant is a specific setting that is saved when a program is executed. Some data input screens allow you to save and execute variants. Variants can also be created in the program maintenance screen of the program. Using variants is a good way to save time because they allow you to execute a routine transaction without having to enter all of the parameters needed by the program every time.

Menu path   SAP, like most client/server applications, utilizes menus to allow a user to navigate through the system. When we refer to or list menu paths in the book, we are starting from the root menu and progressing down through each menu hierarchy to reach the needed transaction. When we refer to only the menu path, we are talking about the Implementation Guide (IMG) menu path. SAP application menu paths are explicitly noted.

Transaction code   A transaction code is a four-character code that is entered in the command field on the toolbar. Transaction codes are not case sensitive. SAP provides two ways of executing a transaction, via a menu path or a transaction code. It is important to note that, unless you are at the main SAP menu or the main menu of a submodule such as G/L, it is necessary to include /N or /O before the transaction code in order to execute a transaction in a different module. For example, if you are currently in the Cost Center accounting module in the screen used to create cost centers and you want to enter a G/L document (transaction code FB01), you must enter /NFB01 or /OFB01 to execute the transaction. /N takes you back to the root menu and then executes the transaction code. /O opens up a new session and then executes the transaction code. Remember, you can only have six open sessions of SAP at once.

T I P   As stated earlier, unless you are at the main SAP menu, or a submodule main menu, it is necessary to include /N or /O before a transaction code in order to execute a transaction in a different module.

Parameter ID   A parameter ID is a special identifier given to some fields in SAP. It can be stored in your user profile with its default values. For example, the parameter ID for company code is BUK. A user who is responsible only for entering documents in company code 1000 would set up the BUK parameter ID with a default of 1000 in their user profile. By specifying this parameter ID, the user will never have to enter the company code in a transaction; the company code will automatically default to 1000. Parameter IDs are stored in the technical information field screen. An explanation of how to display the Technical Information screen is included in "Finding the Table to Configure" later in this chapter.

Batch input session   A batch input session stores values to be entered during a normal system transaction. Some transactions automatically create batch input sessions because of the heavy processing required. To complete the transaction, you must select the batch input session and then run the batch input session manager. Batch input sessions are also the way in which most data transfer programs are executed. A good way to think of a batch input session is to think of it as a macro. A macro uses standard functioning to input data that is stored to automate a repeated task. You can use transaction code SM35 to run and manage batch input sessions.

Jobs   A job is similar to a batch input session in that it executes a standard SAP transaction in the background, usually at night. Jobs are set up and scheduled for processor-intensive transactions and reports. If you do not correctly specify the print parameters on a print request, your print request will be stored as a job. This means that, when you start a print transaction from within SAP and you do not check the Print Immediately box, the print request is stored in the print spool as a job and has to be manually released through the job manager to print. Your company's Basis group usually manages jobs.

User menus You can create your own user menu with your most commonly used transactions. Then you can assign this personalized menu to your user ID in your user preferences. If you are developing a system to be used by a client site, user menus can also be set up for a group of users with limited access to the system. This includes users who might not use the system often enough to remember the menu paths they need to use to execute a transaction.

Distributed systems (ALE) Some SAP installations have more than one productive instance of SAP running at any one time. SAP provides a tool called Application Link Enabling (ALE) to allow two different SAP systems to share data with each other.

TIP In a lot of cases, the FI/CO team acts as the "police" on the project, ensuring that quality business processes are implemented. You must remember that almost everything else that the other modules do affects FI/CO, and sometimes they don't know it. Oftentimes, other modules are only concerned that quantities update correctly and don't really care about the financial updates because they are viewed as an FI/CO responsibility. Unfortunately, the other modules don't always proactively let you know what needs to be checked, so it is up to you to ask and make sure that you have reviewed all financial updates in the system. Mud flows downhill, and FI/CO is in a hole, in a trench, in the bottom of the lowest valley!

A New Approach to System Customization

For many years, organizations struggled with extremely long project timelines in order to develop information systems that met their specific requirements. Most IT projects used structured development methodologies that were very unforgiving in terms of missed or changing business requirements. The development of custom code was a tedious process requiring armies of programmers, as well as significant end-user involvement.

The project timeline was also dragged out because often business owners didn't know what they wanted until they saw it, which led to what is commonly referred to in the IT industry as "analysis paralysis" in projects. Upon project completion, large IT staffs needed to be retained to maintain the custom programming and to update the programs with requirements that may have changed during the long development cycle. Numerous companies also had departmentalized systems, which oftentimes did not share information. These numerous departmental systems became "information silos" within the organization. Often, a report on the same key figure, such as sales volume, would result in different answers, depending upon on which system the query was run.

These disparate and numerous systems also created the need for many distinct interfaces between systems that were not designed to talk with each other. Even with the most elaborate interfaces, it was difficult to provide a truly integrated system to be used throughout the organization. The aforementioned problems with legacy systems—coupled with rapidly changing industries, technologies, and the environmental factors affecting businesses—caused custom programming to become more and more expensive. A fundamental change was needed in information technology. Businesses demanded integrated systems between departments—systems that could accommodate rapidly transforming business and technological changes.

To fulfill the new requirements of information systems, a new breed of software systems, now called Enterprise Resource Planning (ERP), was created. ERP systems provide a single source of data with designed integration between different functional modules (for example, Accounting, Sales and Distribution, Materials Management, Production Planning, etc.) to take full advantage of an enterprise's stored information. A common set of source code was needed for these packages so that changes in technology could be rapidly introduced via upgrades to the programs. To facilitate these requirements, a new way of customizing systems was needed. This new way of customizing systems is known as *table-driven customization*, or *configuration*.

Table-driven customization allows for rapid changes in business requirements with a common set of source code or programs. The common programs are coded to focus on settings in specific tables to make the programs react in various ways to fit different business needs. This is what makes ERP systems, and SAP in particular, so flexible—there are well over 10,000 tables in the SAP database structure! Because table settings instead of old-fashioned hard-coded program logic are what drive program functionality, new and changed business requirements can be rapidly implemented and tested in the system. Table-driven configuration (customization) is at the heart of what the functional SAP consultant delivers.

To benefit from the power of SAP, a careful analysis of your company's current business processes is in order. SAP has streamlined business processes to take full advantage of the most efficient business and technological processes. SAP provides the Business Navigator tool to provide a graphical representation of the SAP process flows and integration across modules. The Business Navigator lists the business objects associated with processes as well as the SAP programs that respond. In addition, the

Business Navigator displays the related SAP documentation for selected objects. The Business Navigator can be displayed in either the Component view or Process Flow view. The Component view shows each process and business object in relation to its functional module. The Process Flow view displays each process in relation to overall business function, regardless of system functional module ownership. This allows you to see the big picture of your business plan.

TIP The Business Navigator can be displayed by following the SAP application menu path Tools➤Business Engineering➤Business Navigator. Transaction code SB10 takes you to the Component view and transaction code SB09 takes you to the Process Flow view. Many companies use the implementation of SAP as an opportunity to reengineer their entire business and develop the most efficient processes available. SAP has invested a great deal of time and money into delivering the most efficient business-friendly processes in the system. If your company doesn't have the time or resources to undertake a full reengineering effort, at the very least, you should use the implementation to change and streamline problem processes in your business. A system implementation is the best opportunity you will ever have for change.

There are many small companies that have neither the time nor the resources to undertake a full business process reengineering project, but they are still implementing SAP. The ASAP (Accelerated SAP) methodology developed by SAP provides an excellent tool for small companies to rapidly implement SAP and take advantage of its integrated business processes. Key incentives for adopting ASAP are that you don't need any modifications to standard SAP source code and you can still take advantage of standard SAP best business processes. This type of quick implementation is proving very successful in many different industries and business segments.

SAP System Environment

It is very important for everyone on the implementation project team to understand the SAP system environment used on the project. A system environment is referred to by some as an *instance*. Others will sometimes refer to a client as an instance. In this book, *environment* and *instance* are used to refer to different systems, such as development, quality assurance/testing environment, and production. In some cases, an SAP term may have, or may seem to have, more than one meaning, depending on which part of the system you are working in. One such term is *client*. As defined in the enterprise structure, it means the organization for which SAP is being configured (for example, the XYZ Corporation, or the example corporation used throughout this book, Extreme Sports). When defined in Basis terms (the SAP technical system), *client* means the different installations of SAP used for a specified purpose. Really, these are the same things, but it is difficult to understand the client concept in this light when you are just starting out in SAP. In the standard project setting, there will be three environments: the development environment, the quality assurance/testing environment (QA), and the production environment. Within each environment there are different clients that are used for specified purposes.

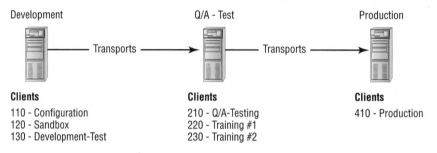

The development environment is where the majority of implementation work takes place. It should have a minimum of three clients: sandbox, configuration, and development-testing. The sandbox client is used to test out configuration ideas and theories at any time. It is also where all system design work should take place. Once you are comfortable with your configuration solution in the sandbox client, you can re-create your solution in the configuration client. The configuration client is also called the transport client. This is where all final configuration that needs to be moved through the testing cycle, and finally into production, takes place. The configuration client has automatic transport recording turned on (covered in a later section of this chapter). Ideally, the configuration client should also be your "golden" client; that is, no transactions or testing should take place in this client. Once a transport has been created, it should be moved to the development-testing client. Once the configuration is in the development-testing client, the transport should be thoroughly unit tested. Usually, only unit testing is conducted in the development system; some projects may conduct integration (string) testing in this client as well. Once the transport has been successfully tested, it is ready to move into the QA environment. Normally, all transports for particular projects or rollout phases are moved into QA at one time.

The QA environment is where all final testing is conducted prior to moving transports to the production environment. Normally, this is where integration (end-to-end business process) testing and user acceptance testing (UAT) is conducted. There is a minimum of one QA client that is used to conduct testing. There may be additional clients you can use in the QA environment to test different transactions for training, data conversion, and user sandboxes. Once the entire project solution has been tested successfully in QA, it is ready to move to production.

The production environment is where all day-to-day business activities occur. This is the client that all end users use to perform their daily job functions. There is usually only one production client per SAP installation. It is very important to move into production only transports that have passed all testing cycles. Production problems are no fun for users or developers.

Transports

Transports are the vehicles by which your configuration settings are moved from client to client and environment to environment. Normally, your configuration client should be the only client that creates transports. Transports in the configuration client are created any time you make a change to a configuration table or program. This is known as automatic recording of transports. The setting to allow for automatic recording of transports is made at the client level in table T000. Although you can make customizing settings in the sandbox, client transports are not automatically created. The sandbox and configuration clients are the only clients in which changes to configuration tables or programs should be allowed.

NOTE Transports are also known as change requests, development requests, and many other names, depending on project methodology and the consulting partner you hire. In this book, we'll always refer to configuration changes as transports.

Once created, your transports should move through the release management strategy used by your implementation project. See the preceding section, "SAP System Environment," for a general explanation of how transports should move from development through to production. Your Basis group should be responsible for the maintenance and movement of transports from client to client. In some small implementation projects, individual consultants are responsible for moving their transports from the configuration client to the development-testing client. We do not recommend this last approach; it should only be undertaken by a small group of very experienced consultants.

> **NOTE**   Most transports record only the changes to the table. However, some transports created by a small number of tables copy the entire table, not just the changes. It is very important that these whole table transports are watched and managed carefully so that only the latest changes are reflected in the target clients. This is especially important once a project is "live" and in maintenance mode. When dealing with whole table transports, you always run the risk of moving into other environments configuration that shouldn't be moved. You can also very easily "leapfrog" transports moved by other developers and overwrite new configuration with old configuration.

You can use the Change Request Query screen to create a transport automatically in a configuration client. A transport number is assigned automatically, but you are free to add the description yourself.

There are two types of transports: *client dependent* and *client independent*. When an environment such as the development environment is created with multiple clients, most objects are copied one for one to be used for each individual client. For example, table T030 contains the settings for automatic account assignment. In the development environment, the sandbox, configuration, and development-testing clients each have their own copy of table T030. Any change to table T030 results in a client-dependent transport—all the T030 tables in the various places reflect the change only after it is transported.

All programs and a small amount of tables are shared among the clients within an environment. These are known as client-independent objects. For example, table (view) V_T021S is client independent, meaning that, when this table is changed in the configuration client, the setting automatically takes effect in all clients in that environment because there is only one V_T021S that is used by all clients in that environment. A change to a client-independent table should be made only in the configuration client; the Basis group controls this setting when it sets up the client. The option to allow client-independent changes is set at the client level in table T000. Sometimes, when testing new design and development in the sandbox, you are required to make a change in the configuration client. It is fine to design in the configuration client as long as you are only making client-independent changes.

Each consultant/developer is responsible for keeping track of their individual transports. Transaction code SE10 allows you to view and manage all transports you have created. You can also view transports created by other developers. This transaction allows viewing of only modifiable (unreleased), only released, or both released and unreleased transports. The default is set to modifiable (unreleased) transports. Figure 1.1 shows the initial screen, Customizing Organizer.

FIGURE 1.1 You can use transaction code SE10 to view and manage transports in the Customizing Organizer screen.

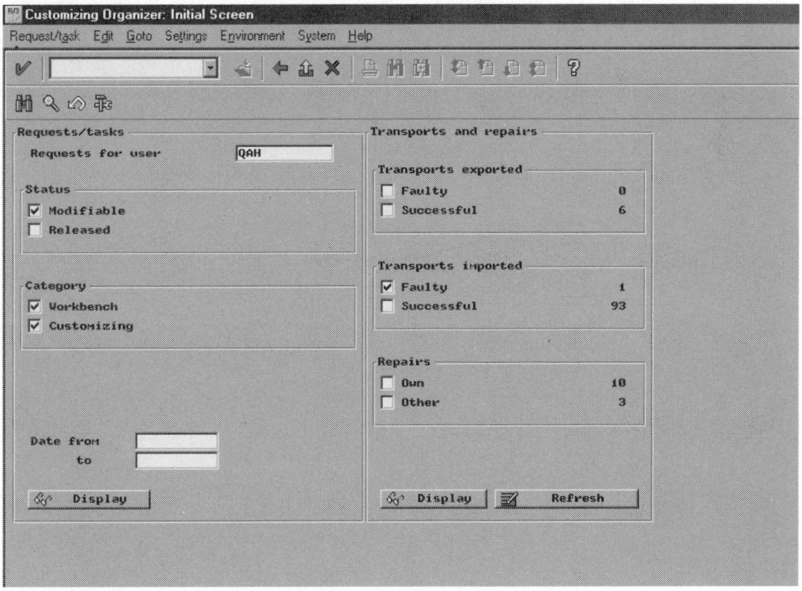

Once you are ready to unit test your configuration, the related transports must be released so that the changes can move from the configuration client to the development-testing client. It is normally the responsibility of the consultant/developer to release their own transports and let the Basis group know that they are ready to move via the procedures set forth in their project. This is an implementation activity, and this transport movement can happen once the system is in production. Remember that it is only necessary to release and move client-dependent transports to the development-testing client. Client-independent transports are already reflected in all clients in the environment. Client-independent transports need to be released and moved only when sending changes from environment to environment. Figure 1.2 shows the listing of transports created by an individual consultant or developer. This screen is obtained by proceeding through the screen displayed by transaction code SE10 (Figure 1.1).

FIGURE 1.2   The transports "owned" by consultant Quentin Hurst

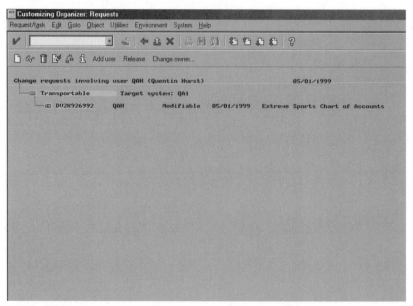

Each transport in the list (as shown in Figure 1.2) can be expanded to show the tasks included in it. Each transport has at least one related task associated to it. The tasks actually contain the table changes. The upper-level transport acts only as a container for these tasks. When you release transports for the Basis group, you must release the individual tasks related to the transport before releasing the upper-level transport. It is important to note that each task always has objects attached to it. It is not necessary to release objects to the Basis group, only the tasks themselves. This is because the tasks carry the objects with them. When you release a task, a snapshot is taken of the key that is contained in the task. The configuration that resides in the snapshot is what is written to the operating system to be transported. It is very important to understand this timing and how it affects your transports if other consultants are configuring the same key. For example, consultant X makes a change to object key 123 on May 1st; on May 30th, consultant Y makes a change to the same object key 123. When consultant X releases his task on June 1st, it contains the changes that consultant Y made on May 30th, not the changes that consultant X made on May 1st. As you can see, communication is a key success factor on any SAP project. Transports are released using the same screen that is generated by following transaction code SE10, selecting the task, and clicking the Release button, as seen Figure 1.3. When you release a task, it is released (copied) to its corresponding transport request. The transport request is then released for export. The transport request is what is actually moved between clients and environments.

FIGURE 1.3   **Releasing a transport**

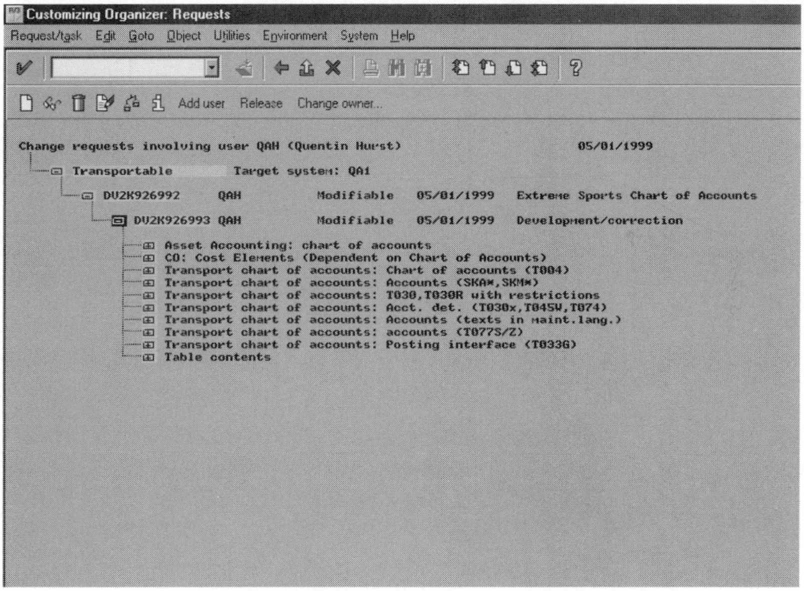

The Implementation Guide (IMG)

The Implementation Guide (IMG) provides step-by-step detail on the configuration settings that need to take place in each module of the SAP system. The IMG is grouped by functional modules and the business processes that occur in each module, as shown in Figure 1.4. It provides the front end to the customizing tables as well as explanations of the functionality affected by each table. The majority of a consultant/developer's time in the design and development phase of a project is spent in the IMG.

FIGURE 1.4   The Implementation Guide (IMG) main screen

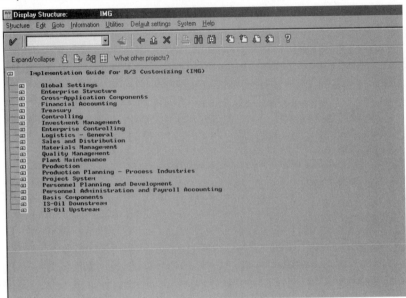

The IMG can be displayed in three different views: the SAP Reference IMG, the Enterprise IMG, and the Project IMG. The SAP Reference IMG comes with your installation of SAP. It contains all components for all modules of SAP. The Enterprise IMG is generated from the SAP Reference IMG. The Enterprise IMG normally contains all modules and their related business processes for your specific instance of SAP and the countries being implemented. It is usually a safe bet that everything from the SAP Reference IMG has been copied to the Enterprise IMG.

T I P   The IMG can be viewed via transaction code SPRO or through the menu path Tools ➢ Business Engineering ➢ Customizing.

The Project IMG is created by the project team manager or by module team leaders. It contains only those modules and business processes that the creator of the Project IMG (generally a single person or the project manager) deems necessary. It is very important to carefully select what is needed and to not forget anything when generating the Project IMG. The Project IMG can also serve as a valuable project management and documentation tool. The status of project tasks can be viewed and exported to Microsoft Project for detailed project tracking. Using the IMG, you can store configuration documentation with related steps and tables.

WARNING   You and your customer will be happier and more productive in the long run if you keep detailed documentation on the configuration settings that are made in the system. It is not necessary to use the IMG as the documentation tool, but it is necessary to document your entire configuration. The only thing worse than trying to figure out someone else's configuration settings is going back and trying to figure out your own!

If your project doesn't use the Project IMG for documentation and status tracking, it is a good idea to use the SAP Reference IMG or the Enterprise IMG to find your configuration steps. You can expect with some certainty that all steps, processes, and tables will be included in the final product. It is difficult to discover what SAP functionality is needed if you do not have access to all of it. SAP has provided an easy view of virtually all configuration tasks, if you include all of the tasks in the IMG. If you forget to include those tasks in the IMG, it is very difficult to try to configure needed functionality. When in doubt, use the SAP Reference IMG. The IMG can display both optional and mandatory activities (see Figure 1.5). By no means must every task in the IMG be completed; the number of tasks and how specific tasks are customized are dependent on the functionality needed by the business processes being used. It is very useful to use the search functionality included in the IMG to find where specific settings are made. To use the search function, click the binoculars icon in the top toolbar of the IMG, as seen in Figure 1.5.

FIGURE 1.5   Using the search functionality in IMG

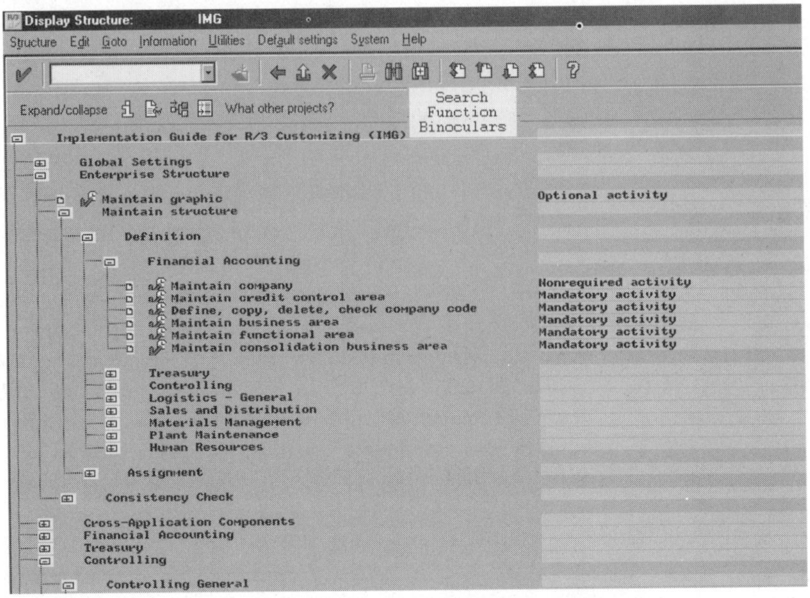

An explanation of the specific tasks can be viewed by double-clicking the name of the step. The level of detail provided in the documentation can be very useful in determining which steps, or tasks, are suitable for your project.

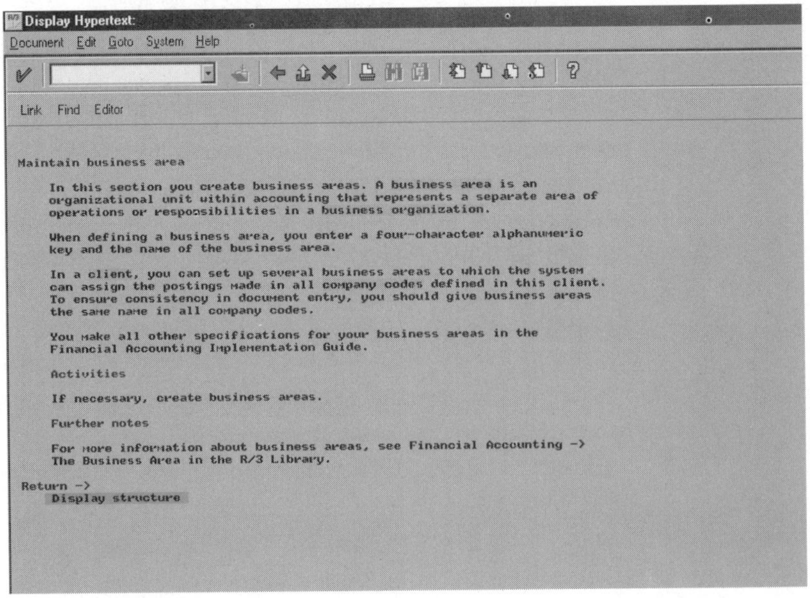

Other Methods of Table Maintenance and Customizing

It is sometimes difficult to find the table you need to customize in the IMG. SAP provides two transaction codes that can be used when you know the name of the table you need to customize and you're not sure where it is in the IMG. Transaction code SM30 is used to access the screen for maintaining tables or table views, shown in Figure 1.6. Although it is more common to refer to customizing objects as tables, most customizing objects are actually *views* of tables. In order for an object to be customized, a maintenance interface must be created for that object. SAP very rarely creates maintenance interfaces on tables themselves. Most of the time, maintenance interfaces are created for table views by SAP for R/3 as delivered. Do not try to create maintenance interfaces for SAP-delivered tables! Transaction code SM30 is used to maintain custom-created (user-defined) tables.

FIGURE 1.6   Transaction code SM30 is for maintaining tables or table views.

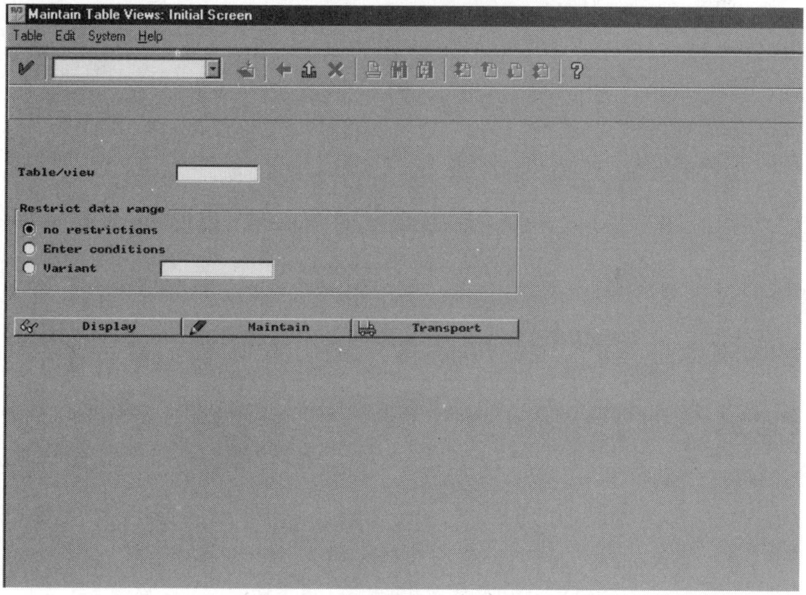

In those instances when you know the table name and not the customizing view name, the transaction code SM31 (Extended Table Maintenance) can be used to access the Table Maintenance screen. Simply enter the table name into the SM31 screen's Table field, and click the View Maintenance button, as displayed in Figure 1.7. This will give you a listing of the views of maintenance interfaces for that table. Then you can click the name of the appropriate view and SAP will take you to the proper configuration screen.

FIGURE 1.7   The Table Maintenance screen is displayed by using transaction code SM31.

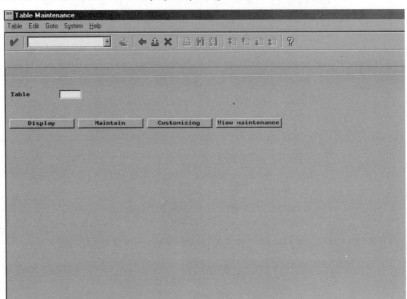

Finding the Table to Configure

Often it may be necessary to find a customizing setting when you're processing a business transaction in the system. The easiest way to accomplish this task is to select on the business transaction the field that contains the setting you wish to customize. In this example, we want to configure company code. Figure 1.8 shows the appropriate screen (the G/L creation transaction that will be covered in Chapter 3). Once the field is selected, press the F1 key or select the SAP help icon. This displays general information about the selected field, as shown in Figure 1.9. You can then select the technical information box or press the F9 key. The Technical Information screen lists the field name and tables of the selected setting (Table RF02H, Field Name BUKRS), as shown in Figure 1.10. Armed with this information, you are now ready to go to the configuration table and make the desired changes.

FIGURE 1.8   The Create G/L Account screen

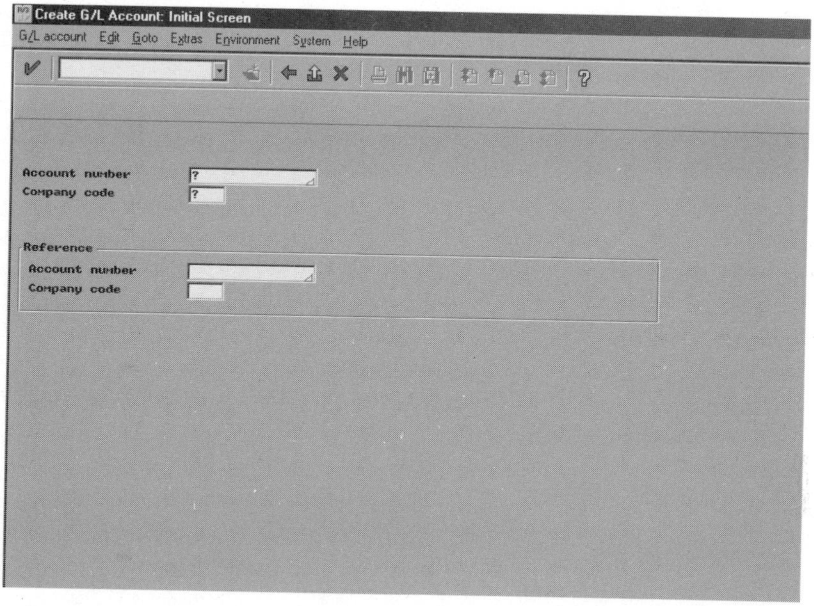

FIGURE 1.9   The Help screen, which is obtained by pressing F1 or the help icon, can give you general information about selected fields.

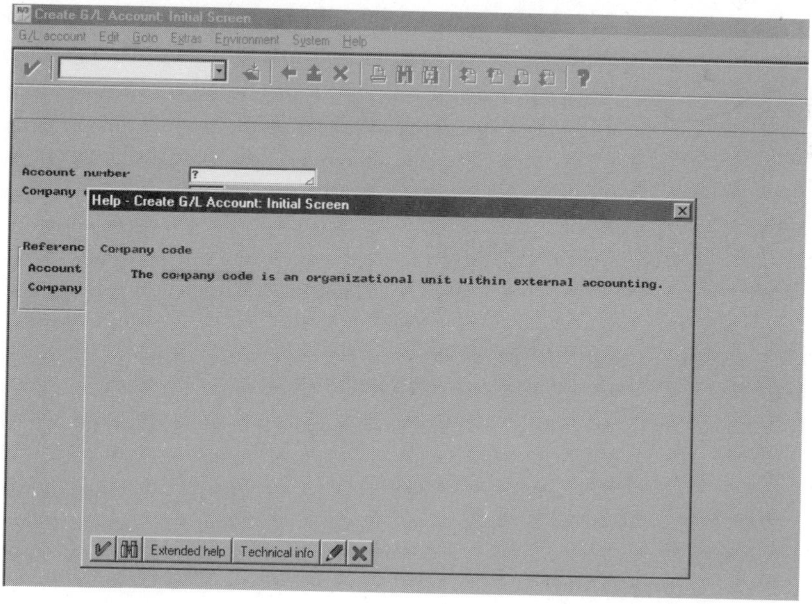

FIGURE 1.10   The table and field names can be discovered by pressing F9 from the Help screen.

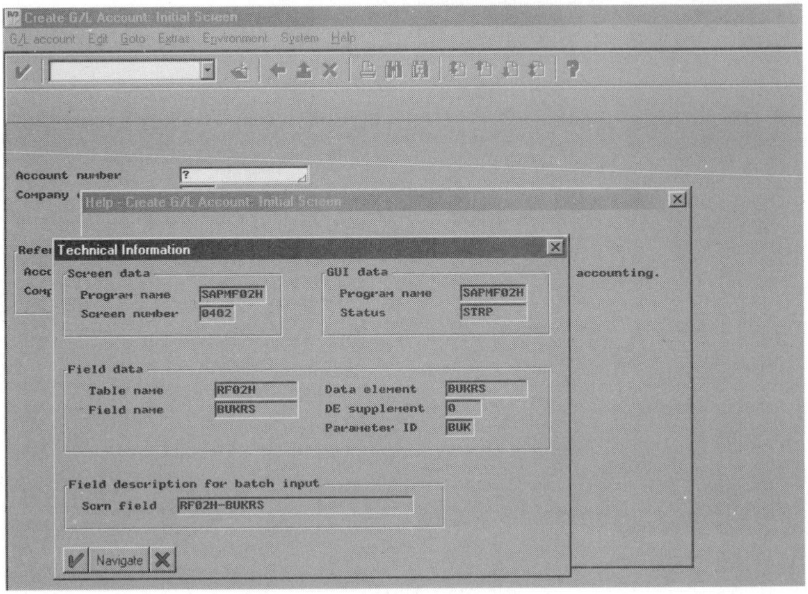

The Dictionary Display is an invaluable tool for viewing table structures as well as finding configuration tables and other pertinent system information. We will use the Dictionary Display to return to the customizing (configuration) table. We will then use transaction code SE12 to display the table that we found named in the Help screen (the data Dictionary Display is shown in Figure 1.11). After you click the Display button, SE12 lists all fields that are included in the table. Locate the field name found in the Help screen (Figure 1.10), BUKRS.

TIP   You can also double-click the field or table name in the Technical Information screen and it will take you into the Dictionary Display transaction for the particular table.

FIGURE 1.11   The table RF02H is displayed using transaction code SE12.

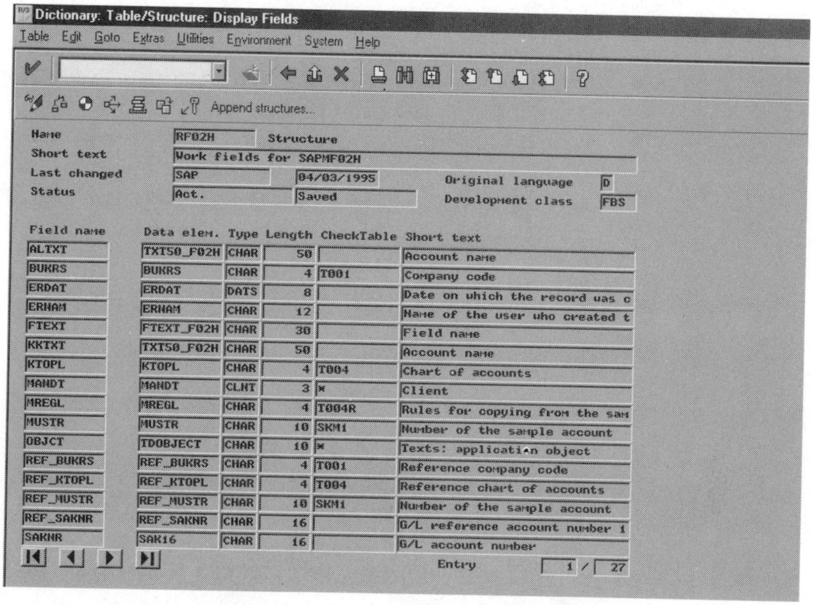

By viewing the structure of table RF02H, you can see that the field name BUKRS has a check table of T001. This is the table that we need to configure. We know that we need to configure table T001 because this is where the primary key for company code (field name BUKRS) resides. In SAP, check tables always refer to the primary table that the field belongs in. If there is no check table next to the field name, you know that this instance of the field is the primary key and not included in the table via a foreign key relationship. In relational database terms, the field BUKRS in table T001 is the foreign key for table RF02H. Because it is the foreign key, you know that table T001 is the table in which BUKRS (a key field) is created and maintained. To find the configuration view you need to access, use transaction SM31 (discussed in the preceding section). Once we have entered T001 in the table name field and clicked the View Maintenance button (see Figure 1.7), a list of configuration views is returned, as shown in the next graphic.

TIP   In relational databases, a "key" field is a unique identifier for a table. This field is used as a reference to the same data in other tables. For example, your employer uses your social security number as a unique identifier for information about you. Rather than listing all the relevant statistics about you in every table, a relational database connects the various kinds of information through a single key field that represents "you." A "foreign" field is another sort of key field, but it's the key field for a "foreign" table. For example, say your employer needs a table containing names and addresses. In this table, the key field might be the last name of the employee. The last name would certainly also be referenced in a table containing social security numbers, but it would be a foreign key there—used only to verify that two people with the same last name stay unique as entities in the various tables.

After double-clicking the appropriate view name, you are taken to the configuration screen for company code setup. From this display, you can click the New Entries button in the toolbar (see Figure 1.12) to create the new company code.

The Databrowser and Common Tables to Display

The databrowser is a useful tool for displaying data table contents. Transaction SE12 is used to display the structure of a table, and the databrowser, which is run via transaction code SE16, displays the contents of a table. Figure 1.13 shows the results of running transaction code SE16 and entering BSEG as the table name. You can choose from the listing of options for narrowing the results that you would like returned to you.

FIGURE 1.12   Creating a new company code configuration screen

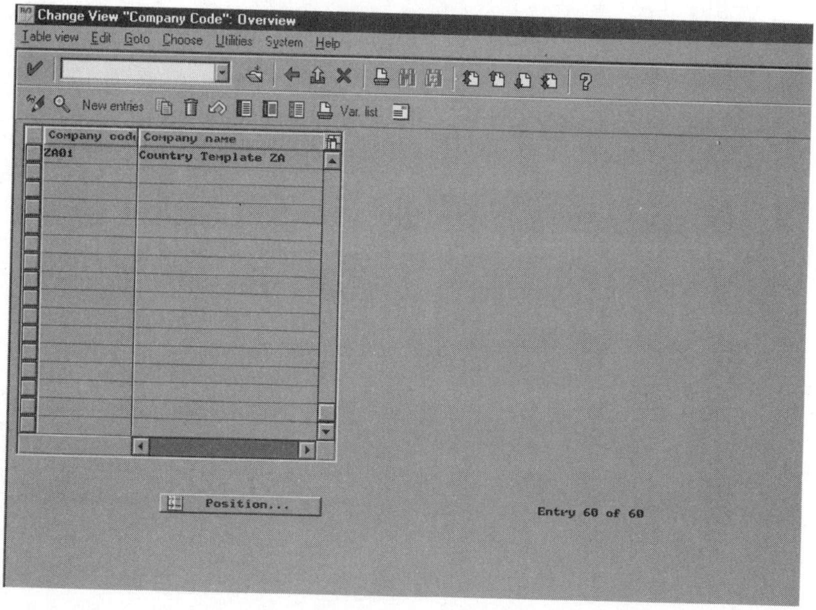

FIGURE 1.13   The options for narrowing the results of transaction code SE16

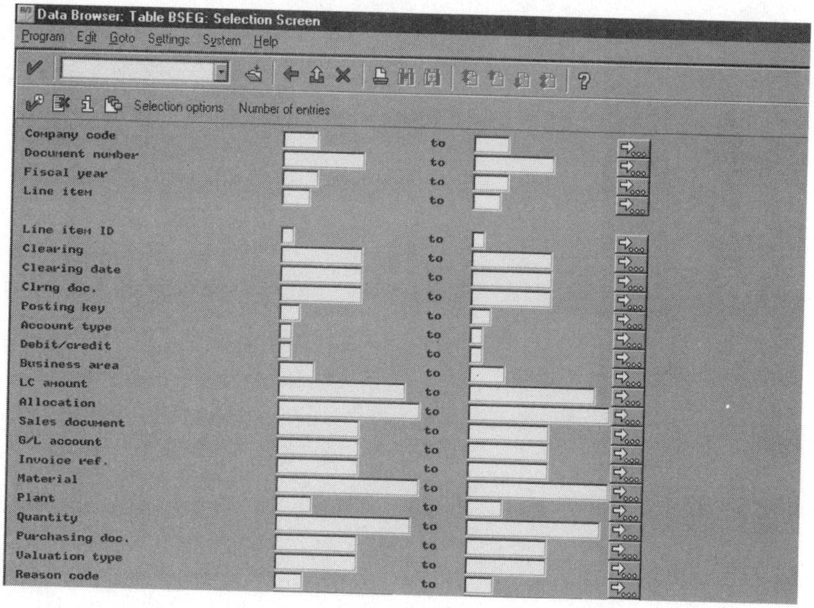

The fields that are automatically displayed for selection criteria aren't the only fields that can be used. By following the menu path Settings ➣ Fields for Selection, you can choose additional fields to select. Be careful, SAP defaults so that only 500 entries

are returned. If you require more than 500 entries, you can change this option via the field at the bottom of the selection screen.

The databrowser can be used to display data from all different types of tables, including summary and line item detail. This is very useful because reports using the Report Painter or Report Writer can only be written against summary-level tables. The Report Painter and Report Writer tools allow you to create customized reports based on users' needs. Most modules in the system can utilize Report Painter and Report Writer to create reports. Report Painter and Report Writer are especially useful for creating FI/CO custom reports. The table that is most commonly displayed by FI/CO team members is BSEG. This table contains all the segment (line item) detail behind every financial transaction in FI. You need to be very careful when displaying BSEG, or any segment-level table, because you can cripple performance on your system if you do not narrow your selection criteria enough. Running wide-ended table displays or queries is also a good way to get locked out of transactions by your friendly neighborhood Basis group, and a good way to feel the wrath of your project team.

The Online Support System (OSS)

The Online Support System (OSS) is a dial-in tool provided by SAP to help solve application problems. Some projects allow individual developers or consultants to log their own OSS problem notes into the online site. In other projects, OSS note inquiries are sent through a central person or group. You'll find that, most of the time, you won't need to log your OSS problem because someone has already logged it on a previous project. All problems that have been sent in and determined to be valid by SAP and then solved by SAP are documented and stored in the OSS system as OSS Notes.

OSS Notes usually supply any additional code to fix program bugs. They may also be "consulting" notes explaining work-arounds in the system for certain functionality. Whichever the case, the information provided in the OSS system is invaluable. If you can't find a needed piece of functionality in the system, always make sure you check OSS to see if it already exists.

T I P   Depending on the technical setup of your client, you may be able to access the OSS system through transaction code OSS1. If this transaction code is unavailable, your Basis group will provide a project-specific OSS setup in your SAP Logon.

To find OSS Notes, click the General button on the first screen presented. From there, click the Find button and you will be presented with a Search Requirement screen. Just fill in the criteria you're looking for (the release of SAP you are working with and the application area) and the applicable OSS Notes will be returned to your screen. If you find a note that applies to the problem at hand, download a copy to your hard drive for yourself, then let one of your Basis teammates know which note you would like applied. Unless you are very experienced, don't try to apply OSS Notes yourself. The Notes often deal with changing and adding to core SAP source code. You do not want your name attached to any changes to SAP programs. Generally speaking, changing SAP programs is not a good idea and shouldn't be done. We will explore this in greater detail in the next section.

In addition to OSS Notes, the OSS system has other purposes. As mentioned before, you can log questions to SAP. Other uses include checking SAP training class schedules, reviewing new information from SAP, and looking up information on Hot Packs, upgrades, and so on.

N O T E   In simple terms, *Hot Packs* are groups of OSS Notes that SAP feels you should apply based on bugs in the system or on additional functionality provided by the notes. Instead of applying individual notes one by one, you can use Hot Packs to apply a group of OSS Notes.

Modifications to SAP Source Code and User-Exits

The golden rule of packaged software and of SAP in particular is **Do *Not* Modify The Source Code!** Always try to live by the golden rule; a modification to SAP source code is a *bad idea*, to say the least. Once you modify the source code of a program, SAP generally will not support the program and related business processes and may not support your entire installation. Source code modifications also make for a nightmare when applying Hot Packs and are even more of a problem when trying to do upgrades. There are some SAP clients who have made modifications to source code and have paid the price: they are now trying to remove the modifications to get back to "core" code in order to regain support from SAP.

If standard SAP functionality just doesn't work for your business, there are other options. SAP has developed specific Industry Solutions (ISs). There are prefabricated ISs for certain industries, such as IS-Aerospace & Defense, IS-Oil, IS-Retail, and many more. One of the existing ISs may work for your business. If not, work with SAP regarding your business needs; they may make—or allow you to make—SAP-supported modifications to your system.

SAP also provides what are called *user-exits* in some standard programs. User-exits allow developers to create their own code that is called by a standard SAP program. Once the custom code has finished, control returns to the standard SAP program for further processing. Contrary to programming modifications, home-brewed user-exits are a good idea. SAP is providing increasing numbers of user-exits in upgrades and new releases. To see if a program already has a user-exit, while displaying the program source code, search for the string "customer-exit". If this string is found, the program already has a user-exit. The transaction code CMOD also contains the customization projects for activating all user-exits. You can search through these projects to see if the functionality you need is included.

Summary

In this chapter, you've been introduced to the basic concepts you'll need to understand to get the most out of the rest of this book. You have reviewed the basic configuration of a three-tiered database and learned about a table-driven approach to designing your own system. You've learned about transports and who has control over the various aspects of preparing and implementing a transport. We walked through the IMG screens and a few tables that will be useful in configuration and customization. And you're more familiar with the sorts of changes that you shouldn't make and how to find out about problems and solutions using the OSS Notes system.

Next, let's look at the structure of the FI Enterprise system and begin to configure the system for our project company, Extreme Sports.

CHAPTER 2

Financial Accounting Enterprise Structure

FEATURING:

▶ **CHART OF ACCOUNTS**

▶ **FISCAL YEAR VARIANT**

▶ **COMPANY CODE CONFIGURATION**

▶ **BUSINESS AREAS**

▶ **FUNCTIONAL AREAS**

▶ **ADVANCED VALIDATION AND SUBSTITUTION CONFIGURATION**

▶ **SALES AND USE TAX**

The Financial Accounting (or *FI*) Enterprise Structure is the key building block to your entire organization. Most other modules in the system build upon the FI Organization Elements that you create in the Enterprise Structure. The configuration that will occur in the rest of the book will all be built upon the base elements that you will configure in this chapter.

It is very important to carefully analyze your organization before setting up the FI Enterprise Structure. It is not only important to have a good picture of how your organization currently looks, but it is also equally important to have an idea of what your organization may look like in the future.

Chart of Accounts

Before configuring any part of the FI Enterprise Structure, it is vital to have already drawn out and agreed upon what your structure will look like. From a purely technical point of view, the order in which you configure the chart of accounts, fiscal year variant, or company codes doesn't matter. For ease of illustration and continuity, we will cover the chart of accounts and fiscal year variant before demonstrating company code configuration.

Settling on a chart of accounts with the users in your client sites is one of the first big hurdles to overcome in a project. Before beginning design sessions on the chart, it is essential that both you and the client personnel responsible for design decisions have a clear understanding of the differences between FI and CO in SAP. The main reporting purpose of FI is for external legal reporting to outside authorities (Securities and Exchange Commission, Internal Revenue Service, etc.). The main reporting purpose of CO is for internal managerial reporting. This is often a very difficult subtlety for users to grasp. The FI versus CO concept is hard to understand for many people because, since the beginning of accounting and accounting information systems, the chart of accounts was the sole reporting tool for both external and internal purposes. Old habits die hard, and this is no exception. Your end-user community is familiar with having thousands of accounts in the chart and coding internal and external reporting logic into the G/L (general ledger) account numbers. It is your job to make them comfortable with a smaller chart of accounts.

NOTE   The main reporting purpose of FI is for external legal reporting to outside authorities (SEC, IRS, etc.). The main reporting purpose of CO is for internal managerial reporting.

With SAP, you don't need thousands of accounts or any logic other than grouping logic (for example, all Assets are in the 100000 to 199999 range) built into the G/L account number. Once you have completed your review of the existing chart for deletions, you are ready to configure in SAP. The easiest way to configure a chart of accounts is to copy an existing chart of accounts. With the default system, SAP delivers the chart of accounts for the U.S., known as CAUS. Let's look at how to copy the SAP-delivered chart of accounts, CAUS, to create the Extreme Sports chart of accounts, EXCA. You can copy CAUS by following the menu path Financial Accounting ➢ General Ledger Accounting ➢ G/L Accounts ➢ Master Data ➢ G/L Account Creation ➢ Copy (Alternative 1) ➢ Copy Chart of Accounts.

COPY CHART OF ACCOUNTS

You can use the following methods to get to the chart of accounts US version configuration screen:

Menu Path: **Financial Accounting ➢ General Ledger Accounting ➢ G/L Accounts ➢ Master Data ➢ G/L Account Creation ➢ Copy (Alternative 1) ➢ Copy Chart of Accounts**

Transaction Code: **OBY7**

To give you a better feel of how to maneuver around in the Implementation Guide (IMG), we have provided a screenshot of the IMG path for this first piece of the configuration in Figure 2.1.

FIGURE 2.1   The IMG path to CAUS creation

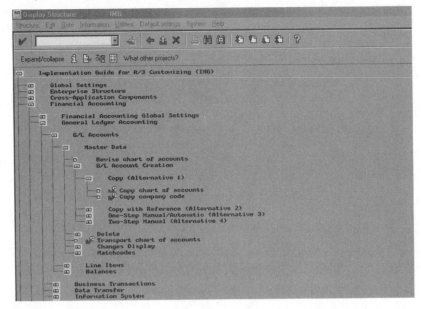

After selecting the execute icon in the IMG, as shown in Figure 2.1, you are provided with the configuration screen shown in Figure 2.2.

FIGURE 2.2   This dialog box allows you to customize the aspects of CAUS to copy.

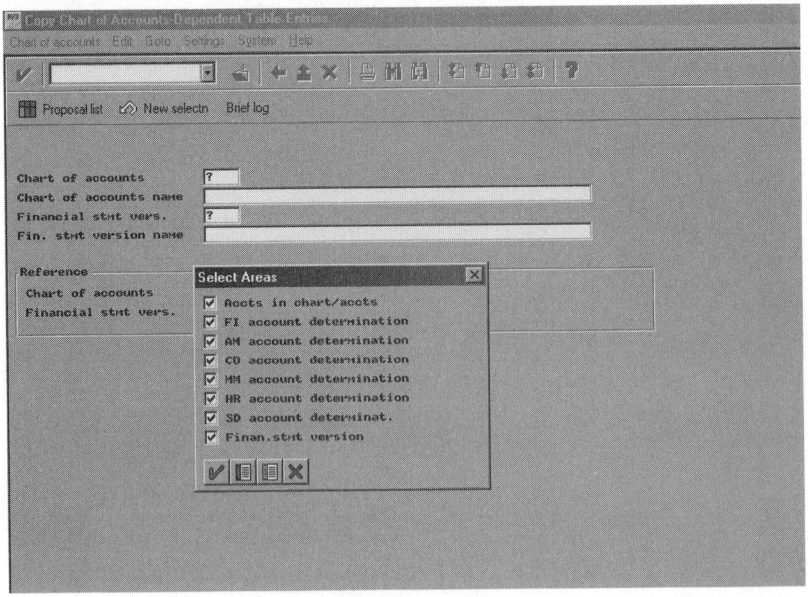

Select the green check mark (shown in Figure 2.2) to copy all selected automatic account determinations from the reference chart of accounts. *Account determinations* (or automatic account assignments) are an important part of the integrated SAP system because every G/L entry will stop flowing through the accounting department if you get this wrong. SAP automatically creates accounting documents from transactions that are carried out by users in other parts of the system (MM, HR, SD, etc.). When you select this option, you have to be very careful before deleting any accounts in your new chart. Deleting an account that is mapped in automatic account assignment can stop business processing cold. Automatic account assignments will be covered in Chapter 3. After pressing Enter (or clicking the green check mark you saw in Figure 2.2), you are presented with your first true configuration screen, shown here in Figure 2.3.

WARNING   Exercise caution when selecting automatic account assignments. Deleting an account that is mapped in automatic account assignment can stop business processing cold. This is because documents created in other parts of the system won't be reflected in your chart. Automatic account assignments will be covered in Chapter 3.

FIGURE 2.3   The configuration screen for the chart of accounts

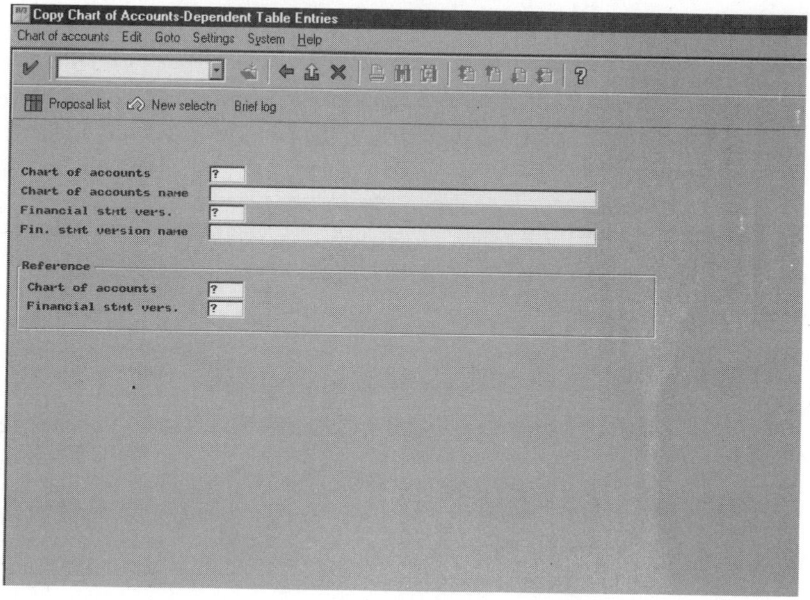

Copy Chart of Accounts-Dependent Table Entries

Chart of accounts   Edit   Goto   Settings   System   Help

Proposal list   New selectn   Brief log

Chart of accounts   ?
Chart of accounts name
Financial stmt vers.   ?
Fin. stmt version name

Reference
Chart of accounts   ?
Financial stmt vers.   ?

You will notice that a number of the fields in the configuration screen contain question marks. A question mark is SAP's indicator that an entry is required. Explanations of the fields displayed in Figure 2.3 are listed here:

Chart of Accounts   Enter the four-digit alphanumeric identifier of the chart of accounts you wish to create. There is no right or wrong way to come up with a chart of account identifier, but usually the entry is all characters.

Chart of Accounts Name   Enter the description for your chart of accounts. The field is alphanumeric and can contain up to 50 characters.

Financial Stmt Vers.   Enter the four-digit alphanumeric identifier of the financial statement version you wish to create. The financial statement version is used by SAP to form your company's standard Balance and Profit and Loss statements. We will cover the configuration of the financial statement version in detail in Chapter 3. For now, you only need to enter a placeholder to be used later.

Fin. Stmt Version Name   Enter a descriptive name for your financial statement version. The entry is alphanumeric and can contain up to 50 characters.

Chart of Accounts   Enter the four-digit alphanumeric identifier of the chart of accounts you wish to copy from. A listing of all available charts can be seen from the drop-down box on this field. To display the drop-down box, single-click on the field.

Financial Stmt Vers.   Enter the four-digit alphanumeric identifier of the financial statement version you wish to copy from. A listing of all available financial statement versions can be seen from the drop-down box on this field.

NOTE   Generally, each SAP-delivered chart of accounts has a corresponding financial statement version already created. Make sure you select the financial statement version that goes with your chart.

The configuration for Extreme Sports appears in Figure 2.4.

FIGURE 2.4   Extreme Sports' chart of accounts

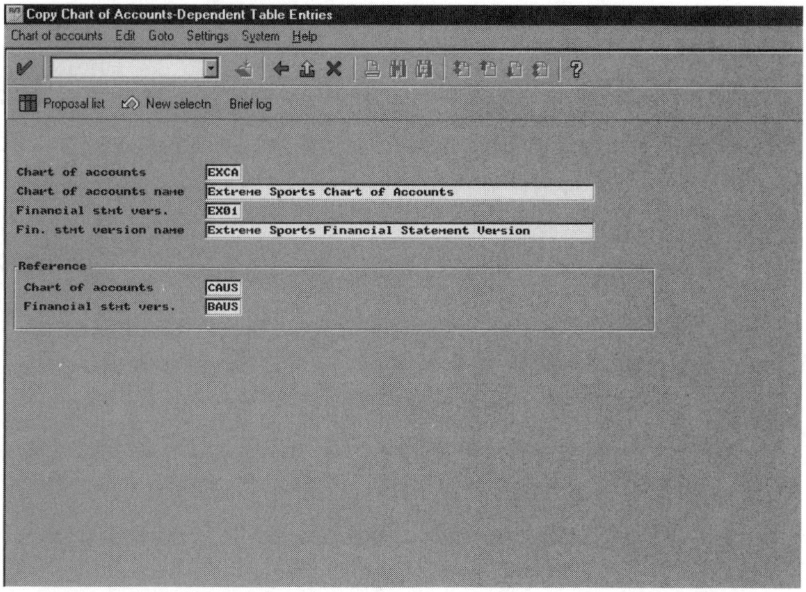

Once you have made all of your entries, click the Proposal List button near the top of the screen, shown in Figure 2.4. You will then be presented with a screen detailing what is going to be copied. To actually create the chart, click the copy icon or execute the following menu path: Chart of Accounts ➢ Copy Chart of Accounts. Your new chart of accounts now exists. The newly created chart is ready to use and will now appear on the drop-down box of all available charts.

EXTREME SPORTS CONFIGURATION ANALYSIS: CHART OF ACCOUNTS

Extreme Sports will utilize a single chart of accounts to be used by all of its company codes. The Mexican subsidiary company (company code 1300) will utilize a country chart of accounts in addition to the standard chart of accounts. The country chart of accounts configuration will be explained in "Company Code Configuration" later in this chapter. Because Extreme Sports is a U.S.-based company, the sample U.S. chart of accounts (CAUS), delivered by SAP, was used to create the Extreme Sports chart of accounts (EXCA). The sample financial statement version (BAUS) that comes with CAUS was used to create the Extreme Sports financial statement version (EX01).

The copy method of creating a chart of accounts is not the only method that can be used. You are also free to create your own chart of accounts—by hand—in the system or to import a chart of accounts from another system. Copying is far and away the easiest method of creating a chart of accounts (or any other configuration for that matter). By copying the chart of accounts, you are also able to copy the automatic account assignments. As discussed earlier, automatic account assignments are vital to the integration of SAP. Let the system do your configuration work for you whenever possible. We will cover the remainder of the chart of accounts configuration in Chapter 3.

Fiscal Year Variant

The *fiscal year variant* determines the posting periods to be used by your client's company. As the name implies, it should be configured to match your client's fiscal year. The fiscal year variant is very flexible and can be configured to match any organization's fiscal calendar.

SAP allows a maximum of 16 posting periods each fiscal year. The 16 periods normally comprise 12 regular posting periods and 4 special posting periods, which can be used for such things as posting audit or tax adjustments to a closed fiscal year. Having four special posting periods gives you a lot of flexibility; you may want to use one special period for each quarterly and year-end audit and/or tax adjustment. When you close a period or year in SAP, you define which regular and which special periods are allowed for posting. Because the default period for each posting is one of the 12 regular posting periods, you can be safe leaving open one or more special periods for postings. To get to the fiscal year variant screen, follow the menu path Financial Accounting ➢ Financial Accounting Global Settings ➢ Fiscal Year ➢ Maintain Fiscal Year Variant (Maintain Shortened Fiscal Year).

DEFINE FISCAL YEAR VARIANTS

You can use the following methods to get to the fiscal year variant screen:

Menu Path: **Financial Accounting ➢ Financial Accounting Global Settings ➢ Fiscal Year ➢ Maintain Fiscal Year Variant (Maintain Shortened Fiscal Year)**

Transaction Code: **OB29**

The fiscal year variant configuration screen is presented in Figure 2.5.

FIGURE 2.5   The fiscal year variant configuration screen

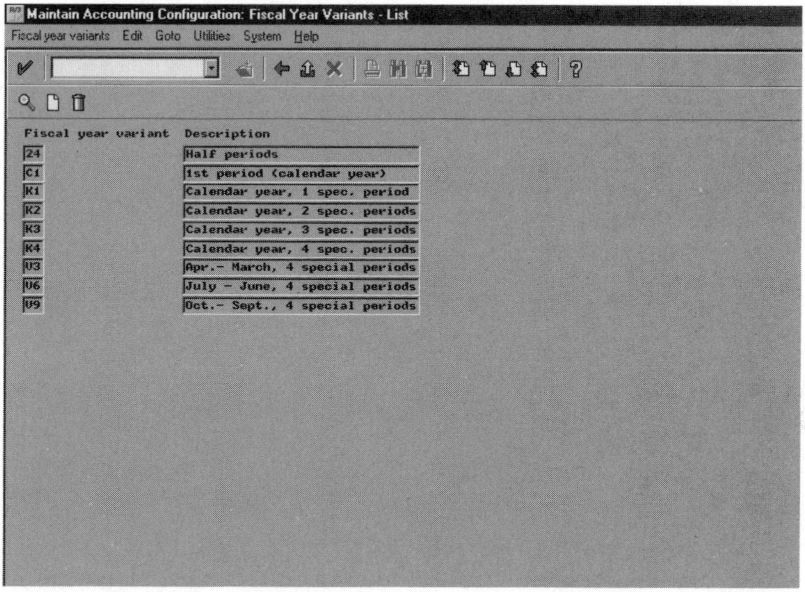

Using the screen presented in Figure 2.5, you can configure your fiscal year variant. As always, it is easier to copy an existing entry than to create one from scratch. With this in mind, we will select the variant we wish to copy (the option called V3 on the screen) and then carry out the copy command. The copy command can be executed in one of two ways: by clicking the copy icon (shown in Figure 2.5) or executing the following menu path: Fiscal Year Variants ➤ Copy ➤ Fiscal Year Variant. The dialog box presented by executing the copy command is shown in Figure 2.6. You will notice that the configuration for Extreme Sports has already been entered. This will be the case throughout the rest of the book. When you enter the transaction in your system, the fields will of course be blank.

FIGURE 2.6   The copy fiscal year variant dialog box

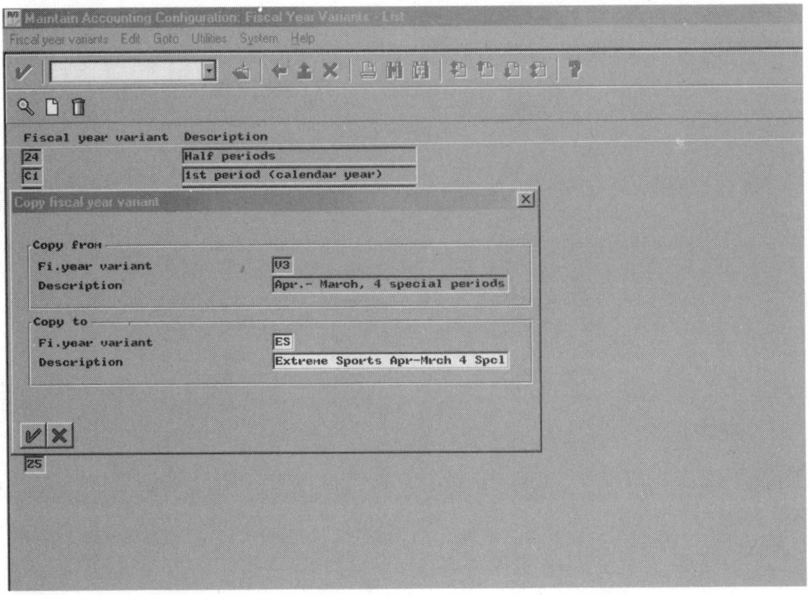

Let's look at how to enter data in the fields by using this list of entry fields:

Fi. Year Variant   Enter the two-digit alphanumeric identifier of your fiscal year variant. SAP-delivered fiscal year variants normally begin with a *K* or a *V*, so avoid using these letters in your variant.

Description   Enter a description of your fiscal year variant. The field is alphanumeric and can contain up to 30 characters.

EXTREME SPORTS FISCAL YEAR VARIANT CONFIGURATION ANALYSIS

Extreme Sports operates on an April-to-March calendar month fiscal year. For this reason, we decided to copy an already existing fiscal year variant that uses an April-to-March fiscal calendar based on calendar months with 12 regular posting periods and 4 special posting periods.

We will now look at the fiscal year variant configuration in more detail. After choosing the check mark and transacting the changes shown in Figure 2.6, we are taken back to the main fiscal year variant configuration screen. Double-click the newly created fiscal year variant, ES. By looking at the configuration, you will be able to figure out how to configure fiscal year variants manually (without copying) should you need to for your project. The configuration detail is presented in Figure 2.7.

FIGURE 2.7 Details of the configuration for fiscal year variant ES

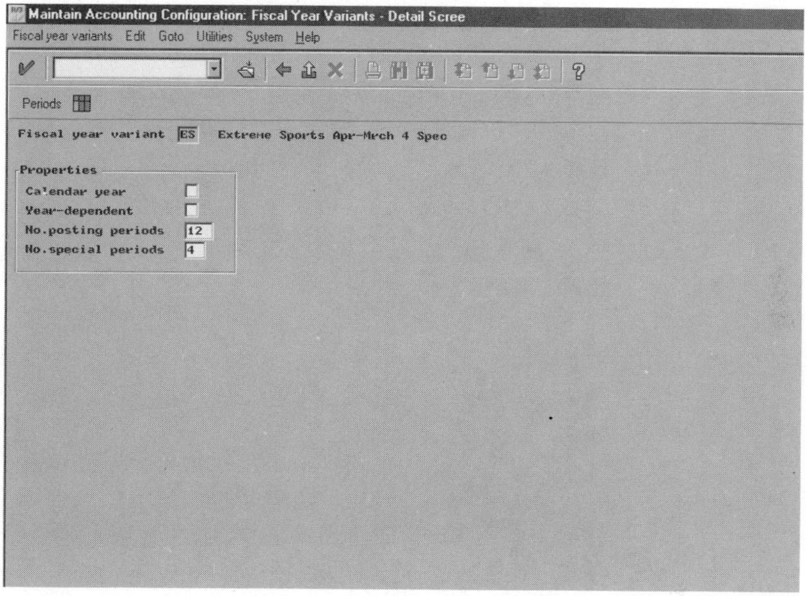

Let's look at the data entry fields:

Calendar Year Set this indicator if your fiscal year is also the calendar year.

Year-Dependent Set this indicator if the closing day of your fiscal year varies from year to year. You would set this indicator if you are using a 4-5-4 accounting calendar, for instance.

No. Posting Periods Enter the number of normal posting periods that are used for each fiscal year. The maximum number of normal posting periods in 1 year is 12. The standard general ledger can accommodate up to 16 periods. Most companies choose to have 12 regular periods and 4 special periods.

No. Special Periods Enter the number of special posting periods that are used for each fiscal year. Four is the recommended maximum number of special posting periods. The standard general ledger can accommodate up to 16 periods. Most companies choose to have 12 regular periods and 4 special periods.

Select the Periods button, shown in Figure 2.7, and you are taken to the fiscal year variant configuration periods screen, shown in Figure 2.8. This screen is used to map calendar months to fiscal months for the variant. If you selected the Year-Dependent field, shown in Figure 2.7, you will be prompted for a year to maintain. It is necessary to maintain the periods screen for each individual year if your variant is year dependent.

FIGURE 2.8   The periods screen

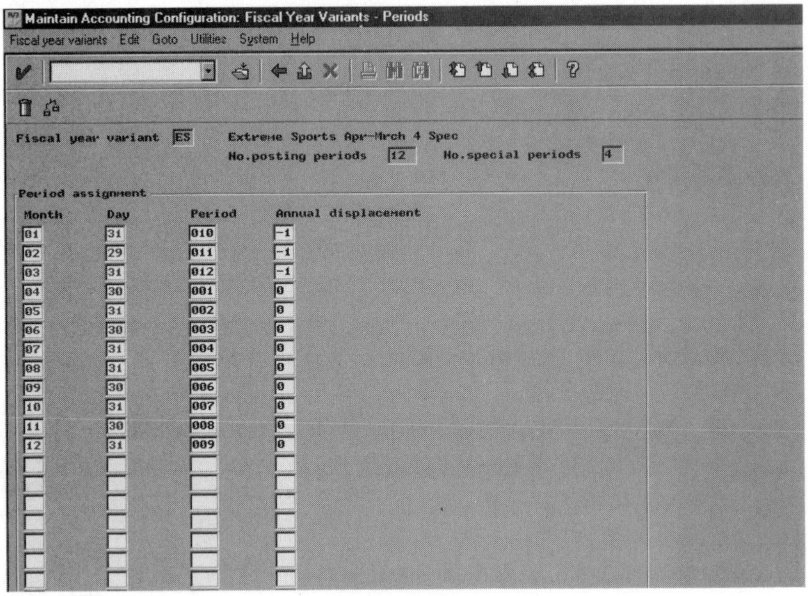

There are four entries on the periods screen:

Month   This entry represents the calendar month for the record being configured.

Day   This entry represents the last calendar day of the accounting period being configured.

Period   This column represents the fiscal posting period that relates to the calendar month and calendar day of the record. Because we are using an April-to-March fiscal year, the first calendar month, January, is posting period 10 of the fiscal year.

Annual Displacement   For fiscal years that do not correspond to calendar years, this entry is used to offset the calendar year to the correct fiscal year, by entering either a –1 or a +1. Using our Extreme Sports example, the first fiscal period (01) for fiscal year 1999 is April (calendar period 04). When we go into a new calendar year in January 2000, we are in posting period 10 of fiscal year 1999. Because of this, all the 1999 fiscal year posting periods that occur in calendar year 2000 require an annual displacement of –1 in order to specify the correct fiscal year. How about that for a Y2K problem!

Posting Period Variant

The *posting period variant* controls which posting periods, both normal and special, are open for each company code. It is possible to have a different posting period variant for each company code in your organization. The posting period is independent of the fiscal year variant. The number of posting period variants is determined by the closing schedules of each of your company codes. Follow the menu path Financial Accounting ➤ Financial Accounting Global Settings ➤ Document ➤ Posting Periods ➤ Define Variants for Open Posting Periods to define the variants.

DEFINE POSTING PERIOD VARIANTS

You can use the following methods to get to the posting period variant configuration screen:

Menu Path: **Financial Accounting ➤ Financial Accounting Global Settings ➤ Document ➤ Posting Periods ➤ Define Variants for Open Posting Periods**

Transaction Code: **OBBO**

The posting period variant configuration screen is presented in Figure 2.9.

FIGURE 2.9   The posting period variant configuration screen

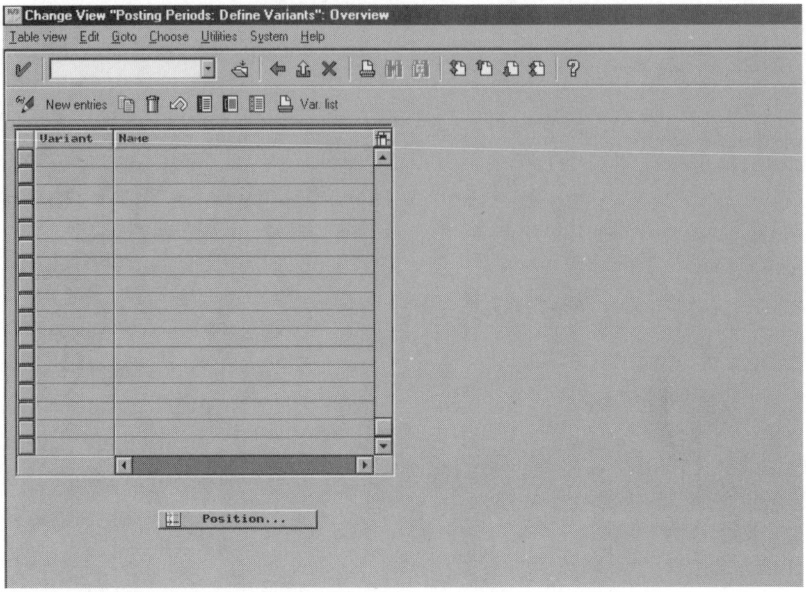

Clicking the New Entries button allows you to configure your posting period variants. Here they are:

Variant   Enter the four-digit alphanumeric identifier for your posting period variant. If you are using separate posting period variants for each company code, it is a good idea to name the variants the same as your company codes.

Name   Enter a descriptive name for your posting period variant. The field is alphanumeric and can contain up to 35 characters.

The fully configured posting period variants for Extreme Sports are presented in Figure 2.10.

FIGURE 2.10   Here's how we configured the Extreme Sports posting periods.

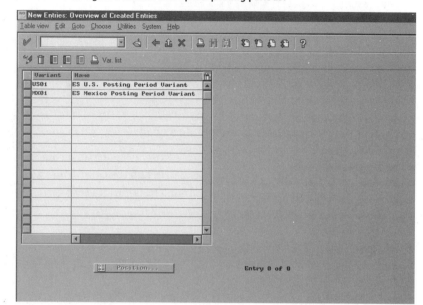

EXTREME SPORTS MULTICOUNTRY POSTING PERIOD VARIANT CONFIGURATION

With the implementation of SAP, Extreme Sports has decided to streamline its back-office functions. Before the SAP implementation, each company within Extreme Sports operated its own accounting department independently. Using SAP, there will only be two accounting departments: one for the U.S.-based companies and one for the Mexican-based company. Because of this change, only two posting period variants, US01 and MX01, are needed because all U.S.-based companies will be closed at the same time and the Mexican-based company (with any additional future Mexican-based companies) will be closed at a different time than the U.S.-based companies.

Company Code Configuration

In SAP, a *company code* is representative of a stand-alone legal entity that requires its own set of accounting records for reporting purposes. It is very important to understand this concept. There are substructures within the system to account for divisions within a company, which we will cover later. We will now set up the company codes for Extreme Sports. An explanation of Extreme Sports and its organizational setup was described in the introduction in the section titled "Case Company Background."

We will begin by configuring Extreme Sports' first company, company code 1000 ES Ski & Surf. Follow the menu path Enterprise Structure ➢ Maintain Structure ➢ Definition ➢ Financial Accounting ➢ Define, Copy, Delete, Check Company Code to add the first company to the system.

COMPANY CODE CREATION

You can use the following methods to get to the screen for adding a company code:

Menu Path: **Enterprise Structure ➢ Maintain Structure ➢ Definition ➢ Financial Accounting ➢ Define, Copy, Delete, Check Company Code**

Transaction Code: **OX02**

The Select Transaction dialog box presents you with an option to choose your own order of activities or to follow the prescribed plan in the dialog box, as seen in Figure 2.11. Double-click the Define Company Code option. Alternatively, you can select the option by clicking once on the Define Company Code text and then clicking the Choose button. (Please note that if the transaction code is entered instead of the menu path, the screen shown in Figure 2.11 is not displayed and you are taken directly to the screen in Figure 2.12.)

You are then presented with the screen that appears in Figure 2.12. You will notice that three options already exist in the system: Country Template SG, SAP America, and Country Template ZA. An alternative way of creating a company code would be to copy one of these entries. You can click the New Entries button to add your own specific requirements. You are then presented with the screen shown in Figure 2.13.

FIGURE 2.11   The Select Transaction dialog box

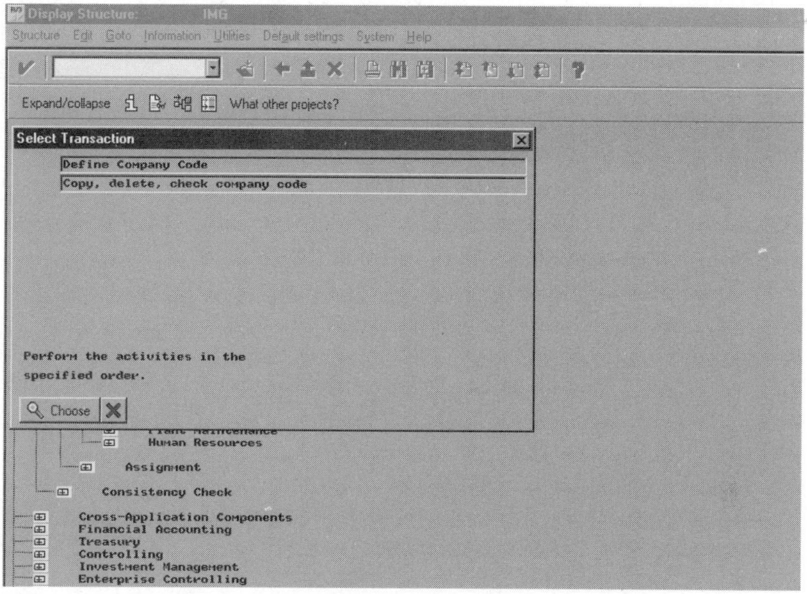

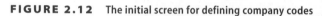

FIGURE 2.12   The initial screen for defining company codes

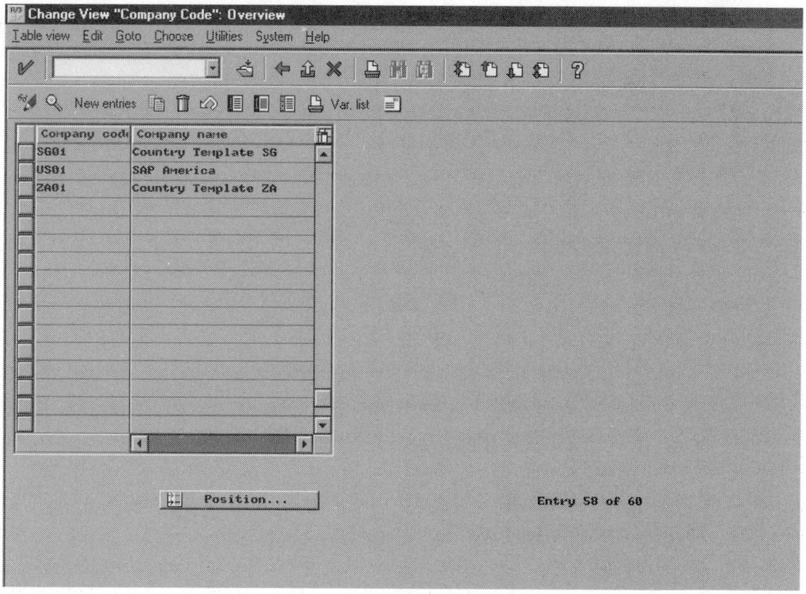

FIGURE 2.13   You can enter your own specific company code options by using the New Entries screen.

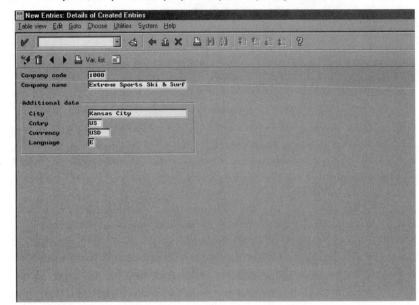

Let's look at this list of data entry fields:

Company Code   Enter the four-digit alphanumeric identifier of your company code. It is usually a good idea to make the company code identifier numeric (1000).

Company Name   Enter a descriptive name for your company code. This field is alphanumeric and can contain up to 25 characters.

City   Enter the name of the city in which your company is located or headquartered. This field is alphanumeric and can contain up to 25 characters.

Cntry   Enter the name of the country in which your company is located. This field must contain one of the two-character SAP country identifiers.

Currency   Enter the currency that your company code will operate with. Make sure to use the pull-down menu on this field to make an entry that is acceptable to the SAP system.

Language   Enter the one-character language ID for the default SAP language display for this company code.

Once you click the save icon, you will be taken to the general address data of the company code, as seen in Figure 2.14. For U.S.-based companies, the Postal Code field is a required field. It is important to note that all address information in the system is stored in table SADR. Much of the required information on the Address screen is repeated from the previous screen, the New Entries screen. Unfortunately, it is very easy to get address information wrong when transporting data. For this reason, it is recommended that you do not transport any address information, but rather maintain the address information by hand in your production client.

NOTE   All address information in the system is stored in table SADR.

FIGURE 2.14   The Address screen for your company information

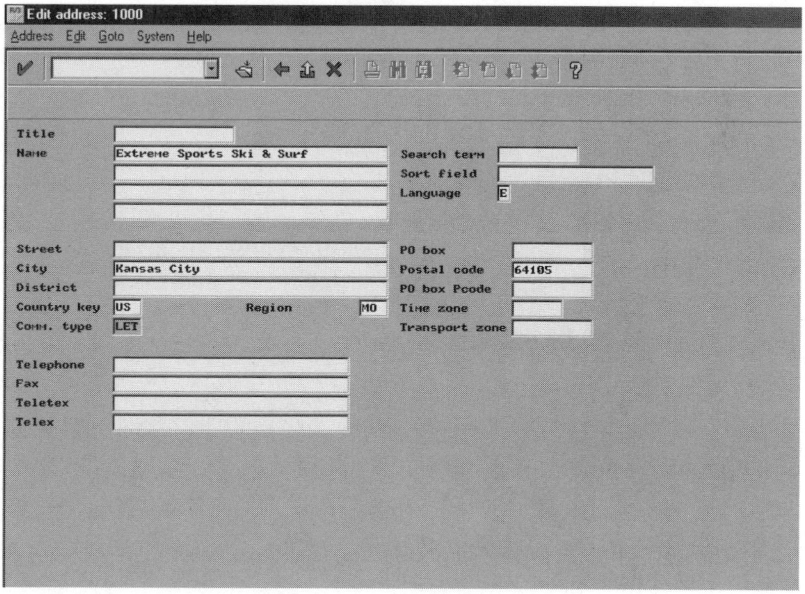

```
Edit address: 1000
Address   Edit   Goto   System   Help

Title
Name          Extreme Sports Ski & Surf         Search term
                                                 Sort field
                                                 Language      E

Street                                           PO box
City          Kansas City                        Postal code   64105
District                                         PO box Pcode
Country key   US             Region        MO    Time zone
Comm. type    LET                                Transport zone

Telephone
Fax
Teletex
Telex
```

EXTREME SPORTS COMPANY CODE CONFIGURATION ANALYSIS: PART 1

Extreme Sports has decided to use all numeric company code identifiers. There are three U.S.-based companies who all use dollars (USD) as their base currency and English (E) for the SAP default logon language. We will cover the configuration of the Mexican-based company code in a later section of this chapter.

We will now enter the *global parameters* for our company code. The configuration screen for global parameters is where we link company code to the chart of accounts, the fiscal year variant, and the posting period variants, among other settings. You can get to this screen by following the menu path Financial Accounting ➢ Financial Accounting Global Settings ➢ Company Code ➢ Enter Global Parameters.

DEFINE COMPANY CODE GLOBAL PARAMETERS

You can use the following methods to reach the screen to enter global parameters:

Menu Path: **Financial Accounting ➢ Financial Accounting Global Settings ➢ Company Code ➢ Enter Global Parameters**

Transaction Code: **OBY6**

The first screen for configuring global parameters contains a listing of all company codes configured in the system. Double-click the company code you want to configure (1000 for Extreme Sports) and you will be taken to the configuration screen shown in Figure 2.15.

FIGURE 2.15   The global parameters configuration screen for Extreme Sports

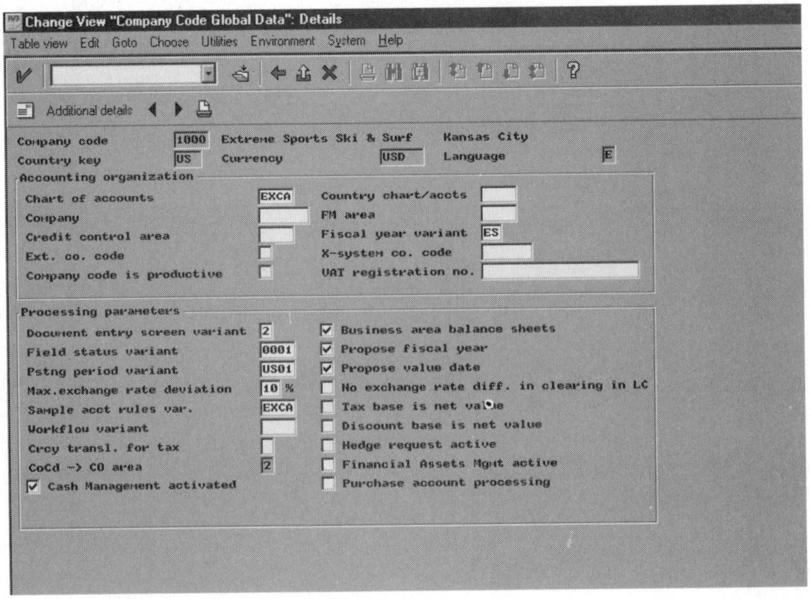

Let's look at this list of data entry fields:

Chart of Accounts   Enter the four-digit identifier of the chart of accounts that you wish to use for this company code. We've already set this up in "Chart of Accounts" earlier in this chapter. It's called EXCA for Extreme Sports.

Country Chart/Accts   If the company code you're configuring has a special country or statutory chart of accounts, enter the four-digit identifier for that chart here. We will make use of this field with our Mexican company code in a later section of this chapter.

Company   A company is generally used in the legal consolidation module to roll up financial statements of several company codes. A company can consist of one or more company codes. It is important to make the distinction and remember that a company is not the same thing as a company code. If you are going to use SAP's consolidation functionality for your organization, enter the six-character alphanumeric company identifier that relates to this company code.

FM Area   *FM Area* is short for Financial Management area. Financial Management areas are used for advanced functions of the Treasury module, more specifically, for funds management. Funds Management functionality allows your client's organization to budget commitments and financial resources. If you are using Funds Management, enter the four-character alphanumeric identifier of the Financial Management area. FM areas can contain more than one company code. If you are using Investment Management along with Funds Management, your FM areas must be assigned to the proper controlling areas (the controlling areas that are assigned to your company codes). This is covered in more detail in the chapter on controlling, Chapter 7, "CO Enterprise Structure."

Credit Control Area   Credit Control Area controls the credit limits (tolerances) for your customers. Enter the four-character alphanumeric identifier of the credit control area for your company code. A credit control area can be linked to many company codes, but a company code can be linked to only one credit control area. We will configure the credit control area in Chapter 5.

Fiscal Year Variant   Enter the two-character alphanumeric identifier of your fiscal year variant. Fiscal year variants were configured and discussed in detail earlier in this chapter.

Ext. Co. Code   This setting is only relevant if you are using ALE. If you are using ALE, check this field; if not leave it blank.

X-System Co. Code   If you checked the Ext. Co. Code indicator, you must enter the corresponding external company code ID (the one that resides in the external system) of this company code ID. For example, company code 1000 might have a corresponding external company code ID of EXSP10 that relates to company code ID 1000 in the other ALE system. Once again, this setting is only relevant if you are using ALE.

Company Code Is Productive   Only make this setting in your production client. Once you set your company code to productive, it is impossible to delete transactional data from your system. It is very handy to be able to wipe out transactional data in your development system, and it is equally important to make sure this indicator is set in your production client so that your business data is not wiped out!

VAT Registration No.   If your company code is subject to European Union (EU) regulations, enter your Value Added Tax (VAT) registration number here.

Document Entry Screen Variant   This setting controls country-specific on-screen fields for accounting documents. The most common U.S. setting is 2; this setting is for countries with withholding tax, like the U.S.

Business Area Balance Sheet   Set this indicator if you want to use business areas for your organization. We will cover business area configuration in detail later in this chapter.

Field Status Variant   The field status variant groups together several field status groups. Field status groups specify which fields are required, optional, or suppressed when processing transactions. Field status groups will be covered in detail in Chapter 3.

Propose Fiscal Year   Setting this field, in effect, makes the fiscal year part of the concatenated key field for looking up document numbers in either display or change mode. It is usually a good idea to set this indicator so you can cycle through document numbers from year to year. Number ranges will be explained in more detail in Chapter 3. Regardless of document number strategy, it is also a good idea to use this field because the more detailed the primary key is, the faster the search will be.

Pstng Period Variant   The posting period variant controls the opening and closing of posting periods for each company code. The posting period variant was discussed in detail earlier in this chapter.

Propose Value Date   Set this indicator if you want the system to make the current date the default date for the value date. Value dating is used for A/P, A/R, and Treasury transactions. In A/P and A/R, the value date is also referred to as the baseline date.

Max. Exchange Rate Deviation   If you are working with more than one currency in your organization, enter the maximum percentage rate in which a foreign currency transaction can deviate from the rates entered in the exchange rate tables. An exchange rate can deviate because SAP gives you the option of specifying an exchange rate when entering a document in a foreign currency. If the exchange rate entered manually on the document deviates from the exchange rate specified in the exchange rate table by more than the percentage specified in this field, a warning message is displayed. The exchange rate tables will be covered in Chapter 6.

No Exchange Rate Diff. in Clearing in LC   When this indicator is set, documents posted in foreign currency (such as pesos) that are cleared in local currency (dollars) will use the local currency value at the time the document is posted in order to determine exchange rate gains or losses. If this indicator is not set, the clearing will use the exchange rate at the date of clearing. In the following example, open item clearing refers to receiving a payment for an invoice created or paying a vendor for a product received. The payment offsets the invoice amount and "clears" both items. For example, company code 1000, whose local currency is U.S. dollars, bills a customer in the foreign currency of pesos, for 500 pesos. At the time the billing document is posted, the exchange rate is .25, thus giving the item a local currency amount of $125. The customer decides to pay the invoice using dollars, in the amount of $125. At the time the payment is received, the exchange rate is .20, giving the local currency value of the open item $100. If, at the time of posting, this indicator is set, no exchange rate gain or loss will be recognized because the payment amount ($125) matches the local currency amount of the document ($125) at the document posting date. If, at the time of posting, this indicator is not set, the system will recognize an exchange rate gain of $25 because the system recalculates the local currency amount of the open item at the time of payment (the new exchange rate of .20).

Sample Acct Rules Var.   This variant determines which field settings are carried over from a sample account to a newly created G/L account. Sample accounts will be discussed in more detail in Chapter 3.

Tax Base Is Net Value   The cash discount is deducted from the total invoice amount to calculate the tax base by means of this setting. Whether this field can be used is based upon the laws of the country where the company conducts business.

For example, let's say an invoice has a total amount of $100 but offers a cash discount of $2 for payment within 10 days. If this indicator is set, the tax base is $98—the total invoice amount ($100) less the cash discount amount ($2). The tax calculation carried out by the system will then be $98 times the applicable tax rate. If this indicator were not set, the tax base would be $100—the total invoice amount. For countries that use tax jurisdictions for their taxing procedure, such as the U.S., any entry in this field is ignored. For these countries, the tax base is configured on the tax jurisdiction code. Taxes will be covered in more detail later in this chapter.

Workflow Variant   If workflow is active in your system, enter the appropriate four-character alphanumeric identifier of the workflow variant. Workflow allows for documents to be routed to other users and processes in the system for approval or further processing.

Discount Base Is Net Value   If this indicator is set, the sales and use taxes are not included in the base-amount calculation for cash discounts. For example, an invoice is received in the amount of $225 and offers a cash discount of 2% if paid within 10 days. Of the total amount of the invoice, $200 relates to materials and $25 relates to sales taxes. If this indicator is set in this example, the cash discount base will be $200, the amount of the materials only, relating to a total payment of $221 ($200 * (1.00 − .02) plus the $25 tax amount). In the same example, if the indicator is not set, the total payment would be $220.50 ($225 * (1.00 − .02)). For countries that use tax jurisdictions for their taxing procedure, any entry in this field is ignored. The discount base is configured on the tax jurisdiction code for countries utilizing the tax jurisdiction taxing procedure.

Crcy Transl. for Tax   If you do not want tax amounts to be translated using the exchange rate defined by the tax base amount, you can use this field to override the tax base setting. This allows you to use an exchange rate for tax amounts that is different than the one used for other amounts on the document. The possible entries are as follows:

- ▶ Code 1: Manual Exchange Rate Entry Possible—This option allows you to manually enter a separate exchange rate to be used for taxes.

- ▶ Code 2: Exchange Rate Determined Using Posting Date—This option uses the exchange rate that is valid on the posting date when the document is cleared.

- ▶ Code 3: Exchange Rate Determined Using Document Date—This option uses the exchange rate that is valid on the document date of the affected transaction.

Hedge Request Active Selecting this indicator makes hedge requests active. A hedge request is an advanced function of the Treasury module. This setting is only valid with releases 4.*x* in the new Treasury Management submodule.

CoCd ⇒ CO Area This indicator is defaulted from the configuration of the controlling area to which this company code is assigned. This setting will be explained in more detail in Chapter 7. The possible entries are as follows:

- Code 1: If the controlling area contains only one company code (no cross-company accounting in controlling)

- Code 2: If the controlling area contains more than one company code (cross-company accounting is active in controlling)

Financial Assets Mgmt Active If you plan on utilizing the fixed assets module within SAP on your project, set this indicator to activate fixed assets. The fixed assets module allows you to track assets, depreciation, asset lives, and so on. The configuration of the Fixed Assets module is beyond the scope of this book.

Cash Management Activated Set this indicator if you are going to use the cash management positions and liquidity forecast functionality within the Treasury module. The cash management position and liquidity forecast will be explained in Chapter 7.

Purchase Account Processing Set this indicator if you wish to utilize purchase accounting. Purchase accounting segments the cost of externally related materials. For example, you would want to utilize purchase account processing if you do not want freight values for moving average-priced materials to be included in your inventory balance.

EXTREME SPORTS COMPANY CODE CONFIGURATION ANALYSIS: PART 2

As you can see from Figure 2.15, we were able to make use of the chart of accounts (EXCA), fiscal year variant (ES), and posting period variant (US01) that were configured earlier. Currently, legal consolidation funds management and fixed assets are beyond the scope of the Extreme Sports project (and the book). The credit control area for Extreme Sports will be configured in Chapter 5. At that time, we will come back and enter in the values.

EXTREME SPORTS COMPANY CODE CONFIGURATION ANALYSIS: PART 2 (CONTINUED)

Extreme Sports has used document entry screen variant 2 because company code 1000 is a U.S.-based company that utilizes withholding taxes. Extreme Sports will also use business areas, which will be discussed in greater detail later in this chapter.

The CFO of Extreme Sports has determined that a 10% exchange rate deviation is acceptable. Extreme Sports will also utilize the standard field status variant 0001, with custom field status groups added to the variant. Field status groups will be covered in detail in Chapter 3. In addition, Extreme Sports wants the system to use the fiscal year as part of the key field for looking up documents because document numbers can be used over from fiscal year to fiscal year if desired. Document number configuration will be explained in Chapter 3. Finally, Extreme Sports wants the system to default to the current date for the baseline date and value date in accounting transactions.

By clicking the Additional Details button, shown in Figure 2.15, you are able to enter the tax identification number of your company code. The completed screen is shown in Figure 2.16.

FIGURE 2.16   The tax identification number code is filled in using the Additional Details button of the global parameters configuration screen.

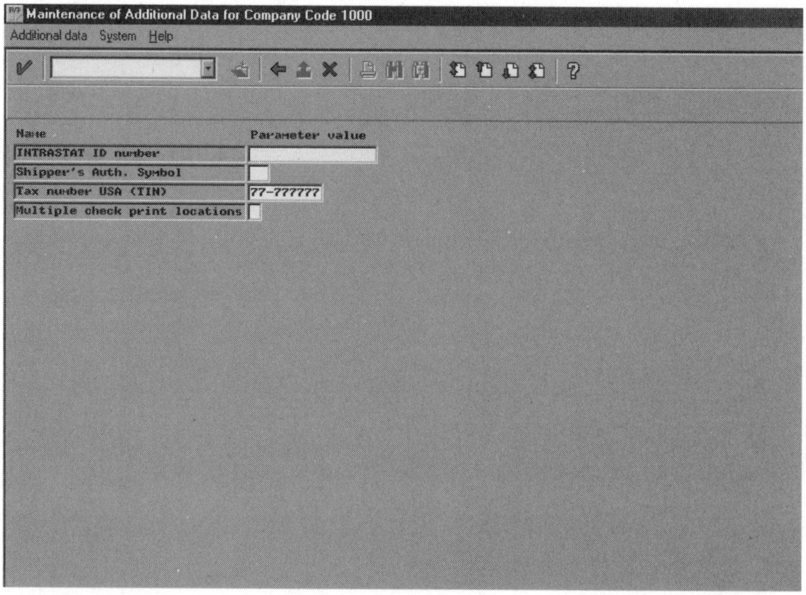

Creating New Companies by Copying Existing Company Code

In the preceding section, we configured company code 1000, ES Ski & Surf. We now need to configure company codes 1100, 1200, and 1400, the U.S. subsidiaries of Extreme Sports. We cover configuration of our Mexican company code 1300 in a later section of this chapter. Fortunately, we did most of the hard work in the preceding section; we now need only to copy our sample company code 1000 to create 1100, 1200, and 1400. We will use the first configuration command you learned earlier in this section by again following the menu path Enterprise Structure ➢ Maintain Structure ➢ Definition ➢ Financial Accounting ➢ Define, Copy, Delete, Check Company Code.

COPY COMPANY CODES

You can use the following methods to get to the Copy Company Code screen:

Menu Path: **Enterprise Structure** ➢ **Maintain Structure** ➢ **Definition** ➢ **Financial Accounting** ➢ **Define, Copy, Delete, Check Company Code**

Transaction Code: **EC01**

We are then presented with the Select Transaction dialog box that you saw in Figure 2.11. (Please note that if you enter the transaction code instead of the menu path, you will be taken directly to the screen in Figure 2.17, skipping over the screen that is shown in Figure 2.11.) This time, after following the menu path, we will select the Copy, Delete, Check Company Code option. The next configuration screen, as shown in Figure 2.17, is displayed.

FIGURE 2.17 The Organizational Unit Company Code screen

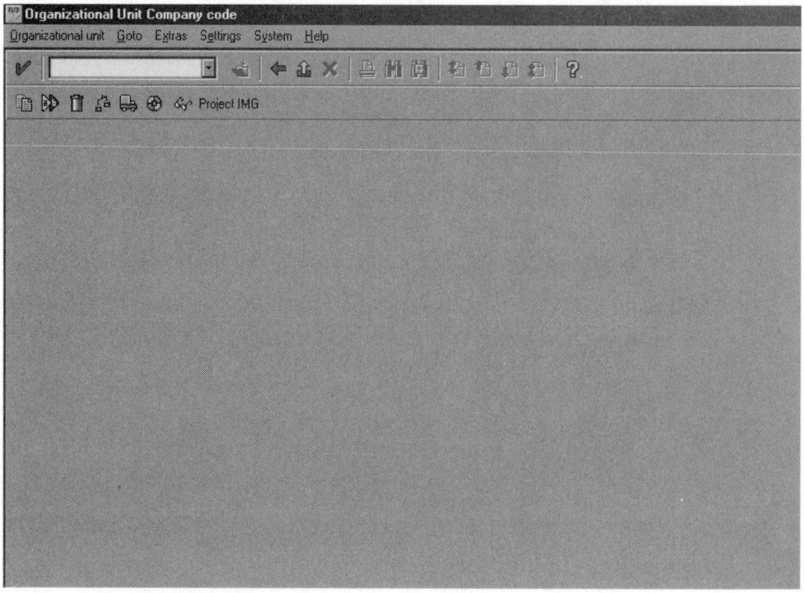

From this screen, you will follow the menu path Organizational Unit ➤ Copy Org Unit. The resulting screen is displayed in Figure 2.18.

FIGURE 2.18 The Copy Org Unit pop-up box

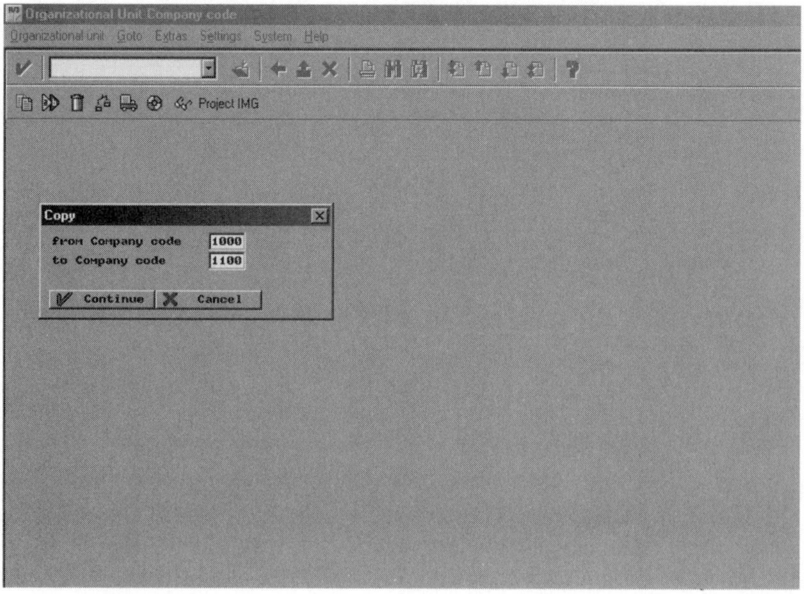

In the pop-up box (displayed in Figure 2.18), enter the Copy From company code and the Copy To company code. We have filled in the From box with company code 1000 (the company code that was configured earlier in the chapter) and the To box with company code 1100 (the company code that we wish to create). We will then repeat the process for the remaining U.S. subsidiaries using company code 1000 as the "from" company code.

The copy transaction copies all of the general and global parameter settings that we entered by hand for company code 1000. The only remaining step is to add the company name and address information. This is done the same way it was done for company code 1000—by using the same transaction code that we just executed—but this time, select the Define Company Code option (remember that the transaction code for defining is OX02). You will then double-click each of the new company codes, which will take you to their respective configuration screens (the configuration screens were explained earlier in this chapter). You can refer to Figure 2.13 to refresh your memory.

Configuring International Companies

In this section, we will configure company code 1300 ES Mexico S.A. The goal in this section is not to present the legal requirements needed to actually configure a Mexican company code, but rather to show the configuration settings you need when dealing with international company codes.

The configuration to set up the Mexican company code is very similar to the configuration for U.S.-based companies. We will only need to change and add a few additional entries to accomplish the company code assignment.

The first step is to define our company code. The same configuration paths and screens used in the U.S. company code configuration are used here. The only changes we will make are to set the country code to MX (Mexico) and the currency code to MXN (pesos).

Because Mexico has different government reporting requirements than the U.S., we will need to create a country chart of accounts to be used by ES Mexico in addition to the normal chart of accounts, EXCA. First, follow the configuration procedures documented in "Chart of Accounts" at the beginning of this chapter. The only difference is that we will copy the SAP-delivered Mexican chart of accounts to our new chart of accounts, EXMX. The chart of accounts EXMX will be used as our country chart of accounts in company code 1300.

You are now ready to enter global parameters for company code 1300. You will use the following configuration screens and paths, which were already demonstrated in "Company Code Configuration" earlier in this chapter. Follow the menu path Financial Accounting ➤ Financial Accounting Global Settings ➤ Company Code ➤ Enter Global Parameters.

DEFINE COMPANY CODE GLOBAL PARAMETERS

You can use the following methods to enter global parameters:

Menu Path: **Financial Accounting** ➤ **Financial Accounting Global Settings** ➤ **Company Code** ➤ **Enter Global Parameters**

Transaction Code: **OBY6**

The configured record for company code 1300 appears in Figure 2.19.

FIGURE 2.19   The configuration for company code 1300

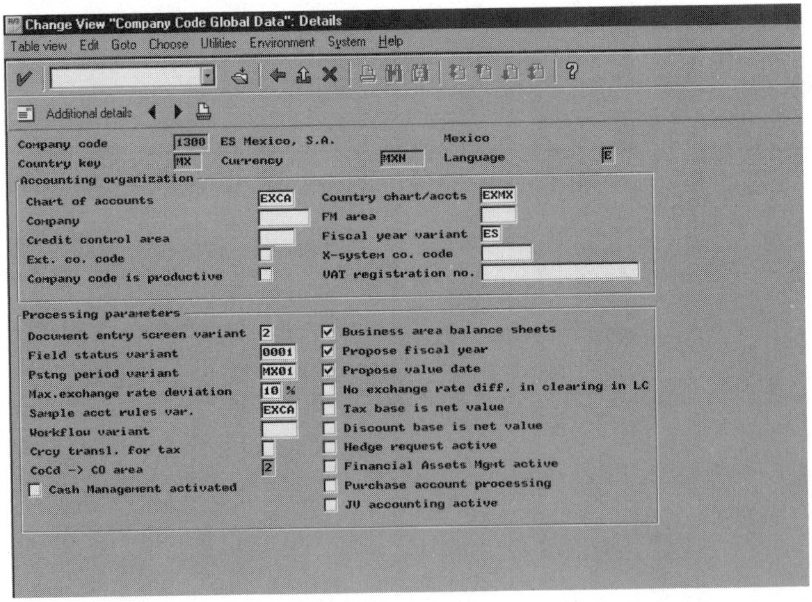

EXTREME SPORTS INTERNATIONAL COMPANY CODE CONFIGURATION ANALYSIS: PART 1

The country chart of accounts was set to EXMX for company code 1300. This will allow Extreme Sports to comply with external reporting obligations to the Mexican government. The link between the regular chart of accounts and the country chart of accounts appears in the alternate account number field of the G/L master record. This will be explained in more detail in Chapter 3.

Because company code 1300 has a different accounting staff than the rest of the company codes, we assigned posting period variant MX01. You will recall from the case company background in the introduction that company code 1400 Extreme Sports Shared Services provides all of the back-office and administrative functions for all U.S.-based subsidiaries of Extreme Sports. This will allow company code 1300 to close its books at a different time than the U.S.-based companies to facilitate Mexican reporting requirements.

N O T E   Sharing services or not is ultimately a business decision. We decided to do this as part of the case company code in order to show the reengineering that occurs in the project and to be able to better demonstrate how to use more than one posting period variant, among other things.

You may have one local currency and up to two parallel currencies in the system. All documents are posted in both the local and parallel currencies. A hard currency is one type of parallel currency that can be used in the system. The configuration for hard currency is done at the country level. The CFO of Extreme Sports is not comfortable with the inflationary pressures on the peso, so we will set up U.S. dollars as the hard currency for Mexico to be used along with the local currency, pesos. To accomplish this, we'll need to follow the menu path Global Settings ➢ Set Countries ➢ Define Countries to reach the screen shown in Figure 2.20.

DEFINE COUNTRIES

You can set country definitions by using one of the following methods:

Menu Path: **Global Settings** ➤ **Set Countries** ➤ **Define Countries**

Transaction Code: **OY01**

FIGURE 2.20   The country configuration screen

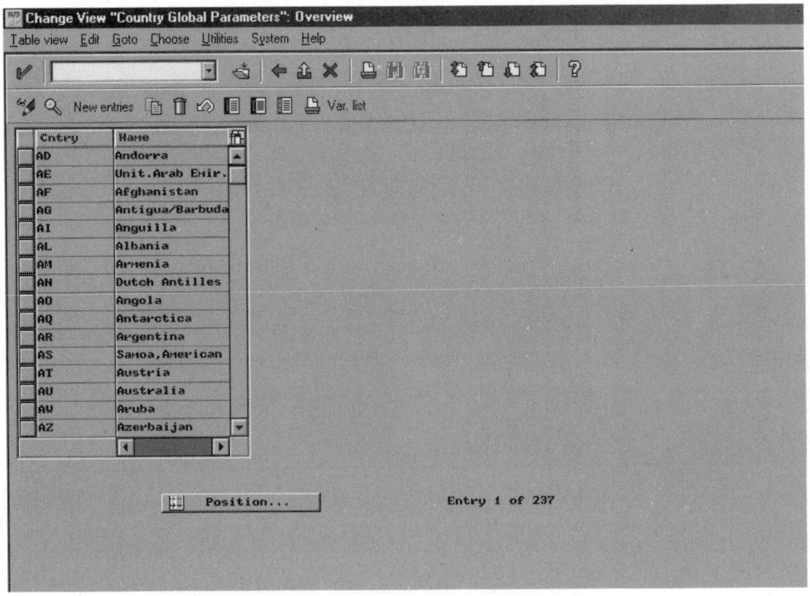

From this screen, select the country (MX). After selecting MX, you can either press Enter or double-click the entry. Next we are presented with the screen to identify the alternative country settings (as shown in Figure 2.21).

FIGURE 2.21 Selecting the alternative country settings

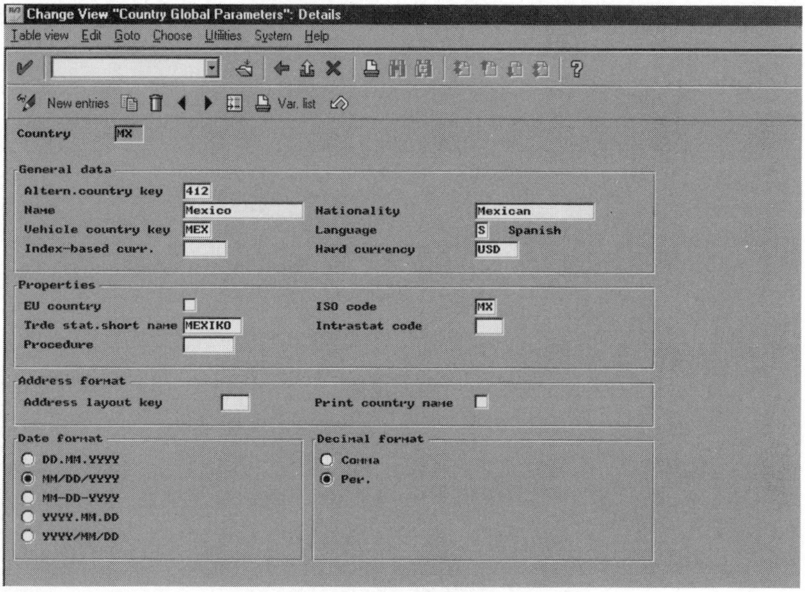

A definition of the field names that we will configure from this screen follows:

Hard Currency Enter the key of the currency you want to set as the hard currency for the country. Hard currencies are used in countries with high inflation to improve the value of transactions. When a hard currency is selected, the document is automatically updated in the local currency and the hard currency.

Index-Based Curr. Index currencies are used for statutory reporting in some countries with very high inflation. The way index currency valuation reporting works depends on the rules of each specific country. Enter the key of the currency that you want to set as the index currency, if applicable, for your country.

Date Format Enter your preference for a date format from the available options. When you are selecting this format, you may want to consider whether Europeans will be using this same database at some future time.

Decimal Format Select whether you would like decimals displayed using periods or commas. Again, you may want to consider whether Europeans will be using this same database at some future time.

Although you have configured for hard currency at the country level, the setting will not be fully activated until it is activated at the company code level. Let's activate the company code's hard currency configuration. To set the parallel currencies, follow the menu path Financial Accounting ➢ Financial Accounting Global Settings ➢ Company Code ➢ Parallel Currencies ➢ Define Additional Local Currencies.

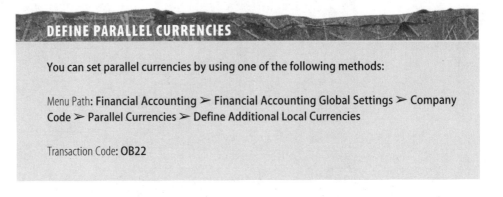

DEFINE PARALLEL CURRENCIES

You can set parallel currencies by using one of the following methods:

Menu Path: Financial Accounting ➢ Financial Accounting Global Settings ➢ Company Code ➢ Parallel Currencies ➢ Define Additional Local Currencies

Transaction Code: OB22

The parallel currencies configuration screen is presented in Figure 2.22.

FIGURE 2.22   Parallel currencies are set using the define additional local currencies screen.

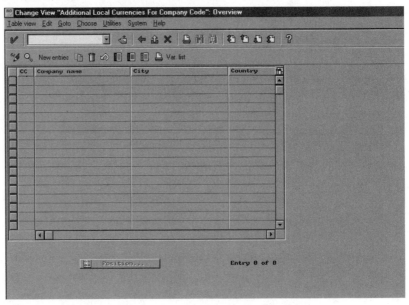

Click the New Entries button to create a new record for your configuration settings. The new entries configuration screen appears (Figure 2.23).

FIGURE 2.23 The new entries screen for configuring alternate local currencies

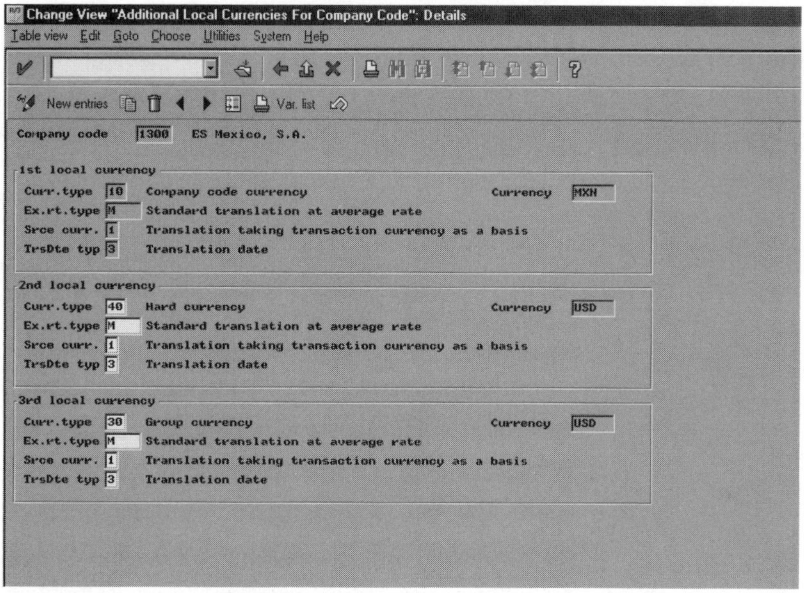

Let's look at this list of data entry fields:

Company Code Enter the four-digit identifier of the company code that you wish to configure.

1st Local Currency These fields will fill in automatically with default information based on the currency defined in the company code definition.

2nd and 3rd Local Currency As explained earlier, each company code can have two additional parallel currencies that can be used in conjunction with local currency defined for the company code.

Curr. Type The currency type field specifies which type of parallel currency you want to configure. The following options are available:

Group Currency Group currencies are defined at the client level in table T000. Group currencies are used to enable cross-company postings in controlling for company codes that use different company code currencies. This concept is explained in more detail in "Reconciliation Ledger" in Chapter 8.

Hard Currency Hard currencies are used for subsidiaries in countries with a lot of inflation. Hard currencies allow you to better valuate transactions in an inflationary economic environment.

Index-Based Currency   Index-based currencies are used for statutory reporting purposes for subsidiaries in some countries that have an extreme amount of inflation.

Global Company Currency   Global company currencies are used for legal consolidation within SAP. Many company codes can be linked to one company that has a global company currency.

Ex. Rt. Type   The exchange rate type determines how foreign currencies are revalued at the time of foreign currency revaluation and translation. The number of possible entries is too numerous to list here.

Srce Curr.   Enter the source currency that the foreign currency is to be translated against. The possible entries are as follows:

1:Translation Taking Transaction Currency as Basis   This option always tries to translate the parallel currency against the transaction currency of the document.

2:Translation Taking First Local Currency as Basis   This option always translates the parallel currency against the first local currency (company code currency).

TrsDte Typ   This setting is used to determine which date is used for foreign currency translations. The available options are as follows:

1:Document Date   Select this option if you want the translation calculation to use the exchange rate that was in effect on the day the document was dated.

2:Posting Date   Select this option if you want the translation calculation to use the exchange rate that was in effect on the posting date in the document.

3:Translation Date   Select this option if you want the translation calculation to use the exchange rate that is in effect on the date of the foreign currency translation.

EXTREME SPORTS INTERNATIONAL COMPANY CODE CONFIGURATION ANALYSIS: PART 2

Extreme Sports has decided to use a hard currency to help offset the inflationary pressures of its Mexican-based company code. U.S. dollars are used as the hard currency. The peso is the company code currency for the Mexican division. Extreme Sports has decided to use the transaction currency as the base currency for translation and to use the translation date to determine the proper exchange rate. Because we have company codes with different currencies using the same controlling area, we also configured a group currency of U.S. dollars for all company codes. The group currency will allow us to make cross-company code postings in the Controlling module. We will also need to make entries for all of the U.S. company codes to add the group currency to their records.

Business Areas

The function of business areas is to create balance sheets and Profit and Loss statements below the company code level. Some common uses of business areas are to produce divisional financial statements or SEC segment-level reporting. It is important to note that business area functionality can be duplicated using Profit Center Accounting. The decision to use or not to use business areas should be made early on in the design phase of your project. Many new projects are leaning away from business areas and toward profit centers, but ultimately, the decision is an individual project decision based on what fits in to the overall system design of the project implementation. Some of the deciding factors are the need to report on business lines across company codes, the need for full balance sheets at the divisional or business line level, as well as the cost and benefits of business areas versus profit centers. Profit Center Accounting will be explained in Chapter 12.

NOTE Business area functionality can be duplicated using Profit Center Accounting. Getting a full balance sheet in Profit Center Accounting is tricky but not impossible.

Business areas are independent of any other FI Enterprise Structure. Therefore, business areas are designed to cut across company codes. (For example, company code 1000 and company code 1100 are both allowed to post transactions to business area AES as is shown in the graphic explaining Extreme Sports in the case company background in this book's introduction.) A common mistake that some companies make is to try to force a one-to-one relationship between the business area and the company code. Having a one-to-one relationship defeats the entire purpose of business areas. The purpose of business areas is to be able to report on similar activities that occur across company codes. There is no residual benefit to configuring business areas in that manner. As a matter of fact, it often causes a lot of reconciliation problems because business areas are not linked to company codes in standard configuration. In the Extreme Sports example, more than one company code produces apparel. To report balance sheet and income statement information on the apparel business line, a business area for apparel will be configured (AES). Let's set up the business areas. First, follow the menu path Enterprise Structure ➢ Maintain Structure ➢ Financial Accounting ➢ Maintain Business Area to get to the screen you'll need.

DEFINE BUSINESS AREAS

You can use the following methods to maintain the business area:

Menu Path: **Enterprise Structure ➢ Maintain Structure ➢ Financial Accounting ➢ Maintain Business Area**

Transaction Code: **OX03**

The fields on the New Entries dialog box (Figure 2.24) are as follows:

Business Area   Enter the alphanumeric identifier of your business area (you can use up to four characters).

Description   Enter a description of the business area identifier just entered. The description can be up to 30 alphanumeric characters.

FIGURE 2.24   The New Entries dialog box for creating the configuration of a business area

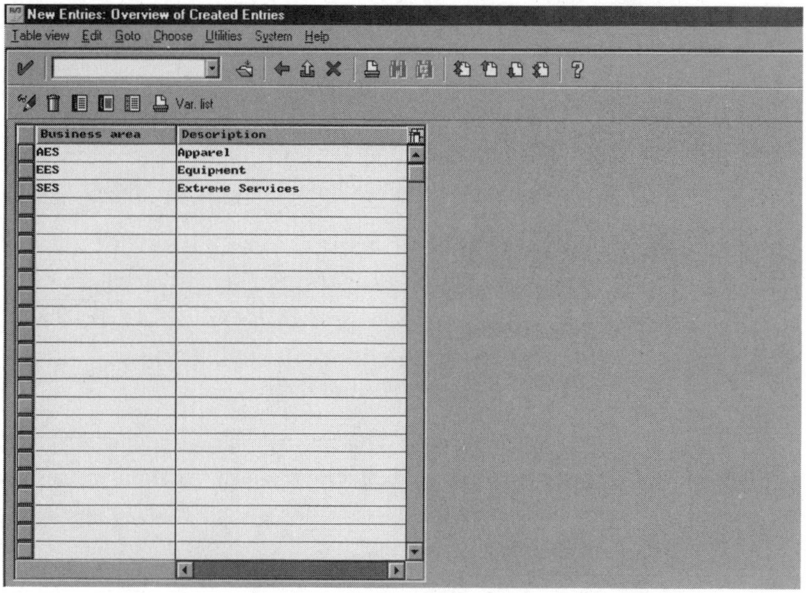

EXTREME SPORTS BUSINESS AREA CONFIGURATION ANALYSIS

Extreme Sports has decided to use three business areas. The CFO has determined that he would like a cross-company balance sheet for both the apparel and equipment industries in which Extreme Sports conducts business activity. In order to better track non-value-added administrative assets and expenses, the services business area was created. The new shared services department that provides centralized administration functions for the organization is being implemented as part of the business process reengineering effort portion of the SAP project implementation. It is important to remember that the idea is for all company codes to share all the business areas. The one exception is that the accounting department wants to ensure that postings from company code 1200 (ES Boats) are only posted to the equipment business area (EES) because this company code only produces equipment and not apparel. We will fulfill this business requirement through a validation of company codes, which will be the subject of the next section.

As you recall from the section "Company Code Configuration" earlier in this chapter, we enabled Business Area Balance Sheets as part of our company code configuration. These are the only settings that we need to make to utilize business areas. In Chapter 3, we'll cover how to set up field status variants to allow the Business Area field on document entry of business transactions in the system. Although business areas are not linked to any other FI Enterprise Structures, they can be linked to other organizational elements in the system, for example:

Plant/Valuation Area & Division   It is very useful to link a business area to a plant/valuation area and division because single plants usually only produce products for one business area (for example, a ball manufacturer would not be likely to also manufacture rock-climbing shoes). This ensures that postings are made to the correct business area.

Plant & Division   This setting is almost identical to the Plant/Valuation Area & Division setting. The decision to use valuation areas is made by your Materials Management (MM) team. You will use this setting when your MM team does not utilize valuation areas.

Sales Area   If your sales organizations are designed to sell a single grouping of products, it may make sense to link business areas to sales areas to ensure that your revenue postings are made to the correct business area.

Cost Centers   Depending on the design of the CO module, it may make sense to map business areas to cost centers. Cost centers are explained in detail in Chapter 9.

Assets   The Fixed Asset module captures fixed asset information. Once you enable the Business Area Balance Sheet indicator in the company code, Business Area becomes a required field in the fixed asset module regardless of how you configure the screen layout for asset classes.

Consolidation Business Areas   If you are utilizing the consolidation functionality of SAP, you can make several business areas into one consolidation business area for reporting purposes.

FI Validations

Validations are used to check settings and return a message if the prerequisite check condition is met. You can use validations to supplement existing SAP logic to fit your business needs. A validation is a valuable tool that can be used in many of the financial and controlling modules. In this section, we will configure an FI validation to fulfill our requirement of allowing postings from company code 1200 to be posted to only business area EES. To maintain the validation, follow the menu path Financial Accounting ➢ Special Purpose Ledger ➢ Tools ➢ Maintain Validation/Substitution/Rules ➢ Maintain Validation.

DEFINE VALIDATIONS

You can use the following methods to get to the validation configuration screen:

Menu Path: **Financial Accounting** ➢ **Special Purpose Ledger** ➢ **Tools** ➢ **Maintain Validation/Substitution/Rules** ➢ **Maintain Validation**

Transaction Code: **GGB0**

From the first validation configuration screen, presented in Figure 2.25, we will follow the next menu path, Validation ➢ Create. We are then taken to the Create Validation screen (shown in Figure 2.26).

FIGURE 2.25   The first validation configuration screen

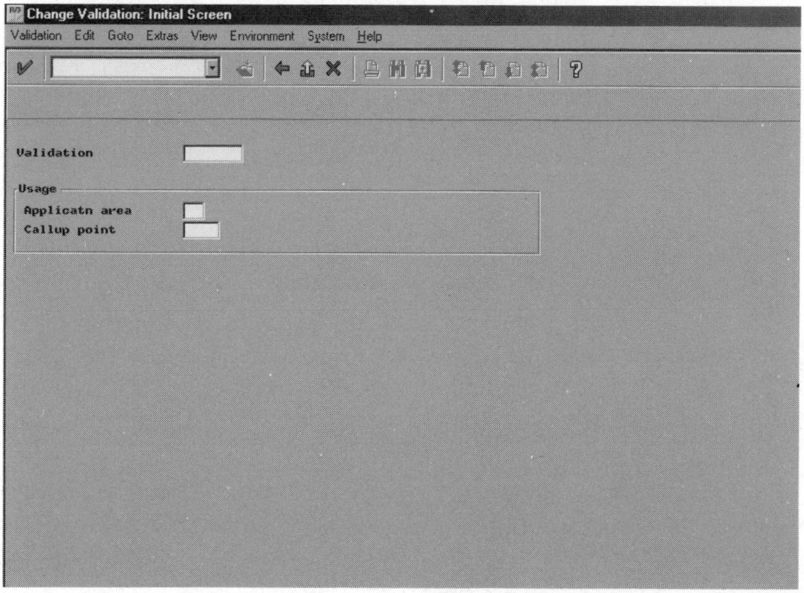

FIGURE 2.26   The Create Validation screen is used to create a validation configuration for business areas.

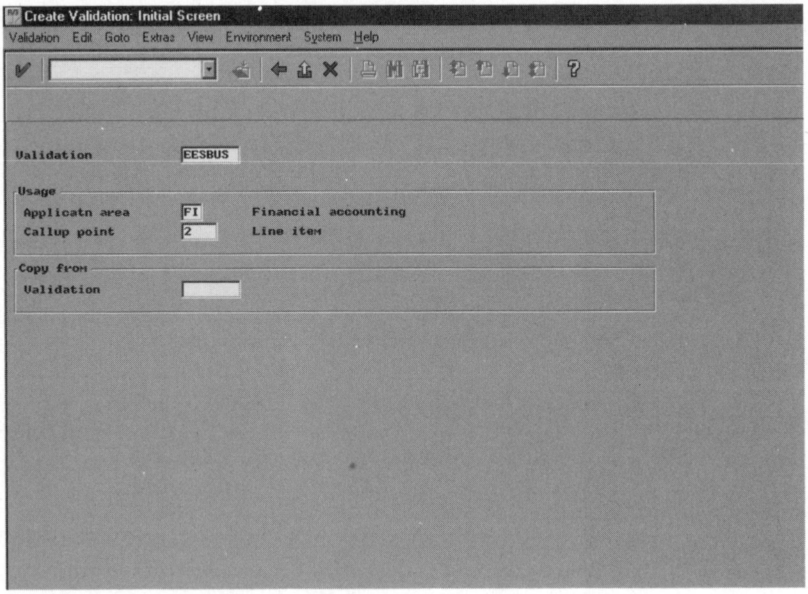

Let's look at the data entry fields:

Validation   Enter the name of the validation you wish to create. The entry can be up to seven characters in length and is alphanumeric.

Application Area   The application area is the module or submodule for which you wish to create the validation. The available options are as follows:

- ▸ AM: Asset Management

- ▸ CO: Controlling

- ▸ FI: Financial Accounting

- ▸ GL: Special Purpose Ledger

- ▸ JV: Joint Venture Accounting

- ▸ KC: Enterprise Controlling—SAP EIS (you can use only substitutions, not validations)

- ▸ LC: Legal Consolidation

- ▸ MC: Management Consolidation

- ▸ PS: Project System

Callup Point   Callup points determine when the validation is run. The callup points that are available are dependent upon the application area that is selected. For the FI application area, the following callup points are available:

▶ 0001 Document Header: Use this callup point to validate entries at the document header level. The entries that are usually available for validation at this point are stored in the BKPF table.

▶ 0002 Line Item: Use this callup point to check line item entries within a document. The entries that are usually available for validation at this point are stored in the BSEG table.

▶ 0003 Complete Document: This is also known as a matrix validation. This callup point checks settings for the document as a whole.

After pressing Enter (or clicking the green check mark), you are taken to the next configuration screen (Figure 2.27). On this screen, you will enter a description of your validation and define the steps that are to be carried out.

FIGURE 2.27   **The validation description screen**

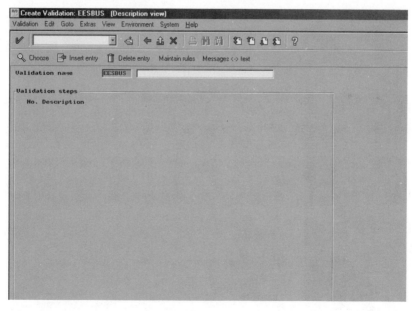

Enter the description of the validation and then click the Insert Entry button to add a step to the validation. Validation steps store the logic and message that the validation will carry out. The new validation step screen is displayed in Figure 2.28.

FIGURE 2.28   Entering a validation step into the business area description

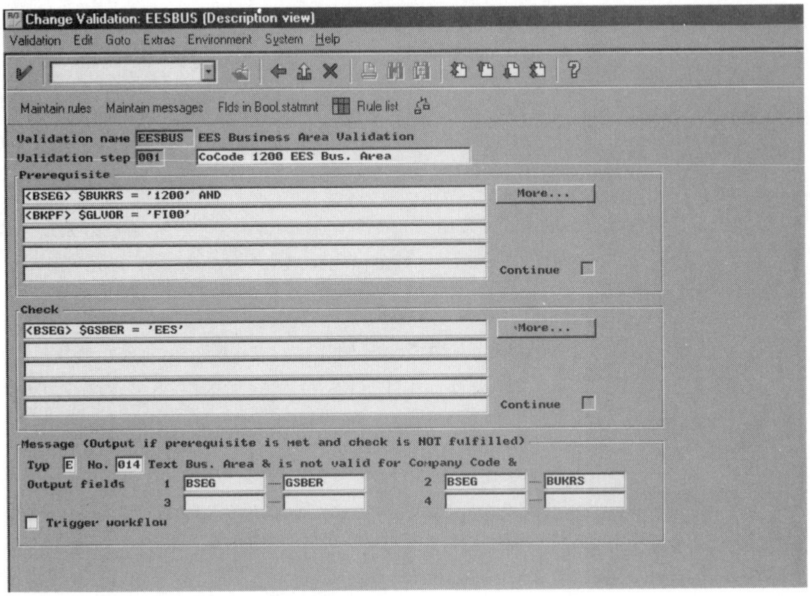

It is important to enter a description for each step next to the step number. These are the major sections of the validation steps and their descriptions:

Prerequisite   Before the validation step is executed, the *prerequisite* must first be met. Prerequisites use Boolean logic to verify that a condition exists. Click the Flds in Bool. Statmnt button to display and select the available fields to be used in your logic. The valid Boolean logic operators are =, >, <, and <>. The entry immediately following the Boolean statement must be put in single quotation marks (' ') unless a set is being used. Sets group together a number of entries. When you use sets, the system needs to match only one of the entries in the set. Sets are defined using Report Writer. The creation of sets will be covered later in this chapter. To link multiple logic steps together, either an AND or an OR is required at the end of each statement line.

Check   If the prerequisite is met, the *check* is carried out. The check also uses Boolean logic to check whether a particular system setting is made.

Message   A message is displayed if the prerequisite is met and the check is not fulfilled. A message can be defined as an Error (E), Warning (W), Cancel (A), or Information (I). You must also select the message to be displayed. You can also create a custom message. If a variable such as & or $ is used, you can specify the field contents to display for each variable. The variable number is determined by the order in which it appears in the message. Select the table name and field name for each variable you would like to populate.

Once you have completed your validation step configuration, make sure you run the check syntax function to see if your Boolean logic has any errors. The check syntax icon is the one that looks like a hanging scale with two monitors on it. You can also execute the menu path Validation ➤ Check. Once you have checked your validation step and there are no errors, click the green arrow to move back a screen to the validation description screen, as in Figure 2.27. Click the save icon to generate the ABAP code that runs your validation.

As you can see from Figure 2.28, we chose to have error message number 14 displayed if the check is not fulfilled. Let's walk through the configuration of custom error message 14. From the new validation step screen (shown in Figure 2.28), click the Maintain Messages button. You are then taken to the Maintain Message Class screen (Figure 2.29). Please note that the message class may be different in your system. You can set the validation program to go against any message class, but only one message class can be active at any one time. The message class stores all of the messages that can be used by validations in your system. Message class configuration will be explained in a later section of this chapter.

FIGURE 2.29   The Maintain Message Class screen

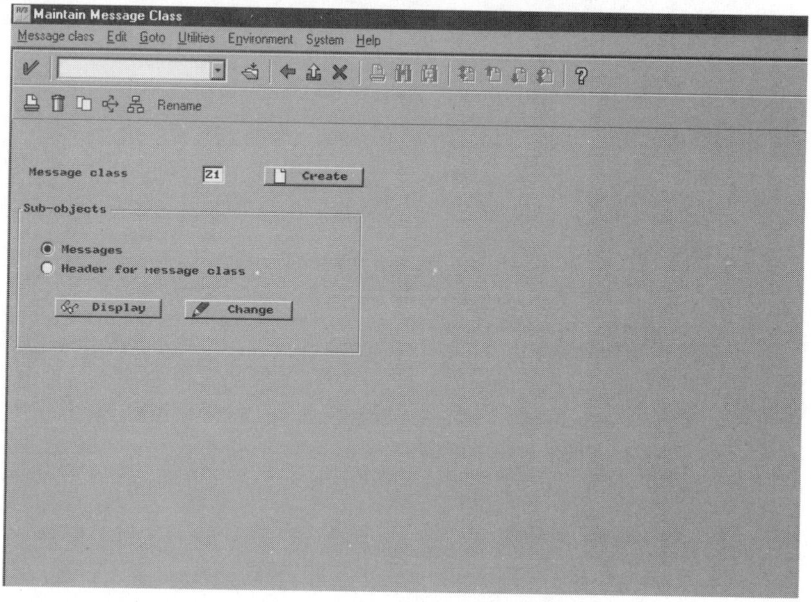

Now, click the Change button in the Sub-Objects section of this screen. This will allow you to add and customize any message you may need. The screen displayed after clicking the Change button (Figure 2.30) is where you'll customize message number 14.

FIGURE 2.30   The message customization screen

```
Maintain Messages: Class Z1
Messages  Edit  Goto  Utilities  System  Help

[✓] [            ▼] [⏎] [← ⬆ ✕] [🖺 🔍 🔍] [🔁 🔁 🔁 🔁] [?]

⌖ Individual maint.   Maintain all   Next free number   Next used   Compact display   Long text

Short text
Person responsiblQAH
Last changed by  QAH
Date             05/15/1999

Message number  [    ]                                     Self-explanator

000  Business Area & is not valid for Company Code & Please Use Bus. Area &    [
001                                                                            [
002                                                                            [
003                                                                            [
004                                                                            [
005                                                                            [
006                                                                            [
007                                                                            [
008                                                                            [
009                                                                            [
010                                                                            [
011                                                                            [
012                                                                            [
013                                                                            [
014  Bus. Area & is not valid for Company Code &                               [
015                                                                            [
016                                                                            [
017                                                                            [
018                                                                            [
019                                                                            [
020                                                                            [
021                                                                            [
022                                                                            [
023                                                                            [
024                                                                            [
025                                                                            [
026                                                                            [
027                                                                            [
028                                                                            [
029                                                                            [
```

EXTREME SPORTS FI VALIDATION CONFIGURATION ANALYSIS

As stated earlier, the accounting department of Extreme Sports has requested that company code 1200 (ES Boats) only be allowed to post the equipment business area (EES) because ES Boats is not involved in creating any apparel merchandise. We configured the prerequisite of the validation to see if the line item is for company code 1200 and if the activity that created the line item is from FI. The check section of our validation verifies that the posting is made to business area EES if the prerequisite is fulfilled. If the check is not true, then our custom message number 14 is displayed as an error that will stop the processing of the transaction.

Now that we have defined and generated the ABAP code for validation, we must now activate the validation. Let's walk through the configuration steps to activate our newly created validation. Get to the appropriate screen by following the menu path

Financial Accounting ➤ Financial Accounting Global Settings ➤ Document ➤ Line Item ➤ Define Validations for Posting.

ACTIVATE FI VALIDATIONS

You can use the following methods to get to the activate FI validations screen:

Menu Path: **Financial Accounting ➤ Financial Accounting Global Settings ➤ Document ➤ Line Item ➤ Define Validations for Posting**

Transaction Code: **OB28 or GGB4**

As is the case with most configuration screens, there are many different ways to get there. The IMG path and transaction code (OB28) take you specifically to the FI validation application area. Using transaction code GGB4, you can manage the activation of all validations in the system for any application area or callup point. Our configuration example will use the FI validation application area screen shown in Figure 2.31.

FIGURE 2.31   The activate FI validation screen

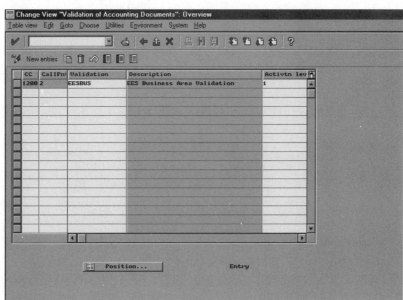

To set the validation for your application, enter values in the following fields:

CC   Enter the four-character identifier company code you want to activate your validation with. Only one validation can be active per company code per callup point. You can add additional steps to your validation in order to carry out more validations.

CallPnt   Enter the callup point you want your validation to be executed with. Callup points were explained in detail earlier in this section.

Validation   Enter the identifier of the validation you wish to activate.

Description   The Description field fills in automatically based on the validation you choose.

Activtn Level   Enter the activation level for the validation:

- ▶ 0: Not Active (validation will not execute)

- ▶ 1: Activated at all levels throughout the system

- ▶ 2: Activated at all levels throughout the system except for batch input

Functional Areas

Functional areas within the FI Enterprise Structure are used to organize your business for Cost of Sales (COS) accounting. Functional areas allow you to segregate and classify different types of costs within one expense account. This makes it possible, for example, to use a single labor account to determine what amount of labor is spent directly on production as opposed to sales or administration. It is possible to report on functional areas from both FI and Profit Center Accounting (functional area information is available in both FI and Profit Center Accounting).

Functional Area Organizational Elements

Let's set up the functional area organizational elements. As always, it is important to have clearly defined your requirements and thought of any existing or future requirements. To get to the maintenance screen for functional areas, follow the menu path Enterprise Structure ➢ Maintain Structure ➢ Definition ➢ Financial Accounting ➢ Maintain Functional Areas.

DEFINE FUNCTIONAL AREAS

You can get to the functional area configuration screen by one of the following methods:

Menu Path: **Enterprise Structure** ➢ **Maintain Structure** ➢ **Definition** ➢ **Financial Accounting** ➢ **Maintain Functional Areas**

Transaction Code: **OKBD**

The functional area configuration screen is presented in Figure 2.32.

FIGURE 2.32   The configuration screen for the functional areas

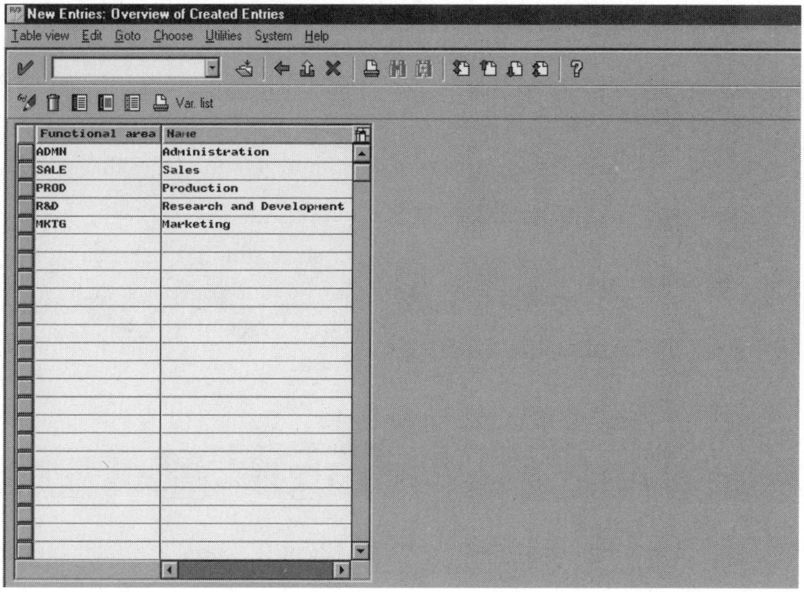

The fields on this screen are as follows:

Functional Area   Enter the four-character alphanumeric identifier for your functional area.

Name   Enter a descriptive name for your functional area. This entry is alphanumeric and can be up to 25 characters long.

EXTREME SPORTS FUNCTIONAL AREA CONFIGURATION ANALYSIS: PART 1

Extreme Sports has determined that it requires five functional areas to classify Cost of Sales accounting. The functional areas are Administration, Sales, Production, Research & Development, and Marketing. By using these functional areas, Extreme Sports will be able to report on an individual expense account using these five categories. Our next piece of configuration will be to enable SAP to populate our postings with functional areas.

Functional Area Substitution

In order to populate your postings with functional areas, you must set up a *substitution*. Substitutions are similar to validations, which were discussed in the "FI Validations" earlier in this chapter. Unlike validations that create on-screen messages to the user, substitutions actually replace and fill in field values behind the scenes without the user's knowledge. Similar to validations, substitutions can be set up for a number of different application areas and callup points. Substitutions are activated on the company code level, so it is important to ensure that you have followed all steps for each company code.

Let's set up a functional area substitution. The menu path and transaction codes are very similar to those used for validations. Follow the menu path Financial Accounting ≻ Special Purpose Ledger ≻ Tools ≻ Maintain Validation/Substitution/ Rules ≻ Maintain Substitution.

DEFINE SUBSTITUTIONS

You can use the following methods to set up the functional area substitution:

Menu Path: **Financial Accounting** ≻ **Special Purpose Ledger** ≻ **Tools** ≻ **Maintain Validation/Substitution/Rules** ≻ **Maintain Substitution**

Transaction Code: **GGB1**

The first substitution configuration screen is shown in Figure 2.33.

FIGURE 2.33   The first substitution configuration screen

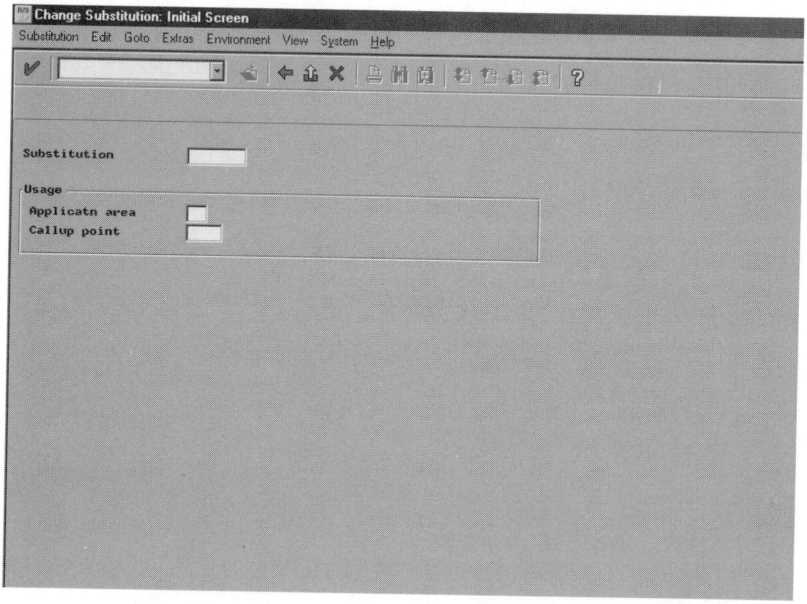

From here, execute the menu path Substitution ➤ Create. You'll be taken to the
screen shown in Figure 2.34.

FIGURE 2.34   The Create Substitution screen

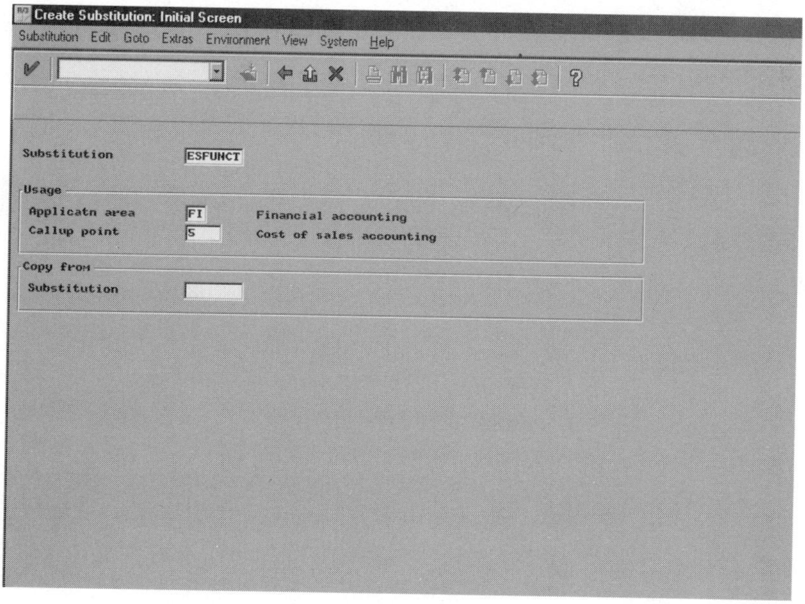

Here are the fields on the Create Substitution screen:

Substitution   Enter the seven-character alphanumeric identifier for your substitution. The identifier can be anything you want it to be.

Application Area   Enter the appropriate area. The application area is the module or submodule that you wish to create the substitution for. The available options are as follows:

AM: Asset Management

CO: Controlling

FI: Financial Accounting

GL: Special Ledger

JV: Joint Venture Accounting

KC: Enterprise Controlling—SAP EIS

PC: Profit Center Accounting

PS: Project Systems

Callup Point   Enter the appropriate callup point. Callup points determine when the substitution is run. The available callup points are dependent upon the application area that is selected. For the FI application area, the following callup points are available:

0001 Document Header: Use this callup point to substitute entries at the document header level. The entries that are usually available for substitution at this point are stored in the BKPF table.

0002 Line Item: Use this callup point to substitute line item entries within a document. The entries that are usually available for substitution at this point are stored in the BSEG table.

0003 Complete Document: This callup point substitutes settings for the document as a whole. This activity is also known as a matrix substitution.

0005 Cost of Sales Accounting: This callup point is used for functional area substitutions

After pressing Enter (or clicking the green check mark), you are taken to the next configuration screen (Figure 2.35). On this screen, you will enter a description of your substitution and define the steps that are to be carried out.

FIGURE 2.35   The blank substitution description screen

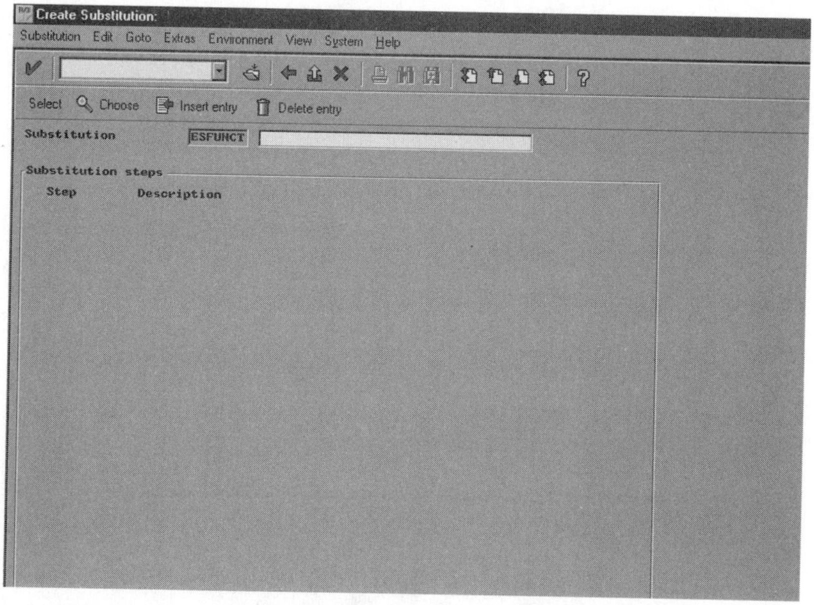

After entering the description of your substitution, click the Insert Entry button to add a step to your substitution. Substitution steps store the logic and field contents that the substitution will use. When you click the Insert Entry button, the dialog box shown in Figure 2.36 appears.

FIGURE 2.36   The Fields for Substitution dialog box

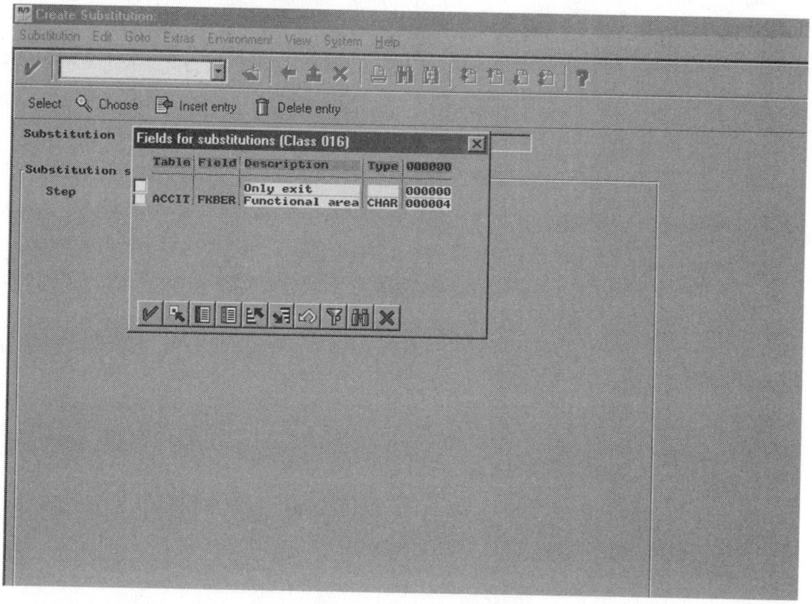

In the Fields for Substitution dialog box, either select the field you wish to substitute or specify that you are going to carry out a user-exit. In this example, we are going to substitute the field ACCIT-FKBER (functional area). Once you have selected this option, you are presented with the substitution prerequisite configuration screen, shown in Figure 2.37.

FIGURE 2.37   The substitution prerequisite configuration screen

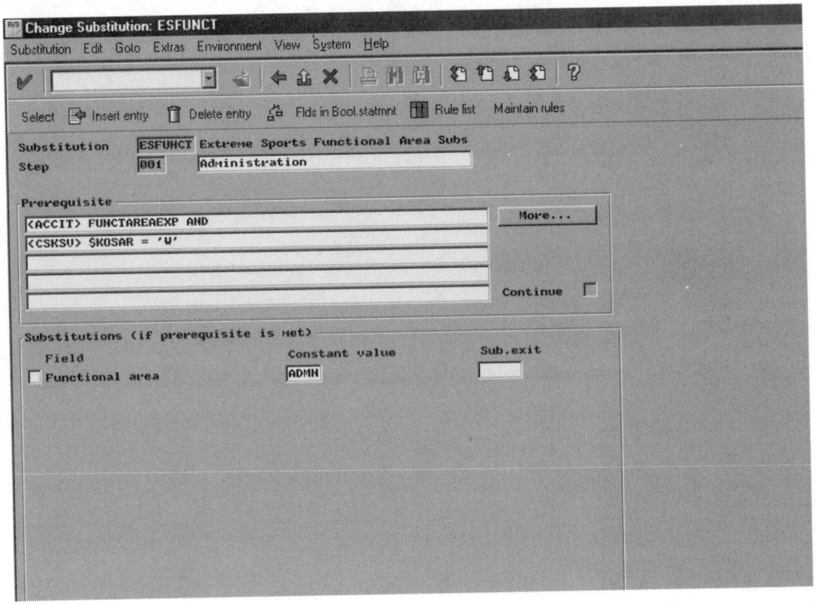

It is important to enter a description for your step next to the step number. The major sections of the substitution steps are as follows:

Prerequisite   The prerequisite uses Boolean logic to determine if a condition is true. If the condition is true, the substitution is carried out. If it the condition is not true, no further processing occurs. Click the Flds in Bool. Statmnt button to display and select the available fields to use in your logic. The valid Boolean logic operators are =, >, <, and <>. The entry immediately following the Boolean statement must be put in singe quotation marks (' ') unless a set is being used. Sets group together of a number of entries. When you use sets, the system needs to match only one of the entries in the set for the prerequisite to be true. Sets are defined using Report Writer. The creation of sets will be covered later in this section. To link multiple logic steps together, either an AND or an OR is required at the end of each statement line.

Substitutions   The Substitutions section is where you tell the system what values to replace. You have the option of either using constant values or using a user-exit to specify values or carry out other logic statements. As you can see from the screen in Figure 2.37, your substituted field (functional area) is automatically displayed.

> **WARNING**   Within validations and substitutions, some of the logic is case sensitive. Be sure to type in your logic using ALL CAPS. The syntax check will not tell you that you have an error if it's in lowercase.

Once you have completed your substitution step configuration, make sure you run the check syntax function to see if your Boolean logic has any errors. The check syntax button is the one at the top of the screen that looks like a hanging scale with two monitors on it. You can also follow the menu path Substitution ➢ Check. Once you have checked your substitution step and there are no errors, click the green arrow to move back a screen to the substitution description screen, as shown in Figure 2.35. Click the save icon to generate the ABAP code to run your substitution. You will soon create additional entries from this screen to populate your other functional areas. The only differences in the new steps will be the cost center category (<CSKSV> $KOSAR) that is mapped to the remaining functional areas.

As you can see from the completed configuration screen shown in Figure 2.37, we used a *set* in order to specify a range of G/L account numbers. Sets simply hold a number of values for a characteristic (field). Sets are used in the same way that arrays are used in standard programming. Although there are several types of sets, we will cover only the simplest, the basic set. A basic set contains several values for a single characteristic (field). To create a set, follow the menu path of your application (not the IMG) Information Systems ➢ Ad Hoc Reports ➢ Report Painter ➢ Report Writer ➢ Set ➢ Create.

CREATE SETS

You can create a set by following one of these methods:

Application Menu Path: Information Systems ➢ Ad Hoc Reports ➢ Report Painter ➢ Report Writer ➢ Set ➢ Create

Transaction Code: GS01

As you can see from the menu path, you will not be using the IMG to create sets. You will use the application menu path to take you to the Report Writer tool. The initial screen for set configuration is presented in Figure 2.38.

FIGURE 2.38   **The Report Writer tool for creating a set**

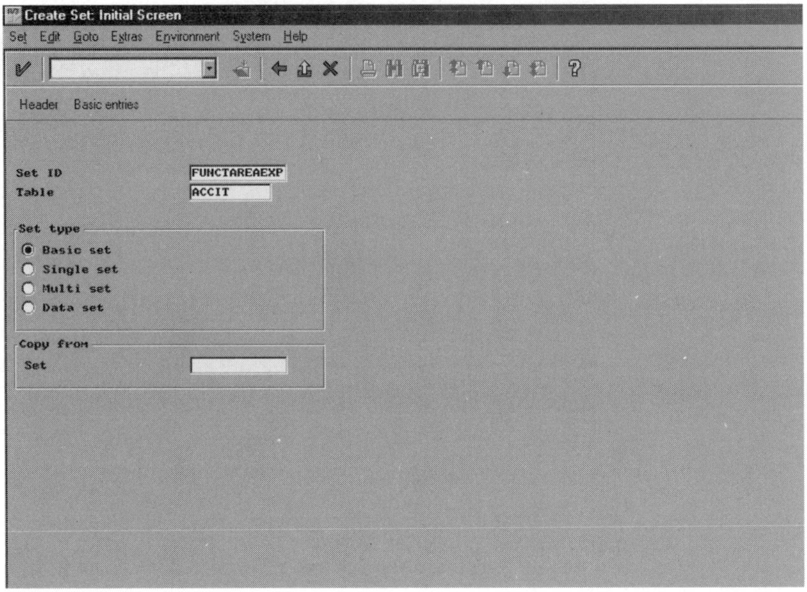

Follow these steps to create a set:

1. Enter the 12-character alphanumeric identifier of your set in the Set ID box. This is the set name that you will refer to when using the set.

2. Enter the name of the table that contains the field you want to create the set for in the Table box. This field and others like it appear in many different tables. It is important to know which table is being used at the time you are using the set. For example, we are creating a set for the field HKONT (G/L account number). HKONT appears in BSEG, COBL, ACCIT, and many other tables. As you already know from selecting the field to substitute earlier, table ACCIT is being read in our substitution, and we will use this table to create our set.

Once you press Enter or click the green check mark, you are presented with the pop-up box shown in Figure 2.39, which guides you through selecting the appropriate field for the set. You can use the drop-down arrow and select from the existing tables, or if you know the field name, you can type it in.

FIGURE 2.39   The Create Set screen

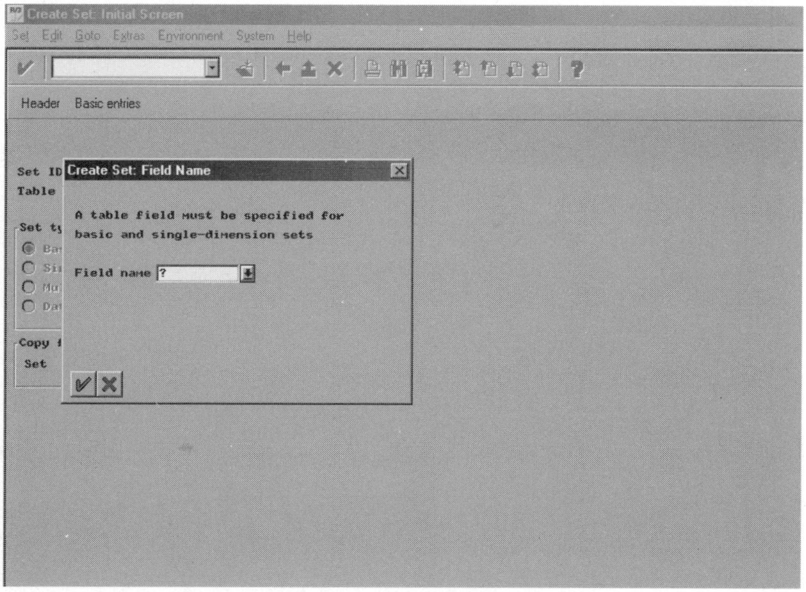

Once you have selected your field name (HKONT) and clicked the green check mark, you are presented with the next configuration screen, shown in Figure 2.40.

FIGURE 2.40   Naming the set field

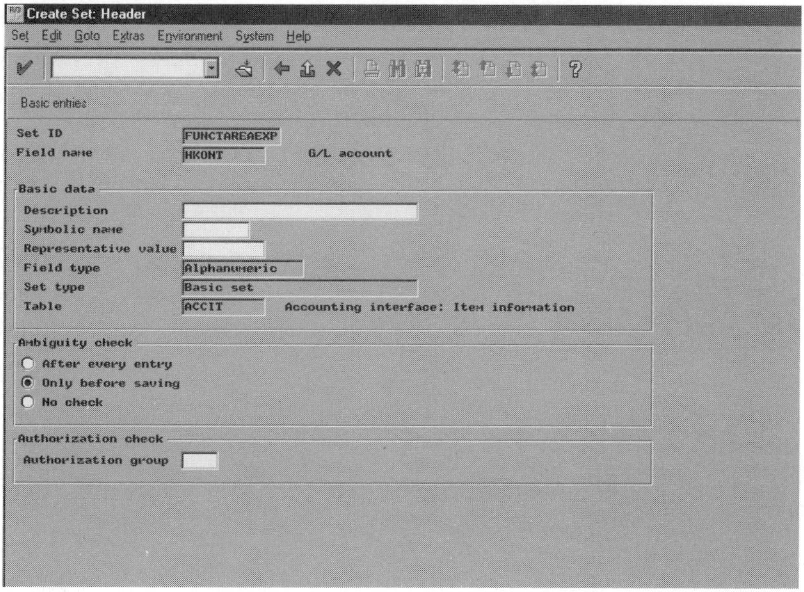

Enter a name in the description field to identify your set. Once you have entered the description, click the Basic Entries button to select the values you wish to include in your set. You are taken to the configuration screen that allows you to set the field's parameters, as shown in Figure 2.41. The screen in Figure 2.41 has already been filled in with the values we would like included in our set.

FIGURE 2.41   The set values screen

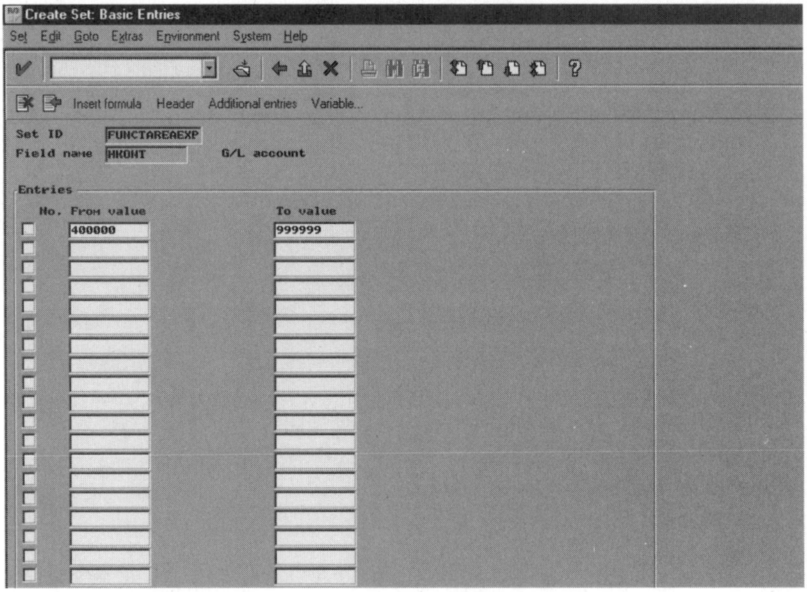

EXTREME SPORTS FUNCTIONAL AREA CONFIGURATION ANALYSIS: PART 2

Extreme Sports has decided to use five different functional areas to analyze individual expense accounts:

Administration

Sales

Production

Research & Development

Marketing

EXTREME SPORTS FUNCTIONAL AREA CONFIGURATION ANALYSIS: PART 2 (CONTINUED)

Extreme Sports will be utilizing cost centers to capture all of its expenses. Because it is using cost centers, we will use an attribute of cost center (cost center type) to populate our functional area on postings. You can use other fields in your substitution, but cost center type makes the most sense for Extreme Sports. A detailed explanation of cost centers will be given in Chapter 9. In the configured substitution, we created and used a set of all expense G/L accounts and the cost center type field (CSKSV-KOSAR). Although only one substitution step was shown, a separate step for each functional area was configured. A mapping of cost center type to functional location follows:

COST CENTER TYPE	FUNCTIONAL AREAS
W: Administration	ADMN
M: Marketing	MKTG
F: Production	PROD
R: R&D	R&D
V: Sales	SALE

Although you have created your substitution and generated the code for your substitution steps, you must still activate the substitution for your company codes. We will activate the same substitution for all of the Extreme Sports company codes. To activate the codes, follow the menu path Financial Accounting ➢ Financial Accounting Global Settings ➢ Company Code ➢ Prepare Cost of Sales Accounting.

ACTIVATE FUNCTIONAL AREA SUBSTITUTION

You can activate the functional area substitution by using one of the following methods:

Menu Path: **Financial Accounting ➢ Financial Accounting Global Settings ➢ Company Code ➢ Prepare Cost of Sales Accounting**

Transaction Code: **OBBZ**

As is the case with most configuration screens, there are many different ways to get there. The IMG path and transaction code (OBBZ) take you specifically to the FI substitution application area for the Cost of Sales accounting callup point. Using transaction code GGB4, you can manage the activation of all substitutions in the system for any application area or callup point. The following configuration example will use the IMG Path (transaction code OBBZ). The screen you'll use to configure the activation is presented in Figure 2.42.

FIGURE 2.42   The configuration screen for the substitution activation

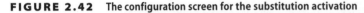

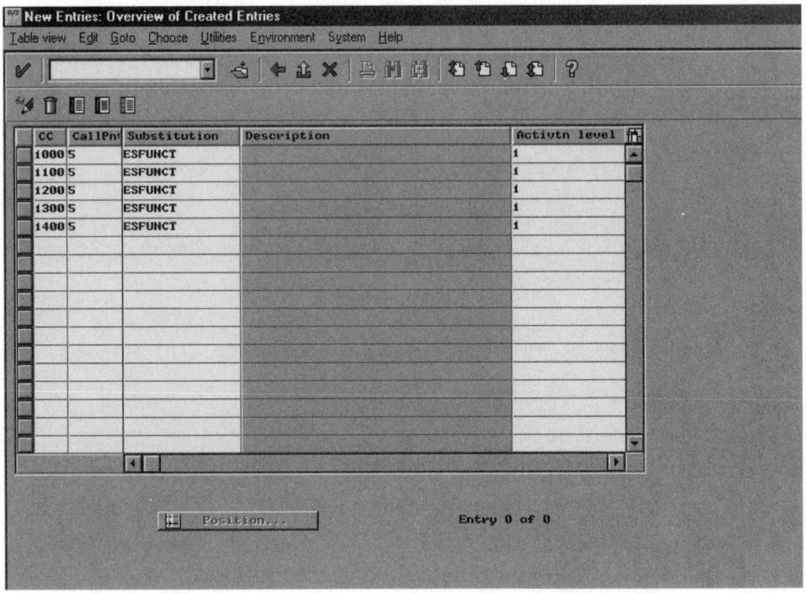

To set the configuration for activating the functional area substitution for the company code, follow these steps:

1. Enter the four-character identifier for the company code (CC) for which you want to activate the substitution. As with validations, you can only have one substitution active per company code per callup point.

2. Enter the callup point (CallPnt) at which you want your substitution to be executed. Callup points were explained in detail earlier in this chapter.

3. Enter the identifier of the substitution that you wish to activate.

4. The description field fills in automatically based on the substitution that you choose.

5. Enter the activation level (Activtn Level) for which you would like to activate the validation. There are three codes to simplify your entry:

0: Not Active (validation will not execute)

1: Activated at all levels throughout the system

2: Activated at all levels throughout the system except for batch input

Advanced Validation and Substitution Configuration

In the previous two sections, we configured an example of both a validation and a substitution. In this next section, you will build upon that knowledge to learn about advanced topics in the configuration of *validations* and *substitutions*.

Validations

The basics of validation were explained earlier in the chapter. You will now learn more about the specific method of adding a message class to your validations.

Message Classes

When you set up your first validation in the system, you will be prompted to provide a message class to be used by all validations. A custom message class should be used. That is, you should create a new message class with a prefix of *Z* to denote a customer-maintained class. To create a new message class, click the Maintain Messages button, as shown in Figure 2.28. You are then taken to the screen shown in Figure 2.29. From this screen, enter a new digit identifier for your message class and click the Create button that is located next to the message class identifier. When new system objects are created, usually only the *Z* and *Y* prefixes are available; all other prefixes are reserved by SAP. If you need to change message classes in the future, from the first validation configuration screen (Figure 2.25), follow the menu path Environment ➤ Change Message Class. Remember, only one message class can be used by all validations in the system.

Substitutions

The basics of substitutions were explained earlier in the chapter. You will now learn more about setting the user-exit program feature of substitutions.

Setting the User-Exit Program

In addition to substituting fixed values, a substitution can call a user-exit to substitute the field or carry out another piece of logic. The substitution user-exits are stored in a form pool (a type of ABAP program). All substitutions use the same ABAP program to store their user-exits. SAP comes delivered with a form pool to be used for the substitution user-exit. You will need to copy this program and give it a name beginning with a *Z* or a *Y* to denote a customer-maintained object. A single user-exit can be called in more than one substitution or substitution step. To get to configuration screen for linking programs to substitutions that you need for this activity, follow the menu path Financial Accounting ➤ Special Purpose Ledger ➤ Basic Settings ➤ User Exits ➤ Maintain Client Dependent User Exits.

LINK PROGRAMS TO SUBSTITUTIONS

You can get to the configuration screen for linking programs to substitutions by using one of the following methods:

Menu Path: **Financial Accounting ➤ Special Purpose Ledger ➤ Basic Settings ➤ User Exits ➤ Maintain Client Dependent User Exits**

Transaction Code: **GCX2**

The configuration screen for linking programs to substitutions is presented in Figure 2.43.

As you can see, application area GBLS is used for our validation and substitution user-exits. When your system is delivered, the exit program provided is named RG******. Do not modify this program or use it for your user-exit. Make a copy of it and put it in the customer name range (Z*******). You will probably need to enlist the help of one of your ABAP teammates in order to copy the program. The ABAPer is also usually responsible for coding the exits that are placed in the program.

FIGURE 2.43   The substitution linking screen

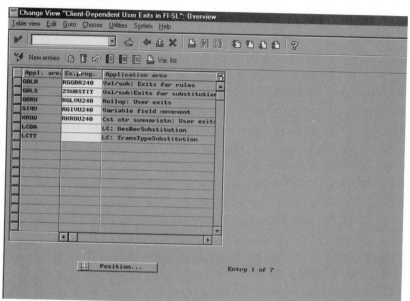

Validations and Substitutions

The advanced features that relate to both validations and substitutions will be explained in this section.

Adding or Deleting Fields to the Boolean Class and Substituted Field List

As you use validations and substitutions, you may find that you want to add a field to be used in Boolean logic or substitution, or you may want to prevent a field from being used. Table GB01 contains a listing of all fields that are currently allowed or disallowed in validations and substitutions. Use the databrowser (transaction code SE16) to display the contents of table GB01. The contents of table GB01 are shown in Figure 2.44.

FIGURE 2.44 The validation and substitution field availability listing

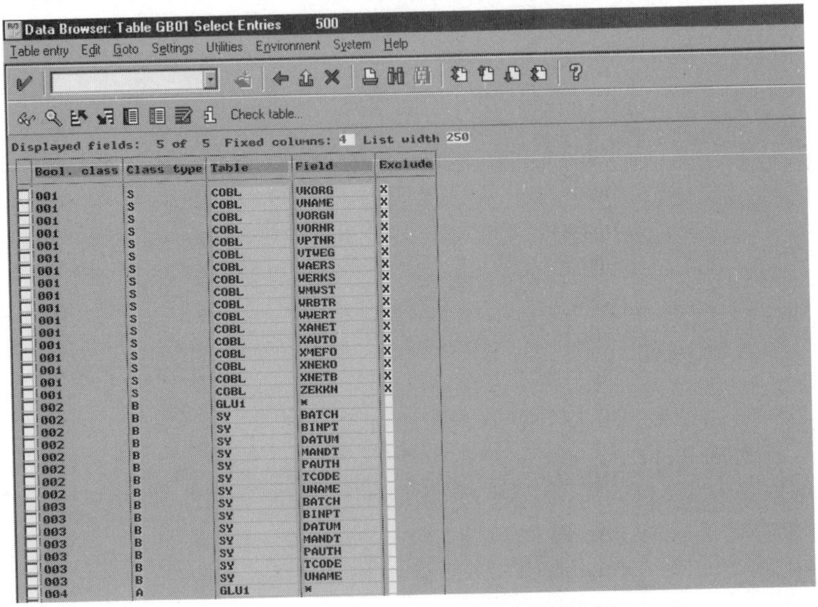

Bool. class	Class type	Table	Field	Exclude
001	S	COBL	VKORG	X
001	S	COBL	VNAME	X
001	S	COBL	VORGN	X
001	S	COBL	VORNR	X
001	S	COBL	VPTNR	X
001	S	COBL	VTWEG	X
001	S	COBL	WAERS	X
001	S	COBL	WERKS	X
001	S	COBL	WMWST	X
001	S	COBL	WRBTR	X
001	S	COBL	WWERT	X
001	S	COBL	XANET	X
001	S	COBL	XAUTO	X
001	S	COBL	XMEFO	X
001	S	COBL	XNEKO	X
001	S	COBL	XNETB	X
001	S	COBL	ZEKKN	X
002	B	GLU1	*	
002	B	SY	BATCH	
002	B	SY	BINPT	
002	B	SY	DATUM	
002	B	SY	MANDT	
002	B	SY	PAUTH	
002	B	SY	TCODE	
002	B	SY	UNAME	
003	B	SY	BATCH	
003	B	SY	BINPT	
003	B	SY	DATUM	
003	B	SY	MANDT	
003	B	SY	PAUTH	
003	B	SY	TCODE	
003	B	SY	UNAME	
004	A	GLU1	*	

An explanation of the fields in table GB01 and their contents follows:

Bool. Class The Boolean class specifies where the field is being used or is excluded. Boolean classes map roughly to the combination of application area and callup point. Here is a partial listing of Boolean classes:

1: Coding Block Used for CO line items

8: Document Header Used for FI items

9: Document Header and Line Item Used for FI items

16: Cost of Sales Accounting Used for functional areas

100: Document Header Used for CO items

Class Type A Class type refers to whether a field is used in Boolean statements, substitution fields, or both. Here's a listing of them:

B Used for fields that are to be used in Boolean statements

S Used for fields that are to be used for substitution

A Used for fields that can be used in both Boolean statements and for substitution

Table The name of the table in which the field you wish to use or exclude resides.

Field   The name of the field you wish to use or exclude.

Exclude   If this field is checked, the field is excluded for use for the class type specified in the record. If this indicator is set, you can not change it, and you can not add the field in the configuration table that adds or excludes fields.

If the field you wish to add is not excluded in GB01, you can add it to the available fields for substitutions. You can maintain view V_GB01C using the table maintenance transaction SM30. You add fields using view V_GB01C. You can only add fields if they are already defined in table GB01 for the Boolean class into which you wish to add the field. The fields in V_GB01C are exactly the same as the fields in table GB01. The only trick is to remember to click the New Entries button. You must click the New Entries button because the entry for the field to be added does not exist in view V_GB01C until you create it.

Testing the Validation or Substitution

SAP provides two special functions to test your validation or substitution. The first function is the Simulate action. To simulate the validation or substitution, you will need to go to the change validation or the change substitution screen (transaction codes GGB0 and GGB1, respectively). From either screen, follow the appropriate menu path, either Validation ➣ Simulate or Substitution ➣ Simulate. A new screen appears as shown in Figure 2.45.

FIGURE 2.45   The simulation screen

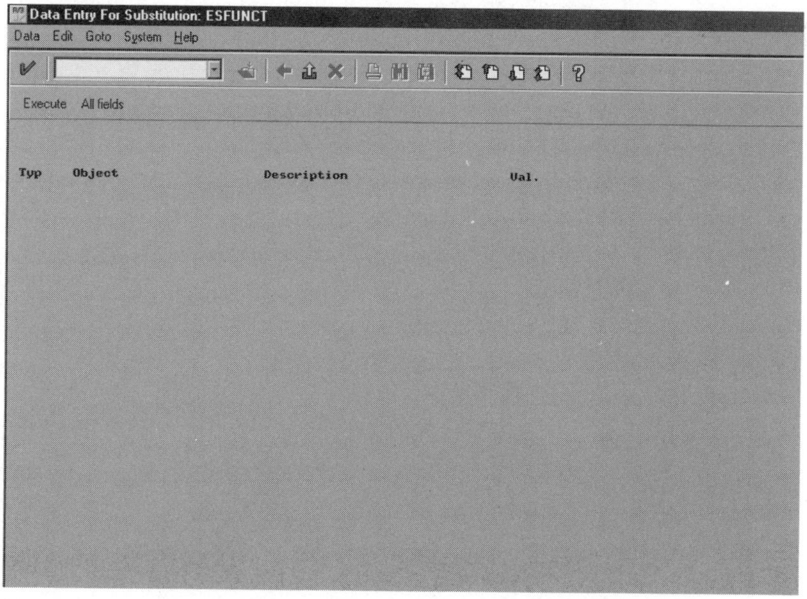

Click the All Fields button at the top of the simulation screen (you can see it in Figure 2.45). You are then presented with an entry screen for all possible fields that your substitution or validation can use. Enter the data you wish to test. Once all the data is entered, click the Execute button. You will then be presented with analysis of how your validation or substitution would act during an actual transaction. The fields that will be displayed will correspond to the substitution or validation based on the application area of the substitution or validation. For example, a substitution that is created for FI line items will display all the fields that are normally available when FI transactions are entered as long as they are available to the substitution.

The second function that can be used to test your validation or substitution is the trace function. Tracing shows the results of your substitution or validation as you are entering actual transactions in the system. This function should only be used in the development environment. To invoke this function, go to the first substitution configuration screen or the first validation configuration screen (transaction codes GGB1 and GGB0 respectively). Enter the name of your substitution or validation and press Enter. You are then taken to the configuration screen where you add new steps or change existing steps in your substitution or validation. From this screen, follow the menu path Extras ➢ Switch On Trace. Once you have tested your validation or substitutions, go back to the configuration screen and follow the menu path Extras ➢ Switch Off Trace.

Transporting Validations and Substitutions

Even when automatic recording of transports is turned on, a transport request for validations and substitutions is not created automatically. You must create the transport by hand. To create the transport, you need to go to the first validation configuration screen or the first substitution configuration screen (transaction codes GGB0 and GGB1 respectively). From this screen, enter the name of the validation or substitution that you wish to transport and then follow the appropriate menu path, either Validation ➢ Transport or Substitution ➢ Transport. You are then presented with the Transport screen for substitutions and validations (Figure 2.46).

FIGURE 2.46   The Transport screen for validations and substitutions

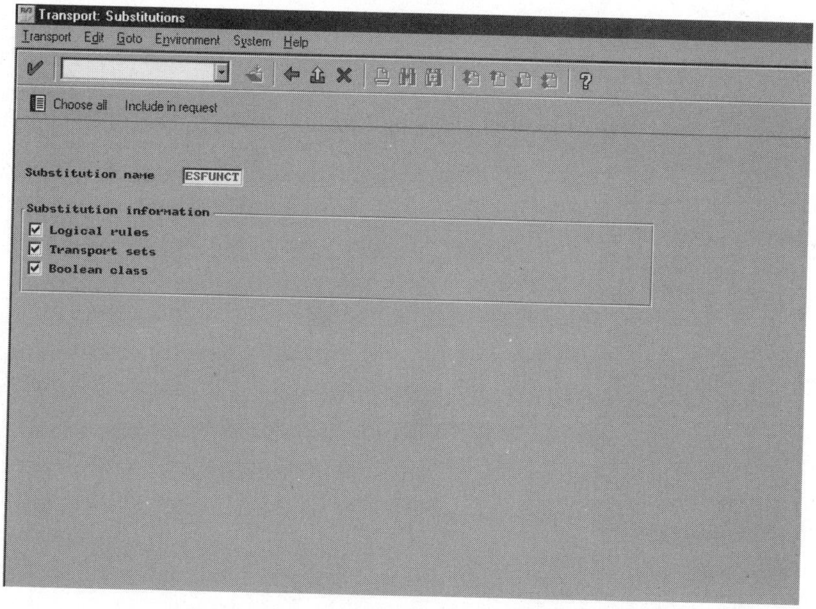

Make sure you select all three options: Logical Rules, Transport Sets, and Boolean Class. Selecting all three options ensures that your entire substitution or validation will be transported. If you don't select all three options, you are in peril of not transporting all of the logic, sets, or Boolean fields that are used in your validation or substitution. Without all three of these elements, your validation or substitution won't work properly. Once you have selected the three options, click the Include in Request button. You will then be presented with the normal transport screen.

Once you have transported your substitution or validation to the target client, you must run a special program in that client to generate the ABAP code and activate the sets. The name of the program is RGUGBR00; it is also affectionately known as the RugBurner program. You will run the program using transaction code SA38. After you click the execute icon in SA38, you are presented with the program settings screen for RGUGBR00 (Figure 2.47). The screen shown in Figure 2.47 has already been filled in with the appropriate settings. Once you have made all the settings, click the execute icon to generate the ABAP code that runs your substitution or validation and to create the sets used by your substitution.

FIGURE 2.47 The RGUGBR00 program settings (the RugBurner program)

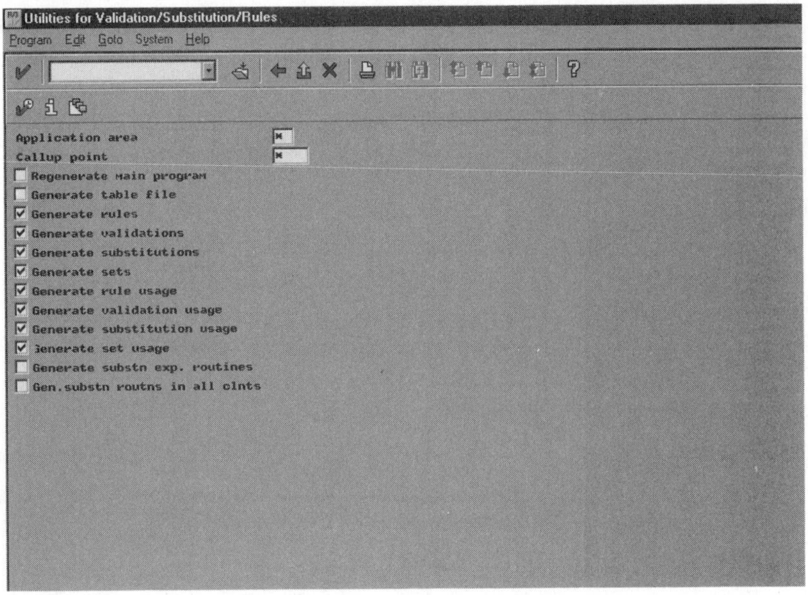

Sales and Use Tax

Settings for *sales* and *use taxes* are made at the country level in SAP. There are standard taxing procedures defined in the R/3 System for many countries. You can also create your own taxing procedure if you want, although this is not recommended. In this section, you will concentrate on U.S. sales and use tax procedures and settings. There are two basic U.S. tax procedures: TAXUSJ and TAXUSX. In TAXUSJ, you create and maintain the tax percentage rates for each taxing jurisdiction by hand. Procedure TAXUSX utilizes a third-party tax system to maintain tax rates in the system. We will cover the basic configuration of TAXUSJ in this section.

The first setting you need to make is assigning a tax procedure to your company's country. In the example that follows, we have already assigned the procedure TAXUSJ to country US. Assign the country by following the menu path Financial Accounting ➢ Financial Accounting Global Settings ➢ Tax on Sales/Purchases ➢ Assign Country to Calculation Procedure.

The assign country to calculation procedure configuration screen is presented in Figure 2.48.

ASSIGN COUNTRY TO TAX CALCULATION PROCEDURE

You can get to the country assignment page by using one of the following methods:

Menu Path: **Financial Accounting** ➢ Financial Accounting Global Settings ➢ Tax on Sales/Purchases ➢ Assign Country to Calculation Procedure

Transaction Code: **OBBG**

FIGURE 2.48 The assign country to calculation procedure configuration screen

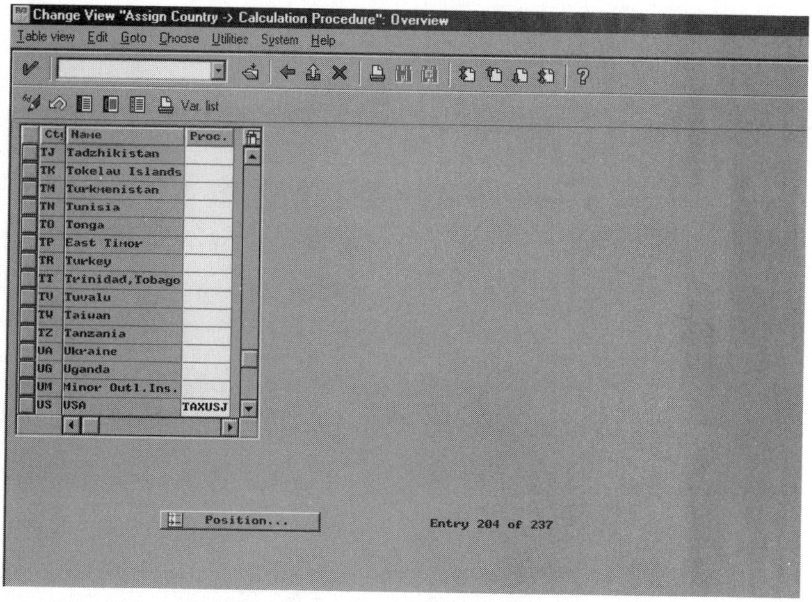

The next step is to set up the structure for the tax jurisdiction codes. The tax jurisdiction codes represent the different taxing authorities to which you submit payments. You can have up to four levels representing State, County, City, and Other in your tax jurisdiction structure. Normally, the tax jurisdiction structure is set up with three levels (Other is for special circumstances). We will now set up our tax jurisdiction structure. First, follow the menu path Financial Accounting ➢ Financial Accounting Global Settings ➢ Tax on Sales/Purchases ➢ Basic Settings ➢ Specify Structure for Tax Jurisdiction Code.

SPECIFY STRUCTURE FOR TAX JURISDICTION CODES

You can also get to the Specify Structure for Tax Jurisdiction Code screen by following these methods:

Menu Path: **Financial Accounting** ➤ **Financial Accounting Global Settings** ➤ **Tax on Sales/Purchases** ➤ **Basic Settings** ➤ **Specify Structure for Tax Jurisdiction Code**

Transaction Code: **OBCO**

Figure 2.49 displays our configured tax jurisdiction structure for Extreme Sports.

FIGURE 2.49 The tax jurisdiction structure

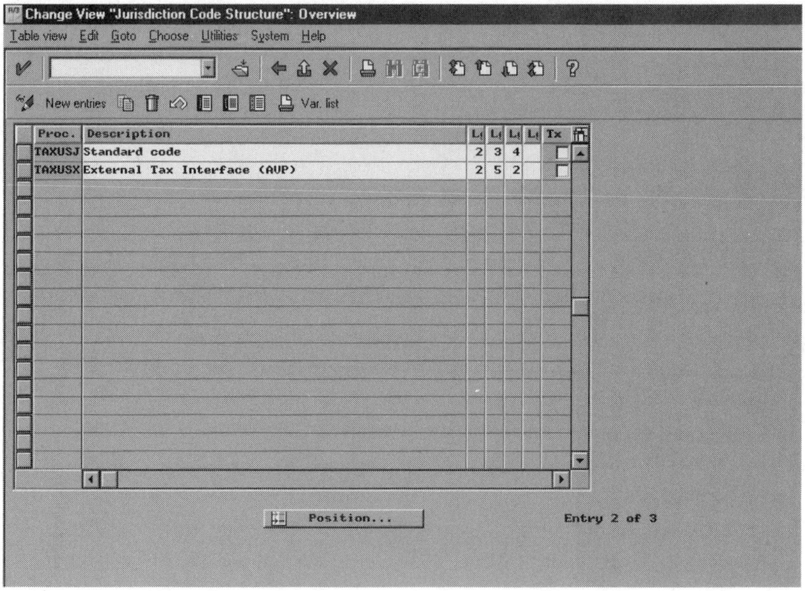

Here's what each of the fields represents:

Procedure   Enter the name of the tax procedure for which you want to configure a tax jurisdiction code structure.

Description   Enter a description of the procedure for which you are configuring a tax jurisdiction code structure.

LG   Enter the character length of the first level of hierarchy within your tax jurisdiction code structure.

LG   Enter the character length of the second level of hierarchy within your tax jurisdiction code structure.

LG   Enter the character length of the third level of hierarchy within your tax jurisdiction code structure.

LG   Enter the character length of the fourth level of hierarchy within your tax jurisdiction code structure.

TX   Set this indicator if you want the system to determine taxes on a line-by-line basis instead of determining them on a cumulative basis per tax jurisdiction code.

EXTREME SPORTS SALES/USE TAX CONFIGURATION ANALYSIS: PART 1

Extreme Sports has decided not to use a third-party tax software program at this point (your company will probably want to use an external system). For this reason, Extreme Sports has opted to use tax procedure TAXUSJ, which uses tax jurisdictions and has rates entered manually. Extreme Sports' tax jurisdiction code structure uses three levels: the first level contains two characters (state), the second level contains three characters (county), and the third level contains four characters (city).

The next step is to configure our tax jurisdiction codes. As stated earlier, the tax jurisdiction codes represent taxing authorities. Using the structure that we configured earlier, we'll use the first two characters to represent state, the next three characters to represent county, and the next four characters to represent city. To set the definition, follow the menu path Financial Accounting ➢ Financial Accounting Global Settings ➢ Tax on Sales/Purchases ➢ Basic Settings ➢ Define Tax Jurisdiction Code.

DEFINE TAX JURISDICTION CODES

You can use the following methods to get to the tax jurisdiction code definition screen:

Menu Path: **Financial Accounting** ➤ Financial Accounting Global Settings ➤ Tax on Sales/Purchases ➤ Basic Settings ➤ Define Tax Jurisdiction Code

Transaction Code: **OBCP**

N O T E   Every nation has a different tax structure. We used the example we knew best, the U.S. You should be able to extrapolate your country's structure according to your country's requirements from this example.

An example of a configured screen appears in Figure 2.50. Before entering the screen, you are prompted to enter the tax procedure that you are setting up tax jurisdictions for. Then as normal, click the New Entries button to configure your settings.

FIGURE 2.50   The configured tax jurisdiction codes

Change View "Tax Jurisdiction": Overview

Table view   Edit   Goto   Choose   Utilities   System   Help

Procedure   TAXUSJ

Tax Jurisdiction

Tax juris.code	Description	Dil	Txt
100000000	Sample entry for jurisdiction on state level	✓	☐
101110000	Sample entry for jurisdiction at county level		
101110001	Sample entry for jurisdiction at city level		
KS0000000	Kansas	✓	☐
KS0010000	Kansas, Riley		
KS0010001	Kansas, Riley, Manhattan		
KS0020000	Kansas, Johnson		
KS0020001	Kansas, Johnson, Stanley		
LA0000000	Louisiana	✓	☐
LA0010000	Louisiana, Grant		
LA0010001	Louisiana, Grant, Pollock		
MO0000000	Missouri	✓	☐
MO0010000	Missouri, Jackson		

Position...   Entry 1 of 17

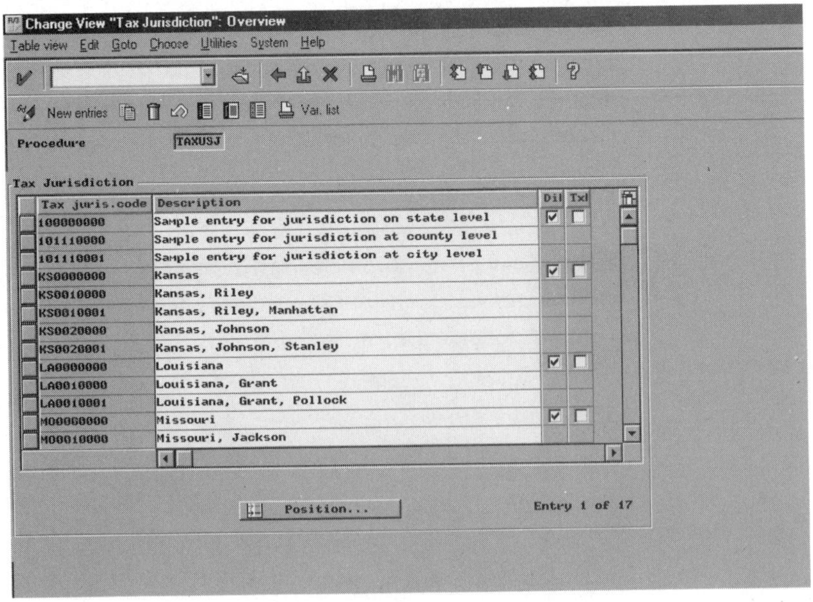

The fields have the following uses:

Tax Juris. Code   Enter the tax jurisdiction code you wish to configure based on the settings you made when you defined the jurisdiction code structure. As you can see from our example, we use KS for all of our Kansas jurisdiction codes. KS0000000 represents the base-level jurisdiction for all of Kansas. KS0001000 represents the base-level jurisdiction for all of Riley County in Kansas. KS00010001 represents our lowest level of jurisdiction, which is the city of Manhattan in the county of Riley and in the state of Kansas.

Description   Enter a descriptive name for your tax jurisdiction code. This entry is alphanumeric and can contain up to 50 characters.

Dil   Set this indicator if you do not want tax amounts included in the base amount used for calculating cash discounts.

Txl   Set this indicator if you want the cash discount amount deducted from the base amount that is used to calculate taxes.

Now that you have determined your tax determination procedure, tax jurisdiction code structure, and tax jurisdiction codes, you need to understand the function of tax codes in the system. Tax codes represent different tax types, such as sales tax charged by the company, sales tax charged to the company, and use tax accrued by the company. The most commonly used tax codes in the system are O1 (output tax charged by the company), O0 (output tax exempt), I1 (input tax charged to the company), I0 (input tax exempt), U1 (use tax accrued by the company), and U0 (use tax exempt). Now that you have an understanding of tax codes, you are ready to enter tax rates in the system. First, follow the menu path Financial Accounting ➤ Financial Accounting Global Settings ➤ Taxes on Sales/Purchases ➤ Calculation ➤ Define Taxes on Sales/Purchases Code.

DEFINE CODES FOR TAXES ON SALES AND PURCHASES

You can use the following methods to define codes for taxes on sales and purchase:

Menu Path: **Financial Accounting** ➤ **Financial Accounting Global Settings** ➤ **Taxes on Sales/Purchases** ➤ **Calculation** ➤ **Define Taxes on Sales/Purchases Code**

Transaction Code: **FTXP**

When first entering this transaction, you are presented with a pop-up screen asking for the country that you are configuring. Once you have entered the country, the configuration screen shown in Figure 2.51 appears.

FIGURE 2.51   The Maintain Tax Code screen

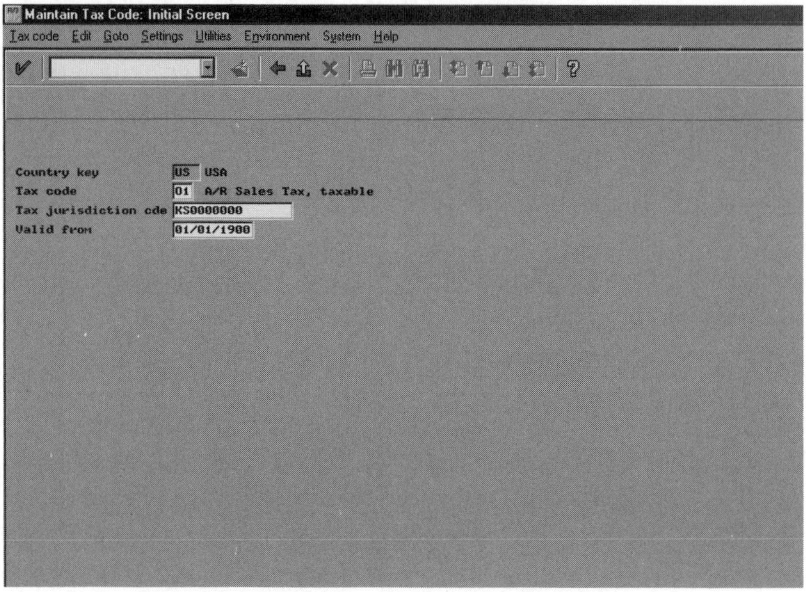

As you can see from Figure 2.51, we are getting ready to enter the tax rate of tax type O1 (Sales Tax) for tax jurisdiction code KS0000000 (state level only). Also, take notice of the validity date field. It is very important to pay attention to this field. Like a lot of settings in SAP, tax rates are time dependent. This will allow you to enter tax rate changes before the specified date and have the changes take effect immediately on the appropriate date. After continuing through the screen in Figure 2.51, you are presented with the screen in Figure 2.52.

Page down the configuration screen (as presented in Figure 2.52) to find the appropriate account keys to configure. Account keys will be covered in detail in Chapter 3. Notice that you can only maintain the first level of the tax jurisdiction code. This is because KS0000000 will be used as the base tax rate for all jurisdiction codes in Kansas. When you enter the tax rate for KS0001000, the Kansas rate will be defaulted in and you will only be able to maintain level 2 for Riley County. This logic continues on down the hierarchy.

FIGURE 2.52   The taxable percentage rate configuration screen

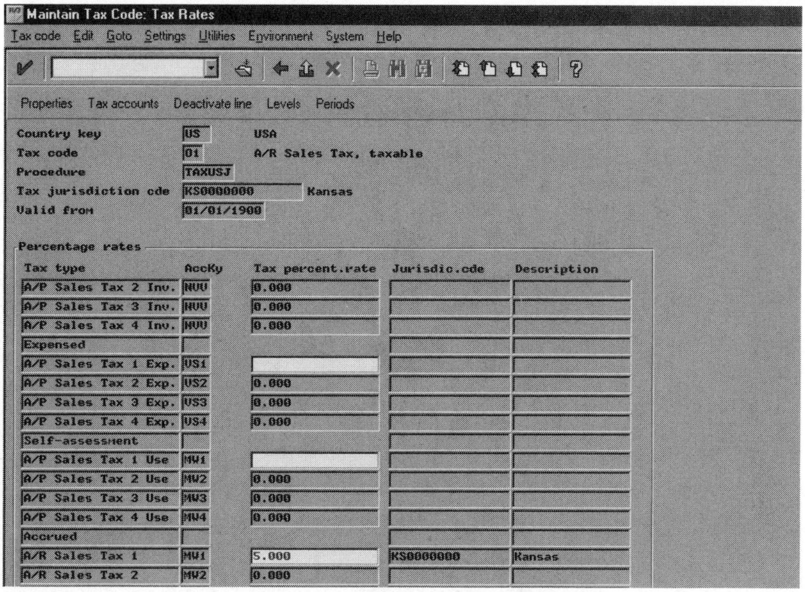

Transporting tax rates can be a very tricky process. Tax rate changes are not automatically recorded in a change request. You have to manually create the transport. It is best to create your transport after all tax rates for all tax codes have been maintained because tax rate transports are very complicated and do not always work as planned. By having a single transport, you minimize the risk of incorrect data getting into the target clients. To create your transport, follow the menu path Tax Code ➤ Transport ➤ Transport ➤ Export. You will be presented with a warning message. Be sure to display the long text of this message; it thoroughly explains the next steps that are needed once the transport reaches the target client. After processing through the warning message, you are allowed to pick which tax codes and jurisdiction codes you wish to transport. As was stated earlier, it is best to transport all of the codes. Once you have moved into a production environment, it is best to have your Basis group make the configuration of tax codes a current setting (a setting that doesn't require configuration access) that can be done directly in the production client. Once your transport has been moved to the production client, you must execute a special program that will create a batch input session to set up your tax codes.

WARNING   Even though you send the tax rate configuration to target clients in a transport, in order to execute the batch input session, the client you're in must be opened up for configuration. Because of this, it is best to create as few tax rate transports as possible. This way, you preserve the integrity of the data as well as lessen the risk of other customizing taking place while you are creating the tax rates

To create the batch input session, you must execute program RFTAXIMP using transaction code SA38. Once you have executed the initial screen in SA38, you are presented with the Import Tax Codes After Transport screen (Figure 2.53).

FIGURE 2.53   The Import Tax Codes After Transport

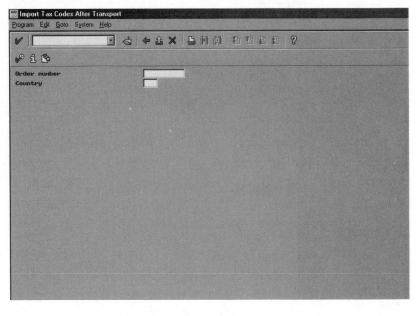

Enter your transport number in the Order Number field and your two-digit country identifier in the Country field (US in our example). After you fill in these fields and execute the program, the program will create a batch input session. To execute the batch input session, execute transaction code SM35.

The next step is to assign tax codes to nontaxable transactions. SAP carries out some system movements that are not tax related but that affect tax-related accounts. To allow proper processing of these movements, we need to assign nontaxable tax codes to each company code. The default nontaxable tax codes are I0 and O0. These codes are maintained at a 0 rate in the system. A 0 rate ensures that no taxes will be calculated ($100 * 0 = 0$). To set the nontaxable tax codes, follow the menu path Financial Accounting ➢ Financial Accounting Global Settings ➢ Taxes on Sales/Purchases ➢ Posting ➢ Allow Tax Codes for Non-Taxable Transactions.

DEFINE TAX CODES FOR NONTAXABLE TRANSACTIONS

You can use the following methods to set the nontaxable codes:

Menu Path: **Financial Accounting** ➢ **Financial Accounting Global Settings** ➢ **Taxes on Sales/Purchases** ➢ **Posting** ➢ **Allow Tax Codes for Non-Taxable Transactions**

Transaction Code: **OBCL**

The fully configured screen appears in Figure 2.54. You almost always want to use I0 and O0 as the settings in this table because this is the intended use of these tax codes (they are nontaxable by definition).

FIGURE 2.54   The configuration of Extreme Sports' nontaxable codes

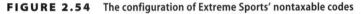

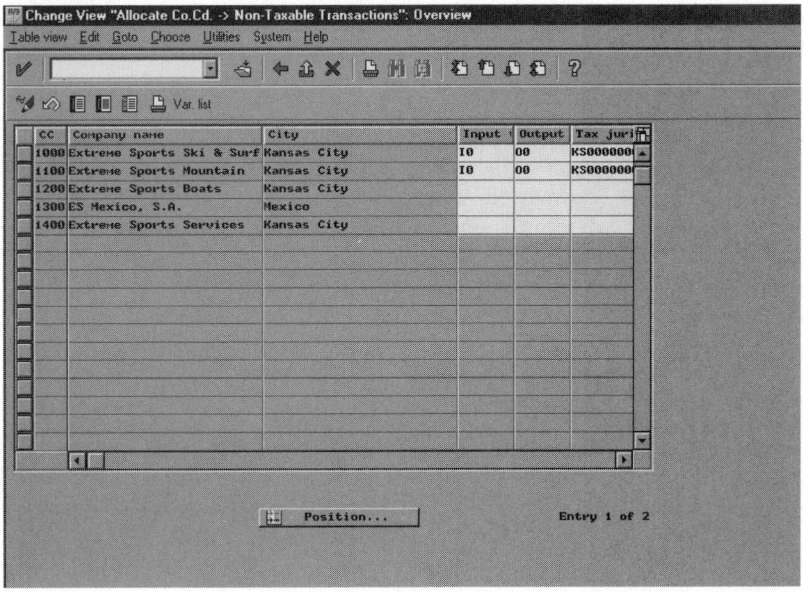

The only remaining task is to assign G/L accounts for taxes using automatic account assignment. Automatic account assignment will be covered in detail in Chapter 3.

Summary

The chapter covered the most important information about the Financial Accounting Enterprise Structure. All of the remaining chapters on FI will build upon the elements that were configured in this chapter. A lot of ground was covered, so it may be necessary to revisit some of the sections several times. As you move forward, you can refer to this list of topics:

Chart of Accounts

Fiscal Year Variant

  Posting Period Variant

Company Code Configuration

  International Company Configuration

Business Areas

  Validations

Functional Areas

  Substitutions

Advanced Validation and Substitution Configuration

Sales and Use Tax

CHAPTER 3

General Ledger

FEATURING:

▶ **CHART OF ACCOUNTS**

▶ **FIELD STATUS GROUPS**

▶ **POSTING KEYS**

▶ **AUTOMATIC ACCOUNT DETERMINATION**

n this chapter, we'll build upon the base chart of accounts configuration that we started as part of the FI Enterprise Structure in Chapter 2. We'll cover a combination of configuration and master data maintenance. It is very important that you understand the master data maintenance explanation because configuration settings affect the available master data options as well as the overall processing of the general ledger (G/L) accounts in the system.

Chart of Accounts

The base configuration for chart of accounts EXCA was done in Chapter 2. We'll now complete the chart of account configuration to make it functional for the production system. As explained in Chapter 2, it is necessary to go through your existing chart of accounts and reduce the number of accounts to only those that are essential. With SAP, there is no need to build logic into the account numbers other than to have similar types of accounts in the same number range as defined for the account group that the G/L account belongs to. Remember, the G/L is no longer your sole reporting system. We will utilize the CO module to implement our controlling/managerial reporting needs. For other types of accounts that require a detailed reconciliation, the allocation field and other posting attributes on the account accommodate accruing or expensing by using several different accounts.

Account Groups

The next step in our chart of accounts configuration is to set up account groups. Account groups determine which fields you can configure on the G/L master record. At the minimum, it is necessary to have at least two account groups, one for balance sheet accounts and one for income statement (Profit and Loss, or P&L) accounts. It is best to have a lot of account groups; the exact number will depend on your business and the overall system design of your project.

Following the menu path Financial Accounting ➤ General Ledger Accounting ➤ G/L Accounts ➤ G/L Account Creation ➤ One-Step Manual/Automatic (Alternative 3) ➤ Define Screen Layout Per Account Group (G/L Accounts), you can define the screen's appearance for account groups. Figure 3.1 shows the account groups that have been configured for chart of accounts EXCA. As you will recall from Chapter 2, when we created the chart, we chose the option to copy the account groups and all automatic account assignments from SAP-delivered examples for the U.S. Extreme Sports has added to and changed some of the standard groupings to fit with its implementation. If you wish to create new account groups, simply click the New Entries button (as seen in the toolbar at the top of Figure 3.1), create an account group identifier, specify the range of accounts that make up the group, and enter a description of the account group.

DEFINE ACCOUNT GROUPS

You can use the following methods to get to the account group design screen:

Menu Path: **Financial Accounting ➢ General Ledger Accounting ➢ G/L Accounts ➢ G/L Account Creation ➢ One-Step Manual/Automatic (Alternative 3) ➢ Define Screen Layout Per Account Group (G/L Accounts)**

Transaction Code: **OBD4**

FIGURE 3.1 **The account groups for EXCA**

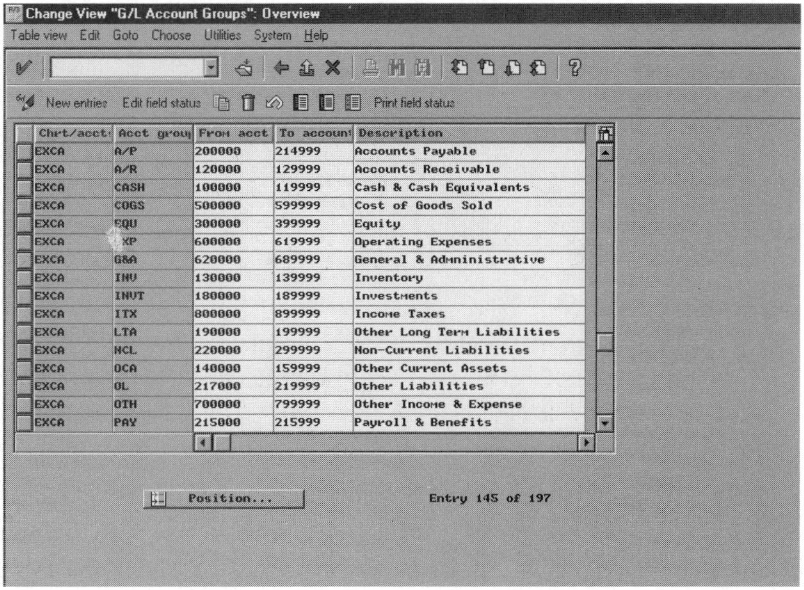

Chrt/acct	Acct grou	From acct	To accoun	Description
EXCA	A/P	200000	214999	Accounts Payable
EXCA	A/R	120000	129999	Accounts Receivable
EXCA	CASH	100000	119999	Cash & Cash Equivalents
EXCA	COGS	500000	599999	Cost of Goods Sold
EXCA	EQU	300000	399999	Equity
EXCA	XP	600000	619999	Operating Expenses
EXCA	G&A	620000	689999	General & Administrative
EXCA	INV	130000	139999	Inventory
EXCA	INVT	180000	189999	Investments
EXCA	ITX	800000	899999	Income Taxes
EXCA	LTA	190000	199999	Other Long Term Liabilities
EXCA	NCL	220000	299999	Non-Current Liabilities
EXCA	OCA	140000	159999	Other Current Assets
EXCA	OL	217000	219999	Other Liabilities
EXCA	OTH	700000	799999	Other Income & Expense
EXCA	PAY	215000	215999	Payroll & Benefits

By double-clicking any of the entries in the account group listing, you can configure the field status for the account group. It is important to note that field statuses appear at four different levels in the system: the account group, the G/L account, the posting key, and the activity. The field status is maintained in different tables and different configuration steps for each of the levels. This section deals only with the account group field status; the other types of field statuses will be covered in later sections of this chapter. The configuration screen for the account group field status is displayed in Figure 3.2. The field status is maintained independently for all account groups. The field status for account groups controls the fields that can be configured in the company code setup of G/L accounts. The configuration of the actual G/L accounts will be covered in greater detail in the next section.

FIGURE 3.2   The configuration screen for the account group field status

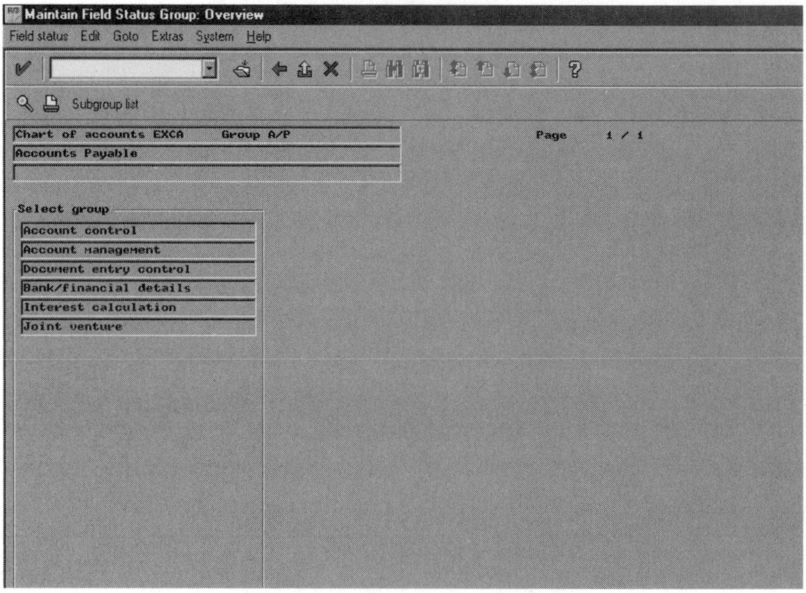

The various fields that can be maintained are grouped into different categories. You can see this in Figure 3.2. The default for all options within the categories is to make the field optional. SAP also provides the ability to make the fields required or suppressed. When dealing with field statuses, the safest thing to do is to keep all fields optional if at all possible; this rule is more important for field statuses at the other levels (the G/L account, the posting key, and the activity) that were mentioned earlier. Figure 3.3 displays the Account Control category for the account group A/P. Because Extreme Sports is not utilizing Application Link Enabling (ALE), it is safe to make the field Account Managed in Ext. System suppressed.

FIGURE 3.3 The field status screen

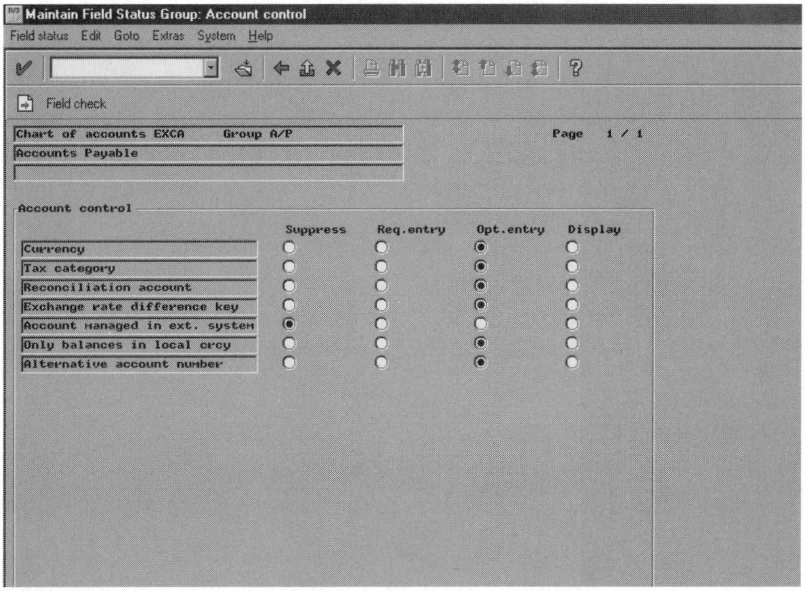

EXTREME SPORTS ACCOUNT GROUP CONFIGURATION ANALYSIS

Extreme Sports decided to add to and modify the account groups that were copied from the standard chart of accounts CAUS when creating the Extreme Sports chart of accounts EXCA. The account groups will control which fields can be configured for various types of accounts when the company code portion of the G/L accounts is set up. The chart of accounts configuration screen for G/L accounts cannot be modified. The account groups will also be used in the standard G/L reporting delivered with SAP.

Configuring G/L Account Master Records

The configuration of G/L accounts is more like maintenance of master records than true configuration. G/L master data requires you to understand the configuration behind the chart of accounts, as well as the system flow of accounting transactions in SAP. The necessary configuration steps that allow you to set up a G/L account have already taken place (in Chapter 2). Setting up the G/L accounts will determine how the G/L accounts act, are reconciled, reported on, and indirectly, how they post in the G/L.

There are several different ways to set up a G/L account in the system. A G/L account can initially be set up in the chart of accounts or in the company code. If you initially set up the G/L account in the company code, it is also set up in the chart of accounts automatically. If you initially set up your G/L account in the chart of accounts, it is available only to the chart. A company code will not be able to post to the account until the account is created (extended) in that company code.

As you will recall from Chapter 2, when the Extreme Sports chart of accounts (EXCA) was created, it was copied from the SAP-delivered chart of accounts (CAUS). Because EXCA was created by copying, all of the accounts that exist in CAUS are already set up at the chart of accounts level in EXCA. Before creating the G/L accounts, let's view a G/L account at the chart of accounts level in order to better understand the configuration that has occurred up to this point.

CHART OF ACCOUNTS DISPLAY

You can get to the display screen of the chart of accounts by using one of the following methods:

Application Menu Path (not IMG): **Accounting** ➢ **Financial Accounting** ➢ **General Ledger** ➢ **Master Records** ➢ **Chart of Accounts** ➢ **Display**

Transaction Code: **FSP3**

Follow the menu path (in SAP, not the IMG) Accounting ➢ Financial Accounting ➢ General Ledger ➢ Master Records ➢ Chart of Accounts ➢ Display to get to the display screen for the chart of accounts, shown in Figure 3.4. In this screen, enter the G/L account (700000) and the company code. The chart of accounts (EXCA) defaults into the transaction based on the company code.

After entering the G/L account and company code to be analyzed, you are presented with the more complex screen that shows the effect of the relationship you just created (Figure 3.5).

FIGURE 3.4 The chart of accounts display screen

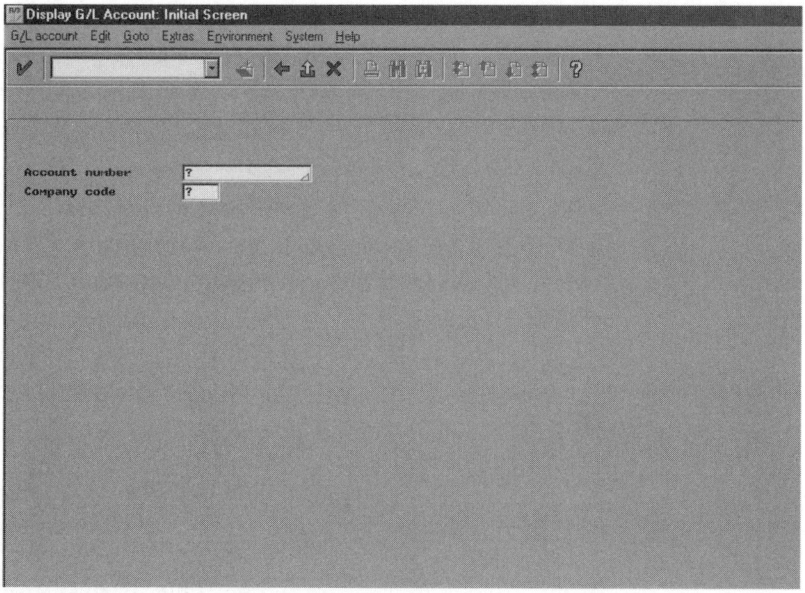

FIGURE 3.5 The chart of accounts G/L account configuration screen

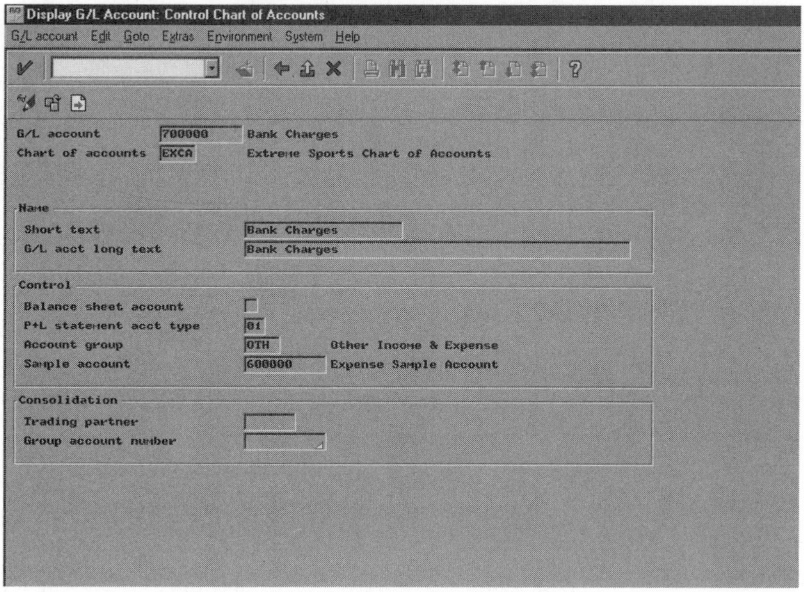

As you can see, the chart of accounts determines a lot of the overriding information for the account. Specifically, this screen is where you give the G/L account a textual name, define whether it is a balance sheet or an income statement account, assign the account group that it belongs to, select the sample account (an optional entry), and enter consolidation information if you are using SAP consolidation functions.

When you set an account as an income statement account, you must choose a variant that determines the retained earnings account that it rolls to. The configuration of the retained earnings account will be shown in the next configuration step. Note the account group that is displayed in Figure 3.5 (OTH). This account group has its field status set so that all fields are optional. This means that when the account is set up at the company code level, all fields will be available for entry, but entry is not required. Sample accounts are optional entries. They are used to copy field values over to the company code screen of a G/L account. Sample accounts will be discussed in detail following the next section.

Retained Earnings

SAP gives you the flexibility to utilize multiple retained earnings accounts (each G/L account will only be assigned to one retained earnings account). Because of this, you are required to enter a variant specifying which retained earnings account to use when you specify an account as an income statement account. Let's try it.

DEFINE RETAINED EARNINGS ACCOUNTS

You can use the following methods to get to the define retained earnings account screen:

Menu Path: **Financial Accounting** ➤ **General Ledger Accounting** ➤ **G/L Accounts** ➤ **One-Step Manual/Automatic (Alternative 3)** ➤ **Define Retained Earnings Account**

Transaction Code: **OB53**

To get to the configuration screen, follow the menu path Financial Accounting ➤ General Ledger Accounting ➤ G/L Accounts ➤ One-Step Manual/Automatic (Alternative 3) ➤ Define Retained Earnings Account. Figure 3.6 displays the retained earnings configuration screen.

FIGURE 3.6   The retained earnings configuration screen

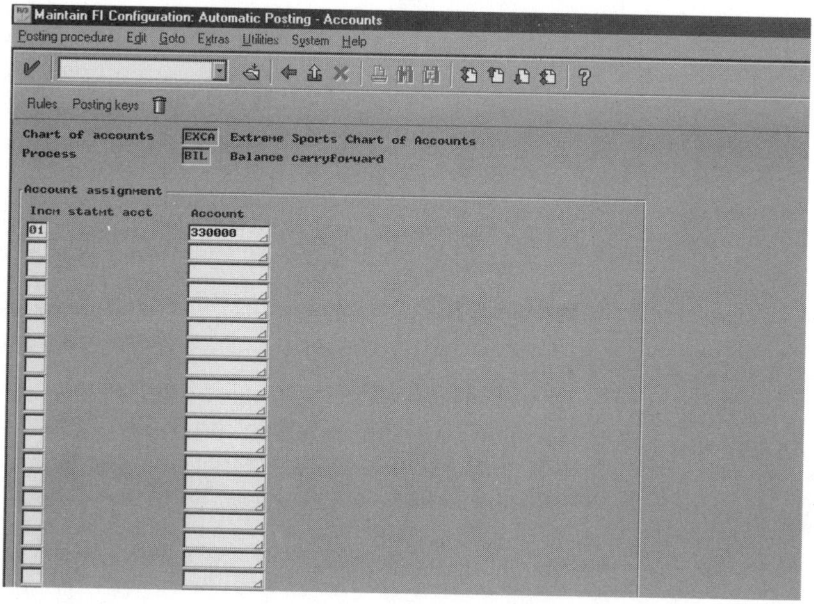

This configuration screen is relatively simple. All you have to do is create a variant ID and specify which account belongs to the variant. As you can see in Figure 3.6, this screen utilizes a process key of BIL (Balance Carryforward). Any account configuration screen that utilizes processes is really a case of automatic account assignment. Table T030 is also a giveaway that what we are doing here is really automatic account assignment. Automatic account assignment will be covered in great detail in a later section, "Automatic Account Determination."

EXTREME SPORTS RETAINED EARNINGS CONFIGURATION ANALYSIS

Extreme Sports requires only one retained earnings account for financial reporting purposes. Because of this requirement, the single retained earnings variant 001 was created to drive all income statement accounts to the retained earnings account 330000. G/L account 330000 is linked to variant 01. When you create an income statement (P&L) account, you are required to choose a retained earnings variant. Because the variant 01 is the only one that is configured in our case example, all income statement accounts drive or "roll to" G/L account 330000. If Extreme Sports decides in the future that its financial reporting needs require additional retained earnings accounts, they can be set up at that time.

Sample Accounts

Sample accounts give you the flexibility to create similar accounts with centrally defined control procedures. Sample accounts copy values over to the company code screen of the G/L account. They are typically used for accounts that you add to your standard chart of accounts (for example, new accounts you set up that are not delivered with a standard chart of accounts). For presentation purposes in this book, we used a standard delivered account to demonstrate sample accounts. There are several configuration steps that need to be followed before you can use sample accounts.

The first step in using sample accounts is to maintain a sample account rules variant. The sample account rules variant is used to link your sample account transfer rules to the proper company codes.

DEFINE SAMPLE ACCOUNT RULE TYPES

You can maintain the list of rule types by using one of the following methods:

Menu Path: **Financial Accounting** ➢ **General Ledger Accounting** ➢ **G/L Accounts** ➢ **Master Data** ➢ **G/L Account Creation** ➢ **Two-Step Manual (Alternative 4)** ➢ **Sample Accounts** ➢ **Maintain List of Rule Types**

Transaction Code: **OB15**

Let's go to the screen for maintaining rule types for transferring sample accounts. To do this, follow the menu path Financial Accounting ➢ General Ledger Accounting ➢ G/L Accounts ➢ Master Data ➢ G/L Account Creation ➢ Two-Step Manual (Alternative 4) ➢ Sample Accounts ➢ Maintain List of Rule Types. Figure 3.7 displays the completed screen for configuring a sample account list of rule types. The rule type variant is a placeholder that will be linked to later configuration steps. There are no additional entries or fields that are behind the displayed rule variant.

The next step is to define the data transfer rule for the rule type variant that was just configured. Follow the menu path Financial Accounting ➢ General Ledger Accounting ➢ G/L Accounts ➢ Master Data ➢ G/L Account Creation ➢ Two-Step Manual (Alternative 4) ➢ Sample Accounts ➢ Define Data Transfer Rules to get to the proper screen.

FIGURE 3.7   Extreme Sports' completed list of rule types configuration screen

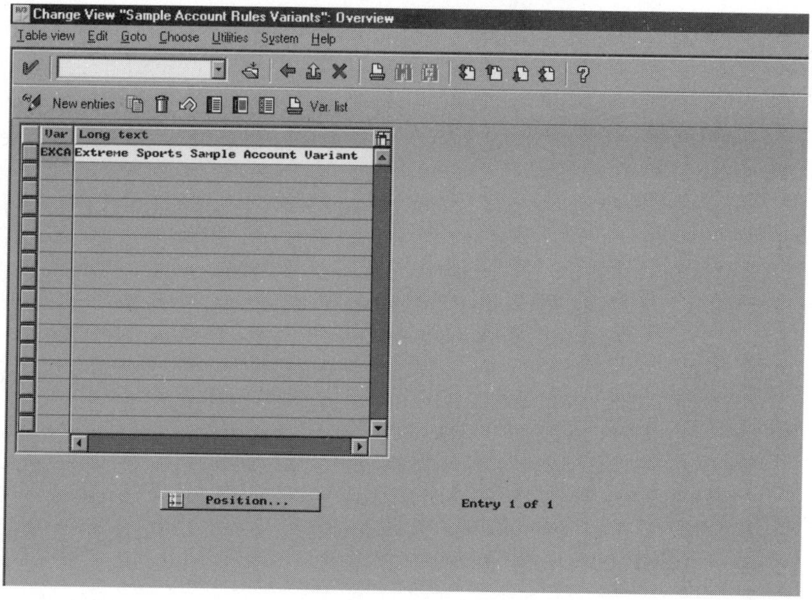

DEFINE DATA TRANSFER RULES

You can use the following methods to get to the screen to define data transfer rules:

Menu Path: **Financial Accounting** ➤ **General Ledger Accounting** ➤ **G/L Accounts** ➤ **Master Data** ➤ **G/L Account Creation** ➤ **Two-Step Manual (Alternative 4)** ➤ **Sample Accounts** ➤ **Define Data Transfer Rules**

Transaction Code: **FSK2**

In Figure 3.8, you can see the proper screen for entering the data transfer rules. Here, you can enter the identifier for the rule type variant that was just configured (EXCA). After entering the identifier and pressing Enter, you are presented with the configuration screen, shown in Figure 3.9.

FIGURE 3.8   The define data transfer rules screen

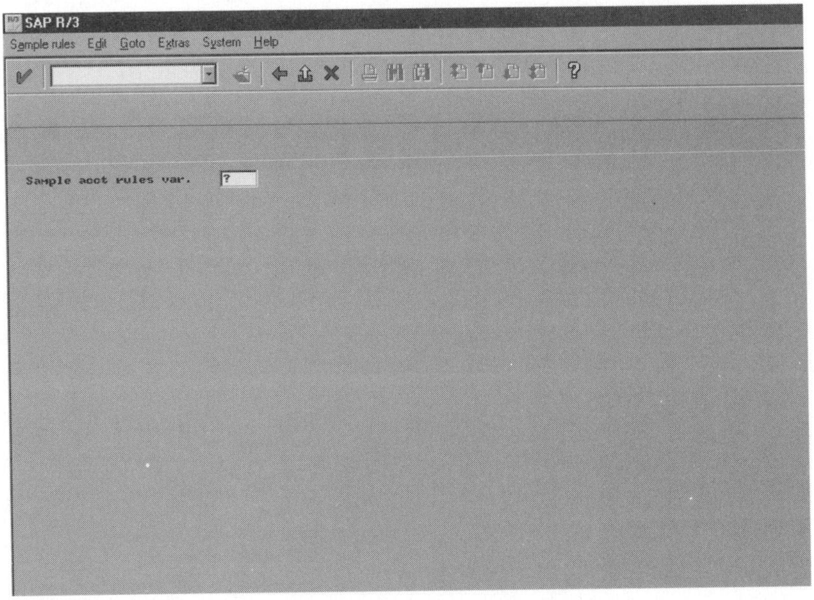

FIGURE 3.9   The configuration screen for data transfer rules

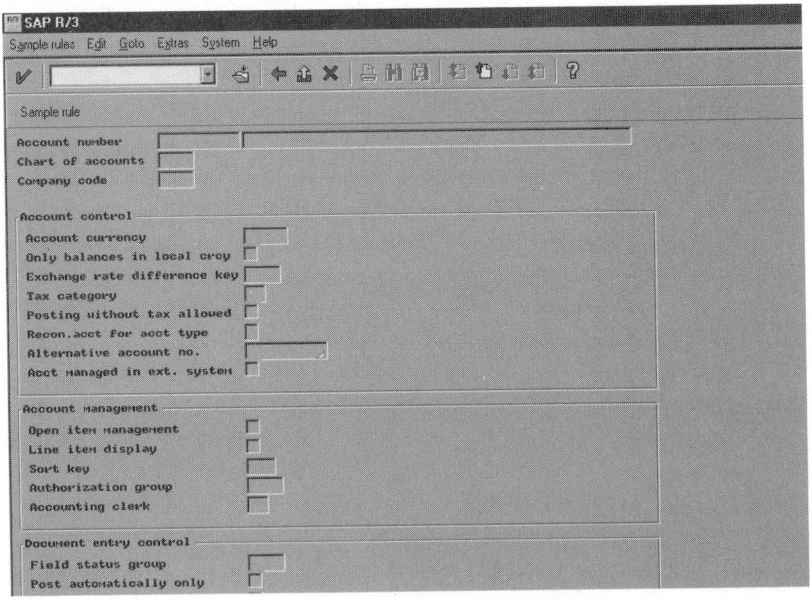

The screen presented in Figure 3.9 is an exact replica of the G/L account company code configuration screen that will be explained later, except we are defining data transfer rules in this screen and values are assigned in the G/L account company code

configuration screen. You'll notice that you have the option of setting data transfer rules for every field on the screen. You are not required to define rules for each field, but you are required to define rules for at least one of the fields. In our example, we set the rule for the Field Status Group field (this is the G/L account field status group, not the account group field status). In order to set this rule, select the Field Status Group field and then click the Sample Rule button. The Sample Rules pop-up dialog box appears.

The dialog box presents three check boxes:

Data in Sample Account Is Transferred   Use this field if you wish to transfer the contents from your sample account and still be able to overwrite what was transferred. If you select any of the other two check boxes, the system will automatically select this check box as well, in order to transfer the data.

Fld Cannot Be Chgd if Contains Set Data   Use this field to transfer data from your sample account and prevent anyone from overwriting the contents of the field if the field contains data. If data is not transferred from the sample account, you can update the field contents manually.

Fld Cannot Be Chgd if Contains Init. Dta   Use this field to transfer data from the sample account and prevent anyone from making an entry in the field if the value of the field is initial (blank). If data (not null) is transferred from your sample account, you can update the field manually after the G/L account has been created.

For Extreme Sports, we're choosing to select both the Data in Sample Accounts Is Transferred and Fld Cannot Be Changed if Contains Init. Dta statuses. Now we have fully configured the transfer rule for the Field Status Group field.

For Extreme Sports' configuration, the Field Status Group field cannot be changed if data is transferred from the sample account. It is important to make sure your sample account data transfer rules are in agreement with your account group field statuses. For example, if you made currency a required field in the account group field status and you didn't define a data transfer rule for this field, you would receive an error when trying to create the account. See what we mean when we said it is best to leave fields optional in the field statuses?!

The final configuration step for sample accounts is to assign rule type variants to company codes. The configuration transaction of allocating a company code to a rule type allows you to complete this step.

ALLOCATE COMPANY CODES TO RULE TYPES

You can use the following methods to get to the screen used to allocate a company code to a rule type:

Menu Path: **Financial Accounting** ➢ **General Ledger Accounting** ➢ **G/L Accounts** ➢ **Master Data** ➢ **G/L Account Creation** ➢ **Two-Step Manual (Alternative 4)** ➢ **Sample Accounts** ➢ **Allocate Company Code to a Rule Type**

Transaction Code: **OB67**

Follow the menu path Financial Accounting ➢ General Ledger Accounting ➢ G/L Accounts ➢ Master Data ➢ G/L Account Creation ➢ Two-Step Manual (Alternative 4) ➢ Sample Accounts ➢ Allocate Company Code to a Rule Type. As you can see in Figure 3.10, all of Extreme Sports' company codes (which were configured in Chapter 2) have been assigned to the sample account rule type variant EXCA. This will provide uniformity in creating the G/L for all company codes that fall under Extreme Sports as it is defined by configuration in R/3.

FIGURE 3.10   The allocate company code to a rule type screen

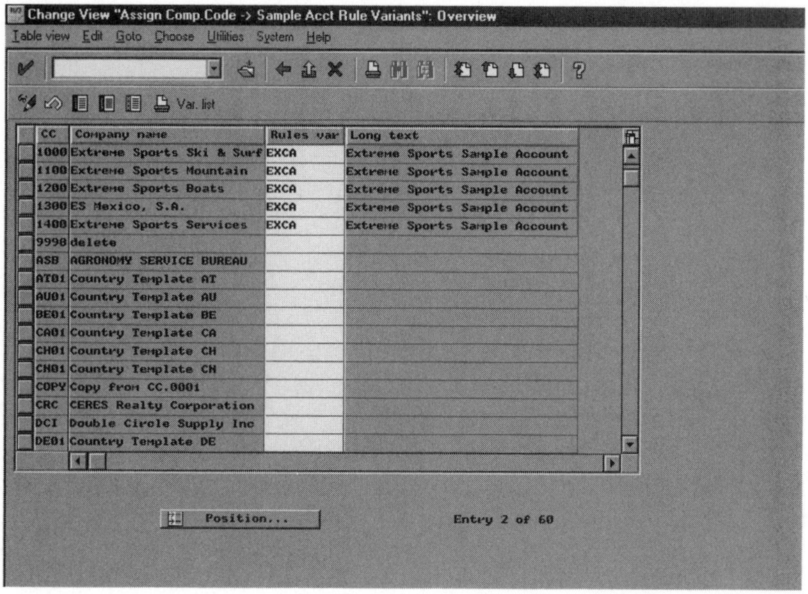

Now that all of the configuration steps are completed, you are ready to create a sample account. The creation of the sample account is actually master data maintenance. In the main SAP screen (not IMG), follow the menu path Accounting ➤ Financial Accounting ➤ General Ledger ➤ Master Records ➤ Sample Account ➤ Create. Figure 3.11 displays the initial sample account creation screen.

CREATE SAMPLE ACCOUNTS

You can get to the screen to create a sample account by using one of the following methods:

Application Menu Path (not IMG): **Accounting** ➤ **Financial Accounting** ➤ **General Ledger** ➤ **Master Records** ➤ **Sample Account** ➤ **Create**

Transaction Code: **FSM1**

FIGURE 3.11   The initial account creation screen

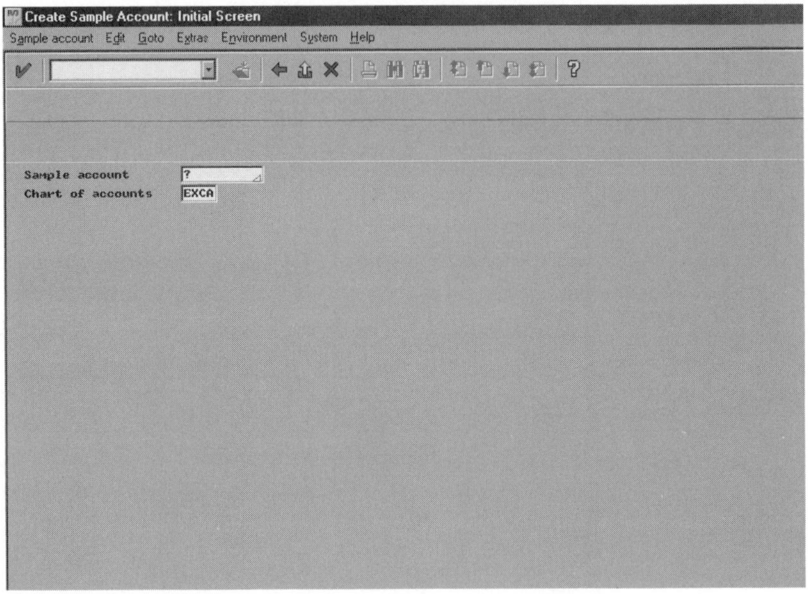

After entering the number (600000) of the sample account that you want to create and pressing Enter, you are presented with the screen in Figure 3.12.

FIGURE 3.12   The sample account data assignment screen

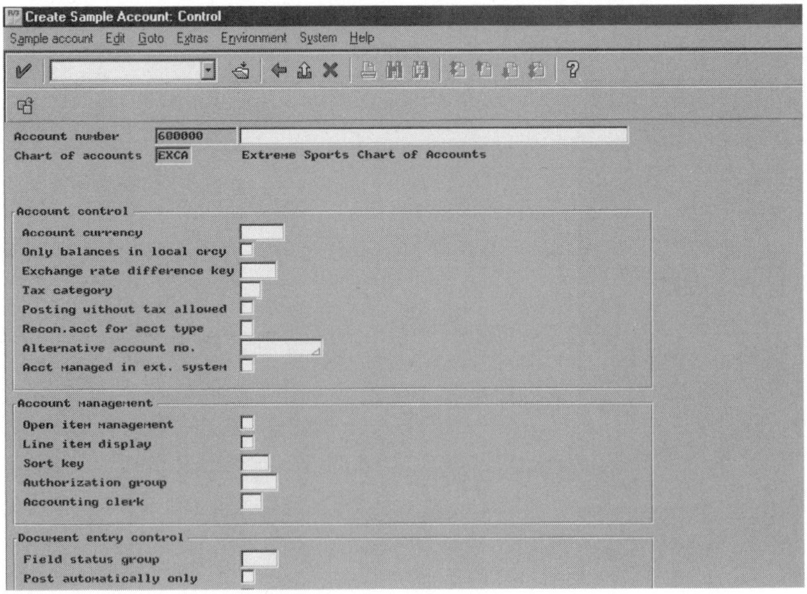

The sample account screen shown in Figure 3.12 is the same as the company code configuration screen that will be displayed when we are creating the actual G/L account in the next section. All of the fields on the screen will be explained when we create the G/L account. As you will recall from the configuration screen for data transfer rules (Figure 3.9), the data will be transferred to the company code screen based on what is filled in for the sample account. For now, you only need to select a field status variant from the drop-down box that is presented on the field. The configured sample account is presented in Figure 3.13.

FIGURE 3.13   The configured sample account

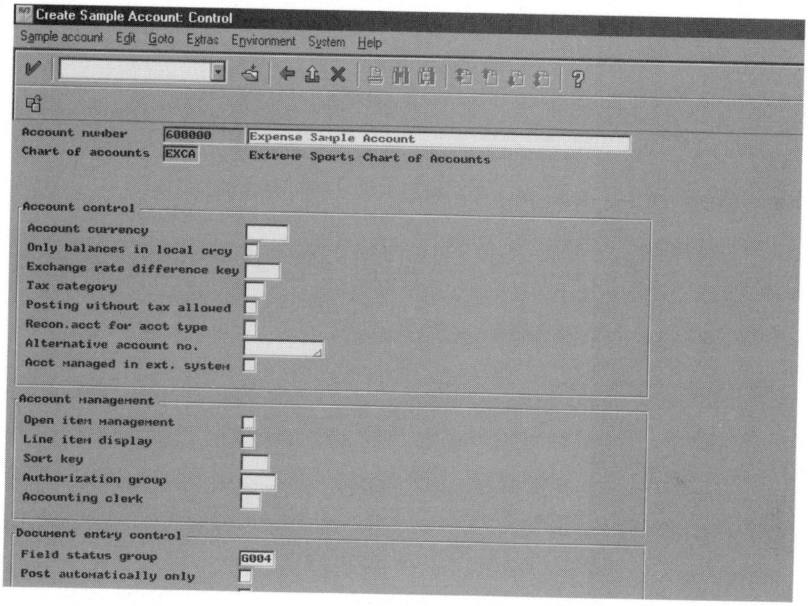

EXTREME SPORTS SAMPLE ACCOUNT CONFIGURATION ANALYSIS

The G/L department at Extreme Sports has decided that they want all expense accounts to be set up uniformly for the field that has been determined to be most important for their requirements (the Field Status Group field). Therefore, sample account 600000 was set up to force all newly created expense accounts to have a field status group of G004. The data transfer rules for this sample account stipulate that the Field Status Group field cannot be changed manually. It is important to note that the sample account will not take effect unless it is specified in the chart of accounts screen of the G/L account creation transaction.

Creating G/L Accounts

Now that the entire prerequisite configuration has been completed, you are ready to create the G/L accounts for your company codes. In this example, an account that already exists in the chart will be created for the company code; therefore, only the company code configuration screen will be displayed. The chart of accounts configuration screen was presented earlier, in Chapter 2. If you create in the company code an account that doesn't exist in the chart of accounts, you will be presented with the chart of accounts screen before being allowed to configure the company code screen. The entry point for both configuration screens is the G/L account master records creation screen.

CREATE G/L ACCOUNT MASTER RECORDS

You can use the following methods to get to the G/L account master records creation screen:

Application Menu Path (not IMG): **Accounting** ➤ **Financial Accounting** ➤ **General Ledger** ➤ **Master Records** ➤ **Create**

Transaction Code: **FS01**

Follow the SAP (not IMG) menu path Accounting ➤ Financial Accounting ➤ General Ledger ➤ Master Records ➤ Create. Figure 3.14 displays the G/L account master records creation screen.

FIGURE 3.14   The G/L account master records creation screen

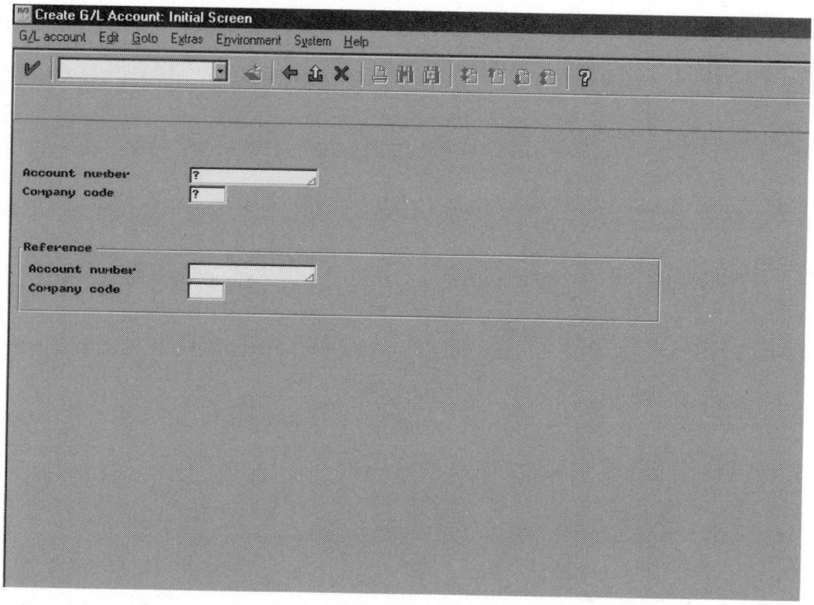

On the G/L account master records creation screen, enter G/L account 700000 and company code 1000 in the appropriate fields to proceed through our example (G/L account 700000 is delivered with CAUS, and company code 1000 relates to Extreme Sports). If the G/L account you are creating already exists in another company code, you can reference that G/L account and company code in the fields in the reference section of the screen, and all the settings will be copied from the reference account. After entering the account number and company code and pressing Enter, you are presented with the G/L company code configuration screen, shown in Figure 3.15 (the screen has been configured for Extreme Sports). It is important to note that the chart of accounts G/L configuration screen (not shown) is valid for all company codes that use that account in the chart. If this screen is changed, the chart of accounts configuration is changed for all company codes. If someone creating the G/L account does not understand this concept, it can lead to problems, such as a company code changing the description of the account for all other company codes. The G/L company code configuration screen can be different for each company code that is using the same chart of accounts.

FIGURE 3.15 The G/L company code configuration screen

![The G/L company code configuration screen]

Create G/L Account: Control Company Code

G/L account   Edit   Goto   Extras   Environment   System   Help

Account number	700000	Bank Charges
Chart of accounts	EXCA	Extreme Sports Chart of Accounts
Company code	1000	Extreme Sports Ski & Surf

Account control

Account currency	USD	American Dollar
Only balances in local crcy	☐	
Exchange rate difference key		
Tax category		
Posting without tax allowed	☑	
Recon.acct for acct type	☐	
Alternative account no.		
Acct managed in ext. system	☐	

Account management

Open item management	☐	
Line item display	☑	
Sort key	001	Posting date
Authorization group		
Accounting clerk	☐	

Document entry control

| Field status group | G004 | Cost accounts |
| Post automatically only | ☐ | |

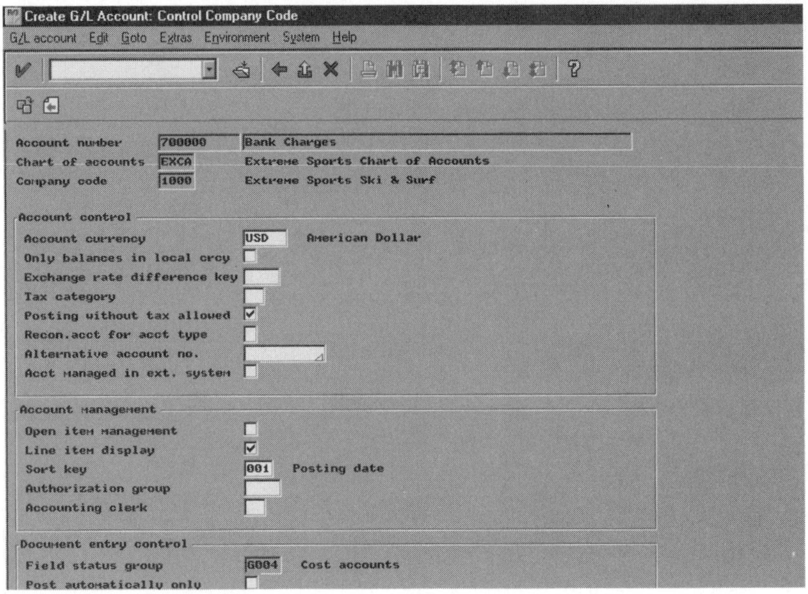

WARNING If you change the chart of accounts configuration when you're configuring the G/L account's company code, all company codes that use the chart of accounts will also be changed.

As you can see in Figure 3.15, field status group G004 Cost Accounts defaulted from the sample account. Based on the sample account data transfer rules, this field cannot be changed. Here's a quick explanation of the fields that appear on the G/L company code configuration screen:

Account Currency Enter the currency in which the account should be managed. You should almost always use the company code currency. By doing so, you can post entries in any currency in the account. If you use anything other than the company code currency, you can only post in the currency that is specified in your entry. Make sure you have all the requirements for the account before setting up this entry because it is difficult to change this setting after the account has been posted to the general ledger.

Only Balances in Local Crcy Set this indicator only if you want the balances in the account to be updated in the local currency. This indicator affects how clearing will work in this account if it is to be managed on an open item basis. *Open item*

basis means that you want to view all individual line items that make up the balance of the account and clear individual line items with offsetting line items so that you can view both open and cleared line items. Open item management is a further reconciliation function. This indicator should usually be set for clearing accounts. If the account is not managed on the open item basis, this indicator is not needed. You must activate this indicator on your GR/IR account in order to allow Goods Receipts transactions to post correctly.

Exchange Rate Difference Key   This key determines which account valuation gains or losses are posted to for the account you are configuring. This indicator is typically only set for accounts that are not managed on an open item basis and are kept in a foreign currency instead of the local currency. The exchange rate difference key is configured in table T030S.

Tax Category   This indicator controls what types of taxes can be posted to with this account. The possible entries based on the standard tax categories in the system are as follows:

- Indicates that only input tax postings are allowed with this account. Input taxes are sales and use taxes paid by the company.

+ Denotes that only output tax postings are allowed with this account. Output taxes are sales taxes charged by the company to its customers.

* Specifies that both input and output tax postings are allowed with this account.

< Signifies input taxes on a tax account. This symbol should only be used for tax accounts.

> Signifies output taxes on a tax account. This symbol should only be used for tax accounts.

Posting Without Tax Allowed   Set this indicator to allow both taxable and nontaxable postings to this account. If you specify a tax category in the earlier field without selecting this indicator, you will not be able to post nontaxable items (without a nontaxable tax category indicator) to this account. Refer back to "Sales and Use Tax" in Chapter 2 for more details.

Recon. Acct for Acct Type   This field denotes that the G/L account being created is a reconciliation account for one of the subledgers. The available selections for this field are listed here:

A   Select this indicator if you are setting up a reconciliation account for the Fixed Assets subledger.

D Select this indicator if you are setting up a reconciliation account for the Customer subledger.

K Select this indicator if you are setting up a reconciliation account for the Vendor subledger.

Alternative Account No. The alternative account number is used when you are using a country chart of accounts for the company code in addition to the regular chart. Enter the account number of the G/L account in the country chart of accounts.

Acct Managed In Ext. System Select this indicator if you are utilizing ALE on your project and want the account managed in one of the other instances.

Open Item Management Select this box if you want to manage the account with open item management. Open item basis means that you want to view all individual line items that make up the balance of the account and clear individual line items with offsetting line items so that you can view both open and cleared line items. Open item management is a further reconciliation function. Open item management allows you to display the open and cleared items and amounts in an account. Open item management should be used if an offsetting entry is made for every line item posted in the account (the account is reconciled and cleared against another account). A good example for the use of open item management is for clearing accounts such as the GR/IR account.

Line Item Display Select this box if you want to be able to see account balances by individual postings to the account. Be careful not to set this indicator on accounts with a very large number of postings. If you selected the Open Item Management indicator, this indicator should also be set. However, setting this indicator does not require that you also make the account open item managed.

Sort Key The sort key determines what is populated in the Allocation field of the G/L line item posting for the account. The system uses the Allocation field to sort postings when displaying the line items of the account. The Allocation field is populated automatically by the system with information from either the document header or line item, or it can be populated manually by the user at the time of document entry. The Allocation field can also be used as a tool to help in the reconciliation process.

Authorization Group   If you want to limit who can make master data changes to this account, populate this field with the authorization group that is needed to change the account. The authorization group is tied to authorization objects, which are tied to user profiles in the system. You should work closely with your Basis team in setting up authorization groups and profiles.

Accounting Clerk   In this field, you can enter the identifier to assign the accounting clerk who will reconcile this account. For example, this might be used to report who is to reconcile certain accounts.

Field Status Group   As you can see from the screen, the field status group G004 has defaulted from the sample account that was created in the preceding section. The field status group controls the account assignments that are made to the account. Specifically, the field status group controls whether postings to cost centers, internal orders, profitability segments, and so on are required, not allowed (suppressed), or optional. The configuration of field status groups will be covered in "Field Status Groups" later in this chapter.

Post Automatically Only   Select this indicator if you do not want users posting manually to this account. When the indicator is selected, only the system can post to this account based on configuration in the account assignment tables. This indicator is normally set on inventory accounts, material variance accounts, and such. Once it is set and postings have been made to the account, be careful about deselecting this indicator. If you deselect it on your inventory accounts, it could cause your G/L account to become out of balance with the material ledger.

Supplement Auto. Postings   With this indicator selected, you can manually update the account assignments (cost centers, internal orders, and so on) for line items that are generated automatically by the system. The field status group on the account will determine what account assignments can be updated manually.

Rec. Acct. Ready for Input   This field indicates that the reconciliation account is ready for posting when you're creating a document. This indicator is used primarily for Fixed Asset reconciliation accounts.

Figure 3.16 displays the rest of the G/L company code configuration screen. The fields are used mostly for G/L cash accounts. Let's take a look at the fields on this screen.

FIGURE 3.16   The rest of the G/L company code configuration screen

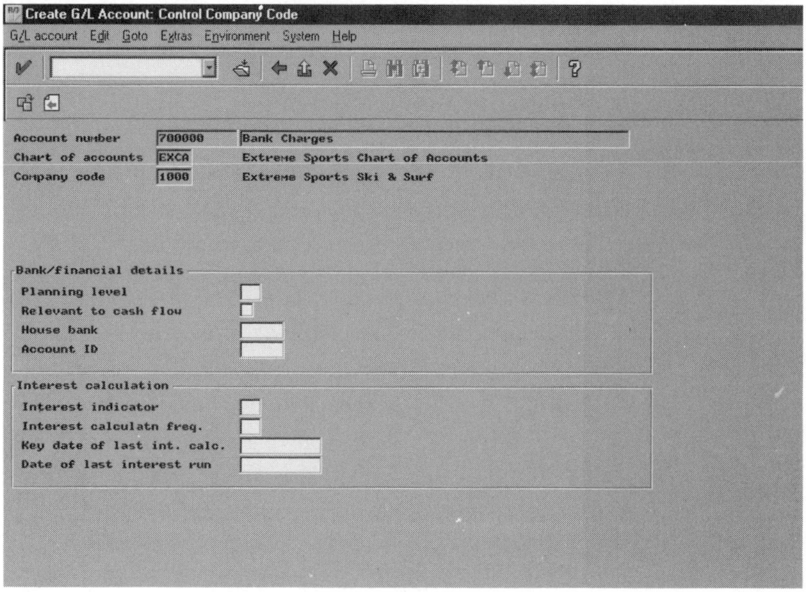

Planning Level   The Planning Level indicator is used in displaying the cash management position in the Treasury submodule. Planning levels denote such things as outgoing payments, incoming payments, and outgoing wires. Planning levels will be covered in more detail in Chapter 6, "Treasury."

Relevant to Cash Flow   This indicator tells the system that the account affects cash flow (receives incoming payments or sends outgoing payments, for example).

House Bank   If you are creating G/L accounts for a bank account, select the house bank that the G/L account belongs to in this field. House banks will be covered in more detail in Chapter 4, "Accounts Payable."

Account ID   If you selected a house bank in the preceding field, select the account ID for the house bank that this G/L account belongs to.

Interest Indicator   If you want to calculate interest on the G/L account (on bank accounts, for instance), select the indicator ID for the interest calculation procedure you want to use.

Interest Calculator Freq.   Select the ID for the interval at which the interest calculation should be run. This should coincide with the interest calculation used by your actual bank.

Key Date of Last Int. Calc.   The system updates this field with the date at which the last interest calculation was run. You should make an entry in this field only if there was an error in the interest calculation.

Date of Last Interest Run   The system stores the last date that interest was posted to this account. You should make an entry in this field only if there was an error when the interest program was processed.

EXTREME SPORTS G/L COMPANY CODE CONFIGURATION ANALYSIS

Because G/L account 700000 is for bank charges, it is not applicable for taxes. That's why the Posting Without Tax Allowed indicator has been set. This setting is for a kind of safety measure because this account will most likely never be used in an A/P transaction. The accounting clerk in charge of this account needs to see all of the individual line items that make up this account. Because the number of postings should not be large, the Line Item Display indicator was chosen. By using the posting date in the Allocation field, it will be easier to analyze the various charges made by the banks. This account may be used in automatic assignment in bank statement configuration, so the Supplement Auto. Postings indicator was set to allow the making of additional account assignments.

Copying and Transporting G/L Accounts

As you read in the preceding section, G/L accounts are set up at the chart and company code level. If your company uses a central account management with a single chart of accounts, it is easy to copy and "sync" up G/L accounts across company codes.

Before trying to transport G/L accounts across clients, you must first transport the chart of accounts. The chart of accounts does not automatically record a transport. To transport the chart of accounts, follow the menu path Financial Accounting ➤ General Ledger Accounting ➤ Data Transfer ➤ Transport Chart of Accounts.

When creating an account in the company code, it is also possible to reference another account in another company code. Refer to the discussion about Figure 3.14 for more information. If you enter a reference to a G/L account number, but you enter a company code that is different than the company code for which the G/L account was created, all entries are copied over to the new company code.

TRANSPORT CHART OF ACCOUNTS

You can get to the Transport Chart of Accounts screen by using one of the following methods:

Menu Path: **Financial Accounting** ➤ **General Ledger Accounting** ➤ **Data Transfer** ➤ **Transport Chart of Accounts**

Transaction Code: **OBY9**

The easiest and quickest way to transfer G/L accounts is during the creation of your initial company code. When creating your first company code, copy the SAP-delivered company code for the country in which your company is located. You are then given the option to copy all G/L accounts and automatic account assignments. This will give you a good head start. From here you can modify the accounts to meet your needs. After modifying all of the accounts, create the rest of your company codes by copying your first company code. You can copy the company code by following the menu path Accounting ➤ Financial Accounting ➤ G/L Accounts ➤ Master Data ➤ G/L Account Creation ➤ Copy (Alternative 1) ➤ Copy Company Code. This configuration path can also be used after your company code has been created (if it did not reference another company code) to copy G/L accounts from one company code to another.

COPY COMPANY CODES

You can use the following methods to copy company codes:

Menu Path: **Accounting** ➤ **Financial Accounting** ➤ **G/L Accounts** ➤ **Master Data** ➤ **G/L Account Creation** ➤ **Copy (Alternative 1)** ➤ **Copy Company Code**

Transaction Code: **OBY2**

SAP delivers two standard programs (RFBISA10 and RFBISA20) for copying G/L accounts between company codes and to "sync" up G/L accounts among clients. A lot of projects allow G/L accounts to be set up directly in production because G/L accounts are master data. If your project does this, be very careful; it is easy to miss settings that differ from client to client. Alternatively, you can set up all G/L accounts in your configuration client and use standard SAP programs to copy the G/L accounts across clients and environments.

The programs RFBISA10 and RFBISA20 appear in the application menu path. The programs can be accessed in the user (application) menu via the following path: Financial Accounting ➢ General Ledger Accounting ➢ Master Records ➢ Compare Company Code ➢ Send (RFBISA10) or Receive (RFBISA20). You can also execute the programs via transaction code SE38 or SA38. The transaction codes SE38 and SA38 allow you to execute ABAP programs. Transaction code SE38 allows you to display the items such as source code, documentation, and variants as well as execute the program. Transaction code SA38 only allows you to execute a program. The example screens in this section will utilize transaction code SA38.

Program RFBISA10 allows you to copy G/L accounts from one company code to another within a client or to create a sequential file that can be uploaded into other clients via the program RFBISA20. Figure 3.17 displays the screen that is shown after executing transaction code SA38.

FIGURE 3.17   Transaction code SA38 allows you to execute a program by entering a program name in the available field.

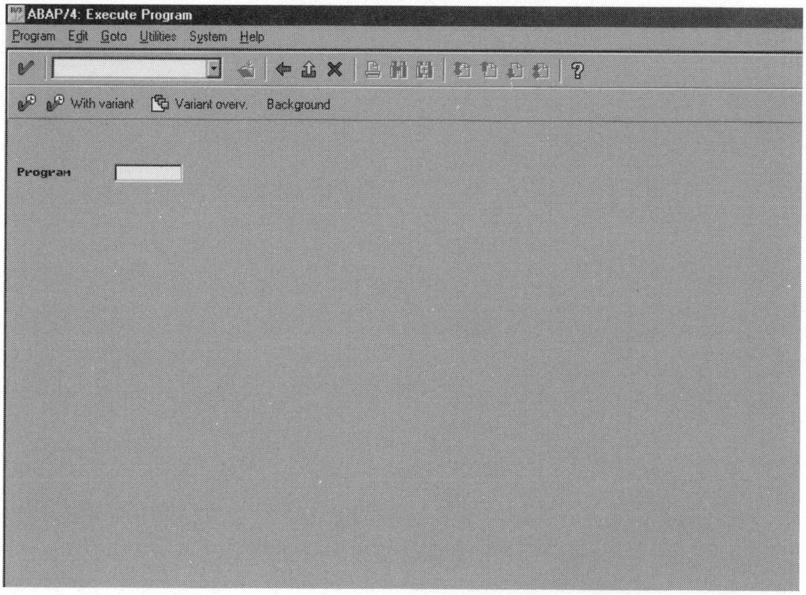

After entering RFBISA10 (to copy a G/L account) in the input box and clicking the execute icon, you are presented with the data entry screen.

The data entry screen gives you many options. You must first decide the range of G/L accounts that you want to transfer, as well as the company code in which those G/L accounts reside. You have the option to transfer master data, block indicators, delete flags, or any combination of these. The program does not automatically transfer the data; it creates a batch input session that must be processed. The default for the batch session name is RFBISA10. You can change the name of the session if you so desire as long as it fits in the field length. Then you must decide if you want to transfer the data to company codes within your client or if you want to transfer the data to other clients. To transfer the data to other company codes in the same client, enter the target company codes in the Transfer Data Directly section. To transfer the data to other clients, enter the filename of the sequential file for the program to write to and make sure there is no data in the Transfer Data Directly section. Figure 3.18 displays the screen and shows the parameters needed to transfer data within the client. After the program runs, you must process the batch input session via transaction code SM35.

FIGURE 3.18   The transfer information has been set using the RFBISA10 program.

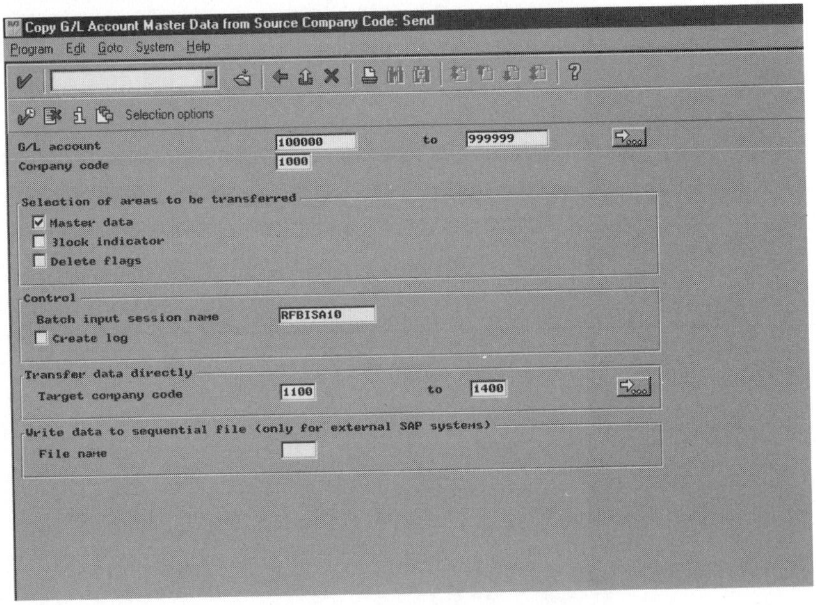

Figure 3.19 displays the parameters needed to transfer data to other clients. The sequential file is written to the application server of the client. When you want to send the G/L accounts to clients in other environments, someone on your Basis team must transfer the file to the proper path on the application server for that environment. Alternatively, if there is an NT or Unix path that can be accessed by all environments, there is an OSS Note you can apply that allows you to point these programs to that path.

FIGURE 3.19   The parameters for transferring data have been set.

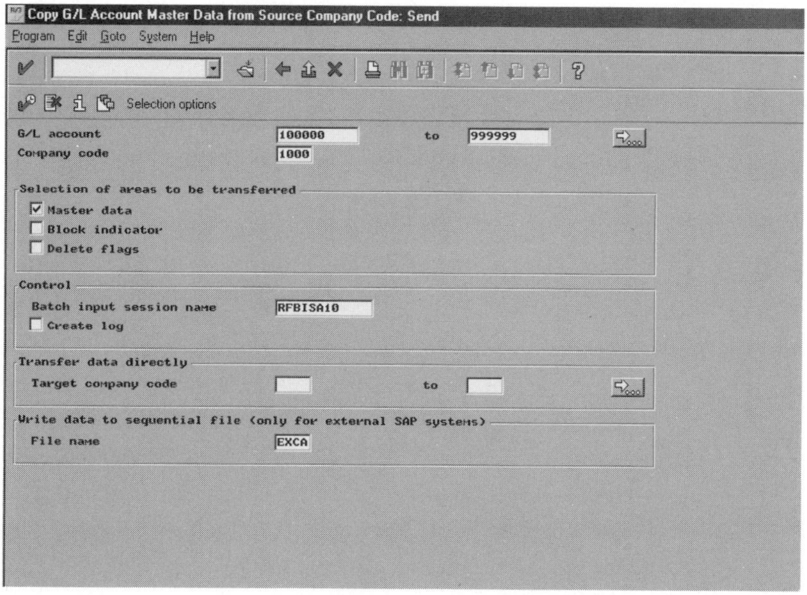

After creating the file, you must run program RFBISA20 in the client into which you are transferring the G/L accounts. Figure 3.20 displays the input screen for program RFBISA20.

FIGURE 3.20   The input screen for RFBISA20

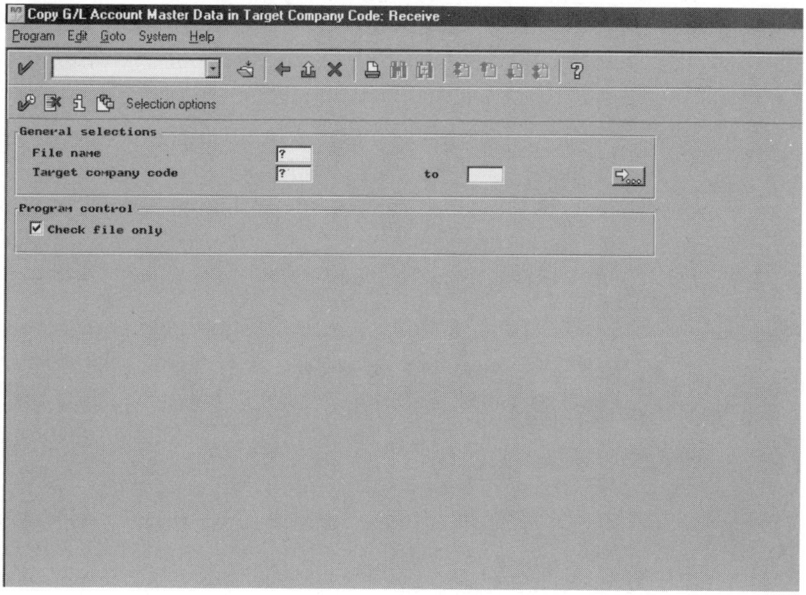

On the RFBISA20 input screen, enter the name of the file that you created when you ran program RFBISA10 in the source client. The next step is to enter the company codes that you would like to update in the target client. You must deselect the Check File Only box in order for the program to update. Much like program RFBISA10, program RFBISA20 does not directly update the records but instead creates a batch input session that must be processed using transaction code SM35.

Field Status Groups

Field status groups control the additional account assignments and other fields that can be posted at the line item level for a G/L account. It is important to remember that the field status of your account must mesh with the field status group of the posting key and/or Materials Management (MM) movement types. A common posting error occurs when a field in the G/L field status group is required and the same field in the MM movement type field status group is suppressed. It is a good idea to keep as many fields as possible optional and make only the most important fields required or suppressed. This kind of "control" will go a long way toward ensuring smooth postings in the system.

You'll recall from Chapter 2 that field status variants are assigned to company codes. Field status groups are assigned to field status variants. Field status variant 0001 is delivered with the system along with several standard field status groups. You can find a listing of these by following the configuration transaction shown in the Define Field Status Groups shortcut box. It is wise not to change the delivered field status groups, but rather to copy the groups and make changes in your version. This way, you'll have a reference of how the groups originated. Alternatively (and probably best), you can copy the delivered field status variant and make changes to the field status groups in your new variant. This way, you do not have to reassign the field status groups in the G/L accounts. The menu path Financial Accounting ➤ Financial Accounting Global Settings ➤ Line Item ➤ Controls ➤ Maintain Field Status Variants will get you to the right screen for configuring field status groups.

Figure 3.21 displays all of the field status variants that are already available in the system. Extreme Sports will make a copy of the delivered field status variant 0001. This copy will allow Extreme Sports to make changes to the field status groups and maintain a reference of the delivered field status groups in the delivered variant.

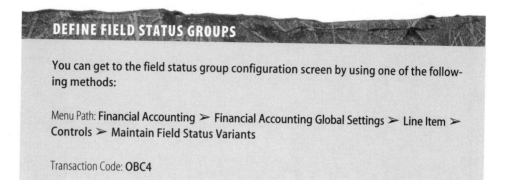

DEFINE FIELD STATUS GROUPS

You can get to the field status group configuration screen by using one of the following methods:

Menu Path: **Financial Accounting** ➤ **Financial Accounting Global Settings** ➤ **Line Item** ➤ **Controls** ➤ **Maintain Field Status Variants**

Transaction Code: **OBC4**

FIGURE 3.21   **The field status group configuration screen**

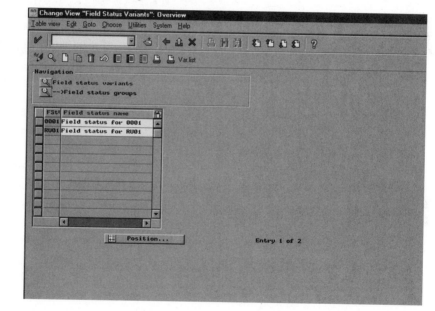

To create the new variant, select the entry for variant 0001 and click the copy button. Then you will need to name your new variant and give it a description. After naming the variant, you will be presented with a pop-up box asking you if you want to copy the dependent entries. Select the Copy All button to copy the field status groups along with the variant. The configured screen should now look like Figure 3.22.

FIGURE 3.22   The configured variant screen

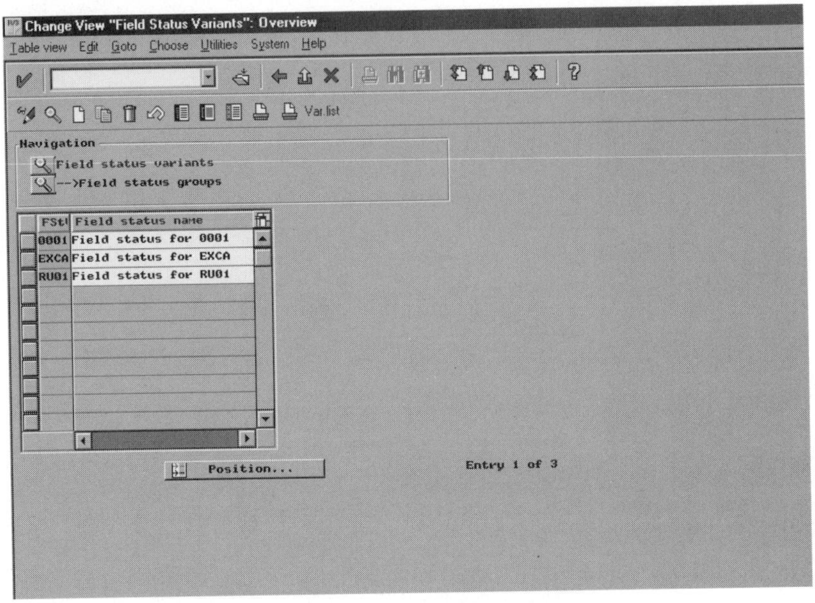

As discussed in Chapter 2, all of Extreme Sports' company codes are assigned to field status variant 0001. You will need to go back to the company code configuration screen and reassign the company codes to field status variant EXCA. Next, you will need to select the entry for variant EXCA on the screen in Figure 3.22. Then, select the magnifying glass that relates to the field status group, or simply double-click the field status variant ID. After doing this, you are presented with the screen shown in Figure 3.23.

Figure 3.23 displays all of the field status groups that belong to that particular field status variant. Select field status group G004. You will remember field status group G004 from the previous section on setting up G/L accounts. After selecting the field status group, you can either double-click the entry or click the Edit Field Status button. After doing this, you are presented with the screen in Figure 3.24.

FIGURE 3.23   The field status groups that belong to the field status variant EXCA

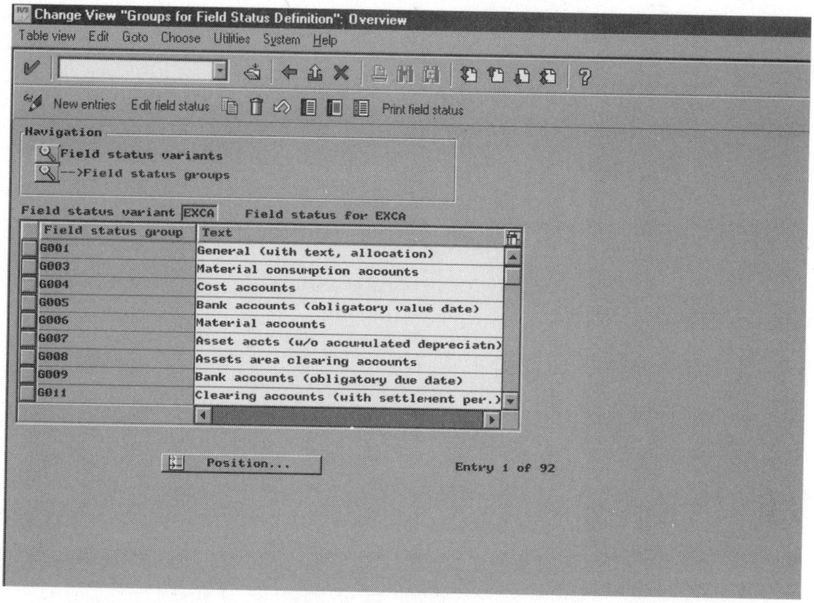

FIGURE 3.24   The field status variants in EXCA for field status group G004

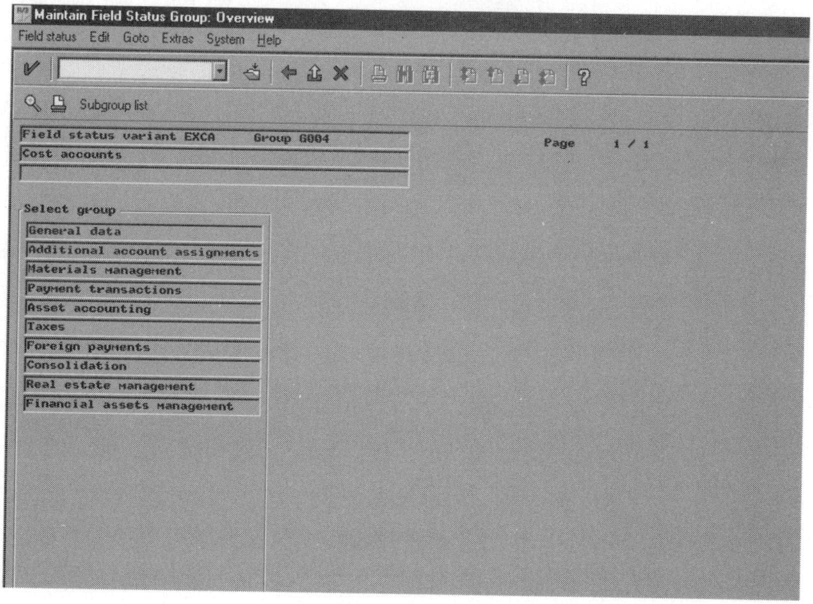

The individual fields are bound together in the groupings, as displayed in Figure 3.24. The highlighted groupings (General Data and Additional Account Assignments are shown in a different color text) represent groupings that have fields set to something other than optional. This highlight is used to point out the optional settings of groupings required for the transactions that SAP intended to be used with the group. After double-clicking the Additional Account Assignments group, you are presented with the screen for selecting the status of each individual field.

As you can see from Figure 3.25, you can choose to suppress each individual field (not available for posting) or make it required or optional. Your safest bet is not modifying the field status group at all, and the next best thing is to keep all fields optional. Extreme Sports wants to ensure that postings go to a business area, so the Business Area field will be changed to required. Figure 3.25 displays the configured additional account assignment grouping for field status group G004.

FIGURE 3.25   The G004 field status modification screen for Extreme Sports shows Business Area as a required field.

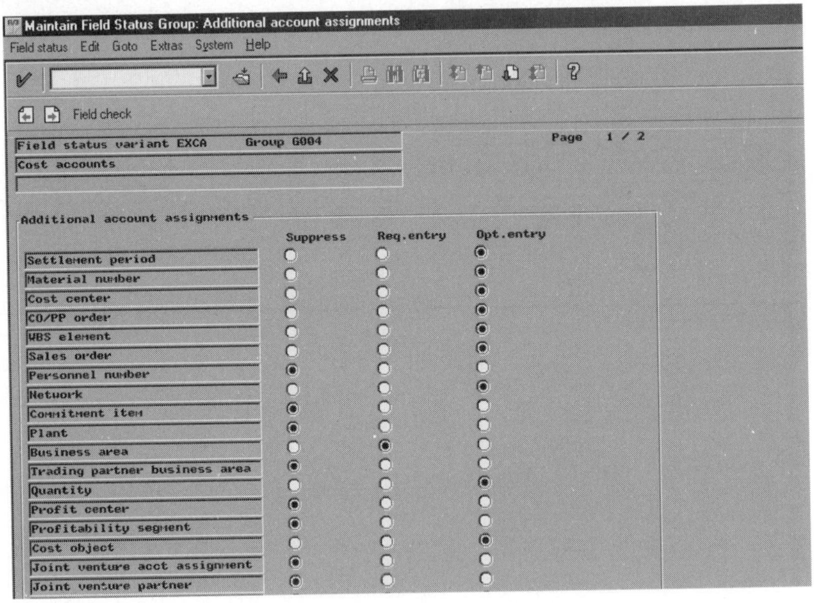

EXTREME SPORTS FIELD STATUS GROUP CONFIGURATION ANALYSIS

Extreme Sports has decided to copy the standard field status variant 0001 and create field status variant EXCA. All of Extreme Sports' company codes will be changed to point to the new field status variant. In the example presented, field status group G004 was modified because the accounting department at Extreme Sports wants to ensure that all postings receive a business area assignment. Because the business area balance sheet will be used to analyze capital requirements of the different business lines, the Business Area field was changed to *required*. This change will involve careful testing with Materials Management transactions (such as material price changes and inventory variances) that post to cost accounts to ensure that this change does not adversely affect processing.

Posting Key Configuration

Posting keys determine whether a line item entry is a debit or a credit as well as the possible field status for the transaction. Modifying the SAP-delivered posting keys is not recommended. You may be able to get by with some changes, such as making additional fields optional on payment-type posting keys, without adversely affecting the system. If a change to a posting key is required, the best possible action is to copy the posting key that needs to be modified and then modify the copy. With these rules in mind, the configuration steps for posting keys are presented here.

DEFINE POSTING KEYS

You can use the following methods to get to the posting key configuration screen:

Menu Path: **Financial Accounting** ➢ **Financial Accounting Global Settings** ➢ **Document** ➢ **Line Item** ➢ **Controls** ➢ **Define Posting Keys**

Transaction Code: **OB41**

The configuration screen you need to use to modify the posting keys appears when you follow the menu path Financial Accounting ➤ Financial Accounting Global Settings ➤ Document ➤ Line Item ➤ Controls ➤ Define Posting Keys.

Figure 3.26 displays all of the posting keys that are configured in the system. The screen reveals the posting key number, description, whether it is a credit or a debit, and the type of account that the posting key is used for (G/L, Customer, Assets, Vendor, and Material). In order to explain the configuration settings, we will create a posting key that is a copy of posting key 40 with modifications to the field status group. Posting keys 40 and 50 are the most commonly used posting keys in financial journal entry postings.

FIGURE 3.26   This screen, Define Posting Keys, displays all the available posting keys in the system.

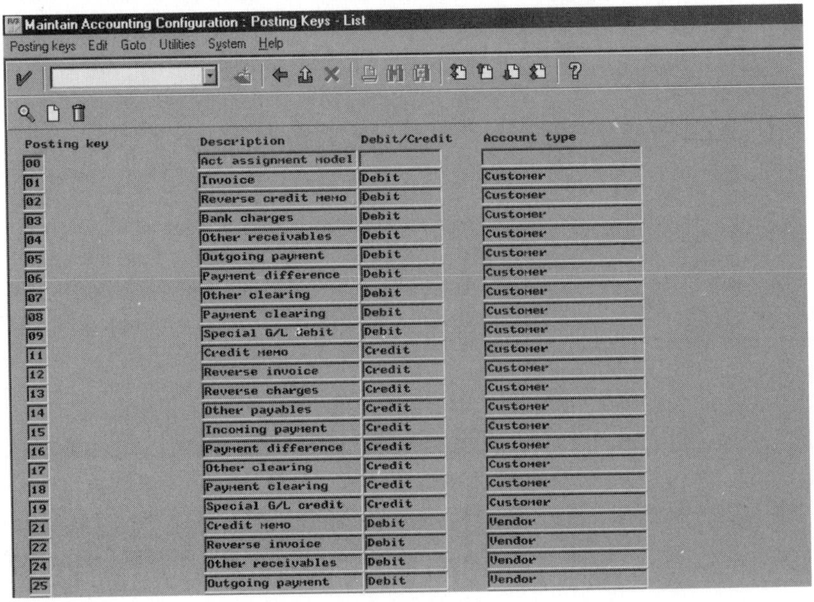

To create the copy of posting key 40, click the create icon on the toolbar. You are then presented with the pop-up box.

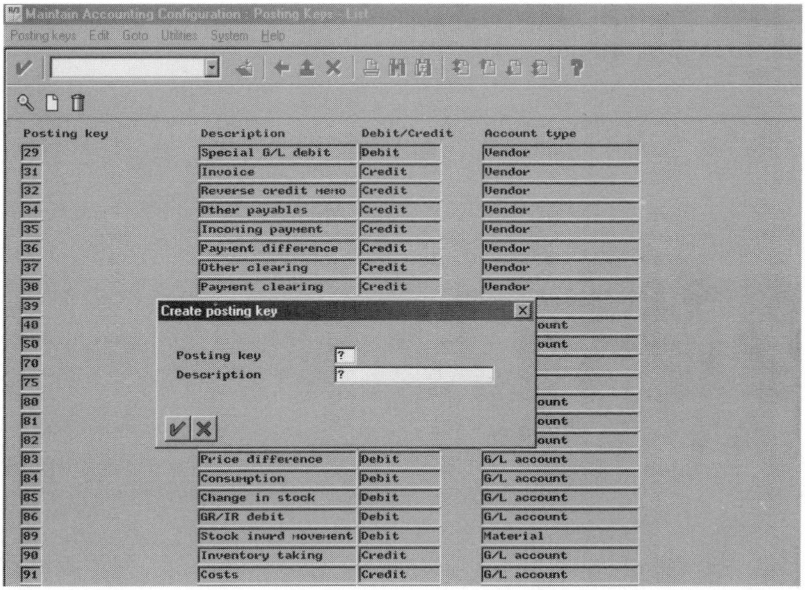

In the pop-up box, enter the ID for your posting key; the entry is alphanumeric. Then enter a description and press the Enter key. The configuration screen, shown in Figure 3.27, appears.

FIGURE 3.27   The fully configured posting key detail for Z1

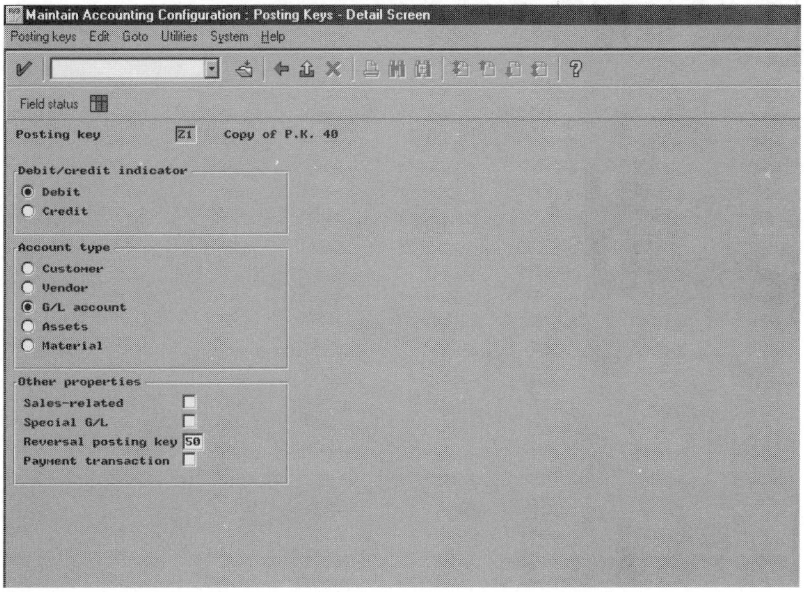

It is important to realize that we are not copying identical data but creating a new posting key. Therefore, you will need to fill in the fields that need to be configured for posting key Z1 by hand. The first thing you must decide is whether your posting key is for a debit or a credit. The next decision to be made is what type of account will be used with the posting key (Customer, Vendor, G/L, Assets, or Material). The fields in the Other Properties section are as follows:

Sales-Related   Select this indicator if the posting key is used when invoicing a customer.

Special G/L   Choose this indicator if the posting key is used for special G/L transactions such as down payments. With this indicator selected, a valid special G/L indicator must be entered on the line item when posting with this key.

Reversal Posting Key   Select the ID of the posting key that will be used on the reversal transaction to back out the entry made by the current posting key.

Payment Transaction   Pick this indicator if the posting key is used for any type of incoming, outgoing, clearing, or residual postings of payments.

The posting key detail configuration settings are now the same for posting keys 40 and Z1. The next step is to modify the field status in posting key Z1 so that it's different than the field status in posting key 40. To configure the field status group, click the Field Status button. You are presented with the screen in Figure 3.28.

FIGURE 3.28   Assigning the field status group for posting key Z1

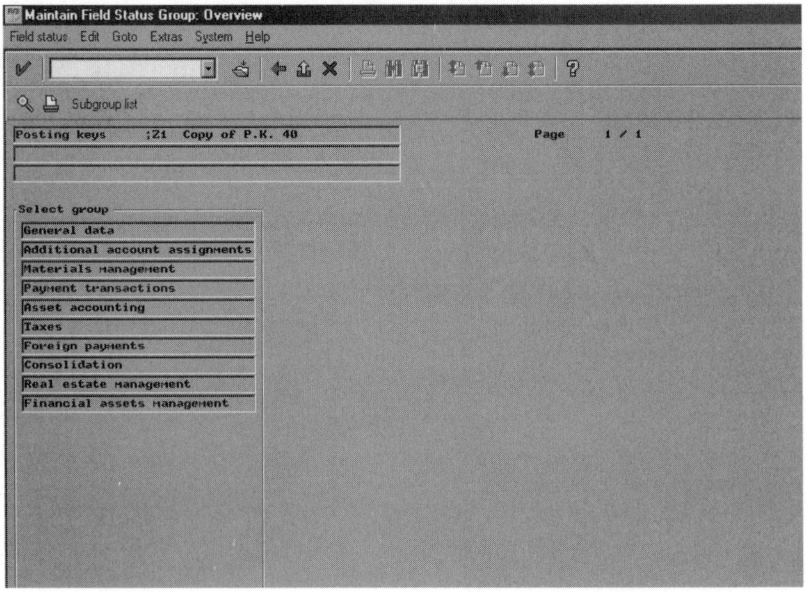

In the field status group for posting key 40, the Reason Code field is suppressed. The Reason Code field is configured in the Payment Transactions grouping. The configuration screen for the Payment Transactions group is displayed in Figure 3.29.

FIGURE 3.29   The Payment Transactions group configuration

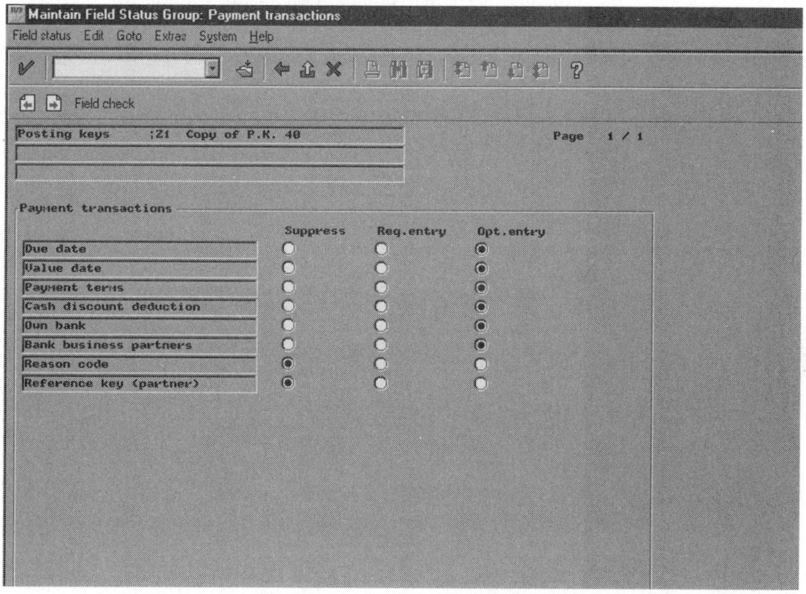

For now, the only change you will make is to click the Opt. Entry radio button for the Reason Code field.

EXTREME SPORTS POSTING KEY CONFIGURATION ANALYSIS

Extreme Sports would like to be able to enter a reason code on a regular debit transaction. To accomplish this with the least risk for adverse system impact, a copy of the standard debit posting key 40 was made. For the new posting key Z1, the field status was changed to make reason code an optional entry.

Automatic Account Determination

Automatic account determination is one of the most powerful tools in SAP. It allows the system to determine the correct G/L account to post to by considering the type of transaction and other factors. This feature provides a lot of flexibility and eliminates the need to hard-code the G/L account in source code.

TIP Automatic account determination is also known as both *automatic posting* and *automatic account assignment* in the SAP system. We will use these terms interchangeably throughout this book.

As stated in "Retained Earnings" earlier in this chapter, all automatic account determination (with the exception of Sales & Distribution) is configured in table T030 and table T001U (for intercompany postings). Table T030 is split into different objects for the various application areas and processing keys. Each object is known as *XXXYY* when viewed on your transport, where *XXX* represents the chart of accounts and *YY* represents the processing key. The processing keys used to determine automatic account assignment are supplied via standard SAP transactions and are updated in BSEG-KTOSL on each FI posting in the system.

When transporting automatic account determinations, it is important to remember that the transport is a whole table transport for that account assignment object (process key). For example, when you make an additional entry to processing key GBB (Offsetting Entry for Inventory Postings), the transport copies all of the entries for the processing key GBB, not just the additional entry that you make.

Whole table transport can become problematic in a multiple-project environment or when your system goes into maintenance mode because it allows someone with an older transport to overwrite changes made by someone with a newer transport. This situation can happen when Consultant X creates and releases a transport on June 15 and Consultant Y then creates and releases a transport on July 22. Consultants Y's transport moves immediately into the production environment on July 22 to fix a production problem. On July 30, Consultant X's transport moves out of the QA environment into production, overwriting all of the configuration that was included in Consultant Y's transport. As you can see, it is very important to have tight control over automatic account assignment in order to avoid problems.

The configuration of automatic account determination is located at various places throughout the IMG to correspond with the application area of the automatic account determination. There is a shortcut transaction code, FBKP, which allows you to configure all automatic account assignments from the same screen. There is no menu path to get to this screen.

CONFIGURE AUTOMATIC ACCOUNT DETERMINATIONS

You can use the following method to configure automatic account determination:

Transaction Code: **FBKP**

Figure 3.30 displays the configuration screen that is presented from the transaction code listed in the shortcut box. Please note that there are additional areas that can be maintained; they will appear on the screen after you page down. In this section, we will cover how automatic account determinations are configured. We will cover several examples of places in the system that require automatic account determination, but not all. In the remaining chapters, we will cover some of the most important automatic account determinations that relate to the topic of the chapter. Because not all automatic account determinations will be explained in this book, it is important to review the IMG for the areas that you are configuring to look for the places that need automatic account assignment. If you miss an automatic account assignment and attempt to execute a business transaction, the system will issue you an error message telling you what processing key needs to be maintained. So it's pretty easy to catch all of them.

FIGURE 3.30   The automatic account determination configuration screen

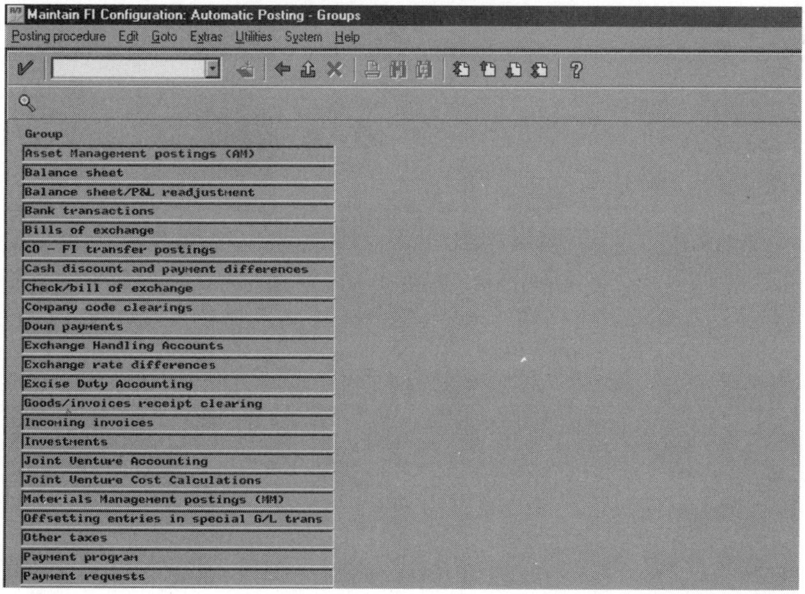

Sales/Use Tax Automatic Account Assignment

As you can see in Figure 3.30, automatic account determination takes place in many areas throughout the system. The first area we'll cover is taxes, which is where we left off in Chapter 2. The tax accounts can be configured by double-clicking the tax group on the screen shown in Figure 3.30 (you'll need to page down to see it) or by following the menu path Financial Accounting ➢ Financial Accounting Global Settings ➢ Tax on Sales/Purchases ➢ Posting ➢ Define Tax Accounts.

DEFINE TAX ACCOUNTS AUTOMATIC ACCOUNT ASSIGNMENTS

You can use the following methods to access the define tax accounts configuration screen:

Menu Path: **Financial Accounting** ➢ **Financial Accounting Global Settings** ➢ **Tax on Sales/Purchases** ➢ **Posting** ➢ **Define Tax Accounts**

Transaction Code: **OB40**

As you can see in Figure 3.31, the account determinations are separated via processing keys that the system uses for different transactions. We will use processing key MW1 as our example of tax automatic account determination.

The main use of processing key MW1 is for sales tax that you charge to your customer's on invoices. To begin configuring, double-click the processing key MW1. You will be presented with a pop-up box asking which chart of accounts you would like to use. After entering the appropriate chart of accounts (EXCA), you are presented with a screen like the one shown in Figure 3.32.

FIGURE 3.31   The account determinations are separated by processing keys for various transactions.

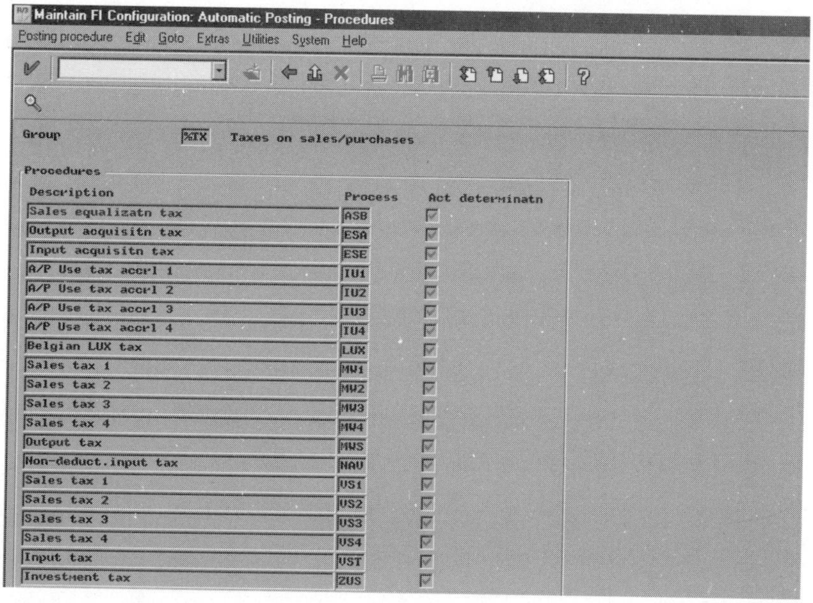

FIGURE 3.32   The rules configuration screen for MW1

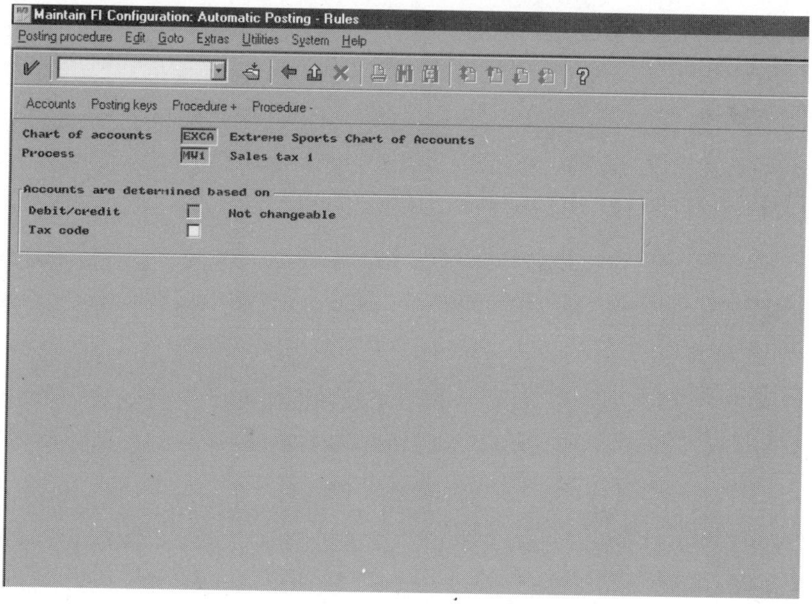

The screen in Figure 3.32 is the rules screen. The rules define at which level the account determination takes place. For tax accounts, the rules can be defined at two possible levels: the debit/credit level and the tax code level. It is important to think carefully about the level at which you want to set your rules because once they are set, they cannot be changed unless all account determinations are first erased. As you can see, the Debit/Credit indicator is grayed out, so it cannot be maintained for this process key. We are able to set the tax code level, which we will do for this example to provide greater flexibility. Once you set this indicator, you should select the save icon to save your rules. Once you do, you are presented with the account determination assignment screen, see Figure 3.33.

FIGURE 3.33   The account determination assignments for Extreme Sports

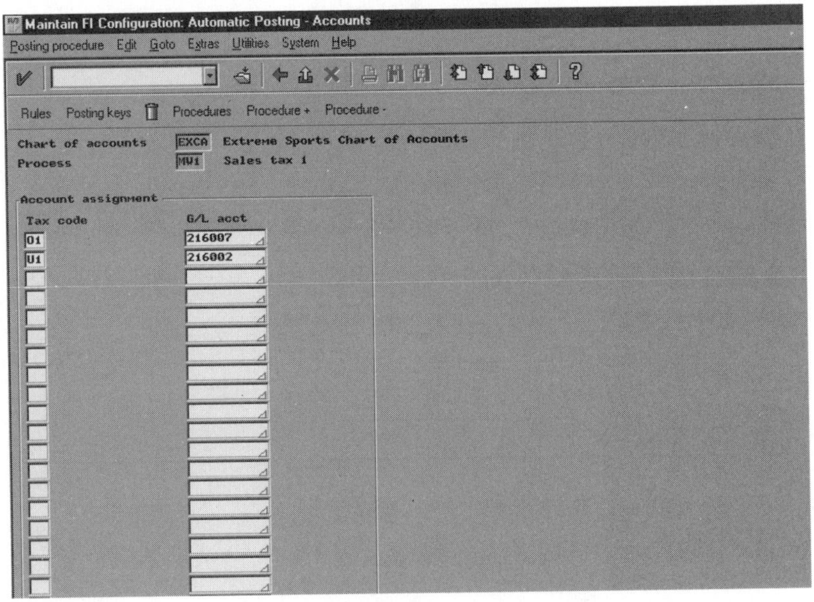

This is where you will assign your account determinations. As you can see, you are required to fill in the Tax Code field as well as the G/L Acct field. This is because we set up the rule for this process key to use tax codes when we set the account rules in the preceding section. In this example for Extreme Sports, the tax codes O1 (for A/R sales tax) and U1 (for use tax) are configured to accrue liabilities to separate accounts. This configuration for Extreme Sports is displayed in Figure 3.33.

The final step for configuring this processing key is to configure the posting keys that will be used when processing this type of transaction. To do so, click the Posting Keys button from either the rules screen (as shown in Figure 3.32) or in the G/L account assignment screen (as shown in Figures 3.33). You are then presented with the screen for assigning debit or credit to your assigned posting key, as displayed in Figure 3.34.

FIGURE 3.34   The posting key needs to have its Debit and Credit settings assigned.

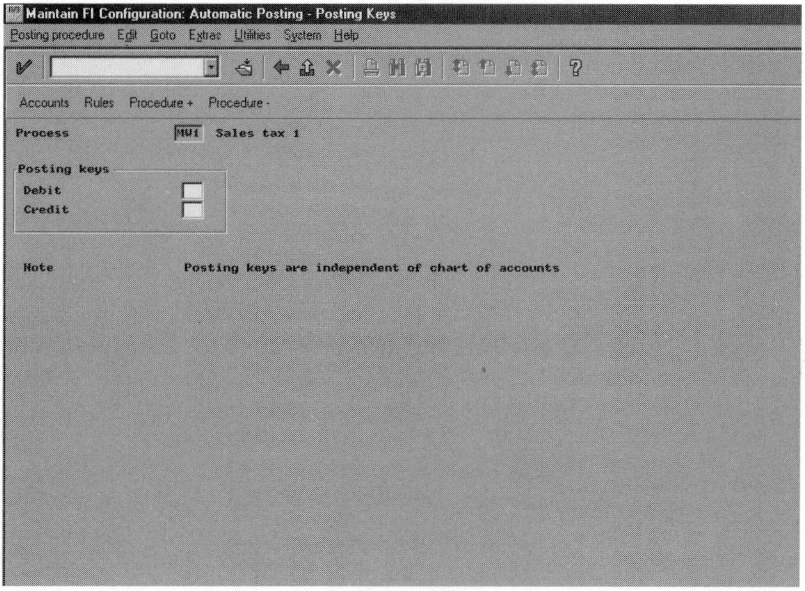

It is important to be aware of the note shown on the screen in Figure 3.34 stating that the posting keys are independent of the chart of accounts. This means that, if your SAP solution includes more than one chart of accounts, the debit and credit posting keys set here will be valid for all charts of accounts. Extreme Sports will use the standard posting keys 40 (debit) and 50 (credit).

Intercompany Posting Automatic Account Assignment

Intercompany postings (also called cross-company code transactions) occur in the system when a single transaction is posted to one or more company codes (this must occur on separate line items). For these postings, an intercompany clearing (payable/receivable) account must be maintained. The configuration screen for determining codes for intercompany accounts can be reached by following the menu path Financial Accounting ➤ General Ledger Accounting ➤ Business Transactions ➤ Prepare Cross-Company Code Transactions.

DEFINE CROSS-COMPANY CODE AUTOMATIC ACCOUNT ASSIGNMENTS

You can change cross-company code transaction configuration by using one of the following methods:

Menu Path: **Financial Accounting** ➤ **General Ledger Accounting** ➤ **Business Transactions** ➤ **Prepare Cross-Company Code Transactions**

Transaction Code: **OBYA**

After finding the configuration transaction screen, you'll get a pop-up box for entering company codes.

In the pop-up box, enter the company codes that you want to configure for intercompany transactions. The screen for configuring the posting keys to specific accounts appears; Figure 3.35 displays the configured intercompany clearing configuration screen for company codes 1000 and 1100.

FIGURE 3.35   The configured intercompany clearing configuration for Extreme Sports

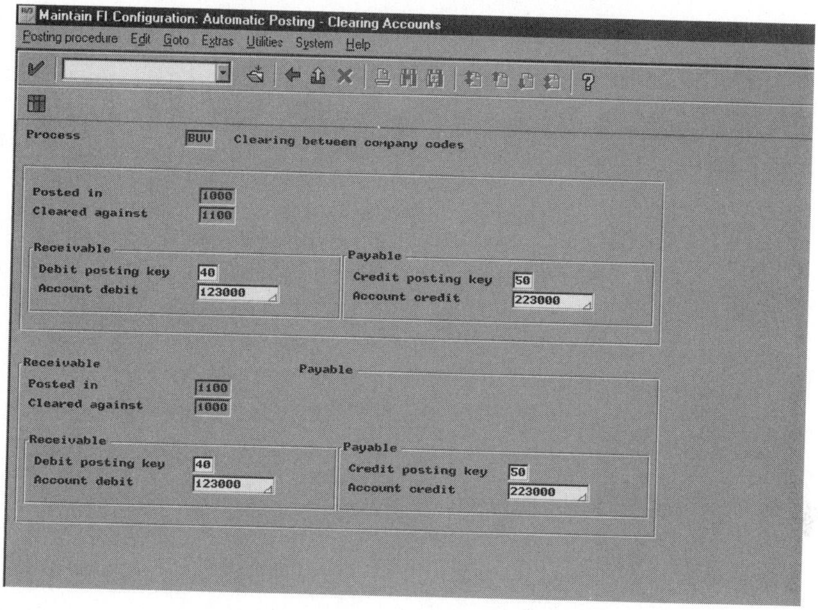

In the configuration screen, you configure the posting keys and intercompany accounts to post to. You will notice that there are two groupings on the screen, one for each combination of intercompany relationships. You need to pay particular attention to the Posted In company code. The Posted In company code represents the company code that the intercompany G/L accounts you designate will be posted *to* for the given Cleared Against company code (for example, the company code for which you are configuring the accounts). You have the option of creating both an intercompany receivable and intercompany payable account or using a single intercompany account for both the payable and the receivable. It is a good idea to use the same G/L account number for both company codes because, in addition to making the clearing less confusing, this will cut down on the number of G/L accounts that are needed.

EXTREME SPORTS INTERCOMPANY ACCOUNT DETERMINATION CONFIGURATION ANALYSIS

The controller of Extreme Sports has determined that there is a need for Extreme Sports to keep track of intercompany payables and receivables separately. Because of this, both an intercompany payable and an intercompany receivable account were set up. Both company codes in an intercompany transaction will use the same G/L account number, thus reducing the number of accounts needed in the chart of accounts. The project team at Extreme Sports will configure the remaining intercompany relationships in the same fashion, as demonstrated in "Materials Management Automatic Account Assignment."

Materials Management Automatic Account Assignment

Materials Management (MM) automatic account determination is a major integration point between FI and MM. It is very important to work with your MM counterparts when configuring this part of the system. Accurate configuration takes a good working knowledge of the different movement types, valuation classes, and transactions that take place in the MM module. A detailed explanation of MM is beyond the scope of this book.

To configure MM's automatic account determination, follow the menu path Financial Accounting ➤ General Ledger Accounting ➤ Business Transactions ➤ Integration ➤ Materials Management ➤ Define Accounts for Material Management.

CONFIGURE MM AUTOMATIC ACCOUNT ASSIGNMENTS

You can get to the MM account definition screen by using one of the following methods:

Menu Path: **Financial Accounting** ➤ **General Ledger Accounting** ➤ **Business Transactions** ➤ **Integration** ➤ **Materials Management** ➤ **Define Accounts for Material Management**

Transaction Code: **OBYC**

Figure 3.36 depicts the configuration screen for all MM account assignments.

FIGURE 3.36   The configuration screen for MM account assignments

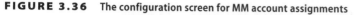

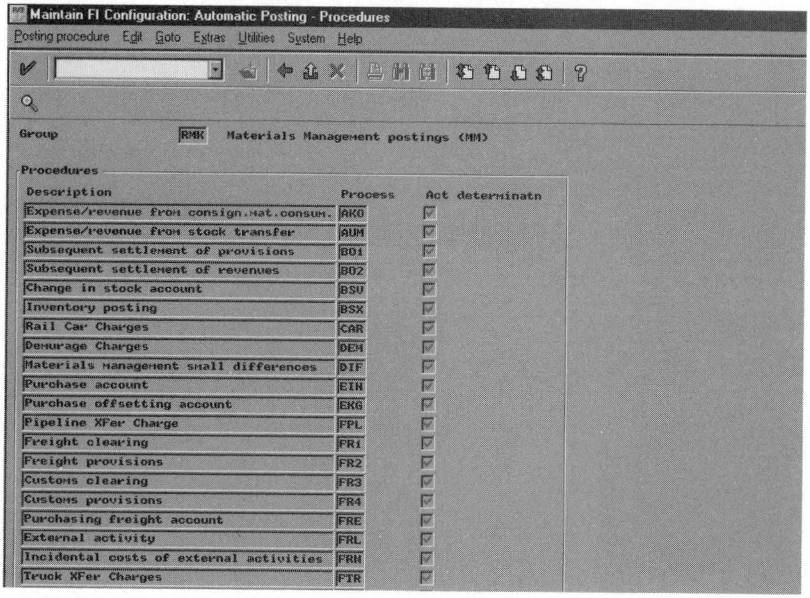

In this example, we will configure the account assignment for the processing key BSX. Processing key BSX is used to determine the inventory account to which MM transactions are posted. For example, you could use it to determine which inventory account to use to increase inventory through a goods receipt or which inventory account to use to decrease inventory through a goods issue. Double-click the processing key BSX, and you are presented with a pop-up screen asking you for the chart of accounts for which you wish to configure the automatic account assignment. After entering the appropriate chart name (EXCA), you are presented with the posting procedure rules screen, shown in Figure 3.37.

Figure 3.37 is the configuration screen for the rules to be used in the automatic account assignment for this processing key (BSX). There are three different control indicators that you can set in your rule: Debit/Credit, Valuation Modif., and Valuation Class.

FIGURE 3.37 The configured posting procedure rules for Extreme Sports

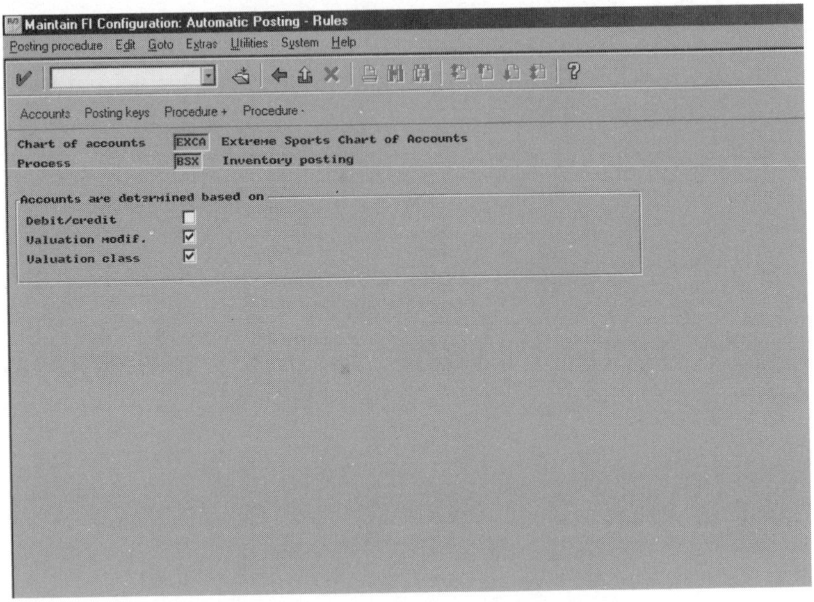

By setting the Debit/Credit indicator, you can assign different accounts to be used by the processing key depending on whether the transaction is debiting or crediting the account. By setting the Valuation Modif. (valuation modifier) indicator, you can use valuation grouping codes to distinguish your account determination. Valuation grouping codes are assigned to production plants; thus, if you want to post the same material to different accounts based upon division assignments, the valuation grouping code will allow you to make these different postings. By setting the Valuation Class indicator, you can assign different G/L accounts based upon the valuation class. Valuation classes are assigned to the material master of each material and signify the type of inventory that material represents, such as a finished good, semifinished good, or maintenance part.

On other processing keys, such as GBB, there is an additional indicator, General Modification, that you can select. The General Modification indicator allows you to configure account modifiers along with the G/L account. Account modifiers are assigned to different movement types, thus allowing you to post to various G/L accounts based on the movement type that is used in the transaction. The configured rules for Extreme Sports' BSX processing key appear in Figure 3.37.

After making the settings, click the Accounts button and the screen in Figure 3.38 appears.

FIGURE 3.38   The account determination screen for valuation grouping code, valuation class, and account has been configured for Extreme Sports.

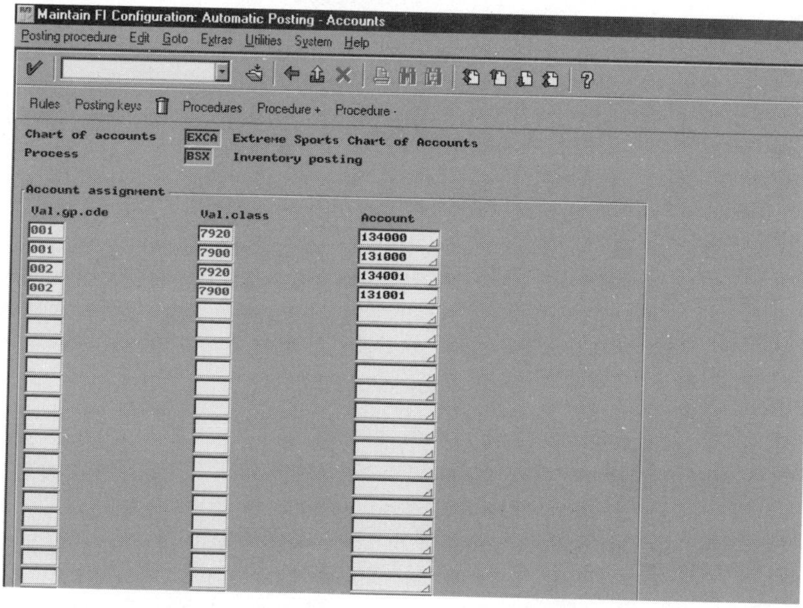

As you can see in Figure 3.38, there are three columns to configure. You'll set the valuation grouping code (which appears because of the valuation modifier settings in the rules), the valuation class (which appears because of the valuation class setting in the rules, and the account. (Only one column appears for the account because the Debit/Credit indicator was not set in the rules. If it had been set, two Account columns would appear.)

EXTREME SPORTS MM AUTOMATIC ACCOUNT DETERMINATION CONFIGURATION ANALYSIS

Extreme Sports needs to keep track of its finished inventory (valuation class 7920) and its raw materials (valuation class 7900) in different accounts based upon whether the account is for apparel or sporting goods. All of the apparel production plants have been assigned to valuation grouping code 001, and all of the sporting equipment production plants have been assigned to valuation grouping code 002. The ability to use valuation classes and valuation grouping codes was set in the configuration for the rules of the processing key.

Sales and Distribution Automatic Account Assignment

As with MM, one of the main integration points between FI and the Sales & Distribution (SD) module is the *automatic account assignment*. SD automatic account assignment is different from all other account assignments in the system. SD account assignment does not use table T030. SD account assignments depend on condition tables and access sequences to determine the correct G/L account. You can set up the condition tables to use different characteristics such as customer class, plant, material group, and account modifiers. Account modifiers are attached to condition types, which are used in the SD pricing procedure. Account modifiers are what allow you to assign different G/L accounts to various condition types. Condition types can be set to be accrual condition types that allow you to make debit and credit postings from a single condition type.

Typically, you will use several different condition tables. After determining which characteristics you need and setting up the condition tables, you configure the access sequence. The access sequence determines the order in which the condition tables are read. Generally, you should go from the most specific condition table (the one with the most characteristics) to the least specific condition table (the one with the least number of characteristics). Some clients choose to have a "General" condition table that has no conditions for G/L accounts only so that all billings are allowed to go through (or post to) the system. There are arguments both for and against this practice; just be aware that it can be very time consuming to fix billings that have gone through the system with the wrong account assignment. If you want to catch all problems before a billing is posted and an invoice is sent to the customer, do not use a "General" condition table. The configuration of condition tables and access sequences is beyond the scope of this book.

N O T E   Using the IMG: **Sales and Distribution** ➢ **Basic Functions** ➢ **Account Assignment** ➢ **Revenue Account Determination**

The configuration path in the note box takes you to the IMG area where you configure condition tables and access sequences, as well as automatic account determinations themselves. The configuration path that appears in the next note takes you only to the account determination screen.

N O T E   Using the IMG: **Financial Accounting** ➤ **General Ledger Accounting** ➤ **Business Transactions** ➤ **Integration** ➤ **Sales and Distribution** ➤ **Prepare Revenue Account Determination**

Financial Statement Versions

Financial statement versions group together related accounts into balance sheet and income statement format for financial reporting purposes. SAP uses the financial statement version assigned to the company code when preparing the standard balance sheet and income statement reports in the system. The grouping in your financial statement version may or may not correspond to the account groupings that were configured earlier. You can assign accounts from different account groups in the same hierarchy nodes (groupings) in the financial statement version. The configuration transaction for financial statement versions is explained in the Define Financial Statement Versions shortcut box.

DEFINE FINANCIAL STATEMENT VERSIONS

You can use the following methods to get to the financial statement versions definition screen:

Menu Path: **Financial Accounting** ➤ **General Ledger Accounting** ➤ **Business Transactions** ➤ **Closing** ➤ **Document** ➤ **Define Financial Statement Versions**

Transaction Code: **OB58**

After entering the appropriate configuration transaction, you are presented with the screen that is shown in Figure 3.39.

FIGURE 3.39   The listing of the financial statement versions

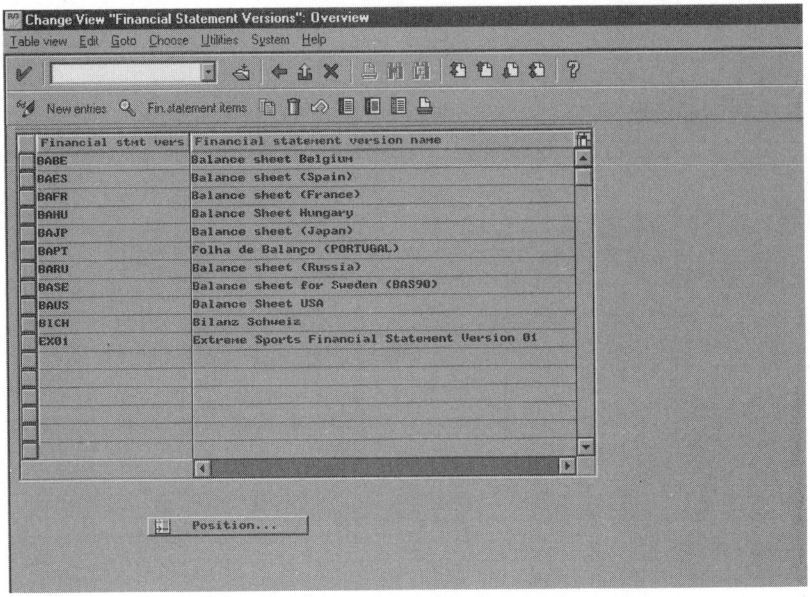

You will recall from Chapter 2 that we've assigned all of Extreme Sports' company codes to financial statement version EX01. After clicking the record for EX01 in the screen shown in Figure 3.39, you are presented with the general specification screen, as shown in Figure 3.40.

FIGURE 3.40   The general specification screen

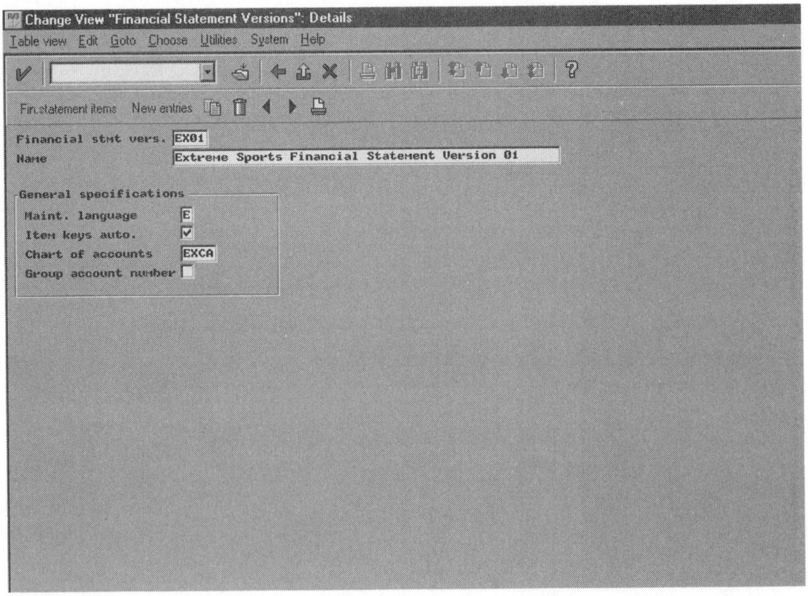

You will notice that there are four configuration settings that can be grouped under the heading General Specifications. They are as follows:

Maint. Language   The maintenance language determines the language in which the financial statement version is kept. For Extreme Sports, the maintenance language is E for English.

Item Keys Auto.   This indicator specifies whether item keys are assigned automatically or manually. Item keys are tied to the hierarchy nodes (financial statement items) in the financial statement version itself. It is recommended that you set this indicator so that item keys are assigned automatically

Chart of Accounts   Enter the chart of accounts that this financial statement version relates to. In our case, the chart of accounts is EXCA.

Group Account Number   Set this indicator if you wish to assign numbers from the group chart of accounts instead of the chart of accounts that was configured in the Chart of Accounts indicator. Group charts of accounts are part of the consolidation function. This setting is only valid if you are using the consolidation functionality of SAP.

Once you have made all of your configuration settings, as shown for Extreme Sports in Figure 3.40, you are ready to configure your financial statement items. Financial statement items are similar to hierarchy nodes. To configure the financial statement items, click the Fin. Statement Items button. You are then presented with a screen like the one shown in Figure 3.41.

FIGURE 3.41   The Extreme Sports Financial Statement Version 01 configuration

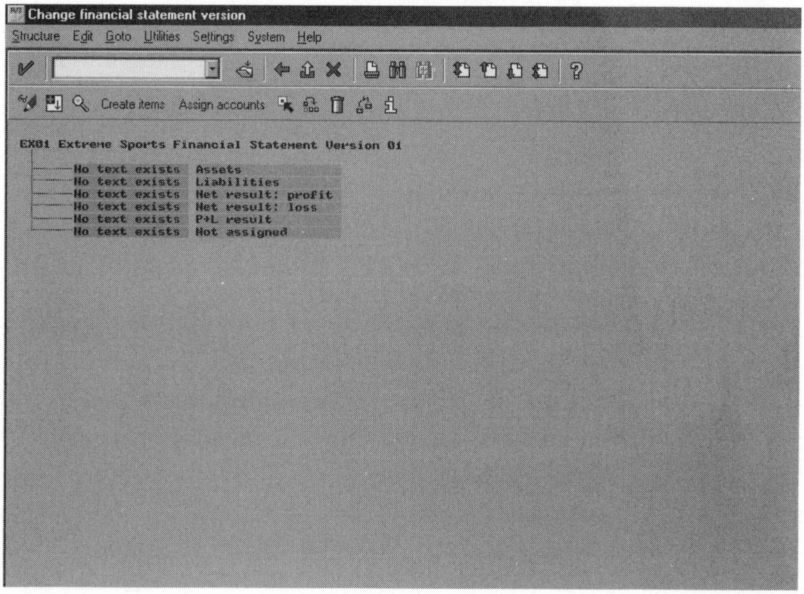

As you can see, only a base skeleton is given to you to work with. Right now, there are no subgroupings or accounts assigned to any of the financial statement items. In our example, the Assets financial statement item will be configured. To start, double-click the Assets financial statement item (hierarchy node). You are presented with the screen that is shown in Figure 3.42.

FIGURE 3.42　The Change Texts dialog box is used to add details to the Assets financial statement.

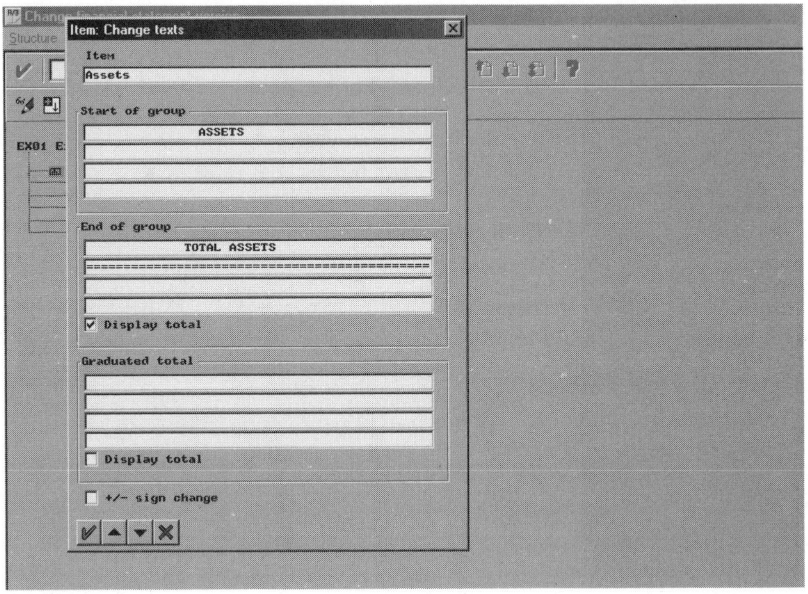

In this screen, you are able to control the textual description of the financial statement item, as well as whether totals are shown for the item and whether the sign should be reversed when displaying the balances in accounts. Reversing the sign of an account causes a credit balance account to display as a debit and vice versa. The fully configured screen for the Assets financial statement item appears in Figure 3.42.

As you can see, the item was named ASSETS in the first line. When this financial statement item is used, the term *ASSETS* will be shown at the beginning of the grouping of Assets accounts. At the end of the group, the term *TOTAL ASSETS,* underscored with a double line, will be shown. The end of the group will also display the total account for the financial statement item. There is no need to display graduated totals because graduated totals are relevant only for income statement accounts. Extreme Sports would also like to display assets using their natural debit balance, so there is no need to set the +/- Sign Change indicator. Now that the Assets financial statement item has been configured, you are ready to assign other subitems to it. To do so, select the Assets financial statement item by clicking on it once. Then click the Create Items button. You are presented with the screen shown in Figure 3.43.

FIGURE 3.43   The Create Items screen

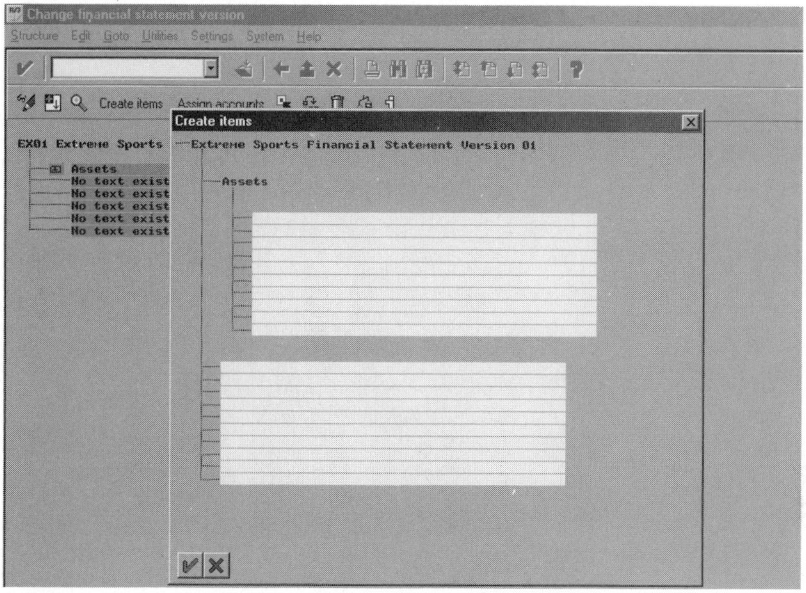

In this screen, enter the subitems you would like to appear under Assets. The subitems can have accounts assigned directly to them or have other subitems attached to them so that they act as hierarchy nodes. The configuration for Extreme Sports appears in Figure 3.44.

FIGURE 3.44   The configuration of some Assets subitems for Extreme Sports

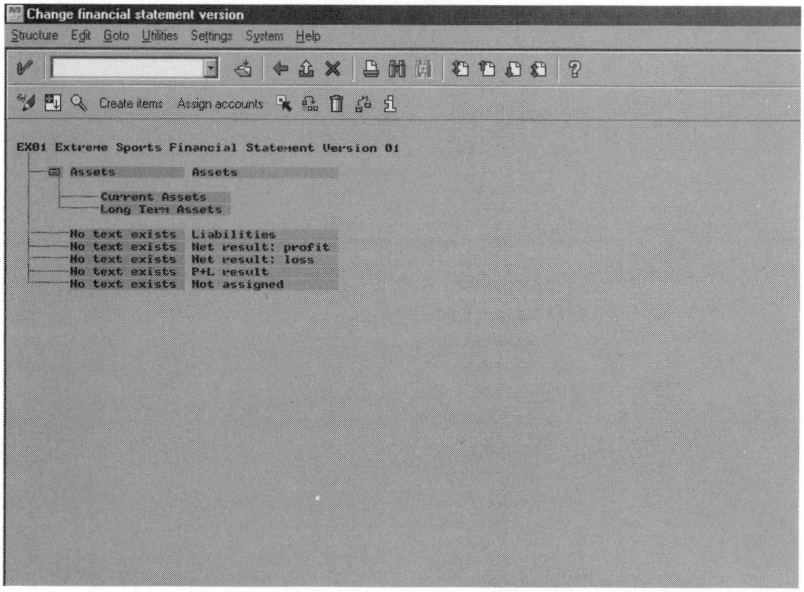

As you can see, only two additional items were attached directly to the existing assets. These two items, Current Assets and Long Term Assets, will have additional items attached to them, and you can have yet more additional items attached to them or, in turn, have G/L accounts assigned to them. You are now ready to configure the items that will appear under the Current Assets item. To attach more items to it, click the Current Assets item and then click the Create Items button, as was done before. You are presented with the Create Items screen, as seen in Figure 3.45.

FIGURE 3.45   The Create Items screen

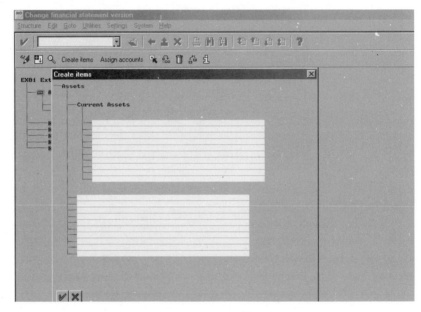

After you enter the additional items needed under Current Assets, the main configuration screen appears, as in Figure 3.46.

Although normally you would want to break out each of the lowest-level items even further later in your project, in this example, we are now ready to assign G/L accounts to the lowest-level financial statement items under Current Assets. To assign G/L accounts, select the item that you want to assign accounts to by single-clicking it (in our example, Cash and Cash Equivalents). After selecting the item, click the Assign Accounts button. You are presented with the screen in Figure 3.47. Yours won't have the elements filled in.

FIGURE 3.46   The configured items now show under Current Assets.

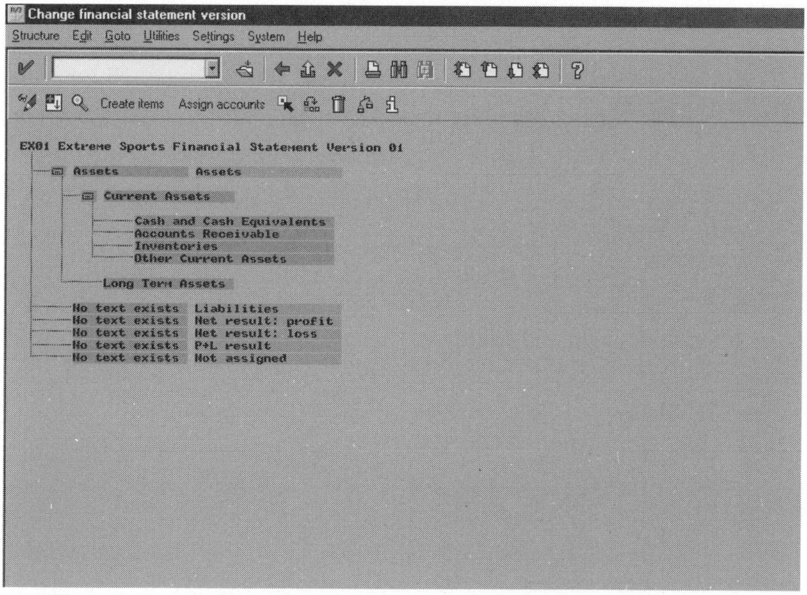

FIGURE 3.47   The Change Accounts dialog box

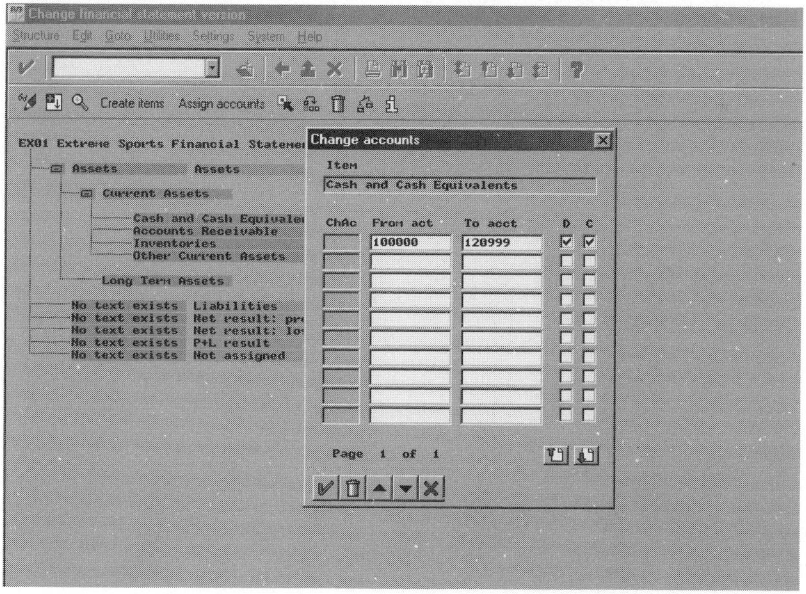

Enter the G/L account number range in the Change Accounts dialog box to display either debit balances, credit balances, or both. It is normally a good idea to set both the debit and credit indicators so that you are picking up all activity in your financial statements. There's nothing that gets the accounting staff more riled up than when the balance sheet doesn't balance. Figure 3.47 displays the configuration for Extreme Sports' Cash and Cash Equivalents grouping on the balance sheet.

Figure 3.48 displays the fully configured Cash and Cash Equivalents portion of Extreme Sports' balance sheet. As you can see, the Cash and Cash Equivalents item now has a range of G/L accounts assigned to it. You can display all the G/L account numbers by clicking on the hierarchy expand/collapse icon next to the range of accounts.

FIGURE 3.48   The configured balance sheet for Extreme Sports

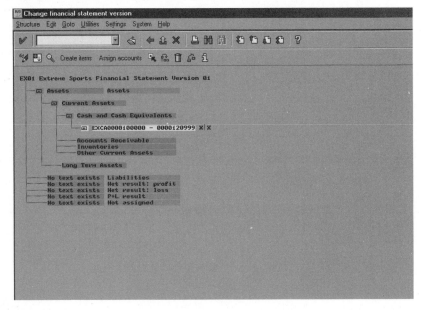

The implementation team will use the technique demonstrated in this section to finish configuring the rest of the financial statement version for both the balance sheet and income statement.

G/L Display Configuration

Now that you have an understanding of the various settings that can be made in G/L accounts, it is time to learn how to incorporate the use of these settings into G/L display functionality. This section will be used specifically to create line item layouts, sort variants, and totals variants to be used in G/L line item display. In addition to these functions, there are other components of line item display that can be configured, such as selection fields, additional fields, and search fields. You will recall from the previous sections that accounts can be set to display line items. Posting and displaying items in an account with line item display turned on allows you the most flexibility in analyzing an individual account.

Line Item Layouts

The first piece of configuration that will be done in this section is a line item layout. Line item layouts display the value of different fields that come from the field status group of the G/L account posted to, fields populated via the G/L company code screen, as well as fields from the accounting document headers and other special fields. Line item layouts are used in the G/L line item display transaction from the application (user) menu. The configuration transaction for line item layouts is presented in the Define Line Layouts shortcut box.

DEFINE LINE LAYOUTS

You can use the following methods to get to the line layout definition screen:

Menu Path: **Financial Accounting** ➤ **General Ledger Accounting** ➤ **G/L Accounts** ➤ **Line Items** ➤ **Line Item Display** ➤ **Define Line Layout**

Transaction Code: **O7Z3**

Follow the menu path Financial Accounting ➤ General Ledger Accounting ➤ G/L Accounts ➤ Line Items ➤ Line Item Display ➤ Define Line Layout to get to the initial configuration screen. Figure 3.49 displays the initial configuration screen.

FIGURE 3.49   The define line layout screen

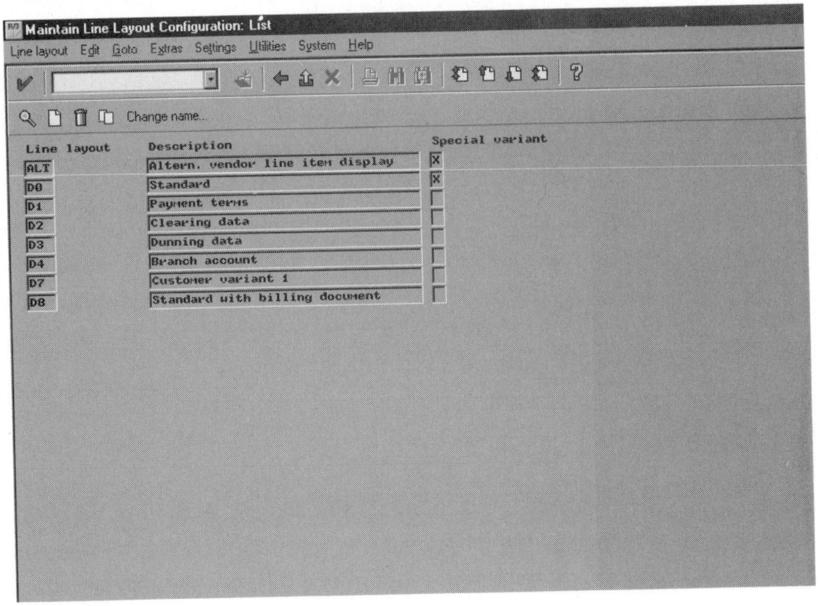

As you can see, SAP comes delivered with several line item layouts. The line item layouts that have an *X* in the far right column (Special Variant) denote that the line item layout uses a special field for its display. Special fields display additional information from places other than the line item display tables (RFPOS), such as the document header, check register, or document line item. Because it is reading from another table, performance may be slower than on other line item layouts that do not use special fields. Special fields will be covered in more detail later in this section.

To create a new line item layout, click the create icon. You are presented with the pop-up box to enter the identifier for the line layout.

Enter a line item layout identifier in the line layout box. The identifier can contain up to three characters. The next step is to give the layout a description and choose whether the line item layout will be used on Customer, Vendor, or G/L accounts. In this example, you will be configuring a G/L line item layout. After entering all of the information in the pop-up box and pressing Enter, you are presented with the blank configuration screen for your line item layout, as shown in Figure 3.50.

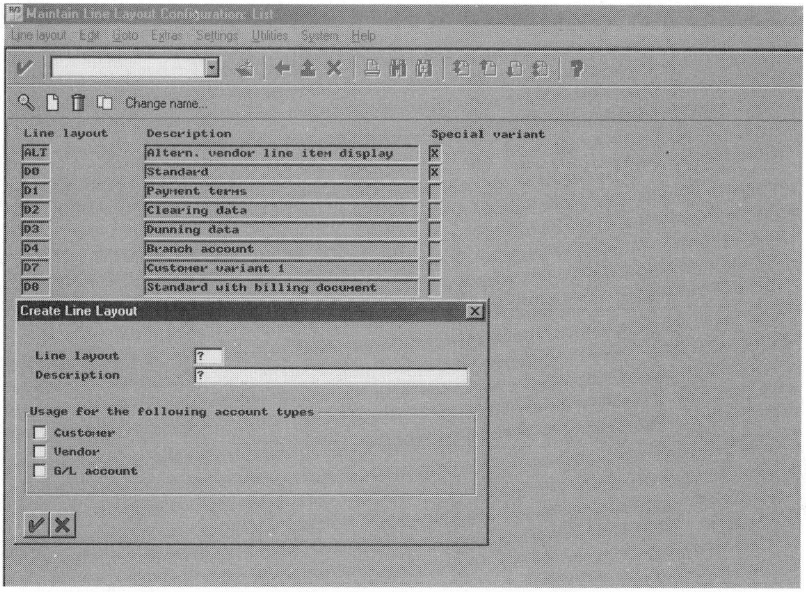

FIGURE 3.50   The blank configuration screen for line item layout

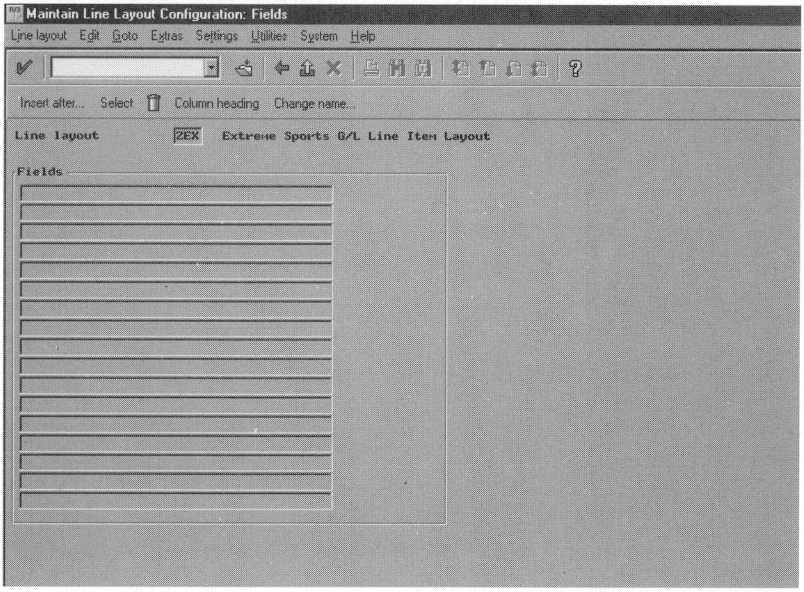

On this screen, select the fields that you would like included on the line item layout. To add fields, click the first of the blank entries under the Fields header. After clicking the entry to select it, click the Insert After button. You'll be presented with a list window.

The list window defaults to show the normal fields you can select from the line item table. Take special notice of the Technical Names On and Special Fields buttons at the bottom of the window. If you click the Technical Names On button, the actual field names from the table are presented next to the description. This feature can be quite helpful because some of the descriptions for different fields are exactly the same. The Special Fields button brings up a list of additional fields that are not in the regular line item tables. As mentioned earlier, special fields may decrease the performance of the line item layout. Once you find the field you want to select, double-click it to add it to your line item layout. Once the field name is added, repeat the process by continuing to click the Insert After button. Line item layouts can contain a maximum of 15 fields and/or a maximum of 130 characters. The fields selected to be displayed in the line item layout default to the maximum size of the data element for the field, with a one-character displacement between fields. You can customize the size of the field, the offset for display, and the character displacement between fields by double-clicking the field. When you do so, you are presented with the Display Format dialog box.

The Display Format fields control the length and display of the field. By entering a number in the Offset field, you can control the position in the field from which the start of the display should begin. For example, placing a 5 in the field will make the field start displaying from the sixth character (it will skip five characters). The Display Length field controls the number of characters that are displayed (cutting off from the end of the field). The Distance field controls the displacement (number of characters) between the end of the preceding field and the start of the current field. After setting the formatting display options for the fields that you have selected, you are ready to configure the column headings of the line item layout. To do so, first click the save icon. Then click the Column Heading button, and the screen displayed in Figure 3.51 appears.

FIGURE 3.51   The column heading configuration screen

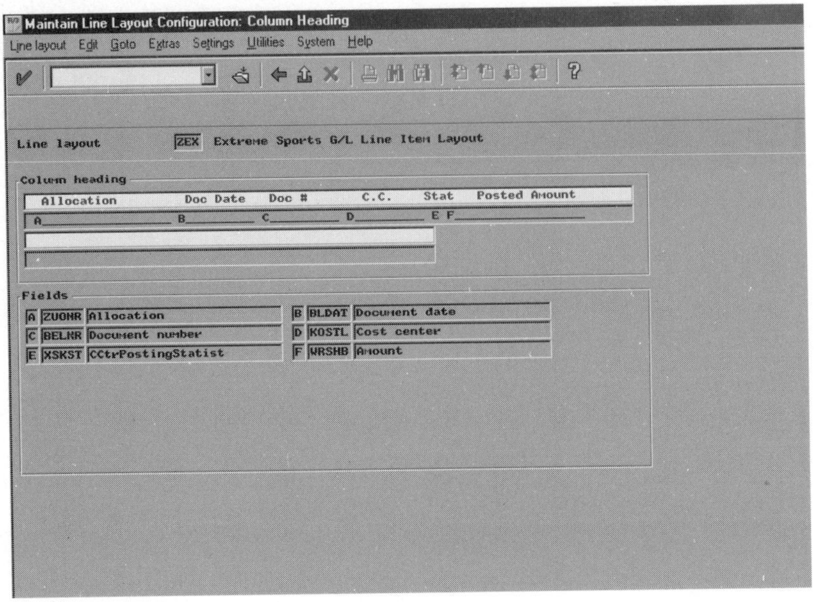

From the screen in Figure 3.51, you can see the fields that were selected for the line item display in the previous steps. Each field is assigned a letter from *A* to *O*, which corresponds to the column heading letters for the fields. In the Column Heading section, enter a description for each of the fields next to the assigned field letter. These are the column headings that will be displayed on the screen when the line item layout is used. Figure 3.51 displays the configured column heading screen for Extreme Sports.

Once you have entered the descriptions, click the save icon. Then use the green arrow to back out to the field configuration screen for the line item layout. Click the save icon once more to save the entire line item layout. If a special field was selected, you will receive an informational/warning message informing you of its selection. Press Enter to complete the save process.

Special Fields

Special fields were used in the line item display subsection. In addition to being used in line item displays, special fields can be used for selecting, finding, and sorting (sort variants) data. SAP comes delivered with several special fields that can be used with no additional configuration. To add additional fields to the special field lists, additional configuration must be undertaken. The configuration transaction for creating additional special fields is begun by following the menu path Financial

Accounting ➤ General Ledger Accounting ➤ G/L Accounts ➤ Line Items ➤ Line Item Display ➤ Define Special Fields For Selecting/Finding/Sorting Data.

ADD SPECIAL FIELDS

You can get to the screen to add special fields by using one of the following methods:

Menu Path: **Financial Accounting ➤ General Ledger Accounting ➤ G/L Accounts ➤ Line Items ➤ Line Item Display ➤ Define Special Fields For Selecting/Finding/Sorting Data**

Transaction Code: **OBVU**

This particular configuration transaction (OBVU) uses table (view) Table: V_T021S. V_T021S is a client-independent table. Refer to Chapter 1 for an explanation of the difference between client-dependent and client-independent tables and transports.

In the configuration screen, shown in Figure 3.52, you are required to enter the table and the field name of the special field you want to add.

FIGURE 3.52 The configuration screen for entering the table and field name of the special field you want to add

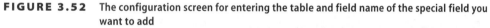

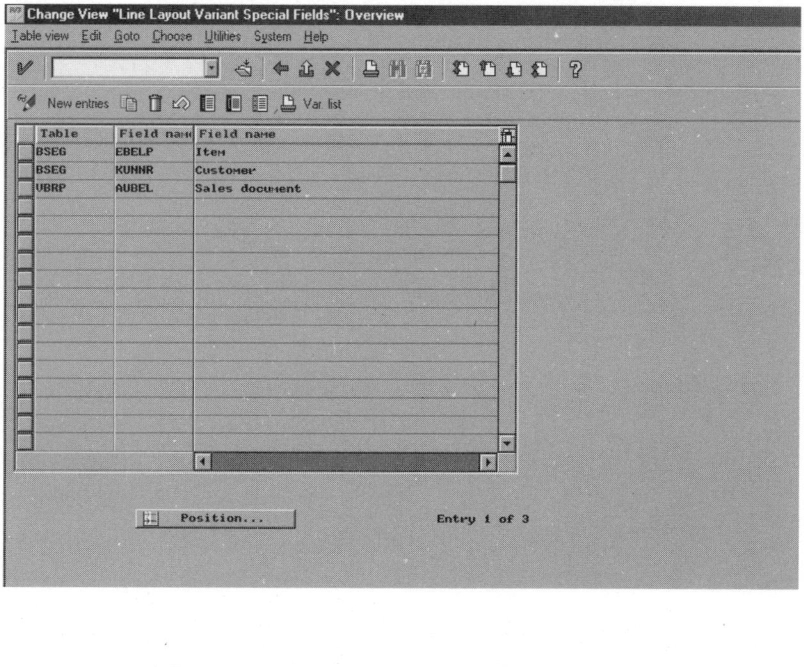

You can choose fields from the following tables:

BKPF	Accounting Document Header
BSEC	One-Time Account Data Document Segment
BSED	Bill of Exchange Fields Document Segment
BSEG	Accounting Document Line Items Segment
PAYR	Payment Transfer Medium File

It is important to note that not all fields from these tables can be selected. You must select one of the fields from the drop-down list. When you decide to use BSEG, you can't select any field that is within BSEG; you must select one of the BSEG fields shown in the drop-down list in the field on the screen.

Sort Variants

Sort variants are used to determine the order in which line items are displayed on the screen while using a line item layout without a totals variant. SAP comes delivered with standard sort variants, but you are also afforded the flexibility to create your own sort variants. You can choose or create configuration commands for sort variants by following the menu path Financial Accounting ➢ General Ledger Accounting ➢ G/L Accounts ➢ Line Items ➢ Line Item Display ➢ Choose Sort Variants.

DEFINE SORT VARIANTS

You can choose or create a configuration command for sort variants by using one of the following methods:

Menu Path: **Financial Accounting** ➢ **General Ledger Accounting** ➢ **G/L Accounts** ➢ **Line Items** ➢ **Line Item Display** ➢ **Choose Sort Variants**

Transaction Code: **07S7**

Figure 3.53 displays the configuration screen for sort variants.

FIGURE 3.53   The configuration screen for sort variants

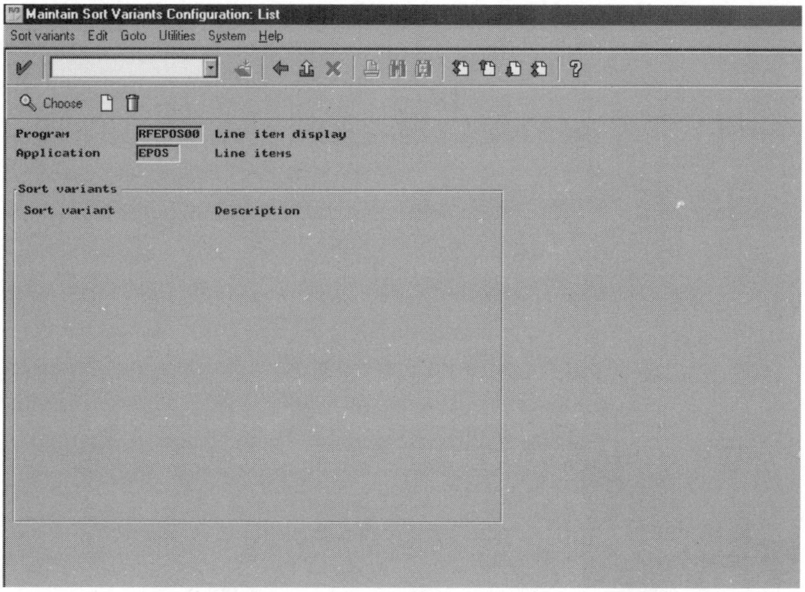

To create a new sort variant, click the create icon. Next you will be asked to enter a three-character identifier for the sort variant as well as a description. After entering the identifier and description and pressing Enter, you are presented with a screen like the one shown in Figure 3.54.

FIGURE 3.54   The sort field configuration screen allows you to set the order in which the fields will be displayed.

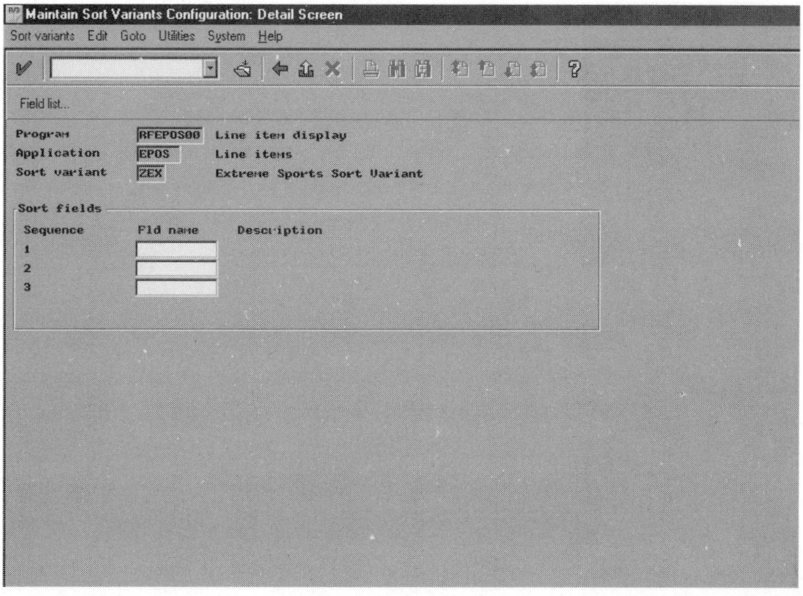

As you can see, you are allowed a maximum of three fields to sort by. The system sorts by field 1 first, then field 2, and then field 3. To select your fields for sorting, use the pull-down button on the field (the pull-down menu will appear when you select the field). You must select one of the fields in the pull-down list. After you've selected the fields that meet your requirements, click the save icon.

Totals Variants

Totals variants are used in lieu of sort variants to display line items and to total and subtotal amounts. For example, you might use a totals variant to total by document type and then by posting date. The described totals variant would subtotal each posting date by document type and display a total for each document type. Follow the menu path Financial Accounting ➢ General Ledger Accounting ➢ G/L Accounts ➢ Line Items ➢ Line Item Display ➢ Define Totals Variants to get to the configuration commands for totals variants.

DEFINE TOTALS VARIANTS

You can use the following methods to get to the configuration commands for setting totals variants:

Menu Path: **Financial Accounting** ➢ **General Ledger Accounting** ➢ **G/L Accounts** ➢ **Line Items** ➢ **Line Item Display** ➢ **Define Totals Variants**

Transaction Code: **O7R1**

In order to create a new totals variant, click the create icon, shown in Figure 3.55. You are then presented with a pop-up box asking for a three-character totals variant identifier as well as a description for the variant. After entering this information and pressing Enter, you are presented with a screen like that in Figure 3.56.

FIGURE 3.55   The totals variant configuration screen

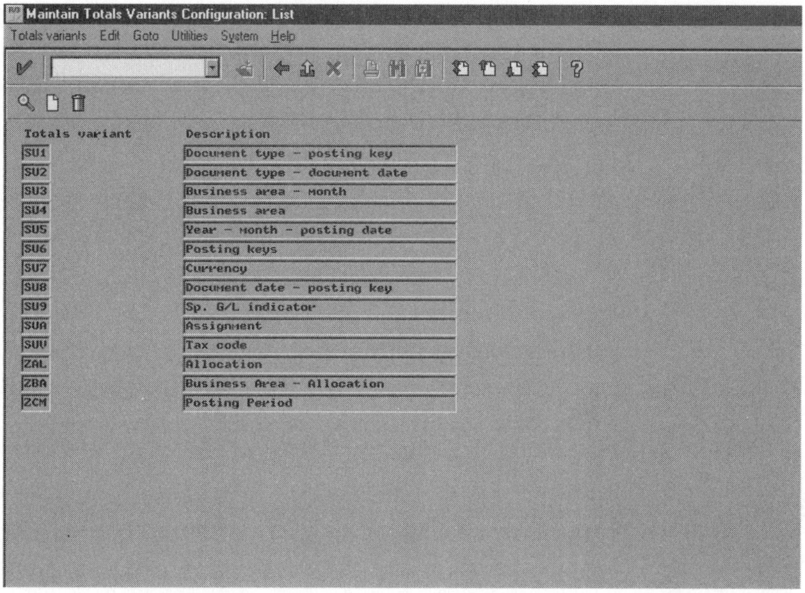

Maintain Totals Variants Configuration: List

Totals variants Edit Goto Utilities System Help

Totals variant	Description
SU1	Document type - posting key
SU2	Document type - document date
SU3	Business area - Month
SU4	Business area
SU5	Year - Month - posting date
SU6	Posting keys
SU7	Currency
SU8	Document date - posting key
SU9	Sp. G/L indicator
SUA	Assignment
SUV	Tax code
ZAL	Allocation
ZBA	Business Area - Allocation
ZCM	Posting Period

FIGURE 3.56   You are allowed to select the way you want the results of a totals variant configuration presented.

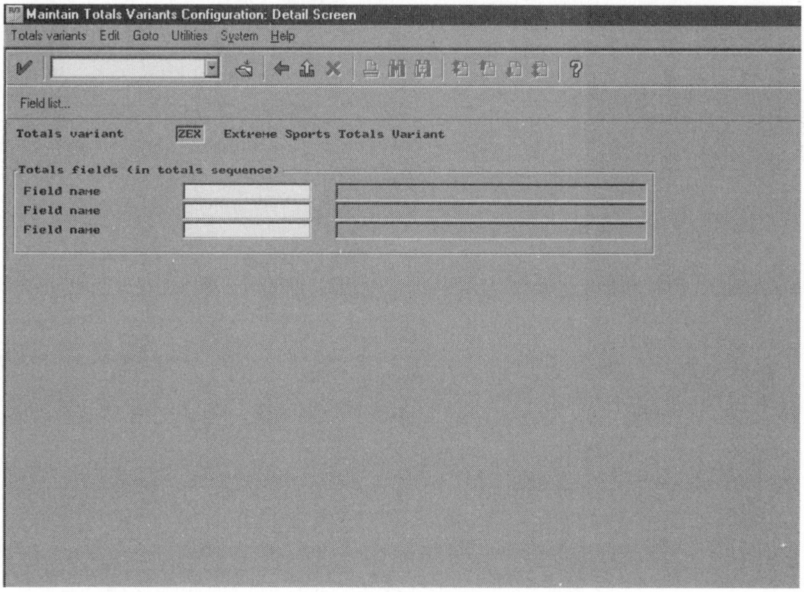

Maintain Totals Variants Configuration: Detail Screen

Totals variants Edit Goto Utilities System Help

Field list...

Totals variant   ZEX   Extreme Sports Totals Variant

Totals fields (in totals sequence)

Field name

Field name

Field name

Like sort variants, totals variants allow you to select up to three fields by which to total. You must select one of the fields from the pull-down box. The system will total by the first field, then the second field, and then the third field; as you can imagine, it is best to go from less detail to more detail when ordering the fields to be used. After entering the fields, click the save icon to record your variant.

Posting Amount Defaults and Tolerance Groups

Now that the entire chart of accounts configuration has taken place, it is time to start thinking about posting transactions in the system. The next step is to set up *posting amount defaults*. Posting amount defaults are stored in *tolerance groups*. Tolerance groups, in turn, are assigned to user IDs. You will need to do a careful analysis of the various tolerance groups that you will need in the system. This process should be part of the overall security and authorization setup of your system. If a tolerance is not explicitly assigned in a user ID, the tolerance group defaults to the group Null (empty) for the company code. It is therefore very important to have the Null tolerance group as the most restrictive tolerance group in your system if you choose to have a Null tolerance group. If you want to ensure that unauthorized persons cannot make postings, do not create a Null tolerance group; then only user IDs with a valid tolerance group assigned to them will be able to make postings. With these concepts in mind, you are ready to configure tolerance groups and posting amount defaults.

NOTE   It is very important to have the Null tolerance group as the most restrictive tolerance group in your system if you choose to have a Null tolerance group. Otherwise, it is possible for unauthorized users to post large amounts to the G/L.

To get to the initial configuration screen for defining tolerance groups (see Figure 3.57) and posting amount defaults, follow the menu path Financial Accounting ➤ Financial Accounting Global Settings ➤ Document ➤ Line Item ➤ Define Tolerance Groups for Employees.

DEFINE TOLERANCE GROUPS

You can use the following methods to get to the tolerance group definition screen:

Menu Path: **Financial Accounting** ➤ **Financial Accounting Global Settings** ➤ **Document** ➤ **Line Item** ➤ **Define Tolerance Groups for Employees**

Transaction Code: **OBA4**

FIGURE 3.57 The configuration screen for defining tolerance groups

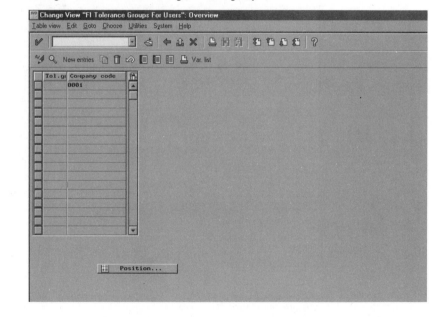

As you can see, SAP comes delivered with a standard tolerance group for the SAP-delivered company code 0001. You must create at least one tolerance group per company code. Postings cannot be made in the system until a tolerance group is configured. Our example will create the Null tolerance group for Extreme Sports' company code 1000. From the configuration screen for defining tolerance groups, click the New Entries button. You are presented with the screen in Figure 3.58.

FIGURE 3.58   The configuration screen for creating a Null tolerance group for Extreme Sports

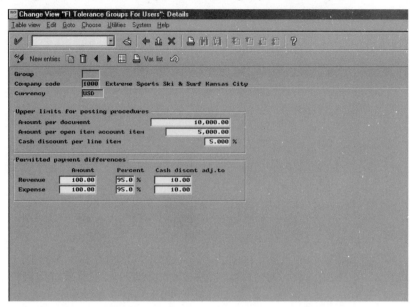

The fields that appear in Figure 3.58 are explained here:

Group   Enter the four-character alphanumeric identifier of the group. In this example for Extreme Sports, we will leave the group field blank (Null).

Company Code   Enter the four-character identifier of the company code to which the tolerance group being configured belongs.

Currency   The company code currency defaults into this field.

Amount per Document   Enter the maximum amount that can be posted in a single accounting document.

Amount per Open Item Account Item   Enter the maximum amount that can be posted to a vendor or customer account. This field restricts the amount that can be paid to a vendor or cleared from receivables for a customer.

Cash Discount per Line Item   Enter the maximum percentage for a cash discount that can be applied to a line item in this field. For example, a cash discount rate of 5% would mean that the maximum cash discount that can be granted on a $100 line item is $5.

Amount, Percent, and Cash Discnt Adj. (both Revenue and Expense)   These fields have to do with the handling of customer overpayments and underpayments to the company. In the Amount field, enter the maximum amount of customer overpayment (revenue fields) or the maximum amount of customer underpayment (expense fields) that can be processed by this tolerance group. In the Percent field, enter the maximum percent of the total payment that can be applied by this tolerance group. The system looks at both the Amount and Percent field when making postings. The system will post differences up to the maximum percent specified as long as it does not go over the amount specified in the Amount field. In the Cash Discnt Adj. (cash discount adjustment) field, enter the amount of the difference that is to be posted to the cash discount account. Typically, this field is set to be a lower figure than the amount field.

To assign user IDs (employees) to tolerance groups, follow the menu path Financial Accounting ➢ Financial Accounting Global Settings ➢ Document ➢ Line Item ➢ Allocate Users to Tolerance Groups, and set the configuration transactions.

ALLOCATE USERS TO TOLERANCE GROUPS

You can allocate users to tolerance groups by using one of the following methods:

Menu Path: **Financial Accounting** ➢ **Financial Accounting Global Settings** ➢ **Document** ➢ **Line Item** ➢ **Allocate Users to Tolerance Groups**

Transaction Code: **OB57**

EXTREME SPORTS POSTING AMOUNT DEFAULT AND TOLERANCE GROUP CONFIGURATION ANALYSIS

Extreme Sports has decided to use several different tolerance groups and assign them to users based on their position in the company. They have also decided to configure the Null tolerance group. This will give Extreme Sports the flexibility to assign tolerance groups only to higher-level accounting staff, with the accounting clerks defaulting to the Null tolerance group. Because of this, the Null tolerance group is the most restrictive tolerance group created for Extreme Sports. Employees assigned to the Null tolerance group can post accounting documents up to $10,000 and clear customer and vendor accounts on items up to $5,000. Employees can grant cash discounts up to 5% of the line item amount. Both revenue and expense payment differences (customer overpayment and underpayment) are set to a maximum of 95.0% up to a total of $100. Amounts up to $10 of the total difference will be applied to the cash discount account.

Number Ranges and Document Types

There is one final piece of configuration that is needed before you can post entries in the system. The final step is setting up *document types* and assigning them to *number ranges*. SAP comes delivered with several different document types that are assigned to different transactions in the system. Each document type must have a number range assigned to it. The number ranges are what determine the document number. The document number, along with fiscal year, is the audit trail that is used in the system. As you are well aware, SAP utilizes the document principle, meaning that every posting in the system is done through a document, thus providing detailed drill-down to the source of all posting entries in the system. Each document in the system must balance before it is posted and cannot be deleted from the system until it is archived to other storage media.

Number Ranges

The first configuration step for this section is to set up number ranges. Because of the nature of number range objects in the system, number ranges are not automatically included in transport requests, even when automatic recording of changes is activated in the client. It is very easy to overlay number range objects and get existing ranges out of sync when you transport number ranges. It is recommended that you do not transport number ranges. Number ranges should be set up individually in each client. Doing so will save a lot of headaches as your project progresses. You set up number ranges by company code and year. Specifying the year as 9999 makes the number range valid for any year.

DEFINE FI NUMBER RANGES

You can get to the screen for defining number ranges by using one of the following methods:

Menu Path: **Financial Accounting** ➢ **Financial Accounting Global Settings** ➢ **Document** ➢ **Document Number Ranges** ➢ **Define Document Number Ranges**

Transaction Code: **FBN1**

Follow the menu path Financial Accounting ➤ Financial Accounting Global Settings ➤ Document ➤ Document Number Ranges ➤ Define Document Number Ranges to get to the initial configuration screen, seen in Figure 3.59.

FIGURE 3.59   The define document number ranges screen

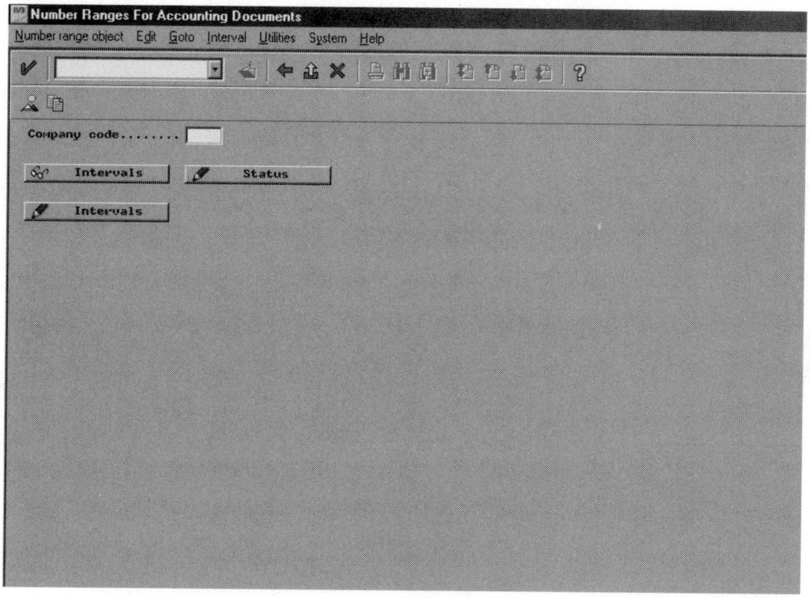

On this screen, enter the company code for which you want to configure number ranges. In our example, we will use company code 1000. After entering the company code, click the change interval button or follow the menu path Interval ➤ Change. You are then presented with the configuration screen shown in Figure 3.60.

FIGURE 3.60   The configuration screen for Extreme Sports' number ranges

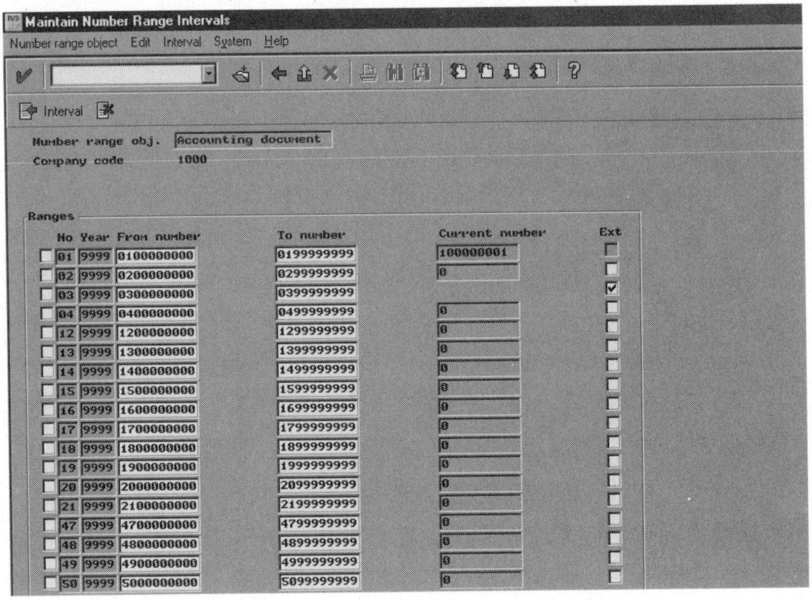

As you can see, Extreme Sports has already configured quite a few number ranges. Each interval is assigned a number, a year, a range of numbers, and an indicator to signify whether the interval should be externally assigned. Externally assigned number ranges require the user or a user-exit to provide the document number to SAP. For internally assigned number ranges, the system determines and fills in the document number based upon the next available number in the range. Let's create a number range to be used by the company code. First, click the insert interval icon, shown in Figure 3.60. You are presented with the pop-up configuration screen.

In the configuration dialog box, you are required to fill in the following fields:

Number   Enter the two-character alphanumeric identifier for the number range.

Year   Enter the last year through which this number range is valid. You can have several different entries for a number range, assigning it to different years. If you enter the year 9999, the number range is valid for all years.

From Number   Enter the first number to be used in the range (lower limit). You can also specify a range to use all characters instead of numbers.

To Number   Enter the last number to be used in the range (upper limit).

Current Number   This field defaults to 0. Do not make an entry in this field unless you do not want the first number that is assigned to be the same as the From Number setting on the interval.

Ext (Externally Assigned)   Select this indicator if you do not want the system to automatically assign a number to the document. Selecting this field makes the user input the document number manually (or a user-exit could possibly populate the field).

After entering information for the fields in the Insert Interval dialog box, press Enter or click the insert icon. Your entry will now appear in the overall number range list that was shown in Figure 3.60.

Document Types

Different document types are used for different transactions throughout the system. The document type controls many things, including the type of account that can be posted to, the number range assigned to it, and required document header fields. SAP comes delivered with several standard document types. For the most part, all you have to do is assign number ranges to each document type. You do have the option of creating new document types if your requirements determine that you need it.

DEFINE FI DOCUMENT TYPES

You can get to the screen to set the document type by using one of the following methods:

Menu Path: **Financial Accounting** ➢ **Financial Accounting Global Settings** ➢ **Document** ➢ **Document Header** ➢ **Document Types**

Transaction Code: **OBA7**

To set the initial configuration screen for document types, seen in Figure 3.61, follow the menu path Financial Accounting ➢ Financial Accounting Global Settings ➢ Document ➢ Document Header ➢ Document Types.

As you can see, there are numerous document types delivered with the system. From this screen, you can change the configuration of an existing document type or create a new document type. In our example, we will look at the configuration for one of the existing document types, SA, a G/L account document. To enter the configuration screen for the document type, double-click the document type identifier. You are presented with the screen shown in Figure 3.62.

FIGURE 3.61   The document types available listing

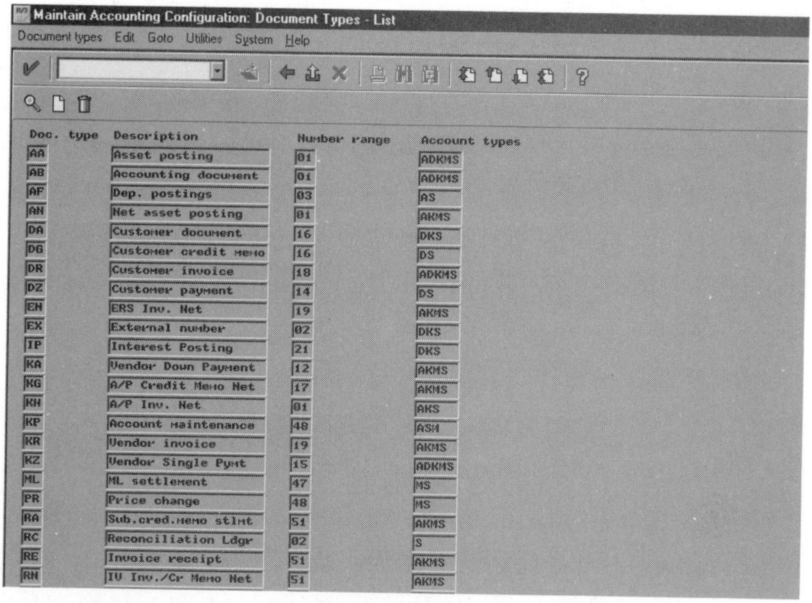

FIGURE 3.62   The document type configuration screen for SA G/L account document

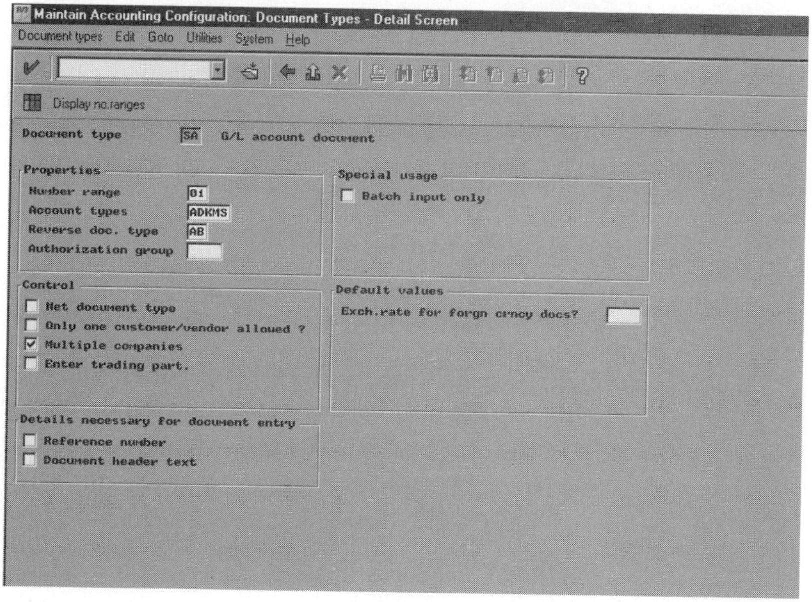

Let's examine the configuration fields:

Number Range Enter a valid number range that you configured in the preceding section. The number range assigned to a document type is valid for all company codes, but the number range must be set up in all company codes before it can be posted to. The number range can be assigned different number intervals in each company code. A number range can be assigned to more than one document type.

Account Types Enter the valid account types that can be posted to through this document. A single account type or any combination of account types can be specified. The valid account types are as follows:

ENTER	DESCRIPTION
A	Assets
D	Customers
K	Vendors
M	Materials
S	G/L Accounts

Reverse Doc. Type In this field, enter the identifier of the document type that should be used to reverse this type of document. The document type specified here will be used when a reversal transaction is undertaken in the system. The reversal document type can be the same document type as the document type being configured or it can be a different document type.

Authorization Group If you want to restrict the document type so that it can only be used by certain users, assign it to an authorization group. Authorization groups are assigned to user IDs via authorization objects. You will need to work closely with your Basis group to determine authorization groups.

Net Document Type This field is only valid for document types used for vendor invoices. Selecting this indicator will reduce the total amount due by the cash discount amount specified by the payment terms on the invoice.

Only One Customer/Vendor Allowed? Select this indicator if only a single customer or vendor should be allowed to be posted to on the document type. Setting this indicator on A/P and Invoicing document types is usually a good idea so that individual transactions exist for each customer or vendor account.

Multiple Companies Select this indicator to allow postings for more than one company code on the document. When a document contains entries for more than one company code, a cross-company code accounting document is automatically created by the system using the automatic account determination that was configured earlier in the cross-company code automatic postings discussion.

Enter Trading Part.   If this indicator is selected, the user is allowed to manually enter the trading partner on the document. Normally, trading partners default in off of one of the vendor master records.

Reference Number   Select this indicator to make the reference number in the document header a required entry. Normally, this indicator is set on document types used for A/P invoices.

Document Header Text   Select this indicator to make the document header text field a required entry.

Batch Input Only   Select this indicator if you want to keep this document type from being used on manual postings. If this indicator is set, only batch input sessions can create documents of this type.

Exch. Rate for Forgn Crncy Docs?   The system uses exchange rate type M (average rate) for documents posted in a foreign currency. The foreign currency translation is automatically done at this rate. If you want to use an exchange rate type other than M (average rate), enter it here. This field contains a pull-down list with all available exchange rate types.

Transaction Default Document Type and Posting Key

The standard accounting transactions delivered with SAP enable you to customize a default document type and posting key for each transaction. SAP comes delivered with standard document types and posting keys. If you wish to change these settings, SAP has the flexibility to allow you to do so. Depending on your requirements, you might find it useful to create several new documents to be used by different transactions. The following configuration will allow you to assign a new document to the proper transaction. Changing the default-posting key is not recommended unless you are very experienced in the system and it is absolutely necessary.

DEFINE DOCUMENT TYPES AND POSTING KEYS

You can use the following methods to get to the screen for defining document types and posting keys:

Menu Path: **Financial Accounting** ➢ **Financial Accounting Global Settings** ➢ **Document** ➢ **Line Item** ➢ **Default Values for Document Processing** ➢ **Define Document Type and Posting Key**

Transaction Code: **OBU1**

To change one of the entries, follow the menu path Financial Accounting ➤ Financial Accounting Global Settings ➤ Document ➤ Line Item ➤ Default Values for Document Processing ➤ Define Document Type and Posting Key. You'll get a screen like the one shown in Figure 3.63. Double-click the appropriate entry. You will then be able to select another document type and posting key from their respective pull-down menus. Please note that this is a client-independent configuration setting. (For more on client-dependent and client-independent settings, see Chapter 1.)

FIGURE 3.63   The configuration screen for defining documents and posting keys

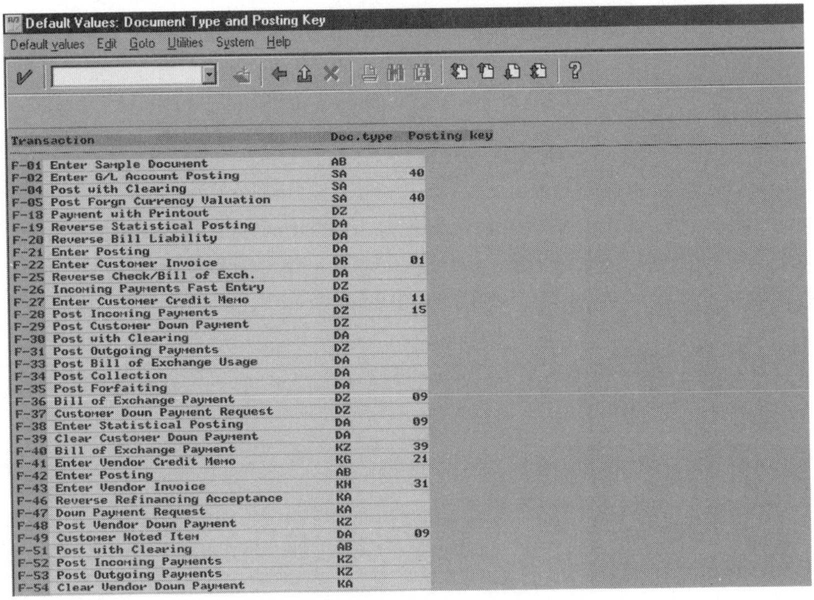

Fast Entry Screens

G/L document fast entry is a popular function with end users. Fast entry screens allow transactions to be posted at a more rapid pace than the usual method. In this section, we will demonstrate how to configure G/L fast entry screens. The configuration transaction for G/L fast entry screens is reached by following the menu path Financial Accounting ➤ Financial Accounting Global Settings ➤ Document ➤ Line Item ➤ Maintain Fast Entry Screens for G/L Account Line Items.

To create a new fast entry screen, click the create icon, shown in the screen in Figure 3.64.

DEFINE FAST ENTRY SCREENS

You can configure a fast entry posting by using one of the following methods:

Menu Path: **Financial Accounting** ➤ **Financial Accounting Global Settings** ➤ **Document** ➤ **Line Item** ➤ **Maintain Fast Entry Screens for G/L Account Line Items**

Transaction Code: **O7E6**

FIGURE 3.64   The fast entry configuration screen

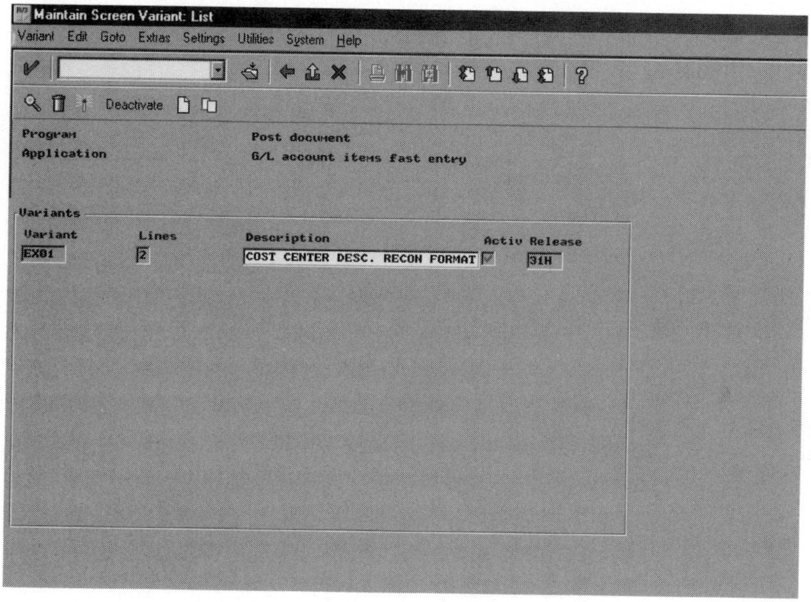

After clicking the create icon, you are presented with a pop-up box asking for a variant name, a description, and the number of lines for the variant. The number of lines defaults to one, and you can have a maximum of three lines. The number of lines determines the number of rows on which the fields for the variant are placed. After entering the required information, you are presented with the screen that shows the array of field names available. You can see the screen for Extreme Sports in Figure 3.65.

FIGURE 3.65   The fields available for fast entry in Extreme Sports

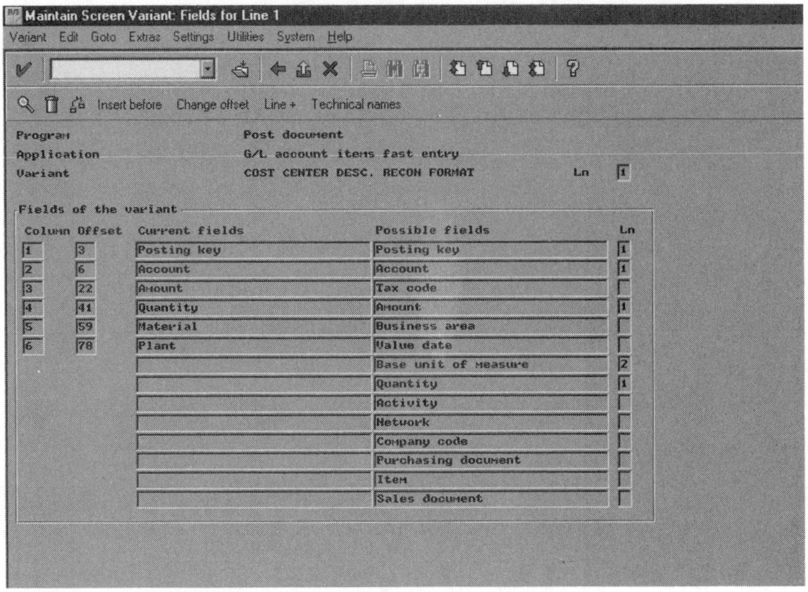

SAP presents you with the names of the fields that can be added. To add a field to your fast entry screen, double-click it. This will move the field over to the Current Fields column. After a field is moved to the Current Fields column, an indicator for the column number appears, as does a configurable field for offset. The offset of a field determines from what position the field starts, beginning from the left margin of the line in the fast entry screen. A fast entry screen line can have a maximum of 82 characters, which means that an entire fast entry screen can have a maximum of 246 characters because each fast entry screen can have up to three lines. The field posting key is required for each fast entry screen. If you set your fast entry screen to have more than one line, once you have entered all of the fields for the first line, click the Line+ button. After entering all of the fields you need, click the save icon.

After saving the fast entry screen, you must activate it in order for it to be available for use. To activate it, select the fast entry screen ID, as shown in Figure 3.64. After selecting the proper fast entry screen ID, click the Activate button. The Activate button is the one that looks like a magic wand.

The configured Extreme Sports fast entry, as it would be used in a G/L account posting transaction, is shown in Figure 3.66. Notice that the available fields for posting appear on two different lines.

FIGURE 3.66   The results of configuring Line 1 for fast entry as you'd see in a G/L account posting

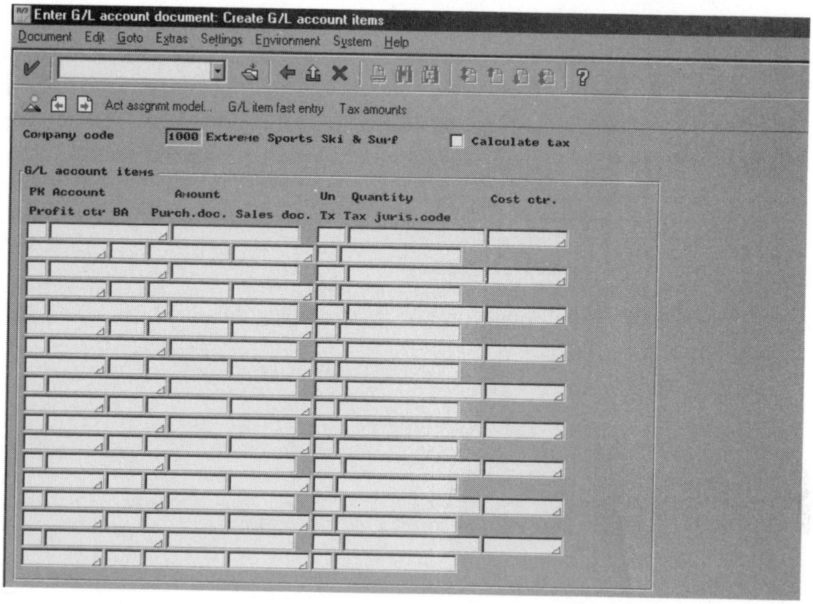

EXTREME SPORTS G/L FAST ENTRY SCREEN CONFIGURATION ANALYSIS

Extreme Sports has decided to configure an all-encompassing G/L fast entry screen for regular G/L entry transactions. Knowing the overall system design and requirements, the appropriate fields for the fast entry screen were selected (Posting Key, Account, Amount, Business Area, Company Code, Tax Code, Tax Jurisdiction Code, Cost Center, Order, Profit Center, Allocation). Because fast entry screens are limited to 82 characters and the fields required for the screen were more than 82 characters, the variant was set up to use two line items. Accounting clerks at Extreme Sports will use the configured fast entry screen when making normal journal entries in the system.

Summary

This chapter covered a combination of configuration and master data maintenance. We finished the configuration of our chart of accounts, as well as created a G/L account. The important concept of automatic account determination was introduced in this chapter. As you work through other chapters, be sure to look for automatic account assignments in the IMG because it would be impossible to cover every needed automatic account assignment in this book. If you remember one thing from this chapter, remember that automatic account assignments act like a whole table transport and that changing the rules on a processing key wipes out all existing account assignments for that key. In addition to these key areas, we also looked at the detailed configuration settings for the following:

Chart of Accounts

    Account Groups

    Configuring G/L Master Records

Copying and Transporting G/L Accounts

Field Status Groups

Posting Keys

Automatic Account Determination

    Sales/Use Tax Automatic Account Assignment

    Intercompany Posting Automatic Account Assignment

    Materials Management Automatic Account Assignment

    Sales & Distribution Automatic Account Assignment

Financial Statement Versions

G/L Display Configuration

    Line Item Layouts

    Special Fields

    Sort Variants

    Totals Variants

Posting Amount Defaults and Tolerance Groups

Number Ranges and Document Types

    Transaction Default Document Type and Posting Key

    Fast Entry Screens

CHAPTER 4

Accounts Payable

FEATURING:

▶ **HOUSE BANKS AND ACCOUNTS**

▶ **PAYMENT PROGRAM CONFIGURATION**

▶ **VENDOR MASTER DATA**

ccounts Payable is the first subledger that will be discussed. The A/P module is tightly integrated with the MM module, the Treasury module, and the A/R module. The A/P module allows you to manage the most complex of A/P transactions. With SAP's A/P system, a company can easily manage its payables to provide the maximum cash discount and available cash position on its liabilities. All types of payments can be used, as well as the additional function of A/P and A/R netting for vendors that are also customers. In addition to the configuration of the A/P module, configuration of house banks and accounts will be discussed.

House Banks and Accounts

The first step in configuring the A/P submodule is to create house banks. House banks are the banks your company uses for banking purposes. Each house bank can have several different bank accounts linked to it. As part of the reengineering phase of your project, it is important to analyze which and how many banks and bank accounts your company uses. Your SAP implementation is a good time to cut down on both the number of banks and the number of accounts that are used. Normally, you will find that, as your organization has grown over the years, it has maintained a relationship with a large number of banks and has a lot of bank accounts based on previous organizational structures, acquisitions, and legacy system constraints.

A house bank is identified by a unique bank key. Bank keys vary in form from country to country. In the U.S., the bank key is known as the A.B.A. (American Banking Association) number. Normally, the system is set up so that each house bank has its own company code. Lately, with the large number of mergers in the U.S. banking industry, it may be necessary to set up for a single banking institution two house banks within a company code. This need arises because some of the larger banks use one A.B.A. number for paper transactions (your company's checks) and another A.B.A. number for electronic transactions. For this scenario, two house banks would be set up for a single physical bank, and two bank accounts linked to the same G/L account would also be created for the single bank account. Once again, this is the exception and not the rule; a thorough understanding of the system is necessary for this technique to be implemented successfully.

The configuration of house banks is relatively simple. It is much like setting up master data in the system. To get to the house bank configuration screen, follow the menu path Financial Accounting ➤ General Ledger Accounting ➤ Bank-Related Accounting ➤ Bank Accounts ➤ Define House Banks.

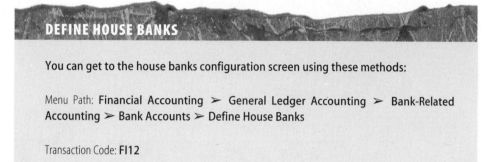

DEFINE HOUSE BANKS

You can get to the house banks configuration screen using these methods:

Menu Path: **Financial Accounting** ➤ **General Ledger Accounting** ➤ **Bank-Related Accounting** ➤ **Bank Accounts** ➤ **Define House Banks**

Transaction Code: **FI12**

The initial configuration screen for house banks is shown in Figure 4.1.

FIGURE 4.1   The initial house banks configuration screen

As you can see, a house bank is tied to a company code, and each bank account is tied to a house bank. The first configuration step is to enter the company code for which the house bank is being configured and click the Create Bank button. After you enter these parameters, a pop-up box appears asking for the house bank identifier and the bank country. The house bank identifier is used by the system as part of the key for the house bank. It is determined by you and should follow the naming standards developed for your project. The house bank identifier is alphanumeric and can be up to five characters in length. The bank country is the country where the bank and your accounts reside. A pull-down menu is available to choose the allowable entries. Enter the house bank identifier and the house bank country and click the execute icon inside the pop-up box. The house bank data configuration screen appears (Figure 4.2).

FIGURE 4.2   **The house bank data configuration screen**

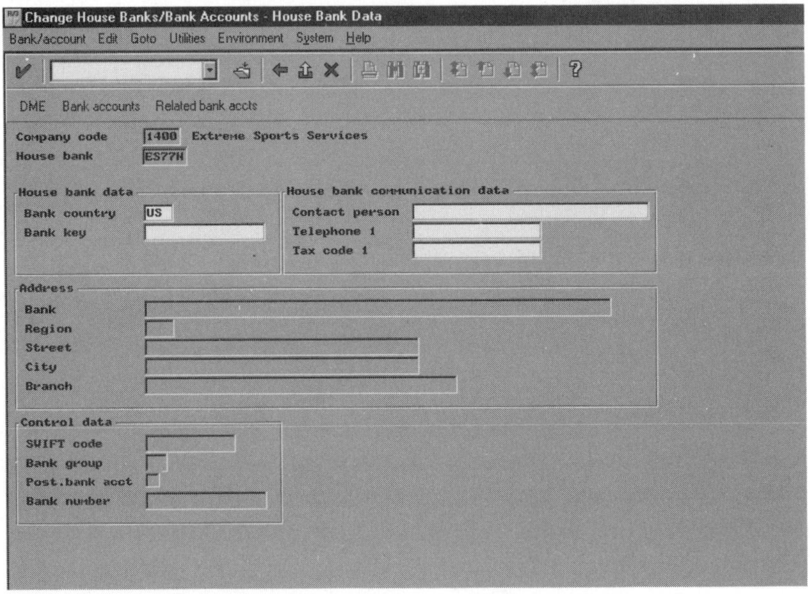

The bank country defaults in from the entry that was made on the pop-up box. Bank Key is a required field. In the U.S., the bank key (also known as the A.B.A. number) is a nine-digit field; the A.B.A. number along with your account number and check number is printed at the bottom of your checks and is known as the MICR (micro-encoding) number. SAP uses an algorithm to ensure that the entry is a valid bank key for the country you've specified. The check algorithm, as well as other settings controlling the bank master data, can be controlled in the global settings of the IMG for your specific country. The settings made here are the default settings for the U.S. Enter the bank key and press Enter. A configuration pop-up screen appears if this is the first time a house bank is being configured for this particular bank key (this pop-up screen contains the grayed-out fields that are shown in Figure 4.2). After entering the information in the pop-up screen, you are returned to the configured house bank data configuration screen (Figure 4.3).

FIGURE 4.3 The configured house bank data configuration screen

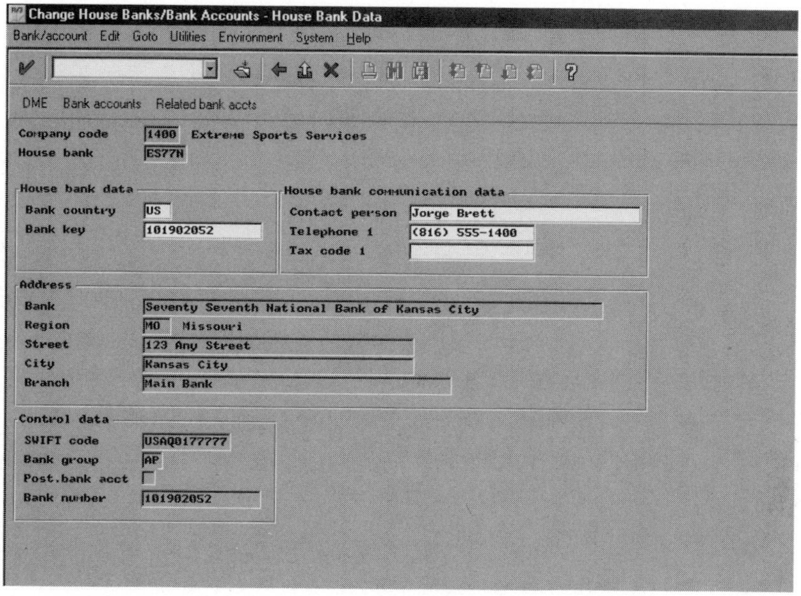

In the screen shown in Figure 4.3, enter the name of the bank in the Bank field. In the Region field, enter the state where the bank is located. The Street, City, and Branch fields are self-explanatory. Within the Control Data section, the SWIFT Code and Bank Group fields are the most important. SWIFT stands for Society of World-wide Interbank Financial Telecommunications. SWIFT codes are used throughout the world to identify banks in international transactions. It is a good idea to enter the SWIFT code of your bank if you want to conduct international business. You define the Bank Group field. Bank groups can be set up to meet your project's needs and are used to help optimize bank selection in the payment program. You can also enter information for the contact person for your company at this bank as well as telephone and tax code information (not required in the U.S.). After entering this information and clicking the Bank Accounts button, you are taken to the list of bank accounts configuration screen, shown in Figure 4.4.

FIGURE 4.4   The list of bank accounts configuration screen

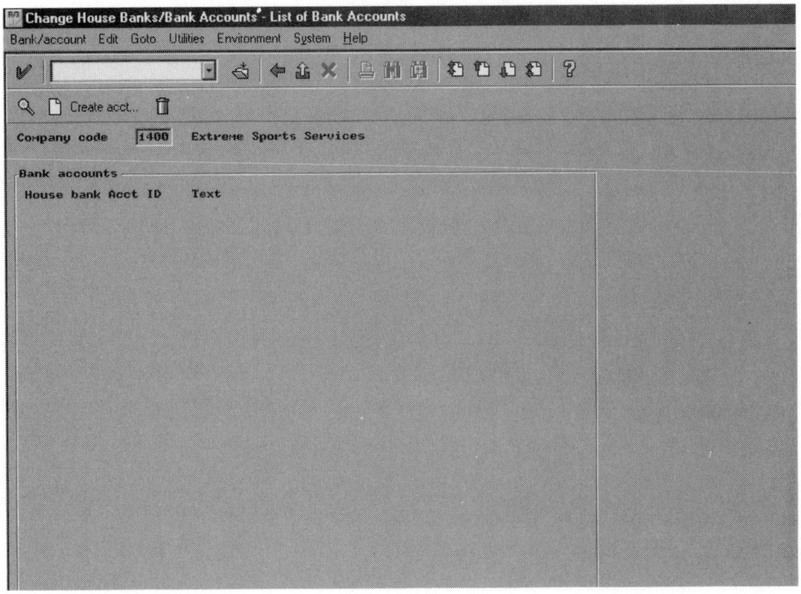

Now that the house bank is fully configured, it is time to create the accounts that go with it. As was stated earlier, each bank account is tied to one house bank. To create a bank account, click the Create Acct button. The Create Bank Account pop-up screen is displayed. Enter the house bank identifier, the account identifier, and a text description for the bank account. Press Enter and you are taken to the bank account data configuration screen shown in Figure 4.5. You are free to define the identifier; it is alphanumeric and can be up to five characters in length.

Let's take a look at the fields on the bank account data configuration screen:

Bank Account   Enter the identifying number of your account at the bank. This entry should correspond to the account number that is given to you on your bank statement.

Altern. Acct No.   This field should only be used when accounts at the same bank use the same account number. Normally, the only way two different accounts will have the same account number is if the bank manages your company's accounts in more than one currency. Do not make an entry in this field unless it is required by your banking relationship. The alternative account number must be different than your normal bank account number.

FIGURE 4.5   The bank account data configuration screen

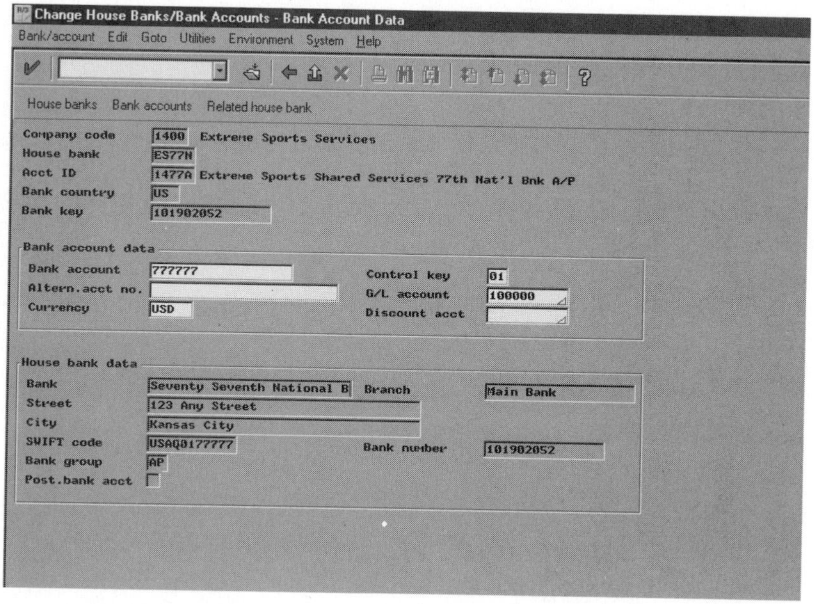

Currency   Enter the currency in which this account is managed. A listing of all valid currencies is available in a drop-down box.

Control Key   For U.S. banks, this is used to identify whether the account is a checking account (01) or a savings account (02). If an entry is not made in this field, the system defaults to checking account (01).

G/L Account   Each bank account has to be tied to a valid G/L account number. The bank account updates the G/L account entered here. The G/L structure for bank accounts will be explained in more detail later.

Discount Acct   If your company utilizes Bill of Exchange functionality, enter the cash discount account for credit memo postings that this bank account should update.

EXTREME SPORTS HOUSE BANK AND ACCOUNT CONFIGURATION ANALYSIS

With the implementation of SAP, Extreme Sports has decided to consolidate its purchasing and A/P departments into a single shared services organization (Extreme Sports Shared Services, company code 1400). For this reason, Extreme Sports' bank and related A/P bank accounts were set up in the Shared Services company code. Because Extreme Sports has several trading partners outside of the U.S., the SWIFT code for the house bank was entered. This will greatly enhance Extreme Sports' ability to conduct electronic banking transactions with the partner banks of its vendors and customers. The use of bank accounts will be configured in a later section.

Bank Account G/L Structure

One of the many benefits that the flexibility of SAP offers is the ability to determine how much confirmed cash, floating cash out, and floating cash in there is for your company on any particular day. To accomplish this, a strategy for the bank account G/L structure must be formed. In order for this to work, there must be *only one* confirmed cash G/L account, with several bank-clearing accounts. For example, a checks outgoing clearing, wire outgoing, ACH out, and deposits clearing need to be set up for each bank account. It is also important to leave yourself room for additional clearing accounts that you may need in the future for additional functionality.

The most flexible and best solution is to have a range of 10 G/L account numbers for each bank account. This solution will give you maximum flexibility; though you probably won't need nine clearing accounts for each bank account at the outset, it gives you the ability to add more in the future should the need arise. This solution also allows you to simplify electronic bank statement transactions. (Electronic bank statement transactions will be explained in detail in Chapter 6.) For Extreme Sports, each confirmed cash balance will end with 0 (for example, G/L account 100000), each deposit clearing account will end with 1(for example, G/L account 100001), each outgoing check clearing account will end with 2, each outgoing ACH account will end with 3, and each outgoing wire account will end with 4. You will notice in Figure 4.5 that Extreme Sports' A/P bank account was assigned to G/L account 100000. Even though it is an account designated for A/P, it still has a confirmed cash balance (100000) and clearing accounts for the different ways in which A/P transactions can be paid.

EXTREME SPORTS BANK ACCOUNT G/L STRUCTURE CONFIGURATION ANALYSIS

Extreme Sports wants the ability to see its confirmed cash balance as well as any incoming deposits or outgoing payments. For this reason, several bank-clearing accounts are set up for each bank account. This functionality is explained in more detail in Chapter 6. The Extreme Sports bank account G/L structure is as follows (the + symbol is a wildcard):

Confirmed Cash	+++++0
Deposit Clearing	+++++1
Outgoing Check Clearing	+++++2
Outgoing ACH Clearing	+++++3
Outgoing Wire Clearing	+++++4

Check Lots and Void Reason Codes

The final step in configuring the A/P bank account is to assign it to a check lot. Extreme Sports has purchased a Micro-Encoding (MICR) printer so that blank check stock can be used for payables. The check lot will determine the check number that is used on payments. To get to the check lots configuration screen, follow the menu path Financial Accounting ➢ Accounts Receivable and Accounts Payable ➢ Business Transactions ➢ Automatic Outgoing Payments ➢ Payment Media ➢ Check Management ➢ Define Number Ranges for Checks.

DEFINE CHECK LOTS

You can get to the check lots configuration screen by using the following methods:

Menu Path: **Financial Accounting** ➢ Accounts Receivable and Accounts Payable ➢ Business Transactions ➢ Automatic Outgoing Payments ➢ Payment Media ➢ Check Management ➢ Define Number Ranges for Checks

Transaction Code: **FCHI**

The Check Lots screen is shown in Figure 4.6.

FIGURE 4.6   The Check Lots screen

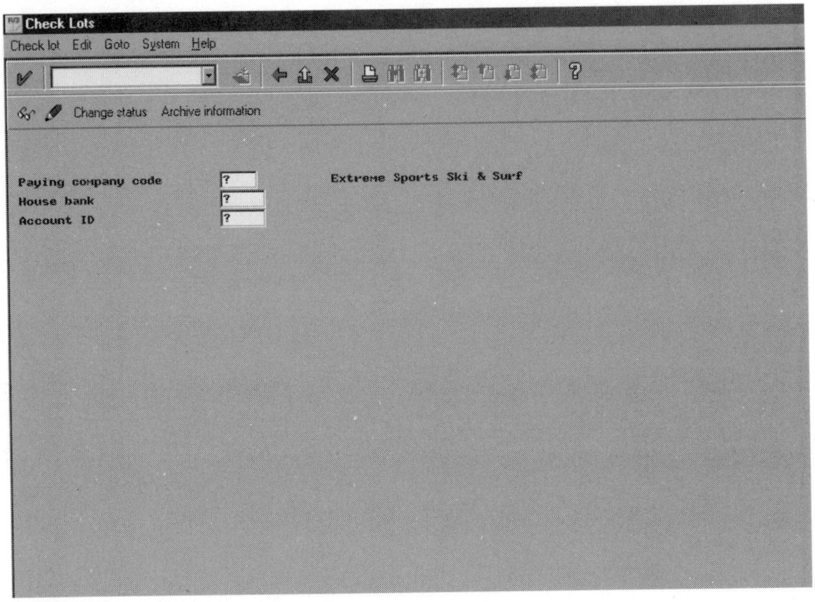

Enter the company code, house bank, and account for which you are creating the check lot and then click the Change Status button. The Maintain Check Lots screen, shown in Figure 4.7 fully configured for Extreme Sports, appears.

FIGURE 4.7   The Maintain Check Lots screen

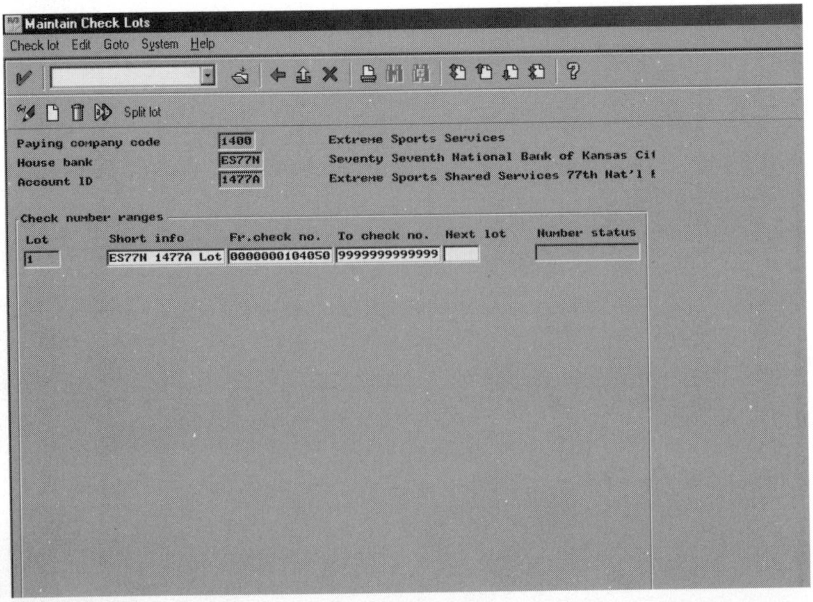

To create a new check lot and assign it to this account, click the create icon. In the pop-up box that appears, enter an identifier for the lot number (numeric only), the check numbers that the lot should begin and end with, as well as the next lot number (if needed). After entering these fields, press Enter.

The next step is to create void reason codes. SAP does not allow the user to void a check without a valid void reason code. You can have as many or as few void reason codes as you need, but you must have at least one. You can display the void reason codes configuration screen by using the menu path Financial Accounting ➢ Accounts Receivable and Accounts Payable ➢ Business Transactions ➢ Automatic Outgoing Payments ➢ Payment Media ➢ Check Management ➢ Define Void Reason Codes.

DEFINE VOID REASON CODES

You can get to the void reason codes configuration screen by using the following methods:

Menu Path: **Financial Accounting** ➢ **Accounts Receivable and Accounts Payable** ➢ **Business Transactions** ➢ **Automatic Outgoing Payments** ➢ **Payment Media** ➢ **Check Management** ➢ **Define Void Reason Codes**

Transaction Code: **FCHV**

The void reason codes configuration screen is shown in Figure 4.8.

FIGURE 4.8   The void reason codes configuration screen

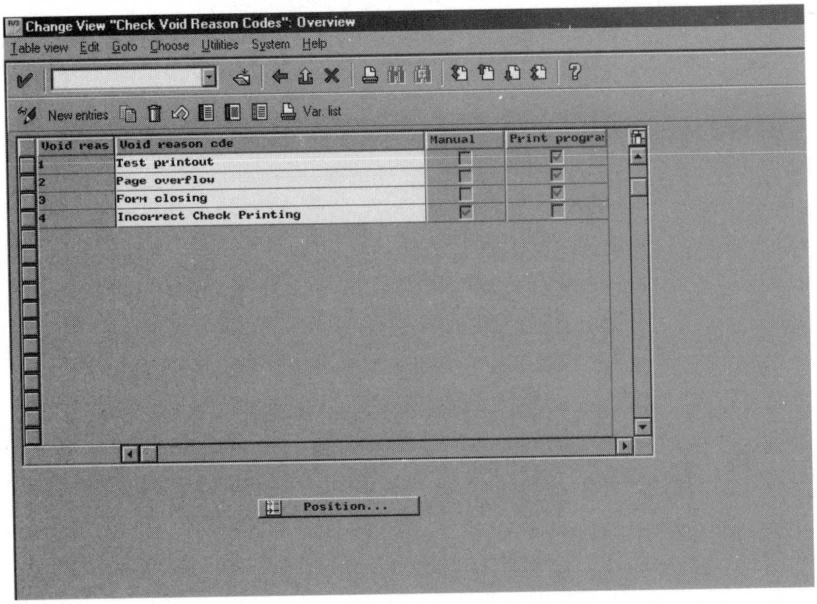

SAP comes delivered with void reason codes 1, 2, and 3 in this version. The payment program uses these void reason codes when it encounters problems with the printer. As you can see from the indicators on the right side of the screen, a void reason code can be used manually or by the print program that is used by the payment program. Any void reason codes you create are automatically set to the manual indicator, which cannot be overwritten (Extreme Sports has configured void reason code 4). To create a new void reason code, click the New Entries button. In the new entries screen that appears, enter a new void reason code identifier (two-digit numeric) and a description. The system activates the manual check box for you.

EXTREME SPORTS CHECK LOTS AND VOID REASON CODES CONFIGURATION ANALYSIS

Check lot 1 was created for one of Extreme Sports' A/P accounts. The lot number is specific to the bank account, so it is not of great importance. The beginning number of the check range was set to what the next check number should be once the cutover is made to SAP. Because Extreme Sports has invested in a MICR printer and will be using blank check stock, the last check number was set to the highest possible limit allowed by the system.

EXTREME SPORTS CHECK LOTS AND VOID REASON CODES CONFIGURATION ANALYSIS (CONTINUED)

The manual void reason code 4 was created for Extreme Sports. This void reason code can be used after checks are printed to void a check number from the system. The project team will create additional void reason codes.

Payment Program Configuration

The configuration of the payment program is where you tell SAP how to process payment transactions in the system. There are a lot of settings that you can configure in the payment program; this provides you with a lot of flexibility in how you process payables in your production system. SAP allows both vendor and customer line items to be paid through the payment program. The ability to pay customers comes in handy when used in conjunction with some of SAP's other standard functionality, such as SD (Sales & Distribution) rebates.

Payment program configuration is a series of steps that are configured within one program (and one main configuration screen). The specific steps that need to be undertaken will be shown in the order needed for configuration. The configuration transaction for the payment program is shown in the following sections. It occurs in table T042 and other variations of table T042 that end in another letter (for example, T042Z, T042E, and so on). To get to the payment program configuration screen, follow the menu path Financial Accounting ➢ Accounts Receivable and Accounts Payable ➢ Business Transactions ➢ Outgoing Payments ➢ Automatic Outgoing Payments ➢ Payment Method/Bank Selection ➢ Configure Payment Program.

PAYMENT PROGRAM CONFIGURATION

You can get to the payment program configuration screen by using the following methods:

Menu Path: **Financial Accounting** ➤ **Accounts Receivable and Accounts Payable** ➤ **Business Transactions** ➤ **Outgoing Payments** ➤ **Automatic Outgoing Payments** ➤ **Payment Method/Bank Selection** ➤ **Configure Payment Program**

Transaction Code: **FBZP**

Figure 4.9 displays the main configuration screen for the payment program. All configuration activities for the payment program will begin from this screen. The configuration steps follow the order of the buttons on the screen, going from left to right.

FIGURE 4.9   The initial payment program configuration screen

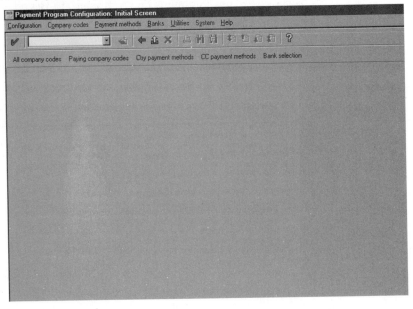

Company Code Data

The first configuration step is to set up your company code(s) so it is available to the payment program. In addition to making the company code available to the payment program, this setting specifies a lot of the general control data for the company code. To carry out this step, select the All Company Codes button displayed in Figure 4.9. You are presented with the screen shown in Figure 4.10.

FIGURE 4.10   The company codes configuration screen

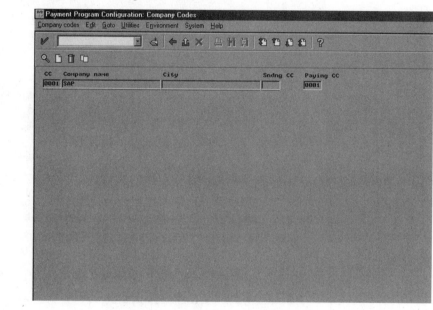

Click the create icon to access a pop-up box in which you enter the company code you wish to make available to the payment program. After entering the company code identifier and pressing Enter, you are presented with the screen shown in Figure 4.11.

FIGURE 4.11   The company code data configuration screen

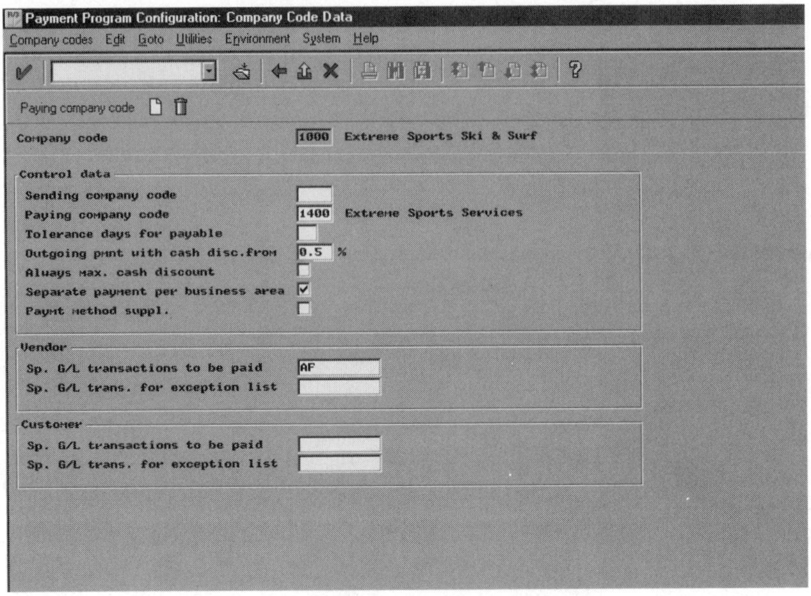

Here is a list of the fields that appear in the company code data configuration screen:

Sending Company Code   Enter the company code identifier by which the vendor you're paying knows your company. This will almost always be the same as the company code you are setting up. Leaving this field blank is the same as entering the company code that you are configuring.

Paying Company Code   Enter the company code identifier of the company that is actually paying the invoices. This is a required entry, even if the paying company code is the same as the company code you are configuring. A lot of companies, such as Extreme Sports, have a centralized A/P function set up in a shared services company. For this type of organizational structure, enter the company code of the shared services company that is actually paying the invoice for the configured company code. When you use this functionality, an intercompany posting is automatically created when invoices are paid.

Tolerance Days for Payable   If your company wants to grant itself "grace days," enter the number of days here. For example, if you enter a 5 in this field, the invoice won't be paid until the due date plus five days.

Outgoing Pmnt with Cash Disc. From   Unless a minimum percentage rate is entered here, SAP will make the payment at the time in which your company would receive the maximum cash discount amount related to its terms of payment on the invoice. If you enter a percentage here, SAP will only take cash discounts equal to or greater than the amount entered. Any cash discount below the entered rate will be ignored, and payment will be made on the next due date. For example, Extreme Sports earns 6% annually (0.5% monthly) on its deposits at the bank. Because most of Extreme Sports' terms are at X% discount rate, net thirty days, it would not want to accept a cash discount below 0.5%.

Example 1   Suppose there is an invoice amount of $5,000 and terms of 2% cash discount if paid in 10 days, otherwise the full amount is due in 30 days. Keeping the money to pay the invoice in the bank for 30 days would allow Extreme Sports to earn $25 in interest ($5,000 * 1.005). Taking the cash discount would save Extreme Sports $100 ($5000 * .02). Clearly, the benefit of the $100 cash discount far exceeds the $25 in interest that could be earned by keeping the money in the bank.

Example 2   Suppose there is an invoice amount of $5,000 and terms of 0.25% cash discount if paid in 10 days, otherwise the full amount is due in 30 days. Keeping the money in the bank for 30 days would allow Extreme Sports to earn $25 in interest ($5,000 * 1.005). Taking the cash discount would save Extreme Sports $12.50 ($5000 * .0025). Clearly the benefit of the $25 earned in interest by not paying the invoice until the end of 30 days far outweighs the cash discount amount of $12.50.

Always Max. Cash Discount   When this indicator is selected, the cash discount amount is always deducted when invoices are paid, even when the payment is after the maximum date specified in the terms to allow a cash discount. For example, an invoice has a baseline date of January 1, 2000 and terms of 2% cash discount if paid in 10 days, otherwise the full amount is due in 30 days. According to the terms, a cash discount can only be taken on the invoice up to January 10th. If this indicator is selected, and the invoice mentioned earlier was paid after January 10th, the cash discount would still be subtracted from the payment, and the full amount of the invoice would be cleared on the paying company's books. Selecting this indicator makes any entry in the Outgoing Pmnt with Cash Disc. From field invalid.

Separate Payment Per Business Area   When this indicator is selected, SAP will group payables by business area. The payables will also be paid by business area (one check is cut for each business area).

Payment Method Suppl.   Select this indicator if you want to utilize payment method supplements. Payment method supplements are freely definable. They can be specified in the vendor and customer master record as well as entered or overwritten on the document. Payment method supplements are used to group documents for payment or to sort checks. They can be useful if your project has unique check sorting requirements.

Vendor Sp. G/L Transactions to Be Paid   In this field, enter the letter(s) of the special type of G/L postings that can be paid for vendors. The available special transactions are as follows:

A	Down Payment Request
B	Financial Assets Down Payment
D	Discount
E	Unchecked Invoice
F	Initial Down Payment Request
G	Guarantee
H	Security Deposit
I	Intangible Asset Down Payment
M	Tangible Asset Down Payment
O	Amortization Down Payment
P	Payment Request
S	Check/Bill of Exchange
V	Stocks Down Payment
W	Bill of Exchange (rediscountable)

Vendor Sp. G/L Trans. for Exception List   In this field, enter the letter(s) of the special type of G/L postings that should be output to the exception list when the payment program is run. If a type of special G/L transaction is not entered in this field or in the Sp. G/L Transactions to Be Paid field, the payment program will totally ignore these transactions. The listing of special G/L transactions is the same as the list for the preceding field.

Customer Sp. G/L Transactions to Be Paid   In this field, enter the letter(s) of the special type of G/L postings that can be paid for customers. The available special transactions are as follows:

A	Down Payment
B	Bill of Exchange Receivable
E	Reserve for Bad Debt

F   Down Payment Request

G   Guarantee

H   Security Deposit

P   Payment Request

Q   B/E Residual Risk

R   B/E Payment Request

S   Check/Bill of Exchange

T   Down Payment

W   Bill of Exchange Receivable

X   Prepayment Posting

Y   Prepayment Request

Z   Interest Due

Customer Sp. G/L Trans. for Exception List   In this field, enter the letter(s) of the special type of G/L postings that should be output to the exception list when the payment program is run. If a type of special G/L transaction is not entered in this field or in the Sp. G/L Transactions to Be Paid field, the payment program will totally ignore these transactions. The listing of special G/L transactions is the same as the list for the preceding field.

EXTREME SPORTS PAYMENT PROGRAM COMPANY CODE DATA CONFIGURATION ANALYSIS

The shared services organization of Extreme Sports (company code 1400) will be in charge of A/P for Extreme Sports' U.S.-based operations. Extreme Sports Mexico (company code 1300) will be responsible for its own A/P process. Because the shared services organization will be paying all invoices, company code 1400 (Extreme Sports Services) was entered as the paying company code for company code 1000 (Extreme Sports Ski & Surf). Utilizing this approach will cause SAP to automatically create an intercompany posting between company code 1000 and company code 1400 when payments are made.

The minimum cash discount amount to be taken was set to 0.5%. Please refer to the explanation of the Outgoing Pmnt with Cash Disc. From field for a review of why this setting was made.

EXTREME SPORTS PAYMENT PROGRAM COMPANY CODE DATA CONFIGURATION ANALYSIS (CONTINUED)

Because Extreme Sports is utilizing business area functionality, the indicator was set to group and pay invoices by business area. This will help with the clearing and reconciliation of business area liabilities.

Some of Extreme Sports' business partners require down payments on materials. Because of this, special G/L transactions of A (Down Payment) and F (Down Payment Request) were configured so that these transactions would be paid on vendor line items. Extreme Sports does not currently have any special G/L transactions that should be paid for customers, so the customer special G/L transaction field was left blank.

Paying Company Code Data

The second step to configuring the payment program is to set up parameters for the *paying company codes*. You will recall from the preceding section that the sending company code does not necessarily need to be the paying company code. For our example, company code 1400 is the paying company code for all of Extreme Sports' U.S.-based operations. Because of this, we will only need to set up company code 1400 as a paying company code. The project team at Extreme Sports will set up company code 1300 (Extreme Sports, Mexico) as a paying company code for Mexican-based operations at a later date.

From the main payment program configuration screen displayed in Figure 4.9, click the Paying Company Codes button. The paying company codes configuration screen, shown in Figure 4.12, appears.

Although company code 1400 was set up as the paying company code for company code 1000 in the first payment program configuration step, it is still not set up as a paying company code. To configure company code 1400 as a paying company code, click the create icon. A pop-up window appears asking you to configure the company code identifier of the paying company code. After you enter the appropriate identifier and press Enter, the paying company code data configuration screen appears (Figure 4.13).

FIGURE 4.12 The paying company codes configuration screen

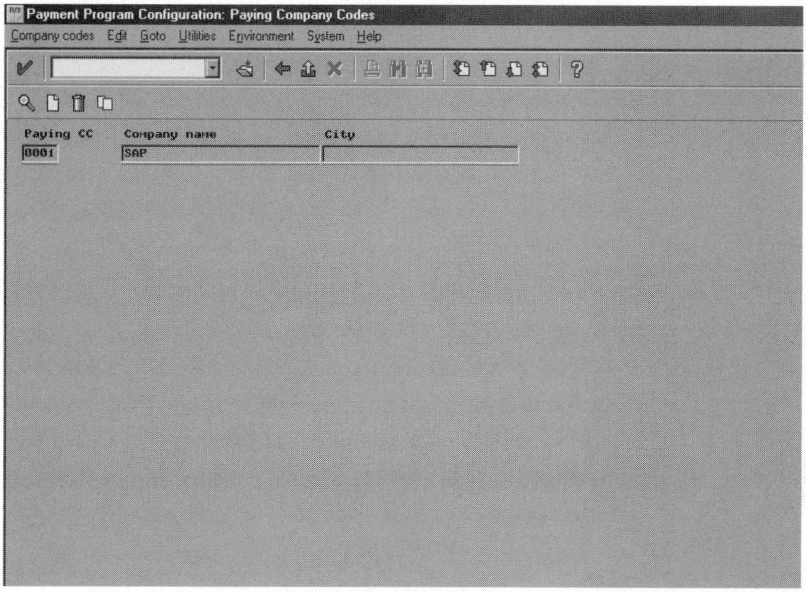

FIGURE 4.13 The paying company code data configuration screen

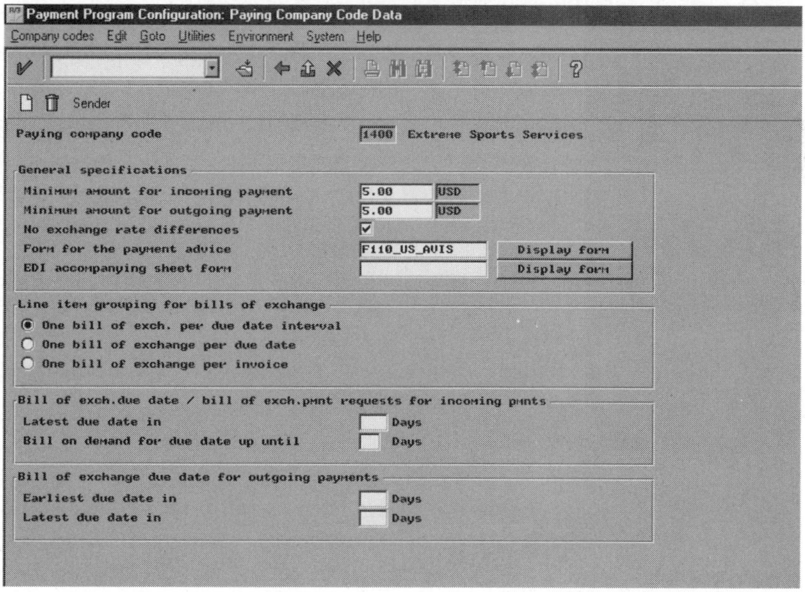

Here is an explanation of some of the key fields in Figure 4.13:

Minimum Amount for Incoming Payment   If you want to stop the system from generating debit memos for amounts below a certain threshold, enter the threshold amount here. Only debit memos with an amount equal to or above the amount entered in this field will be generated by the system. All debit memos under this amount will be generated in an exception list after processing. Once there are enough line items to put the customer over the threshold amount, all line items will be included in the debit memo.

Minimum Amount for Outgoing Payment   If you want to stop the system from generating checks for amounts below a certain threshold, enter the threshold amount here. Only checks with an amount equal to or above the amount entered in this field will be generated for payment by the system. All checks under this amount will be generated in an exception list after processing. Once there are enough line items to put the customer over the threshold amount, all line items will be included in the check.

No Exchange Rate Differences   If you do not want the system to generate exchange rate differences when paying invoices, set this indicator. If this indicator is left blank, exchange rate differences will be posted for each individual transaction affected by foreign currencies.

Form for the Payment Advice   Enter the identifier of the SAPScript to be used for creating payment advices. Payment advices are sent to vendors along with checks to explain the product or service for which the check is issued. (The creation of SAPScripts is beyond the scope of this book. SAP does deliver for each form several standard SAPScripts that can be used or referenced to create a custom form.)

EDI Accompanying Sheet Form   Enter the identifier of the SAPScript that is to be used to create the correspondence sheet that accompanies EDI transactions.

The remaining fields on the screen in Figure 4.13 all have to do with Bills of Exchange. Each setting is self-explanatory if you are using the Bill of Exchange functionality.

EXTREME SPORTS PAYING COMPANY CODE DATA CONFIGURATION ANALYSIS

Extreme Sports has determined that it is too costly to process payments below $5. For this reason, $5 was set as the minimum amount for incoming and outgoing payments. Extreme Sports does not want to recognize foreign currency gains and losses on individual payment transactions, so the No Exchange Rate Differences indicator was set. Layout set F110_US_AVIS was set as the form for the payment advice. Later, an ABAP project team member will copy and then modify the layout set to meet Extreme Sports' requirements. Bill of Exchange functionality is not utilized by Extreme Sports.

Country Payment Methods

The third step in configuring the payment program is to set up *country payment methods*. Country payment methods specify which payment methods (checks, wires, ACH, etc.) can be used by company codes in a specific country. The country payment method configuration specifies the general control parameters for a payment method. To configure the country payment methods, click the Ctry Payment Methods button shown in Figure 4.9. The screen shown in Figure 4.14 appears.

FIGURE 4.14   The country payment methods configuration screen

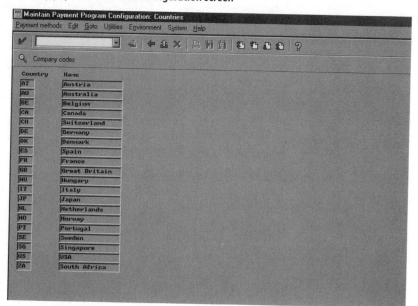

Select the country you wish to configure by double-clicking its identifier. When you double-click the appropriate country (U.S. in our example), the screen shown in Figure 4.15 appears.

FIGURE 4.15   The country payment methods list screen

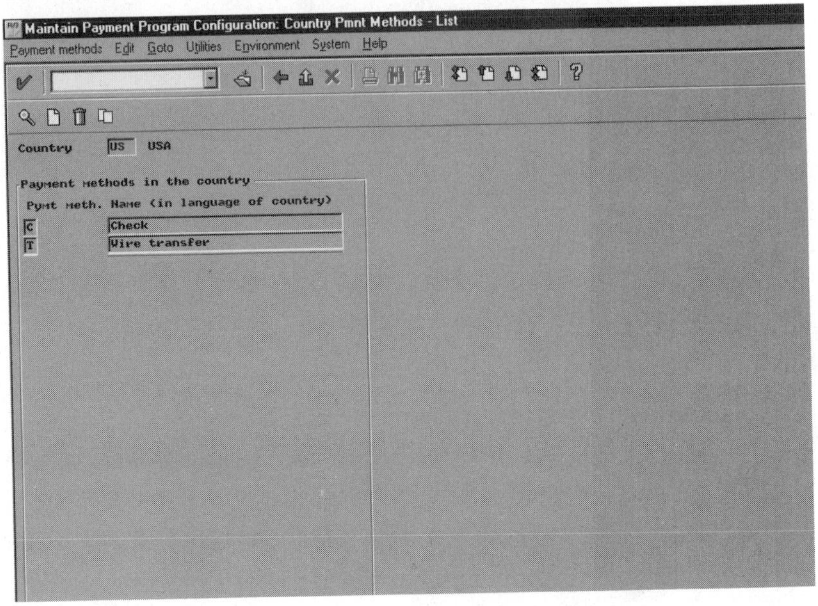

As you can see, SAP is delivered with the most popular payment types for each country. You can also create your own specialized payment types. The most popular payment type in the U.S. is payment by check. You can access the configuration settings for the check (payment type C) by double-clicking the payment type identifier for checks, C. When you do so, the country payment methods detail screen is displayed (Figure 4.16).

FIGURE 4.16   The country payment methods detail screen

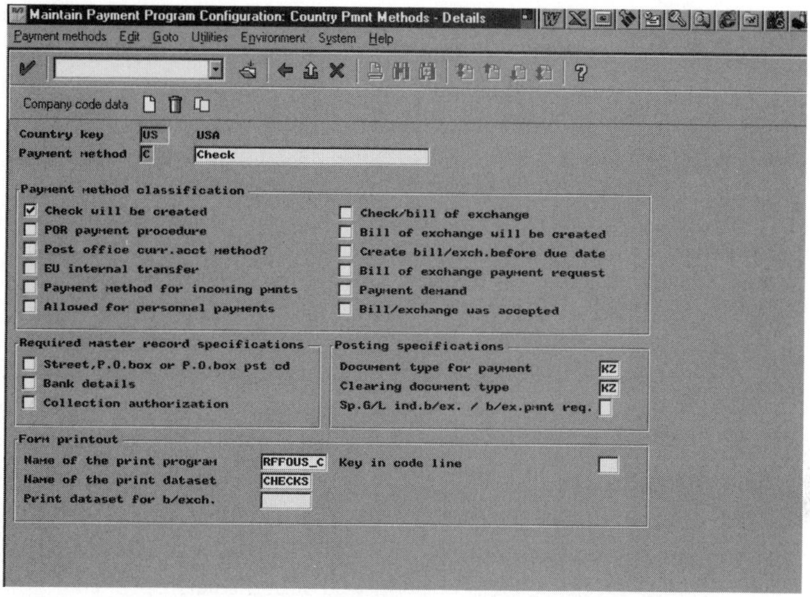

The fields in the country payment methods detail screen are grouped into four categories; the category explanations as well as the most important fields in each category are listed here:

Payment Method Classification   These fields control the type of payment that is made as well as special country-specific processing methods that are used by the payment type. The most important indicators for normal payment types are Check Will Be Created, Payment Method for Incoming Pmnts, and Allowed for Personnel Payments. If the payment type is supposed to create a physical check, the Check Will Be Created indicator must be activated. For payment types that are set up for incoming payments, the Payment Method for Incoming Pmnts indicator must be active (this is used primarily with other treasury activities). To allow the SAP Human Resources module to use a payment type, the Allowed for Personnel Payments indicator must be activated. It is a good idea not to allow the normal check payment type (C) to be used for payroll transactions. So that you can better reconcile and control A/P and payroll checks, a new payment type for payroll checks (P) should be created. Payment type P should be a copy of C with the Allowed for Personnel Payments indicator activated.

Required Master Record Specifications   These fields specify what master data must be filled out on the individual customer or vendor master record for a payment to be made by this payment type. If the master data fields activated in this grouping are not filled out on the customer or vendor master record, the line items are output to an exception list.

Posting Specifications   These fields control how payments update (post) in the system. The document types for payment and reversal of payments are specified here as well as the special G/L indicator that is updated when Bills of Exchange are processed.

Form Printout   These fields control how the output of the payment program is created. The most important field in this grouping is Name of the Print Program. To find the correct print program for your payment type in your country, do a search of SAP programs that begin RFFO*. The programs for your country are usually RFFO++*, where ++ is the two-character identifier for your country. The check printing program for the U.S. is RFFOUS_C, and the program for wires and ACH transfers is RFFOUS_T. The name of the print dataset is used when the checks are spooled instead of immediately printed.

EXTREME SPORTS COUNTRY PAYMENT METHODS CONFIGURATION ANALYSIS

The U.S. payment type for checks (C) was configured in this section. Because physical checks will be created with this payment type, the Check Will Be Created indicator was activated. Extreme Sports wants the ability to easily see what checks are A/P and what checks are payroll, so the Allowed for Personnel Payments indicator was not activated.

Extreme Sports will make important fields required in the actual setup of vendor master records, not in the payment types. For this reason, none of the fields in the Required Master Record Specifications section were activated. Making fields required in the actual setup for master records will cut down on exception processing by Extreme Sports' staff.

Document type KZ (Vendor Payment) was set for both the payment document type and the clearing document type. Any document type that allows postings to both vendor and G/L accounts can be used.

EXTREME SPORTS COUNTRY PAYMENT METHODS CONFIGURATION ANALYSIS (CONTINUED)

The SAP standard U.S. check printing program (RFFOUS_C) was set for use by this payment type. If the standard SAP program does not meet all of your requirements, the program can be copied and modified. The name Checks was used for the print dataset so the print job can be easily found if the checks are spooled instead of imme-diately printed.

Company Code Payment Methods

The fourth step to configuring the payment program is to make further specifica-tions to the payment types that were created in the preceding section (country pay-ment types). The *company code payment methods* allow further control of how the payment method works in the system. To configure the company code payment methods, click the CC Payment Methods button shown in Figure 4.9. The screen shown in Figure 4.17 appears.

FIGURE 4.17   The company codes payment methods configuration screen

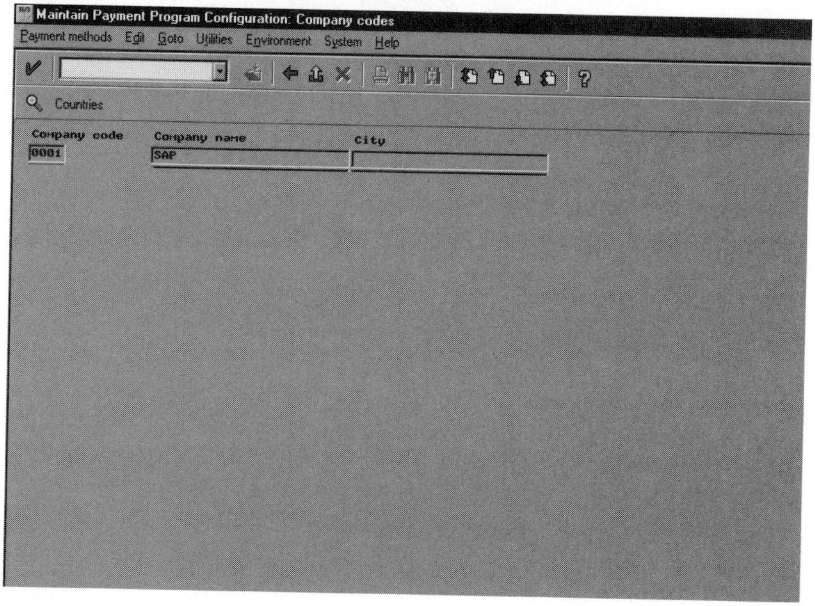

As you can see, we must once again set up company code 1400, this time to extend country payment methods to it. From the screen in Figure 4.17, execute the following menu path: Edit ➢ New Company Code. A pop-up window prompts you for the identifier of the new company code and the company code to copy from (if you wish to copy from an existing company code). After you enter the company code identifier and press Enter, the screen shown in Figure 4.18 appears.

FIGURE 4.18   The company code payment methods list screen

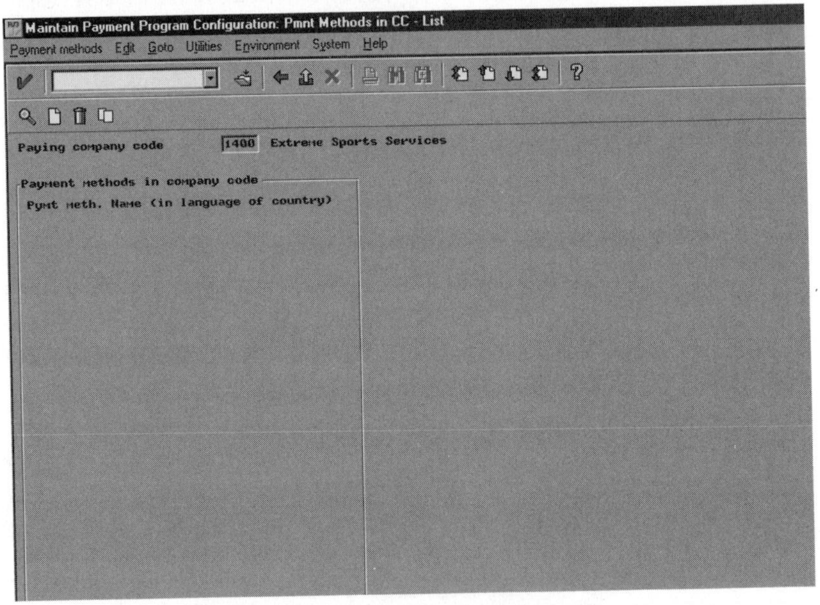

You'll notice that this company code (1400) has not been maintained yet. The payment methods for the company code's country need to be extended to the company code. To extend the payment methods, click the create icon. A pop-up window will appear and ask you to enter the payment method you want to create (extended) in the company code. After you enter the appropriate payment method (C) or select the available payment for the country from the pull-down menu, the screen shown in Figure 4.19 appears.

FIGURE 4.19   The company code payment methods general data configuration screen

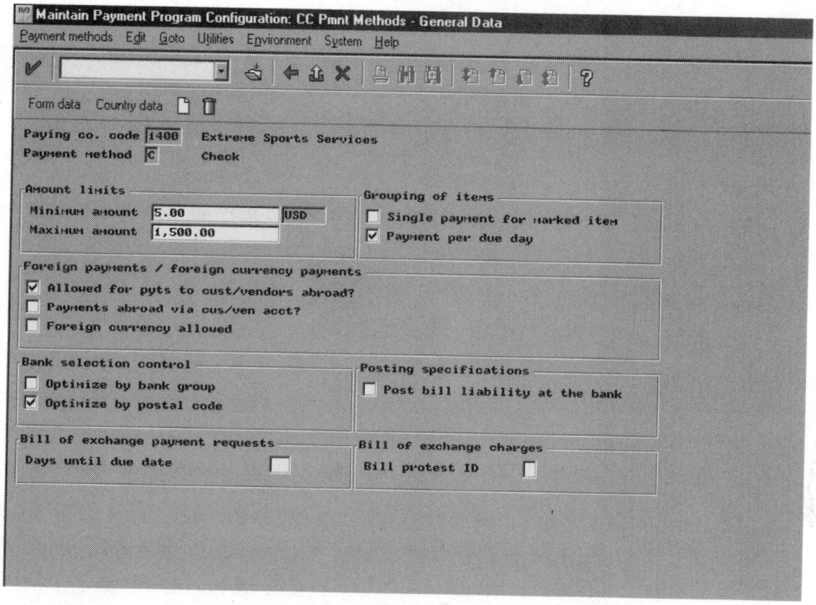

Here's an explanation of the fields (with the exception of Bill of Exchange fields) that appear in the company code payment methods general data configuration screen:

Minimum Amount   You will recall from the subsection on company code data that a minimum amount for payment was already configured. The Minimum Amount field on this screen controls the minimum amount for the payment method on items that are not explicitly assigned a payment type. This field has no effect on items that are assigned a payment type on the document or vendor master record. The table below shows whether the payment method Minimum Amount field would work on each line item, assuming a minimum amount entry of $4.

Vendor Master Record Payment Type	C	-	-	-
Document Payment Type	-	C	-	-
A/P Amount	$2.00	$2.00	$2.00	$4.25
Payment Method Minimum Amount Field Used?	No	No	Yes	No

Maximum Amount   Enter the maximum amount that can be paid by this payment method on items that are not explicitly assigned a payment method. This field has no effect on items that are assigned a payment type on the document or vendor master record. Review the explanation of the minimum amount field to determine how the processing will work.

Single Payment for Marked Item   Activate this field if you want to create an individual payment for each line item assigned this payment type. If this field is not activated, the payment program will group together all open items for a vendor or customer and pay them on a single payment. If you have only a small group of vendors that require individual payment for each invoice, an easier method is to activate the single payment field in the vendor master record of the affected vendors. This approach is much easier than creating a new payment method for single payments; this will be explained further in "Vendor Master Data" later in this chapter.

Payment per Due Day   Activate this field if you want to group together items by payment date. This features means that only items with the same due date for a vendor will be grouped together for payment. Normally, all items, regardless of due date for vendors, are grouped together. The functionality of this field is better explained in the following example, in which Extreme Sports has six individual line items with vendor A:

DUE DATE	AMOUNT	PAYMENT GROUPING
10/03/1999	$500	1
10/19/1999	$200	3
10/03/1999	$700	1
10/04/1999	$876	2
10/03/1999	$589	1
10/19/1999	$250	3

If the Payment per Due Day functionality was activated, there would be three separate payments to vendor A because the six line items are due on three separate days. Payment 1 (10/03/1999 due date) would be in the amount of $1,789, Payment 2 (10/04/1999 due date) would be in the amount of $876, and Payment 3 (10/19/1999 due date) would be in the amount of $450.

Allowed for Pyts to Cust/Vendors Abroad?   Select this indicator if you want to allow the payment method to be used with vendors and customers who do not reside in the home country of the company code.

Payments Abroad via Cus/Ven Acct?   Select this indicator if you want to be able to use bank-to-bank payment communication for customer and vendors who reside abroad and wish to be paid at a bank in their home country. The bank must be set up in the vendor master record in order for the bank-to-bank communication to occur.

Foreign Currency Allowed   Select this indicator if you want the ability to pay invoices in a currency other than your company code currency. Be careful not to allow payments in foreign currency on checks if your check stock denominates in your home currency.

Optimize by Bank Group   Activate this indicator if you want SAP to determine the paying bank based on the best match of your company's house banks and the vendor's banks. You will recall from the section on house banks that there was a Bank Group field on the house bank master data. SAP will look at the entries in the Bank Group field for all affected banks (paying company and vendor) and determine the best match for quicker processing of payments. This functionality is particularly useful in electronic payment types (wires, ACH, etc.).

Optimize by Postal Code   Activate this indicator if you want SAP to determine the paying bank by looking at the zip code of the vendor being paid. This functionality will be configured in the next section.

EXTREME SPORTS COMPANY CODE PAYMENT METHOD CONFIGURATION ANALYSIS

The payment method C (for checks) was configured in this section. Extreme Sports decided to keep the minimum overall payment amount for items not explicitly assigned to this payment method. A maximum of amount $1,500 was configured for items not explicitly assigned this payment method.

To make sure cash discounts are maximized, the Payment per Due Day indicator was activated. This will allow invoices to be held as long as possible before payment.

This payment method is also allowed for payments to customers and vendors that are not based in the company code's country (U.S.A.) because of a reciprocity agreement with some Canadian banks, allowing Extreme Sports' Canadian vendors to cash U.S. checks.

EXTREME SPORTS COMPANY CODE PAYMENT METHOD CONFIGURATION ANALYSIS (CONTINUED)

Bank selection will be optimized by postal code. SAP will look at the vendor's zip code and determine the appropriate house bank to use for payment based on configuration settings that map ranges of zip codes to house banks.

Bank Selection

The fifth and final step in configuring the payment program is determining the *bank selection* procedure. The step is actually a series of smaller steps that build upon one another. To configure the bank selection, click the Bank Selection button shown in Figure 4.9. The initial bank selection configuration screen shown in Figure 4.20 will appear.

FIGURE 4.20 The initial bank selection configuration screen

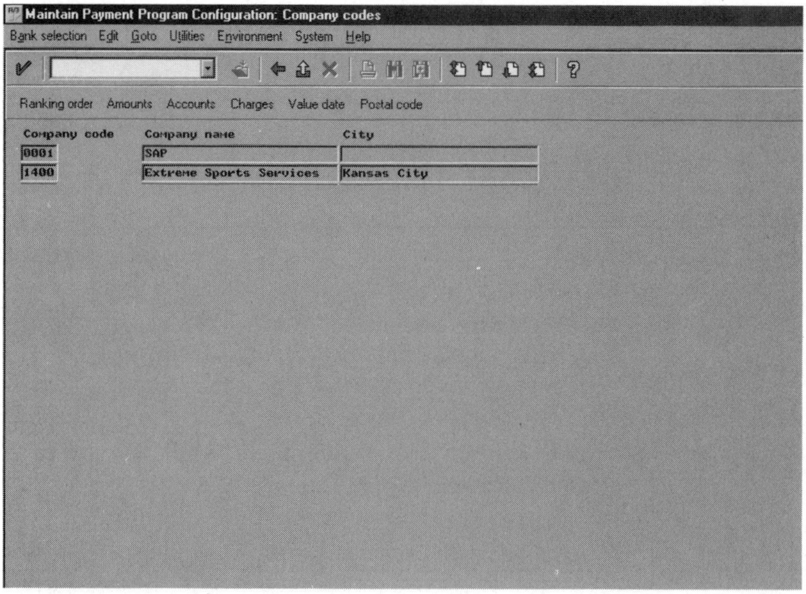

Payment Method Bank Selection

On the screen in Figure 4.20, double-click the paying company code (1400) for which you wish to configure bank selection. The payment method bank selection screen, shown in Figure 4.21, appears.

FIGURE 4.21 The payment method bank selection screen

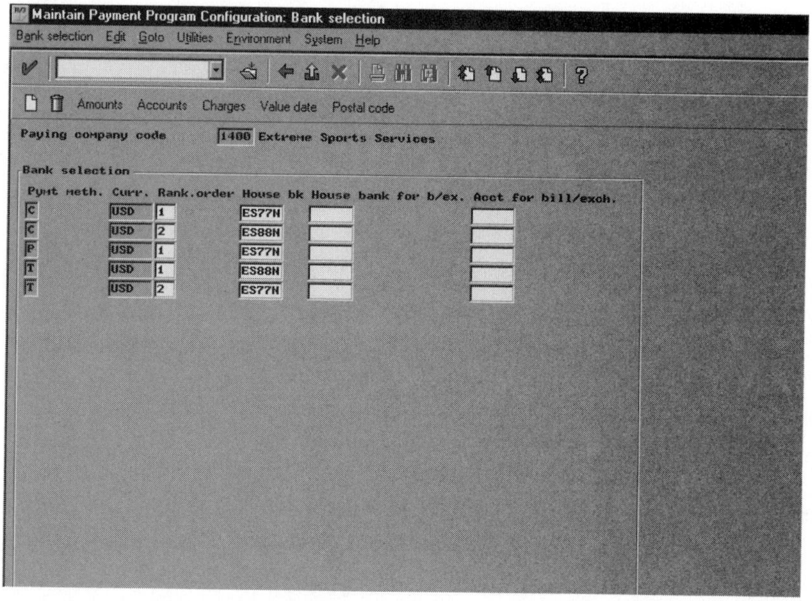

The payment method has been configured for Extreme Sports, but when the screen first appears, there will be no existing information for the company code you are configuring. To configure the information, click the create icon. A pop-up window is displayed. Within the pop-up window, insert the appropriate payment method (C), currency (USD), ranking order, and house bank in the proper fields. The ranking order determines which bank should be selected for the given payment method if the other forms of bank selection fail. For example, if postal code bank optimization is being used and the vendor has a zip code that does not fall within a configured range, SAP will use the bank with the highest-ranking order (starting from 1) with the available funds to pay the invoice. If you do not utilize bank selection optimization by either bank group or postal code, this is the only way SAP knows how to select the bank.

EXTREME SPORTS PAYMENT METHOD BANK SELECTION CONFIGURATION ANALYSIS

Extreme Sports utilizes two different banks for payment activities (ES77N and ES88N). For payment method C, house bank ES77N should be the first bank selection if the postal code optimization is unable to select a bank; house bank ES88N should be the second bank selected. The only way house bank ES88N would be selected in this case is if house bank ES77N did not have the available funds to make the payment.

EXTREME SPORTS PAYMENT METHOD BANK SELECTION CONFIGURATION ANALYSIS (CONTINUED)

As you can see from the screen in Figure 4.21, two additional payment methods were created for company code 1400: P for payroll checks and T for wires. House bank ES88N was configured to be the first bank selected for payment method T, and ES77N was configured to be the second bank available for selection. Payment method P was assigned only to house bank ES77N because Extreme Sports has only one payroll account.

Bank Account Determination

The next step in configuring bank selection is to configure the accounts that are to be used by the house banks you just set up for payment method bank selection. To configure the bank accounts, click the Accounts button shown in Figure 4.21. The screen shown in Figure 4.22 will appear.

FIGURE 4.22   The bank account determination screen

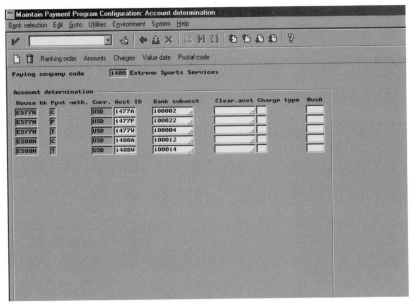

Figure 4.22 shows the bank account determination screen configured for Extreme Sports, but when the screen first appears, there won't be any bank accounts set up for the company code you're using. To make the proper bank accounts available, click the create icon. The pop-up window shown in Figure 4.23 appears.

FIGURE 4.23 The Create pop-up window

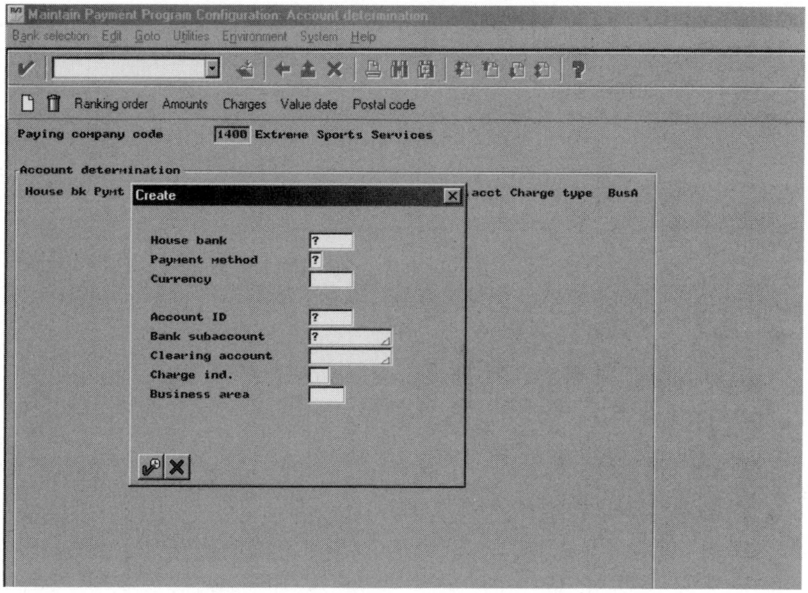

The fields that appear in Figure 4.23 are explained here:

House Bank Enter the identifier for the house bank where the bank account you wish to configure resides. Make sure all accounts configured in this screen belong to house banks that were set up in the payment method bank selection screen.

Payment Method Enter the payment method with which the bank account is to be used. Payment methods were configured in "Payment Method Bank Selection."

Currency Enter the currency identifier used by the bank account.

Account ID Enter the identifier for the bank account that is to be configured. House bank IDs were configured in "House Banks and Accounts."

Bank Subaccount Enter the G/L account to which the payment posting for the bank account is to be made. This account should be the clearing account that should be used by the payment method for which you are using the account. Refer back to "Bank Account G/L Structure" earlier in this chapter for an explanation of the different bank clearing accounts used by Extreme Sports.

Clearing Account If the bank account that you are configuring is using a Bill of Exchange payment method, enter the clearing account that is to be used.

Charge Ind.   Some payment methods, such as Bills of Exchange, utilize charges on payments. If your payment requires a charge, enter a charge indicator here. Generally, this field is not used for U.S. payment methods.

Business Area   Enter the business area that is to be posted to for this bank account. If you configured separation of payment per business area in the company code configuration of the payment program, this entry is ignored.

EXTREME SPORTS BANK ACCOUNT DETERMINATION CONFIGURATION ANALYSIS

The bank accounts that are to be used by Extreme Sports were configured in this section. Notice the bank subaccounts that were used and how they relate to the information in "Bank Account G/L Structure" earlier in this chapter. Also be aware that some of the bank accounts, such as those used for payment methods C and T, are physically one bank account with several G/L subaccounts to simplify bank statement processing.

Amounts

Now that the appropriate bank accounts have been configured, it is time to maintain the available amounts they can use. To configure the amounts for bank accounts, click the Amounts button shown in Figure 4.22. You are presented with the planned amounts configuration screen, shown in Figure 4.24.

As you can see, information has not been maintained for company code 1400. To configure the amount per bank account information, click the create icon. A pop-up box appears. Within the pop-up box, enter the identifiers for the house bank and bank account as well as the currency of the bank account. The Days until Value Date field is generally only used for Bill of Exchange payment methods; this allows you to post payment before the due date. For payment methods other than Bill of Exchange, enter **999** in the Days until Value Date field. The 999 entry in effect nullifies this field when processing is taking place. Enter the maximum amount of money in the configured bank account that you want to be available to the payment program. You can enter all 9s in this field to make all amounts in the account available for use by the payment program.

FIGURE 4.24   The planned amounts screen

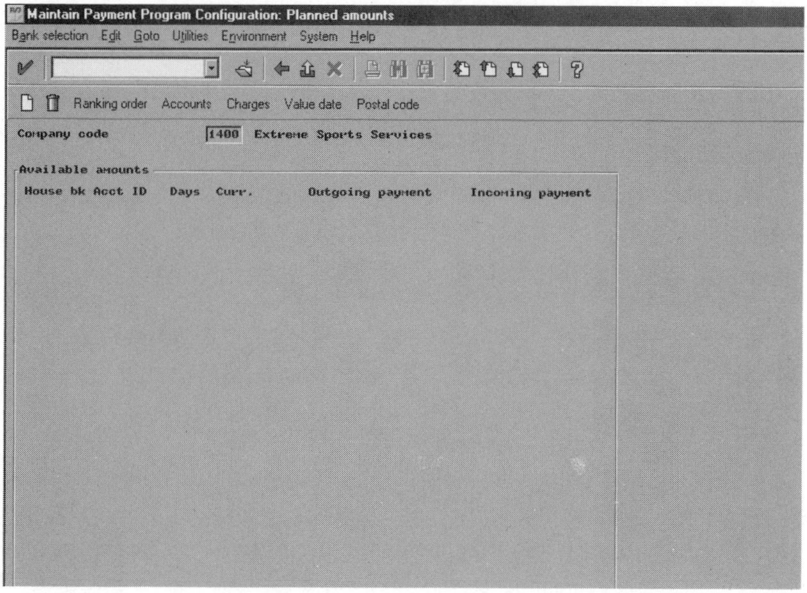

The fully configured planned amounts screen for Extreme Sports is shown in Figure 4.25.

FIGURE 4.25   The fully configured planned amounts screen for Extreme Sports

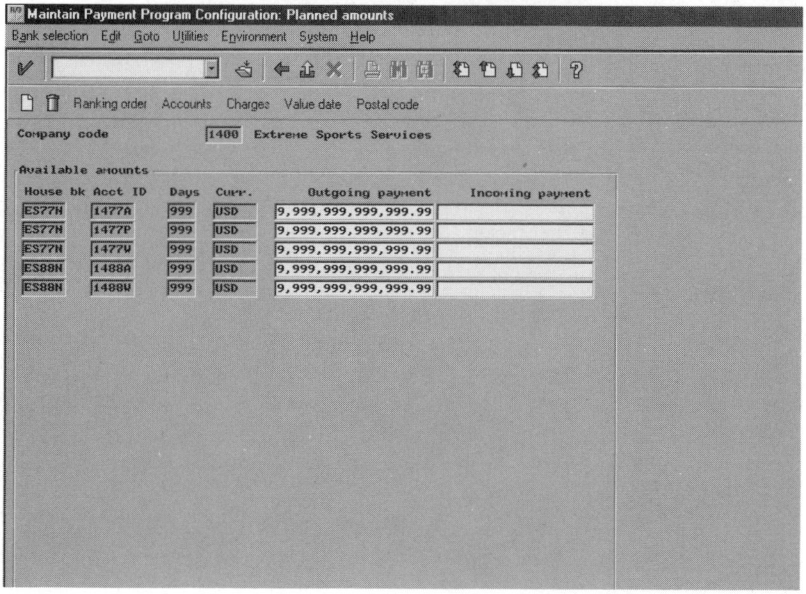

EXTREME SPORTS AMOUNTS CONFIGURATION ANALYSIS

Because Extreme Sports does not utilize the Bill of Exchange payment method, the value date for all of Extreme Sports' bank accounts was set to 999. Extreme Sports' cash strategy is to have separate A/P and Payroll accounts that are segregated from all other activities. For this reason, the available amount for outgoing payment was set to $9,999,999,999,999.99 so that all funds in these accounts are available for use by the payment program.

Value Dates

Another important step in configuration of the payment program is to maintain *value dates* for the payment methods used by your company. A value date is used as an average of the number of days it takes for a payment to clear the bank. The value date is important because it determines the amount available per due date to the payment program as well as for cash management and liquidity forecasting in the Treasury module. To configure value dates, click the Value Date button shown in Figure 4.25. The value date configuration screen appears (Figure 4.26).

FIGURE 4.26   The value date screen

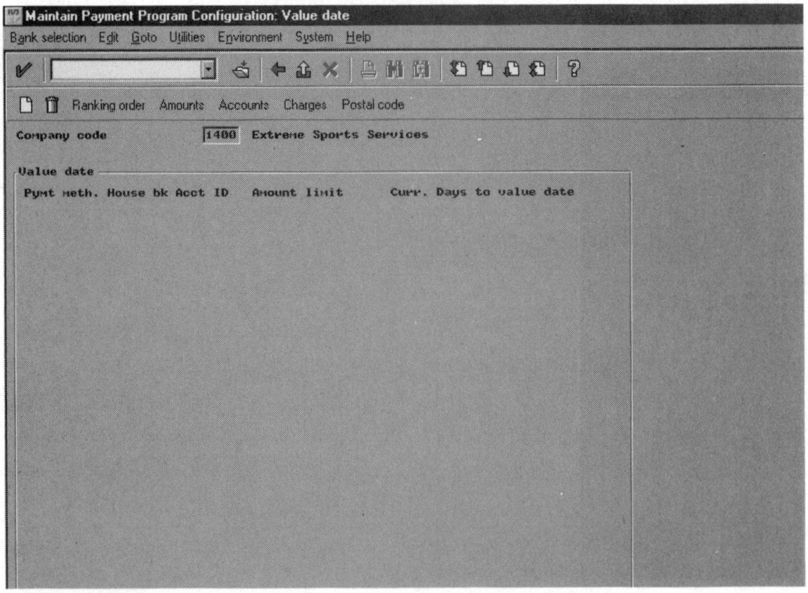

Value dates have not yet been maintained for company code 1400. To configure value dates, click the create icon. A pop-up screen appears. You will be able to tell from the pop-up screen that value dates are unique per payment method, house bank, bank account, and marginal amount. The marginal amount is the maximum amount up to which the value date is valid. This functionality is useful if a payment that is over a certain amount takes longer to process through the bank than payments of lower amounts. The number of days entered in the Days to Value Date field is added to the payment date to derive the value date. The fully configured value date screen for Extreme Sports is shown in Figure 4.27.

FIGURE 4.27   The fully configured value date screen for Extreme Sports

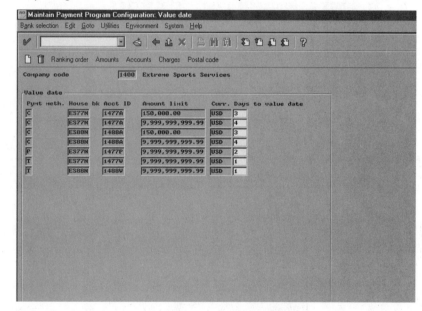

EXTREME SPORTS VALUE DATE CONFIGURATION ANALYSIS

On average, Extreme Sports has determined that it takes three days for A/P checks under $150,000 to be cleared through the bank. For A/P checks over $150,000, it generally takes four days. It takes an average of two days for payroll checks to clear the banks. The bank clears all U.S. wire transactions on the next business day.

EXTREME SPORTS VALUE DATE CONFIGURATION ANALYSIS (CONTINUED)

The value date will be used to forecast available cash balances to the payment program as well as cash management and liquidity forecasts in the Treasury module. Once there is more history in the system, SAP has the functionality to determine value dates for each individual vendor. When this information is in the system, the value date here will be used only if there is no information for a vendor.

Bank Optimization via Postal Codes

You will recall from the configuration of the paying company code that bank selection optimization via postal codes was activated. The functionality for selecting a bank from the zip code on the vendor master record will be configured in this section. To configure postal code functionality, click the Postal Code button shown in Figure 4.27. The configuration screen shown in Figure 4.28 appears. (The screen in Figure 4.28 has been configured for Extreme sports.)

FIGURE 4.28   The bank optimization via postal codes configuration screen

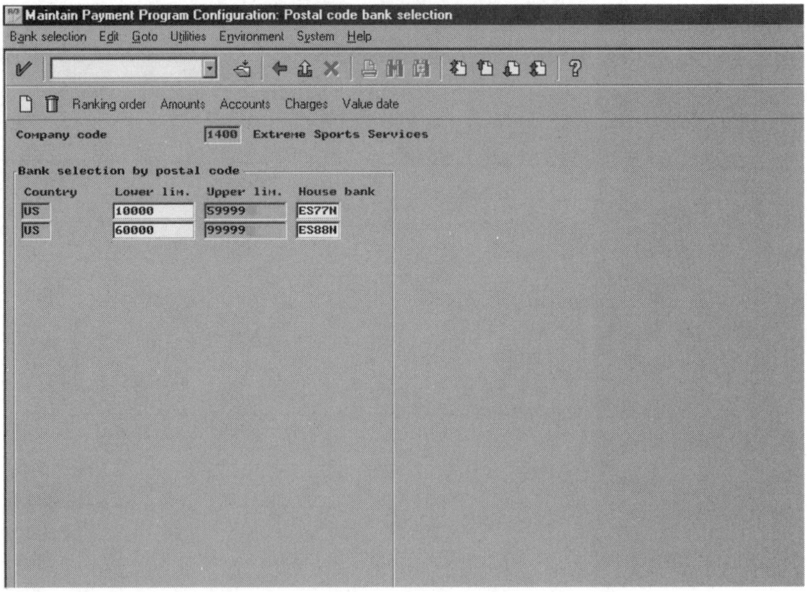

To enter the necessary data to use this functionality, click the create icon. A pop-up window is displayed. The fields to configure in the pop-up window are for country, postal code (zip code) lower limit, postal code (zip code) upper limit, and the house bank that is to be used for the range of zip codes in the country being configured. This configuration is very simple and self-explanatory.

EXTREME SPORTS BANK OPTIMIZATION VIA POSTAL CODES CONFIGURATION ANALYSIS

Extreme Sports has opted for a simplified bank optimization via zip codes at this time. For purpose of this book, it is assumed that all zip codes from 10000 to 59999 lie west of the Mississippi and all postal codes from 60000 up lie east of the Mississippi, with house bank ES77N based in Kansas City and house bank ES88N based in New York. This allows Extreme Sports to match bank payments to geographic regions as an added benefit to its vendors (which will allow vendors to cash Extreme Sports' payments faster).

Vendor Master Data

Before you begin configuration of *vendor master data*, it is necessary to have a strategy. You should know ahead of time how you would like to use your vendor master data and how you will convert vendors from your legacy system, as well as the integration points that vendor master data has with MM, Treasury, and A/R. Much like the G/L, vendor master data is a combination of configuration and master data maintenance.

A key concept in the configuration of vendor master data is *vendor groups*. Vendor groups allow you to have separate purposes and field statuses for different types of vendors. For example, you could have a group for regular vendors, a group for 1099 vendors, and a group for one-time vendors. By separating these different types of vendors into different vendor groups, you can make different fields required, optional, or suppressed for each of the groups.

Vendor Groups

The first step in configuring vendor master data is to create your vendor groups. Once you have gathered all of your requirements and know what the groups should be, you are ready to begin. You can display the configuration screen for creating vendor groups by using the menu path Financial Accounting ➤ Accounts Receivable and Accounts Payable ➤ Vendor Accounts ➤ Master Records ➤ Preparation for Creating Vendor Master Records ➤ Define Account Groups with Screen Layout (Vendors).

DEFINE VENDOR GROUPS

You can get to the vendor groups configuration screen by using the following methods:

Menu Path: **Financial Accounting ➤ Accounts Receivable and Accounts Payable ➤ Vendor Accounts ➤ Master Records ➤ Preparation for Creating Vendor Master Records ➤ Define Account Groups with Screen Layout (Vendors)**

Transaction Code: **OBD3**

After entering the configuration transactions, you are presented with the screen shown in Figure 4.29.

FIGURE 4.29   The initial vendor groups configuration screen

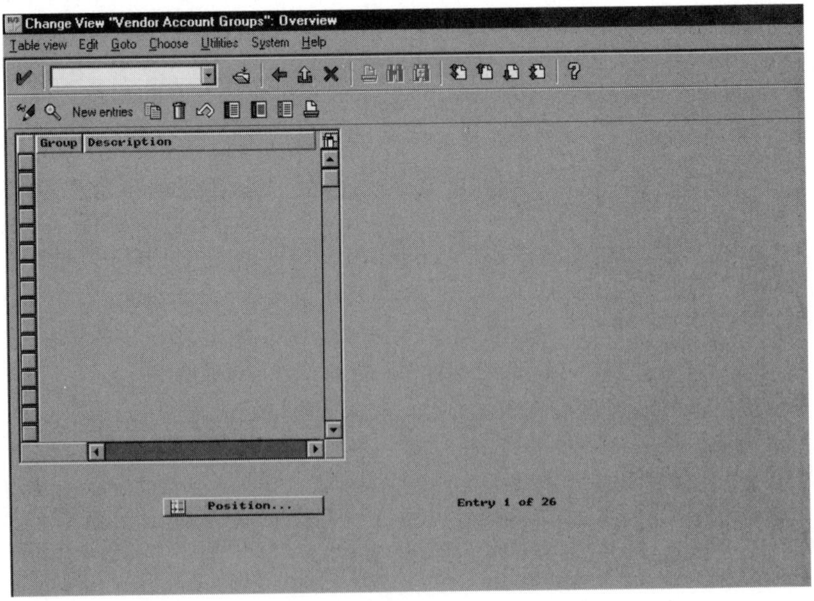

From the initial vendor groups configuration screen, click the New Entries button to access the screen shown in Figure 4.30.

FIGURE 4.30   The vendor groups new entries screen

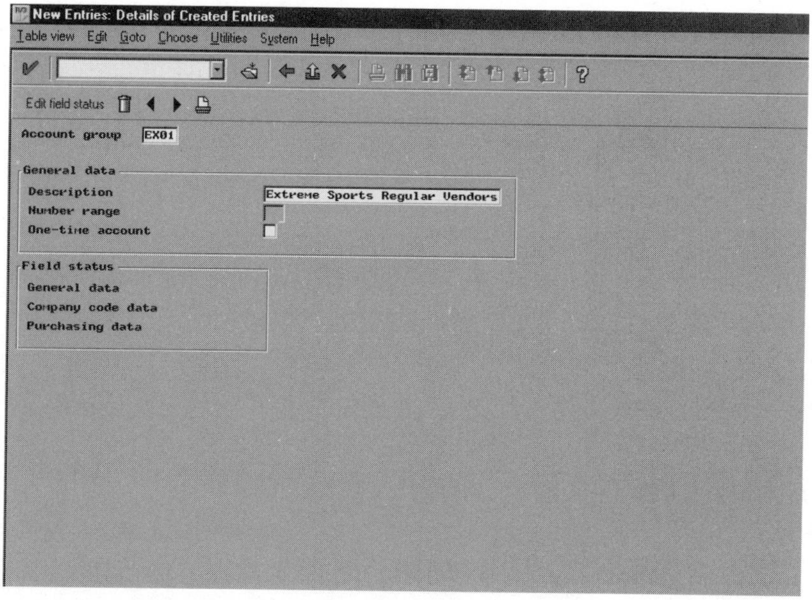

Here is a list of the fields that appear in the vendor groups new entries screen:

Account Group   Enter a four-character alphanumeric identifier for the vendor group you are creating.

Description   Enter a descriptive name for the vendor group you are creating.

Number Range   This field shows the number range assigned to this vendor group. This field is not configurable from this screen. Number ranges will be assigned to vendor groups in a later section.

One-Time Account   Select this indicator if you want this vendor group to be used for one-time vendors. One-time accounts are used for vendors that you may use only once and for which you do not want to store a unique vendor master record. Only one vendor master record is needed for all one-time vendors. The name, address, and other important information needed for payment are entered on the document when you specify a one-time vendor number. You should only need one one-time vendor account group for your company.

Field Status The concept of field statuses should be familiar to you from your work on the general ledger in Chapter 3. The field statuses on this screen control which fields are optional, required, and suppressed when a vendor master record is created.

The first page of the configuration screens and the most important fields for each category of vendor group field status are covered in the following sections.

Vendor Group Field Status

Now we will explore in detail the different kinds of data that you configure from the Field Status section of the vendor groups new entries screen. To access a field status group, double-click the field status group name on the bottom left-hand corner of the screen.

General Data The first screen for the configuration of the *General Data* section of the vendor group field status appears in Figure 4.31. The fields in this section are valid for the vendor master data regardless of the company code using it.

FIGURE 4.31   The initial general data configuration screen

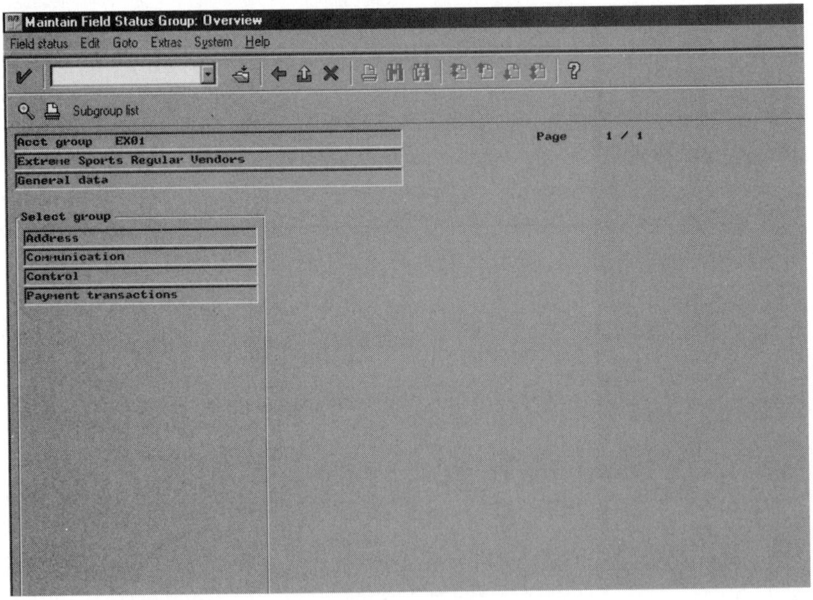

Explanations of the subsections of the general data field status, as well as some of the most important fields to consider in each subsection, are listed here:

Address   The Address section contains the fields that capture the mailing address information about the vendor. It is generally a good idea to make the Name, Location (city), Region (state), and Country fields required so that you don't have incomplete information about your vendors.

Communication   The Communication section contains fields that capture information such as telephone numbers, fax numbers, and so on. These fields are relatively self-explanatory, and it's easy to determine if you need to fill them out.

Control   The Control section contains many important fields that capture how the vendor master record is processed. Here's a listing of the most important fields in this section:

Customer   In this field, you can tell the system that this vendor is also a customer (by entering the customer number). This allows you to do A/P-A/R netting if you so desire.

Tax Codes   These fields are important in determining the type of tax used on invoices for these vendors (Sales or Use Tax) and in specifying 1099 vendors.

Payment Transactions   The fields in this section help with the processing of the payment program:

Bank Details   The fields pertaining to bank details allow you to specify where the vendor's bank wishes to receive payment. This helps with payment program optimization by bank group as well as electronic payment transactions.

Alternative Payee Account   If you have some vendors you do not pay directly, this field helps to facilitate that transaction.

Company Code Data   The first screen for the configuration of the *Company Code Data* section of the vendor group field status appears in Figure 4.32. All fields in this section are valid at the company code level only. This means that, as vendors are extended across several company codes, the fields in this section can have different values based on the company code using the vendor master data.

FIGURE 4.32　The initial company code data configuration screen

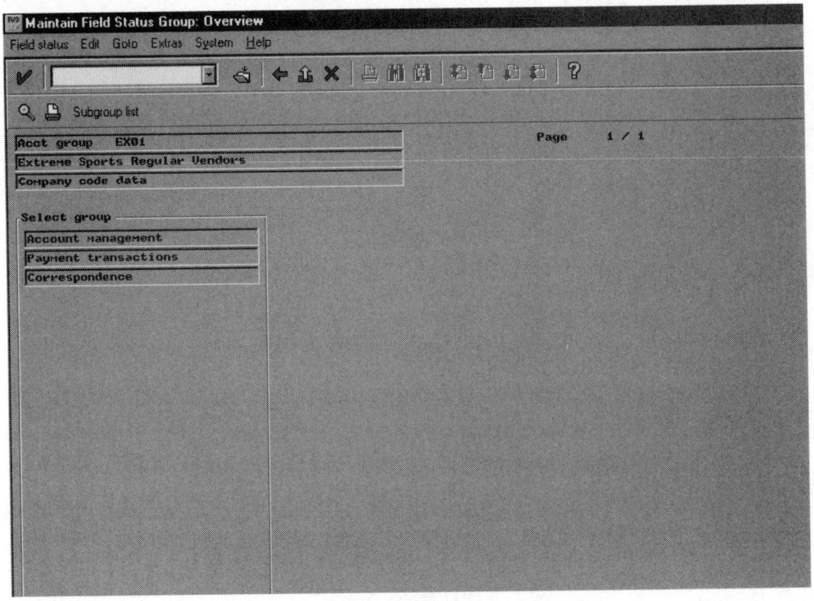

Explanations of the subsections of the company code data field status, as well as the most important fields to consider in each subsection, are listed here:

Account Management　The Account Management fields control how vendor master data updates the general ledger. They are as follows:

Reconciliation Account　As you are aware, the A/P system is a subledger. The reconciliation account is the G/L account updated by A/P transactions using this vendor account. Different vendors or vendor groups can update different reconciliation accounts.

Planning Group　The planning group is a major integration point between A/P and Treasury. The planning group updates the payable section in the liquidity-forecast functionality of the Treasury module. (The liquidity-forecast report will be covered in Chapter 6.) If you want to utilize the treasury functions within SAP, make this field mandatory.

Previous Account Number　This field can be used to capture the legacy vendor number in SAP. It is especially useful in the initial time after Go-Live when the system is looking up vendors. A match key can be created to look up vendor numbers based on this field.

Payment Transactions   The fields in this section help with the processing of the payment program based on specific settings for the company code in which the vendor can be used. The settings for these fields can vary from company code to company code, whereas the payment transaction subgrouping in the General Data section cannot. Here are the settings and their definitions:

Terms of Payment   You can specify the default payment terms that the vendor grants your company in this field. The default terms of payment can be overridden at the document level when the invoice is entered.

Double Invoice Validation   When this indicator is set, the system checks to see if the invoice being entered has previously been entered. It is a good idea to make the reference document field required on the document type that is used for A/P invoices. The vendor's invoice number should be entered in the Reference Document field. The use of the Reference Document field allows this indicator to work for non–P.O.-related invoices.

Payment Block   Using this field, you can block all invoices for this vendor from being paid automatically by the payment program.

Payment Methods   You can specify which payment method(s) is valid for this vendor's invoices. Payment methods were configured in the payment program.

Clearing with Customer   Select this indicator if you want to clear open A/P accounts with open A/R accounts for this vendor if the vendor is also a customer. The customer number can be specified in the General Data section.

Cashed Checks Duration   The system updates this field based on the history of how long it takes for checks cut to this vendor to clear the bank. The program that updates this field is contained in the Treasury module.

Individual Payment   Select this indicator if individual checks should be cut for each invoice that relates to this vendor.

Correspondence   The fields in this section allow you to store additional information for contact with the vendor as well as enable and specify dunning information with the vendor:

Account at Vendor   Your customer number at the vendor is stored in this field. This can greatly help your A/P clerks in researching open A/P issues.

Purchasing Data   The first screen for the configuration of the Purchasing Data section of the vendor group field status appears in Figure 4.33. These fields deal mainly with MM functionality. How you configure the fields in this section will depend greatly upon the purchasing strategy that is designed and agreed upon between you and your MM group. These fields are another major integration point between FI and MM.

FIGURE 4.33   The initial purchasing data configuration screen

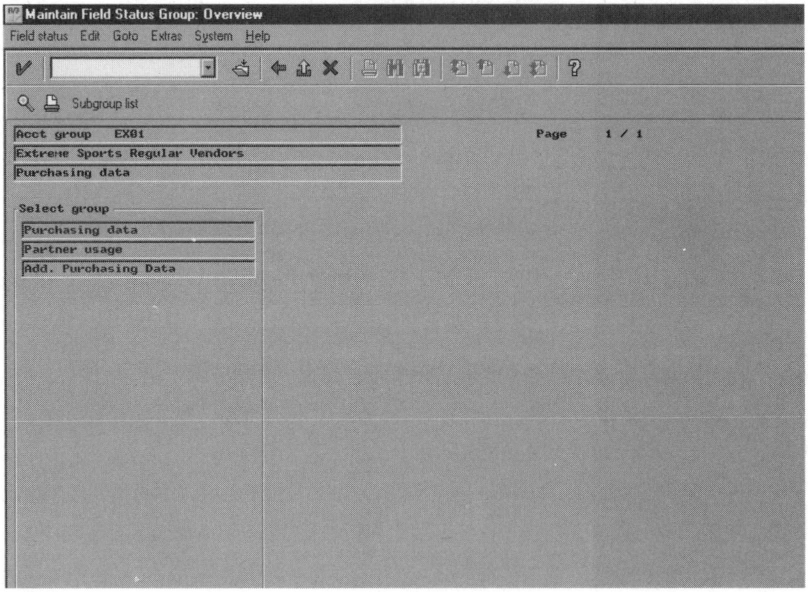

EXTREME SPORTS VENDOR GROUP CONFIGURATION ANALYSIS

The regular vendor account group for Extreme Sports was configured in this section. The vendor group identifier EX01 was configured for this group. The One-Time Account indicator was not activated because a separate one-time vendor account group will be configured for Extreme Sports.

Assigning Number Ranges to Vendor Account Groups

In this section, you will create a new number range and assign the number range to the vendor account group that was just configured. Number ranges can be set up as external (user assigns a number) or internal (system assigns a number).

TIP It is a good idea to initially make all of your vendor account groups externally assigned. This will help in the conversion of your vendor accounts from your legacy system to SAP. This way, the conversion program can be run into each client and you know that the vendor numbers will be the same for production. After your final conversion run into your production client, the number range can be changed to internal.

To get to the vendor account number ranges configuration screen, follow the menu path Financial Accounting ➢ Accounts Receivable and Accounts Payable ➢ Vendor Accounts ➢ Master Records ➢ Preparation for Creating Vendor Master Records ➢ Create Number Ranges for Vendor Accounts.

CREATE NUMBER RANGES FOR VENDOR ACCOUNT GROUPS

You can get to the vendor account number range configuration screen using the following methods:

Menu Path: **Financial Accounting** ➢ **Accounts Receivable and Accounts Payable** ➢ **Vendor Accounts** ➢ **Master Records** ➢ **Preparation for Creating Vendor Master Records** ➢ **Create Number Ranges for Vendor Accounts**

Transaction Code: **XKN1**

After entering the configuration transaction, you are presented with the screen shown in Figure 4.34.

FIGURE 4.34   The vendor account number ranges configuration screen

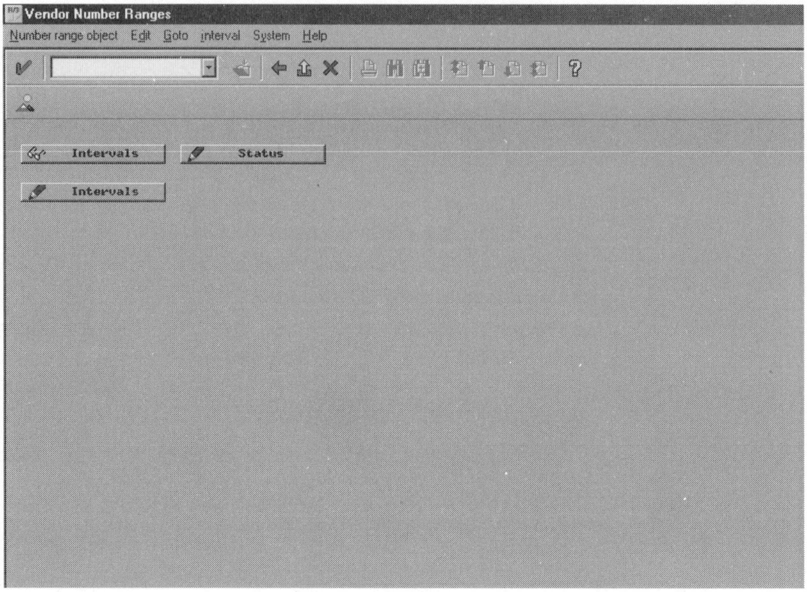

Click the Maintain Number Range Intervals button. You are then presented with the screen shown in Figure 4.35.

FIGURE 4.35   The number range intervals screen

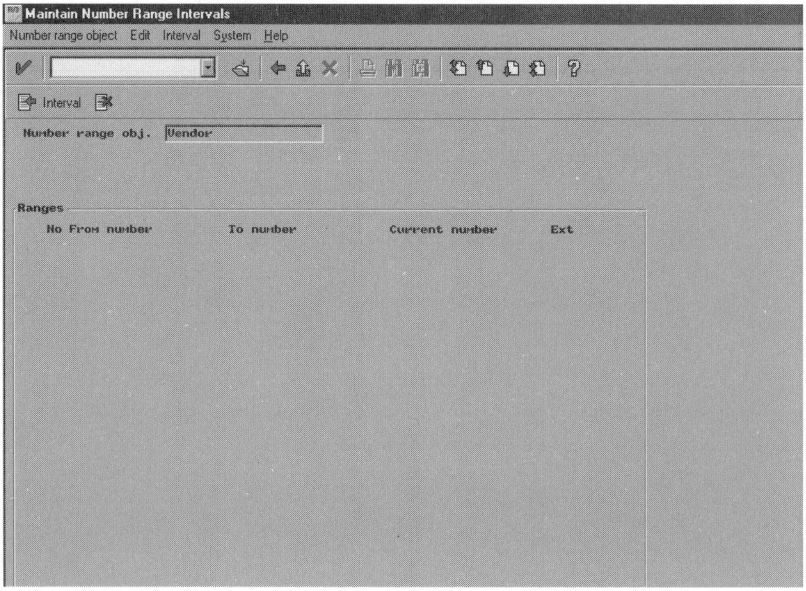

From the screen displayed in Figure 4.35, click the insert interval icon. You are presented with the screen shown in Figure 4.36.

FIGURE 4.36 The Insert Interval pop-up box

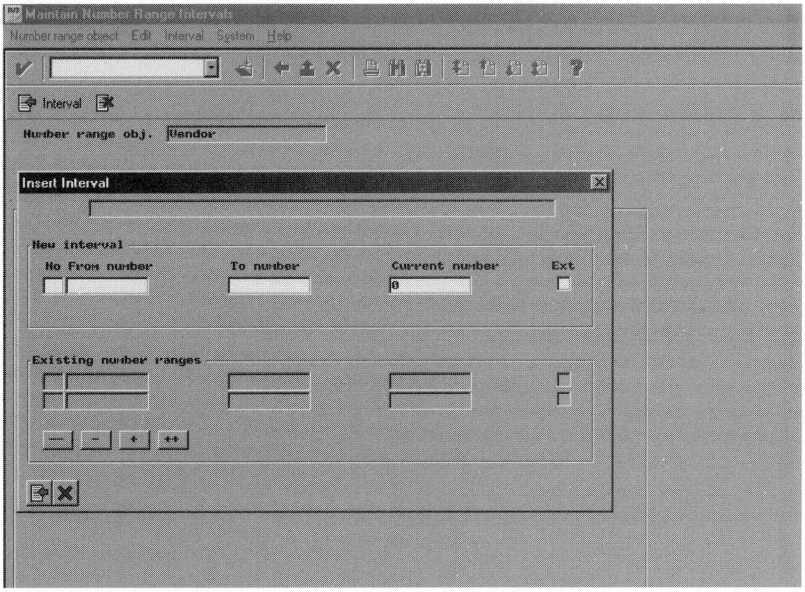

In the fields in Figure 4.36, enter an identifier for the number range, the number where the range should start (From Number), and the number where the range should stop (To Number). Update the current number (if internal number assignment is used), and activate the external indicator if you want the user to specify the vendor number. After entering this information, click the insert icon. The configured number range for Extreme Sports is shown in Figure 4.37.

FIGURE 4.37   The configured number range intervals screen for Extreme Sports

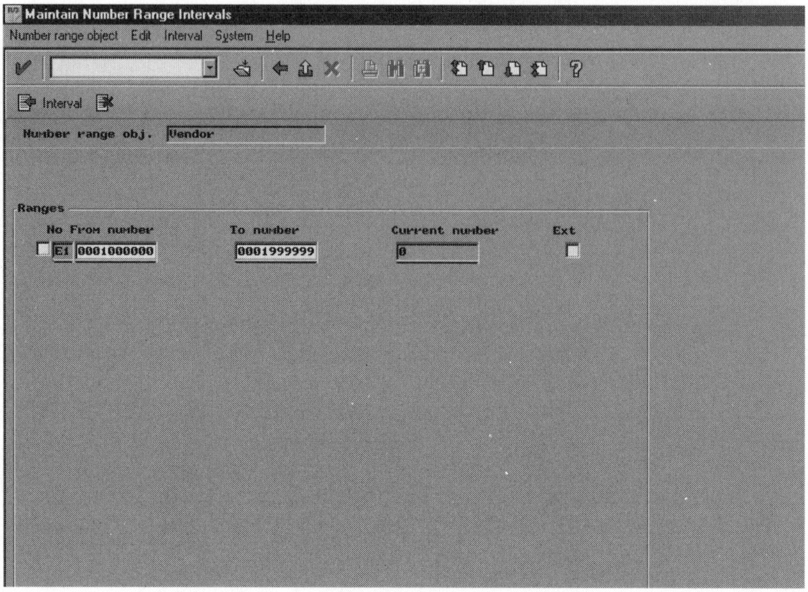

The next step is to assign the number range that was just created to the vendor group just created. Remember that number ranges are not automatically included in transports and should be created manually in each client. The configuration transaction for assigning number ranges to vendor groups is displayed using the menu path Financial Accounting ➢ Accounts Receivable and Accounts Payable ➢ Vendor Accounts ➢ Master Records ➢ Preparation for Creating Vendor Master Records ➢ Allocate Number Ranges for Vendor Accounts.

ASSIGN NUMBER RANGES TO VENDOR GROUPS

You can get to the configuration screen for assigning number ranges to vendor groups by using the following methods:

Menu Path: **Financial Accounting ➢ Accounts Receivable and Accounts Payable ➢ Vendor Accounts ➢ Master Records ➢ Preparation for Creating Vendor Master Records ➢ Allocate Number Ranges for Vendor Accounts**

Transaction Code: **OBAS**

The configuration screen for assigning number ranges to vendor account groups is shown in Figure 4.38. Enter the number range you would like to assign to the vendor group.

FIGURE 4.38   The configuration screen for assigning number ranges to vendor account groups

FIGURE 4.38   The configuration screen for assigning number ranges to vendor account groups

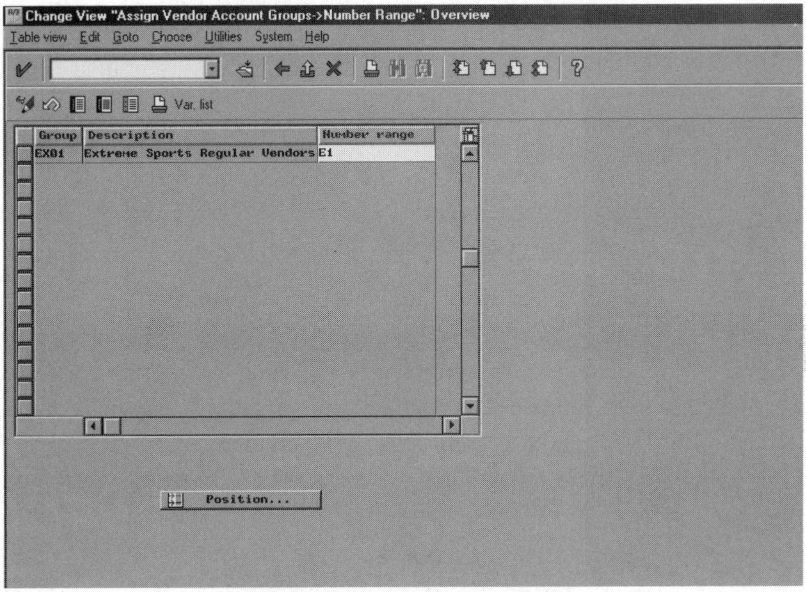

EXTREME SPORTS VENDOR GROUP NUMBER RANGE ASSIGNMENT

Extreme Sports created number range E1 with internal number assignment to be used for vendor group EX01, which is for normal vendors. Utilizing internal number assignment for normal vendors will speed up the process of creating new normal vendors.

Creating Vendor Master Data

There are several ways to create vendor master data in the system. In particular, there are two ways to create vendor master data in the FI-AP area. Vendor master records can be created for the company code or centrally. When you select company code creation, only the general and accounting screens are available for data population. When you select the option to create them centrally, all the general, accounting, and

MM purchasing screens are available for configuration. Creating vendor master data centrally requires a good amount of coordination with your MM group.

Just as there are two ways to create vendor master data, there are two ways to enter invoices in the system. You can enter non–P.O.-related invoices directly in the A/P system. Non–P.O.-related invoices are usually for services such as utilities and telephone and for insurance bills. The other way to enter invoices is through the MM module. Invoices entered through the MM module are P.O.-related invoices. The MM module can be configured to require either two-way or three-way matching. Three-way matching ensures that each P.O. has matching G.R. (Goods Receipt) and I.R. (Invoice Receipt). P.O.-related invoices are usually done for production and maintenance materials. Using P.O.-related invoices allows you to use a lot of functionality included in the MM module.

SAP delivers two programs that allow you to extend vendor master records to company codes other than the company code where the vendor master record was created. These programs are very similar to the programs that are used to extend G/L accounts. You can get to the program that copies vendor master records from company code to company code by using the application menu path Accounting ➢ Financial Accounting ➢ Accounts Payable ➢ Compare ➢ Company Codes ➢ Send.

COPY VENDOR MASTER RECORDS

You can get to the vendor master record copy program by using the following methods:

Program: **RFBIKR10**

Application Menu Path: **Accounting** ➢ **Financial Accounting** ➢ **Accounts Payable** ➢ **Compare** ➢ **Company Codes** ➢ **Send**

Transaction Code: **FK15**

The screen for the vendor master record copy program (RFBIKR10) is shown in Figure 4.39.

FIGURE 4.39   The vendor master record copy program (RFBIKR10) screen

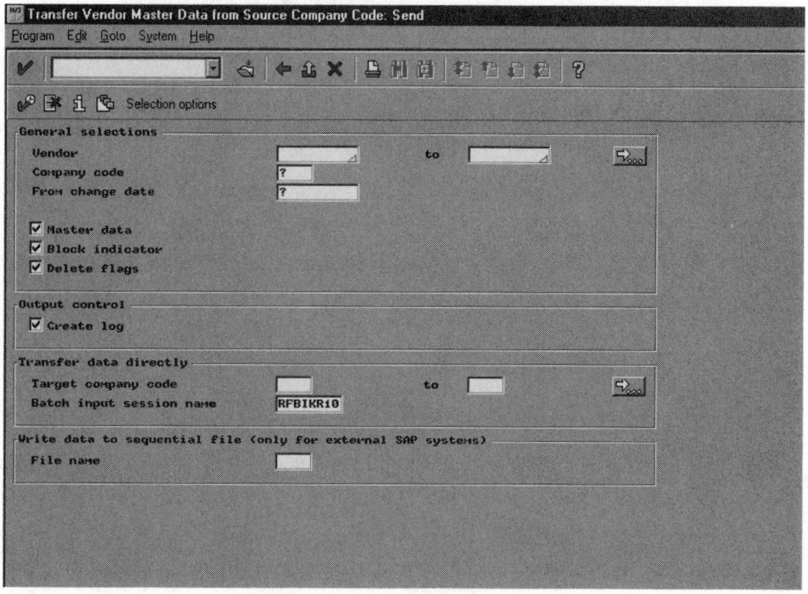

As we mentioned earlier, this program works in much the same manner as the G/L copy program (RFBISA10). Using this program (RFBIKR10), you can either create a batch input session that can be executed in the same client, or you can create an external file that can be run into other clients.

You can get to the program that imports the file created by the vendor master copy program (RFBIKR20) using the application menu path Accounting ➢ Financial Accounting ➢ Accounts Payable ➢ Compare ➢ Company Codes ➢ Receive.

The vendor master copy file import program (RFBIKR20) screen is shown in Figure 4.40.

IMPORT VENDOR MASTER RECORDS

You can get the vendor master copy file import program by using the following methods:

Program: **RFBIKR20**

Application Menu Path: **Accounting** ➤ **Financial Accounting** ➤ **Accounts Payable** ➤ **Compare** ➤ **Company Codes** ➤ **Receive**

Transaction Code: **FK16**

FIGURE 4.40 The vendor master copy file import program (RFBIKR20) screen

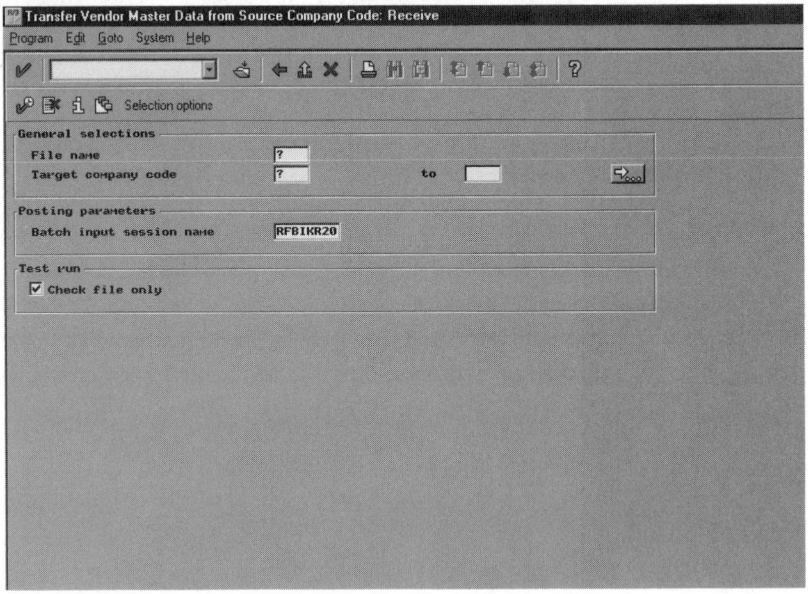

Summary

In this chapter, we covered the configuration of the Accounts Payable module. You learned that the proper master data configuration (house banks, bank accounts, and vendor master data) is vital to a finely tuned A/P module. The paramount of A/P configuration is the payment program. We covered configuration of the payment program step by step, allowing you to learn how to best configure the program for your company. Specifically, we covered the following topics in this chapter:

House Banks and Accounts

    Bank Account G/L Structuring

    Check Lots and Void Reason Codes

Payment Program Configuration

    Company Code Data

    Paying Company Code Data

    Country Payment Methods

    Company Code Payment Methods

    Bank Selection

Vendor Master Data

    Vendor Groups

    Vendor Group Field Status

    Assigning Number Ranges to Vendor Account Groups

    Creating Vendor Master Data

CHAPTER 5

Accounts Receivable

FEATURING:

▶ TERMS OF PAYMENT AND INTEREST CALCULATION

▶ REASON CODES

▶ OVERALL A/R AND EMPLOYEE TOLERANCES

▶ CREDIT MANAGEMENT

▶ CUSTOMER MASTER RECORDS

The Accounts Receivable subledger (A/R) allows you to effectively manage your customer accounts and unpaid invoices. The A/R submodule has lots of options and is very flexible. In addition to strictly A/R topics, credit management will also be covered in this chapter. Credit management allows you to grant customers' credit according to your business terms and risk aversion.

Terms of Payment and Interest Calculation

Terms of payment involve the discount amounts and the related time frames for payment you send to your customers. The configuration for terms of payment is the same for both A/R and A/P. The same terms of payment can be used for both A/R (customer) and A/P (vendor) accounts. To configure terms of payment, follow the menu path Financial Accounting ➤ Accounts Receivable and Accounts Payable ➤ Business Transactions ➤ Outgoing Invoices/Credit Memos ➤ Maintain Terms of Payment.

DEFINE TERMS OF PAYMENT

You can get to the terms of payment configuration screen by using these methods:

Menu Path: **Financial Accounting** ➤ **Accounts Receivable and Accounts Payable** ➤ **Business Transactions** ➤ **Outgoing Invoices/Credit Memos** ➤ **Maintain Terms of Payment**

Transaction Code: **OBB8**

After entering the configuration transaction listed in the shortcut box, you are presented with the terms of payment overview screen, shown in Figure 5.1

FIGURE 5.1   The terms of payment overview screen

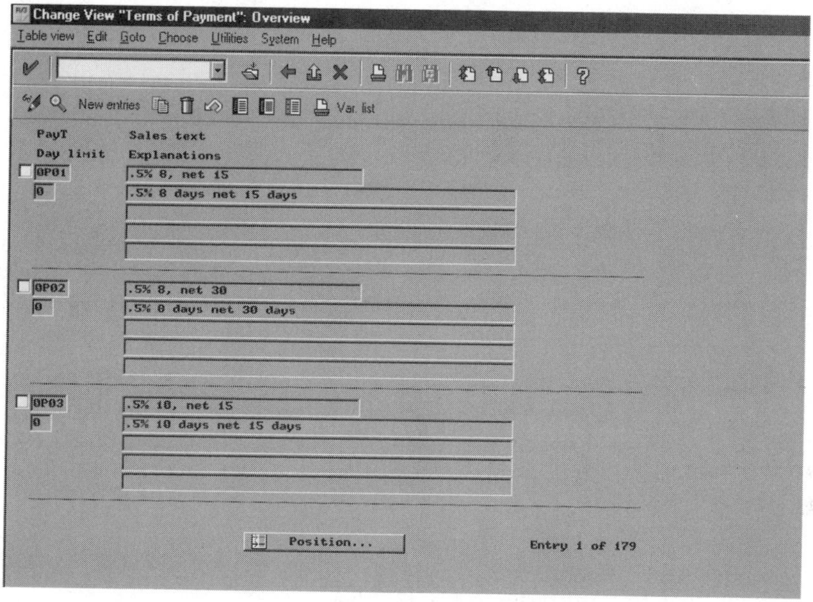

To create a new payment term, click the New Entries button. The payment terms
new entry screen, shown in Figure 5.2, appears.

FIGURE 5.2   The payment terms new entry screen

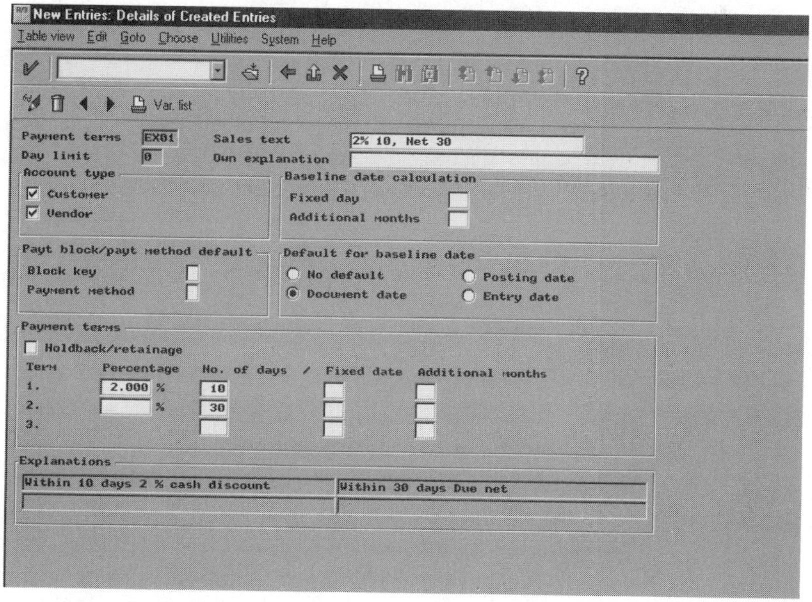

Here is an explanation of the fields in the payment terms new entry screen:

Payment Terms   Enter a four-character alphanumeric identifier for your payment term key.

Sales Text   Enter a short text explanation of the key. Your entry is limited to 30 characters.

Day Limit   This field is only valid if your terms of payment depend on the day of the month. For example, an invoice billed on or before the 10th of the month is due on the 25th of the same month, and an invoice billed after the 10th is due on the 5th of the next month. Given this example, a 10 would be entered in this field because the terms are good until the 10th day of the month.

Own Explanation   This field is used to give a detailed explanation of the payment terms. This field should be used only if you want to override the explanation that is automatically generated by the system. The system explanation is shown in the bottom fields, in the Explanations section.

Customer   Select this indicator if you want the payment term to be used for customer accounts (A/R).

Vendor   Select this indicator if you want the payment term to be used for vendor accounts (A/P).

Fixed Day   Use this field if you want to override the default baseline date proposed by the system. If you want to utilize this functionality, enter the calendar day that should be used for the baseline date.

Additional Months   Use this field in conjunction with the Fixed Day field. Enter the number of months that should be added to the calendar month of the proposed baseline date. The baseline date then becomes the combination of the Fixed Day field and the Additional Months field.

Block Key   If this term of payment should propose a block key—which blocks goods issue for delivery (A/R) or payment (A/P)—enter the block key here. The block key takes effect only if the terms of payment key is entered in the customer or vendor master record. If this payment term is inserted in the line item of the document, the block key is not defaulted in.

Payment Method   If you want to specify a specific payment method (other than that specified in the customer or vendor master record) with this term of payment, enter the payment method identifier here.

Default for Baseline Date   Select the radio button that corresponds to the baseline date you want to default to when using this term of payment. You can choose between No Default, Document Date, Posting Date (the date that the document posts in the system; this can be the same, or it can vary from the document date), or Entry Date (the system prompts you for the baseline date when the document is entered).

Holdback/Retainage   Select this indicator to allow the system to automatically break out a single line item into multiple line items with different due dates based on the payment term. The system prompts you for the breakout when an FI document is entered.

Percentage   Enter the percentage rate that is to be used for the discount.

No. of Days   Enter the number of days out from the baseline date for which the percentage discount is valid.

Fixed Date   Enter the day of the month the discount ends if you do not want to use the baseline date.

Additional Months   If you want to add month(s) to the baseline date month to determine the length of time the discount is valid, enter the number of additional month(s) in this field.

Explanations   The system defaults an explanation of the payment term in this field based on of the percentage discount and length of time the discount is valid. An entry in the Own Explanation field overwrites the system-derived explanation.

EXTREME SPORTS TERMS OF PAYMENT CONFIGURATION ANALYSIS

Extreme Sports' terms of payment key, EX01, was configured to meet one of the terms it grants for cash discount. Both customer and vendor accounts can use EX01. This way, Extreme Sports can use the key on the invoices they send out, and if a vendor uses the same terms for Extreme Sports' invoices due, this key can be used in the vendor master record. The default baseline date for this key is the document date. This means that the calculation for cash discount and overall due date will begin from the document date entered in the system. You can see in the Payment Terms section that a cash discount of 2% is granted if the invoice is paid within 10 days (of the document date of the invoice). If the invoice is not paid within 10 days, the full amount of the invoice is due in 30 days. The sales text is set to read "2% 10, Net 30," so that, when invoices and customer master records are created, the user can easily determine what type of cash discount this terms of payment key is granting. The Explanations section at the bottom of the screen is automatically generated by the system based on the configuration that was done in the screen.

Interest Calculation

The next feature that will be configured for Extreme Sports is the *interest calculation* procedure. Interest calculation allows you to charge interest on overdue customer accounts. The system keeps track of the date of the last interest run and stores it in the customer master record.

The first step to configuring interest calculation is to create an *interest indicator*. For interest to be calculated on a customer, the interest indicator must be stored in the customer master record. Interest can be calculated by using line items or overall account balances. The line item calculation will be used in this example. If you want to calculate interest on a G/L account such as confirmed cash, you would calculate the interest based on the account balance. To get to the configuration screen for interest indicators, follow the menu path Financial Accounting ➣ Accounts Receivable and Accounts Payable ➣ Business Transactions ➣ Interest Calculation ➣ Interest Calculation Global Settings ➣ Define Interest Calculation Types.

DEFINE INTEREST CALCULATION TYPES

You can get to the interest indicator configuration screen by using these methods:

Menu Path: **Financial Accounting** ➣ **Accounts Receivable and Accounts Payable** ➣ **Business Transactions** ➣ **Interest Calculation** ➣ **Interest Calculation Global Settings** ➣ **Define Interest Calculation Types**

Transaction Code: **OB46**

The interest settlement (calculation type) overview screen, shown in Figure 5.3, is displayed by entering the configuration transaction shown in the Define Interest Calculation Types shortcut box.

FIGURE 5.3   The interest settlement (calculation type) overview screen

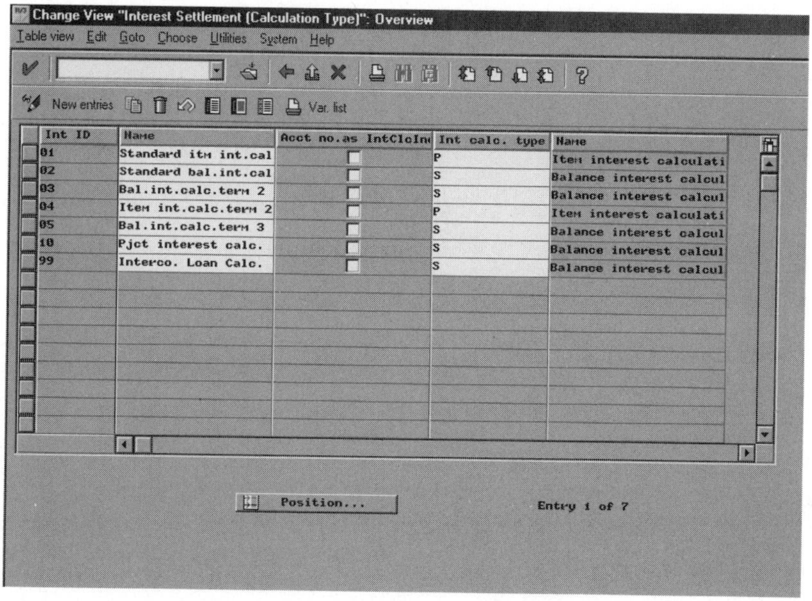

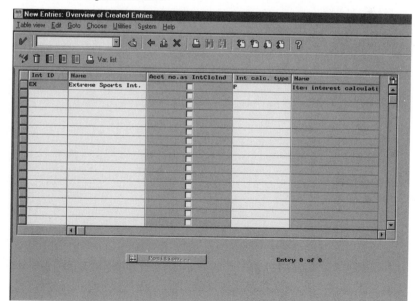

To create a new interest indicator, click the New Entries button. You are then presented with the new entries configuration screen, shown in Figure 5.4.

FIGURE 5.4   The new entries configuration screen

Here is a list of explanations for the fields that appear in the new entries configuration screen:

Int ID   Enter a two-character alphanumeric identifier to be used for your interest indicator.

Name   Enter a descriptive name for your interest indicator.

Acct No. as IntClcInd   If you want to use the customer account number as the interest indicator, activate this field. The field must contain 10 characters, so you may have to enter leading zeros.

Int Calc. Type   Select either P or S from the drop-down box. P signifies that this interest indicator will calculate interest based on line items. S signifies that this interest indicator will calculate interest based on account balances.

EXTREME SPORTS INTEREST INDICATOR CONFIGURATION ANALYSIS

The interest indicator EX was configured for Extreme Sports. It will be used for overdue accounts receivable interest calculations. Therefore, the interest calculation type of P was used so that the interest would be calculated off of individual line items. Because interest indicators can also be used on normal G/L accounts such as confirmed cash, the S option is also given so that interest can be calculated off of account balances.

Now that the interest indicator has been created, the next step is to make it available to the interest run program. When you make the interest indicator available to the interest run program, you also specify additional characteristics about how you want the indicator to function. Follow the menu path Financial Accounting ➢ Accounts Receivable and Accounts Payable ➢ Business Transactions ➢ Interest Calculation ➢ Interest Calculation Global Settings ➢ Prepare Interest on Arrears Calculation to get to the configuration screen to make the interest indicator available to the interest run program.

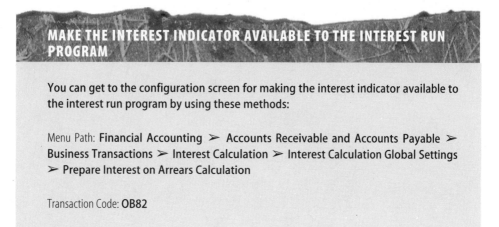

MAKE THE INTEREST INDICATOR AVAILABLE TO THE INTEREST RUN PROGRAM

You can get to the configuration screen for making the interest indicator available to the interest run program by using these methods:

Menu Path: **Financial Accounting** ➤ **Accounts Receivable and Accounts Payable** ➤ **Business Transactions** ➤ **Interest Calculation** ➤ **Interest Calculation Global Settings** ➤ **Prepare Interest on Arrears Calculation**

Transaction Code: **OB82**

The configuration screen for making the interest indicator available to the interest run program is shown in Figure 5.5.

FIGURE 5.5   The initial interest run program configuration screen

To make your interest indicator available to the interest run program, click the New Entries button. The screen shown in Figures 5.6 and 5.7 is displayed (Figure 5.7 is the bottom half of the screen shown in Figure 5.6).

FIGURE 5.6   The top half of the interest run program configuration screen

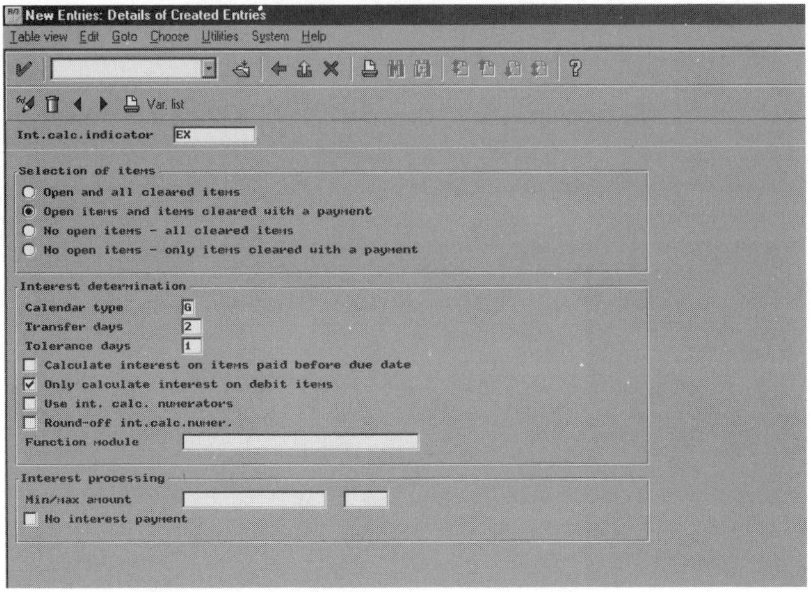

FIGURE 5.7   The bottom half of the interest run program configuration screen

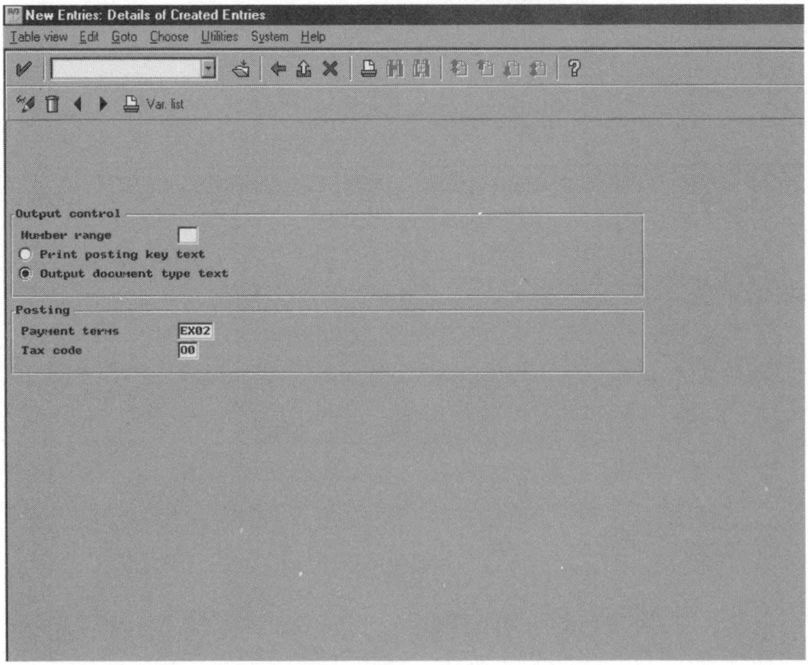

Here is an explanation of the fields in the interest run program configuration screen:

Int. Calc. Indicator   Enter the identifier of the interest indicator you created earlier (see Figure 5.4).

Selection of Items   The radio buttons in this section determine the line items on which interest is calculated. The program will try to select all available line items that have become past due since the date of the last interest run based on the parameter selected here. The available entries are as follows:

Open and All Cleared Items   If you select this radio button, all line items (both open and cleared), regardless of the clearing method, are selected for interest calculation—this option is all inclusive. For example, if an invoice has already been cleared by a payment but the payment did not fall within the terms of payment, interest is still calculated on the invoice. The same rule applies for invoices cleared with a credit memo.

Open Items and Items Cleared with a Payment   If you select this radio button, all open line items and line items cleared by a payment transaction are selected for interest calculation. In this example, invoice line items cleared by a credit memo would not be selected for interest calculation—only those invoice line items cleared by a payment would be selected.

No Open Items—All Cleared Items   If you select this radio button, only cleared items are selected for interest calculation. All cleared items are selected regardless of how they were cleared. Open items are not selected with this option.

No Open Items—Only Items Cleared with a Payment   If you select this radio button, only line items cleared by a payment will be selected for interest calculation. Line items cleared by any other method and open line items are ignored.

Calendar Type   The calendar type determines the number of days per period that interest is calculated. The available options are as follows:

B (Bank Calendar)   The bank calendar uses 360 days as the basis for a year and 30 days as the basis for a month.

F (French Calendar)   The French calendar uses 360 days as the basis for a year and the exact number of days in the month as the basis for a month.

G (Gregorian Calendar)   The Gregorian calendar uses 365 days as the basis for a year and the exact number of days in the month as the basis for a month.

J (Japanese Calendar)   The Japanese calendar uses either 365 or 366 days (depending on leap years) as the basis for a year and 30 days as the basis for a month.

Transfer Days   Transfer days represent the number of days it takes for the customer's payment to reach your company and be applied. For example, you can use transfer days to figure out the average number of days it takes a customer's check to reach your company or your company's lockbox through the mail. Transfer days are deducted from overdue up until the point that they would result in a late payment being paid early. Transfer days only affect cleared line items; they have no effect on open line items. Assume, for example, that an invoice is paid four days late. If two transfer days have been granted in this configuration step, when interest calculation is run, SAP treats the invoice as being only two days late (four days overdue minus two tolerance days). If an invoice was cleared with a payment two days late and three transfer days have been granted in this configuration step, when interest calculation is run, SAP treats the invoice as being paid on the due date (not before the due date as the calculation of two days overdue minus three tolerance days might lead you to believe).

Tolerance Days   Tolerance days are also known as the grace period, or grace days. They are subtracted from overdue days to determine whether or not interest should be calculated. For example, if an item is one day overdue and one tolerance day is granted, it will be treated as paid on the due date, and no interest will be calculated. However, if an item is five days overdue and one tolerance day is granted, the item is treated as four days overdue, but five days worth of interest would be calculated. Transfer days are subtracted before grace days when interest calculation is run.

Calculate Interest on Items Paid before Due Date   If you select this indicator, interest is also calculated on items paid before their due date. The result of this calculation is credit interest, which will decrease the customer's A/R balance. This is the opposite of the most common reason for calculating interest—debit interest that increases the customer's A/R balance.

Only Calculate Interest on Debit Items   If you select this indicator, interest is only calculated on debit line items (invoices and debit memos). If you do not select this indicator, interest is also calculated on credit line items (credit memos), and this credit interest is offset against the debit interest from invoices.

Use Int. Calc. Numerators   This option is not normally needed. If this indicator is activated, the system first determines the numerators that are to be used for the calculation and then carries out the rest of the interest calculation.

Round-Off Int. Calc. Numer.   If you have activated interest calculation numerators in the preceding field, you can activate this indicator to allow the system to automatically round off the numerators that are used in the calculation.

Function Module   If you do not want to use the standard interest calculation procedure in SAP, you can program your own function module to calculate interest. Enter the name of the module in this field.

Min/Max Amount   You can keep the system from posting insignificant amounts of interest by entering a minimum/maximum amount here. If the amount of interest calculated is larger than the minimum/maximum amount entered here, the interest is posted. If the amount of interest calculated is smaller than the minimum/maximum amount entered here, the interest is not posted.

No Interest Payment   If you are calculating interest on credit items as well as debit items, you can select this indicator if you do not want to create an interest settlement when credit interest is paid back to the customer.

Number Range   SAP will post interest using a normal accounting document. However, you have the option of also creating an interest form that becomes a reference document to the interest posting. If you wish to create an interest form, enter the document number range that should be used by the form. Use transaction code OB84 to define the form that should be used by your company code for interest forms.

Print Posting Key Text   If you decide to use interest forms, you can activate this indicator to output the posting key text on the line item that is created on the interest form.

Output Document Type Text   If you decide to use interest forms, you can activate this indicator to output the document type text on the line item that is created on the interest form.

Payment Terms   Enter the terms of payment that should be used for the interest posting. The interest posting does not automatically take on the terms of payment for the line item causing the interest posting.

Tax Code   Enter the tax code that should be used by the system when making the interest posting. Normally, you should enter an exempt tax code (a tax code maintained with a 0% rate).

EXTREME SPORTS—MAKING THE INTEREST INDICATOR AVAILABLE TO THE INTEREST RUN PROGRAM CONFIGURATION ANALYSIS

In this step, we have made interest indicator EX, which was configured earlier, available to the line item interest calculation program. There is a separate configuration step to make interest indicators available to the account balance interest calculation program. Interest indicator EX will select all open items and only cleared items that were cleared with a payment. This means that items cleared by a credit memo or other means will not be selected for interest. This fits in well with Extreme Sports' customer service philosophy because items cleared with a credit memo normally arise due to some type of dispute with the customer, in which case Extreme Sports has decided that the customer is correct. Extreme Sports decided that calculating interest on an invoice that was disputed, and might later be issued credit, would not work well with its business model.

The Gregorian calendar is used for the basis of calculating interest. Analysis done by Extreme Sports has determined that it normally takes two days for a check to travel from the customer's office to Extreme Sports' lockbox. Because of this, Extreme Sports has granted two transfer days. Extreme Sports has also decided to grant one tolerance day per invoice and to calculate interest only on debit items (invoices and debit memos) because this is the standard U.S. business practice followed by all of Extreme Sports' subsidiaries. The payment term EX02 was configured for use with interest postings. Payment term EX02 does not grant any cash discount—all line items with EX02 are due in full in 30 days. Tax code O0 was configured for use with interest postings. Tax code O0 is maintained with a 0% rate. This will work well because interest postings are nontaxable in the U.S.

Now that the interest indicator has been made available to the interest calculation program, the next step is to determine the interest rate that will be used by the calculation. The first step in determining the interest rate is to define a reference interest rate. Reference interest rates are a key by which specific interest rates are assigned to specific periods. Examples of reference interest rates include LIBOR, Prime, Fed Funds Rate, 30-Year Bond Rate, and so on. To create a reference interest rate, follow the menu path Financial Accounting ➢ Accounts Receivable and Accounts Payable ➢ Business Transactions ➢ Interest Calculation ➢ Interest Calculation ➢ Define Reference Interest Rates.

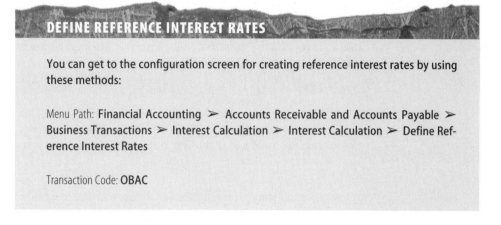

DEFINE REFERENCE INTEREST RATES

You can get to the configuration screen for creating reference interest rates by using these methods:

Menu Path: Financial Accounting ➢ Accounts Receivable and Accounts Payable ➢ Business Transactions ➢ Interest Calculation ➢ Interest Calculation ➢ Define Reference Interest Rates

Transaction Code: **OBAC**

After executing the transaction listed in the Define Reference Interest Rates shortcut box and clicking the New Entries button, you are taken to the reference interest rate new entries screen, shown in Figure 5.8.

FIGURE 5.8   The reference interest rate new entries screen

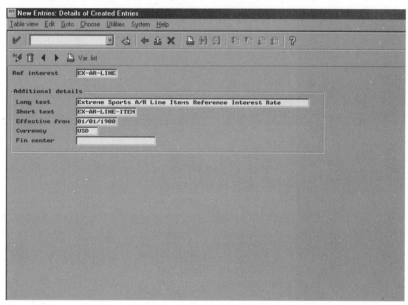

The fields on the reference interest rate new entries screen are as follows:

Ref Interest   Enter a 10-character identifier to be used for the reference interest rate key.

Long Text   Enter a long text description that can be used to give detailed information about the reference interest rate key.

Short Text   Enter a short text description that can be used to give information about the reference interest rate key.

Effective From   Enter the first date that the reference interest rate can be used. Like most things in SAP, reference interest rates are time dependent. Make sure you set this date so it is available in all periods in which you may want to use it. It is always safer to make it available much earlier than you think you will need it.

Currency   Enter the currency identifier key that this reference interest rate uses.

Fin Center   If you are utilizing the cash budget management functionality within the Treasury module, enter the financial center that this reference interest rate belongs to.

Now that a reference interest rate has been created, the next step is to assign our interest indicator to our reference interest rate. The relationship between interest indicator and reference interest rate is time dependent. Because it is time dependent, you can configure your interest indicator to use different reference interest rates in the future. The assignment of interest indicators to reference interest rates is done by following the menu path Financial Accounting ➢ Accounts Receivable and Accounts Payable ➢ Business Transactions ➢ Interest Calculation ➢ Interest Calculation ➢ Define Time Dependent Terms.

ASSIGN REFERENCE INTEREST RATES TO INTEREST INDICATORS

You can use the following methods to get to the configuration screen for assigning reference interest rates to interest indicators:

Menu Path: **Financial Accounting** ➢ **Accounts Receivable and Accounts Payable** ➢ **Business Transactions** ➢ **Interest Calculation** ➢ **Interest Calculation** ➢ **Define Time Dependent Terms**

Transaction Code: **OB81**

Following the configuration methods for assigning reference interest rate to interest indicators takes you to the screen shown in Figure 5.9.

FIGURE 5.9   The reference interest rate configuration screen

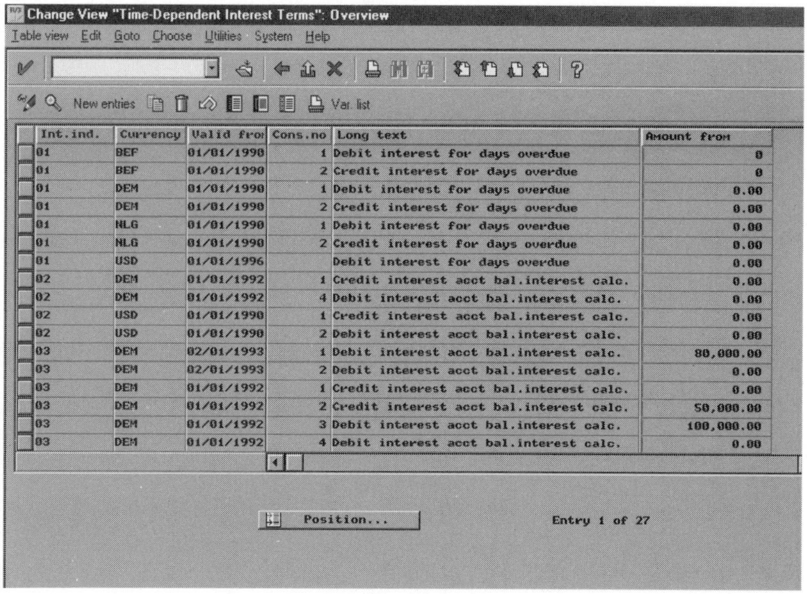

After clicking the New Entries button, you are taken to the time-dependent interest terms configuration screen, shown in Figure 5.10.

FIGURE 5.10   The time-dependent interest terms configuration screen

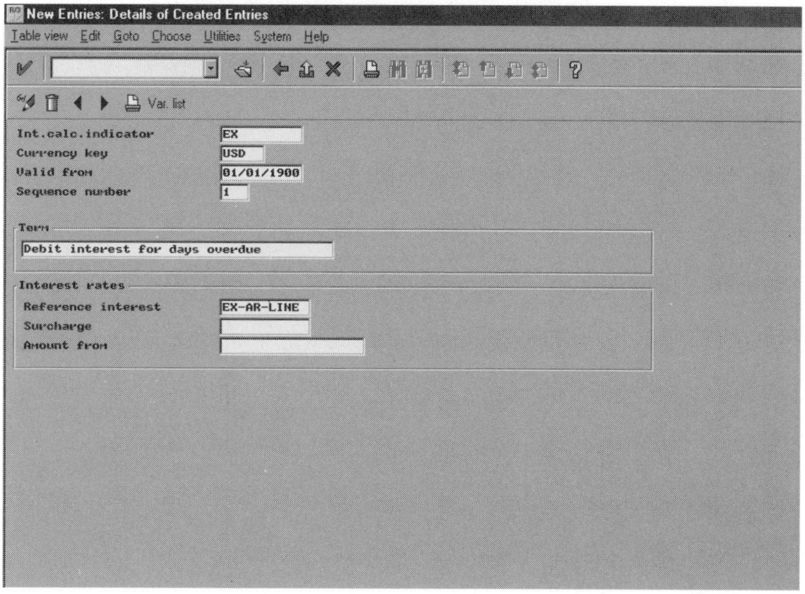

The fields on the screen shown in Figure 5.10 are listed here:

Int. Calc. Indicator   Enter the interest indicator identifier to which you wish to assign a reference interest rate.

Currency Key   Enter the currency key identifier that is to be used in the interest calculation.

Valid From   Enter the first date this relationship is valid. If in the future you want to assign the interest indicator to a different reference interest rate, you can create a new record with a Valid From date that is later than the Valid From date in the first record. In this case, the Valid From date on the first record will only be valid until the Valid From date on the second rate. Beginning at the Valid From date on the second record, the new reference interest rate is used.

Sequence Number   If you are calculating interest based upon account balances instead of line items, you can enter the sequence number that is to be used. This field, in combination with the Amount From field, allows you to use more than one interest rate based upon the amount of the account balance and the sequence in which reference interest rates are assigned. If you are using line item interest calculation, always enter 1 in this field.

Term   Use the pull-down box on this field to select the appropriate entry. This field determines what the interest indicator/reference interest rate relationship is used for (credit interest for days overdue, credit interest for account balances, debit interest for days overdue, or debit interest for account balances).

Reference Interest   Select the reference interest rate key you want to assign to the interest indicator entered in the first field.

Surcharge   You can charge an additional percentage rate on top of the reference interest rate by entering a percentage rate in this field. If the reference interest rate is not maintained or contains 0%, only the surcharge rate is used in interest calculation.

Amount From   If you are calculating interest based upon account balances, you can set the minimum amount for which this reference interest rate is valid. You can then create new records with different amounts and sequence numbers so that you can use different reference interest rates based upon the account balance.

The final configuration step needed to make the interest calculation program work is to determine how and to which accounts the interest program will post. The interest calculation program does not use the automatic account determination features that we discussed in Chapter 3. It uses its own posting interface to determine the accounts instead of using process keys. However, the posting interface functions in the same way account determination via process keys functions. To define your account determination for interest calculation, execute the menu path Financial Accounting ➢ Accounts Receivable and Accounts Payable ➢ Business Transactions ➢ Interest Calculation ➢ Interest Posting ➢ Prepare Interest on Arrears Calculation (Customers).

INTEREST CALCULATION ACCOUNT ASSIGNMENT

You can get to the configuration screen for interest calculation account assignment by using the following methods:

Menu Path: **Financial Accounting** ➢ **Accounts Receivable and Accounts Payable** ➢ **Business Transactions** ➢ **Interest Calculation** ➢ **Interest Posting** ➢ **Prepare Interest on Arrears Calculation (Customers)**

Transaction Code: **OBV1**

After executing one of these configuration methods, you are taken to the interest calculation account assignment configuration screen, shown in Figure 5.11.

FIGURE 5.11   The interest calculation account assignment screen

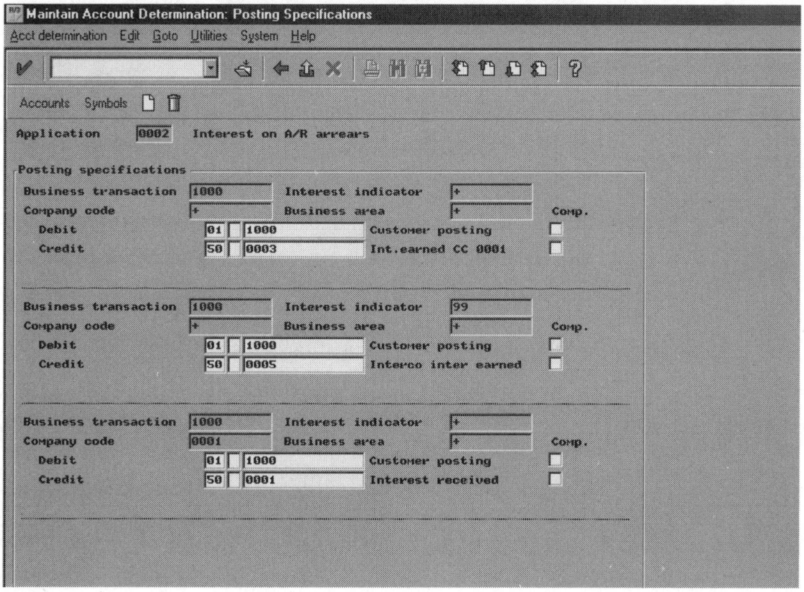

The screen in Figure 5.11 might look like hieroglyphics at first, but once you understand how it functions, it is not difficult at all. Instead of directly indicating G/L accounts, it uses symbols, which represent different G/L accounts. To create or view the symbols that can be used, click the Symbols button. You are then taken to the account symbols configuration screen, shown in Figure 5.12.

FIGURE 5.12   The account symbols configuration screen

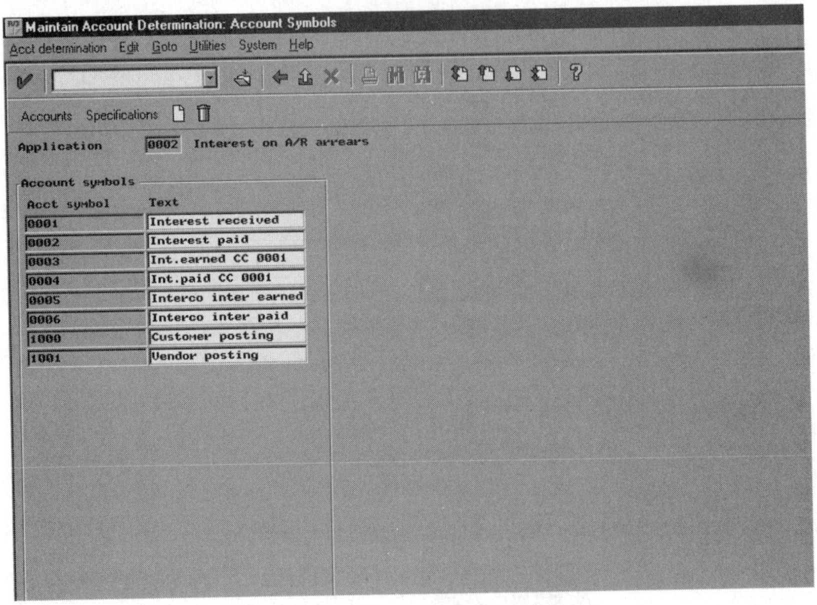

SAP is delivered with some standard symbols. The most important are 1000 for customer postings and 1001 for vendor postings. G/L accounts do not need to be assigned to symbols 1000 and 1001 because they will post automatically against the correct master record. Extreme Sports will use the delivered account symbols. The next step is to assign G/L accounts to the account symbols. To do so, click the Accounts button. A pop-up box appears asking you for the chart of accounts you want to use. Enter the appropriate chart of accounts (EXCA), and you are then presented with the account determination accounts configuration screen, shown in Figure 5.13.

The configuration for assigning G/L accounts to account symbols is very straightforward. All you need to do is select the account symbol, specify the currency, and assign the account symbol to an existing G/L account. We are now ready to complete our account determination. From the screen shown in Figure 5.13, execute the menu path Goto ➢ Posting Specs. You are taken back to the interest calculation account assignment screen shown in Figure 5.11. From this screen, click the create icon. The pop-up box shown in Figure 5.14 appears.

FIGURE 5.13 The account determination accounts configuration screen

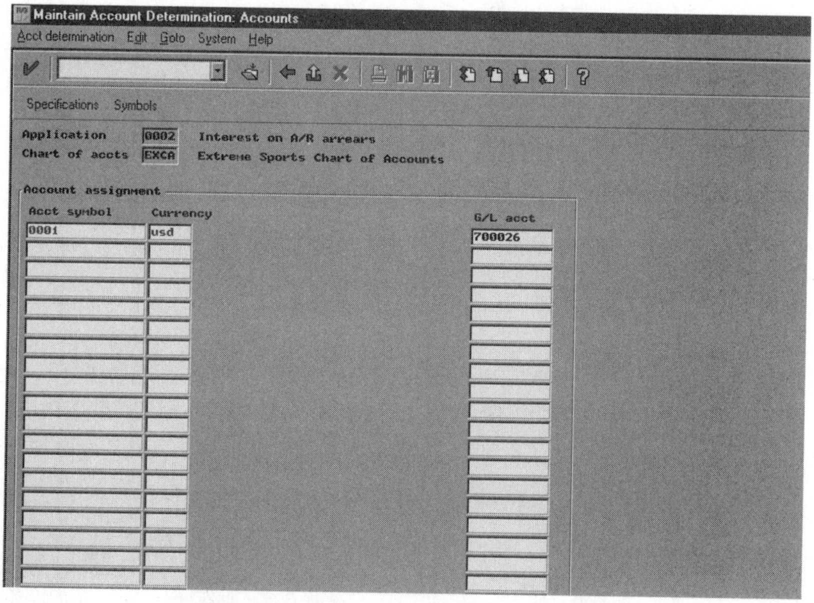

FIGURE 5.14 The Create New Posting Procedure pop-up box

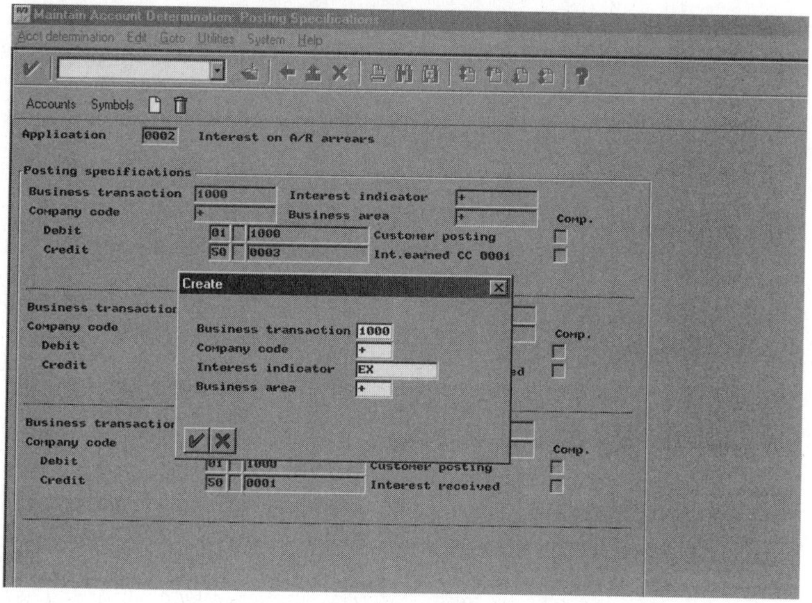

The first field that needs to be filled in is the Business Transaction field. You have two options to choose from: business transaction 1000 or business transaction 2000.

Business transaction 1000 is for interest *received* by your company and business transaction 2000 is for interest *paid* by your company. The next field to be configured is the Company Code field. You can either enter a specific company code or the wildcard character + to symbolize all company codes. After making your settings in the Company Code field, you need to select the interest indicator that this account assignment is for. Once again, you can enter a specific interest indicator or use the + wildcard character. The last field to be configured is the Business Area field. As before, you can enter a specific business area or the + wildcard character. After filling in all the fields in the pop-up box, press the Enter key. You are taken to the account determination posting specifications detail screen, shown in Figure 5.15.

FIGURE 5.15   The account determination posting specifications detail screen

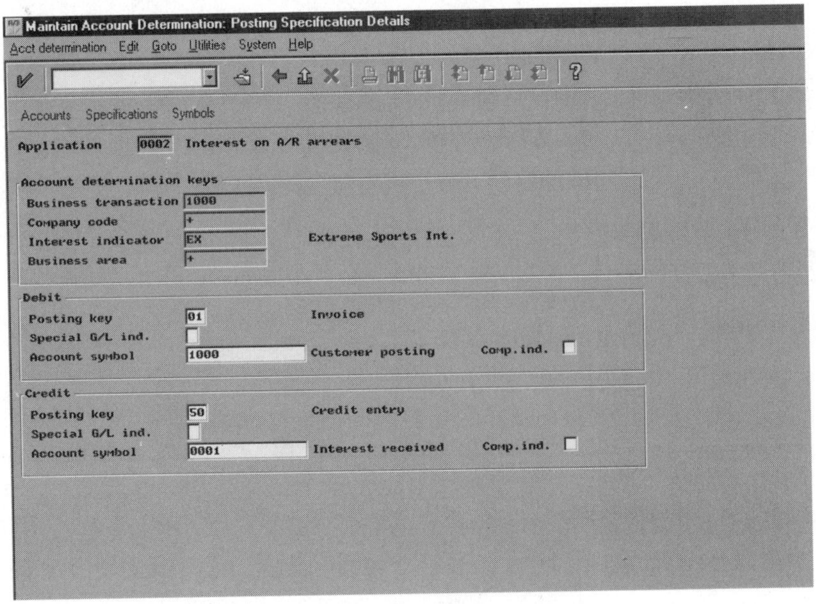

Next, you need to specify the posting key and account symbols to be used for the debit and credit for the interest calculation posting. You have the option of using a special G/L indicator if needed. Selecting the Comp. Ind. indicator compresses the line items before posting (for example, it combines several line items into one per account).

The last step required to run interest calculation for A/R line items is to maintain the interest rates for the reference interest rate to which you have assigned your interest indicator. Maintaining the interest rates is very simple. You only need to enter the correct rate and the valid from date for your reference interest rate. Maintaining the

EXTREME SPORTS INTEREST CALCULATION AUTOMATIC ACCOUNT ASSIGNMENT CONFIGURATION ANALYSIS

The standard account symbols 0001 and 1000 were used for Extreme Sports' automatic account assignment procedure for the interest posting. Account symbol 1000 always represents the customer master record and is not assigned to a specific G/L account for this reason. Extreme Sports configured account symbol 0001 to map to G/L account 700026 (interest received). The standard customer debit posting key 01 was used to debit (increase) the customer account balance. The credit posting key 50 was used to credit (increase) the interest received G/L account 700026. This automatic account assignment is available for use by all company codes and business areas, but it is only valid for the interest indicator EX. The business transaction 1000 represents the interest received transaction.

reference interest is not truly a configuration activity. You would not want to transport the interest rates from your development to your production client because this would be too tedious and time consuming. Because of this, SAP has made maintaining the reference interest rate a current setting, much like opening and closing posting periods, entering exchange rates, and so on. To maintain your reference interest rate, follow the SAP application menu path Accounting ➢ Financial Accounting ➢ General Ledger ➢ Environment ➢ Current Settings ➢ Enter Reference Interest Values.

Reason Codes

Reason codes are used to segregate different reasons for underpayment and overpayment on A/R line items. With a reason code, you can define whether the difference should be charged off to a G/L account or if a residual posting should be made. Residual postings clear the line item being paid and create a new open line item for the difference between the total amount of the line item and the payment amount.

An example of a residual posting would be as follows: A customer pays $700 against invoice #123, which has a total due amount of $1,000. Invoice #123 with a total due amount of $1,000 is cleared against the customer account, and new residual posting for $300 ($1,000 invoice amount – $700 payment amount) is created. Residual postings made via reason codes are treated as disputed amounts and therefore do not figure against the customer's available credit. (Credit management will be discussed later in this chapter.) Reason codes are valid for only one company code. They can also be configured to generate correspondence to the customer, informing them of the residual item and how it is being treated by your company or should be treated by their company. To create reason codes, follow the menu path Financial Accounting ➤ Accounts Receivable and Accounts Payable ➤ Business Transactions ➤ Incoming Payments ➤ Payment Receipt Global Settings ➤ Overpayment/Underpayment ➤ Define Reason Codes.

DEFINE REASON CODES

You can get to the configuration screen for creating reason codes by using the following methods:

Menu Path: **Financial Accounting** ➤ **Accounts Receivable and Accounts Payable** ➤ **Business Transactions** ➤ **Incoming Payments** ➤ **Payment Receipt Global Settings** ➤ **Overpayment/Underpayment** ➤ **Define Reason Codes**

Transaction Code: **OBBE**

After executing this configuration transaction, you are presented with a pop-up box asking you for the company code for which you want to configure reason codes. Remember that reason codes are valid for only one company code. After entering the appropriate company code (1000 in our example), you are taken to the reason code configuration screen shown in Figure 5.16.

As you can see, three reason codes have already been configured for Extreme Sports' company code 1000. Explanation of the fields shown in Figure 5.16 are listed here:

RCd   Enter the three-character identifier of your reason code. This field is alphanumeric.

Short Text   Enter a short text description for what this reason code represents. This field can be 20 characters long.

Long Text   Enter a long text description for what this reason code represents. This field can be 40 characters long.

CorrT   Select one of the correspondence identifiers from the pull-down window if you wish to generate a letter to your customer for line items with this reason code. SAP comes with several correspondence types that can be used or copied and changed. The creation of new correspondence types is usually the responsibility of an ABAPer who is knowledgeable in SAPScript. The creation of correspondence types is beyond the scope of this book.

C   Activate this indicator if you want line items assigned to this reason code to charge off the difference between the payment amount and the invoice amount to a G/L account. This indicator will take any payment difference (over or under) to a miscellaneous income and expense account and totally clear the customer line item. The assignment of the G/L account will be explained later in this chapter.

D   Activate this indicator if you want line items assigned to this reason code to create a residual posting on the customer account. As explained earlier, a residual posting clears the original line item in total and creates on the customer account a new line item for the difference between the invoice amount and the payment amount.

FIGURE 5.16   The reason code configuration screen

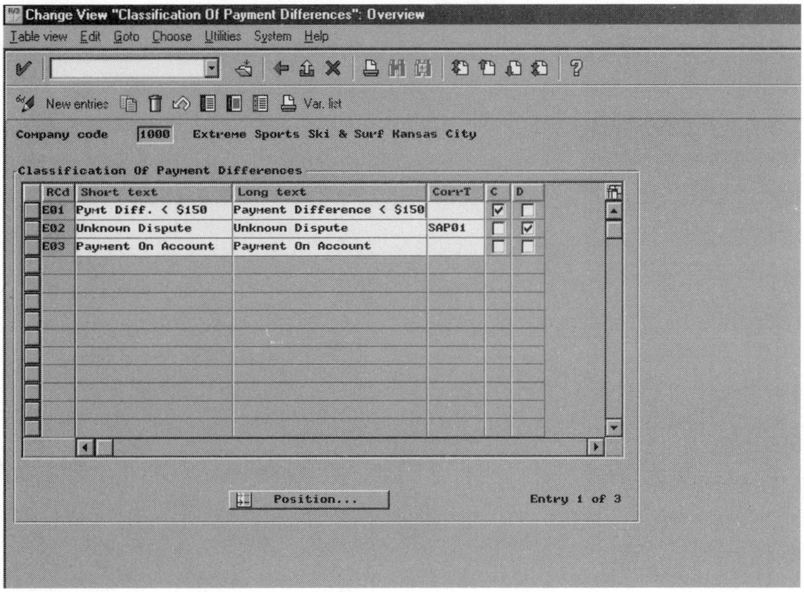

EXTREME SPORTS REASON CODE CONFIGURATION ANALYSIS

Extreme Sports has created three reason codes (E01, E02, and E03) to use with company code 1000. Reason code E01 is used for payment differences (overpayments and underpayments) of less than $150. These differences are written off to a G/L account. Reason code E02 is used for unknown payment differences. Reason code E02 is configured to create a residual posting and send out a letter (correspondence) to the customer inquiring about the difference. Reason code E03 is used for payments on account. This reason code is not configured to write off to a G/L account or create a residual line item because the invoice that it is supposed to clear is unknown.

Reason Code Conversion Versions

Some industries, such as the apparel industry, have a large amount of customer deductions on invoices that are paid. Deductions are in essence an underpayment of an invoice. There are numerous business reasons for deductions. In the industries where deductions (short-pays) are common practice, it is normally customary to clear the underlying invoice and create a residual item to follow up. The residual item is then either written off to a G/L account based on the type of deduction, or the customer is informed via correspondence that they are still liable for the underpayment (an invalid deduction). In the deduction situation, it would be very cumbersome to have a large number of on-account postings when using lockbox (autocash) functionality. SAP's lockbox functionality will be covered in Chapter 6.

The short version of lockbox functionality is that payment differences on an invoice result in an on-account posting for the entire check without clearing a line item, or if the payment amount doesn't match the invoice amount, the payment is distributed across the oldest invoices. It is a good idea to configure a reason code that will be used for creating deductions (residual postings) that can be used by the lockbox. This is accomplished through reason code conversion versions. Reason code conversion versions allow customer reason codes to be mapped to your SAP reason codes to create the desired effect (residual postings or G/L account write-offs) and to mark the line item with your proper reason code. It is also a good idea to write a lockbox preprocessing program to include a generic reason code on every line item that doesn't already have a reason code. This will allow for smooth processing of your lockbox cash application.

The first step is to create a reason code conversion version to be used by your customers. The reason code conversion version is assigned to the customer master record in your system. You can have more than one reason code conversion version per company code. The fields to be updated in the customer master record will be covered later in this chapter. To create a reason code conversion version, follow the menu path Financial Accounting ➢ Accounts Receivable and Accounts Payable ➢ Business Transactions ➢ Incoming Payments ➢ Payment Receipt Global Settings ➢ Overpayment/Underpayment ➢ Define Reason Code Conversion Version.

DEFINE REASON CODE CONVERSION VERSIONS

You can get to the configuration screen for creating reason code conversion versions by using the following methods:

Menu Path: **Financial Accounting** ➢ **Accounts Receivable and Accounts Payable** ➢ **Business Transactions** ➢ **Incoming Payments** ➢ **Payment Receipt Global Settings** ➢ **Overpayment/Underpayment** ➢ **Define Reason Code Conversion Version**

Transaction Code: **OBCR**

The reason code conversion version configuration screen shown in Figure 5.17 is displayed after following one of the previously mentioned configuration methods.

FIGURE 5.17 The reason code conversion version configuration screen

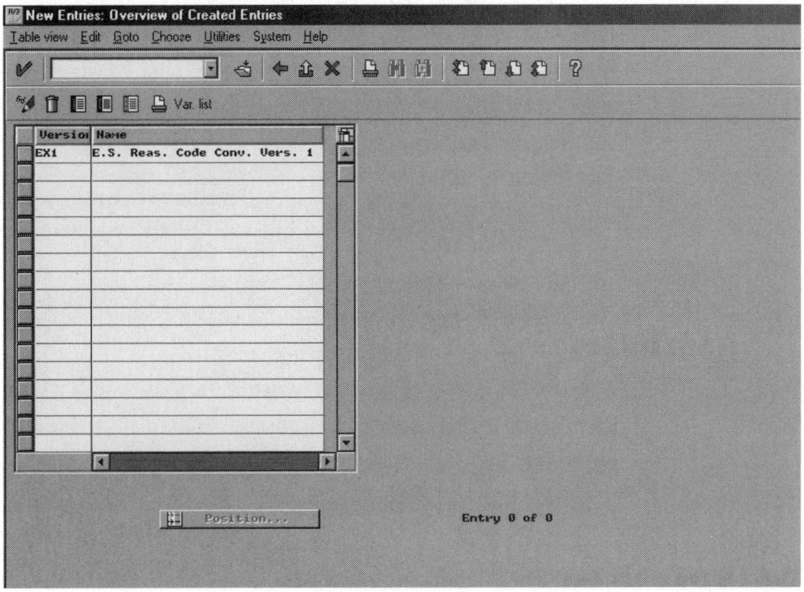

The configuration of reason code conversion versions is very simple. You only need to create a three-character identifier and a textual description of your version.

The final configuration step that is needed to make reason code conversion versions work is to map customer (external) reason codes to your SAP (internal) reason codes. To do so, follow the menu path Financial Accounting ➤ Accounts Receivable and Accounts Payable ➤ Business Transactions ➤ Incoming Payments ➤ Payment Receipt Global Settings ➤ Overpayment/Underpayment ➤ Define Conversion of Payment Difference Reason Codes.

MAP EXTERNAL REASON CODES TO INTERNAL REASON CODES

You can get to the configuration screen for mapping customer (external) reason codes to SAP (internal) reason codes by using the following methods:

Menu Path: **Financial Accounting** ➤ **Accounts Receivable and Accounts Payable** ➤ **Business Transactions** ➤ **Incoming Payments** ➤ **Payment Receipt Global Settings** ➤ **Overpayment/Underpayment** ➤ **Define Conversion of Payment Difference Reason Codes**

Transaction Code: **OBCS**

After executing one of these configuration methods, you are presented with the reason code conversion screen shown in Figure 5.18. Before the screen is actually displayed, you are prompted to enter the company code you are mapping.

N O T E   The mapping of reason codes is done on a company code level.

FIGURE 5.18   The reason code conversion screen

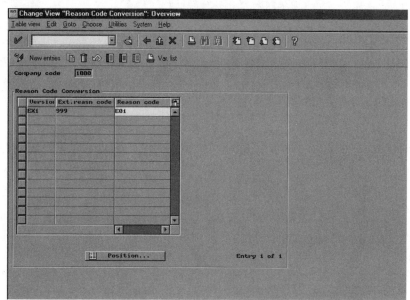

EXTREME SPORTS REASON CODE CONVERSION VERSION CONFIGURATION ANALYSIS

Reason code conversion version EX1 was created for Extreme Sports. The reason code conversion version will be set up in Extreme Sports' customer master records to allow easier lockbox cash application processing. External reason code 999 was mapped to SAP reason code E01 for company code 1000. In Extreme Sports' lockbox preprocessing program, reason code 999 will be inserted on any line item that doesn't have a reason code. This will allow the lockbox program to create residual postings for payment differences of over $150. Remember that another reason code charges off any payment difference less than $150. As the implementation progresses, Extreme Sports will communicate with its major customers to get a listing of their reason codes so they can be mapped to Extreme Sports' reason codes.

Default Account Assignments

In this section, we will cover some of the most important automatic account determinations that relate to A/R. You will recall that automatic account determinations for G/L functionality was covered in Chapter 3.

Overpayments/Underpayments

You will recall from the previous section on reason codes that you can configure a reason code to create a residual posting or to post to a G/L account. You are now ready to determine what G/L accounts are posted to for each individual reason code. The payment differences that arise from the use of reason codes are referred to as overpayments/underpayments in the system (as well as in real life). To assign G/L accounts to post reason codes to, follow the menu path Financial Accounting ➤ Accounts Receivable and Accounts Payable ➤ Business Transactions ➤ Incoming Payments ➤ Payment Receipt Global Settings ➤ Define Accounts for Overpayments/Underpayments.

ASSIGN G/L ACCOUNTS TO REASON CODES

You can get to the configuration screen for assigning G/L accounts to reason codes for the purposes of overpayment/underpayment postings by using the following methods:

Menu Path: **Financial Accounting** ➤ **Accounts Receivable and Accounts Payable** ➤ **Business Transactions** ➤ **Incoming Payments** ➤ **Payment Receipt Global Settings** ➤ **Define Accounts for Overpayments/Underpayments**

Transaction Code: **OBXL**

After executing one of these configuration methods, you are prompted to enter the chart of accounts that you want to use for the automatic account determination. After entering the appropriate chart of accounts (EXCA), you are presented with the payment differences by reason automatic posting rules screen, shown in Figure 5.19.

FIGURE 5.19   The payment differences by reason automatic posting rules screen

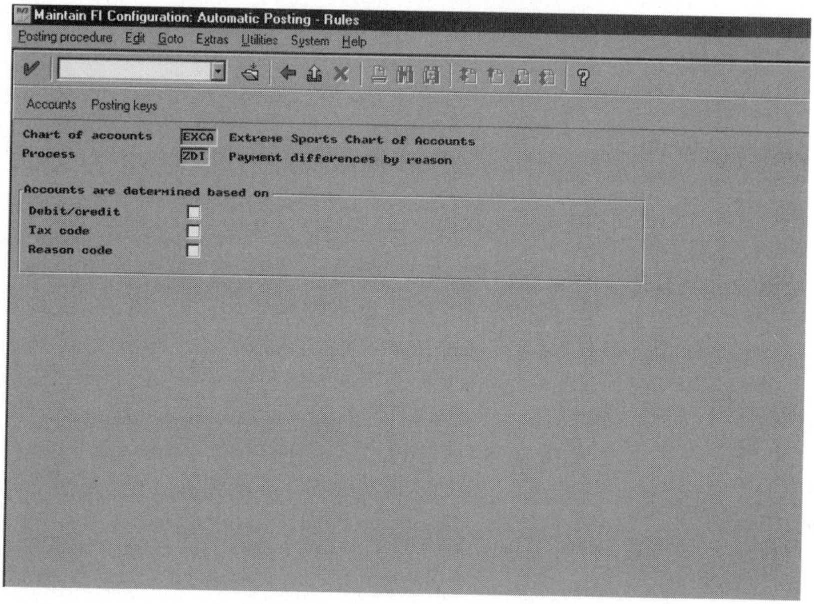

Overpayment/underpayment automatic account assignment uses processing key ZDI. You have the option of assigning G/L accounts based on debit/credit postings, tax code, reason code, or a combination thereof. In addition, account determination is always determined via the chart of accounts first. Using the chart of accounts to distinguish account determination is nonconfigurable. After selecting the indicators you wish to use (Debit/Credit and Reason Code in our example), you must maintain the posting keys that are to be used. To set the posting keys, click the Posting Keys button. (The process of setting the posting keys was shown in detail in Chapter 3; please refer to that chapter for a detailed explanation.) Once you have set your posting keys, you are ready to assign your G/L accounts. You can assign the G/L accounts by clicking the Accounts button shown in Figure 5.19. Alternatively, once the rules for the processing key and the posting key have been maintained, when you enter one of the configuration methods for this step, the G/L assignment screen for overpayments/underpayments, shown in Figure 5.20, is defaulted.

FIGURE 5.20   The G/L assignment screen for overpayments/underpayments

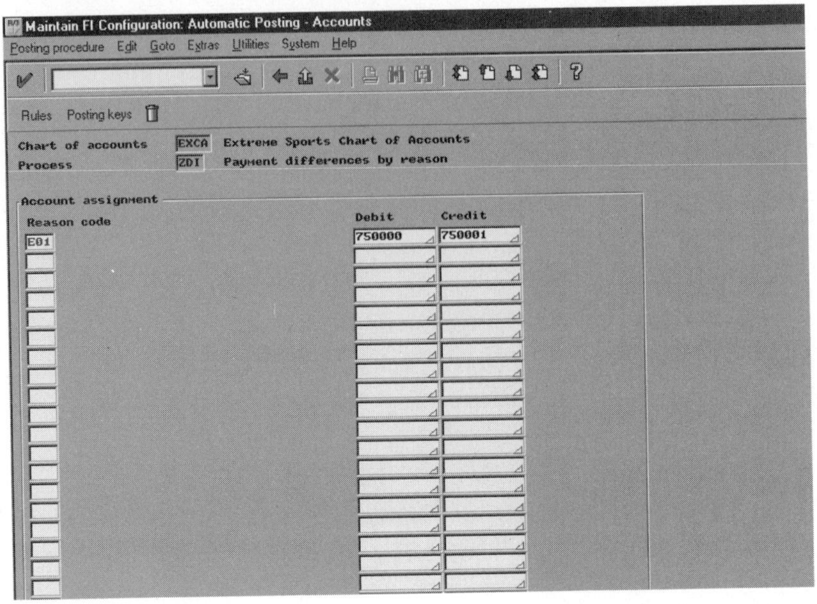

You'll notice that we have maintained the missing configuration for reason codes by assigning reason code E01 to G/L account 750000 for debits and G/L account 750001 for credits. This configuration will allow Extreme Sports to track all underpayments in G/L account 750000. An underpayment will result in a debit on this account and will allow Extreme Sports to track all overpayments in G/L account 750001 because an overpayment will result in a credit on this account.

Cash Discounts

If your company grants cash discount terms to its customers, it is necessary to define the cash discount account that will be used by automatic account assignment. The cash discount account is debited when payments of the gross amount less the cash discount amount are received within the specified time period for which the cash discount is allowed. This happens to the customer account clearing transaction (applying the cash against the appropriate customer invoice). To configure the cash discount account, follow the menu path Financial Accounting ➢ Accounts Receivable and Accounts Payable ➢ Business Transactions ➢ Incoming Payments ➢ Payment Receipt Global Settings ➢ Define Accounts for Cash Discount Granted.

DEFINE CASH DISCOUNT ACCOUNTS

You can configure the cash discount amount by using the following methods:

Menu Path: **Financial Accounting** ➤ **Accounts Receivable and Accounts Payable** ➤ **Business Transactions** ➤ **Incoming Payments** ➤ **Payment Receipt Global Settings** ➤ **Define Accounts for Cash Discount Granted**

Transaction Code: **OBXI**

Figure 5.21 shows the account determination configuration screen for cash discount granted. The rules for the processing key SKT and the posting key are not shown in this example. The only option you have for rules is to assign G/L accounts based on tax codes. As you can see, all cash discounts taken by Extreme Sports' customers will be posted to account 440000.

FIGURE 5.21   The account determination configuration screen for cash discount granted

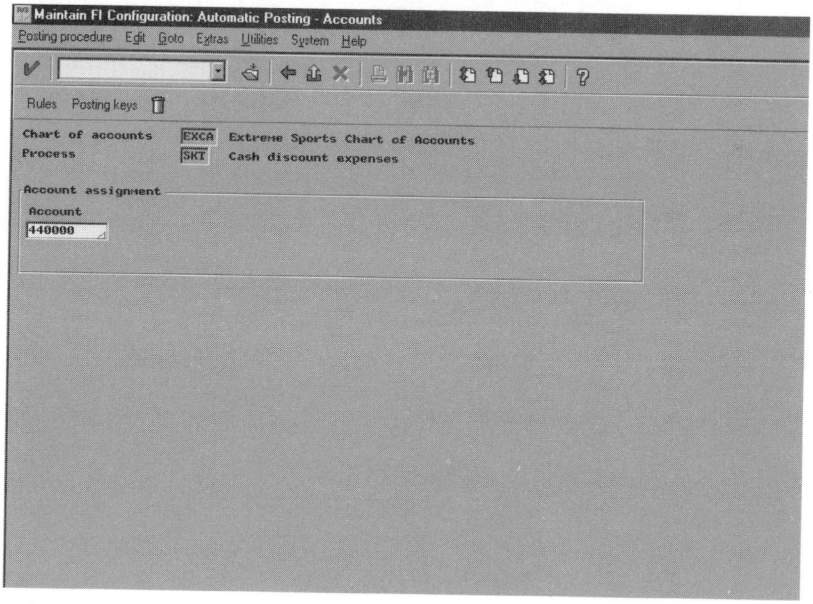

Overall A/R and Employee Tolerances

You will recall from Chapter 3 that the employee tolerance group Null was configured for Extreme Sports. In the configuration of tolerance groups, you can set the maximum amount that employees can clear against a customer account, the maximum cash discount percentage amount that can be applied to a customer invoice, and the maximum payment difference in percentage terms up to an overall dollar amount. Please review "Posting Amount Defaults and Tolerance Groups" in Chapter 3 for more information on employee tolerance groups.

In addition to employee tolerance groups, there are also what are known as *customer tolerance groups*. Customer tolerance groups are assigned to customer master records, which will be covered later in this chapter. Customer tolerance groups allow you to specify the maximum payment difference that can be charged off to a G/L account, the maximum cash discount percentage amount, and the maximum allowable payment difference in percentage terms up to a total dollar amount. As with employee tolerance groups, you can specify a null customer tolerance that will be valid for all customers that do not explicitly have a different tolerance group assigned to them via their customer master record. To configure customer tolerance groups, follow the menu path Financial Accounting ➤ Accounts Receivable and Accounts Payable ➤ Business Transactions ➤ Manual Payment Receipt ➤ Define Tolerances (Customers).

DEFINE CUSTOMER TOLERANCE GROUPS

You can use the following methods to get to the configuration screen for creating customer tolerance groups:

Menu Path: Financial Accounting ➤ Accounts Receivable and Accounts Payable ➤ Business Transactions ➤ Manual Payment Receipt ➤ Define Tolerances (Customers)

Transaction Code: OBA3

After following one of these configuration methods and then clicking the New Entries button on the screen that appears, you are taken to the create new customer tolerance group configuration screen, shown in Figure 5.22.

FIGURE 5.22   The create new customer tolerance group configuration screen

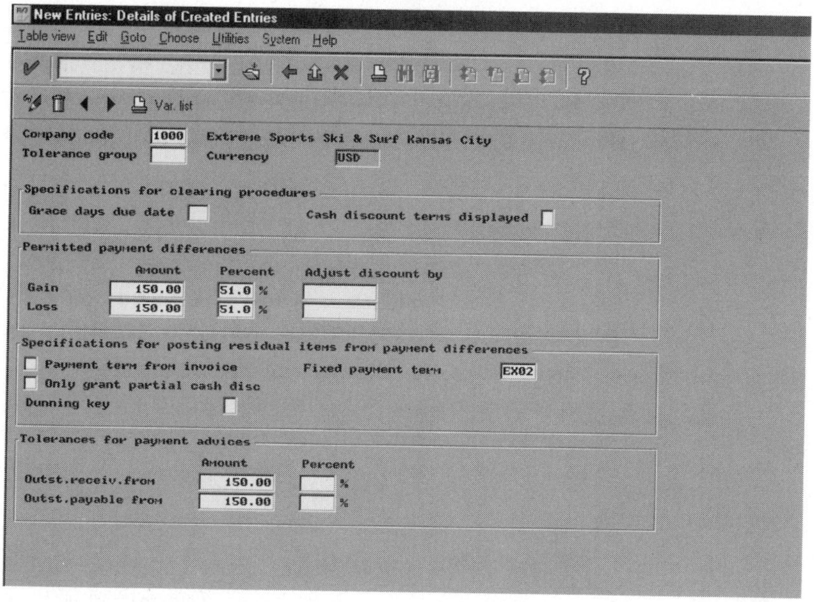

The fields in the create new customer tolerance group configuration screen are explained here:

Company Code   Enter the four-character identifier of the company code you want this customer tolerance group assigned to. A tolerance group can be assigned to only one company code.

Tolerance Group   Enter the four-character identifier to distinguish this customer tolerance group. The naming convention of the tolerance group is up to you. If you leave this field blank (or null), this tolerance group is valid for all customer master records that are in this company code and aren't explicitly assigned a named tolerance group.

Currency   The currency key identifier defaults into this field based on of the company code (company code currency).

Grace Days Due Date   If you wish to grant grace days to your customers (beyond the grace days granted in the payment term), enter the number of grace days here.

Cash Discount Terms Displayed   You can change the cash discount terms that are displayed when the line item is cleared by entering the appropriate indicator here. Leaving the field blank makes the cash discount term default to the cash discount term on the line item.

Permitted Payment Differences:

Amount   Enter the maximum payment difference that can be written off to a G/L account. You will recall from earlier in the chapter that we configured a reason code and assigned the reason code to the proper G/L accounts for payment differences of less than $150. You can specify different amounts for overpayments (Gain) and underpayments (Loss).

Percent   For small dollar invoices, you can limit the maximum amount that can be written off by entering a percentage in this field. The system will take the total invoice amount times this percentage to come up the maximum allowable amount up to $150. For example, if 51% is entered in this field and an invoice of $200 is being paid, the maximum allowable amount to write off would be $102 ($200 * 51%). You can specify different percentages for overpayments (Gain) and underpayments (Loss).

Adjust Discount By   In this field, you can enter an amount that is equal to or less than the number that was entered in the Amount field. The amount entered in this field will be treated as a cash discount as long as the cash discount rules you set up in the employee tolerance group allow the amount entered to be handled as a cash discount.

Specifications for Posting Residual Items from Payment Differences:

Payment Term from Invoice   Activate this indicator if you want the residual posting that is creating during clearing to assume the payment term on the invoice from which the residual item was created.

Only Grant Partial Cash Disc   Activate this indicator if you do not want to grant the full cash discount amount when a residual item is paid.

Fixed Payment Term   You can signify a specific payment term that should be used on all residual postings by entering the payment term identifier in this field.

Dunning Key   If you are using dunning (sending out past due letters), you can enter the dunning key to be used by all residual postings.

Tolerances for Payment Advices:

Amount   A residual item is automatically created for any payment difference amount greater than the amount entered here. Normally, the amount entered in the field should equal the amount entered in the Amount field in the Permitted Payment Differences section. Different amounts can be specified for overpayments (outstanding receivables) and underpayments (outstanding payables).

Percent   You can enter a percentage rate that is used in conjunction with the Amount field when the system is deciding to generate residual items. This means that a residual item can be created for less than the amount entered in the Amount field depending on the invoice amount. For example, if 52% is entered in this field and an invoice in the amount of $200 is being a paid, a residual item posting would be created for any payment difference of $104 ($200 * 52%) or greater.

EXTREME SPORTS OVERALL A/R AND EMPLOYEE TOLERANCES

Accounts Receivable tolerances comprise two parts: employee tolerances and customer tolerances. Employee tolerances were covered in detail in Chapter 3. The customer tolerance group Null (blank) was configured for Extreme Sports company code 1000 in this section. The Null customer tolerance group for Extreme Sports was configured so that any payment difference equal to or less than $150—only payment differences that exceed 51% of the invoice amount—are eligible to write off the entire $150. The fixed payment term EX02 was configured for use on all residual postings. Payment term EX02 does not grant a cash discount and is due within 30 days. Any payment differences greater than $150 will automatically create a residual line item posting to the customer account.

Credit Management

SAP's *credit management functionality* allows you to grant credit terms according to your business practices. Based on the credit limit and open A/R value for your customer, SAP can automatically block deliveries from being sent to customers who exceed the credit limit you have set for them. There is a question as to who really owns credit management on a project—FI or SD. According to SAP, both do. There are vital pieces of credit management configuration in both modules. We will cover the configuration of credit management in the FI module.

As with some of the other areas in SAP that we have looked at, there are several separate pieces of interrelated configuration that must be completed. There is not a set order in which these components must be configured—we will show them in the order that we feel makes the most sense to the flow of the book. With this in mind, the first piece of credit management that will be configured is the credit control area.

A company code can only be assigned to one credit control area. A credit control area can, however, be assigned to more than one company code. To create a credit control area, follow the menu path Enterprise Structure ➤ Maintain Structure ➤ Definition ➤ Financial Accounting ➤ Maintain Credit Control Area.

DEFINE CREDIT CONTROL AREAS

You can get to the configuration screen for creating credit control areas by using the following methods:

Menu Path: **Enterprise Structure ➤ Maintain Structure ➤ Definition ➤ Financial Accounting ➤ Maintain Credit Control Area**

Transaction Code: **OB45**

After following one of the configuration methods and clicking the New Entries button on the overview screen that is displayed, you are presented with the create new credit control area configuration screen, shown in Figure 5.23.

FIGURE 5.23   The create new credit control area configuration screen

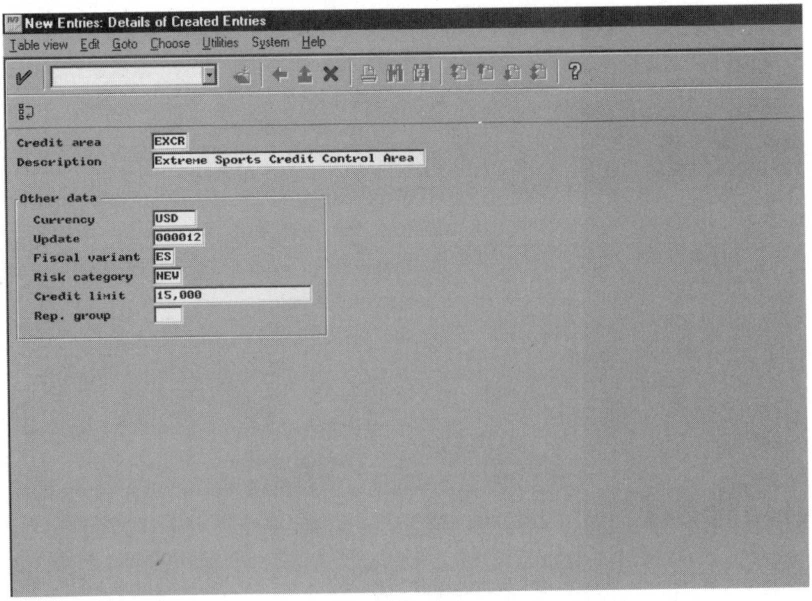

Here is a detailed list of the fields that appear in the create new credit control area configuration screen:

Credit Area   Enter a four-character identifier for your credit control area.

Description   Enter a long text description for your credit control area.

Currency   Enter the currency identifier for the monetary unit that will be used by this credit control area.

Update   The equation for available credit is credit limit less the sum of open orders, open deliveries, open billings, and the A/R account balance. Open billings are used because it is possible for a billing (invoice) to be created and not be passed to accounting due to a posting error. Once a billing is passed on to accounting, the open billing balance decreases and the A/R balance increases. This field controls how SAP updates the values for open orders, open deliveries, and open billings from SD documents. The following choices are available in this field:

Null (Blank)   Leaving this field blank (null) causes SAP to ignore SD documents when determining available credit. If this option is selected, available credit equals the credit limit less the A/R account balance of the customer.

000012   This option is the most robust. If the system cannot use the algorithm due to the way master data is set up (a material on the order is not relevant for delivery), the system will determine the best remaining algorithm to increase the value elements for available credit. This algorithm causes the open orders value to increase with SD sales orders (for delivery-relevant items only); once the sales order has a valid delivery against it, the open sales order value is decreased and the open delivery value is increased. Once the delivery has been billed (invoiced), the open delivery value decreases and the open billing value increases. Once the billing is posted successfully to accounting (this is instantaneous unless there is a problem with the invoice), the open billing value is decreased and the A/R balance is increased.

000015   If this algorithm is used, sales orders are ignored. When a delivery is created, the open delivery value and the open billing value increase. Once the billing document is posted in accounting, the open billing value and open delivery value are decreased while the A/R balance increases.

000018   If this algorithm is used—when a sales order is created—the open delivery value increases. When the billing occurs, the open delivery value decreases and the open billing value increases. Once the billing document is posted in accounting, the open billing value decreases and the A/R balance increases.

Fiscal Variant   Enter the identifier of the fiscal year variant that will be used by this credit control area. Remember that a credit control area can be assigned to more than one company code. Therefore, all company codes assigned to the credit control area must have the same fiscal year variant (the one that matches this entry).

Risk Category   If you want all new customer master records to default in a risk category, enter the appropriate risk category here. Risk categories will be explained later in this section.

Credit Limit   If you want all new customer master records to default in a credit limit, enter the appropriate credit limit here.

Rep. Group   If you want all new customer master records to default in a credit representative group, enter the appropriate credit representative group here. Credit representative groups will be explained later in this section.

N O T E   Until credit master data has been entered for a customer, the customer has no credit limit. Credit master data is not created until one of the main credit elements is maintained for the customer: risk category, credit limit, and/or credit representative group. If you want to ensure that all new customers have a credit limit, it is a good idea to make one of the main credit elements default in from the credit control area configuration.

Now that you have created your credit control area, the next step is to assign the newly created credit control area to the company codes that you would like use with it. Remember, a credit control area can be assigned to several company codes, but a company code can only be assigned to one credit control area. You assign credit control areas to company codes in the global parameters configuration of company codes (transaction code OBY6). You can revisit Chapter 2 for an in-depth explanation of company code global parameters and see where this field is assigned.

After assigning your credit control area to the proper company codes, you are ready to define credit risk categories for your credit control area. You will recall from the explanation of credit control area configuration that we have already assigned a credit risk category of New to the credit control area. As mentioned at the beginning of this section, there is no set order for the configuration steps with the exception of creating the credit control area. Do not be confused; we have not already assigned a credit risk category to the credit control area. Credit risk categories provide a way to

EXTREME SPORTS CREDIT CONTROL AREA CONFIGURATION ANALYSIS

Credit control area EXCR was created for Extreme Sports. Credit control area EXCR is configured to use U.S. dollars as its currency and Extreme Sports fiscal year variant ES. Algorithm 000012 was selected for the credit update controls. This algorithm provides the most updates to open values that are in the system and is used to determine available credit. If the system cannot use algorithm 000012 for any reason, it will select the next most encompassing algorithm to update open values. All new customer records will default in with risk category New and a credit limit of $15,000. In addition to ensuring that all customers have a credit limit in the system, defaulting in this information causes credit master data to automatically be created for the customer. If a customer does not have a credit limit, it is impossible for SAP to perform credit checking.

group together customers with a similar credit rating (credit risk). You can run credit reports off of credit risk categories to analyze how well your credit management policies are working with each risk category. You assign the credit risk category to the credit management screens of the customer master record. To create credit risk categories, follow the menu path Financial Accounting ➢ Accounts Receivable and Accounts Payable ➢ Credit Management ➢ Credit Control Account ➢ Define Risk Categories.

DEFINE CREDIT RISK CATEGORIES

You can use the following methods to create new credit risk categories:

Menu Path: **Financial Accounting ➢ Accounts Receivable and Accounts Payable ➢ Credit Management ➢ Credit Control Account ➢ Define Risk Categories**

Transaction Code: **OB01**

After following one of these configuration methods and clicking the New Entries button on the screen that appears, you are presented with the define new credit risk categories configuration screen, shown in Figure 5.24.

FIGURE 5.24   The define new credit risk categories configuration screen

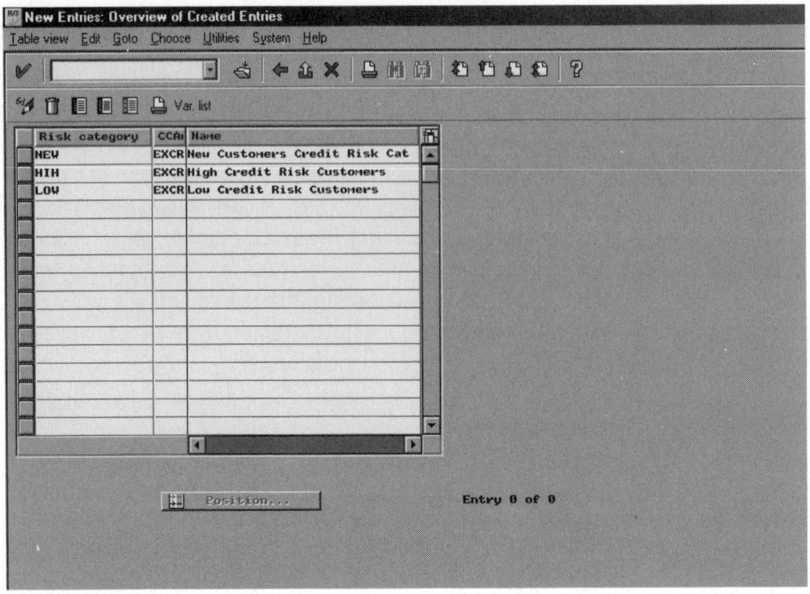

The configuration of credit risk categories is very simple. You only need to create a three-character risk category, select the credit control area you want to assign it to, and then give the credit risk category a description.

You are now ready to create credit representative groups. You assign credit representative groups in the credit management screens of the customer master record. The credit representative groups relate to the credit representative or credit manager that is assigned to the customer account. To create credit representative groups, follow the menu path Financial Accounting ➢ Accounts Receivable and Accounts Payable ➢ Credit Management ➢ Credit Control Account ➢ Define Accounting Clerk Groups.

The create new credit representative groups configuration screen, shown in Figure 5.25, appears after you follow one of the configuration transactions and click the New Entries button.

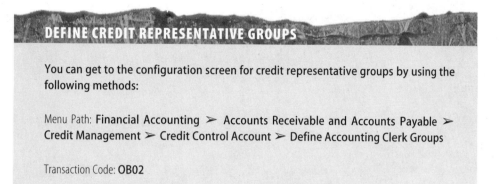

DEFINE CREDIT REPRESENTATIVE GROUPS

You can get to the configuration screen for credit representative groups by using the following methods:

Menu Path: **Financial Accounting** ➤ Accounts Receivable and Accounts Payable ➤ Credit Management ➤ Credit Control Account ➤ Define Accounting Clerk Groups

Transaction Code: **OB02**

FIGURE 5.25   The create new credit representative groups configuration screen

As you can see, the configuration for credit representative groups is straightforward. You only need to create a three-character credit representative group identifier, assign the identifier to your credit control area, and give the credit representative group a long text name.

Once you have created your credit representative groups, you can assign employees to them. To do so, follow the menu path Financial Accounting ➤ Accounts Receivable and Accounts Payable ➤ Credit Management ➤ Credit Control Account ➤ Define Credit Representatives.

ASSIGN EMPLOYEES TO CREDIT REPRESENTATIVE GROUPS

You can assign employees to credit representative groups by using the following methods:

Menu Path: **Financial Accounting** ➢ **Accounts Receivable and Accounts Payable** ➢ **Credit Management** ➢ **Credit Control Account** ➢ **Define Credit representatives**

Transaction Code: **OB51**

The assign employees to credit representative group configuration screen, shown in Figure 5.26, appears when you follow one of these configuration transactions and then click the New Entries button.

FIGURE 5.26   The assign employees to credit representative group configuration screen

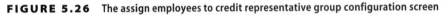

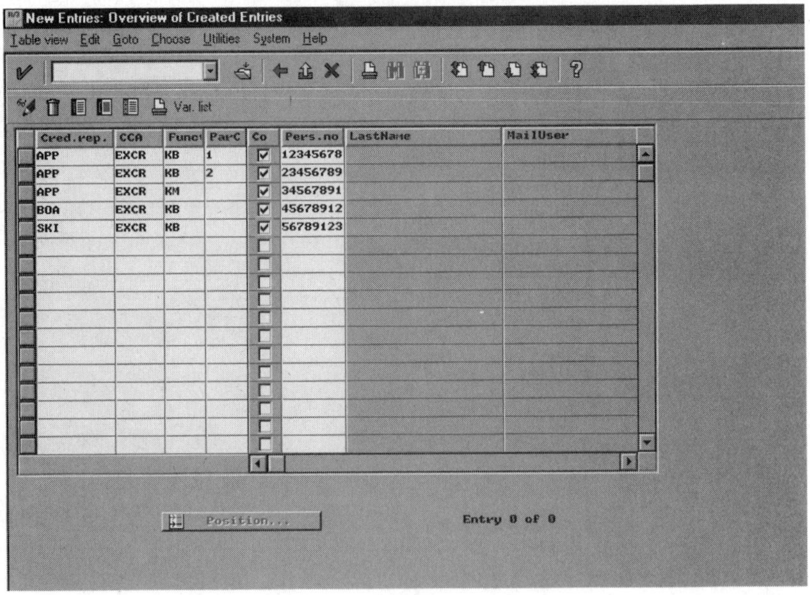

Here's an explanation of the fields that are displayed in Figure 5.26:

Cred. Rep.   Enter the credit representative group to which you want to assign an employee. Credit representative groups were created in the preceding step.

CCA   Enter the credit control group that the credit representative group belongs to.

Funct   Enter the SD partner function that assigns the employee as the credit representative for your company. The two standard delivered SAP partner functions that are used for this purpose are KB (credit representative) and KM (credit manager). A credit representative group can have both a credit representative and a credit manager assigned to it.

ParC   If you have assigned the same partner function more than once to a credit representative group, there are several employees that are assigned to the credit representative group. You can enter the numerical sequence (1, 2, 3, etc.) that the system should use when assigning them.

Cp   Activate this indicator if you want the ability to copy the employee number into SD documents.

Pers. No   Enter the employee number of the person that you wish to assign to this credit representative group for this partner function. The employee number is the personnel number assigned to the employee in the HR module. After you enter the personnel number, the last name and the R/Mail user ID of the employee default into the LastName and MailUser fields respectively.

EXTREME SPORTS CREDIT REPRESENTATIVE GROUP AND CREDIT REPRESENTATIVE CONFIGURATION ANALYSIS

Extreme Sports created credit representative groups for its three major business lines: apparel (APP), boats (BOA), and ski equipment (SKI). Employees of Extreme Sports were assigned to each credit representative group. Credit representative group APP (apparel) has two employees assigned to the credit representative partner function. Employee number 12345678 is assigned first and employee number 23456789 is assigned second in each document. In addition to the two credit representatives, a credit manager (partner function KM) is also assigned to the apparel credit representative group (APP). The remaining credit representative groups (BOA and SKI) each has employees assigned as credit representatives.

The final step on the FI side of credit management is to define your days in arrears calculation. SAP allows you to set the grouping of days outstanding and how the due date is calculated for analysis purposes. To create a days in arrears calculation, follow the menu path Financial Accounting ➤ Accounts Receivable and Accounts Payable

> Credit Management > Business Transaction: Credit Monitoring > Define Intervals for Days in Arrears for Credit Management.

DEFINE DAYS IN ARREARS CALCULATION

You can use the following methods to get to the configuration screen for maintaining the days in arrears calculation:

Menu Path: **Financial Accounting** > **Accounts Receivable and Accounts Payable** > **Credit Management** > **Business Transaction: Credit Monitoring** > **Define Intervals for Days in Arrears for Credit Management**

Transaction Code: **OB39**

The define new days in arrears calculation configuration screen is shown in Figure 5.27. This screen appears when you enter one of the configuration transactions and click the New Entries button.

FIGURE 5.27   The define new days in arrears calculation configuration screen

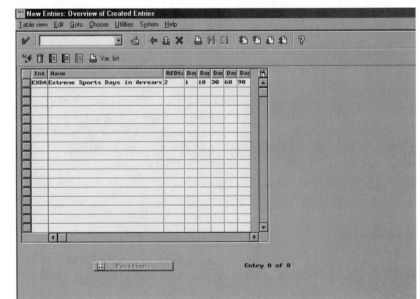

Here are the explanations of the fields that are displayed in Figure 5.27:

Int   Enter a four-character identifier for your days in arrears calculation. You will select this identifier when running custom SAP A/R and credit management reports.

Name   Enter a textual description of your days in arrears calculation indicator.

RfDte   This field defines the reference date that is used as the due date in the calculation. You have two options to choose from:

1   The cash discount due date

2   The net due date

Day   There are five Day fields. In the first Day field, enter a number that represents the last day of the days outstanding that you want to analyze. For example, if you enter a 15 in the first day field, SAP will group items that are 0–15 days overdue. Because there are five Day fields, there are six day groupings because the last Day field serves as the lower indicator. If you enter 90 in the last Day field, a grouping of all items that are at least 90 days past due is created.

Once you have completed the FI configuration of credit management, it is time to take a look at the SD configuration of credit management. As an FI configurer, you may or may not be responsible for the SD configuration of credit management. Whether you are responsible or not, it is important to work closely with the SD team in configuring the remaining pieces. So, what are the remaining pieces? In the SD configuration (configuration that falls under SD in the IMG), you can use sales order type and delivery type to define whether automatic credit checking should occur. You can then use risk category and order or delivery type to further define how stringent the credit check should be and whether a warning message, a warning message with a delivery block, an error message, or just a delivery block should be automatically created if the customer's credit limit is exceeded. If you want to know more, you can look at the activities that fall under the menu path Sales and Distribution ➢ Basic Functions ➢ Credit Processing.

Customer Master Records

Before you begin configuration of customer master data, it is necessary to have a strategy. You should plan how you would like to use customer master data and how you will convert customers from your legacy system, as well as the integration points that vendor master data has with SD Treasury and A/P. Much like the G/L, customer master data is a combination of configuration and master data maintenance.

A key concept in the configuration of customer master data is customer groups. Customer groups allow you to have separate purposes and field statuses for different types of customers. SD uses partner functions, which segregate different purposes for customer master data, such as the sold-to party, the ship-to party, the bill-to party, and so on. It is important to work closely with SD and have a good design between FI and SD so that master data fulfills the needs of both modules. Also, by separating these different types of customers into different customer groups, you can make different fields required, optional, or suppressed for each of the groups.

We will not go into detail in this section on how to actually create the customer master record but will instead focus on the configuration that allows you to create customer master records. However, it is important to remember that customer master records can be maintained from the FI point of view or centrally (just like vendor master data). It is also important to note that when you maintain customer accounts centrally, you are still not able to maintain the credit screens for the customer. To create the credit views of the customer, you must specifically select the Maintain Credit option on the A/R master data menu.

Customer Groups

The first step in configuring customer master data is to create *customer groups*. As mentioned earlier, customer groups are used to segregate different types of customers as well as segregate customers by SD partner function. To create customer groups, follow the menu path Financial Accounting ➤ Accounts Receivable and Accounts Payable ➤ Customer Accounts ➤ Master Records ➤ Preparations for Creating Customer Master Records ➤ Define Account Groups with Screen Layout (Customers).

The create new customer account group configuration screen shown in Figure 5.28 is displayed after you enter one of the configuration methods and click the New Entries button. SAP comes with some standard customer account groups for SD partner functions and other needed groupings. We will explore a custom customer account group for demonstration purposes.

DEFINE CUSTOMER GROUPS

You can get to the configuration screen for customer account groups by using the following methods:

Menu Path: Financial Accounting ➢ Accounts Receivable and Accounts Payable ➢ Customer Accounts ➢ Master Records ➢ Preparations for Creating Customer Master Records ➢ Define Account Groups with Screen Layout (Customers)

Transaction Code: OBD2

FIGURE 5.28   The create new customer account group configuration screen

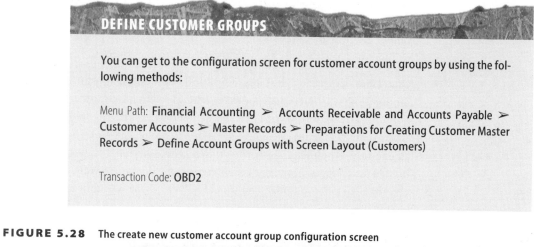

The fields shown in Figure 5.28 are explained here:

Account Group   Enter a four-character identifier by which to distinguish your customer account group.

Description   Enter a long text description of what this customer account group is used for.

Number Range   You assign customer account groups to number ranges. A separate configuration step is needed to do so. This step is very similar to assigning vendor account groups to number ranges. For more details, please refer to the last section in Chapter 4, which covers assigning account groups to number ranges.

One-Time Account   Select this indicator if you want this customer group to be for one-time customers. One-time accounts are used for customers you may use only once and for whom you do not want to store a unique customer master record (such as miscellaneous cash sales). Only one customer master record is needed for all one-time customers. The name, address, and other important information needed for creating an invoice are entered on the document when you specify a one-time customer number. You should only need one one-time customer account group for your company.

Output Determ. Proc.   The billing process produces different outputs that are sent to the customer, such as invoices, past due notices, order acknowledgement, and so on. Using the output determination procedure, you can determine which fields are available for output and in what order they can be output. You can select from the following options when populating this field:

Null (Blank)   No output determination procedure is used.

DB0001   This output determination procedure is used for sold-to parties.

DB0002   This output determination procedure is used for ship-to parties.

DB0003   This output determination procedure is used for bill-to parties.

DB0004   This output determination procedure is used for payers of the invoice.

Field Status   The concept of field statuses should be familiar to you from your work on the general ledger in Chapter 3 and with A/P vendors in Chapter 4. The field statuses on this screen control which fields are optional, required, and suppressed when you're creating a customer master record.

Customer Group Field Status

The first page of the configuration screen, and the most important fields for each category of customer group field statuses, will be explained in the following sections.

General Data   The first screen for the customer group field status appears in Figure 5.29. You can get to this screen by double-clicking the General Data text or clicking the Edit Field Status button—both shown in Figure 5.28. The settings made in the general data field status are valid for customer master records created in this customer account group regardless of company code or sales organization.

FIGURE 5.29 The first general data field status screen for customer groups

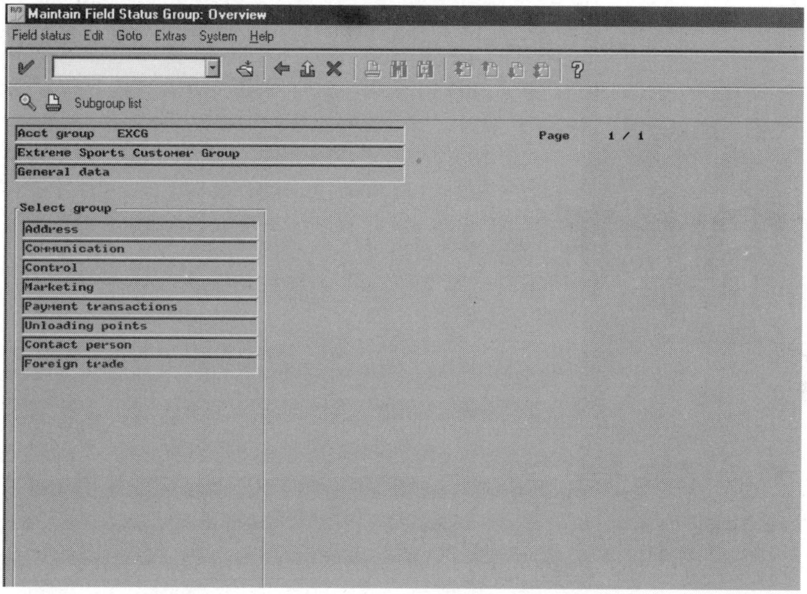

Explanations of the subsections of the general data field status as well as the most important fields to consider in each subsection are listed here:

Address   The Address section contains fields for name, street address, P.O. box, and so on. It is a good idea to make the customer name and address fields required for entry.

Communication   The Communication section contains fields that capture such information as telephone numbers and fax numbers. These fields are relatively self-explanatory, and it's easy to determine if you need them based on your requirements.

Control   The Control section contains many important fields that capture how the customer master record is processed. Here's a listing of the most important fields in this section:

Vendor   By utilizing this field, you can tell the system that this customer is also a vendor (by entering the vendor number). This allows you to do A/P-A/R netting if you so desire.

Tax Codes   These fields are important in determining the tax and tax jurisdiction from which sales taxes on invoices are generated.

Marketing   The Marketing section contains fields that can help you capture marketing information about your customers. Some of the fields that are included are Nielson ID, Industry Sector, and Fiscal Year of the Customer.

Payment Transactions   These fields help in receiving payment from customers. You can capture information about the customer's banks and accounts to help with electronic payment transactions. You can also specify alternate payers if the customer has more than one partner function that may pay an invoice.

Unloading Points   The Unloading Points fields help you to determine where customers receive shipments as well as the times the customers' docks are open for receiving goods.

Contact Person   The Contact Person fields allow you to keep information about your frequent contacts as well as their function in the organization.

Foreign Trade   The Foreign Trade fields allow you to capture information about the different countries that this customer may have you ship goods to or buy from. You can specify by country whether the customer is blocked for export due to government regulations such as denial orders, specially designated nationals, or overall boycotts.

Company Code Data   The first screen for the configuration of the Company Code Data section of the customer group field status appears in Figure 5.30. All fields in this section are valid at the company code level only. This means that, as customers are extended across several company codes, the fields in this section can have different values based on the company code using the customer master data.

FIGURE 5.30 The first company code field status screen for customer groups

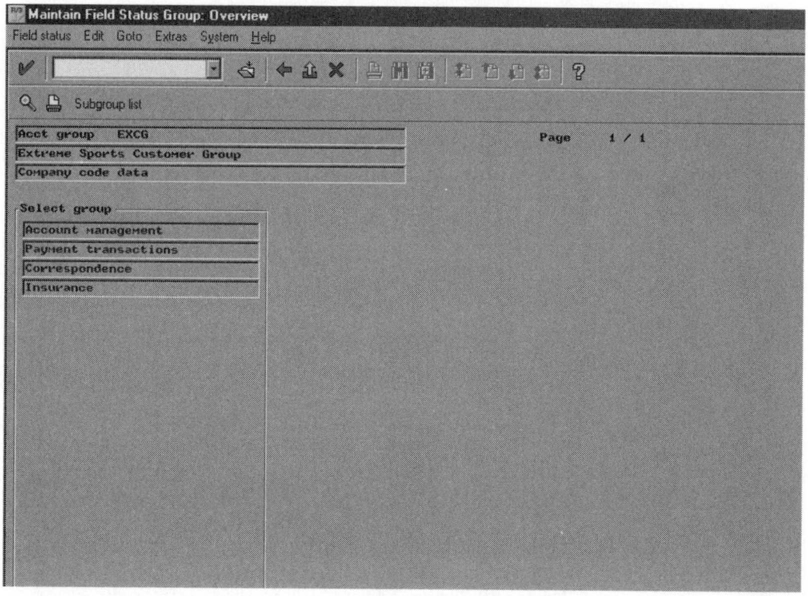

Here's a listing of the subsections of the company code data field status as well as the most important fields to consider in each subsection:

Account Management The Account Management fields control how vendor master data updates the general ledger:

Reconciliation Account As you are aware, the A/R system is a subledger. The reconciliation account is the G/L account updated by the A/R transactions using this customer account. Different customers or customer groups can update different reconciliation accounts.

Planning Group The planning group is a major integration point between A/R and Treasury. The planning group updates the receivable section in the liquidity-forecast functionality of the Treasury module. The liquidity-forecast report will be covered in Chapter 6. If you want to utilize the treasury functions within SAP, make this field mandatory.

Previous Account Number This field can be used to capture the legacy customer number in SAP. This field is especially useful in the initial time after Go-Live when users are looking up customers. A match key can be created to look up customer numbers based on this field.

Payment Transactions   The Payment Transactions fields help in processing customer payments. Some of the most important customer payment transactions are explained here:

Terms of Payment   Use this field to give the customer a default terms of payment key to occur on all invoices. The terms of payment key can be overridden in the document line item.

Clearing with Vendor   Activating this field allows you to activate A/P-A/R netting. If a customer is both a customer and a vendor, you can net the two accounts to create either one payable or one receivable.

Tolerance Group   Using this field, you can indicate the customer tolerance group you would like to assign this customer to. Customer tolerance groups were created earlier in the chapter.

Lockbox   If you are going to use lockbox functionality to apply cash and clear receivable, you can enter the lockbox that this customer is assigned to in this field. Lockboxes will be explained in Chapter 6.

Correspondence   The fields in this section allow you to store additional information for contact with the customer as well as enable and specify dunning information with the customer:

Account at Customer   Your vendor number at the customer is stored in this field. This can greatly help your A/R clerks in researching open A/R issues.

Insurance   The Insurance field group allows you to use fields to store information about export credit insurance.

Sales Data   The first screen for sales data field status appears in Figure 5.31. The fields stored in the sales data field status are valid for combinations of sales organizations, distribution channels, and divisions. These fields have an impact on the functionality of the SD module, so it is a good idea to work in close coordination with your SD group when defining rules for these fields.

FIGURE 5.31   The first screen of the sales data field status for customer groups

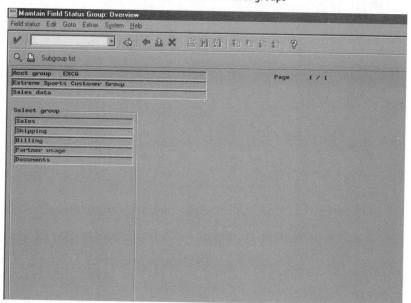

EXTREME SPORTS CUSTOMER ACCOUNT GROUP CONFIGURATION ANALYSIS

The customer account group EXCG was created for Extreme Sports. The output determination procedure DB0004 was used because payer partners will be set up using this customer account group. The One-Time Account indicator was not activated for this customer account group because a separate one-time customer account group will be created for Extreme Sports at a later time.

Summary

In this chapter, we covered the configuration of the A/R subledger, including credit management. Like all aspects within SAP, master data is vital to ensuring that processing goes smoothly. Specifically, we covered the following topics:

Terms of Payment and Interest Calculation

Reason Codes

Reason Code Conversion Versions

Default Account Assignments

Overpayments/Underpayments

Cash Discounts

Overall A/R and Employee Tolerances

Customer Tolerance Groups

Credit Management

Credit Control Areas

Assigning Credit Control Areas to Company Codes

Credit Risk Categories

Credit Representative Groups

Credit Representatives

Intervals For Days in Arrears

Customer Master Records

Integration with SD

Customer Groups

Customer Group Field Statuses

CHAPTER 6

Treasury

FEATURING:

▶ **LOCKBOX PROCESSING**

▶ **BANK ACCOUNT G/L STRUCTURE REVISITED**

▶ **LIQUIDITY FORECAST, CASH MANAGEMENT POSITION, AND CASH CONCENTRATION**

▶ **BANK STATEMENT PROCESSING**

▶ **EXCHANGE RATES**

The Treasury module within SAP gives you the ability to manage and forecast your cash requirements on a very detailed level. It is integrated with the A/P, A/R, MM, and SD submodules and modules. Using SAP's Treasury functionality, you can utilize lockbox (autocash) electronic processing to apply cash received and clear accounts receivable. You can also forecast projected cash on hand and cash flow needs based on outstanding payables, receivables, purchase orders, and sales orders. SAP also provides you with the ability to use electronic bank statement processing to reduce the time it takes to reconcile your cash accounts.

Lockbox Processing

The predominant way payments are made in the U.S. is by checks. Lockboxes help in the speedy deposit of funds and clearance of customer accounts. Lockbox functionality is also sometimes referred to as autocash. Lockboxes are special depository accounts set up at a bank to which customers remit their invoice payments. At least daily, the bank will submit to your company an electronic file listing all deposits and the invoices they are paid against. Your company then has the ability to upload all deposits into SAP, automatically update its cash balance, and clear customer accounts (A/R).

Some companies have a single lockbox, whereas others set up lockboxes at different locations throughout the country in order to decrease the time it takes to receive customer payments. The number of lockboxes used and the location of the lockboxes are purely business decisions.

Lockbox File Formats

SAP supports both U.S. lockbox file formats—BAI and BAI2. Although BAI and BAI2 are touted as standard file formats, you will quickly find that each bank has its own "standard" BAI or BAI2 format. It is therefore important to work with your bank and test its files to ensure that they are compliant with SAP's file format. If you find that the bank's file format is not compatible, most banks are pretty good about working with you to meet your file format needs. Alternatively, you can also have someone on your ABAP team write a preprocessing program that converts the bank's file format to SAP's file format. Lockbox processing is a major integration point between Treasury and A/R.

As was mentioned earlier, BAI and BAI2 are the preferred lockbox file formats in the U.S. The main difference between BAI and BAI2 is the detail in which check and invoice information is captured and submitted. BAI records the total check amount and up to three invoices to which the check should be applied. This makes it somewhat difficult when customers pay more than one invoice with a check and may be making partial payments against each invoice. BAI2 records information about the check and then allows as many detail records as are needed to explain what amounts are paid against what invoices and to list the deduction amount against the invoice and the reason code. If you're trying to decide which format to use, it is normally better to use BAI2 because you have a greater probability of producing automatic matches in the processing and because it allows you to record deduction information and create the proper residual postings. To find out the details about the structure of each file format, you can view the SAP structures (using transaction code SE11 or SE12) that make up the file format. The structures are listed here:

BAI

FLB01	Header Record
FLB02	Service Record
FLB04	Overflow Record
FLB05	Detail Header Record
FLB06	Detail Record
FLB07	Batch Total Record
FLB08	Lockbox Total Record
FLB09	Trailer Record

BAI2

FLB01	Header Record
FLB02	Service Record
FLB24	Overflow Record
FLB05	Detail Header Record
FLB26	Detail Record
FLB07	Batch Total Record
FLB08	Lockbox Total Record
FLB09	Trailer Record

Lockbox Configuration

Now that you have a solid understanding of lockboxes and the different file formats that can be used, you are ready to begin configuring them. Your first step is to set up lockboxes that can be referenced in customer master accounts and used by invoices as part of the remit-to information. Although this particular step has no effect on how actual lockbox files are processed, it is important because lockboxes can be referenced and used in this way so customers know where to send their payments. To create a lockbox account to be included in customer master records and invoice remit-to information, follow the menu path Financial Accounting ➢ General Ledger Accounting ➢ Bank-Related Accounting ➢ Bank Accounts ➢ Define Lockbox Accounts at House Banks.

DEFINE LOCKBOXES

You can use the following methods to get to the configuration screen for creating lockbox accounts for customer master records and invoice remit-to information:

Menu Path: **Financial Accounting** ➢ **General Ledger Accounting** ➢ **Bank-Related Accounting** ➢ **Bank Accounts** ➢ **Define Lockbox Accounts at House Banks**

Transaction Code: **OB10**

You can display the create lockbox at house bank configuration screen shown in Figure 6.1 by following one of the configuration methods and then clicking the New Entries button.

You need to enter information in the four fields in the create lockbox at house bank configuration screen:

- ▶ The company code for the company to which the lockbox belongs
- ▶ A name for the lockbox, to be used in the customer master record
- ▶ The name of the house bank to which the lockbox belongs
- ▶ The lockbox number (account number) at the house bank

Once you enter all of the information and click the save icon, you are presented with the Edit Address screen, shown in Figure 6.2. You can also get to the Edit Address screen by clicking the address icon, which looks like an envelope, on the toolbar shown in Figure 6.1.

FIGURE 6.1   The create lockbox at house bank configuration screen

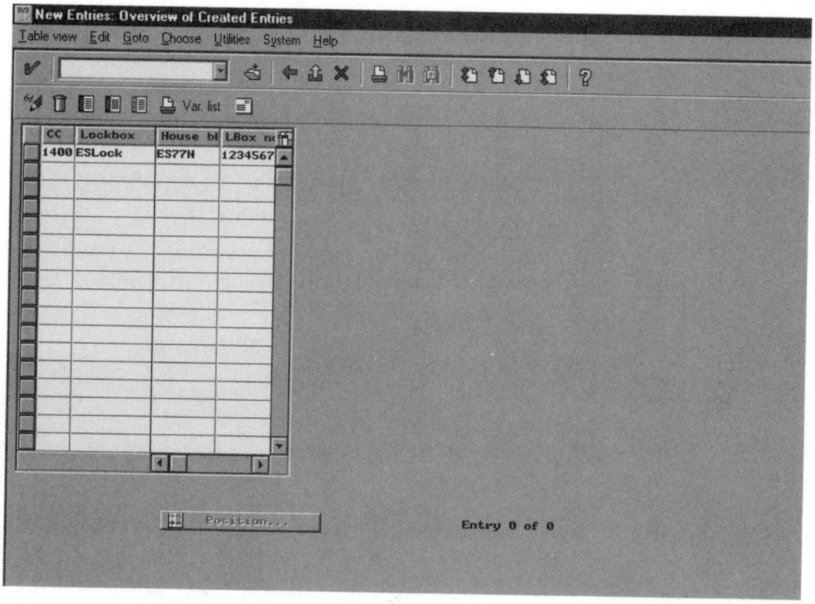

FIGURE 6.2   The Edit Address screen

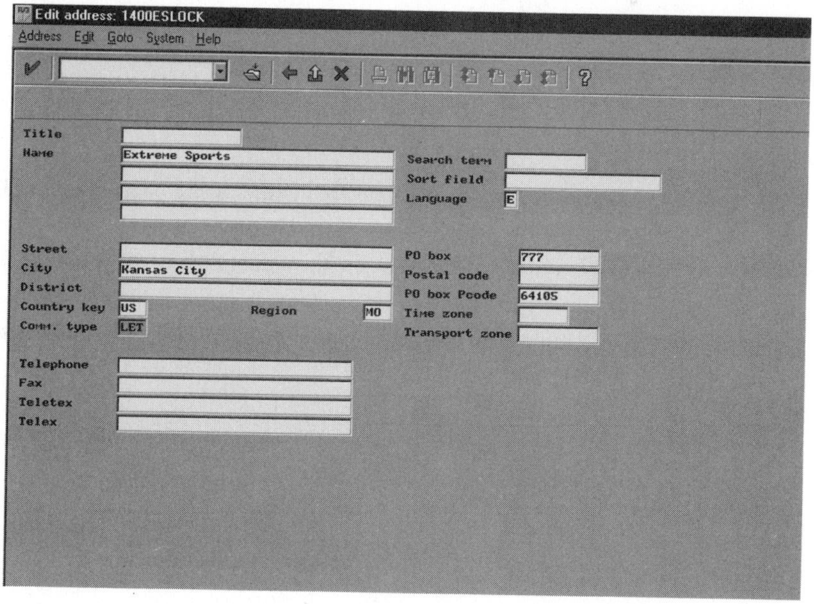

In the Edit Address screen, you need to enter your company name and the address of the lockbox to which payments should be made. Most lockbox mailing addresses are set up as P.O. boxes by the bank. This address information will be used in the remit-to information of invoices the system creates so that customers know where to mail their payments.

Now that you have created lockboxes for customer accounts, you are ready to define the control parameters that will be used by the lockbox processing program. You only need to set up a control parameter for the file format you are using. In our Extreme Sports example, we will be using the BAI2 format. To create the control parameter for lockbox processing, follow the menu path Treasury ➢ Cash Management ➢ Business Transactions ➢ Lockbox ➢ Define Control Parameters.

DEFINE LOCKBOX CONTROL PARAMETERS

You can use the following methods to get to the configuration screen for defining lockbox control parameters:

Menu Path: **Treasury ➢ Cash Management ➢ Business Transactions ➢ Lockbox ➢ Define Control Parameters**

Transaction Code: **OBAY**

Once you execute one of the configuration methods, you are presented with the autocash control parameters configuration screen, shown in Figure 6.3.

As you can see, SAP is delivered with control parameters for both the BAI and BAI2 formats. The only procedure that is supported is Lockbox. With that under your belts, you are ready to define the control parameters for the BAI2 format that Extreme Sports will be using. To change the control parameters, double-click the BAI2 entry. You are presented with the BAI2 control parameters configuration screen, shown in Figure 6.4.

FIGURE 6.3   The autocash control parameters configuration screen

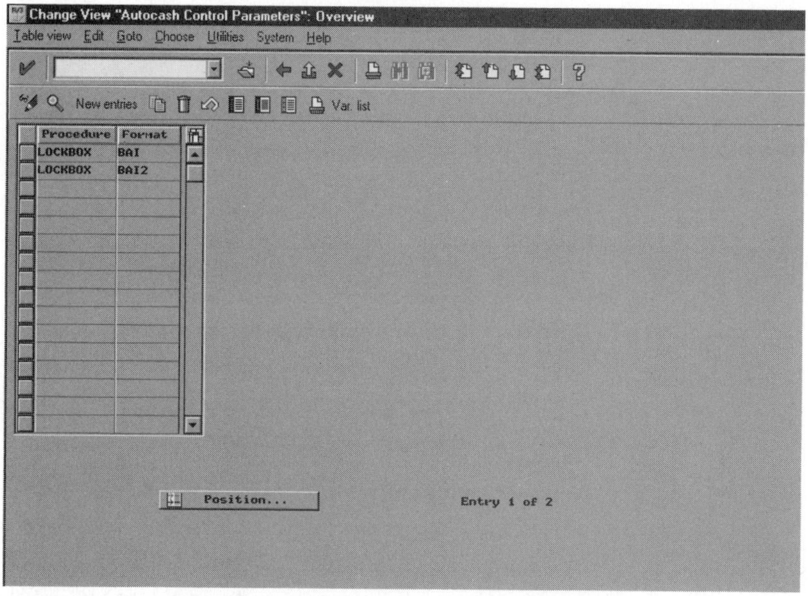

FIGURE 6.4   The BAI2 control parameters configuration screen

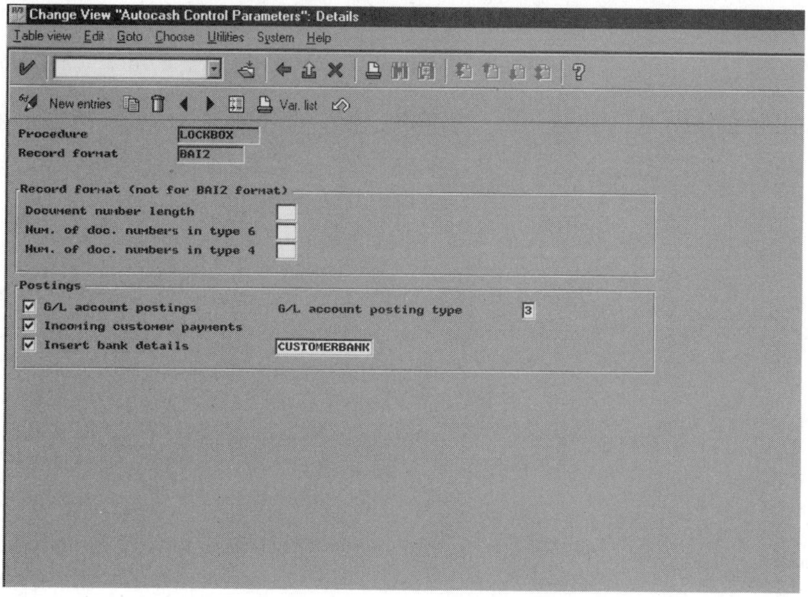

The fields that are shown in Figure 6.4 are explained in the following list:

Procedure   As was mentioned earlier, the only procedure that is currently supported is Lockbox.

Record Format   The two record formats that are currently supported are BAI and BAI2. Enter the format you wish to use for lockbox processing.

Document Number Length   This field is only applicable for the BAI record format. Enter the document number length that will be entered in the file. The default document number length for SAP is 10.

Num. of Doc. Numbers in Type 6   This field is only applicable for the BAI record format. Enter the number of documents that are entered on each line of record type 6 in the BAI file format. This field is not needed in BAI2 format because each invoice has its own record type 6 line.

Num. of Doc. Numbers in Type 4   This field is only applicable for the BAI record format. Enter the number of documents that are entered on each line of record type 4 in the BAI file format. This field is not needed in BAI2 format because document numbers are only entered in record type 6 fields.

G/L Account Postings   Activate this indicator to make postings to your cash account in the G/L for deposits. Activating this field is recommended.

Incoming Customer Payments   Activate this indicator to make postings to the A/R subledger in order to clear customer accounts and create residual postings. Activating this field is recommended.

Insert Bank Details   Activate this indicator if you want to create a batch input session that updates the bank details of master records for customers who have either changed bank information or did not have bank information maintained for them. In the text box next to this field, enter the names of the batch input sessions you're creating. The bank detail information is an important part of the lockbox algorithm because, if the invoice can't be found, the check can be applied to the customer's account based on the MICR (bank account information) in the check.

G/L Account Posting Type   If you activated G/L Account Postings, you need to select the level at which the postings are made. The available options are as follows:

1   This option creates a posting to the G/L account for every check in the file (one per check).

2 This option creates one posting to the G/L account for the entire lockbox file (the sum of all checks).

3 This option creates a posting to the G/L account for each batch. A single lockbox file may have more than one batch recorded in it. The bank makes deposits to your accounts based upon batches. Therefore, this option makes a lot of sense if you want to be able to easily reconcile your bank statement because the postings made to the G/L will match the deposit records of the bank. This option is only available in releases before 4.6 if you apply OSS Note number 0140631.

NOTE Beginning in version 4.*x*, there is an additional check box for partial payments. If this check box is activated, all short-pays clear the invoice amount and create a residual item for the difference between the invoice amount and the amount paid.

EXTREME SPORTS LOCKBOX CONTROL PARAMETERS CONFIGURATION ANALYSIS

Extreme Sports has decided to use the BAI2 format for lockbox processing. It wants the lockbox program to update the cash deposit G/L account and update the A/R sub-ledger with customer clearings and residual postings. In addition, it wants the lockbox program to create one G/L entry to the cash account for every batch total in the lockbox file. This will make it much easier for Extreme Sports to automatically update its bank statements with electronic bank statement processing (which will be covered later in this chapter). If a check from a customer is received with new bank information, or if a customer does not have bank information in their customer master record, Extreme Sports wants the lockbox program to create a batch input session that will update the bank details in the customer master record.

Now that you have created lockbox control parameters, you are ready to define in more detail how each lockbox account should update SAP—posting data. To define the posting data for your lockbox, follow the menu path Treasury ➢ Cash Management ➢ Business Transactions ➢ Lockbox ➢ Define Posting Data.

DEFINE LOCKBOX POSTING DATA

You can get to the configuration screen for defining lockbox posting data by using the following methods:

Menu Path: **Treasury** ➤ **Cash Management** ➤ **Business Transactions** ➤ **Lockbox** ➤ **Define Posting Data**

Transaction Code: **OBAX**

After following one of the configuration transactions and clicking the New Entries button, you are taken to the lockbox posting data configuration screen, shown in Figure 6.5.

FIGURE 6.5   The lockbox posting data configuration screen

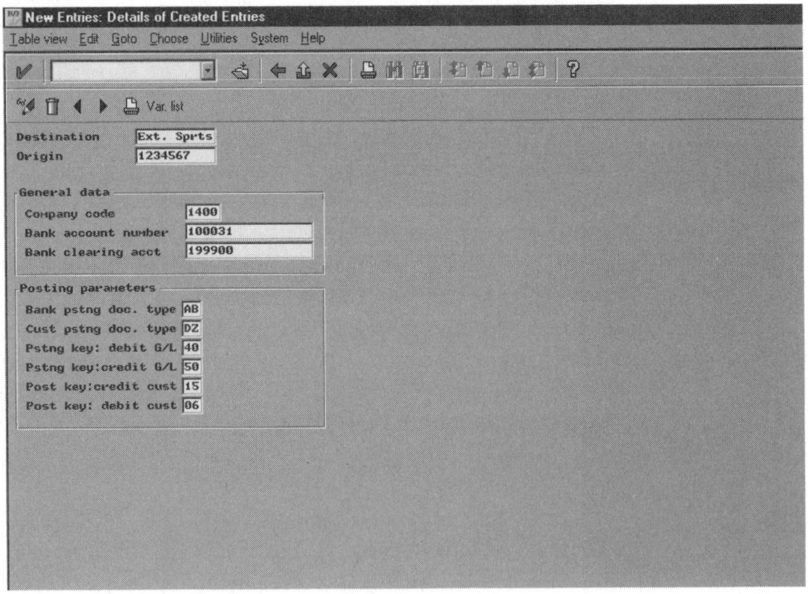

The fields that appear in Figure 6.5 are explained here:

Destination   The Destination field should contain the destination code the bank submits to you in your lockbox file.

Origin   The Origin field should contain your lockbox (bank account) number at the bank.

Company Code   Enter the identifier of the company code to which this lockbox account belongs.

Bank Account Number   The name of this field is quite deceptive. Instead of entering the bank account number, you need to enter the G/L account that the cash deposits should update. (Bank account G/L structure was covered in Chapter 4 and will be revisited later in this chapter).

Bank Clearing Acct   Enter the G/L account number of the clearing account you want to post to in the lockbox posting routing. The initial entry made by the lockbox program is to debit the cash deposit clearing account and credit a bank clearing account. The system then debits the bank clearing account and credits the customer A/R account for all customer matches it is able to make. If the system cannot find a customer match, the credit remains in the clearing account for the A/R clerks to research and apply to a customer account.

Bank Pstng Doc. Type   Enter the identifier of the document type you would like to use for the G/L posting that debits the deposit clearing account and credits the bank clearing account.

Cust Pstng Doc. Type   Enter the identifier of the document type you would like to use for the customer credit posting and the debit to the bank clearing account.

Pstng Key: Debit G/L   Enter the posting key that should be used to debit the G/L accounts that are posted to in the lockbox transaction.

Pstng Key: Credit G/L   Enter the posting key that should be used to credit the G/L accounts that are posted to in the lockbox transaction.

Post Key: Credit Cust   Enter the posting key that should be used to credit the customer account in the lockbox posting transaction.

Post Key: Debit Cust   Enter the posting key that should be used to debit the customer account in the lockbox posting transaction.

EXTREME SPORTS LOCKBOX POSTING DATA CONFIGURATION ANALYSIS

Extreme Sports configured the posting data for its lockbox in this example. The destination code used by the bank in lockbox transmission is Ext. Sprts; the origin or bank account number for this lockbox is 1234567. The lockbox belongs to Extreme Sports' company code 1400—Extreme Services. Extreme Services handles all accounting functions for Extreme Sports' U.S.-based operations. The deposit clearing account used by the lockbox is 100031 (bank account G/L structure was covered in Chapter 4 and will be revisited later in this chapter). The bank clearing account 199900 is being used. After a lockbox run, the only postings that will be left in this account are for checks that could not be applied to a customer account. The postings left in the bank clearing account need to be researched by the accounting staff and cleared against a customer account. Standard SAP document types and posting keys will be used for lockbox postings.

Lockbox Processing in SAP

SAP gives you the option of using one of two standard algorithms for lockbox processing. A common misperception is that you can create your own algorithm. You cannot; you have to use one of the SAP-delivered algorithms. The algorithm will determine what data is used from the lockbox file and in what order so that the proper invoice and customer account can be credited. The algorithm also determines how checks that can be matched to a customer account but cannot be applied toward specific invoices are handled. Program RFEBLB00 is the lockbox processing program. It is a good idea to look at the documentation for RFEBLB00 (transaction code SE38)—it provides a lot of good information about lockbox processing and the data SAP expects. This program also contains user-exits. You will recall from Chapter 1 that user-exits are SAP-delivered calls in which you can place your own ABAP code to manipulate the transaction. Although you can't create your own algorithm, you can manipulate it to an extent by using user-exits. The two algorithms that can be used are 001 and 003. If you have checks that cannot be applied against a specific invoice, but for which the customer account is known, SAP posts them on the customer account without reference to any specific invoice. Using algorithm 003, SAP distributes the check across open invoices, beginning at the oldest invoice and working its way forward until the check amount is fully distributed.

Bank Account G/L Structure Revisited

In this section, we will revisit the bank account G/L structure that we began in Chapter 4. In this section and the sections that follow, you will see how it ties in with Treasury functionality.

One of the many benefits of the flexibility of SAP is the ability to determine how much confirmed cash, floating cash out, and floating cash in there is for your company on any particular day. To accomplish this, a strategy for the bank account G/L structure must be formed. In order for this to work, there must be only one confirmed cash G/L account, with several bank clearing accounts per bank account. For example, a checks outgoing clearing, a wire outgoing, an ACH out, a deposits clearing, and so on need to be set up for each bank account. It is also important to leave yourself room for additional clearing accounts you may need in the future for additional functionality.

The most flexible and best solution is to have a range of 10 G/L account numbers for each bank account. This solution will give you maximum flexibility; though you probably won't need nine clearing accounts for each bank account at the offset, it gives you the ability to expand and add more in the future should the need arise. This solution will allow you to view all confirmed cash and floating cash in and out in your liquidity forecast and cash management position. The bank clearing accounts also simplify the processing of electronic bank statements. We will look at the configuration of the liquidity forecast, cash management positions, and electronic bank statement later in this chapter. For Extreme Sports, each confirmed cash balance will end with 0 (e.g., G/L account 100000), each deposit clearing account will end in 1 (e.g., G/L account 100001), each outgoing check clearing account will end in 2, each outgoing ACH account will end in 3, and each outgoing wire account will end in 4.

The use of the bank account G/L structure can be seen through the following example. When Extreme Sports executes the payment program and cuts checks for open payables, the check clearing account is credited and the vendor A/P account is debited. The check amount will remain in the check clearing account until it clears the bank. This allows Extreme Sports to monitor its real confirmed cash balance and have insight into float created by transactions that have not yet cleared the bank. Once the check clears the bank, the check clearing account will be debited and the confirmed cash balance account will be credited (this occurs during electronic bank statement processing).

EXTREME SPORTS BANK ACCOUNT G/L STRUCTURE CONFIGURATION ANALYSIS

Extreme Sports wants the ability to see its confirmed cash balance as well as any incoming deposits or outgoing payments. For this reason, several bank clearing accounts are set up for each bank account. The implementation of this functionality will be used in the liquidity forecast, cash management position, and electronic bank statement. The Extreme Sports bank account G/L structure is as follows (the + symbol is a wildcard):

Confirmed Cash	+++++0
Deposit Clearing	+++++1
Outgoing Check Clearing	+++++2
Outgoing ACH Clearing	+++++3
Outgoing Wire Clearing	+++++4

Liquidity Forecast, Cash Management Position, and Cash Concentration

In this section, we will cover the configuration that is needed for the liquidity forecast, cash management position, and cash concentration functionality of the Treasury module. Each step that is covered is not necessarily needed for all three pieces of functionality—we will point out what pieces of the functionality each step is applicable to as it is covered.

So what exactly does each piece of functionality do? The liquidity forecast allows you to predict future cash inflows and outflows—such as A/P transactions that become due, purchase orders, purchase requisitions, A/R items that are expected to be paid, and sales orders—based upon information from other modules. This allows you to see the expected net cash inflow or outflow on any given day out into the future. You can also view this information by the risk level and other factors by which you segregate your customers and vendors. Cash management position allows you to see what your bank account activity was on any given date as well as predict the cash balance on given day based on planned bank and payment transactions. You can also view your predicted net cash flow on any given day by combining the liquidity forecast and cash management position in the same report (this is a standard option available on the cash management position/liquidity forecast report). Cash concentration allows you to drive (or sweep) the account balance of one or several source bank accounts to a single target bank account. This functionality is useful if your company has several different bank accounts and wishes to sweep all account balances nightly (or some other time interval) into one central account. A good example of this is the use of lockboxes—you would probably want to sweep the account balance of your lockbox account to a central bank account nightly. Cash concentration also produces the documentation to send to the bank. Although many banks can do this automatically, using SAP to instruct the bank ensures that the accounts are reconciled.

Source Symbols

The first setting we need to make is to define the source symbols that are to be used. Source symbols are the highest level of the treasury hierarchy that is used in the cash management position and liquidity forecast. The main purpose of source symbols is to define the module (FI, MM, SD) from which the underlying transactions originated. Follow the menu path Treasury ≻ Cash Management ≻ Basic Settings ≻ Define Source Symbols to get to the configuration screen for source symbols.

DEFINE SOURCE SYMBOLS

You can use the following methods to get to the configuration screen for defining source symbols:

Menu Path: **Treasury** ≻ **Cash Management** ≻ **Basic Settings** ≻ **Define Source Symbols**

Transaction Code: **OT05**

After entering one of the configuration transactions, you are presented with the source symbols for cash management configuration screen, shown in Figure 6.6.

FIGURE 6.6   The source symbols for cash management configuration screen

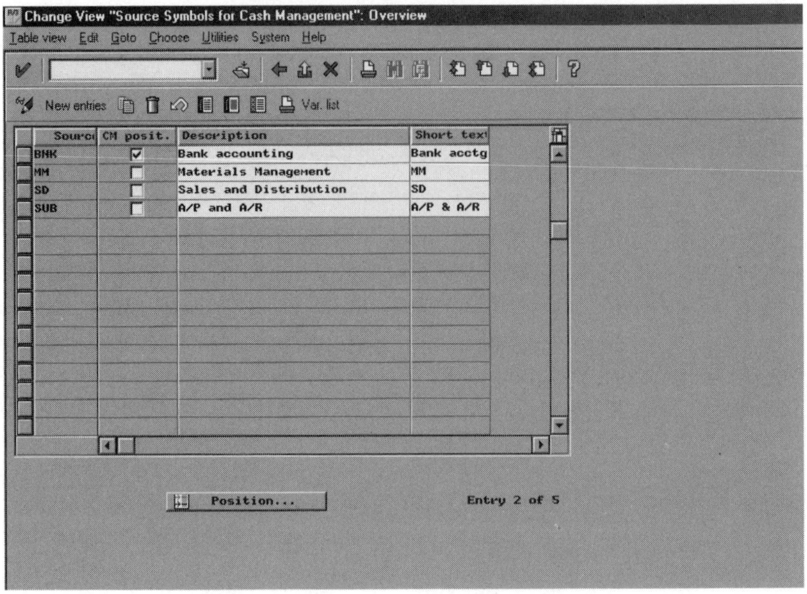

As you can see, Extreme Sports has created the following source symbols: BNK, MM, SD, and SUB. They will be used in the cash management position and liquidity forecast. You can see that the configuration is very simple; you only need to define an identifier (up to three-characters long), a long text name, and a short text name. The CM Posit. field should be updated if you want the source symbol to update the cash management position. If this field is not activated, the symbol is used by the liquidity forecast functionality.

EXTREME SPORTS SOURCE SYMBOL CONFIGURATION ANALYSIS

Source symbols are the highest level of the hierarchy that you can view in the cash management position and liquidity forecast reports. The source symbols represent the module in which the transaction that updated the report originated. The following source symbols were created for Extreme Sports:

BNK   This source symbol is used to group transactions from bank accounts. It is configured to update the cash management position.

EXTREME SPORTS SOURCE SYMBOL CONFIGURATION ANALYSIS (CONTINUED)

MM   This source symbol is used to group together transactions that originate in the MM module (purchase requisitions, purchase orders, etc.). It is configured to update the liquidity forecast. Once an invoice is received, the transaction drops out of the MM source symbol and is included in the SUB source symbol because it is now an open payable.

SD   This source symbol is used to group together transactions that originate in the SD module (sales orders). It is configured to update the liquidity forecast. Once an invoice is billed to a customer, the transaction drops out of the SD source symbol and is included in the SUB source symbol because it is now an open receivable.

SUB   This source symbol is used to group together transactions that originate in one of the subledgers (A/P or A/R). It is configured to update the liquidity forecast.

Planning Levels

The next piece of configuration that is needed is to create planning levels. Planning levels are used to further subdivide the postings that are made to the source symbols we created earlier. Planning level F0 comes delivered with SAP and is used to update bank accounts (source symbol BNK)—the confirmed cash balance only. Although this entry may not already be created in the system, the SAP source code looks for this level, so be sure to use it for its intended purposes. SAP further recommends that planning levels F1 and F2 be used for customer and vendor accounts and that levels B1-Bn be used for bank clearing accounts. You can get to the configuration screen for planning levels by following the menu path Treasury ➤ Master Data ➤ Subledger Accounts ➤ Define Planning Levels.

DEFINE PLANNING LEVELS

You can get the configuration screen for planning levels by using the following methods:

Menu Path: **Treasury ➤ Master Data ➤ Subledger Accounts ➤ Define Planning Levels**

Transaction Code: **OT14**

After executing one of the configuration transactions and clicking the New Entries button, you are presented with the create planning levels configuration screen, shown in Figure 6.7.

FIGURE 6.7   The create planning levels configuration screen

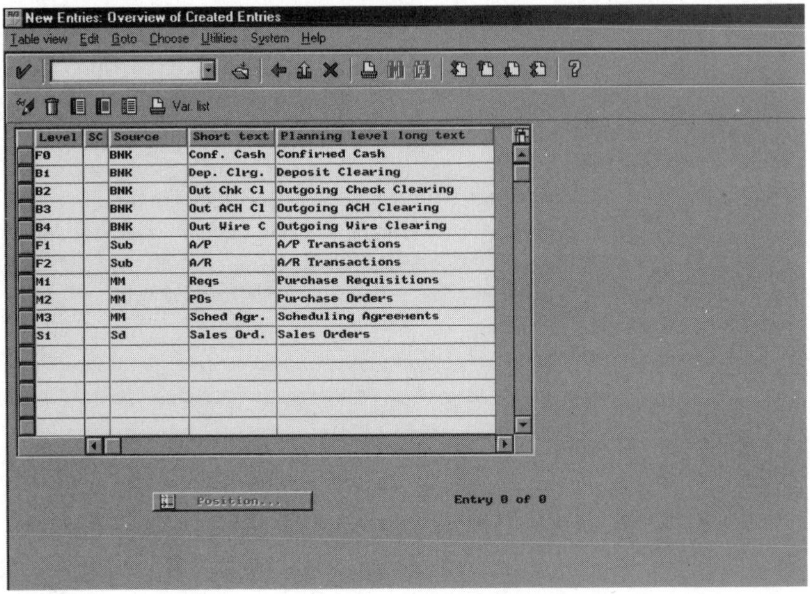

The configuration of planning levels is fairly straightforward. You need to enter a two-character planning level identifier, the source symbol the planning level belongs to, a short text description, and a long text description. The SC field allows you to manipulate the signs (+ or −) in which transaction figures are displayed in the cash management position or liquidity forecast report. There are three available options for the SC field:

null   The natural sign is displayed.

+   The amounts are displayed as positive.

−   The amounts are always displayed as negative.

For the planning levels that were created for bank accounts (F0, B1, B2, B3, B4), the planning level indicator needs to be maintained in the Planning Level field of the bank account grouping in the company code screen of the G/L account in which the bank account is assigned. You can refer back to Chapter 3 for more information on how to create a G/L account. The planning levels for MM and SD transactions need to be assigned to internal transactions—this will be covered later in this chapter.

EXTREME SPORTS PLANNING LEVEL CONFIGURATION ANALYSIS

In this section, planning levels were created for confirmed cash balances, deposit clearing, outgoing check clearing, outgoing ACH clearing, outgoing wire clearing, A/P, A/R, purchase requisitions, purchase orders, purchasing scheduling agreements, and sales orders. The planning level is the next level below the source symbol, and therefore, each planning level is allocated to a single source symbol. The natural sign will be displayed for all of Extreme Sports' planning levels. The G/L accounts that are tied to bank accounts will be maintained so that the proper planning level (F0, B1, B2, B3, or B4) is maintained in each account and will be updated properly.

Planning Groups

Planning groups are used to segregate customers and vendors into different groups. Normally, they are set up according to risk, size of vendor, payment method, or some other sort of characteristic. Planning groups are a level below planning levels, and each planning group is tied to a single planning level. The planning groups created in this step are assigned to customer and vendor master records—this is how the planning group is updated in the Treasury submodule. It is important to note that the only planning levels that are directly updated without a planning group are planning levels that are tied to bank accounts (source symbol BNK) and updated via MM or SD transactions. The assignment of MM and SD planning levels to transactions will be explained later in this chapter. It is a good idea to follow a naming convention in the creation of your planning group, such as beginning all vendor planning groups with *O* for outgoing and beginning all customer planning groups with *I* for incoming. The following menu path allows you to create planning groups: Treasury ➢ Master Data ➢ Subledger Accounts ➢ Define Planning Groups.

DEFINE PLANNING GROUPS

You can get to the configuration screen for planning groups by using the following configuration methods:

Menu Path: **Treasury** ➢ **Master Data** ➢ **Subledger Accounts** ➢ **Define Planning Groups**

Transaction Code: **OT13**

After entering one of the configuration methods and clicking the New Entries button, you are taken to the create planning groups configuration screen, shown in Figure 6.8.

FIGURE 6.8   The create planning groups configuration screen

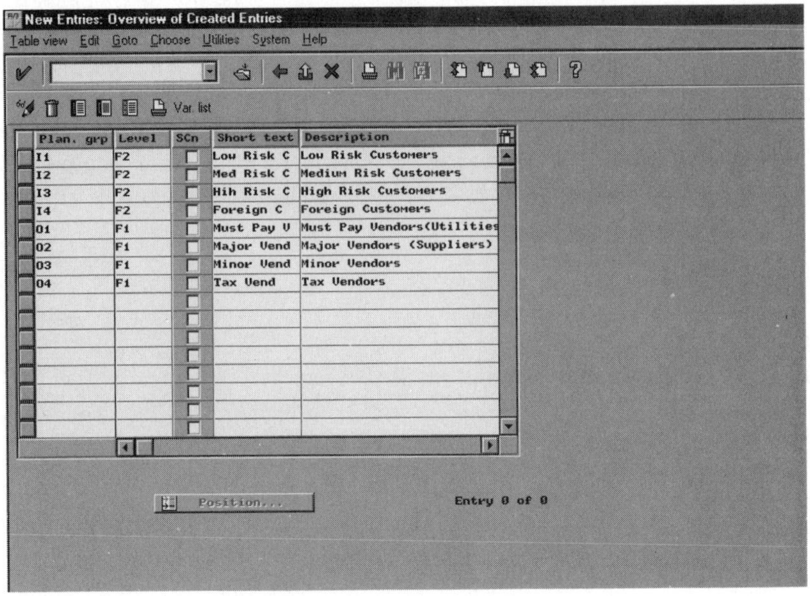

Let's take a look at the fields in this screen:

Plan. Grp   Enter an identifier for the planning group that you wish to create. The planning group will be allocated to customer and vendor master records. It is a good idea to come up with a naming convention, such as beginning the names of all planning groups for customers with *I* for incoming payments. For your most important customers and vendors, you can enter the customer or vendor account number in this field to further improve your ability to analyze the liquidity forecast reports.

Level   Enter the identifier of the planning level that this planning group belongs to. Each planning group can be assigned to only one planning level. This is how subledger planning levels are updated.

SCn   By activating this indicator, you can make the Planning Date and Planning Level fields available for manual entry when creating or changing documents in the system—this option allows you to override the default planning level that you assign in this table.

Short Text   Enter a short text description of what this planning group is to be used for.

Long Text   Enter a long text description of what this planning group is to be used for.

EXTREME SPORTS PLANNING GROUP CONFIGURATION ANALYSIS

Extreme Sports created several planning groups that will be assigned to customer and vendor accounts (master records). The planning groups will allow Extreme Sports to better segregate information within its liquidity forecast report. Each planning group is assigned to a specific planning level. Extreme Sports decided to not allow users to overwrite the default planning date and planning level—this will allow for more consistent information and central control over planning group assignment.

Assigning Internal MM and SD Transactions to Planning Levels

As was discussed earlier, internal MM and SD transactions need to be assigned to the planning levels. You will recall that planning levels M1 (Purchase Requisitions), M2 (Purchase Orders), M3 (Purchasing Scheduling Agreements), and S1 (Sales Orders) were created earlier in the chapter. We will now assign SAP internal transaction indicators to these planning levels. You can get to the configuration screen for assigning SAP internal transactions to planning levels by following the menu path Treasury ➢ Cash Management ➢ Structuring ➢ Define Planning Levels for Logistics.

DEFINE PLANNING LEVELS FOR LOGISTICS

You can get to the configuration screen for assigning SAP internal transactions to planning levels by using the following methods:

Menu Path: **Treasury** ➢ **Cash Management** ➢ **Structuring** ➢ **Define Planning Levels for Logistics**

Transaction Code: **OT47**

After entering one of the configuration transactions, you are taken to the allocate transactions for MM and SD transactions configuration screen, shown in Figure 6.9.

FIGURE 6.9   The allocate transactions for MM and SD transactions configuration screen

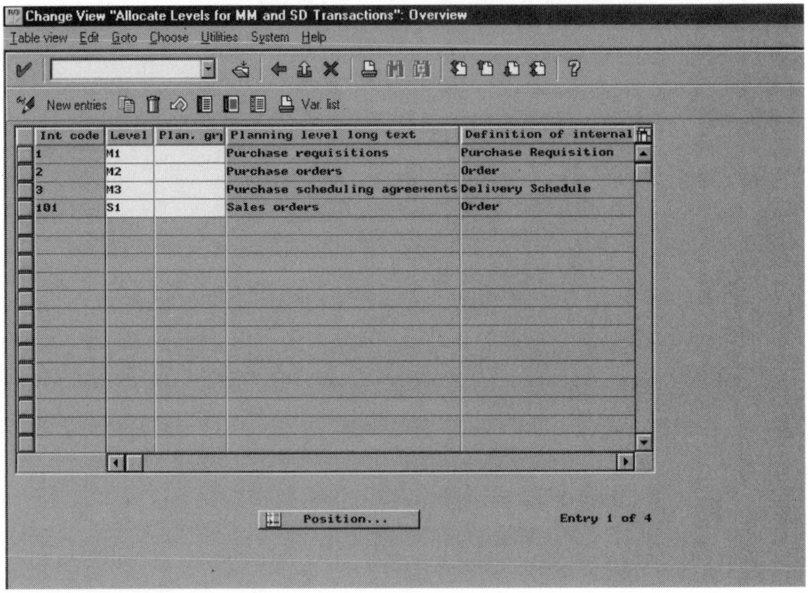

The following internal codes (transactions) are used by SAP:

1   Purchase Requisitions

2   Purchase Orders

3   Delivery Schedule (Purchasing Scheduling Agreements)

101   Sales Orders

You need to assign each internal code to the corresponding planning level that you created earlier in the chapter. Once you do so, the long text for each element (internal code and planning level) is displayed on the screen. You can also assign each internal code to a planning group that is assigned to the planning level you are assigning—this setting is generally not needed because not much information beyond planning level can be derived from these MM and SD transactions.

EXTREME SPORTS ASSIGNING INTERNAL MM AND SD TRANSACTIONS TO PLANNING LEVELS

The internal codes for each of the four activities that can be allocated to Treasury from MM and SD were assigned to their corresponding planning levels, which were created earlier. As you can see in Figure 6.9, there should be a 1:1 relationship between internal code and planning level. Planning groups were not entered because any useful information below planning level cannot be derived from MM and SD transactions.

Treasury Groupings

Groupings are required in order to run the cash management position, liquidity forecast, or cash concentration in the system. Groupings for the cash management position are used to determine what bank accounts and bank clearing accounts will be presented. Groupings for the liquidity forecast determine what subledger accounts are presented as well as what information from MM and SD is updated in the report. Groupings for cash concentration determine the source accounts (accounts that money is taken out of) and the target account (account that the money is put into). To create groupings, follow the menu path Treasury ➢ Cash Management ➢ Structuring ➢ Groupings ➢ Maintain Structure.

DEFINE TREASURY GROUPINGS

You can get to the configuration screen for treasury groupings by using the following methods:

Menu Path: **Treasury ➢ Cash Management ➢ Structuring ➢ Groupings ➢ Maintain Structure**

Transaction Code: **OT17**

After following one of the configuration transactions and clicking the New Entries button, you are taken to the create new treasury groupings configuration screen, shown in Figure 6.10.

FIGURE 6.10   The create new treasury groupings configuration screen

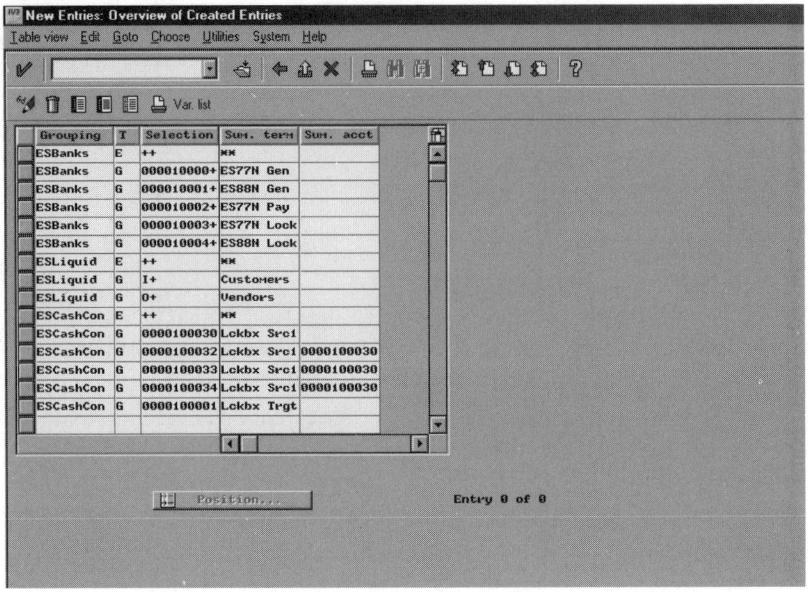

Here is an explanation of the fields in Figure 6.10:

Grouping   Enter the name of the grouping you're creating. You can choose any name you like; it should be a name that describes the type of Treasury information you're grouping together.

T   This field represents line type. Line type specifies whether the entry is a level or a group—the two possible choices are E for level and G for group. Each group must be part of a level, and each level can have many groups (but it must have at least one). The level combines the groups that fall underneath it so that the correct groups are selected and viewed by the cash management position, liquidity forecast, and cash concentration selection screens.

Selection   In the Selection field, you should enter a ++ if the line type is E (level). This will allow group selections that fall under it to be used by the level. If the line type is G, you can enter the G/L account that is to be displayed, the planning level, or the planning group that is to be displayed. A + functions as a wildcard so you don't have to make as many entries to include all the needed G/L accounts or planning levels. If you are using a G/L account, be sure to include the leading zeros (if you specified a 6-character account in your chart, you need to enter 4 leading zeros because the SAP-delivered data element for account number is 10 characters long).

Sum. Term   Enter the textual name that you want to be displayed on the report screen for the related G/L account or planning level that was entered in the Selection field.

Sum. Acct   This field is used for cash concentration groupings only. If you want to include bank clearing accounts in the source accounts for cash concentration, you can use this field to enter the confirmed cash G/L account for the bank; that way, cash concentration occurs through the confirmed cash G/L account only but incorporates the balances from the clearing accounts.

EXTREME SPORTS TREASURY GROUPINGS CONFIGURATION ANALYSIS

Three different treasury groupings (ESBanks, ESLiquid, and ESCashCon) were configured for Extreme Sports in this section. Each grouping will be individually analyzed below.

ESBanks

This grouping will be used for the cash management position. As with all lines that are line type E, the selection ++ and summarization term ** are used so that all lines with line type G that fall under this level are included in the total for the grouping. As you will recall from Extreme Sports' G/L bank account structure, each bank account is allocated 10 G/L accounts (+++++0 to +++++9) that are used for the confirmed cash balance and bank clearing accounts. Therefore, only one line type G is needed for each bank account because the wildcard character + can be used. All general, payroll, and lockbox accounts for Extreme Sports are included in this grouping.

ESLiquid

This grouping will be used for the liquidity forecast. The selection fields for this grouping are I+ for all customer-related postings and O+ for all vendor-related postings (review the earlier sections on planning groups and levels to see where this logic was configured). Because the customer and vendor planning groups are assigned to each customer and vendor master record, all planning levels that are tied to these planning groups are included (A/R, A/P, Purchase Requisitions, Purchase Orders, Purchasing Scheduling Agreements, and Sales Orders) in the liquidity forecast. It is the planning levels that are first displayed on the liquidity forecast screen; you can then drill down into each planning level to see the amounts by planning groups. The sum of the planning groups make up the balance of the planning level.

EXTREME SPORTS TREASURY GROUPINGS CONFIGURATION ANALYSIS (CONTINUED)

ESCashCon

This grouping will be used for cash concentration functionality. The confirmed cash balance, check clearing, ACH clearing, and wire clearing accounts are used as the source accounts. The summarization account 100030 (lockbox confirmed cash) is used by all bank clearing accounts so that cash concentration occurs through G/L account 100030 but includes the balances of accounts 100030, 100032, 100033, and 100034. You will notice that the deposit clearing account is not included as one of the source accounts—this is because Extreme Sports doesn't want to transfer cash that has not cleared the bank yet. It is common practice for banks to post deposits on your account but not make the cash available for a period of some days until it has cleared through a bank clearing house. The target account 100001 (General Bank Deposit Clearing Account) is also included in the grouping. This is where all of the cash from the source accounts will be swept into after cash concentration has run.

Treasury Grouping Headers

Before the treasury groupings that were configured in the preceding section can be used, headers must be created for them. Headers are merely textual descriptions that are displayed in the report header screen when a grouping is used. To create headers for your treasury groupings, follow the menu path Treasury ➤ Cash Management ➤ Structuring ➤ Groupings ➤ Maintain Headers.

DEFINE TREASURY GROUPING HEADERS

You can use the following configuration methods to get to the configuration screen for treasury grouping headers:

Menu Path: **Treasury ➤ Cash Management ➤ Structuring ➤ Groupings ➤ Maintain Headers**

Transaction Code: **OT18**

After entering one of the configuration methods and clicking the New Entries button, you are presented with the create treasury grouping headers configuration screen, shown in Figure 6.11.

FIGURE 6.11   The create treasury grouping headers configuration screen

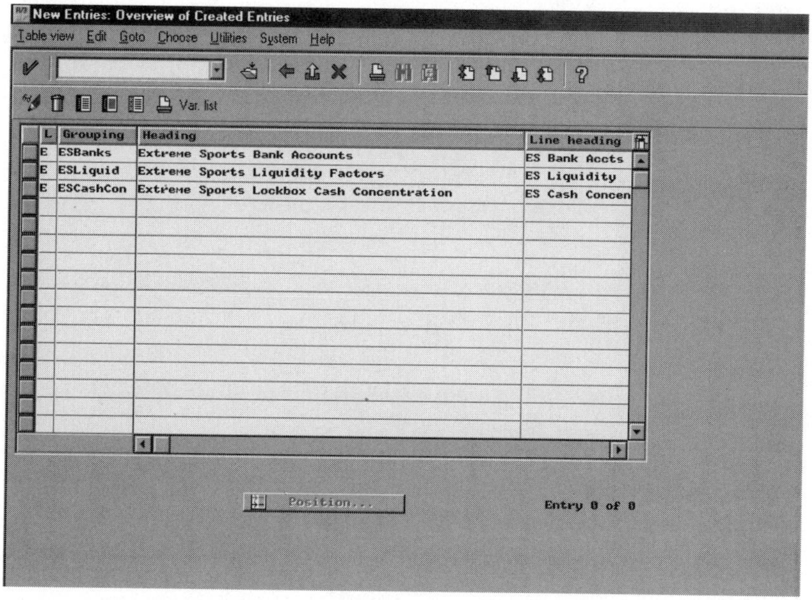

As you can see, there isn't much to creating treasury grouping headers. You only need to enter the language key for the language you are using in the L field (language field), the grouping name that you created in the treasury grouping configuration step, and the textual name that you want displayed on the overall report heading and report line heading in the cash management position, liquidity forecast, and cash concentration reports.

Cash Management Account Names

In the Treasury module, you are not limited to displaying only the G/L account number description; you can create your own descriptive name that can be displayed instead of the G/L account number on the treasury reports. The configuration that allows you to do this is the cash management account name configuration step. To create cash management account names, follow the menu path Treasury ➢ Cash Management ➢ Structuring ➢ Define Cash Management Account Name.

DEFINE CASH MANAGEMENT ACCOUNT NAME

You can get to the cash management account name configuration screen using the following methods:

Menu Path: **Treasury** ➤ **Cash Management** ➤ **Structuring** ➤ **Define Cash Management Account Name**

Transaction Code: **OT16**

Enter one of the configuration transactions. You are presented with a pop-up box asking for the company code for which you want to configure cash management account names. After entering the appropriate company code identifier (1400 in our example), you are taken to the cash management account name configuration screen, shown in Figure 6.12.

FIGURE 6.12   The cash management account name configuration screen

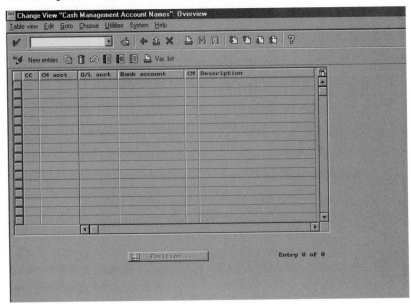

From the screen presented in Figure 6.12, click the New Entries button. You are then taken to the create cash management account names configuration screen, shown in Figure 6.13.

FIGURE 6.13   The create cash management account names configuration screen

CC	CM acct	G/L acct	Bank account	C	Description
1400	ES77NGCASH	100000			ES77N Gen Confirmed Cash Bal
1400	ES77NGDEP	100001			ES77N Gen Deposits Clearing
1400	ES77NGCHK	100002			ES77N Gen Check Clearing
1400	ES77NGACH	100003			ES77N Gen ACH Clearing
1400	ES77NGWIRE	100004			ES77N Gen Wire Clearing
1400	ES77NPCASH	100020			ES77N Pay Confirmed Cash Bal
1400	ES77NPDEP	100021			ES77N Pay Deposits Clearing
1400	ES77NPCHK	100022			ES77N Pay Check Clearing
1400	ES77NPACH	100023			ES77N Pay ACH Clearing
1400	ES77NPWIRE	100024			ES77N Pay Wire Clearing
1400	ES88NGCASH	100010			ES88N Gen Confirmed Cash Bal
1400	ES88NGDEP	100011			ES88N Gen Deposits Clearing
1400	ES88NGCHK	100012			ES88N Gen Check Clearing
1400	ES88NGACH	100013			ES88N Gen ACH Clearing
1400	ES88NGWIRE	100014			ES88N Gen Wire Clearing
1400	ES77NLCASH	100030			ES77N Lockbox Confirmed Cash

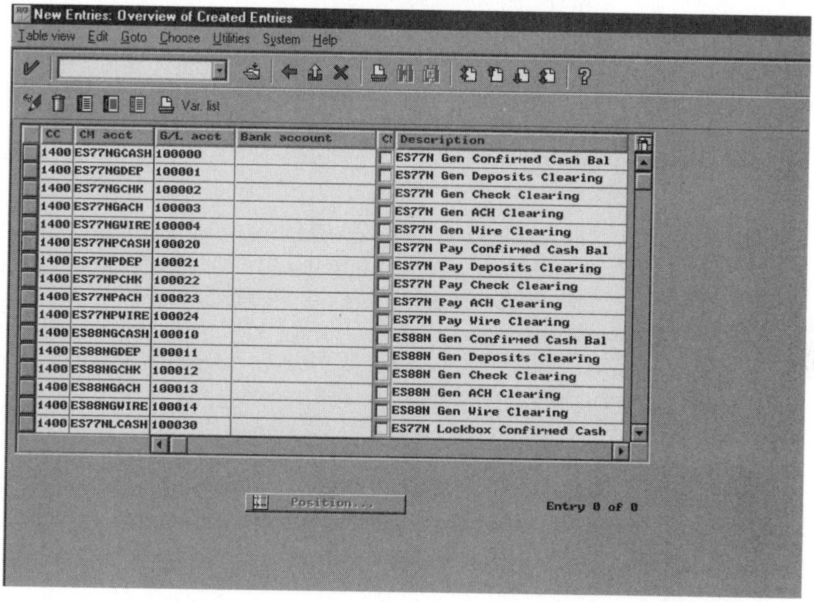

Let's take a look at the fields in this screen:

CC   The company code identifier is defaulted in this field from the entry made in the pop-up box that appears after you enter the configuration transaction code.

CM Acct   Use this field to enter a descriptive name for the account. The name will be displayed on the report screen instead of the G/L account number.

G/L Acct   Enter the number of the G/L account for which the cash management account name is to be used.

Bank Account   In this field, you can enter the bank account number that this cash management account name is related to. Entering the bank account number is optional. It can be useful to enter the bank account for internal bank accounts. Internal bank accounts do not have related G/L accounts—they are available only in the Treasury module and are usually used only for one-time transactions.

CMF   By activating this indicator, you are telling SAP that this cash management account name is for an internal bank account. If you select this indicator, there should not be an entry in the G/L Acct field.

Description   Enter a long text description of the cash management account in this field.

EXTREME SPORTS CASH MANAGEMENT ACCOUNT NAME CONFIGURATION ANALYSIS

In this configuration step, cash management account names were created for all of Extreme Sports' bank accounts (including clearing accounts). The cash management account name instead of the G/L account number will be displayed in the Treasury screens. A naming strategy was used for the cash management account name: The first five characters represent the house bank (i.e., ES77N), the next character represents the account (i.e., G for general, P for payroll, and L for lockbox), and the remaining characters identify the type of clearing account or whether it was the confirmed cash balance (i.e., CASH for confirmed cash balance and DEP for deposits clearing). Thus, the first entry, ES77NGCASH, represents Extreme Sports' 77th National Bank general account confirmed cash balance.

Activating Company Code Treasury Updates

The final piece of configuration that is needed to make cash management position, liquidity forecast, and cash concentration work is to activate treasury updates (cash management activator) for all of your company codes. To do so, you need to activate the Cash Management indicator in the global parameters screen of the company codes. You can refer back to Chapter 2 to get more information on maintaining the global parameters for company codes. You also need to specify that MM and SD data should be updated for each company code. Activating MM and SD data, as well as activating treasury updates for the company code, is accomplished by using the menu path (transaction code OT29) Treasury ➢ Cash Management ➢ Tools ➢ Define Production Startup. The configuration screen is extremely simple; you just need to click each activator for each company code.

Bank Statement Processing

SAP provides you with the functionality to configure bank statement processing that matches how your bank processes your statements. You configure electronic bank statement processing, manual bank statement processing, or both. In this section, we will focus on electronic bank statement processing. Once you know how to configure electronic bank statement processing, manual bank statement processing is a snap to configure. As its name applies, electronic bank statement processing entails processing an electronic file received from your bank in order to reconcile your bank account statements. SAP supports several different electronic file formats for electronic bank statement processing, such as Multi-Cash and BAI. We will focus on the BAI format—it is important to note that this is not the same BAI format as the lockbox BAI file format.

Transaction Types

The first step in electronic bank statement configuration is to create transaction types. Transaction types are tied to house banks. Transaction types will store all of the posting rules and BAI codes that are used by the house bank. (Posting rules and BAI codes will be covered later in this section.) To create transaction types, follow the menu path Treasury ➤ Cash Management ➤ Business Transactions ➤ Electronic Bank Statement ➤ Create Transaction Types.

DEFINE ELECTRONIC BANK STATEMENT TRANSACTION TYPES

You can configure electronic bank transaction types by using the following methods:

Menu Path: **Treasury** ➤ **Cash Management** ➤ **Business Transactions** ➤ **Electronic Bank Statement** ➤ **Create Transaction Types**

Transaction Code: **OBBY**

Follow one of the configuration methods and click the New Entries button to access the create new transaction types configuration screen, shown in Figure 6.14.

FIGURE 6.14   **The create new transaction types configuration screen**

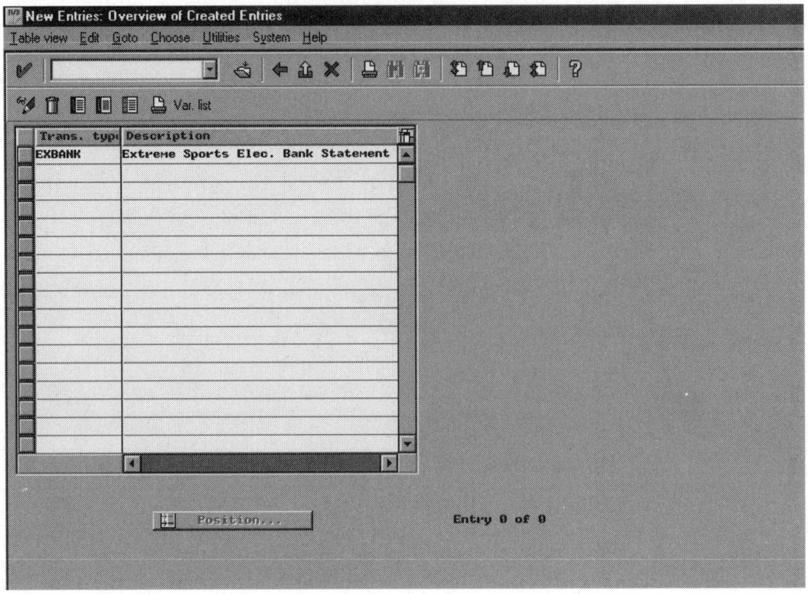

The configuration of transaction types is fairly simple, as shown in Figure 6.14. The only fields that need to be configured are the fields for the transaction type indicator and a description of the transaction type. Additional pieces of configuration will be tied to the transaction type later in this section. Because of Extreme Sports' bank account G/L structure, only one transaction type is needed for use by all of Extreme Sports' house banks. This will become more readily apparent as we delve into later configuration steps.

Now that transaction types have been created, we need to assign transaction type EXBANK to all of Extreme Sports' house bank accounts. Tying the transaction type to the house bank account will allow the system to know what posting rules to use as well as what each BAI code means when the file is processed. To assign transaction types to house banks, follow the menu path Treasury ➢ Cash Management ➢ Business Transactions ➢ Electronic Bank Statement ➢ Allocate Banks to Transaction Types.

ASSIGN TRANSACTION TYPES TO HOUSE BANKS

You can get to the configuration for screen for tying transaction types to house banks by using the following configuration methods:

Menu Path: **Treasury** ➤ **Cash Management** ➤ **Business Transactions** ➤ **Electronic Bank Statement** ➤ **Allocate Banks to Transaction Types**

Transaction Code: **OT55**

After following one of the configuration transactions and clicking the New Entries button, you are presented with the assign transaction types to house bank accounts configuration screen, shown in Figure 6.15.

FIGURE 6.15   **The assign transaction types to house bank accounts configuration screen**

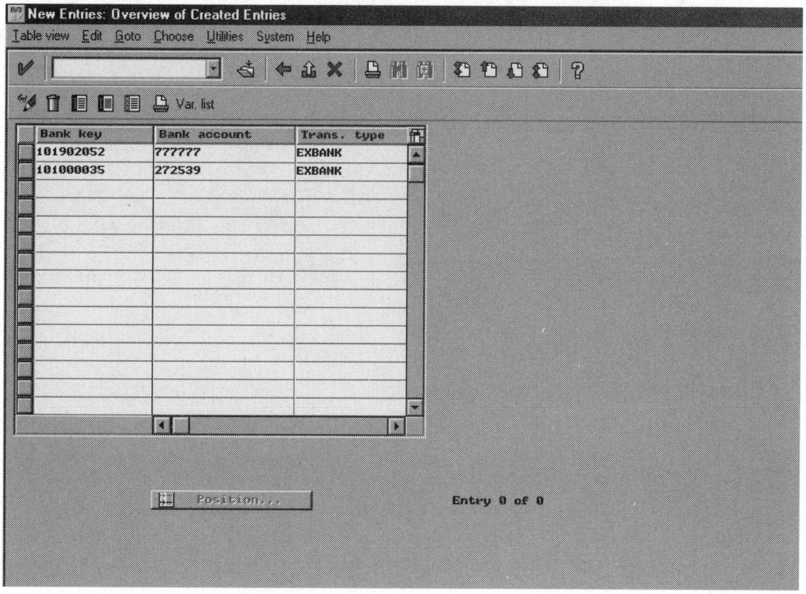

As you can see, you are required to enter the bank key (A.B.A. number), the bank account, and then finally the transaction type that should be used by that bank account. In this example, we have assigned two of Extreme Sports' house banks' (ES77N and ES88N) general accounts to transaction type EXBANK, which was configured earlier.

Keys for Posting Rules

Now that transaction types have been created and allocated to bank accounts, we are ready to configure keys for posting rules. Keys represent different transactions that occur at the bank (deposits, checks, wires, ACHs)—later in this section, the keys created in this step will be allocated to external bank keys (BAI codes) and to posting rules. To create keys for posting rules, follow the menu path Treasury ➢ Cash Management ➢ Business Transactions ➢ Electronic Bank Statement ➢ Create Keys for Posting Rules (Electronic Bank Statement).

DEFINE ELECTRONIC BANK STATEMENT POSTING RULES

You can get the configuration screen to create keys for posting rules by using the following configuration methods:

Menu Path: **Treasury** ➢ **Cash Management** ➢ **Business Transactions** ➢ **Electronic Bank Statement** ➢ **Create Keys for Posting Rules (Electronic Bank Statement)**

Transaction Code: **OT57**

Enter one of the configuration transactions and then click the New Entries button to access the create keys for posting rules configuration screen, shown in Figure 6.16.

There are two fields you need to configure in this screen:

Posting Rule   This field contains the key field identifier for the posting rule. The key can be up to four characters long.

Text   Enter a description of what the posting rule is used for in this field.

FIGURE 6.16 The create keys for posting rules configuration screen

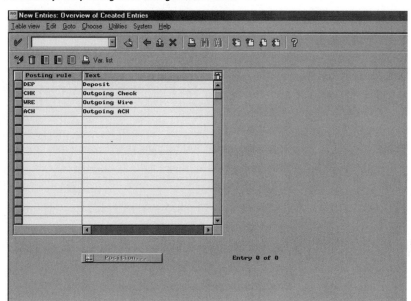

EXTREME SPORTS CREATE KEYS FOR POSTING RULES CONFIGURATION ANALYSIS

In this section, keys for posting rules were created for the most common bank activities—deposits, outgoing checks, outgoing wires, and outgoing ACH. These keys will be assigned to external transactions and thus to posting keys in the next section.

Mapping External Transaction Codes to Posting Rules

Now that we have created our own internal posting rules, we are ready to map external transaction codes (BAI codes in our example) to them. The external transaction code is the code that the bank sends in its file to uniquely represent a transaction—such as a deposit, outgoing check, and so on. It is important to get a listing of all external transactions from your bank so that you have every possible transaction accounted for in your system. This will keep you from having fallouts in electronic bank statement processing from unmapped transaction codes. To map external transaction codes to our internal posting rules (keys), follow the menu path Treasury ➤ Cash Management ➤ Business Transactions ➤ Electronic Bank Statement ➤ Allocate External Transactions to Posting Rules.

MAP EXTERNAL TRANSACTION CODES TO INTERNAL POSTING RULES

You can get to the configuration screen for mapping external transaction codes to internal posting rules (keys) by using the following methods:

Menu Path: **Treasury** ➤ **Cash Management** ➤ **Business Transactions** ➤ **Electronic Bank Statement** ➤ **Allocate External Transactions to Posting Rules**

Transaction Code: **OT51**

After entering one of the configuration transactions, you are presented with a pop-up box asking for the transaction type for which you are mapping external transaction codes (transaction type EXBANK in our example). Once you have entered the transaction type, you are taken to the external transactions for electronic bank statement configuration screen, shown in Figure 6.17.

FIGURE 6.17   The external transactions for electronic bank statement configuration screen

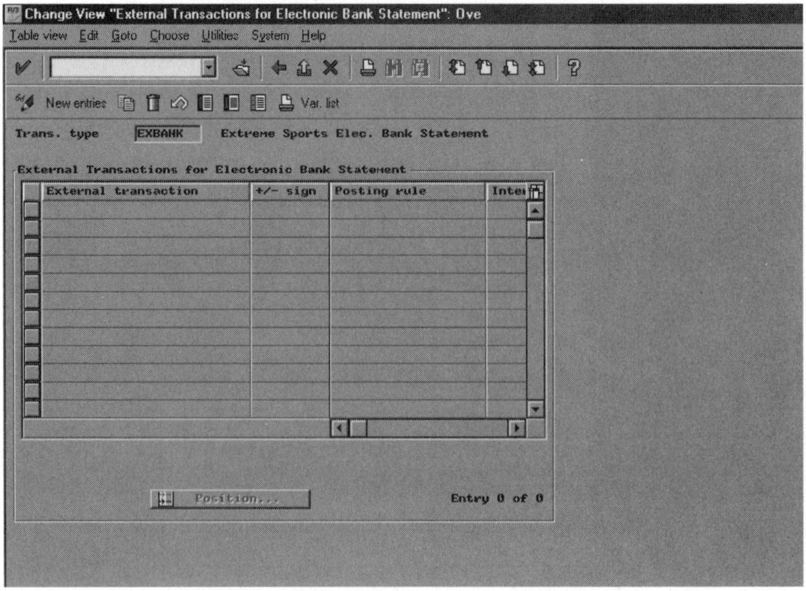

Click the New Entries button and the create new entries for external transactions configuration screen, shown in Figure 6.18, appears.

FIGURE 6.18   The create new entries for external transactions configuration screen

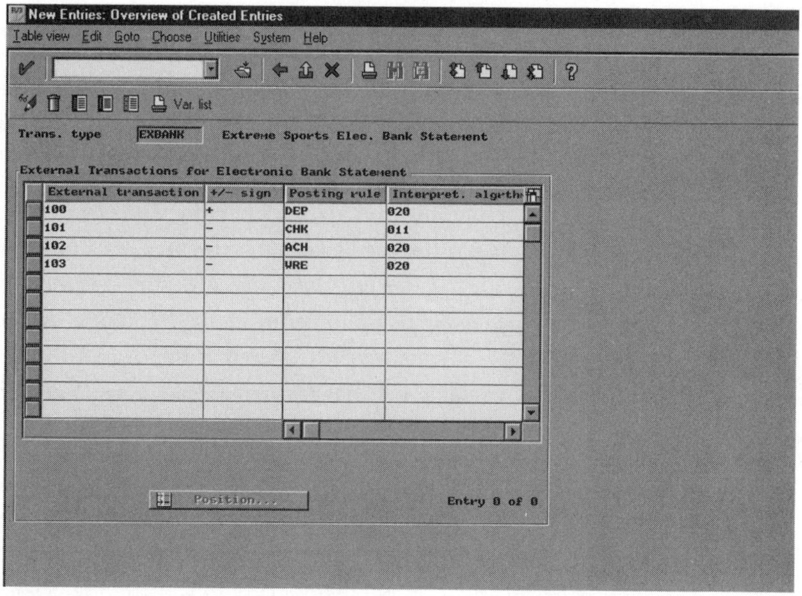

The fields in this screen are as follows:

External Transaction   Enter the external transaction code that your bank uses. This external transaction code will be mapped to an internal posting rule.

+/– Sign   The +/– sign represents whether the transaction results in increased cash (+) or decreased cash (–). Enter either a + or a – in this field.

Posting Rule   Enter the internal posting rule key that relates to the external transaction code entered earlier. Posting rules were configured in the preceding section.

Interpret. Algrthm   SAP comes delivered with several different interpretative algorithms. The algorithm specifies how SAP searches in the system to clear the underlying transaction (Customer Invoice, Outgoing Check/A/P Invoice, etc.). The algorithm uses the information in the Note to Payee field of the electronic bank statement to search in SAP for the matching transactions. The available algorithms currently in use are as follows:

000 (No Algorithm)   Select this entry if want to use a custom algorithm that you have developed in a user-exit.

001 (Standard Algorithm)   This algorithm uses the information in the Note to Payee field to search for either SAP document numbers or reference document numbers. If you use this algorithm, you must enter the valid document number ranges and reference document numbers ranges to be searched on the electronic bank statement processing selection screen. You have to be very careful with how you enter the number ranges due to leading zeros that may entered in the Note to Payee field. It is probably a better idea to use algorithm 011 to carry out this type of search because the user is not required to enter document number ranges with algorithm 011.

011 (Outgoing Check: Check Number Different from Document Number) This algorithm can be used if you want the system to interpret the contents of the Note to Payee field as the check number you sent. The system then finds the correct document number from the check number. This algorithm assumes that the check number is different from the SAP document number. The system will search for matches based on the document number or reference document number.

012 (Outgoing Check: Check Number Same as Document Number)   This algorithm can be used if you want the system to interpret the contents of the Note to Payee field as both the check number and the document number. This algorithm assumes that the SAP document number is the same as the check number you sent.

013 (Outgoing Check: Check Number Either the Same or Not the Same as the Document Number)   This algorithm is a combination of algorithms 011 and 012. The check number can be used to look up the document number, or it can be assumed that the check number equals the document number.

019 (Reference Number DME Administration)   If you use a payment method that uses DME (Data Medium Exchange), such as a Bill of Exchange, you can use the DME information submitted in the Note to Payee field to find the correct document in SAP. This algorithm typically is not used in the United States.

020 (Document Number Search)   This algorithm functions the same way algorithm 011 functions, except this algorithm will search for document number only, not reference document number.

021 (Reference Document Number Search)   This algorithm functions the same way algorithm 011 functions, except that this algorithm will search for reference document number only, not document number.

Processing Type   You can't see this field in Figure 6.18, but it is on the screen when you scroll over to the right. Currently this field is used only for English banking transactions.

EXTREME SPORTS MAPPING EXTERNAL TRANSACTION CODES TO POSTING RULES CONFIGURATION ANALYSIS

Extreme Sports received a listing of the external transaction codes (BAI codes) used by its banks. In this configuration step, the external transaction codes were mapped to internal posting rules that were created earlier.

External transaction code 100 is used by Extreme Sports' banks to signify deposit transactions. Because of this external transaction, code 100 was mapped to posting rule DEP (deposits) with a + sign because it increases Extreme Sports' cash balance. Interpretative algorithm 020 was used so that the system would use the Note to Payee field to find the related SAP document number in the system (customer invoice). This algorithm assumes that the invoice number sent by Extreme Sports will be entered in the Note to Payee field.

External transaction code 101 is used by Extreme Sports' banks to signify outgoing check transactions. Because of this, external transaction code 101 was mapped to posting rule CHK (outgoing checks) with a – sign because it decreases Extreme Sports' cash balance. Interpretative algorithm 011 was used so the system would use the Note to Payee field to find the related SAP document number via a document number search or reference document number search. This algorithm assumes that the check number issued by Extreme Sports is entered in the Note to Payee field in the electronic file.

The logic for the two remaining external transaction codes follow the logic that was used for external transaction codes 100 and 101.

Posting Rules Automatic Account Assignment

The final configuration step for electronic bank statement processing is to assign posting logic (automatic account assignment) to the posting rule keys that were created earlier in this chapter. In the preceding configuration step, we mapped external transaction codes to posting rules. In this step, we tell the system how to post each transaction based on the posting rule. The configuration in this section is very similar to the configuration that was performed for the interest calculation account assignment in Chapter 5 instead of the normal G/L automatic account assignment configuration covered in Chapter 3. To assign posting logic to posting rules (automatic account assignment), follow the menu path Treasury ➢ Cash Management ➢ Business Transactions ➢ Electronic Bank Statement ➢ Define Posting Rules for Electronic Bank Statement.

DEFINE ELECTRONIC BANK STATEMENT POSTING RULES

You can get to the configuration screen for assigning posting logic to posting rules (automatic account assignment) by using the following configuration methods:

Menu Path: **Treasury ➢ Cash Management ➢ Business Transactions ➢ Electronic Bank Statement ➢ Define Posting Rules for Electronic Bank Statement**

Transaction Code: **OT59**

Enter one of the configuration transactions to access the posting rule account determination screen, shown in Figure 6.19.

FIGURE 6.19   The posting rule account determination screen

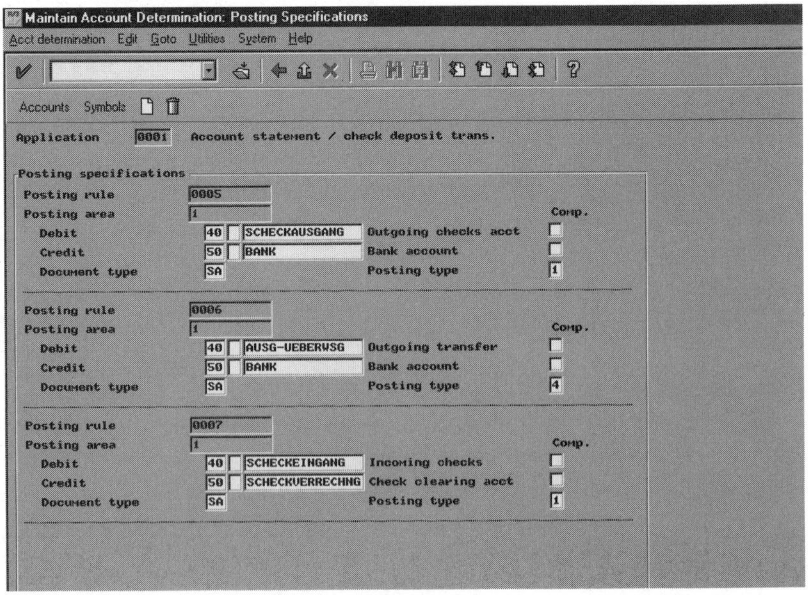

The posting rule account determination screen might look like hieroglyphics at first. But once you understand how it functions, it is not difficult at all. Instead of directly indicating the G/L accounts to be used, you use symbols, which represent different G/L accounts. To create or view the symbols that can be used, click the Symbols button. When you do so, you are taken to the Maintain Account Determination: Account Symbols screen, shown in Figure 6.20.

FIGURE 6.20 The Maintain Account Determination: Account Symbols configuration screen

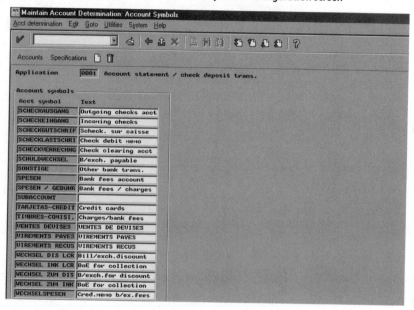

As you can see, several account symbols come delivered with the system. To create your own account symbols, click the create icon. A pop-up box is displayed asking you for the account symbol and a textual description for it. Once you have created your account symbols, click the save icon. Now you are ready to assign the symbols to G/L accounts. To do so, click the Accounts button shown in Figure 6.20. You are then prompted to enter the chart of accounts that you would like to use. After you enter the appropriate chart of accounts identifier (EXCA in our case), the Maintain Account Determination: Accounts configuration screen appears (see Figure 6.21).

FIGURE 6.21   The Maintain Account Determination: Accounts configuration screen

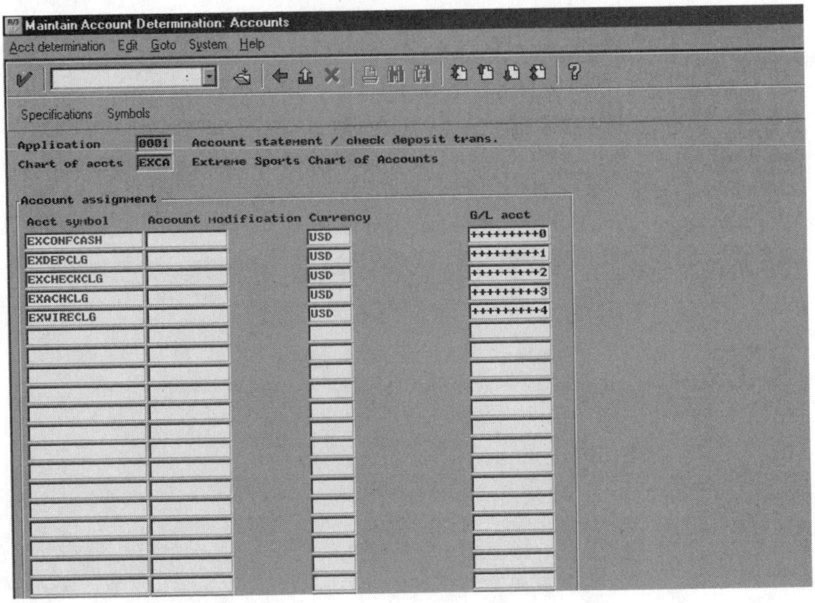

The fields displayed in Figure 6.21 are explained here:

Acct Symbol   Enter the account symbol identifier that you created in the preceding configuration step.

Account Modification   You can specify your own modification key in this field. The modification key is used when an account symbol can be directed to more than one G/L account. The account modifier determines which G/L account to post to.

Currency   Enter the currency identifier that you want to use with this account symbol and G/L account. You can enter the wildcard character + in this field to make the assigned G/L account valid for all currencies.

G/L Acct   Enter the G/L account you would like assigned to the source symbol. The wildcard character + can be used to simplify the data entry in this field in accordance with your bank account G/L structure. You can now see the beauty of the G/L account structure defined for Extreme Sports—each defined clearing and confirmed cash account, regardless of the G/L account series it is assigned to, ends with the same digit. This greatly cuts down on the number of account symbols and posting rules that need to be configured.

Now that G/L accounts are assigned to account symbols, you can create your posting specifications for each posting rule. First, you must save the G/L account mapping by clicking the save icon. Next, click the Specifications button. You are returned to the posting rule account determination screen (Figure 6.19). Click the create icon and you are presented with the pop-up box shown in Figure 6.22.

FIGURE 6.22   The Create New Posting Specifications pop-up box

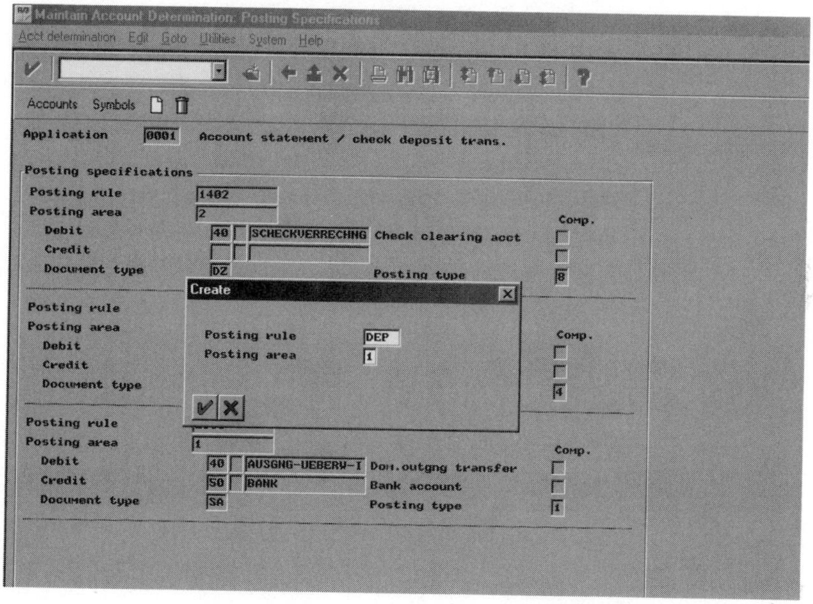

In the pop-up box, enter the identifier of the posting rule for which you want to create the account determination and also specify whether the posting area is bank accounting (1) or subledger accounting (2). In most cases, you will choose bank accounting because normally the electronic bank statement is reconciling items that have already cleared in the subledger (due to payment processing or lockbox processing, which clears the underlying invoice that created the receivable). After entering this information, click the green checkmark. You are presented with the posting specifications detail screen, shown in Figure 6.23.

FIGURE 6.23   The posting specifications detail screen

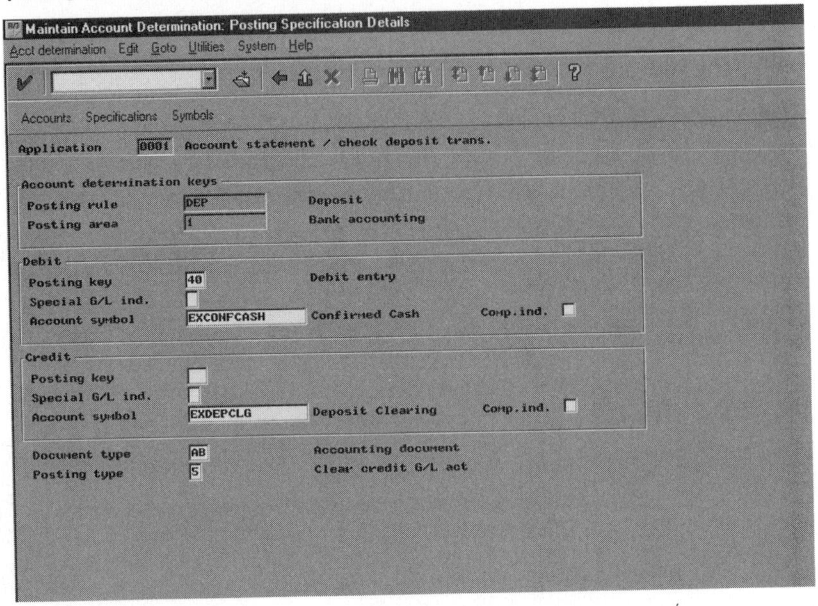

As you can see, you need to specify the posting key and account symbols to be used for the debit and credit entries for the electronic bank statement posting rule posting. You have the option of using a special G/L indicator if needed. Selecting the Comp. Ind. indicator compresses the line items before posting (i.e., combines several line items into one per account). You also need to specify the document type to be used for the posting along with the posting type. The available posting types are as follows:

1   Post to a G/L account.

2   Post to a subledger account in the debit. This can be used only for posting area 2 (subledger accounting).

3   Post to a subledger account in the debit. This can be used only for posting area 2 (subledger accounting).

4   Clear G/L account in debit. If you select this indicator, do not specify a debit posting key (leave the field blank).

5   Clear G/L account in credit. If you select this indicator, do not specify a credit posting key (leave the field blank).

6   Clear subledger account in debit. This can be used only for posting area 2 (subledger accounting). If you select this indicator, do not specify a debit posting key (leave the field blank).

7   Clear subledger account in credit. This can be used only for posting area 2 (subledger accounting). If you select this indicator, do not specify a credit posting key (leave the field blank).

The posting specifications for posting rule CHK (outgoing check clearing) is shown in Figure 6.24.

FIGURE 6.24   Posting specifications for posting rule CHK (outgoing check clearing)

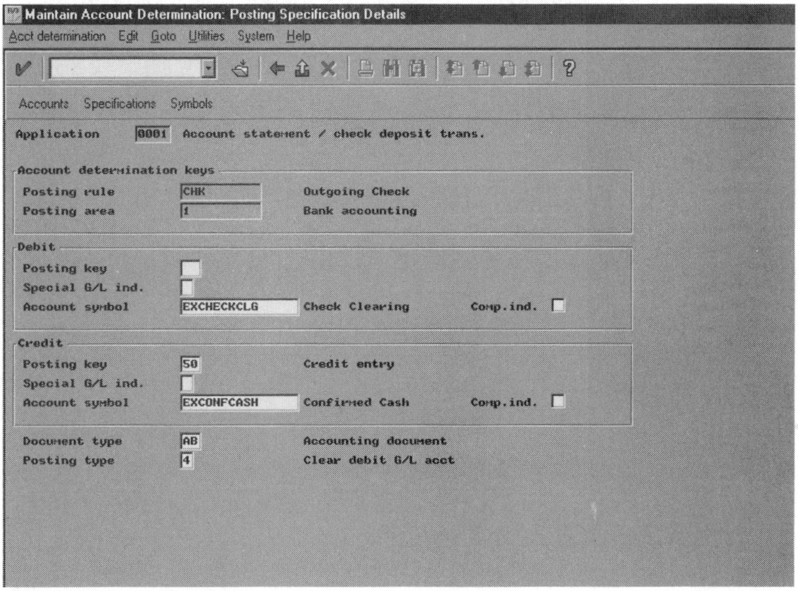

EXTREME SPORTS POSTING RULES AUTOMATIC ACCOUNT ASSIGNMENT CONFIGURATION ANALYSIS

In this configuration step, automatic account determination was configured for the posting rules that were configured earlier. Because external transaction codes were mapped to posting rules, the electronic bank statement will be able to post to the proper accounts based on the automatic account determination configured here. Account symbols were created for confirmed cash, deposit clearing, check clearing, ACH clearing, and wire clearing accounts. Each account symbol was assigned to a G/L account. Because of Extreme Sports' bank account G/L structure, only one account symbol was needed for each type of clearing account (all confirmed cash accounts end in 0, all deposit clearing accounts ends in 1, etc.).

EXTREME SPORTS POSTING RULES AUTOMATIC ACCOUNT ASSIGNMENT CONFIGURATION ANALYSIS (CONTINUED)

The posting specifications (automatic account determination) for posting rule DEP were configured. Extreme Sports is utilizing lockbox functionality, so only postings to the bank account (G/L accounts) are required because the lockbox makes the needed posting to the A/R subledger to clear customer accounts. The DEP posting rule debits the confirmed cash account (+++++0) and credits (and clears) the deposit clearing account (+++++1). Because posting type 5 (clear G/L account on credit posting) was used, a credit posting key was not specified—the system will automatically determine the correct posting key.

The posting specifications (automatic account determination) for posting rule CHK were also configured. The payment program automatically clears the A/P subledger when a check is written by Extreme Sports. The CHK posting rule debits (and clears) the check clearing account (+++++2) and credits the confirmed cash account (+++++0). Because posting type 4 (clear G/L account on debit posting) was used, a debit posting key was not specified—the system will automatically determine the correct posting key.

Exchange Rates

To carry out foreign currency translations and to properly work in more than once currency within SAP, exchange rates must be maintained. SAP provides tools that greatly simplify the maintenance of exchange rates within the system.

SAP comes delivered with several exchange rate types. The most commonly used exchange rate types are M (average rate), G (buying rate), and B (selling rate). If you need to create more exchange rate types or modify the delivered exchange rate types, you can do so by following menu path Financial Accounting ➢ Legal Consolidation ➢ Currency Translation ➢ Exchange Rates ➢ Set Up Exchange Rate Types. You can also get to the screen by using transaction code OC47. For each exchange rate type, you can specify whether inverse exchange rates can be used. Inverse exchange rates are used if, for example, an exchange rate for pesos to dollars is defined (3 pesos to 1 dollar) and maintained but an exchange rate for dollars to pesos is not maintained. If a translation from dollars to pesos needs to occur, then the inverse of the pesos to dollars exchange rate (1/3 of a dollar to 1 peso) is used.

After you have determined the exchange rate types you want to use, you need to define the currency relationships for which you want to maintain exchange rates. To specify currency relationships for exchange rate maintenance, follow the menu path Accounting ➤ Legal Consolidation ➤ Currency Translation ➤ Exchange Rates ➤ Specify Translation Ratios.

DEFINE TRANSLATION RATIOS

You can get to the configuration screen for specifying currency relationships for exchange rate maintenance by using the following configuration methods:

Menu Path: **Accounting** ➤ **Legal Consolidation** ➤ **Currency Translation** ➤ **Exchange Rates** ➤ **Specify Translation Ratios**

Transaction Code: **GCRF**

After executing one of the configuration transactions and clicking the New Entries button, you are taken to the maintain new currency relationships for exchange rates configuration screen, shown in Figure 6.25.

FIGURE 6.25   The maintain new currency relationships for exchange rates configuration screen

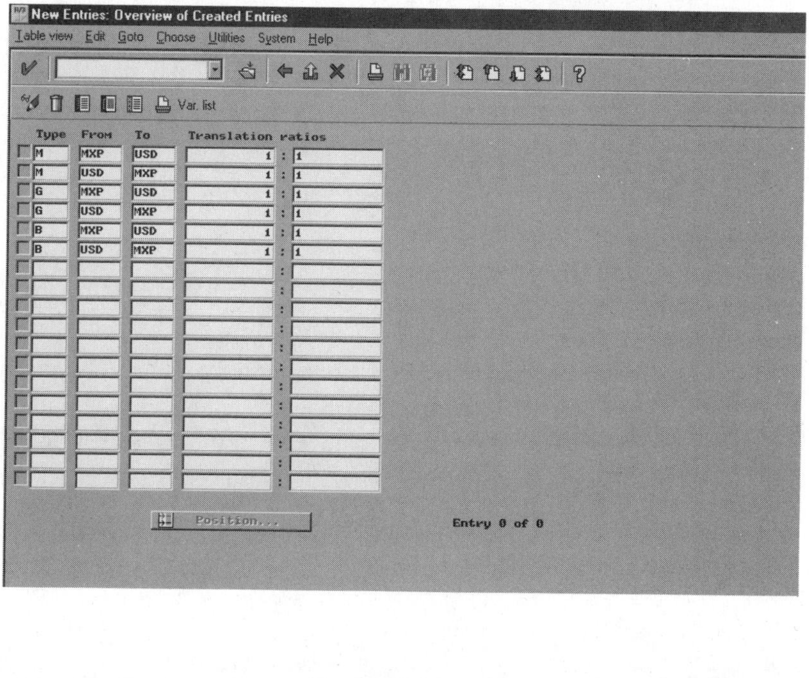

As you can see, you need to specify for each relationship the from and to (from pesos to dollars or from dollars to pesos, etc.) currencies, the exchange rate type you want to maintain values for, and the translation ratio. Normally, it is a good idea to keep the translation ratio at 1:1 because this is how most exchange rates are quoted; it is also a lot simpler to know that you always use a 1:1 relationship when viewing the exchange rates so that you can instantly decipher what the proper exchange rate is. Once you have maintained the currency relationships for which you want to maintain exchange rates, you are ready to enter the proper exchange rates in the exchange rate table (TCURR).

The first method of maintaining the exchange rate table (TCURR) is by hand. The maintenance of exchange rates is a current setting (much like maintaining G/L posting periods) that can be maintained in production by authorized users (it is not configuration). You can get to the screen for maintaining exchange rates through the current settings of either the G/L modules or the Treasury module. The application menu path for maintaining exchange rates through the Treasury module is Accounting ➤ Treasury ➤ Cash Management ➤ Basic Functions ➤ Environment ➤ Current Settings ➤ Enter Exchange Rates.

ENTER EXCHANGE RATES

You can get to the screen for maintaining exchange rates by using the following methods:

Application Menu Path: **Accounting ➤ Treasury ➤ Cash Management ➤ Basic Functions ➤ Environment ➤ Current Settings ➤ Enter Exchange Rates**

Transaction Code: **OB08**

Execute one of the transactions and then click the New Entries button to access the exchange rate maintenance screen, shown in Figure 6.26.

You maintain the exchange rates for the currency relationships for each exchange rate type that you specified in the preceding step. Like most data within in SAP, exchange rates are date sensitive. Enter the earliest date for which an exchange rate is valid, and the rate will be valid until a later date is entered for that currency relationship and exchange rate type.

FIGURE 6.26   The exchange rate maintenance screen

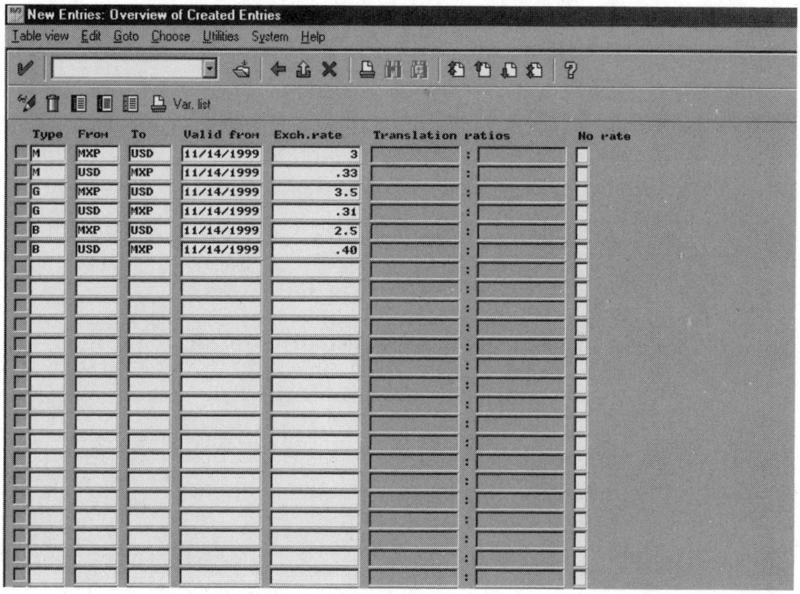

In addition to giving you the ability to maintain exchange rates manually, SAP comes delivered with a program that automatically updates the exchange rate table (TCURR). The program name is RFDEV310. You can execute the program by following the application menu path Accounting ➤ Treasury ➤ Cash Management ➤ Basic Functions ➤ Tools ➤ Load Exchange Rates. This program can also be executed via transaction code FF:1. Program RFDEV310 comes with excellent documentation that can be reviewed online. The program uses the multicash format to upload exchange rates. You will need to work with your financial data provider to get the data in a multicash format the program can use. This program uploads exchange rates for the standard delivered exchange rate types—M (average rate), G (buying rate), and B (selling rate).

Summary

In this chapter, we covered the configuration needed to carry out the basic functions of the Treasury module. We looked at how lockbox processing can be used and configured, and we went over the configuration needed for the cash management position, liquidity forecast, and cash concentration functions of the Treasury module.

The configuration of electronic bank statements and exchange rates was also covered. Finally, we looked at the integration points between Treasury and the A/R subledger, A/P subledger, MM, and SD. Specifically, the following topics were covered in this chapter:

Lockbox Processing

    Lockbox File Formats

    Lockbox Configuration

    Lockbox Processing in SAP

Bank Account G/L Structure Revisited

Liquidity Forecast, Cash Management Position, and Cash Concentration

    Source Symbols

    Planning Levels

    Planning Groups

    Assigning Internal MM and SD Transactions to Planning Levels

    Treasury Groupings

    Treasury Grouping Headers

    Cash Management Account Names

    Activating Company Code Treasury Updates

Bank Statement Processing

    Transaction Types

    Keys for Posting Rules

    Mapping External Transaction Codes to Posting Rules

    Posting Rules Automatic Account Assignment

Exchange Rates

    Exchange Rate Types

    Currency Relationships

    Maintaining Exchange Rates

CHAPTER 7

Controlling (CO) Enterprise Structure

FEATURING:

▶ CONTROLLING AREA DEFINITION

▶ ACTIVATING COMPONENTS/CONTROL INDICATORS

▶ ASSIGNING COMPANY CODES TO CONTROLLING AREA

▶ ASSIGNING NUMBER RANGE TO CONTROLLING AREA

▶ OPERATING CONCERN DEFINITION

▶ MAINTAINING CO VERSIONS

The enterprise structure is the foundation upon which all SAP configuration is built. We discussed and presented configuration for the FI Enterprise Structure in Chapter 2. It is not necessary to complete the CO Enterprise Structure if the CO module is not in your work plan. As described earlier, the configuration covered in the book will include most of the CO module. Therefore, the two sections that define the CO Enterprise Structure are the controlling area and the operating concern.

This chapter will show you in detail how to establish both sections. The word *establish* is appropriate because the configuration work is done piecemeal and is covered in more than one chapter of this book. In many instances, SAP requires that you perform configuration tasks in a specific order. Development of the controlling area and operating concern falls into this category.

The Controlling Area

The controlling area is the central organizational unit within the CO module. It is representative of a contained cost accounting environment where costs and revenues can be managed. If you utilize CO, you must configure at least one controlling area.

Prior to beginning any configuration, it is important to understand the relationships between FI and CO and between the controlling area and the operating concern. The operating concern will be explained in greater detail in a later section, but briefly, it is the environment within which CO-PA, or Profitability Analysis, operates. It is the first step in completing CO-PA configuration.

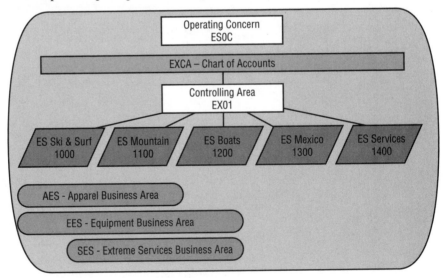

You can see that the link between FI and CO is established through the assignment of company codes to a controlling area. A controlling area can contain multiple company code assignments. Note that, in contrast, a single company code can be assigned to only one controlling area.

The relationship between the controlling area and operating concern is established in much the same manner. An operating concern may contain multiple controlling areas, but a controlling area may be assigned to only one operating concern.

Also, if you are thinking of creating more than one controlling area, keep in mind that there can be no cross-controlling area or cross-operating concern postings in the system. A cross-controlling area or cross-operating concern posting would be similar in nature to a cross-company code posting. Each side of a debit/credit entry would take place in a different controlling area or operating concern.

Controlling Area Definition

Establishing the controlling area is the first step in completing CO configuration. Additional steps include activating the components you will use within the controlling area and assigning company codes. To get to the controlling area maintenance screen, follow the menu path Enterprise Structure ➢ Maintain Structure ➢ Definition ➢ Controlling ➢ Maintain Controlling Area.

CONTROLLING AREA MAINTENANCE

You can get to the controlling area maintenance screen by using one of the following methods:

Menu Path: **Enterprise Structure** ➢ **Maintain Structure** ➢ **Definition** ➢ **Controlling** ➢ **Maintain Controlling Area**

Transaction Code: **OX06**

After you enter the configuration transaction listed in the shortcut box, the controlling area maintenance screen, shown in Figure 7.1, appears.

FIGURE 7.1   The controlling area maintenance screen

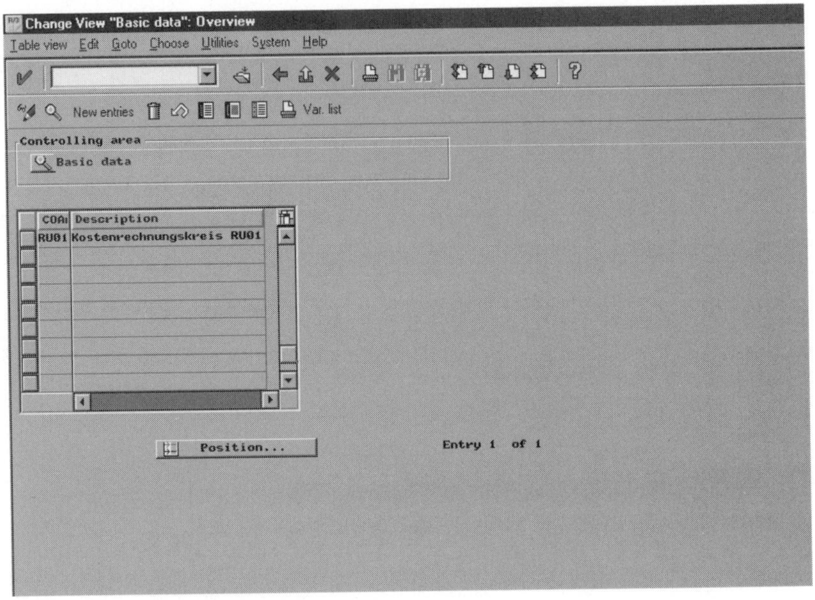

Select the New Entries button to access the controlling area details configuration screen, shown in Figure 7.2.

FIGURE 7.2   The controlling area details configuration screen

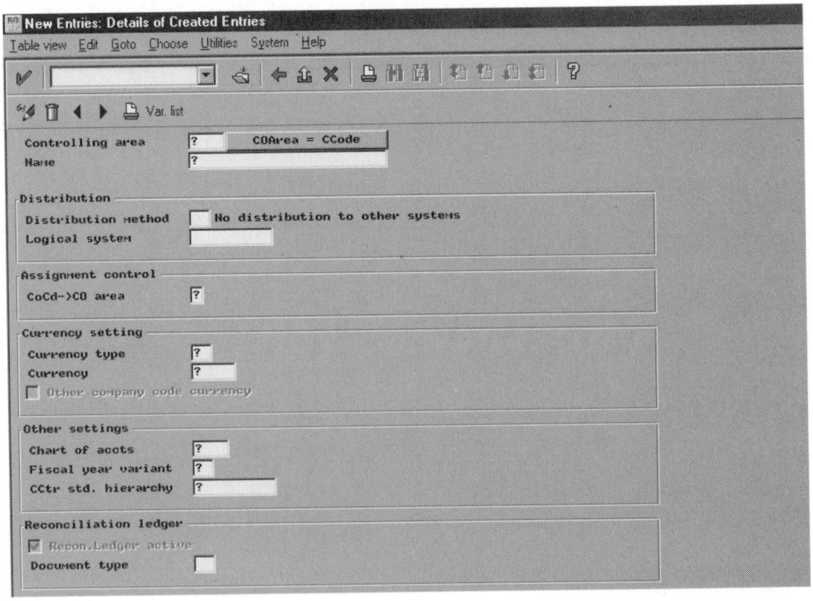

N O T E   You'll notice that a number of the fields contain question marks. A question mark is SAP's indicator that an entry is required.

Let's examine the fields:

Controlling Area   Enter the four-digit alphanumeric identifier of your controlling area. If your controlling area will contain just one company code, select the COArea = CCode button. When prompted, enter the company code ID.

Name   Enter a description of your controlling area.

Distribution Method   This field is relevant only if you are using SAP's Application Link Enabling (ALE) to link multiple R/3 systems together. If you are not using ALE, leave this field blank.

Logical System   This is relevant only if ALE is utilized. Enter the name of the central system for the controlling area.

CoCd->CO Area   This field is used to define the relationship between the company code and the controlling area. You will have identified this relationship when you determined the controlling area ID. The options for this field are as follows:

1 (Controlling Area Same as Company Code)   Use this if you have a one-to-one relationship between company code and controlling area.

2 (Cross-Company Cost Accounting)   Use this if your controlling area will have two or more company codes assigned to it. This setting will activate cross-company cost accounting within the controlling area.

Currency Type   This setting defines the type of currency used throughout the controlling area. Currency settings can be confusing. If you selected 1 in the CoCd-> CO Area field, R/3 uses the default setting of 10, Company Code Currency. If you selected 2, or Cross-Company Cost Accounting, your choices expand. Use the pull-down menu and the following options will appear:

10 (Company Code Currency)   Use this only if all the company codes assigned use the same currency.

20 (Any Currency!)   This selection offers the greatest amount of flexibility when choosing a controlling area currency. All other selections impose artificial constraints.

30 (Group Currency)   This is currency maintained at the client level. Use this option to reconcile FI and CO ledgers.

40 (Hard Currency)   This can be used if the assigned company codes are from the same country and use the same index-based or group currency. This option is often used in countries where inflation is very high.

50 (Index-Based Currency)   This is often used in countries where inflation is high or unstable. The currency is fabricated and is used to support external (outside the company) reporting only.

60 (Global Company)   Use this only if you have global companies configured. In addition, each of the companies assigned to the controlling area must belong to the same company or use the same currency.

N O T E   In many cases, and in the case of Extreme Sports, currency type 20 is selected.

Currency   The entry made for currency type may influence your selection of a currency. Remember that you are defining the default currency for the controlling area only.

Chart of Accts (COA)   Each controlling area can utilize only one chart of accounts. If you selected 1 in the CoCd->CO Area field, the system populates this field automatically with the company chart. If not, you must manually enter the chart name. Remember that all company codes assigned to the controlling area must use the same chart the controlling area uses.

Fiscal Year Variant   The variant must be the same for the assigned company codes and the controlling area.

N O T E   These definitions are unique to the controlling area. Company code currency assignments, exchange rates, and currency translation are covered in Chapter 2.

When you've filled out all the fields, save the controlling area definitions. The controlling area details configuration screen configured for Extreme Sports is shown in Figure 7.3.

FIGURE 7.3 The controlling area details configuration screen configured for Extreme Sports

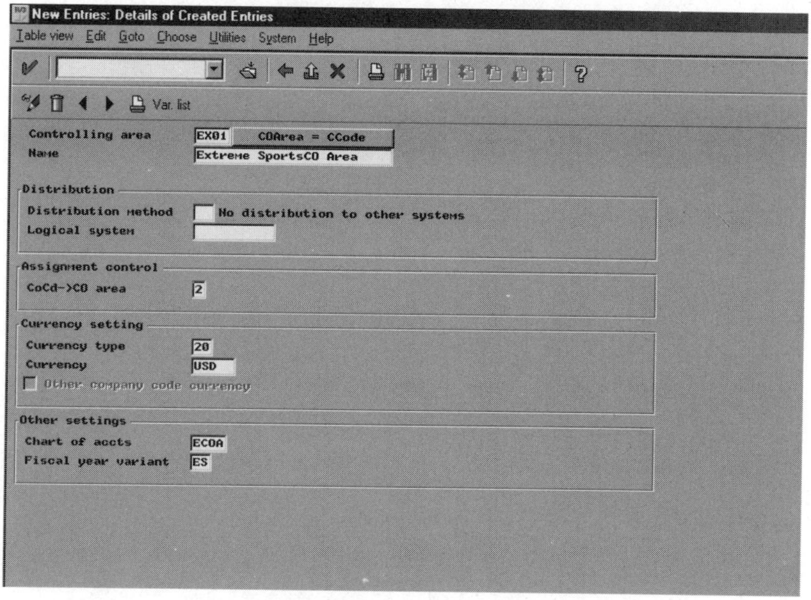

EXTREME SPORTS CONTROLLING AREA DEFINITION CONFIGURATION ANALYSIS

The organizational structure for Extreme Sports includes multiple company codes and therefore needs to maintain cross-company cost accounting. Extreme Sports is a U.S.-based company and maintains its books in U.S. dollars. It has a Mexican subsidiary that operates in pesos, and it is anticipating a foreign sales expansion into Europe. The company's SAP solution does not include ALE.

Activate Component/Control Indicators

After establishing the controlling area, it becomes important to activate the components of CO that are relevant to your project. To activate the components, you must move to the Controlling section of the IMG. Do this by following the menu path Controlling ➢ Controlling General ➢ Organization ➢ Maintain Controlling Area.

ACTIVATE RELEVANT CO COMPONENTS WITHIN THE CONTROLLING AREA

You can get to the controlling area maintenance screen by using the following methods:

Menu Path: **Controlling** ➤ **Controlling General** ➤ **Organization** ➤ **Maintain Controlling Area**

Transaction Code: **OKKP**

Follow the menu path or enter the transaction code. The controlling area maintenance screen, shown in Figure 7.4, appears.

FIGURE 7.4   The controlling area maintenance screen

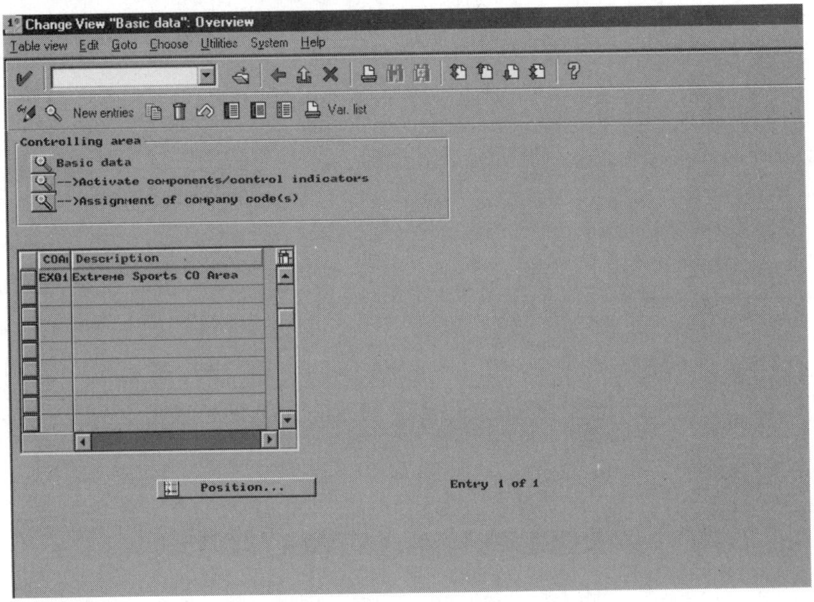

This screen looks similar to the one you used to create the controlling area. In fact, it is the same screen with a few additions. The Activate Components/Control Indicators and Assignment of Company Code(s) buttons now appear in the Controlling Area box.

Components are activated and defined within the controlling area through a fiscal year assignment. You decide whether to establish one parameter that covers all years (for example, from 1999 to 9999) or to maintain a new variant each year (for example, from 1999 to 1999).

The next step is to finish the basic data configuration for your new controlling area. Once you've completed that, you'll assign a cost center standard hierarchy. The hierarchy will not be completed until Chapter 9, "Cost Center Accounting," but to complete the controlling area, it's important to define the hierarchy.

Double-click the newly created controlling area found in the description box in the middle of the screen. The controlling area details configuration screen, shown in Figure 7.5, appears.

FIGURE 7.5   The controlling area details configuration screen

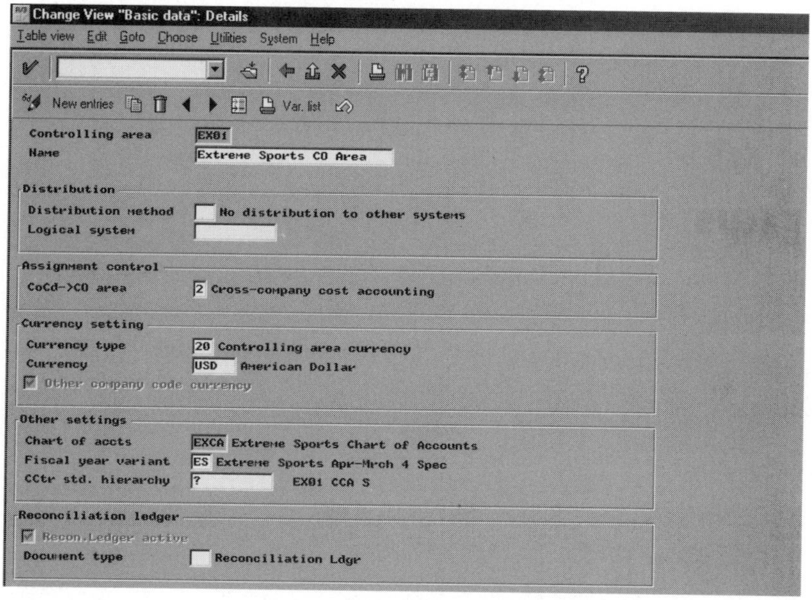

In the CCtr Std. Hierarchy field, enter the name you want to give your cost center standard hierarchy. If the hierarchy you enter is new, a box will pop up and ask you if you want SAP to create the hierarchy for you. Select Yes. If you select No, the screen will revert to the original setting and the standard hierarchy will not be defined. It is important that this step be completed before moving on to the next step.

When you've defined the hierarchy, save the controlling area. Click the green arrow to move back to the controlling area maintenance screen. Select the Activate Components/ Control Indicators button. The control indicators configuration screen appears (see Figure 7.6).

FIGURE 7.6   The control indicators configuration screen

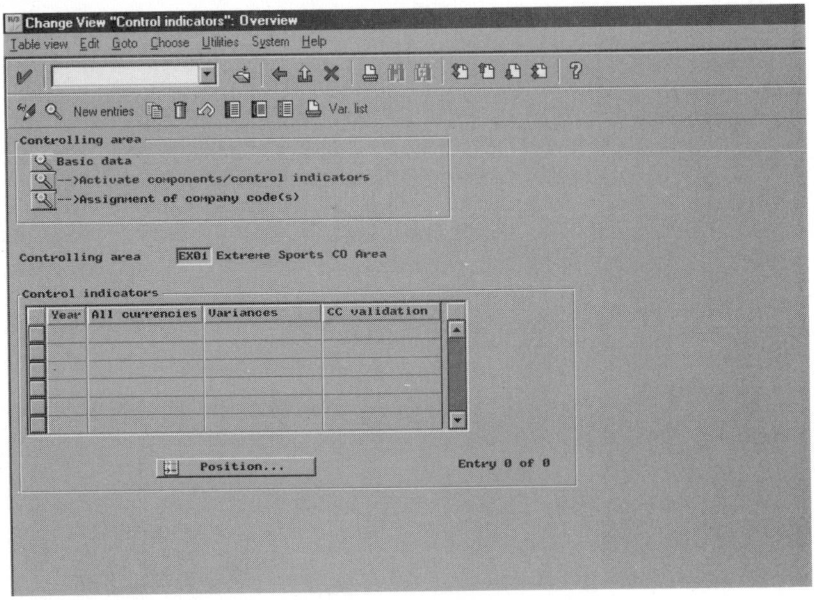

Click the New Entries button to access the control indicators detail configuration screen, shown in Figure 7.7.

FIGURE 7.7   The control indicators detail configuration screen

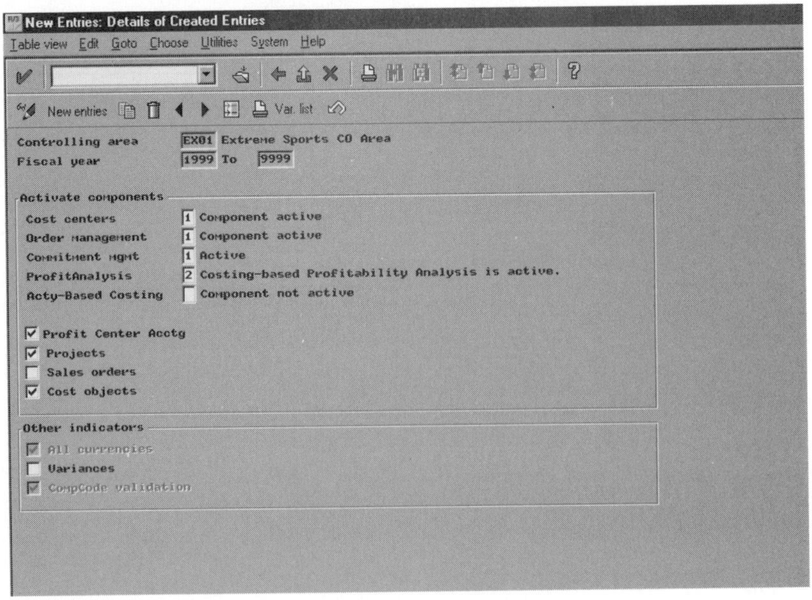

Here are the fields on this screen:

Fiscal Year   Enter the fiscal year when the activation settings become valid.

Cost Centers   If you leave the box empty, Cost Center Accounting (CCA) is not activated. The possible entries from the drop-down list are as follows:

1   CCA is fully activated.

2   CCA is not activated, but you can use cost centers as account assignment objects. The cost center is validated/checked against the master data table. CO is not updated. Utilize this setting if you do not want CCA active today but may want to activate it with the same cost center master data at some point in the future. You can then subsequently post all the cost center data to the CO files. Cost centers must be created in full.

3   CCA is not activated, but you can use cost centers as account assignment objects. The main difference is that cost centers do not have to be completed in full.

Order Management   If you leave this box empty, Internal Order Accounting is inactive. Here are the other options for this field:

1   Internal Order Accounting is fully activated.

2   Internal Order Accounting is not activated, but you can use orders as account assignment objects. The order is then validated/checked against the master data, including whether the order has been released for postings. CO is not updated. Utilize this setting if you do not want internal orders active today but may want to activate them at some point in the future. You can then subsequently post all the internal order data to the CO files.

3   Internal Order Accounting is not activated, but you can use internal orders as account assignment objects. The system doesn't check internal orders to see whether postings can occur; it only checks to see if they exist.

Commitment Mgmt   Use this field to determine whether commitments (for example, purchase requisitions and purchase orders) are updated for the controlling area. Leave this empty if you do not want to activate this function. Select 1 if you want commitment management activated.

ProfitAnalysis   Use this field to define whether and how Profitability Analysis (CO-PA) is activated. SAP provides two types of CO-PA: account-based and costing-based. Of the two, costing-based is more flexible and therefore more popular. Originally, only costing-based CO-PA existed. However, many accountants thought is was important to easily tie to the G/L, so SAP developed account-based

CO-PA. Leave this field blank if CO-PA should not be activated. The options from the drop-down list are as follows:

1   Only costing-based CO-PA is activated.

2   Only account-based CO-PA is activated.

3   Both account and costing-based CO-PA is activated.

Acty-Based Costing (ABC)   With this field, you can choose whether activity-based costing should be activated within your system. (ABC will not be discussed in detail within any chapter of this book. However, we will provide an explanation of the settings. It is our recommendation that anyone interested in learning more about ABC, or product costing, attend a relevant SAP course.) Leave this blank if ABC should not be activated. There are two other options for this field:

1   ABC is activated with restrictions. Allocations are posted as statistical entries on the cost object. The real posting would go to another CO object like a cost center. (The differences between real and statistical postings are covered in Chapter 8.)

2   ABC is activated without restrictions.

Profit Center Acctg (PCA)   Select this field if you want PCA to be activated. (Profit Center Accounting will be discussed and configured in Chapter 12.)

Projects   If you are utilizing Project Systems, this setting becomes important. Project Systems integrates with CO through Work Breakdown Structure (WBS) elements and networks. (Project Systems will not be covered in this book. For further information on the impact of Project Systems to the controlling area, we recommend that you attend an SAP course on the matter.) If you activate Projects in the controlling area, you can use WBS elements and networks as real account assignment objects and CO data is recorded. If this field is not activated, project data within CO is not updated.

Sales Orders   If you are utilizing make-to-order production, this setting becomes important. If you are not, leave this blank. If it's activated, all revenues and costs will post to the sales order item.

Cost Objects   If you are using repetitive manufacturing within your product cost environment, this setting becomes relevant. Repetitive manufacturing uses cost objects to plan and track production costs.

All Currencies   This setting will often default from your controlling area definition. If it's activated, the system will update CO values in the transaction currency and the object currency. If it's inactive, only the controlling area currency is used to update CO values.

Variances   Activate this if you want SAP to calculate and post as a line item variances from each primary cost posting. Variances occur when the actual costs are less than or greater than planned costs. Actual and planned cost variances result when the actual price of the resource is less than or greater than the planned price.

CompCode Validation   This setting will automatically activate if cross-company code cost accounting is activated in the controlling area definition. If active, the setting will ensure that both sides of an accounting or purchasing transaction generate from a cost center in the same company code. And, using the same criteria, it ensures that all inventory activities are posted properly in both company codes.

When you're finished configuring the control indicators, save your settings. You will notice that SAP has filled 9999 in the Valid To field of the fiscal year range. The settings are valid until year 9999 or until you make an entry for a new fiscal year.

If you want to make a change to any of the settings for the next fiscal year, create a new entry in the Control Indicators table. By entering a new fiscal year in the table, you ensure that the validity date for the prior entry becomes the last fiscal year before the new entry. Table 7.1 provides you with an example of multiple fiscal year assignments. The first entry for 1999 was originally valid until the aforementioned year 9999. A new fiscal year entry was then defined for 2002, which immediately changed the prior setting's validity period end date to 2001.

TABLE 7.1   Control Indicator Validity Period

Maintain Fiscal Year	Validity Period
1999	1999—2001
2002	2002—2005
2006	2006—9999

Component activation is complete and you can now begin to assign your company codes.

EXTREME SPORTS COMPONENT/CONTROL INDICATOR ACTIVATION CONFIGURATION ANALYSIS

Extreme Sports will be using Cost Center Accounting, Internal Orders, Profit Center Accounting, and repetitive manufacturing. Because the company will be using Cost Center Accounting, we had to identify a standard hierarchy, EX01CCAHR. In addition, the company wants to track purchase order commitments. Extreme Sports has decided not to include Project Systems or ABC in this rollout of SAP. Because it is not interested in ABC, it has no desire to track variances.

Assign Company Codes to Controlling Area

The FI-to-CO integration occurs when you assign a company code to a controlling area. If, in your controlling area definition, you determined that there would be no cross-company code cost accounting, the company code assignment would default from the entry made. Remember that you entered a company code when you decided on a controlling area ID (see "Controlling Area Definition" earlier in this chapter).

If you are using cross-company code cost accounting, proceed with the configuration steps that follow. Many of the initial steps are similar to those taken when activating the controlling area components. To get to the proper screen, follow the menu path Controlling ➢ Controlling General ➢ Organization ➢ Maintain Controlling Area.

ASSIGN COMPANY CODES TO THE CONTROLLING AREA THROUGH CONTROLLING AREA MAINTENANCE

You can get to the controlling area maintenance screen by using these methods:

Menu Path: **Controlling** ➢ **Controlling General** ➢ **Organization** ➢ **Maintain Controlling Area**

Transaction Code: **OKKP**

Either place your cursor on the controlling area you want to maintain, or select the button next to your controlling area. Do not double-click the controlling area. If you do, the basic data details screen will appear. Click the green arrow to back out of the screen if necessary.

Select the Assignment of Company Codes button. The initial assignment of company codes screen appears (see Figure 7.8).

FIGURE 7.8   The initial screen to assign company codes to the controlling area

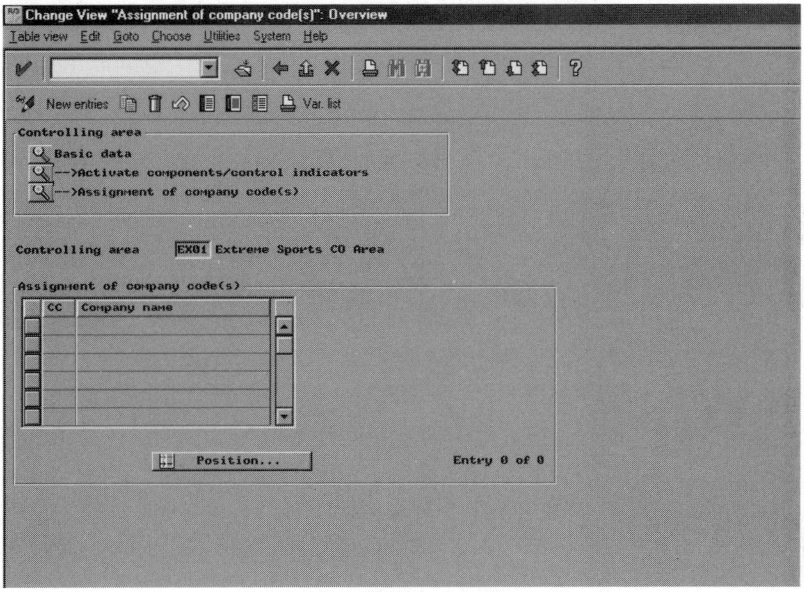

Click the New Entries button in the header. The screen shown in Figure 7.9 appears. You will notice that the company code entry column in the assignment box is empty and ready for postings. Enter company code IDs that you want assigned and save your entries.

FIGURE 7.9   The completed assignment of company codes to controlling area

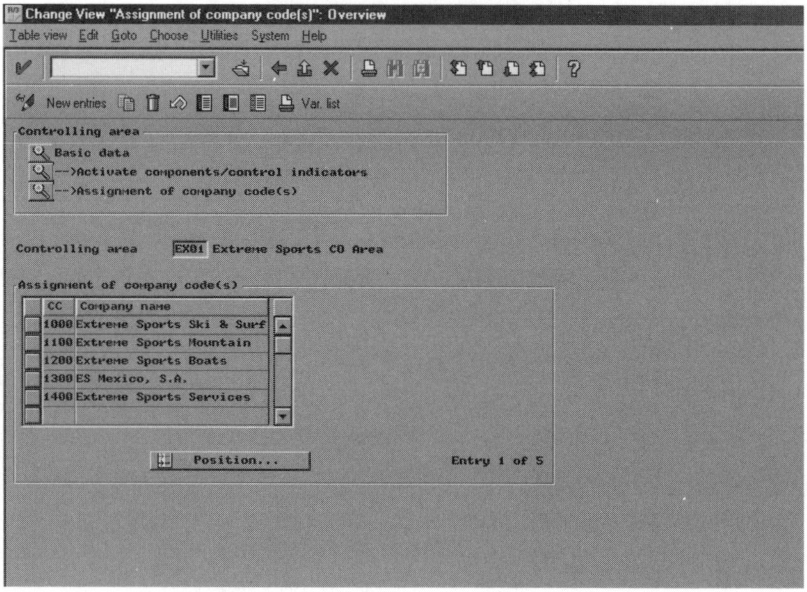

EXTREME SPORTS COMPANY CODE ASSIGNMENT CONFIGURATION ANALYSIS

Extreme Sports maintains five separate legal entities. They are company codes 1000, Extreme Sports Ski & Surf; 1100, Extreme Sports Mountain; 1200, Extreme Sports Boats; 1300, ES Mexico, S.A; and 1400, Extreme Sports Services.

Assign Number Ranges to Controlling Area

Within SAP, all postings are tracked through the assignment of a document number. The document number assigned is dependent upon a couple of factors: the activity used to update the CO file and the number range assigned within the controlling area. Number range assignments can be internally generated by SAP or flagged to allow external (manual) updates. We recommend letting SAP generate the numbering internally.

N O T E Be aware that you should not be transporting your number ranges between clients. There is a potential to accidentally wipe out an existing document range or to accidentally reset the interval status. If this were to occur, your system could possibly contain two documents with the same number in the same fiscal year. Manually entering the ranges in each client prevents any inadvertent duplication.

To maintain the number ranges, follow the menu path Controlling ➢ Controlling General ➢ Organization ➢ Maintain Number Ranges for CO Documents.

MAINTAIN NUMBER RANGES

You can use the following methods to get to the Number Range for CO Documents maintenance screen:

Menu Path: **Controlling** ➢ **Controlling General** ➢ **Organization** ➢ **Maintain Number Ranges for CO Documents**

Transaction Code: **KANK**

After you follow the menu path or use the transaction code, the Number Ranges for CO Document screen appears (see Figure 7.10).

In this section, you'll perform the following tasks:

▶ Set up Number Range Assignment Groups.

▶ Assign activities as necessary.

▶ Create Number Range Intervals.

There are two methods for creating your assignment groups: copy from an existing controlling area or create a new group from scratch. It is far easier to copy a group, so we recommend this approach. Any defaults carried over with the copied group can be augmented later. These augmentations would be necessary if you wanted a specific activity, like assessments, to post to a document number range other than the SAP default.

FIGURE 7.10 The Number Ranges for CO Document screen

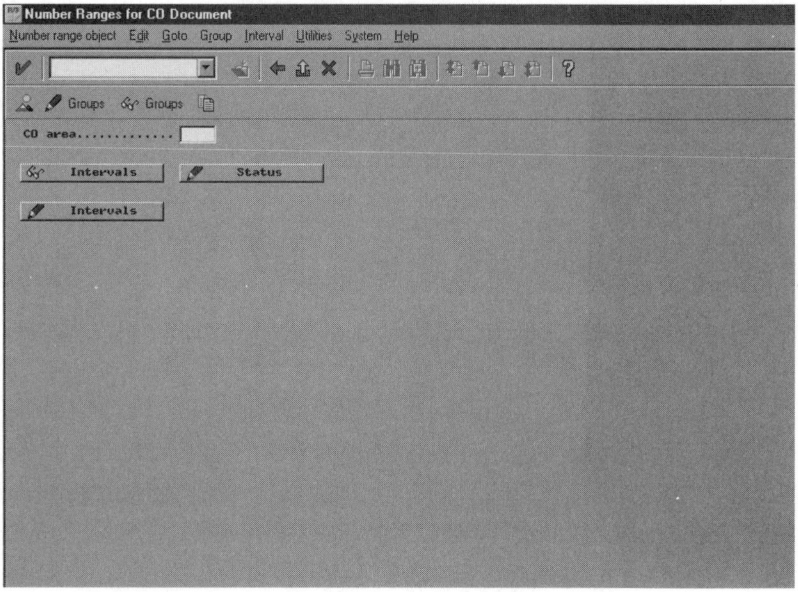

Set Up Number Range Assignment Groups: Copy

In the Number Ranges for CO Document screen, you'll select the proper areas for copying. Follow these steps to set up for copying:

1. In the CO Area field, enter the ID of the controlling area to be copied. Controlling area 0001 is delivered with the system and can be used to copy.

2. Click the copy icon. The pop-up box shown in Figure 7.11 appears.

3. In the To box, enter the name of the receiving controlling area and press Enter. If the copy was successful, you will receive a message at the bottom of the screen that reads "CO area 0001 copied to *XXXX*," where *XXXX* refers to the recipient controlling area.

4. To maintain your number range groups, select the group maintain icon on the Number Ranges for CO Document screen (Figure 7.10). The Maintain Number Range Groups screen appears (see Figure 7.12). You will notice that all the activity assignments are copied from CO area 0001.

FIGURE 7.11 The Copy pop-up box

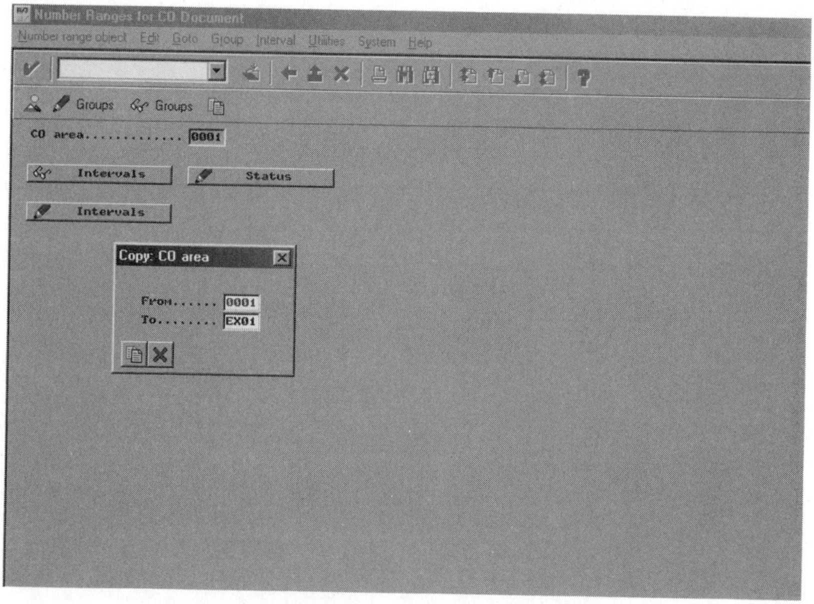

FIGURE 7.12 The Maintain Number Range Groups screen

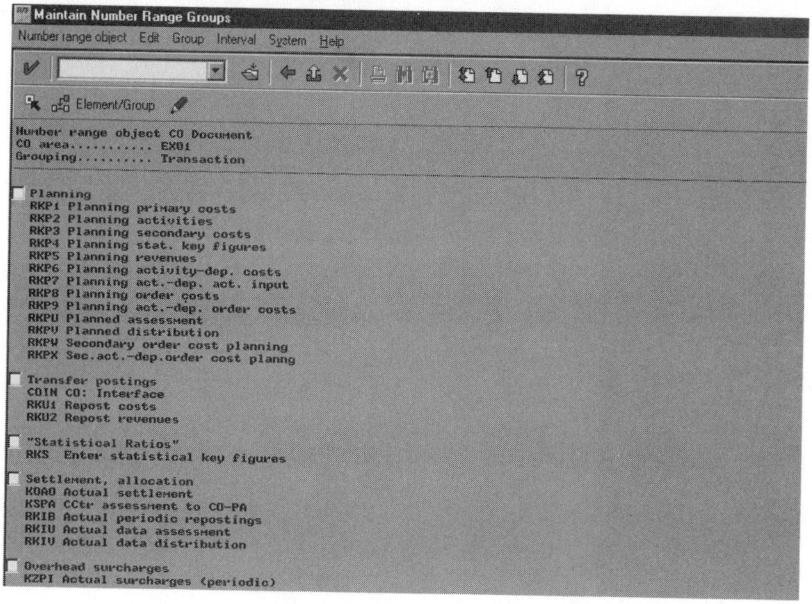

5. Scroll to the bottom of the screen. As you do so, review the activity assignments. At the bottom, you will find all the activities that have not yet been assigned, as shown in Figure 7.13. Depending on your solution, some of these unassigned activities may be relevant.

FIGURE 7.13   The Not Assigned section of the Maintain Number Range Groups screen

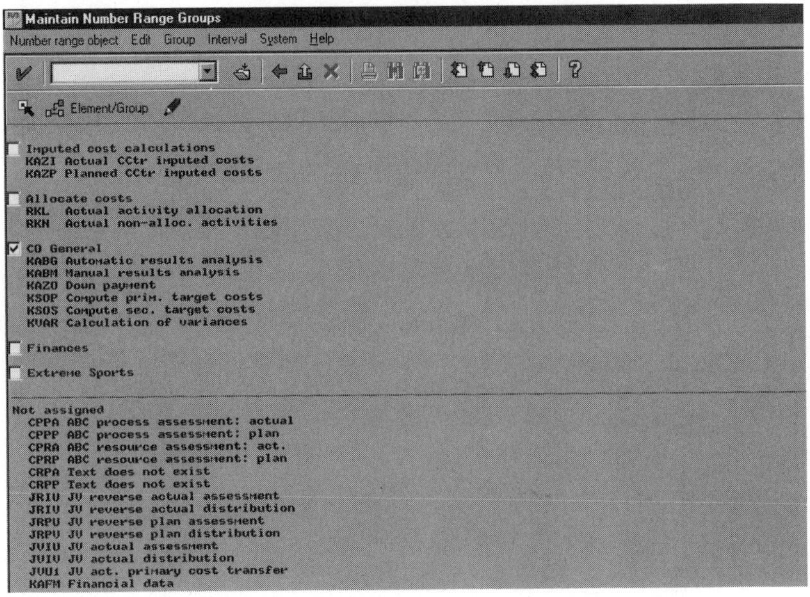

6. To move an unassigned activity to a range group, place your cursor on the activity and choose the select element icon (the icon that looks like an arrow pointing at a box). You will notice that the activity becomes highlighted.

7. Place a check next to the activity group to which you want the activity assigned (see Figure 7.13). Select the Element/Group button. The activity moves from the Not Assigned section to your new activity group. Repeat this assignment as often as necessary.

Set Up Number Range Assignment Groups: Manual

To create a new range group, select Group ➢ Insert (F6) on the Maintain Number Range Groups screen. The Insert Group window appears (see Figure 7.14).

FIGURE 7.14   The Insert Group window

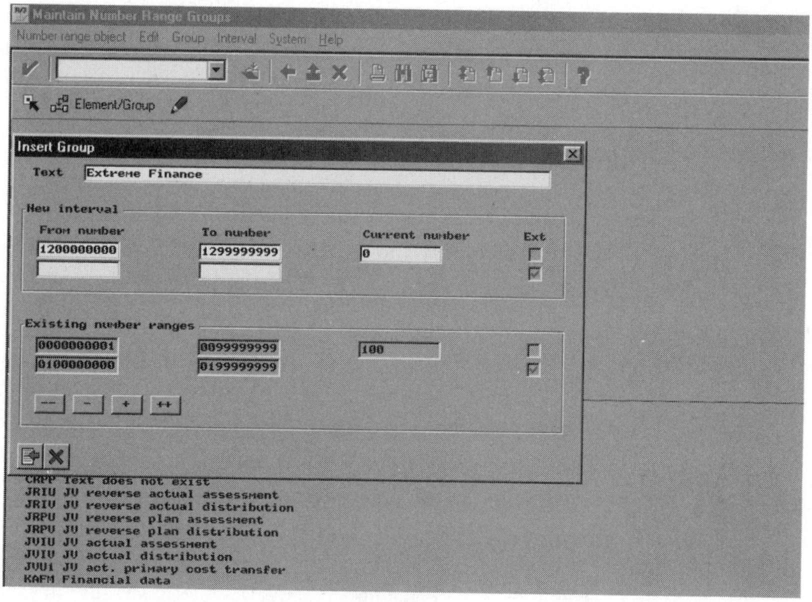

Maintain Number Range Groups

Number range object   Edit   Group   Interval   System   Help

Element/Group

Insert Group

Text   Extreme Finance

New interval

From number	To number	Current number	Ext
1200000000	1299999999	0	☐
			☑

Existing number ranges

0000000001	0099999999	100	☐
0100000000	0199999999		☑

CRP Text does not exist
JRIU JU reverse actual assessment
JRIU JU reverse actual distribution
JRPU JU reverse plan assessment
JRPU JU reverse plan distribution
JUIU JU actual assessment
JUIU JU actual distribution
JUU1 JU act. primary cost transfer
KAFM Financial data

Follow these steps to create a new range group:

1. In the Text field, enter the name of the new group.

2. Enter the number range that will support the new range group in the From Number and To Number fields. Be sure that the new number range does not overlap an existing range. SAP will do a check automatically. To view the existing number ranges, drop to the Existing Number Ranges section and scroll using the + and – keys. When you're finished entering the number ranges, press Enter. The insert box disappears and you are returned to the Maintain Number Range Groups screen.

NOTE If you copy from group 0001, the first number range interval you enter will default to the range group named Finances. Repeat steps 1 and 2 again to get a new group and number range assignment.

Review the new number range by scrolling down until you see your new group. If you place your cursor on the new group and select the Maintain button, the number range assigned to the group will appear. When all number range groups have been created, save the assignments.

To get a listing of activities, assigned and unassigned, grouped by controlling area, be sure you are at the Number Ranges for CO Documents screen. Select the Overview button found on the icon bar and an activity overview screen will appear. To exit, just green arrow back once.

Change the Number Range Status

From this same screen (Number Ranges for CO Documents shown in Figure 7.10), it is possible to review and maintain the number range status for any number interval in the controlling area. To do so, follow these steps:

1. Enter a controlling area ID in the CO Area field.

2. Select the maintain status icon found in the center of the screen (it is identified with a pencil symbol and the word *Status*). A list of the number intervals appears (see Figure 7.15). From this list, you can reset any range to 0 or adjust the number to something more appropriate.

NOTE Resetting number ranges is not recommended in your live production client.

FIGURE 7.15 The Maintain Number Range Intervals screen

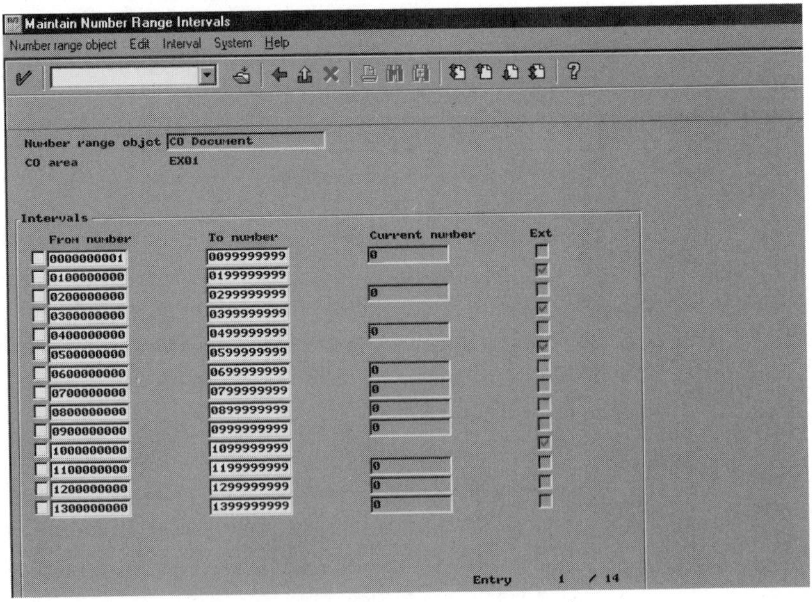

Maintain Number Range Intervals

Number range object   Edit   Interval   System   Help

Number range object CO Document
CO area   EX01

Intervals

From number	To number	Current number	Ext
0000000001	0099999999	0	☐
0100000000	0199999999		☑
0200000000	0299999999	0	☐
0300000000	0399999999		☑
0400000000	0499999999	0	☐
0500000000	0599999999		☑
0600000000	0699999999	0	☐
0700000000	0799999999	0	☐
0800000000	0899999999	0	☐
0900000000	0999999999	0	☐
1000000000	1099999999		☑
1100000000	1199999999	0	☐
1200000000	1299999999	0	☐
1300000000	1399999999	0	☐

Entry   1 / 14

Once you are satisfied with the number range groups and number interval assignments, the controlling area number assignment process is complete.

EXTREME SPORTS CONTROLLING AREA CONFIGURATION ANALYSIS

Upon reviewing the activity groupings, Extreme Sports determined that it could maintain its controlling operations by using most of the standard range and number interval definitions taken from the copy of 0001. Any maintenance to the activity assignments will be minimal.

The Operating Concern

If you have chosen to implement either account-based or costing-based Profitability Analysis (CO-PA), you must configure an operating concern. The operating concern is the main organizational unit within CO-PA. It is utilized as a management tool to analyze specific markets or business segments. As with the controlling area, we will complete the configuration in two steps. With this first step you will establish a name and description for the operating concern. Complete configuration will take place in Chapter 11.

Be aware that much of your operating concern configuration is client independent. The configuration completed in one client will have an impact on all clients in your development instance.

Operating Concern Definition

To change the operating concern using the maintain operating concern screen, follow the menu path Enterprise Structure ➤ Maintain Structure ➤ Definition ➤ Controlling ➤ Maintain Operating Concern.

MAINTAIN OPERATING CONCERN

You can change the operating concern by using the following methods:

Menu Path: Enterprise Structure ➤ Maintain Structure ➤ Definition ➤ Controlling ➤ Maintain Operating Concern

Transaction Code: **KEP8**

In the maintain operating concern screen, shown in Figure 7.16, select the New Entries button. An empty operating concern entries table will appear with the following fields requiring entry:

Operating Concern ID   Enter a four-character alphanumeric key.

Name of Operating Concern   Enter the description of your operating concern.

FIGURE 7.16   The maintain operating concern screen

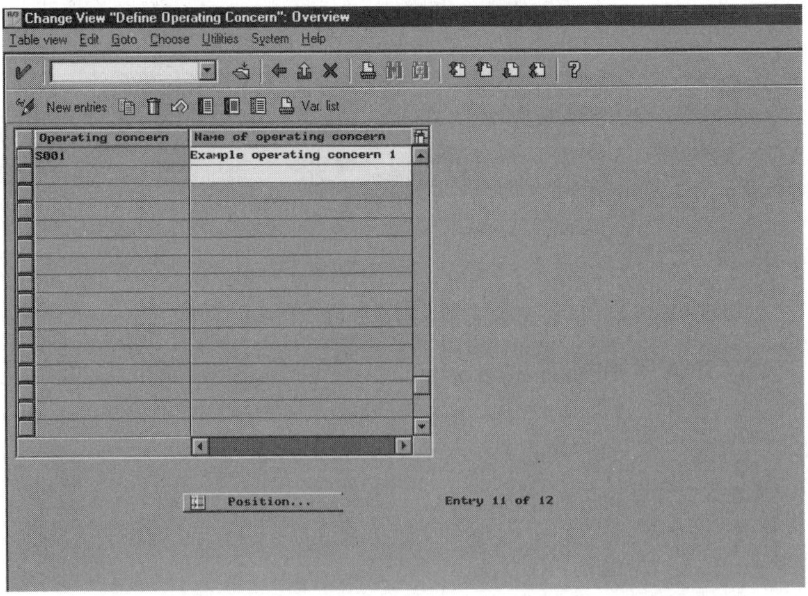

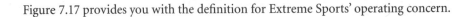

Figure 7.17 provides you with the definition for Extreme Sports' operating concern.

FIGURE 7.17   The saved operating concern data

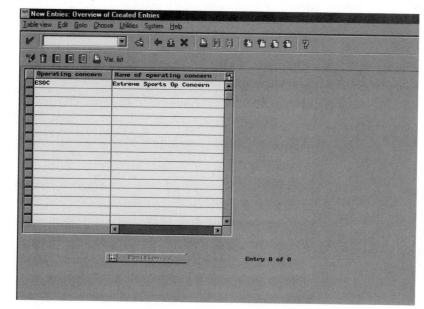

When you've entered the information, save the operating concern data. The first phase of the operating concern configuration is complete.

Maintain CO Versions

Prior to entering transactional data into your production system, you must maintain a version to support planned and actual activity. Version 0 is generated automatically within the system when you create the controlling area. Version 0 is the only version where actual transaction data is posted. SAP allows you to maintain numerous planning versions, and all versions are controlling area independent. This means that all versions are maintained at the client level and thus are available to any controlling area in the client. Please note that controlling area and operating concern level configuration settings can be different.

To complete the base CO enterprise configuration, you will need to configure version 0 for the current fiscal year and Profit Center Accounting. Additional version configuration will take place when Profitability Analysis is addressed in Chapter 11.

To maintain the version, follow the menu path Controlling ➢ Controlling General ➢ Organization ➢ Maintain Versions.

VERSION CONFIGURATION SCREEN

You can get to the screen to maintain a version by using the following methods:

Menu Path: **Controlling** ➢ **Controlling General** ➢ **Organization** ➢ **Maintain Versions**

Transaction Code: **OKEQ**

The maintain version configuration screen, shown in Figure 7.18, is divided into two sections: a Navigation section and a General Version Definition section. In the Navigation section there are six areas to maintain:

▶ General CO version

▶ Settings for operating concern

▶ Settings for Profit Center Accounting

▶ Settings in controlling area

▶ Settings for fiscal year

▶ Delta Version—used with ABC

To make the controlling area functional for version 0, you need to define the CO version and maintain activities for the fiscal year. Begin the process by setting the default controlling area:

1. Choose Extras ➢ Set CO Area.

2. Enter the controlling area ID you are maintaining.

Because version 0 is generated within the controlling area, the settings for the fiscal year will be configured next. When version 0 is generated, SAP makes the version available for five years by default. Should the need arise, additional years can be added once the last year expires.

Fiscal Year Version Parameters

To maintain the version parameters, select version 0 in the General Version Definition section of the maintain version configuration screen. Scroll through the Navigation section to step 5, Settings for the Fiscal Year, using the page up/down buttons found in the middle of the screen. Select the detail icon next to the section and the fiscal year version parameters screen appears. Select New Entries and a new fiscal year dependent version details screen appears (see Figure 7.19).

FIGURE 7.18 The maintain version configuration screen

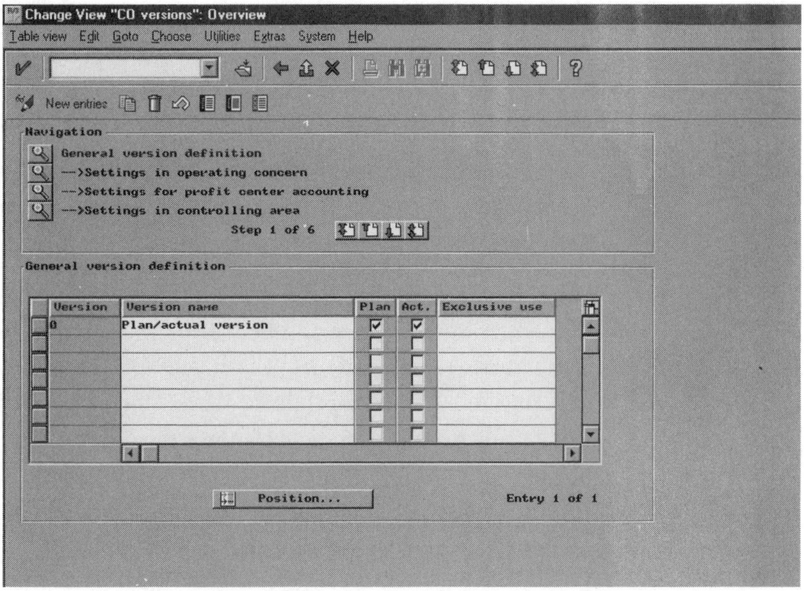

FIGURE 7.19 The new fiscal year dependent version details screen

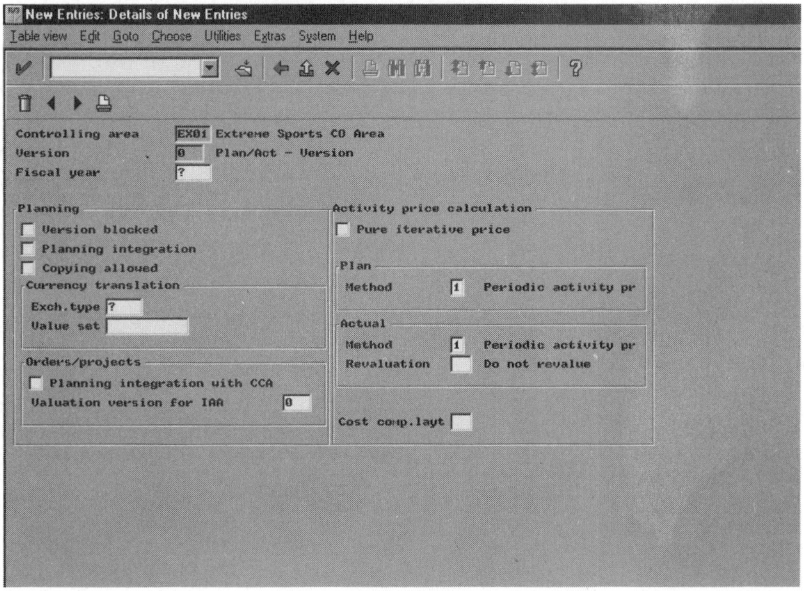

Let's look at the fields in the fiscal year version detail screen:

Fiscal Year   Enter the fiscal year for which you are maintaining the version. You will have to maintain a version for each year.

Version Blocked   If this field is active, planning is locked. This setting is useful if you want to freeze plan values after a certain date.

Planning Integration   Activate this field if you want to transfer plan data from cost centers to Profit Center Accounting or to special ledgers. Although no plan data exists in this version yet, you can change this setting. If plan data has been posted, the integration indicator can be activated through transaction KP96: Activate line items and planning integration. Once this field is activated, SAP posts previously planned line items.

Copying Allowed   Select this field if you want to copy plan versions to one another. We recommend that you activate the setting because of the flexibility it adds to your planning capabilities. With Copying Allowed activated, a company could easily maintain multiple planning scenarios, copying the information from one to another and then making version-specific changes. Upon completion and approval of the plan, the final version could quickly be copied back to version 0 and used in reporting and analysis.

Exch. Type   Enter the key for how you will store exchange rates in the Exchange Type system. P—Standard translation for cost planning—is used most frequently.

Value Set   Enter a date in the Value Set field if you want the same date used for all planning translations. If this field is left blank, SAP will determine the exchange rate on a period-by-period basis. Leave this blank if you want SAP to track any exchange rate fluctuations.

Planning Integration with CCA   This field refers to integration with internal orders and WBS elements. If this field is activated, any planned order settlements will be picked up in Cost Center Accounting. In addition, any planned assessments, distributions, or indirect activity allocations from cost centers to orders/WBS elements will be permitted.

Also, if Planning Integration with CCA is activated, integration could occur between orders/WBS elements and PCA and/or special ledgers.

Valuation Version for IAA   IAA stands for Indirect Activity Allocation. This field can be set only if Planning Integration with CCA is inactive. The default version from SAP is 0.

Pure Iterative Price   This field should be activated if you wish to maintain parallel activity prices within one version. The requirement for activation is that you must manually set the allocation prices during your activity type planning. If this field is not activated, SAP only calculates the prices resulting from your activity planning.

Plan Method   Use this field to choose a method for activity price planning. SAP provides three methods: periodic, average, and cumulative.

Actual Method   Similar to Plan Method, use Actual Method to choose the type of activity for price calculations. SAP offers three types of actual activity price calculations: periodic, average, and cumulative.

Revaluation   Use this field to decide whether actual activities are revaluated or not. If it's checked, you can determine whether actual activity is revaluated using only an actual price or both the actual and the planned price.

Cost Comp. Layt   If activity pricing is used in Product Costing or Cost Center Accounting and you are using a cost component layout, enter the desired layout key in the Cost Comp. Layt box.

When you have completed your settings, save the version (see Figure 7.20). The next step is to maintain the version settings for Profit Center Accounting.

FIGURE 7.20   Extreme Sports' CO settings

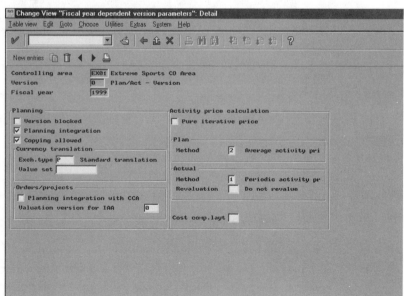

Profit Center Accounting Version Parameters

While in the CO Versions change maintenance transaction OKEQ, select the version you wish to maintain and choose Settings for Profit Center Accounting. The EC-PCA Fiscal Year Dependent Version parameters screen appears. Figure 7.21 shows this screen configured for Extreme Sports.

FIGURE 7.21   The EC-PCA Fiscal Year Dependent Version parameters screen

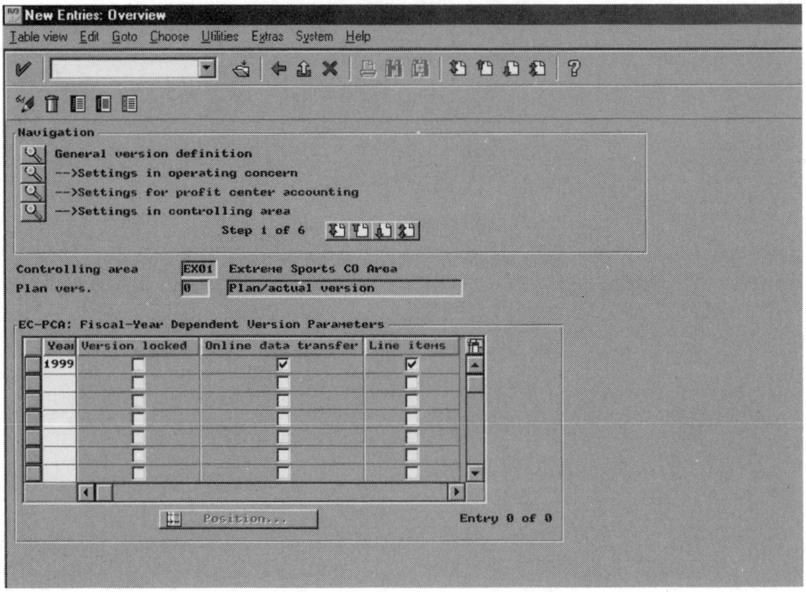

Select New Entries. In the Version Parameters box, there are several fields to complete:

Fiscal Year   Enter the fiscal year for which the settings are valid.

Version Locked   Activate Version Locked if the version should be protected from entries or changes.

Online Data Transfer   If this field is activated, all transactions will update PCA automatically. If it's not activated, postings will have to be transferred manually through special transactions.

Line Items   Activate Line Items if you want to use line item postings for all planning transactions.

When finished, save your settings. That screen concludes the version maintenance for now. As stated earlier, additional maintenance will be covered in later chapters.

EXTREME SPORTS CO VERSION CONFIGURATION ANALYSIS

Extreme Sports requires that only cost center planning roll to the assigned profit center for P&L reporting. The company would like to recognize exchange rate fluctuations in its plan versus actual estimates. The company would also like to have the ability to copy any version. Extreme Sports anticipates having multiple planning versions to support various "what-if" scenarios. When planning is complete, version 1 will be locked and used for Plan to Forecast comparisons. Plan version 0 will then become a forecast version to be changed periodically.

Summary

Chapter 7 is probably the single most important chapter you will cover in CO configuration. Within this chapter, we developed the foundation for the entire CO structure. All other chapters from this point forward will use the configuration discussed here. It may be necessary, as you get further into the system development, to revisit some of the topics covered in this chapter.

Much of the SAP configuration is trial and error. It is not uncommon to develop two or three controlling areas before the right mix of settings are found. Do not be afraid to try different ideas. People find more solutions on the fifth attempt than the first.

For your reference, the following topics were covered in this chapter:

The Controlling Area

Controlling Area Definition

Activate Component/Control Indicators

Assign Company Codes to Controlling Area

Assign Number Ranges to Controlling Area

The Operating Concern

Operating Concern Definition

Maintain CO Versions

CHAPTER 8

Cost Element Accounting

FEATURING:

W ithin the Controlling module are four distinct master data types: cost elements, cost centers, activity types, and statistical key figures. Each is tightly integrated with the others to provide the basis for transactional postings in Controlling. At the center of all the transactional activity are cost elements.

Each posting in cost accounting is linked to a cost element and at least one controlling object, such as a cost center or internal order. Cost elements are also links to the general ledger in the FI module because no primary cost element can exist without its identical twin first being created in FI. The exception to the rule is the relationship that imputed cost elements share with the chart of accounts and the ledger within FI. Imputed cost elements are primary elements, but they are created only in Controlling.

SAP also accommodates internal CO activity through secondary cost elements. Although not linked to general ledger accounts, they are just as important. To keep all the internal CO activity in sync with the FI ledger, Cost Element Accounting utilizes the reconciliation ledger.

To begin, you need to establish the primary cost elements in the CO module.

Cost Element Types

There are two distinct cost element types within the Controlling (CO) module: primary and secondary. In simple terms, primary cost elements can be directly posted to, whereas secondary cost elements must be acted upon by another transaction that will determine the cost element for you. An example of such a transaction is a cost center assessment. Another technical distinction is that a primary cost element is linked to a G/L account that must be created first in the FI chart of accounts. A secondary cost element can be created only in Controlling.

Both primary and secondary cost element types can be broken down further to cost element categories. Categories allow SAP to determine when a cost element should be uniquely utilized within Controlling.

Primary Cost Element Categories

The primary cost element categories will be the first to be defined (recall that the primary cost elements are used for direct postings and must be accompanied by a G/L account in FI).

The categories are as follows:

01: General Primary Cost Elements   Used to capture all primary cost accounting transactions.

03: Imputed Cost Elements, Cost Element Percentage Method   Used in Cost Center Accounting to post calculated imputed costs. Create in CO only.

04: Imputed Cost Elements, Target = Actual Method   Used in Cost Center Accounting to post calculated imputed costs. Create in CO only.

11: Revenue Elements   Used to post revenue in Controlling. Revenues are tracked in Profitability Analysis within Controlling and in Profit Center Accounting in Enterprise Controlling.

12: Sales Deductions   Used by CO to track any sales adjustments or deductions.

N O T E   If you open revenue postings on a cost center, you can use categories 11 and 12 to update the cost center balance. The cost center balance will be updated statistically. SAP will still require a real cost object, either a profitability segment or a sales order.

22: External Settlements   Used to post any settlement to an object outside of Controlling. An example of such a transaction is settlement from an internal order to a G/L account.

90: Financial Accounting Balance Sheet Accounts   *This category has been removed from the options after version 3.0D.*

Secondary Cost Elements Categories

Secondary cost elements are used strictly for internal CO postings like assessments and settlements. The categories for each type are described here:

21: Internal Settlements   Used to track internal settlement activity. An example of internal settlement is settlement from an internal order to a cost center.

31: Results Analysis   Used to track results analysis activity from an internal order or project.

41: Overhead   Used to allocate indirect costs from cost centers to orders.

42: Assessment   Used during assessment to allocate costs.

43: Indirect Activity Allocation   Used to allocate costs, like labor and overhead in a maintenance order, during internal activity postings.

80: Internal Revenue   Used to track internal revenue allocations within CO.

81: Change in stock from internal shipments.

82: Deliveries from other profit centers   Should be used only to track allocations within Profit Center Accounting.

Automatic Cost Element Creation

Primary cost elements can be created either manually or through an automatic batch run. The automated approach is recommended when you're first creating your cost elements because it is the quickest solution. The first of three steps in the process is to define the relationship between the account range and category. The second step is creation of a batch input session, and the third is executing the session.

Define Default Settings

To define default settings, follow the menu path Controlling ➤ Overhead Cost Controlling ➤ Cost and Revenue Element Accounting ➤ Master Data ➤ Cost Elements ➤ Automatic Creation of Primary and Secondary Cost Elements ➤ Make Default Settings.

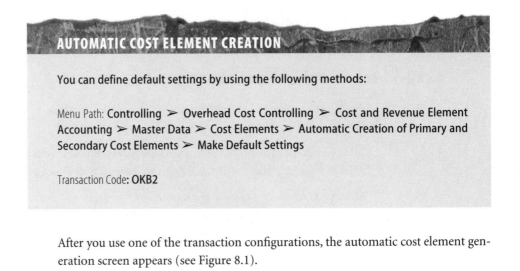

AUTOMATIC COST ELEMENT CREATION

You can define default settings by using the following methods:

Menu Path: **Controlling** ➤ **Overhead Cost Controlling** ➤ **Cost and Revenue Element Accounting** ➤ **Master Data** ➤ **Cost Elements** ➤ **Automatic Creation of Primary and Secondary Cost Elements** ➤ **Make Default Settings**

Transaction Code: **OKB2**

After you use one of the transaction configurations, the automatic cost element generation screen appears (see Figure 8.1).

FIGURE 8.1   The automatic cost element generation screen

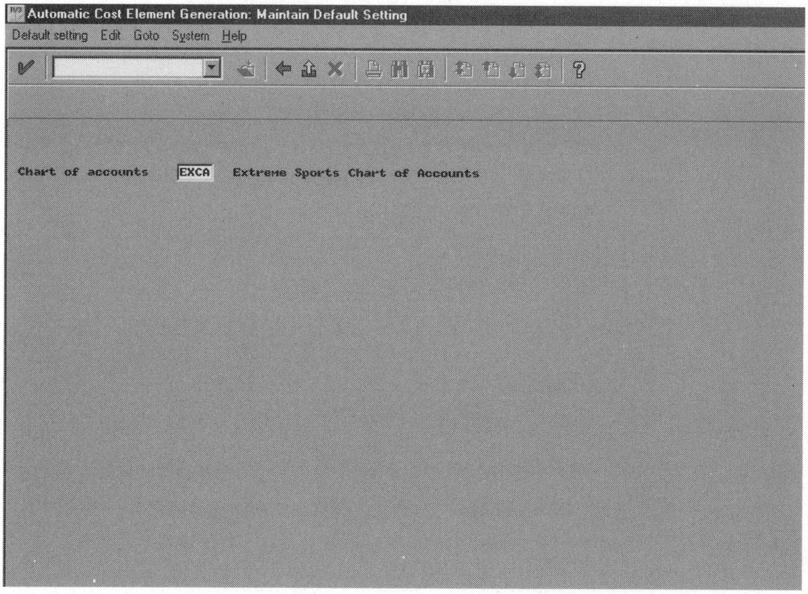

Enter the name of the chart of accounts from which you want to generate your cost elements and press Enter. The automatic cost element generation default setting screen appears (see Figure 8.2). We've already entered the fields we want to configure for Extreme Sports.

FIGURE 8.2   The automatic cost element generation default setting screen

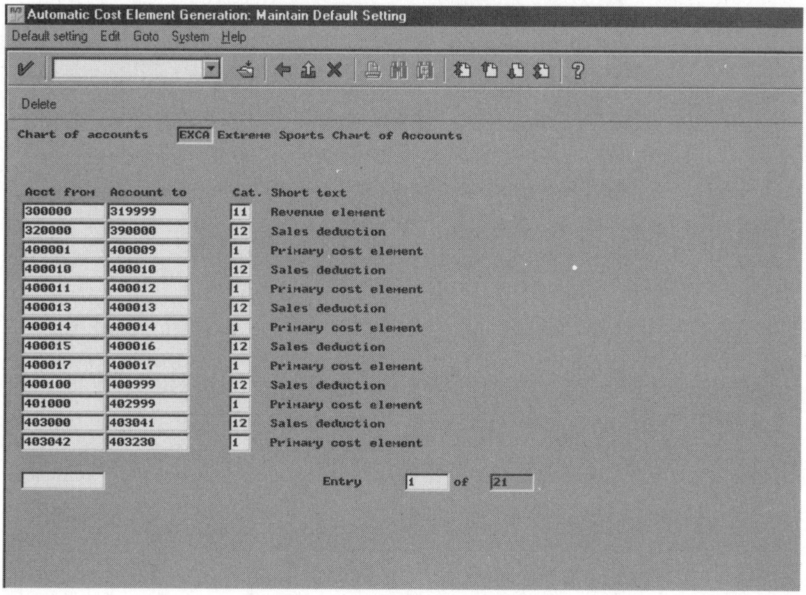

Here are the fields on the screen in Figure 8.2:

Acct From   Enter the beginning account range for a specific category.

Account To   Enter the ending account range for a specific category.

NOTE   The account ranges do not have to be in numerical order. The system will adjust them accordingly.

Cat.   Enter the cost element category that relates to the corresponding account range (see "Cost Element Types" earlier in this chapter).

Short Text   The short text will default from the category assignment in the preceding field.

Remember to use the possible entries key (F4) or the drop-down arrow on the field to search for accounts. To add new lines, use the path Edit ➢ New Entries. When you're finished, save the default settings.

TIP   Remember, you can copy only revenue and cost elements from the chart of accounts. No balance sheet accounts can be copied to Controlling.

Define Batch Input Session

Once the default settings are complete, you must create the cost element creation batch run session. To do so, follow the menu path Controlling ➢ Overhead Cost Controlling ➢ Cost and Revenue Element Accounting ➢ Master Data ➢ Cost Elements ➢ Automatic Creation of Primary and Secondary Cost Elements ➢ Create Batch Input Session. The Create Batch Input Session screen appears (see Figure 8.3). You will want to change most of the default settings.

FIGURE 8.3   The Create Batch Input Session screen

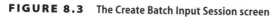

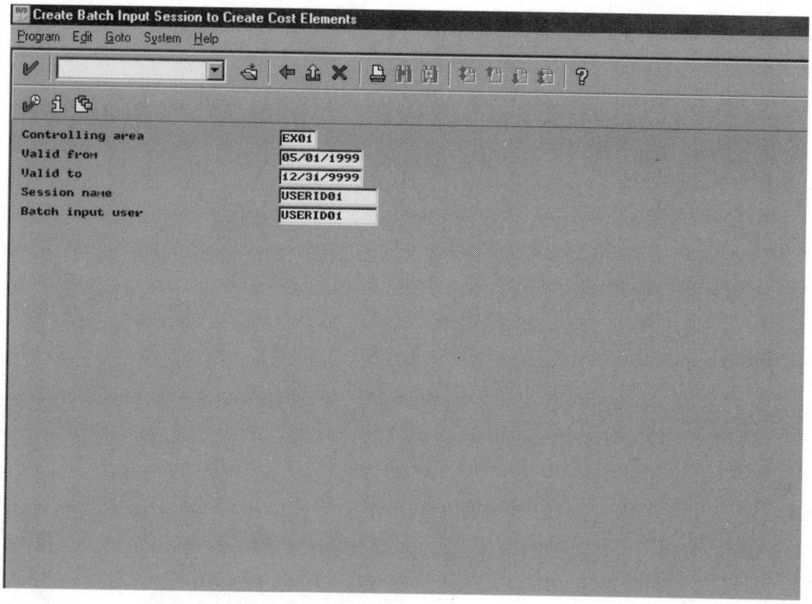

Create Batch Input Session to Create Cost Elements

Program Edit Goto System Help

Controlling area	EX01
Valid from	05/01/1999
Valid to	12/31/9999
Session name	USERID01
Batch input user	USERID01

CREATION OF THE COST ELEMENT CREATION BATCH RUN SESSION

You can create the cost element creation batch run session by using the following methods:

Menu Path: Controlling ➢ Overhead Cost Controlling ➢ Cost and Revenue Element Accounting ➢ Master Data ➢ Cost Elements ➢ Automatic Creation of Primary and Secondary Cost Elements ➢ Create Batch Input Session

Transaction Code: OKB3

Let's examine the fields:

Controlling Area   Enter the ID of the controlling area in which the cost elements should be created.

Valid From   Enter the date from which the cost element will be valid.

WARNING Be sure the From date is set early enough to provide an adequate time frame for any history loads or allocations.

Valid To Enter the date until which the cost element will be valid.

Session Name The user ID of the person creating the session will default as the name of the batch session. Because of the specific use of the batch session, any session name you use will be sufficient.

Batch Input User The user ID of the person creating the session will default as the name of the batch session. As with Session Name, any entry will be sufficient.

You have the option to save the session as a variant. The Save as Variant screen will appear (see Figure 8.4).

FIGURE 8.4 The Save as Variant screen

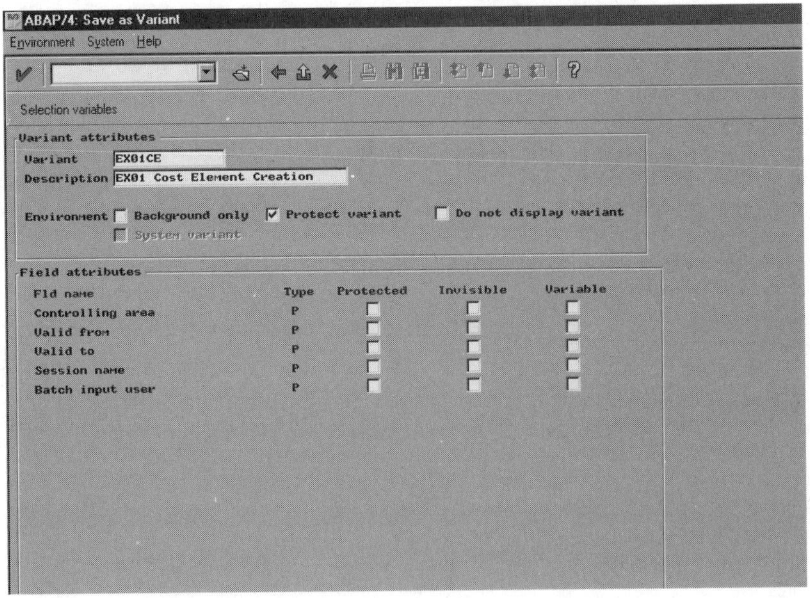

NOTE Saving the settings as a variant is an option. It may be useful if you anticipate using the settings more than once or using them as an automated batch task.

Here are the fields on the Save as Variant screen:

Variant   Enter the name of the variant.

Description   Enter a description of the variant.

Environment   Select as many of the boxes as are relevant for your variant. An entry is not required. The options are as follows:

Background Only   If this check box is selected, the variant can run only in the background.

Protect Variant   If this check box is selected, the variant can be changed only by the person who created it or by the last person to change it.

Do Not Display Variant   If this field is selected, the variant view is restricted to only the variant directory.

Field Attributes   Select as many of the boxes as are relevant for your variant. An entry is not required. The options are as follows:

Protected   If this check box is selected, the value of the field cannot be altered at runtime. For example, if this field is activated for the Controlling Area field, the value of the controlling area is displayed but cannot be changed in the session.

Invisible   If this check box is selected, the field is not visible when the variant is used.

Variable   If this check box is selected, the values of the field are provided through a variable. Selections manually applied to the variant on the selection screen will be overwritten with the variable value.

When all decisions are made, save the variant. The screen will return to the Create Batch Input Session screen (see Figure 8.3).

Create the batch input session by selecting the execute icon. A session log detailing the cost elements to be created will appear (see Figure 8.5). Be sure to review the log for anything that may have been left out. Or, more important, check for cost elements that have been accidentally included. Once master data has been created in the system, it will exist until the validity period expires.

FIGURE 8.5 The session log for the batch input session needs to be carefully checked.

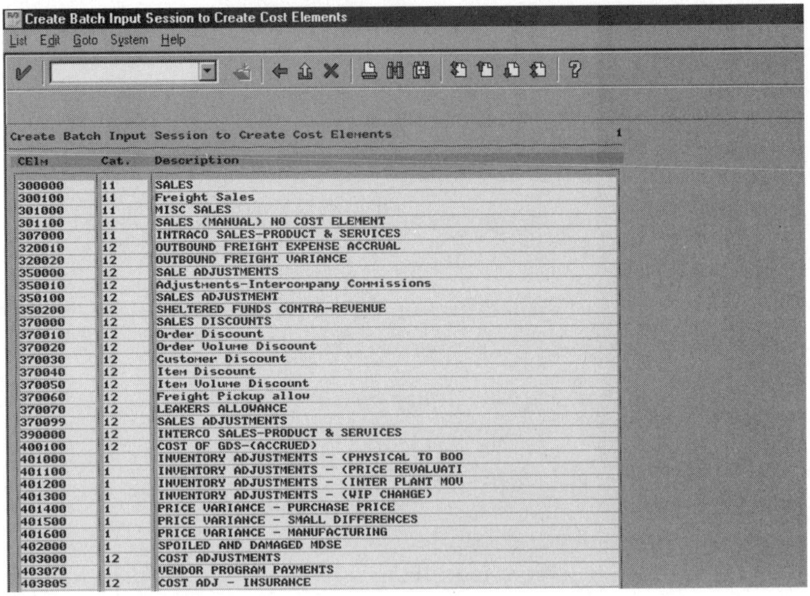

CElm	Cat.	Description
300000	11	SALES
300100	11	Freight Sales
301000	11	MISC SALES
301100	11	SALES (MANUAL) NO COST ELEMENT
307000	11	INTRACO SALES-PRODUCT & SERVICES
320010	12	OUTBOUND FREIGHT EXPENSE ACCRUAL
320020	12	OUTBOUND FREIGHT VARIANCE
350000	12	SALE ADJUSTMENTS
350010	12	Adjustments-Intercompany Commissions
350100	12	SALES ADJUSTMENT
350200	12	SHELTERED FUNDS CONTRA-REVENUE
370000	12	SALES DISCOUNTS
370010	12	Order Discount
370020	12	Order Volume Discount
370030	12	Customer Discount
370040	12	Item Discount
370050	12	Item Volume Discount
370060	12	Freight Pickup allow
370070	12	LEAKERS ALLOWANCE
370099	12	SALES ADJUSTMENTS
390000	12	INTERCO SALES-PRODUCT & SERVICES
400100	12	COST OF GDS-(ACCRUED)
401000	1	INVENTORY ADJUSTMENTS - (PHYSICAL TO BOO
401100	1	INVENTORY ADJUSTMENTS - (PRICE REVALUATI
401200	1	INVENTORY ADJUSTMENTS - (INTER PLANT MOV
401300	1	INVENTORY ADJUSTMENTS - (WIP CHANGE)
401400	1	PRICE VARIANCE - PURCHASE PRICE
401500	1	PRICE VARIANCE - SMALL DIFFERENCES
401600	1	PRICE VARIANCE - MANUFACTURING
402000	1	SPOILED AND DAMAGED MDSE
403000	12	COST ADJUSTMENTS
403070	1	VENDOR PROGRAM PAYMENTS
403805	12	COST ADJ - INSURANCE

Execute Batch Input Session

You can run the batch job online or in the background. For performance reasons, it is recommended that the program be run in either background or display-error-only mode. Correct any fallout or errors after processing. When running a batch online, you can correct any errors as they appear.

Follow the menu path Controlling ➢ Overhead Cost Controlling ➢ Cost and Revenue Element Accounting ➢ Master Data ➢ Cost Elements ➢ Automatic Creation of Primary and Secondary Cost Elements ➢ Execute Batch Input Session.

TIP The SM35 transaction can be used to run any batch session and is not limited to just cost element creation.

Use the menu path or transaction code to access the batch input execution screen, shown in Figure 8.6.

EXECUTION OF THE COST ELEMENT CREATION BATCH INPUT SESSION

You can run the batch by using the following methods:

Menu Path: **Controlling** ➤ **Overhead Cost Controlling** ➤ **Cost and Revenue Element Accounting** ➤ **Master Data** ➤ **Cost Elements** ➤ **Automatic Creation of Primary and Secondary Cost Elements** ➤ **Execute Batch Input Session**

Transaction Code: **SM35**

FIGURE 8.6 The batch input execution screen

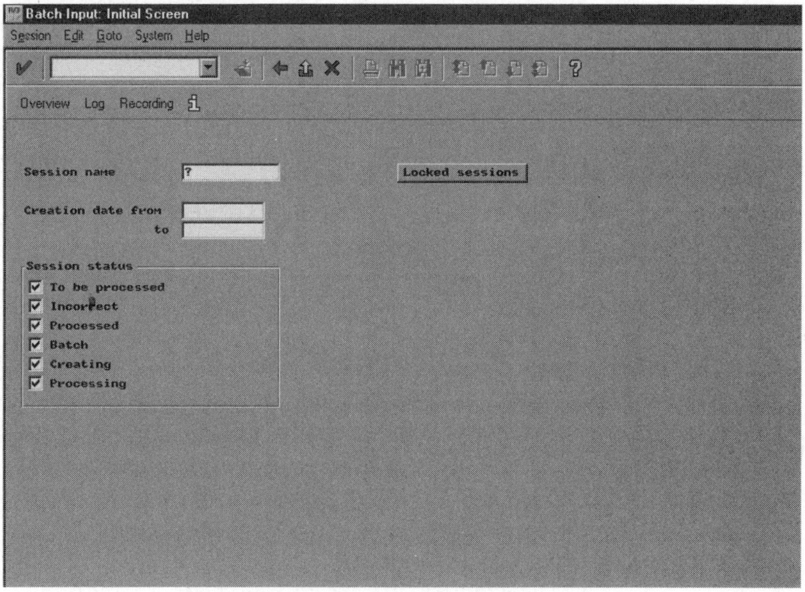

Let's look at the options on this screen:

Session Name Enter the name of the cost element creation batch.

Creation Date From/To This option is used to restrict the batch sessions by date. If you have multiple batch sessions, this allows you to narrow the choices of which session should run.

Session Status   These settings help to limit the number of sessions that appear in the overview. The settings represent the six potential statuses of a batch session. The default settings are appropriate.

Select the Overview button to display the batch session. A listing of potential batch sessions will appear (see Figure 8.7).

FIGURE 8.7   A listing of potential batch sessions appears when you select the Overview button.

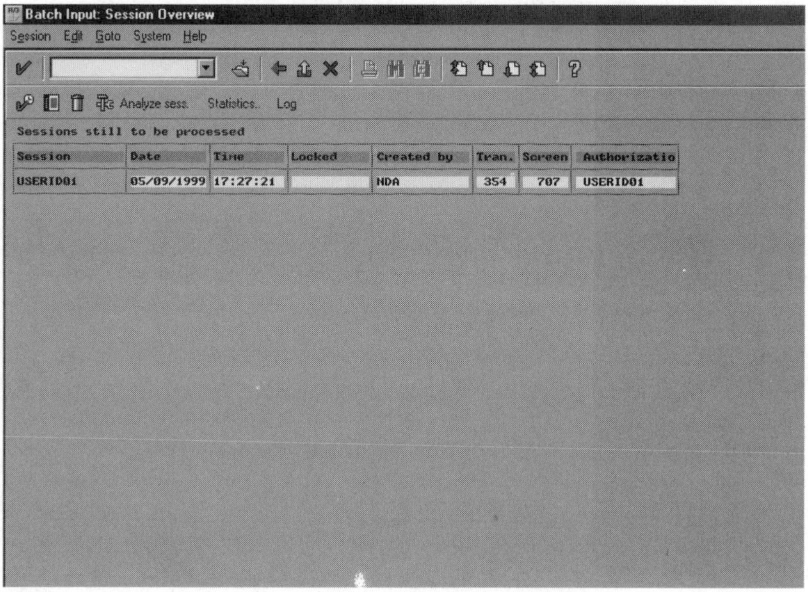

Select the session you wish to run and then execute the batch session. In Extreme Sports' case, there is only one session to choose. A box requesting information on how to run the session will appear (see Figure 8.8).

To run the batch in the background, select Background from the dialog box and enter a target system in the Destination box. Use the drop-down arrow if you are not sure of your system IDs. If the Destination box is left blank, SAP will select the next available system. Leave all other settings as they defaulted and click the Process button.

FIGURE 8.8   The Process Session dialog box

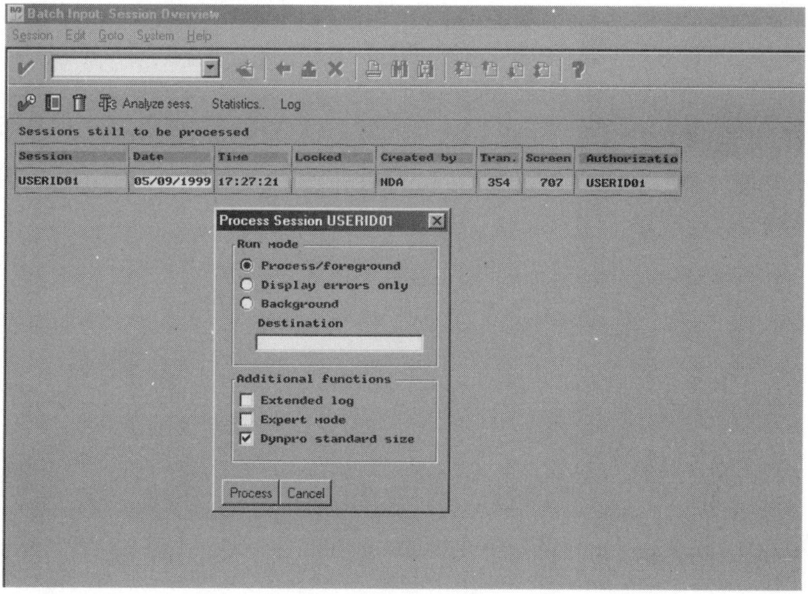

To review the job status, select Goto ➢ Background ➢ Job Overview. If an error occurs when the batch is run in the background, the job will terminate. If that happens, correct the error online and continue processing the session. To analyze the session, select the Analyze Sess. button. From the screen that appears, you can review the transactions that occurred.

Once the batch has completed without error, automated primary cost element creation is complete. There will be a need to manually create additional primary and all the secondary cost elements to support your configuration. The manual creation process is not configuration; it is processed though the user menu in the Cost Element Accounting module.

Manual Cost Element Creation

SAP allows primary and secondary cost element creation from many places within the system. The most direct location is the user menu in the Cost Element Accounting module. Because primary cost elements were created earlier in batch sessions, the creation of secondary cost elements will be described in this section. In either case, the processes are identical.

Remember that secondary cost elements are used to track internal CO movements and are not tied to the chart of accounts. Potential uses for secondary cost elements include the following:

▶ Cost center assessments

▶ Internal order settlements

▶ Internal allocation of overhead to maintenance orders

Secondary cost elements are not restricted to a number range, so be aware of the number you are using.

To create a secondary cost element, follow the SAP (not IMG) menu path Accounting ➤ Controlling ➤ Cost Elements ➤ Master Data ➤ Cost Elements ➤ Create Secondary (or Primary) Cost Elements.

PRIMARY AND SECONDARY COST ELEMENT CREATION

You can use the following methods to create a secondary cost element:

Application Menu Path: **Accounting** ➤ **Controlling** ➤ **Cost Elements** ➤ **Master Data** ➤ **Cost Elements** ➤ **Create Secondary (or Primary) Cost Elements**

Transaction Code: **KA06 (KA01 for Primary Elements)**

After you use one of the configuration transactions, the initial create secondary cost element screen appears (see Figure 8.9).

FIGURE 8.9   The initial create secondary cost element screen

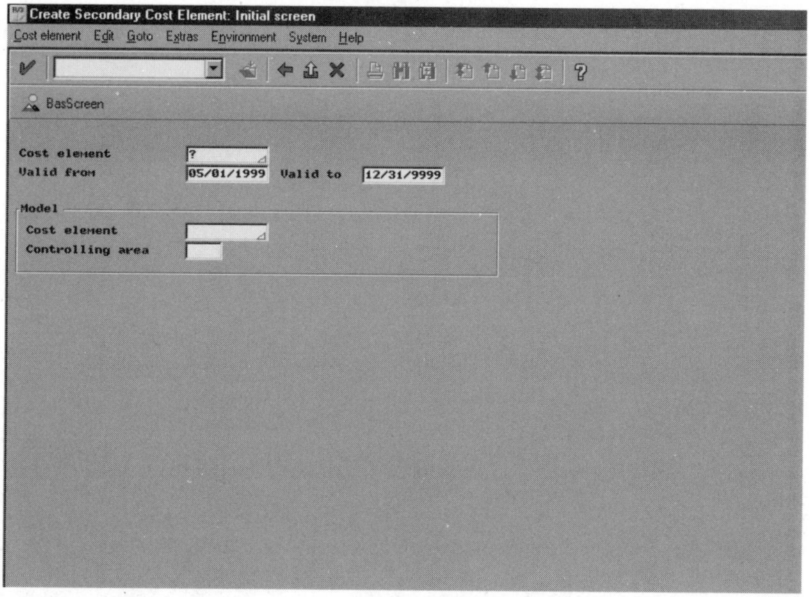

Create Secondary Cost Element: Initial screen
Cost element   Edit   Goto   Extras   Environment   System   Help

BasScreen

Cost element   ?
Valid from   05/01/1999   Valid to   12/31/9999

Model
  Cost element   _
  Controlling area _

NOTE   Be sure that you have predetermined the proper controlling area. If it has not been previously set, SAP will offer a prompt to set one. If you wish to change the designated controlling area, from the Cost/Revenue Element Accounting main screen (transaction code CEMN), use the menu path Environment ➢ Set CO Area.

Let's look at the fields in this screen:

Cost Element   Enter the number of the secondary cost element.

TIP   It will be helpful to segregate the secondary cost elements from the primary by using distinct account ranges for each. For example, internal settlement elements could fall into a 900000 range.

Valid From/To   Enter the validity period of the cost element. You cannot delete the element while it exists within this period of time.

Model   These fields are optional. You can use a cost element from another controlling area as a model when building your element. If you choose to do so, enter the appropriate information in the following fields:

Cost Element   Enter the number of the cost element to copy.

Controlling Area   Enter the ID of the controlling area where the model cost element exists.

NOTE   For primary cost elements, the model element and controlling area must be assigned to the same chart your controlling area is assigned to. You can copy a secondary cost element from any controlling area in the client.

When you've filled in the fields, press Enter. The create secondary cost element configuration screen appears (see Figure 8.10).

FIGURE 8.10   The create secondary cost element configuration screen filled out for Extreme Sports

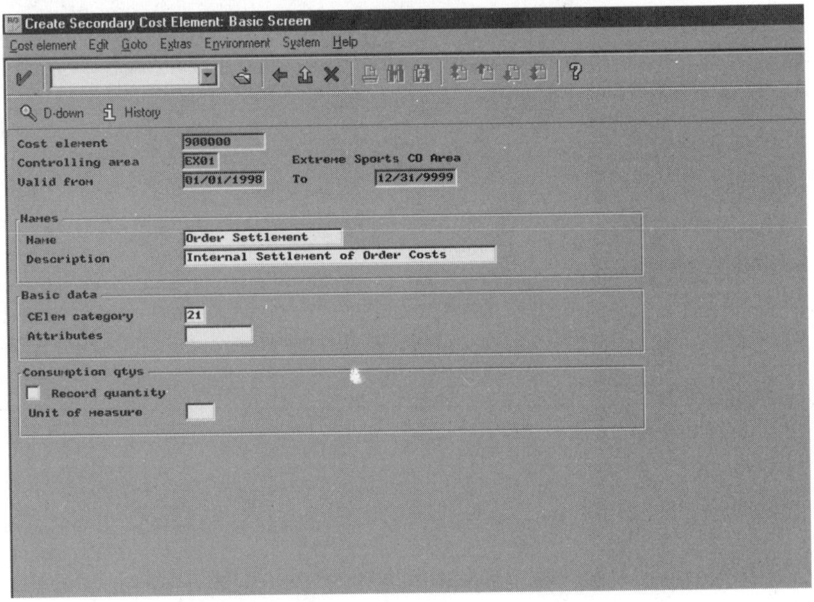

![Create Secondary Cost Element: Basic Screen showing Cost element 900000, Controlling area EX01 Extreme Sports CD Area, Valid from 01/01/1998 To 12/31/9999, Name Order Settlement, Description Internal Settlement of Order Costs, CElem category 21]

You need to fill in these fields:

Name   Enter the name of the cost element.

Description   Enter a description of the cost element.

CElem Category   Enter the category of the cost element. Use the drop-down box or refer to "Cost Element Types" earlier in this chapter for a listing of possible entries. Remember that the cost element category limits the account's use to specific business transactions, so choose carefully.

Attributes   This field is optional. Attributes help to further classify cost elements, but they have no control functionality. That is to say, the attributes do not limit business transactions. Cost element attributes are maintained in the IMG.

Record Quantity   Select this check box if you want to track quantities, as well as currencies, for the cost element.

Unit of Measure   If you select Record Quantity, you must provide a unit of measure with which to track the quantities.

When configuration is complete, save the cost element (see Figure 8.10 for the filled-out version for Extreme Sports).

EXTREME SPORTS COST ELEMENT CONFIGURATION ANALYSIS

The Extreme Sports FI/CO configuration and master data team decided to not use cost element attributes to classify their cost elements. There was no present need for differentiation in this manner. In addition, the team made a decision to not track quantities in any cost element, whether it is a primary or a secondary element. They chose to use other cost objects, like cost centers and orders, to meet their quantity-tracking requirements.

Imputed Costs

Throughout a fiscal year, certain expenses may not accrue in a timely manner, whether they relate to a project, an employee bonus, or a tax bill. To assist in smoothing these irregular costs across multiple periods within the cost accounting environment, SAP provides two methods:

▶ Recurring entries

▶ Imputed cost calculation

The distinct difference between the two methods stems from the origin of the postings. The recurring entry posting originates in the FI module, and the imputed cost calculation originates within the CO module. Although both methods are appropriate, a benefit of the imputed cost calculation is its use of actual costs to generate the posting. The recurring entry is fixed at the time of its creation and cannot augment the account, posting key, or amount.

Simply stated, the imputed cost calculation accrues a cost based on some surcharge percentage and posts to the cost object (cost center or order) of your choice. No FI update is made at the time of the actual CO imputed cost calculation. When the actual irregular cost is incurred, the transaction will initiate in FI and credit CO for costs already imputed and posted. The net effect in activity is smoothed over any number of periods and offset with a one-time charge. Any differences in the total amount of imputed charges in CO will be taken against the operating profit of the entity charged.

SAP provides two types of imputed cost calculations:

► Cost element % method

► Target = Actual method

Of the two processes, the cost element % method is easier to maintain and understand, and it will be described in detail. The Target = Actual method is more difficult and requires some level of activity-based planning. The configuration for Target = Actual will not be demonstrated.

Cost Element % Method

The configuration of the cost element % method is a two-step process:

1. Create the imputed cost element that will be used to post the costs.

2. Maintain the overhead costing sheet for the controlling area.

Imputed Cost Element Creation

An imputed cost element is a primary cost element and thus requires a G/L account prior to its creation. Refer to Chapter 3 for the exact configuration steps to manually create a G/L account.

N O T E   The G/L account(s) should be set up as an expense account(s). Also, remember to extend the account(s) to all the company codes that will use the calculation.

For the steps necessary to manually create the primary cost element, refer to "Manual Cost Element Creation" earlier in this chapter. The cost element category to be applied here is 03. Be sure to create the cost elements first because the accounts are necessary to complete the overhead costing sheet.

TIP It is likely that multiple accounts will be required in most circumstances. Thinking ahead about how and to what level of detail you want the activity tracked will speed up the process.

Overhead Costing Sheet Creation: Manual

The overhead costing sheet configuration is tied directly to a controlling area because of the link to cost elements, cost centers, and internal orders. All of these are controlling area–specific objects. During the configuration process, you will assign your controlling area to a costing sheet. You may assign more than one controlling area to a costing sheet because the master data configuration is controlling area specific.

NOTE There can only be one active costing sheet per controlling area. If you require multiple versions, subsheets may be used.

To assist you with the manual configuration of the costing sheet, the costing sheet requirements for Extreme Sports will be described. As you progress through this section, the Extreme Sports solution will be documented.

EXTREME SPORTS COSTING SHEET DEFINITION CONFIGURATION ANALYSIS

Extreme Sports has decided to use imputed costs to help cost center managers plan taxes and benefits for its staff. Additionally, it wants to accrue a charge on each of its sales cost centers for a bonus to be paid at different points throughout the fiscal year. The bonus is calculated as a percentage of salaries and is charged to the cost center.

Follow the menu path Controlling ➢ Overhead Cost Controlling ➢ Cost and Revenue Element Accounting ➢ Imputed Cost Calculation ➢ Cost Element Percentage Method ➢ Maintain Overhead Cost Sheet to create the overhead costing sheet.

MANUAL OVERHEAD COSTING SHEET CREATION FOR IMPUTED COST CALCULATION

You can use the following methods to create an overhead costing sheet:

Menu Path: **Controlling** ➤ **Overhead Cost Controlling** ➤ **Cost and Revenue Element Accounting** ➤ **Imputed Cost Calculation** ➤ **Cost Element Percentage Method** ➤ **Maintain Overhead Cost Sheet**

Transaction Code: **KSAZ**

After you use one of the transaction configurations, the overhead costing sheet configuration screen appears (see Figure 8.11).

FIGURE 8.11   The overhead costing sheet configuration screen

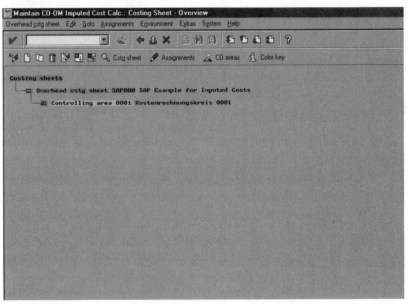

If the table has not been maintained for any other controlling area or costing sheet, only the SAP-delivered sheet, SAP000, will be present. Rather than augment the existing template, we recommend that you either copy SAP000 to something you can update or create your own.

To create a new costing sheet, select the create costing sheet icon (F7).

An ID box will appear to ask for the costing sheet ID and description, as shown in Figure 8.12. The ID is alphanumeric and can be up to six characters long. Enter the information and select Save. An empty screen will appear (see Figure 8.13).

FIGURE 8.12   A new costing sheet can be created using the dialog box generated by pressing F7.

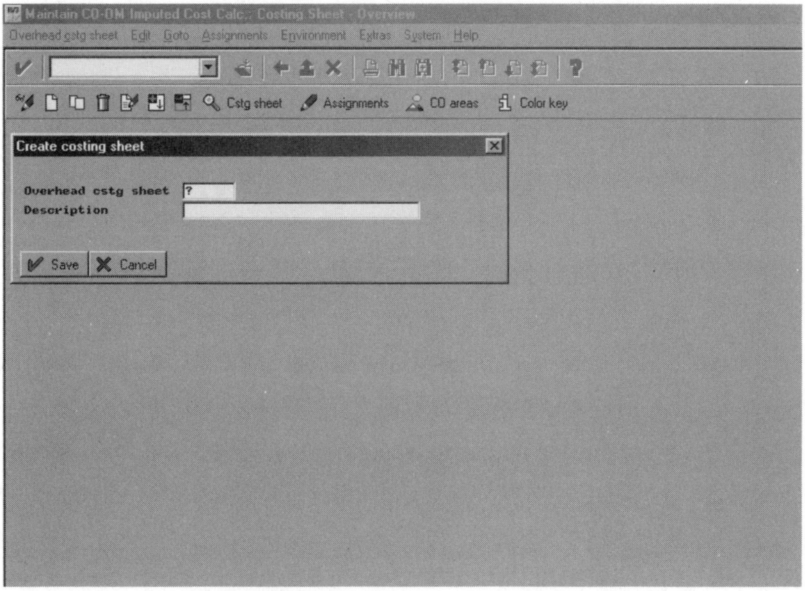

FIGURE 8.13   An empty costing sheet detail configuration screen

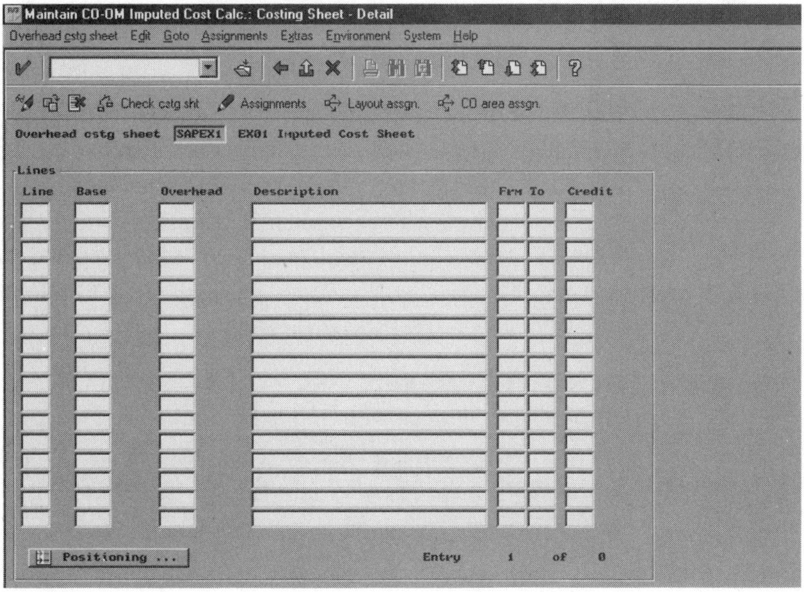

Let's review the columns found within the Lines section:

Line   Enter a three-digit numeric ID. Be sure to make the frequency of the line items large enough to accommodate for the insertion of additional line items (for example, 010, 020, 030).

Base   Enter a four-character ID denoting the calculation base for the costing sheet. The calculation base determines the cost elements to be used.

Overhead   Enter a four-character ID denoting the overhead surcharges. It is here that cost centers and surcharge percentages are applied to the formula.

Description   Enter a text description of the line, base, or overhead item.

Frm/To   Enter a range of reference rows to be used in conjunction with the surcharge percentages.

Credit   Enter a three-character ID. The credit is used to assign the offset to the imputed cost posting, once it's calculated, to a company code, business area, and cost center/order. The imputed cost element to be charged is assigned to the credit.

Creating the costing sheet is a building process. First, define your calculation base. Then, define your percentage charges, and finally, define what objects will receive the charge.

Enter a Line Item and a Base ID   A few bases are delivered with the system. Use the drop-down box to review and choose one. For Extreme Sports, we will calculate a new base called EX-1—Wages. Enter **EX-1** in the Base field and press Enter.

Because EX-1 is a new base, a Create Calculation box appears (see Figure 8.14). Give the base a name and select Create.

Notice that the new base appears in the detail screen (Figure 8.13). From the configuration requirements stated earlier, we know that Extreme Sports does not require additional bases. It is a good idea to place a total line in your costing sheet. A total line clearly defines where the calculation base ends, and it can be used as a reference row for surcharge calculation. To enter a total line, enter a line number, a description, and a range of rows, if applicable, in the Frm/To columns. After pressing Enter, you will notice that the line turns red.

Overhead Surcharge Calculations   As with the base, certain overhead surcharges were delivered with the system and can be used. In the case of Extreme Sports, two new overhead IDs will be created: EXBN (Benefits) and EXBS (Bonus). Enter **EXBN** in the Overhead column field and press Enter. The Create Surcharge screen appears, as shown in Figure 8.15.

FIGURE 8.14   The Create Calculation Base screen

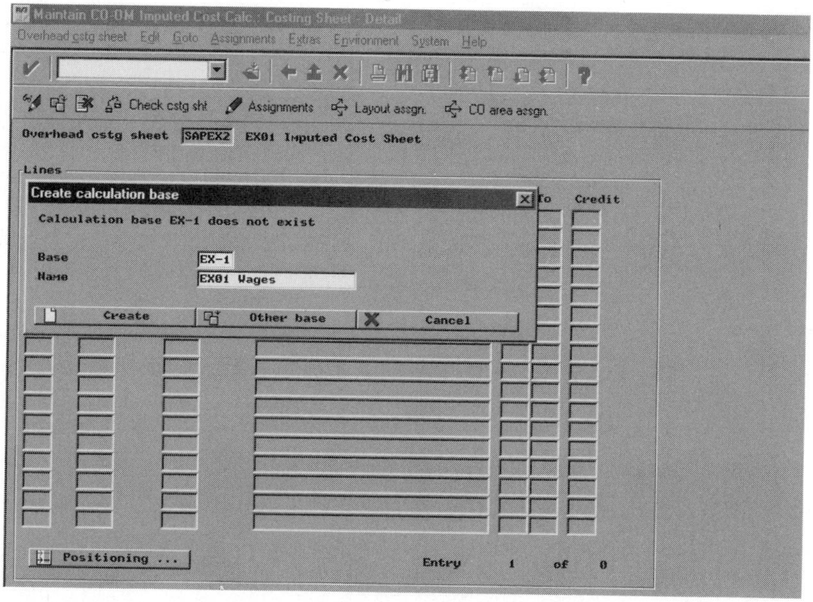

FIGURE 8.15   The Create Surcharge dialog box

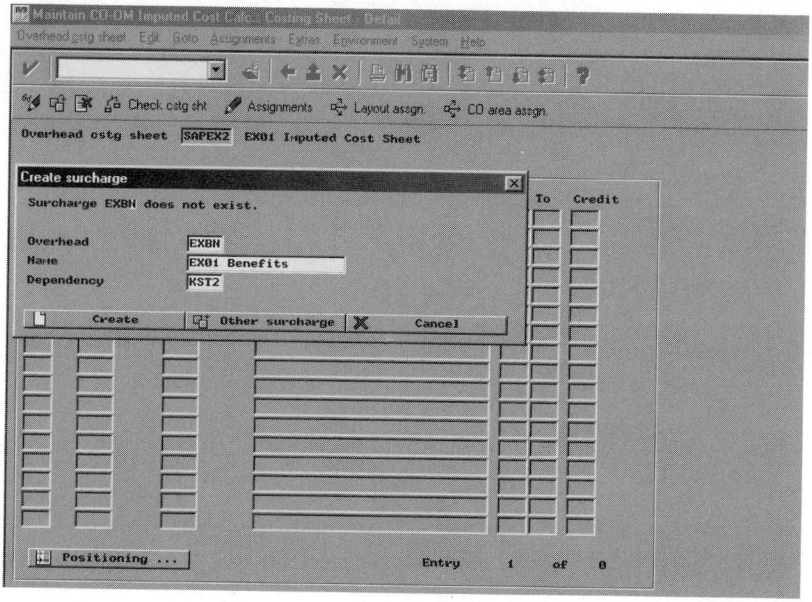

Enter a description of the surcharge and a dependency. Dependencies define the access sequence of the surcharge calculation. Many useful dependencies come pre-defined. For example, by selecting the dependency KST2 (Cost Center/Controlling Area), you will be able to assign an overall controlling area rate, as well as a varying rate, to individual cost centers. When all your selections are complete, select Create.

TIP For a quicker process, repeat the surcharge creation steps for additional overhead charges now. Maintenance will be easier later.

Enter the line item(s) to be used for the calculation base in the Frm/To columns. In Extreme Sports' case, line 100 is selected for all bases.

The credit will supply the costing sheet with the object to be posted with the credit entry during the planning/actual posting process. Some credit IDs are supplied with the system. To create a new ID, enter the ID number, such as EX1 for Extreme Sports, in the Credit field and press Enter. The Create Credit box appears, as shown in Figure 8.16. Enter a description and select Create.

FIGURE 8.16   The Create Credit dialog box

![The Create Credit dialog box screenshot showing the Maintain CO-OM Imputed Cost Calc.: Costing Sheet - Detail window. The Overhead cstg sheet is SAPEX2 EX01 Imputed Cost Sheet. A "Create credit" dialog box reads "Credit EX1 does not exist" with Credit field "EX1" and Name field "EX01 – Benefits", and buttons Create, Other credit, and Cancel.]

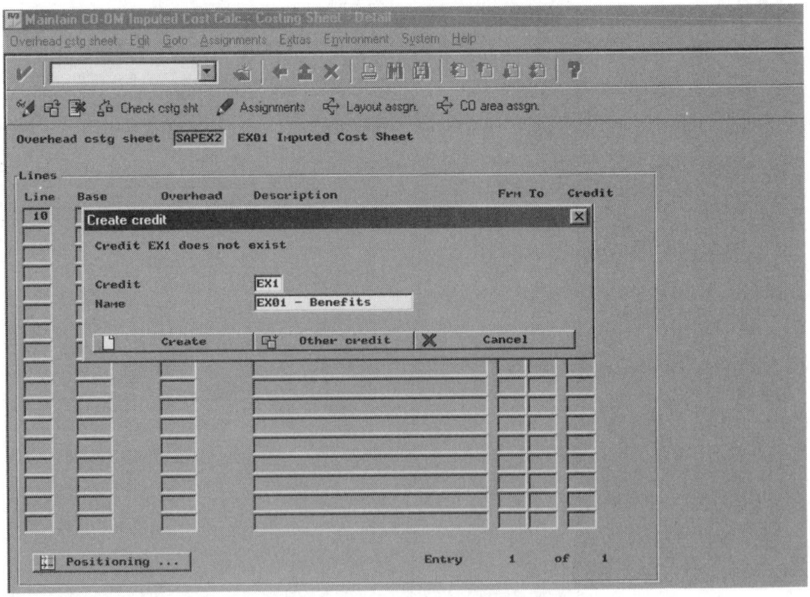

Repeat the process as often as required for your solution. In the case of Extreme Sports, the credit EX2 (Bonus) will also be created. The basics for the overhead costing sheet are now complete. Before you continue, save the sheet. You are now ready to assign the costing sheet and maintain the detail configuration.

 NOTE A warning may appear, stating that a controlling area has not been defined. You will be assigning the controlling area next. It's a really good idea to just be safe and save as you go.

Assign the Costing Sheet to a Controlling Area

At the costing sheet detail configuration screen (see Figure 8.13), select the Assignments button. The Select Assignment screen appears (see Figure 8.17).

FIGURE 8.17   The Select Assignments screen

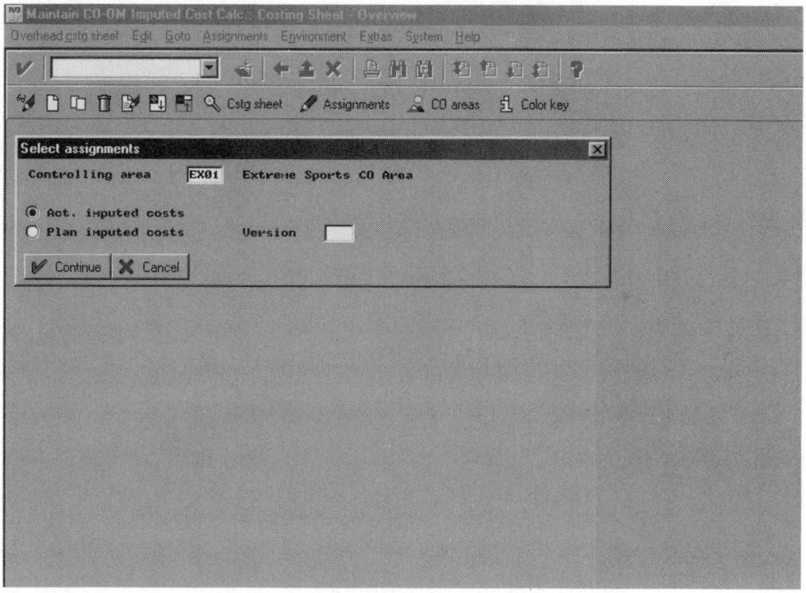

![Screenshot of the Maintain CO-OM Imputed Cost Calc: Costing Sheet - Overview window showing the Select assignments dialog box. Controlling area: EX01 Extreme Sports CO Area. Radio buttons for Act. imputed costs (selected) and Plan imputed costs. Version field. Continue and Cancel buttons.]

There are four fields to fill out on this screen:

Controlling Area   Enter the controlling area that will receive the costing sheet.

Act./Plan Imputed Costs   Imputed costs can be used for posting plan or actual activity. The assignments are made individually; if you want to maintain both actual and plan postings, two assignments must be made.

Version   For the plan assignment, enter a version you would like posted.

Choose Continue. The assignments detail screen appears (see Figure 8.18). Validity periods for the costing sheet assignment are determined here.

FIGURE 8.18 The assignments detail screen

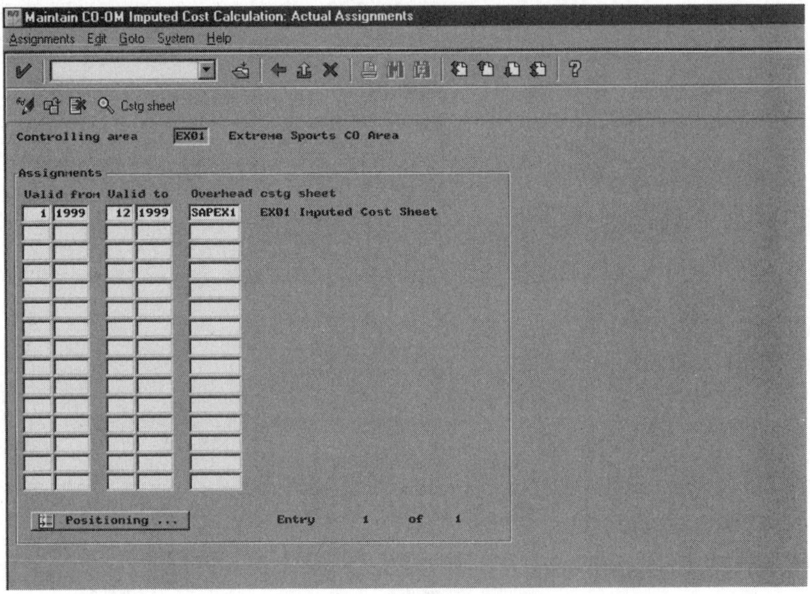

The fields on this screen are as follows:

Valid From/To Enter the range of dates for which the costing sheet assignment will be valid. Remember that only one costing sheet can be valid at any one time for a controlling area. If you want to assign more than one costing sheet, be sure the validity periods do not overlap.

Overhead Cstg Sheet Enter the ID of the costing sheet to be assigned.

When all the assignments are complete, save the settings. Click the green arrow to move back to the costing sheet detail screen. Repeat the steps, if necessary, to assign validity periods for both the actual and planned imputed cost calculations. For Extreme Sports, both will be made.

Maintain the Base Calculation

To make the cost element assignment to the base calculation ID (EX-1), double-click the ID. The cost element assignment screen, shown in Figure 8.19, will appear.

FIGURE 8.19   You can review your settings after clicking the save icon in the cost element assignment screen.

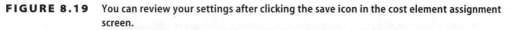

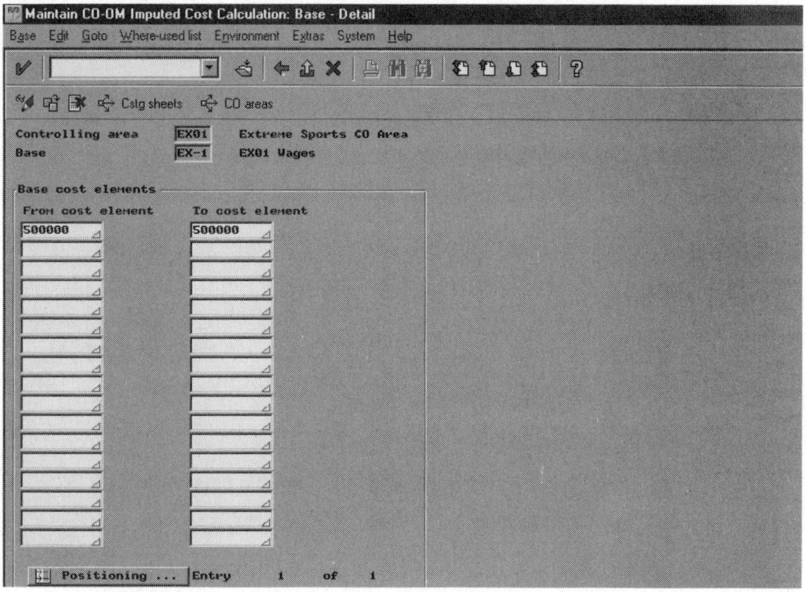

Enter either a single cost element or a varying range of cost elements in the From/To Cost Elements fields and then save the settings. Click the green arrow to move back to the costing sheet detail configuration screen.

Maintain the Overhead Surcharge

To assign the overhead rates and make any cost center–specific percentage assignments, double-click the overhead ID (e.g., EXBN or EXBS). The surcharge assignment screen appears, shown in Figure 8.20. Notice in the Condition section that there's a Controlling Area/Surcharge Type setting and a Controlling Area/Surcharge Type/Cost Center setting.

FIGURE 8.20 The saved settings for controlling area/surcharge

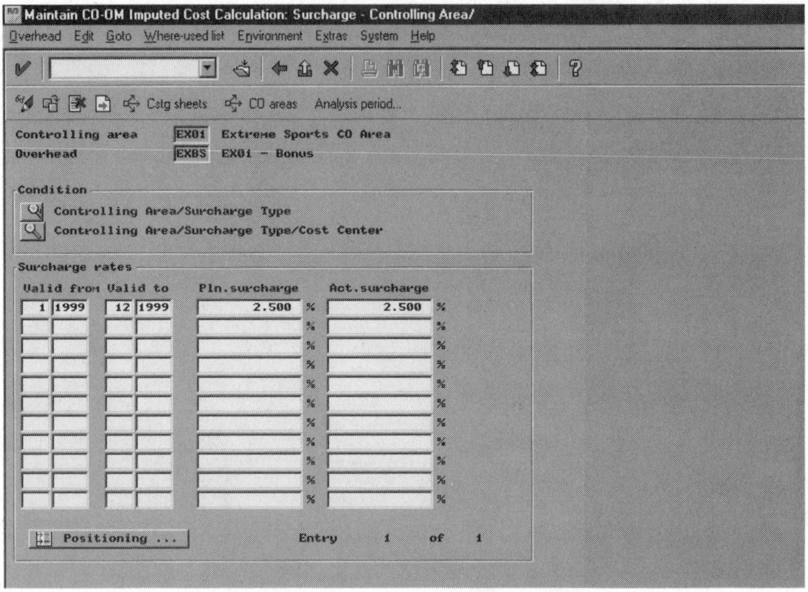

If you want to have a blanket rate for all cost centers in the controlling area, maintain only the Controlling Area/Surcharge section. However, if you would like to override the rate with a special rate for specific cost centers, maintain the Controlling Area/ Surcharge/Cost Center section. You will find both buttons in the Condition section of the screen (see Figure 8.20).

The fields on the controlling area/surcharge screen are as follows:

Valid From/To Enter the valid period range for the surcharge percentages.

Pln. Surcharge If you will be using the plan imputed cost calculation during planning, enter the monthly rate at which you want overhead charged to a cost center.

Act. Surcharge If you will be using the actual imputed cost calculation during period end closing, enter the monthly rate at which you want overhead charged to a cost center.

Save the settings when you're finished. To apply specific rates to select cost centers, select the Controlling Area/Surcharge Type/Cost Center condition button.

NOTE If you wish to apply specific rates to cost centers, you will have to save the controlling area rates first.

The fields found on the controlling area/surcharge/cost center screen include the following:

Cost Center   Enter the number of the cost center to receive the special rate. Enter as many lines as you need.

Valid From/To   Enter the validity period for the cost center/rate relationship. It is possible for a single cost center to have multiple rates within a fiscal year if you properly sequence the validity periods.

Pln. Surcharge   If you will be using the planned imputed cost calculation during planning, enter the monthly rate at which you want overhead charged to a cost center.

Act. Surcharge   If you will be using the actual imputed cost calculation during a period end closing, enter the monthly rate at which you want overhead charged to a cost center.

The saved controlling area/surcharge/cost center configuration is shown in Figure 8.21. Save the settings and click the green arrow to move back to the costing sheet detail configuration screen to maintain the credit IDs.

FIGURE 8.21   The saved controlling area/surcharge/cost center configuration

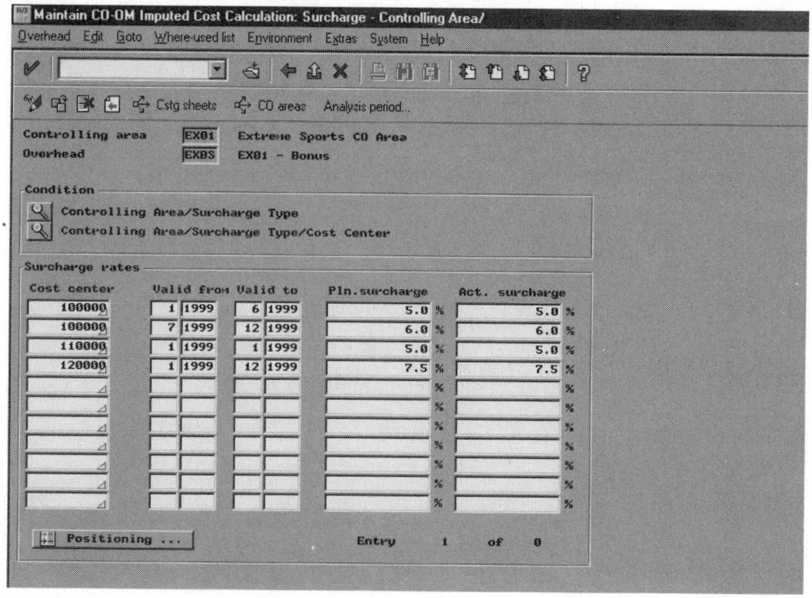

Maintain Credit Calculations

The credit assignment determines which cost object will receive the offsetting credit entry when the imputed costs are posted. Double-click on any of the credit IDs created. The credit detail configuration screen appears (see Figure 8.22).

FIGURE 8.22   The credit detail screen filled out for Extreme Sports

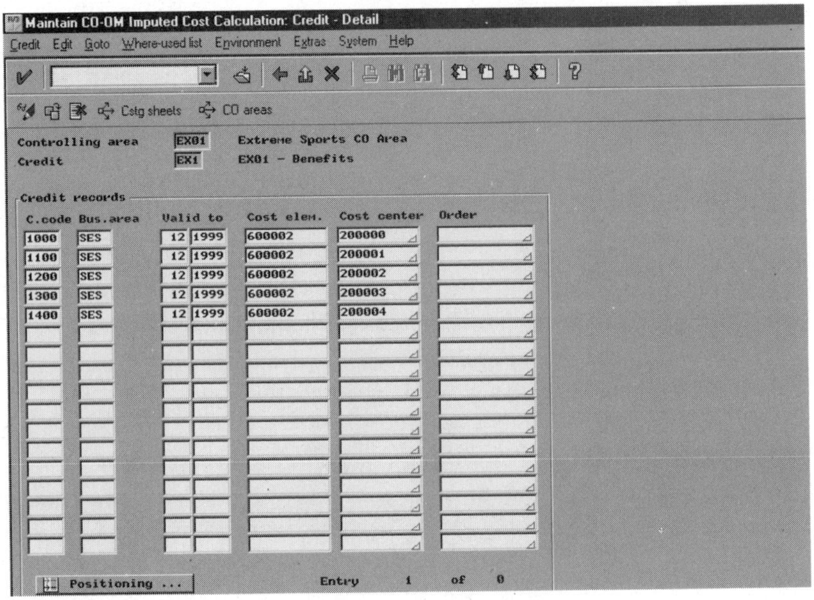

Let's take a look at the fields on this screen:

C. Code   Enter the company code ID to receive the credit entry. The company code should correspond with the cost center assignment in the row.

Bus. Area   Enter the business area ID if you are tracking activity in this manner. Remember that business areas can receive cross-company code postings.

Valid To   Enter the fiscal month and year that represents the last valid period for the credit assignment.

Cost Elem.   Enter the imputed cost element that will receive both the credit and debit imputed cost posting. The cost element chosen here will post to the cost centers selected in the preceding section (see Figure 8.21).

Cost Center   Enter the ID of the cost center, if used, that will receive the offsetting credit posting. The cost center chosen should be the same one that receives the debit cost object assignment when the actual expense is incurred in FI.

Order   Enter the ID of the order, if used, that will receive the offsetting credit posting. The order category of the object will be 02 and must be configured specifically for this purpose. Be sure that the same order receives the debit cost object assignment when the expense is incurred in FI.

TIP   You can have only one unique combination of cost element to cost center or order per validity period.

When configuration is complete, save the settings (Figure 8.22 shows the credit detail screen filled out for Extreme Sports). The imputed cost calculation settings are complete and ready for testing. Experiment with different combinations of settings until the desired posting results are achieved. To test the settings, run the imputed cost calculation for either cost center/order planning or actual postings.

Overhead Costing Sheet Creation: Copy

An alternative to creating a new costing sheet is to copy the SAP-delivered sheet SAP000 and use it as a template.

TIP   Copying SAP-delivered objects and making adjustments to the copies is always recommended.

To copy the SAP-delivered sheet SAP000, follow the menu path Controlling ➤ Overhead Cost Controlling ➤ Cost and Revenue Element Accounting ➤ Imputed Cost Calculation ➤ Cost Element Percentage Method ➤ Maintain Overhead Cost Sheet.

COPYING OF AN OVERHEAD COSTING SHEET CREATION FOR IMPUTED COST CALCULATION

You can get to the overhead cost maintenance screen by using the following methods:

Menu Path: **Controlling** ➤ **Overhead Cost Controlling** ➤ **Cost and Revenue Element Accounting** ➤ **Imputed Cost Calculation** ➤ **Cost Element Percentage Method** ➤ **Maintain Overhead Cost Sheet**

Transaction Code: **KSAZ**

In the cost maintenance screen that appears, place the cursor on the overhead costing sheet line and select the Copy Costing Sheet button (F6). The Copy Costing Sheet input box will appear (see Figure 8.23). Enter an alphanumeric ID and description for your costing sheet. You can use up to six characters. When finished, select Save.

FIGURE 8.23 The Copy Costing Sheet dialog box

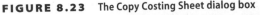

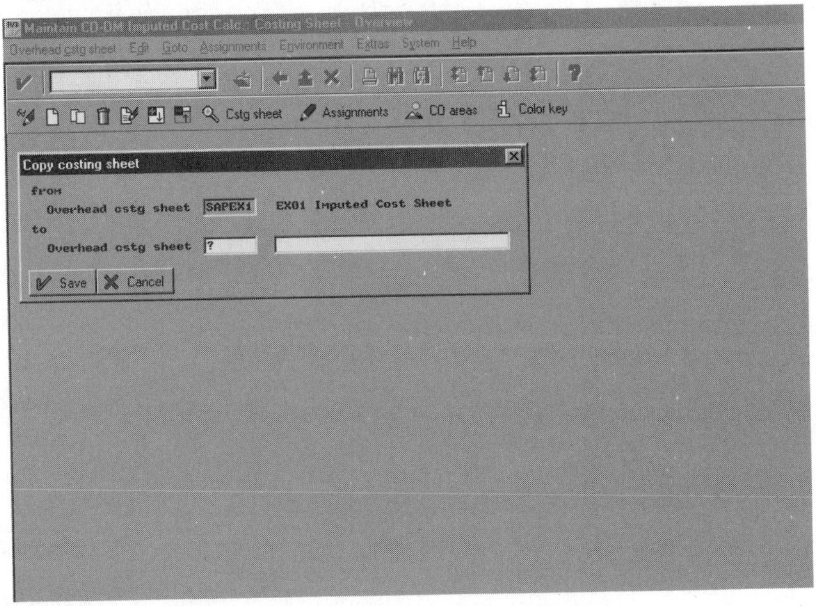

The imputed costing sheet detail screen will appear. Because you copied an existing sheet, some default entries show up. If the entries do not meet your requirements, they can be easily deleted. From this point, refer to the sections earlier in this chapter on manual costing sheet creation for assistance in maintaining the copied template.

Reconciliation Ledger

One of the more important areas of CO configuration is the development of the reconciliation ledger. Among its many uses is the ability to keep activity within the FI G/L in balance with the CO module. The reconciliation ledger tracks all activity within the CO module at a summarized level (to be used for reporting and reconciliation purposes). Activities that occur in CO can be reported by object class and/or object type (shown in Tables 8.1 and 8.2).

TABLE 8.1   Object Classes

Object Classes	Description
OCOST	Overhead costs
INVST	Investments
PRODT	Production
PROFT	Profit and sales

TABLE 8.2   Object Types

Object Types
Cost center
Order
Cost object
Network
Reconciliation object
Sales document item
Project structure
Business process

It is important to understand how each classification can be used. Object types are used within the various CO information systems to report summary and line item activity. Some object types can support many different object classes, and others can support just one. The object types cost center, cost object, reconciliation object, and sales document all have fixed class assignments that cannot be varied. All other object types can have classes assigned by the users. There are a few rules to keep in mind:

▶ Cost center will always be associated with OCOST.

▶ Cost object will always be associated with PRODT.

▶ Reconciliation object will always be associated with PROFT.

▶ Sales document will always be associated with PRODT.

Like the object type, the object class is also used for reconciliation ledger reporting. By correctly identifying the object class on all object types, you can get an accurate view of all operating activity within the CO module. A good example of the need for accuracy in the assignment is the INVST class.

INVST can be used to identify and report all capitalization activity for a controlling area. When costs are capitalized through an investment internal order in CO, depending on the settlement configuration, the original debited account may not receive the offsetting credit during settlement. The result on the FI side is a trial balance with some capitalized costs reported in its operating account balances. If the object class INVST is used properly, an accountant could use the reconciliation ledger to determine how much of an operating account balance was capitalized.

The reconciliation ledger is utilized as a conduit for the FI G/L to access the cost accounting assignment on all its operating postings. Remember that the only organizational unit posted to in FI is the company code.

PURPOSES OF THE RECONCILIATION LEDGER: EXAMPLE #1

When you need to drill back from the FI G/L to find which cost center was posted to on an expense account, the reconciliation ledger is accessed.

The need to have a CO-to-FI reconciliation process is a result of cross-company code, cross-business area, or cross-functional area activity that may occur in the CO module. Order settlement or confirmation, cost center assessment, or other internal CO movement may initiate these postings. When costs are moved internally within CO, the FI G/L is not updated because of CO's use of secondary cost elements to facilitate the postings.

The first two steps in reconciliation ledger configuration are to activate the ledger within the controlling area and assign a document type. If you have an existing controlling area that does not have the reconciliation ledger activated, follow the instructions in the next section. For all newly created controlling areas, the reconciliation ledger is automatically activated.

PURPOSES OF THE RECONCILIATION LEDGER: EXAMPLE #2

A goods receipt posting of $100 has occurred on internal order 1, which is assigned to company code 1. One hundred percent of the value of internal order 1 is settled to internal order 2, which is assigned to company code 2. A settlement cost element is used for the settlement posting. When an order settlement is run, internal order 1 is credited ($100) and internal order 2 is debited $100. The balances of internal order 1 and internal order 2 are $0 and $100 respectively. However, the balances of company code 1 and 2 remain as they were prior to settlement. The reason: The settlement activity was internal to CO. No FI update occurred.

To place the FI company codes back in balance, the CO-FI reconciliation posting transaction should be run. The resulting FI postings would credit company code 1 for ($100) and debit company code 2 for $100. The internal CO activity will now have been accounted for in FI, and the company codes are now in balance.

Activate Reconciliation Ledger

To get to the Activate Reconciliation Ledger screen, follow the menu path Controlling ➤ Overhead Cost Controlling ➤ Cost and Revenue Element Accounting ➤ Reconciliation Ledger ➤ Activate Reconciliation Ledger.

ACTIVATE THE RECONCILIATION LEDGER

You can get to the Activate Reconciliation Ledge screen by using these methods:

Menu Path: **Controlling** ➤ **Overhead Cost Controlling** ➤ **Cost and Revenue Element Accounting** ➤ **Reconciliation Ledger** ➤ **Activate Reconciliation Ledger**

Transaction Code: **KALA**

The Activate Reconciliation Ledger screen appears (see Figure 8.24).

FIGURE 8.24   The Activate Reconciliation Ledger screen

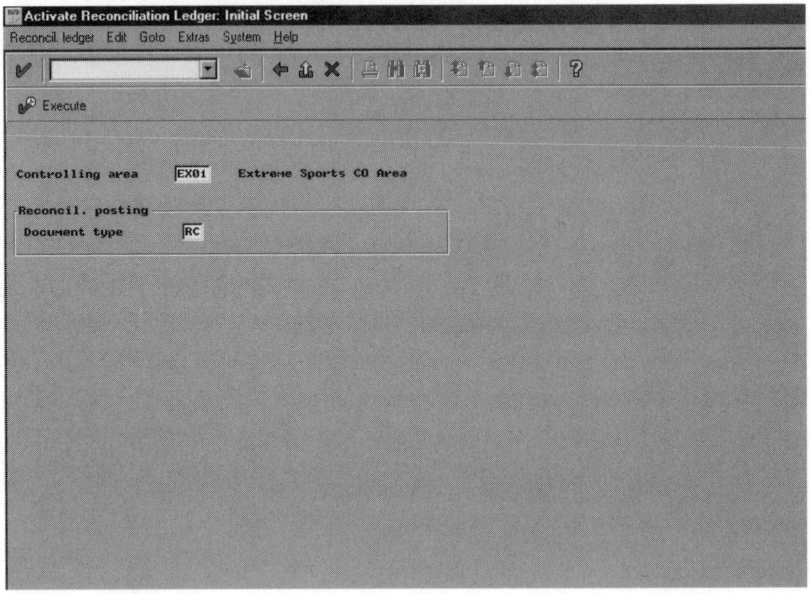

The fields in this screen are as follows:

Controlling Area   Enter the ID of the controlling area in which you wish to activate the reconciliation ledger.

Document Type   Enter the ID of the document type with which you want all reconciliation postings marked. Review the section on document types found in Chapter 3 for some insight into document type configuration. It may be helpful, for analysis purposes, to provide reconciliation postings with their own document type.

Execute the settings when complete. If you were unsure and attempted to activate a previously activated reconciliation ledger, the system will return an error. If not, the ledger is now activated.

For newly created controlling areas, the reconciliation ledger will have been automatically activated, but a document type will not yet be maintained. The assignment of the reconciliation document type to the controlling area will complete the controlling area and basic data settings. To maintain the assignment of the controlling area, follow the menu path Controlling ➢ Controlling General ➢ Organization ➢ Maintain Controlling Area.

The basic data overview screen appears. The screen should look familiar; it was accessed during the base controlling area configuration in Chapter 7. Double-click

ASSIGNMENT OF THE RECONCILIATION DOCUMENT TYPE TO THE CONTROLLING AREA

You can get to the screen used to maintain the controlling area by the following methods:

Menu Path: **Controlling** ➢ **Controlling General** ➢ **Organization** ➢ **Maintain Controlling Area**

Transaction Code: **OKKP**

the controlling area to be maintained. When the basic data screen appears (Figure 8.25), scroll down until you find the field Document Type. Enter the ID of the reconciliation document type you prefer. The document type selected will provide the number range for the FI update, so choose carefully. If you like, you can configure a new document type to allow for the analysis of reconciliation postings in this manner (see Chapter 3). Save the settings when complete.

FIGURE 8.25   The basic data screen

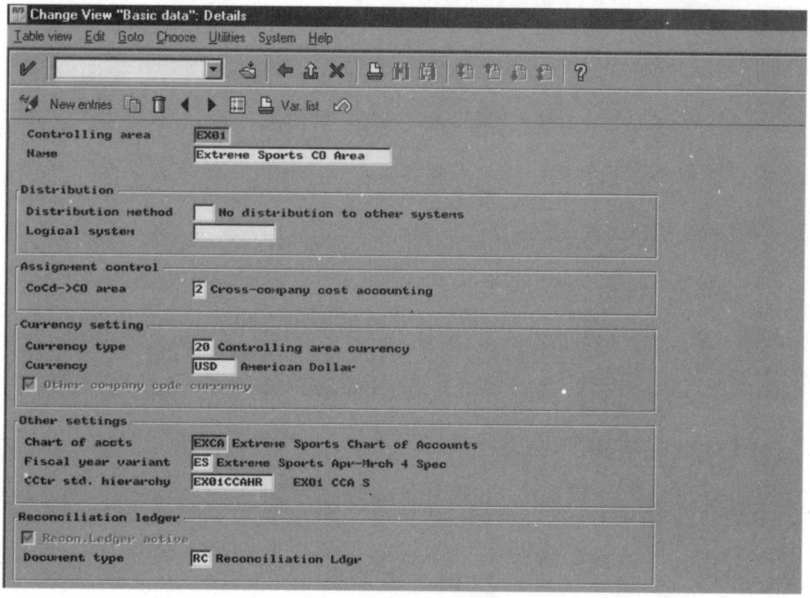

Clearing Account Creation

The reconciliation ledger requires, at minimum, two clearing accounts to post: one intercompany clearing balance sheet account and one reconciliation expense account. There is also the option to add varying layers of account assignment complexity to the configuration, which will be discussed later in this chapter. The intercompany clearing account configuration was discussed in Chapter 3 and should be complete. See Figure 8.26 for a review.

FIGURE 8.26   The intercompany clearing account has already been configured.

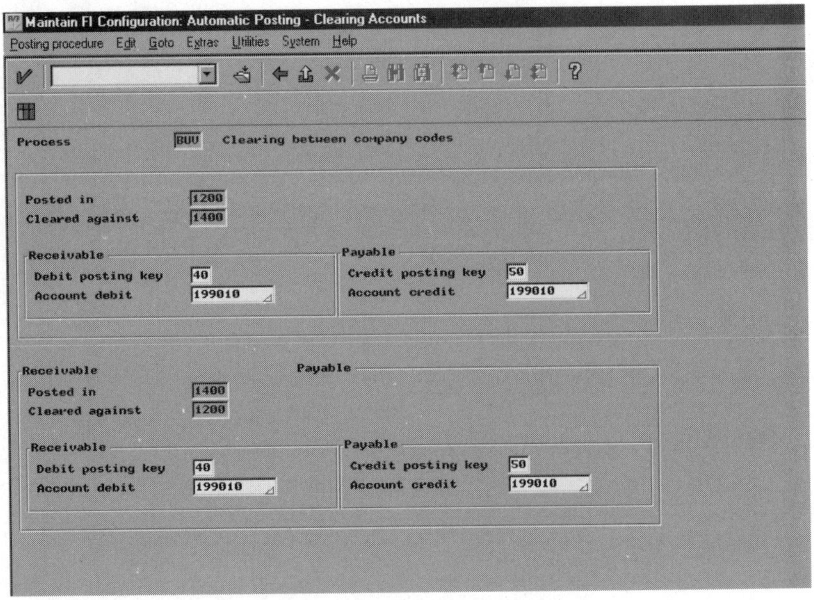

During the CO-to-FI reconciliation process, the intercompany clearing accounts will be automatically credited and debited. The offset to the intercompany clearing will be the expense account you are about to create. Keep in mind that the account(s) must be represented in the FI P&L (Profit and Loss) for the operating activity to be properly reported. Ask yourself some questions before creating the accounts:

▶ How does management want to see reconciliation activity reported?

▶ Do I need to segregate the reconciliation postings by activity or object class?

▶ How much cross-company code, cross-business area, or cross-functional area activity do I anticipate?

Answering these questions up front will ease the remaining configuration process.

Extreme Sports has decided to add some complexity and track reconciliation activity with three accounts: The first will be used to report Investment settlement postings, the second will report production activity, and the third will catch everything else.

Refer to Chapter 3 for the steps to create a G/L account. Here are some notes to be aware of when creating the account:

▶ It is recommended that you use a special account group when creating the reconciliation accounts. The unique account range will make it easier to pick up the activity in reporting.

▶ The account should be created as a P&L account.

▶ Remember to extend the account to all the company codes within the controlling area.

▶ Do not create a corresponding cost element. Reconciliation postings occur only in FI.

An example of one of the accounts to be used by Extreme Sports can be seen in Figure 8.27.

FIGURE 8.27   One of the accounts in Extreme Sports' G/L

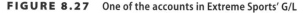

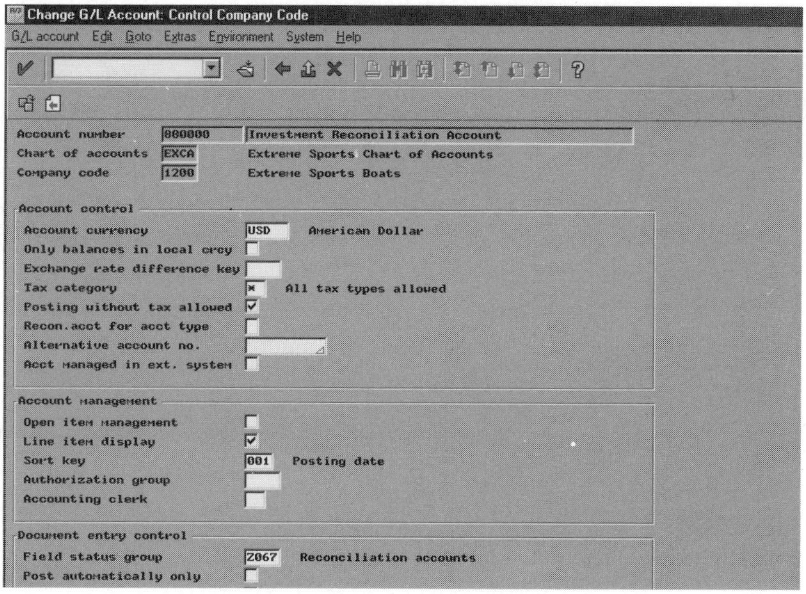

When all accounts have been created and extended to the company codes, you can begin defining the accounts for automatic posting.

EXTREME SPORTS RECONCILIATION ACCOUNTS CONFIGURATION ANALYSIS

Extreme Sports will be using three accounts to track reconciliation activity:

880000   Investment Reconciliation

880100   Production Reconciliation

880110   CO-FI General Reconciliation

Management prefers to see the activities segregated on the company code P&L.

Maintain Accounts for Automatic Reconciliation Posting

Automatic account assignment was discussed in detail in Chapter 3. The same concepts apply to automatic reconciliation postings. Depending on the level of detail required, adjustment account usage can vary from just one account to over one hundred accounts for all postings. In most cases, one is too few, and in all cases, one hundred is too many. Somewhere in between is more appropriate. But how do you determine how many accounts to use? A good place to find the answer is to look at the rules applicable to the process key.

Rules are indicators that you set to control how automated postings can occur in the system. Refer back to Chapter 3, if you need to, in which process keys and rules were discussed in greater detail. A process key provides a unique set of rules that control how the system can be updated. The process key for reconciliation ledger activity is CO1. Potentially, there are four indicators that can be set for CO1: Debit/Credit, Costing Scope (Object Class), CO Transaction (Activity), or Default.

In addition, any combination of the rules can be activated to provide even greater complexity. More will be explained as the configuration is described. Begin by entering the reconciliation account assignment repository after following the menu path Controlling ➢ Overhead Cost Controlling ➢ Cost and Revenue Element Accounting ➢ Reconciliation Ledger ➢ Maintain Adjustment Accounts for Reconciliation Postings ➢ Define Accounts for Automatic Postings.

A pop-up box will appear, asking for the chart of accounts to be entered. Adjustment account activity for the reconciliation ledger is maintained at the chart level and is thus active for the entire client. Keep this in mind when account choices are being made.

MAINTAIN THE CO-FI AUTOMATIC ACCOUNT ASSIGNMENT CONFIGURATION

You can define accounts for automatic postings by using the following methods:

Menu Path: **Controlling** ➢ **Overhead Cost Controlling** ➢ **Cost and Revenue Element Accounting** ➢ **Reconciliation Ledger** ➢ **Maintain Adjustment Accounts for Reconciliation Postings** ➢ **Define accounts for Automatic Postings.**

Transaction: **OBYB**

N O T E   The settings for the reconciliation adjustment accounts are maintained at the chart of accounts level— they are controlling area independent.

Enter the name of the chart of accounts in the field requested and press Enter. The automatic posting configuration screen appears (see Figure 8.28).

FIGURE 8.28   The automatic posting configuration screen

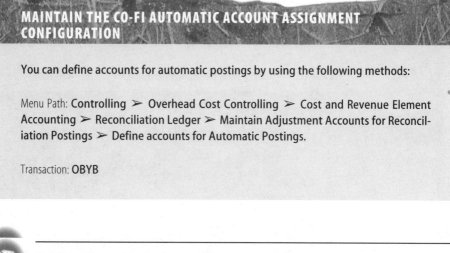

Because no rules indicators have been set, the default rule of one account setting is active. If only one adjustment account is desired for all reconciliation activity, enter the account on this screen and click the save icon. If not, select the Rules button. The automatic posting rules configuration screen appears (see Figure 8.29).

FIGURE 8.29   **The automatic posting rules configuration screen**

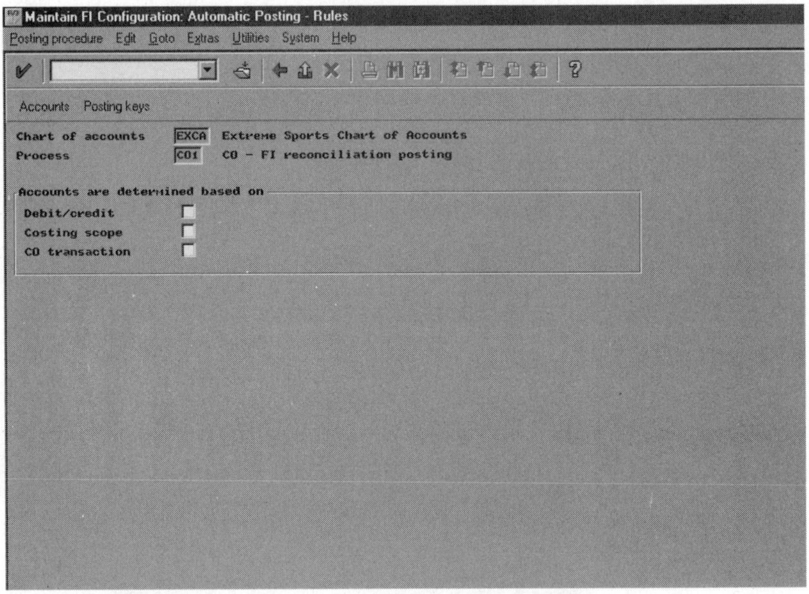

Any one of the rules indicators can be set individually or in combination with any of the others. In the following descriptions of the settings, *level* refers to the amount of detail associated with an account assignment rule. The highest level can be associated with a minimal amount of choice and maintenance. Here are descriptions of the various settings:

Debit/Credit   At a high level, this setting allows for potentially two accounts to be assigned: one debit account and one credit account. If Debit/Credit is set, SAP will provide you with two fields to fill.

Costing Scope   The next level of detail down from Debit/Credit. You define an adjustment account for each of the four object classes: Investment, Production, Profitability, and Overhead Cost.

CO Transaction   The lowest level. Adjustment accounts are assigned at the CO activity level. An example of a CO activity would be KOAO: Order Settlement.

When activating combinations of these rules, keep in mind the maintenance level involved:

Activate Debit/Credit and Costing Scope   You must maintain an adjustment account for both the debit and credit posting for each object class. There are eight assignments in total.

Activate Debit/Credit and CO Transaction   You must maintain an adjustment account for both debit and credit postings for each CO activity. With 25 CO activities times the 2 debit/credit indicators, there are 50 assignments in total.

Activate Costing Scope and CO Transaction   You must maintain an adjustment account for each unique grouping of CO activity and object class. With 25 activities times 4 object classes, there are 100 assignments in total.

Activate all rules   You must maintain adjustment accounts for each unique grouping of Debit/Credit indicator/object class/CO Transaction. The total number of potential assignments is 200.

The complexity certainly builds quickly. Whatever you decide, select one, some, or none, and click the save icon. In the case of Extreme Sports, costing scope will be selected to allow tracking by object class. The account assignment screen appears (see Figure 8.30).

FIGURE 8.30   The account assignment screen

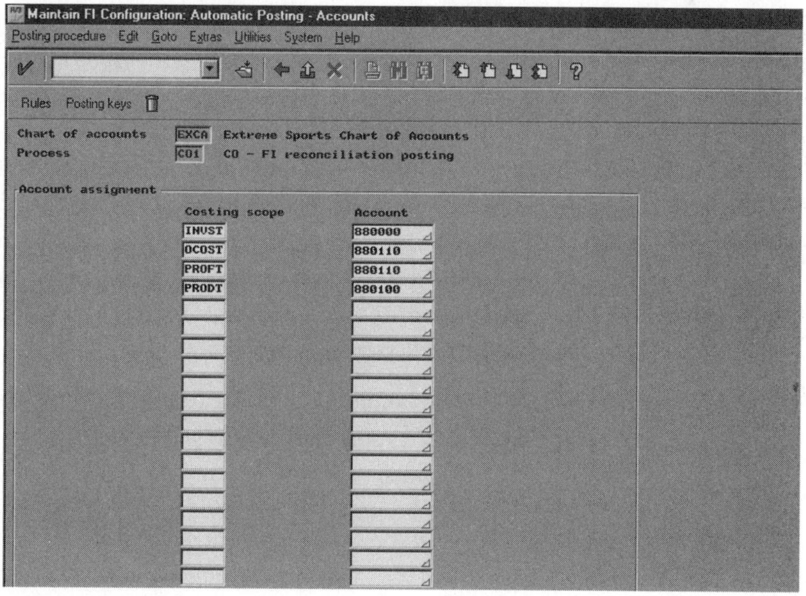

Make the following entries:

Costing Scope   Enter the relevant cost objects one time each in a field.

Account   Enter the proper adjustment account.

When you're finished, save the settings. At this point, reconciliation ledger account assignment activity is complete. The final step in the CO-FI reconciliation ledger configuration is the assigning of a number range.

WARNING   Once the adjustment account settings are made, changes should be carefully thought through. Until you make postings with these settings, changes are acceptable. After activity has occurred and you make a rule change, all prior account assignments are lost forever.

EXTREME SPORTS RECONCILIATION ACCOUNTS CONFIGURATION ANALYSIS

As stated earlier in the chapter, Extreme Sports has decided to track its activity at only the object class level. Capitalized cost transfers between companies are now easily segregated from the production cost transfers.

Assign Reconciliation Activity to a Number Range

As with every activity in the CO module, a number range must be assigned to the reconciliation postings. The number range assignment is at the controlling area level. Use the following menu path to begin: Controlling ➤ Overhead Cost Controlling ➤ Cost and Revenue Element Accounting ➤ Reconciliation Ledger ➤ Maintain Adjustment Accounts for Reconciliation Postings ➤ Determine Document Number Range for Reconciliation Postings.

After you use of the configuration transactions, the reconciliation ledger document number range screen appears (see Figure 8.31).

ASSIGNMENT OF THE RECONCILIATION LEDGER DOCUMENT NUMBER RANGE

You can set the number range by using the following methods:

Menu Path: **Controlling** ➤ **Overhead Cost Controlling** ➤ **Cost and Revenue Element Accounting** ➤ **Reconciliation Ledger** ➤ **Maintain Adjustment Accounts for Reconciliation Postings** ➤ **Determine Document Number Range for Reconciliation Postings**

Transaction: **OK13**

FIGURE 8.31   The reconciliation ledger document number range screen

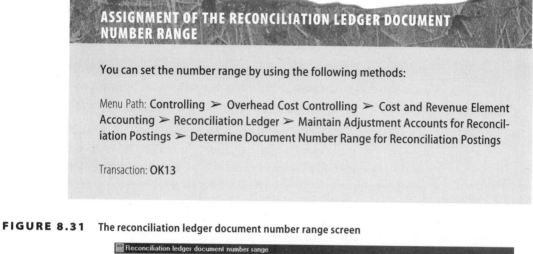

There are two methods to assigning a number range interval: create your own or copy an existing range. The recommended approach is to copy from an existing controlling area if one is available. To copy the interval, select the copy icon. A pop up box labeled Copy: CO Area will appear (see Figure 8.32).

Enter the following data:

From   Enter the ID of the controlling area to provide the range.

To   Enter the ID of the controlling area to receive the number range interval.

Select copy when complete. A memo box may appear, warning you that number ranges should not be transported but rather maintained manually within each client. Press Enter to complete the transaction. The number range has been copied.

If you are maintaining the first controlling area in your client, you must manually create the interval. A similar process occurred when you maintained the controlling area document number range in Chapter 7. In the reconciliation ledger document number range screen, enter the ID for the controlling area to receive the interval in the CO Area field.

FIGURE 8.32   The Copy: CO Area dialog box

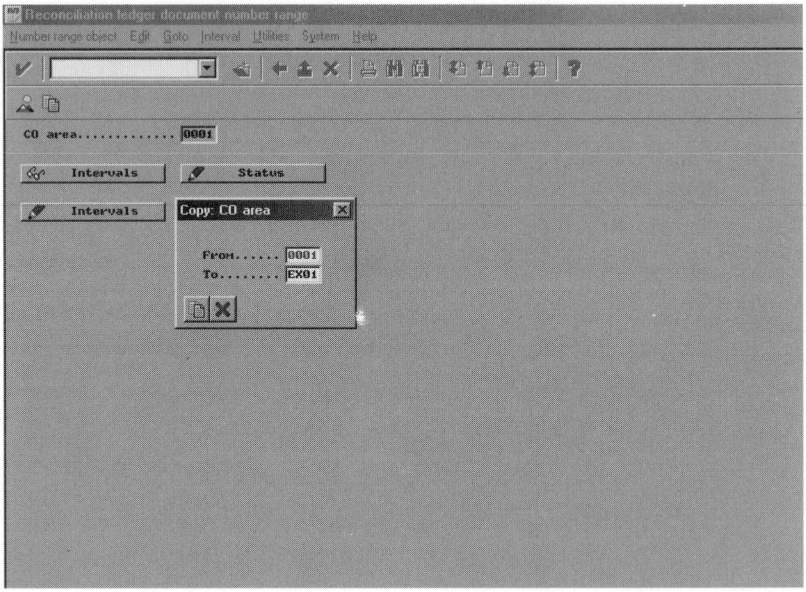

Select the Change Intervals button found in the middle of the screen. The Maintain Number Range Intervals screen appears. Select the Insert Interval button to maintain the number range, and an interval entry box will appear (see Figure 8.33).

FIGURE 8.33   The Insert Interval screen

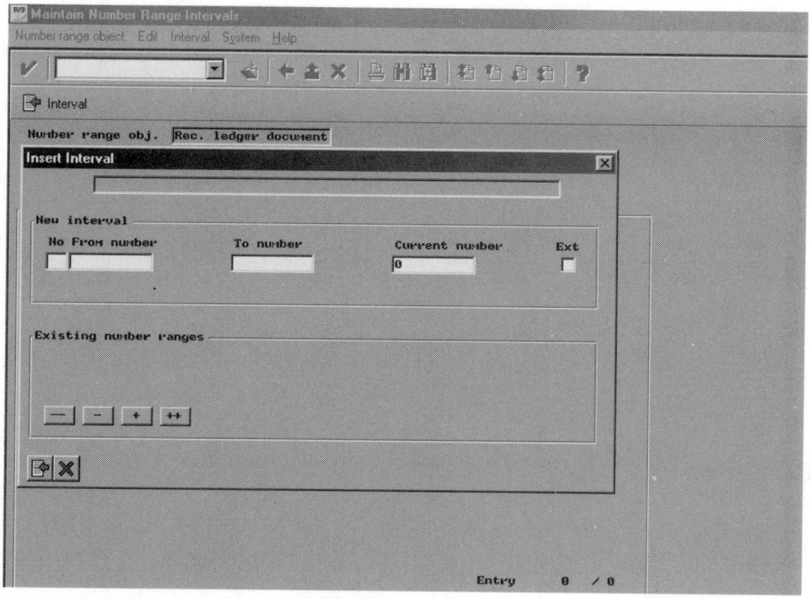

Here are the fields in the Insert Interval screen:

No   Enter the two-digit alphanumeric ID of the number range.

From Number   Enter the lower end of the number range. Use up to 10 digits.

To Number   Enter the upper limit of the number range. Again, use up to 10 digits.

Current Number   If you would like to start at a number other than the From number, enter that number here.

Ext   Select whether you would like the user to determine the document number at the time of entry.

TIP   Whenever possible, allow the system to determine the number range.

When the settings are complete, select the Insert button or press Enter. The number range interval will appear (see Figure 8.34). Save the settings when complete.

FIGURE 8.34   The number range object screen

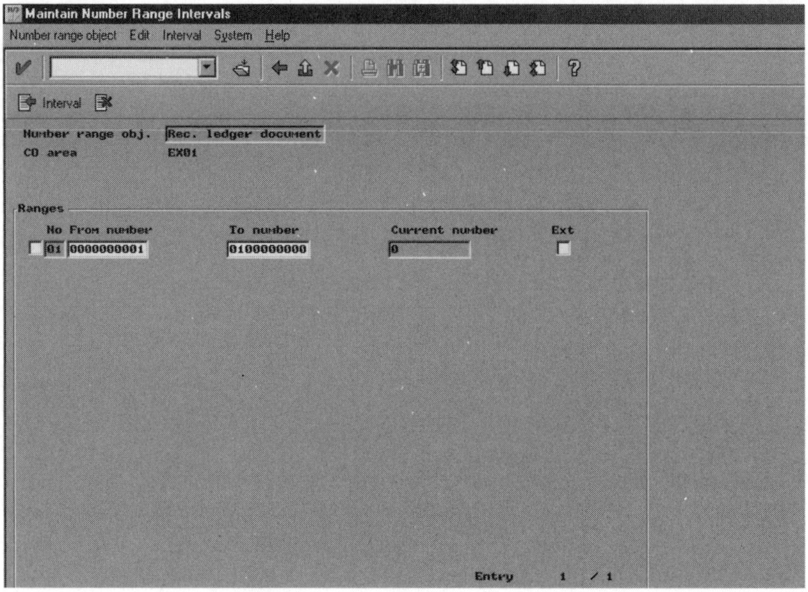

Reconciliation ledger configuration is finished. The system is now capable of success-fully running the CO-FI reconciliation transaction. Although understanding how to configure the CO-FI reconciliation is important, it is equally important to know how the resulting transactions flow. The next section will touch briefly on this subject.

Reconciliation Ledger Cost Flows

When thinking about reconciliation postings, remember that updates occur only in the FI module. No postings will occur in CO as a result of the CO-FI transaction. The reason is that the cross-company, cross-business area, or cross-functional area activity has already happened in CO. The purpose of the reconciliation ledger is to put FI back in balance with CO, not the other way around. To illustrate, Figure 8.35 gives an example of how a cross-company order settlement in CO is balanced in FI.

Notice how the cross-company settlement, Step 2, does not require a posting to an intercompany account. CO tracks only cost accounting activity. All balance sheet activity is maintained in the FI ledger only. CO will allow a two-sided entry, with each side residing in a different company code. The same scenario could be detailed for both business area and functional area postings. When the CO-FI reconciliation transaction is run, as seen in Step 3, the intercompany postings are made automatically. There is no need to keep the companies in balance through manual journal entries.

FIGURE 8.35   The cross-company order settlement flows from CO to FI and balances.

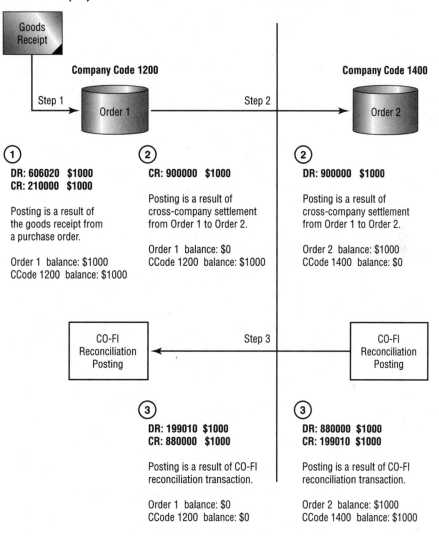

Now that the reconciliation postings have been detailed, a further discussion of CO cost accounting updates is in order.

Explanation of CO Updates

One of the more difficult SAP topics to learn is how costs flow through the CO module. The concepts of object type, object class, and real versus statistical postings are foreign to most individuals. The key to understanding this is to recognize that CO activity is tracked for management reporting only. It is not subject to statutory accounting or reporting requirements. The CO module is governed by the rules of cost accounting assignments and internal/external movements. Of these concepts, internal CO activity movements are possibly the most difficult to understand.

Internal CO movements include, among others, order settlement, cost center assessments, and internal activity allocations. Internal movements are defined as those activities that move cost from one object type to another, without any FI update. External movements can involve movements from an object type in CO to an object in FI. An example would be a settlement from an internal order to a fixed asset. Because the movement is external to CO, a real G/L account would have to be involved for an FI update to occur.

Real vs. Statistical Postings

The flexibility of SAP can be observed when you look at the software's ability to track cost accounting information. A complete account assignment in CO includes both a cost element and a real cost object. It is the cardinal rule in SAP that every cost accounting transaction must have one, and only one, real cost object assignment. Only real postings are reported in the CO reconciliation ledger. Examples of real cost objects include the following:

- ▶ Cost center
- ▶ Real internal order
- ▶ Profitability segment
- ▶ Sales order

Extending its reporting capabilities, SAP also allows you to assign a second cost object to any cost accounting transaction. Now, the cardinal rule doesn't change when you add the second cost object. Only one of the objects will receive a real posting. The second object's posting is not real, but instead is considered statistical. The uses for statistical activity are limited to analysis and reporting. They cannot be acted upon directly by any other SAP transaction. All updates must occur in conjunction with a real object posting.

AN EXAMPLE OF REAL VS. STATISTICAL POSTINGS

A journal entry is made to correct some expense activity on cost center 1000. Within the transaction, costs are credited to cost center 1000 and debited to both cost center 2000 and internal order 3000. Two real cost objects are included in the debit side of the transaction. Only one of these objects can receive the posting in the CO reconciliation ledger. The other will receive a statistical posting. In this case, cost center 2000 will be the recipient of the statistical update.

To support two real objects being included in a single transaction, SAP has hard-coded the real-versus-statistical relationship. SAP will determine which object receives the real update and which receives the statistical update. The relationship is fixed and cannot be acted upon by the user. The following are some of these posting relationships:

Cost center and internal order   The order receives the real posting.

Cost center and sales order   The sales order receives the real posting.

Cost center and project   The project receives the real posting.

Profitability segment and any other object   The profitability segment *always* receives the real posting.

Internal order and sales order   To post to both, the internal order must be statistical.

With any rule, there is always an exception. In certain instances, it is possible that a transaction could have three cost object assignments when one of the cost objects is statistical. If you were to create a journal entry to debit a cost center, profitability segment, and a statistical internal order, the transaction would post because the internal order is statistical. A statistical object maintains special properties that preclude it from being recognized during the transaction.

Like a real object, a statistical object can be used in all reporting and analysis functions. It cannot be posted to directly, however. The differences between a statistical posting to a real object and a statistical posting to a statistical object are minimal. The main variance is the object type. Real objects can be used individually. Statistical objects must be accompanied by a real object assignment in any transaction.

SAP differentiates real versus statistical posting by tagging each CO transaction with a value type. There are numerous value types available in the system, many of which will be discussed in later chapters. Here is a quick list of recognized types:

- ▶ Actual costs

- ▶ Plan costs

- ▶ Actual statistical costs

- ▶ Plan statistical costs

- ▶ Commitments

- ▶ Variances

- ▶ Target costs

Notice that SAP segregates statistical postings. In this manner, the system allows for distinct reporting of actual real and actual statistical costs.

T I P   When line item activity within CO is analyzed, the value type can be displayed for each item. Actual line items will have a value type of 04. Statistical items will have a value type of 11.

Corrections and Other Topics

When you're making corrections that involve statistical updates, it is always recommended that you reverse the original document. If reversal is not possible, it is important that any manual corrections include all the objects originally posted. If you are tracking activity through statistical postings, you must have a unique reporting requirement. If an object is missed during the correction, the reporting will be inaccurate.

A second recommendation is to not post operating expenses directly to Profitability Analysis (CO-PA). Remember, when posting to a cost center in CCA, and a segment in CO-PA, the CO-PA posting is always real. If an error was found, the manual correction activity can be cumbersome because of the level of detail required to properly update CO-PA. The recommended approach to transferring costs to CO-PA from CCA is through cost center assessments. Assessments will be covered in detail in Chapter 9.

Summary

This chapter provided a solid background into the basics of overhead cost controlling. Understanding the cost accounting effects of the various settings will be invaluable as you continue your configuration. Remember to pay attention to object types when creating new cost objects. The benefit from proper definition will be seen in the reconciliation ledger reporting. Also keep in mind the established cost object relationships when posting to two cost objects simultaneously in a single transaction. The topics covered included:

Cost Element Types

    Primary Cost Element Categories

    Secondary Cost Elements Categories

Automatic Cost Element Creation

    Define Default Settings

    Define Batch Input Session

    Execute Batch Input Session

Manual Cost Element Creation

Imputed Costs

    Cost Element % Method

    Overhead Costing Sheet Creation: Copy

Reconciliation Ledger

    Activate Reconciliation Ledger

    Clearing Account Creation

    Maintain Accounts for Automatic Reconciliation Posting

    Assign Reconciliation Activity to a Number Range

    Reconciliation Ledger Cost Flows

Explanation of CO Updates

    Real vs. Statistical Postings

    Corrections and Other Topics

CHAPTER 9

Cost Center Accounting

FEATURING:

▶ COST CENTER ACCOUNTING CONFIGURATION

▶ COST CENTER ACCOUNTING STANDARD HIERARCHY

▶ ACTIVITY TYPES AND STATISTICAL KEY FIGURES

▶ ASSESSMENTS, DISTRIBUTIONS, AND REPOSTINGS

▶ COST CENTER ACCOUNTING: PLANNING

▶ AUTOMATIC ACCOUNT ASSIGNMENT IN CO

C ost Center Accounting (CCA) is utilized within SAP to collect and report operating activity within an organizational unit. Within CCA, operational expenses are captured by three separate master data objects: cost centers, activity types, and statistical key figures. Cost centers are maintained within a hierarchy that is representative of the implementing company's internal reporting/accountability structure. The hierarchy development is central to all cost accounting reporting within the CO module and will be discussed early in the chapter.

Understanding the differences between master data and transactional data is important, and the key topics will be outlined. A key piece of functionality within CCA is the ability to process allocations quickly. Through assessments and distributions, the user has the ability to quickly process hundreds of cost allocations across numerous organizational units. In addition, planning and its entire infrastructure are vital to an effective operational accounting environment and will be dealt with in detail. Lastly, the concept of CO automatic account assignment will be explored, and configuration will be documented.

The process will begin with an introduction to Cost Center Accounting.

Introduction to Cost Center Accounting Configuration

Configuration of the Cost Center Accounting (CCA) module is a combination of table settings and master data development. The key to properly marrying the two is a good understanding of the organization's reporting requirements. How are operating costs supposed to flow through the organization? Does the company collect costs centrally and allocate at the end of the month, or should costs flow directly to the responsibility center? As with most things dealing with SAP, it depends.

The key development area within the CCA module is the standard hierarchy. The standard hierarchy will become your main tool for reporting operating costs. All cost centers must be assigned to a node on the hierarchy. In addition to cost centers, activity types may be developed to assist in calculating internal activity costs. Activity types are assigned to a cost center and, with the help of the activity rates, utilize actual activity quantities to determine the activity cost per cost center.

A third piece of master data used in CCA is the statistical key figure. Key figures are used to track quantities and values for various operating activities. The statistical nature of the master data allows the user to manipulate the data without causing inconsistencies. Uses for key figures range from reporting/analysis to utilization as a tracing factor in allocations.

Cost Center Accounting Standard Hierarchy

Prior to creating any cost centers within your controlling area, you must first complete the standard hierarchy. The standard hierarchy is the central cost center hierarchy created in your system and acts as the one repository for all cost centers. Additional, or alternatively, hierarchies may be created to meet planning or reporting requirements. The hierarchy name is defined when the controlling area is created (see "The Controlling Area" in Chapter 7) and is utilized as the top node. Cost centers cannot be assigned at this level, so further development will be required.

Keep in mind that the standard hierarchy should be developed with the initial intent of supporting your reporting environment. If certain cost centers should be uniquely grouped to support management reporting, reflect this in your hierarchy design. Cost centers can be assigned only at the lowest node level within the hierarchy. Each time a cost center is created, a hierarchy node assignment is required on the master record. The requirement of an assignment thus assures you that all cost centers will be applied to one and only one node within your hierarchy.

TIP Before beginning development, spend time querying management about any upcoming changes to their organizational structure. Then develop a hierarchy outline on a spreadsheet and seek sign-off. This may save needless development time.

The standard hierarchy, like most master data, can be developed from either the user menu or the IMG. To begin, follow the user menu path Accounting ➤ Controlling ➤ Cost Centers ➤ Master Data ➤ Standard Hierarchy ➤ Change.

COST CENTER ACCOUNTING STANDARD HIERARCHY CREATION/ MAINTENANCE

You can get to the screen to develop the standard hierarchy by using the following methods:

Application Menu Path: **Accounting ➤ Controlling ➤ Cost Centers ➤ Master Data ➤ Standard Hierarchy ➤ Change**

Transaction Code: **KSH2**

The change cost center group structure screen will appear (see Figure 9.1).

FIGURE 9.1   The change cost center group structure screen

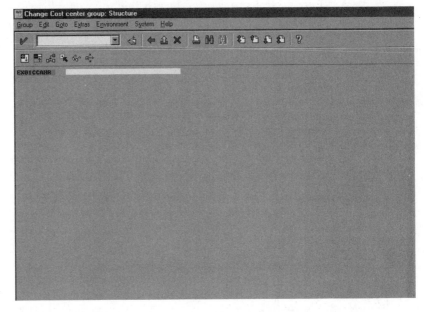

If the hierarchy has not yet been maintained, only the top node will be displayed. Enter a standard hierarchy description into the empty field next to the node, if applicable.

Adding New Hierarchy Nodes

The next step is to add new hierarchy nodes. From the change cost center group structure screen, begin adding nodes by placing the cursor on the node that will be augmented. In the case of a new hierarchy, place the cursor on the top node. By placing your cursor on a node, you are identifying that node as the focal point. Click the Insert Group button and the Insert Group pop-up box appears (see Figure 9.2).

Notice that the ID of the node you selected with your cursor appears in the Superior-Node field. The superior node becomes the basis for the new node's assignment to the hierarchy.

FIGURE 9.2   The Insert Group pop-up box

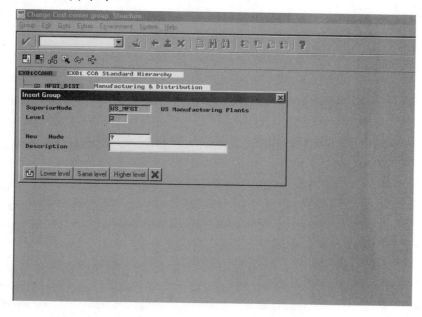

TIP   The node IDs are maintained at the client level and therefore must be unique across all controlling areas within the client.

Let's take a look at the fields in this screen:

SuperiorNode   This field identifies the node that will be the basis for the new node's assignment to the hierarchy. Entry in the field is not possible.

Level   This field identifies the level of the hierarchy on which the superior node exists. As you add lower levels to the hierarchy, the number will increase. Entry in the field is not possible.

New Node   Enter the character ID of the new node group. The ID can be up to 11 characters in length. Remember that the group node ID can be used later in reporting and/or planning, so be sure to use an ID name that easily identifies the cost center group.

Description   Enter the description of the node group.

Lower Level/Same Level/Higher Level   At the bottom of the Insert Group box, you'll find four buttons (when you're entering the first node on the hierarchy, only the Lower Level button appears):

Same Level   If the node you are adding is to be represented on the same level as the superior node, select Same Level.

Lower Level   If the node is to be represented subordinate to the superior node, select Lower Level.

Higher Level   If the node is to become a superior node to the one selected, select Higher Level.

After selecting one of the buttons, you will notice that the new node replaces the preceding node in the SuperiorNode field. Continue adding nodes, deciding whether the node will be subordinate or on the same level.

TIP   It is recommended that the hierarchy be built from the top down—that is, build each level completly, then continue to the next. You will find it quicker to add a string of Same Level nodes than to repeatedly build depth with lower level nodes.

Close/Enter icon   Select the close icon to complete an insertion step. You will notice that the nodes have been added to the standard hierarchy, as shown in Figure 9.3.

FIGURE 9.3   The nodes have been added to the standard hierarchy.

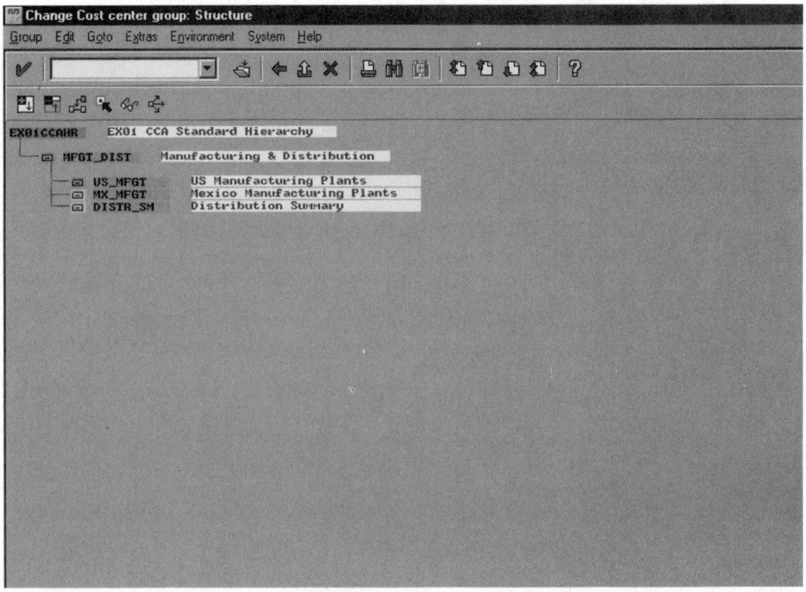

Repeat the steps until the hierarchy is complete. Be sure to save when complete.

Changing/Moving/Deleting Hierarchy Nodes

In the same way that nodes can be added, they can be moved, altered, or deleted. The process is simple and repeatable, even after cost centers have been assigned. To move an existing node, select the node from the standard hierarchy change screen.

ENTERING THE STANDARD HIERARCHY CHANGE SCREEN

You can use the following methods to get to the standard hierarchy change screen:

Application Menu Path: **Accounting** ➢ **Controlling** ➢ **Cost Centers** ➢ **Master Data** ➢ **Standard Hierarchy** ➢ **Change**

Transaction Code: **KSH2**

The change cost center group structure screen appears. Select the node you want to augment by placing the cursor on the specific node and clicking the Select button. You will notice that the standard header information is replaced with new options, as shown in Figure 9.4.

FIGURE 9.4   Selection of hierarchy node OPS_SUM

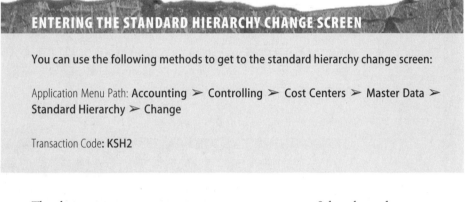

The new options are as follows:

Delete Selection   Use this button to "unselect" the node.

Same Level   If you place your cursor on a new node and select this button, the selected node will move so that it's adjacent to the new node and on the same level.

Lower Level   This button is similar to the Same Level button in function. Place your cursor on the node to which you want the previously selected node to roll up and select the button. The selected node becomes subordinate.

Remove   Use this button to delete the selected node from the hierarchy.

In Figure 9.4, the node OPS_SUM is subordinate to CORP_SUM. It was selected and moved so that it's subordinate to the SHARED_SVC node. The result, shown in Figure 9.5, is that OPS_SUM now rolls up into SHARED_SVC. When your changes are complete, be sure to save the hierarchy.

FIGURE 9.5   Movement of hierarchy node OPS_SUM

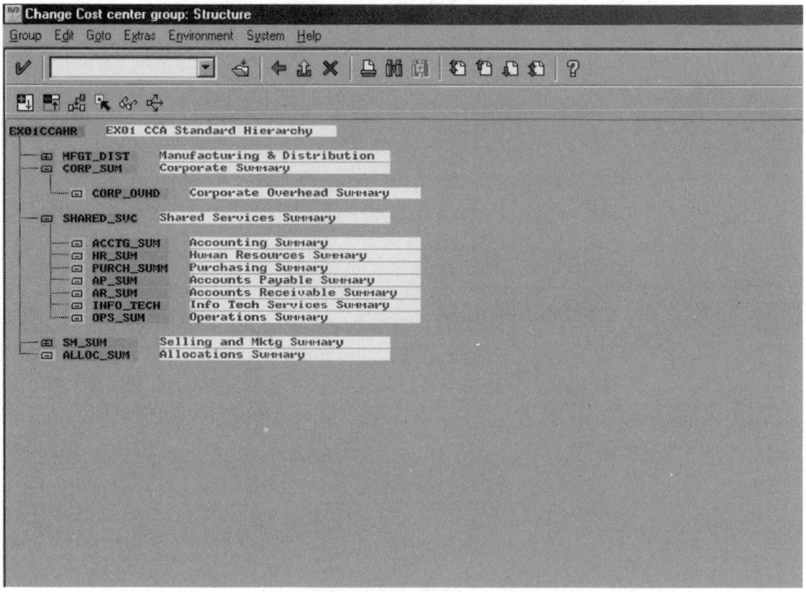

TIP   All changes, except for node removal, can be made after cost centers have been assigned. To remove a node from the hierarchy, it must not have any cost center assignments.

EXTREME SPORTS COST CENTER STANDARD HIERARCHY CONFIGURATION ANALYSIS

Extreme Sports has an uncomplicated operating structure. The majority of overhead expenses are captured within the shared service organization and assessed at period close to the respective profitability centers. All overhead allocations will occur within Cost Center Accounting to ensure that an audit trail exists. Another option for Extreme Sports would be to allocate somewhere between a portion of and all of its costs through Profit Center Accounting.

Controlling Area/Profit Center Accounting Maintenance

If Profit Center Accounting is active within your controlling area, as it is within Extreme Sports' EX01, you must first create a standard hierarchy and assign a dummy profit center. (Further hierarchy development will be discussed in Chapter 12.) Before proceeding, be sure to set the controlling area to the one you will be maintaining. To do so, follow the IMG menu path Enterprise Controlling ➤ Profit Center Accounting ➤ Basic Settings ➤ Maintain Controlling Area.

MAINTAIN THE PCA CONTROLLING AREA SETTINGS

You can use the following methods to get to the screen to maintain controlling areas:

Menu Path: **Enterprise Controlling** ➤ **Profit Center Accounting** ➤ **Basic Settings** ➤ **Maintain Controlling Area**

Transaction Code: **OKE5**

After you use one of these transaction configurations, the EC-PCA controlling area settings screen appears, as shown in Figure 9.6.

FIGURE 9.6   The EC-PCA controlling area settings screen

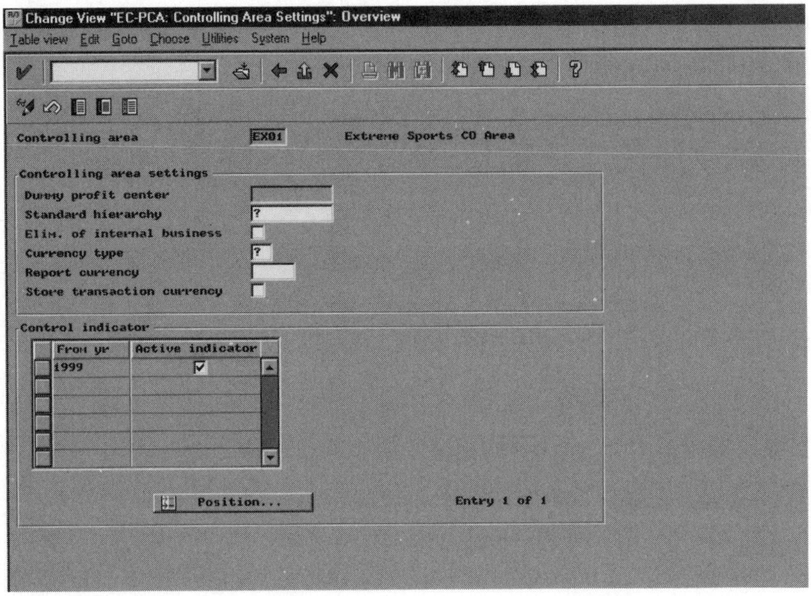

Notice that two fields, Standard Hierarchy and Currency Type, are required. The others are optional:

Dummy Profit Center   The field is grayed out. The dummy profit center is the default profit center for the entire controlling area. It will capture all postings that do not have a profit center account assignment. Additionally, the dummy will serve as the default for assignment on the cost center master record if one is not manually assigned. An entry cannot be made into the field from this screen. The assignment is made when the master record is created. A special transaction is used to create the dummy profit center. There can only be one dummy profit center per controlling area.

TIP   The standard hierarchy must be defined and built prior to creating the dummy profit center. The dummy, like all profit centers, must have a node to reside upon.

Standard Hierarchy   Just as you did for the CCA standard hierarchy, enter the name of the PCA hierarchy. The name can be up to 10 characters in length.

Elim. of Internal Business   Activate this field if it is your desire to eliminate internal activity between two or more account assignment objects that are assigned to the same profit center. For example, a profit center, P1000, has assigned to itself a production order, O2000, and a cost center, C2000. Standard direct labor is confirmed on the order, with the associated labor credit going to cost center C2000. By eliminating internal activity volumes, no PCA document will be produced.

Currency Type   Select the currency type in which all PCA transactions will be maintained. The currency options include the following:

10   Controlling area currency

20   Group currency

90   Profit center currency

If you select 90, Profit center currency, you must identify the currency type. You assign the currency for type 90 in the Report Currency field. In addition, all standard PCA reports will display information in the default currency type identified here.

Report Currency   This field is required if you selected currency type 90. If either the controlling area or group currency type is selected, leave the field blank. If this field is completed, SAP will store transaction data in the currency identified here.

Store Transaction Currency   If you want the transaction currency stored in PCA, flag this field. Data volumes will increase, but if the transaction currency is different from the controlling area or profit center currency, it may be important for reporting.

Control Indicator   The system will display the current year as the default From fiscal year. All settings are good from this year forward. If you make changes, SAP will identify a new From range.

When this screen is configured, save the settings. Figure 9.7 shows the completed PCA controlling area settings. You can now maintain the PCA standard hierarchy.

FIGURE 9.7   The completed PCA controlling area settings

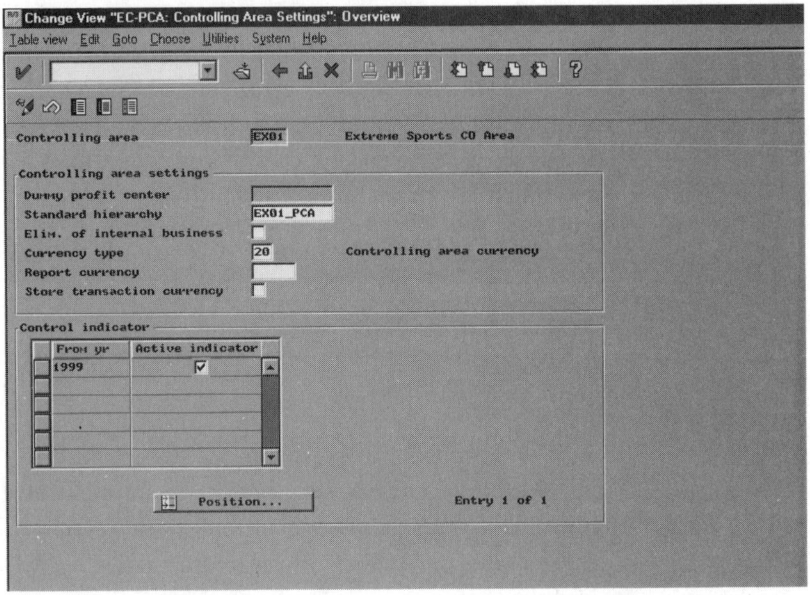

Profit Center Accounting—Creating the Standard Hierarchy

The method for creating and maintaining the PCA standard hierarchy is identical to the processes involved in upkeep of the CCA hierarchy. The keystrokes and movements for adding, moving, and deleting nodes are the same for both hierarchies. Just as there is one CCA standard hierarchy, there is only one PCA standard hierarchy.

Another similarity is that the PCA hierarchy can be created or maintained from either the IMG or the user menu. The IMG menu path is Enterprise Controlling ➤ Master Data ➤ Maintain Standard Hierarchy.

MAINTAIN THE PCA STANDARD HIERARCHY

You can use the following methods to create and maintain the PCA hierarchy:

Menu Path: **Enterprise Controlling ➤ Master Data ➤ Maintain Standard Hierarchy**

Transaction Code: **KCH2**

Please refer to "Changing/Moving/Deleting Hierarchy Nodes" earlier in this chapter for tips on how to maintain hierarchy nodes.

Creating the Dummy Profit Center

The dummy profit center is created by using a special transaction code. Although it shares many of the same attributes as a normal profit center, the indicator flag identifying it as the dummy can only be activated by using either this code or the menu path Enterprise Controlling ➢ Profit Center Accounting ➢ Master Data ➢ Maintain Dummy Profit Center.

CREATING THE DUMMY PROFIT CENTER

To activate the dummy profit center, use the following methods:

Menu Path: **Enterprise Controlling** ➢ **Profit Center Accounting** ➢ **Master Data** ➢ **Maintain Dummy Profit Center**

Transaction Code: **KE59**

A window will appear asking if you want to create the dummy or change a profit center. Select the Create the Dummy Profit Center option. The initial create dummy profit center screen appears. Enter the name of the dummy and press Enter. The create dummy profit center basic configuration screen appears.

Notice that the Valid From and Valid To dates have defaulted into the master record. Because there is only one dummy profit center, the valid dates must cover the entire existence of the active system. Complete the remaining open fields:

Name   Enter the name of the dummy profit center.

Description   Enter a description of the dummy profit center.

Person in Charge   Enter the name of the individual assigned with the responsibility of managing the dummy.

Department   Enter the name or a description of the department to which the person in charge belongs, if desired.

Profit Center Area   Enter the node ID on the PCA standard hierarchy where the dummy is to be assigned.

Dummy Profit Center   This setting is a flag that identifies that this profit center is the dummy. The setting will default as active.

When the fields are filled in, save the master record. The dummy is now active, as shown in Figure 9.8, and postings can begin to occur within PCA.

FIGURE 9.8   The dummy profit center is now active.

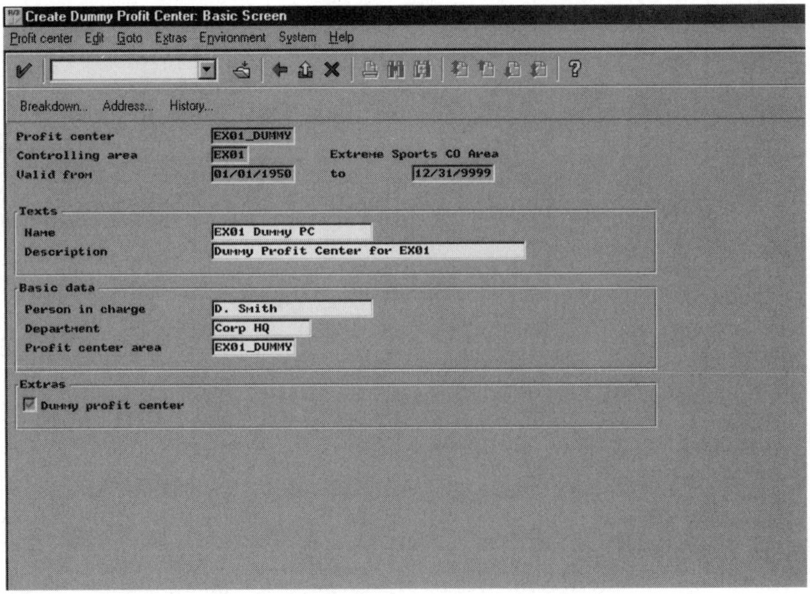

EXTREME SPORTS PROFIT CENTER ACCOUNTING MAINTENANCE CONFIGURATION ANALYSIS

Extreme Sports is using Profit Center Accounting to capture and report its profitability by division. Therefore, because it is active within the controlling area, the profit center standard hierarchy was developed and a dummy profit center was created.

Cost Center Basics

Before creating the cost center master record, there are a few configuration settings that must be considered:

- ▶ Cost center categories or types
- ▶ Time-dependent fields
- ▶ Profit Center Accounting (PCA) relevance

The relevance of PCA stems from the activation settings found on the controlling area. If PCA is active for your controlling area, SAP expects a profit center assignment on the cost center master record. If you attempt to save the cost center without this assignment, the system will give you a warning. Complete Profit Center Accounting configuration will be covered in detail in Chapter 12, but PCA-relevant controlling area configuration must be completed prior to adding any cost centers.

TIP   If PCA is active, it is highly recommended that you always assign a profit center to the cost center master record. Inconsistencies will surely occur if the assignment is not made.

Additionally, the following two tables are relevant when maintaining cost center master data (you can review all necessary setting for each table using the databrowser):

CSKS   Contains all cost center master data field settings (for example, Cost Center Category, Hierarchy Assignment)

CSKT   Contains all cost center text field settings (for example, Cost Center Description, Short Text)

Cost Center Categories

The uses of cost center categories are threefold:

- ▶ They deliver default control indicator values to the cost center master record during cost center creation.
- ▶ They are assigned to the activity type master record as the key to which types of cost centers can use a given activity type.
- ▶ They can be used during functional area assignment, reporting, and evaluations and as search criteria.

SAP delivers standard categories like Sales, Administration, and Production for your immediate use. You can, however, make changes to the standards, or you can create as many of your own categories as you like. To create/change/display the cost center categories, use the menu path Controlling ➢ Overhead Cost Controlling ➢ Cost Center Accounting ➢ Master Data ➢ Cost Centers ➢ Maintain Cost Center Categories.

COST CENTER CATEGORY MAINTENANCE

You can use the following methods to create/change/display the cost center categories:

Menu Path: **Controlling** ➢ **Overhead Cost Controlling** ➢ **Cost Center Accounting** ➢ **Master Data** ➢ **Cost Centers** ➢ **Maintain Cost Center Categories**

Transaction Code: **OKA2**

The cost center types configuration screen appears (see Figure 9.9). Notice the various table settings. To create a new category, click the New Entries button. An empty category table will appear.

FIGURE 9.9 The cost center types configuration screen

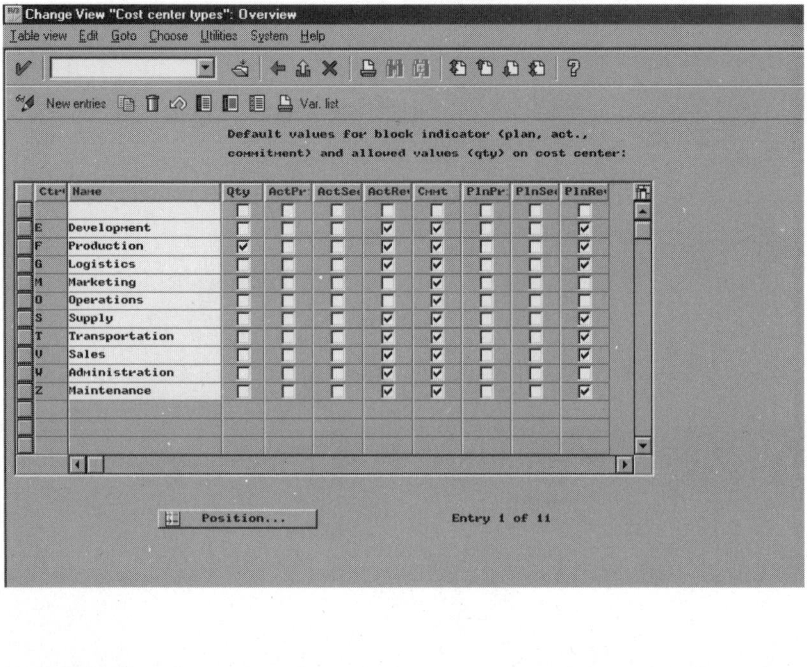

NOTE   Remember, when you begin to make the block indicator settings, an *X* in the column signals that you want that activity blocked. Leave the column field empty if the posting described is desired.

Here are the fields you need to configure on this screen:

Category Indicator   Enter the category ID. This field is alphanumeric, but only one character in length.

Name   Enter a description that corresponds to the category indicator.

Qty   If this field is checked, the cost center will retain quantity information.

ActPr   This field determines if actual primary costs can be tracked. Usually left empty for most categories.

ActSec   This field determines if actual secondary costs can be tracked. Also almost always left empty.

ActRev   If this field is activated, revenues cannot be posted to the cost center with this category. If it's not active, revenues can be posted to the cost center, but only statistically.

Cmmt   This field determines if commitments can be tracked on the cost center. If commitment management is activated for the controlling area, you should strongly consider allowing commitment update postings.

PlnPr   If this field is activated, the cost center category is blocked from planning costs.

Pln Sec   If this field is activated, the cost center category is blocked from planning secondary costs.

PlnRev   If this field is activated, the cost center category cannot be planned with revenue.

Something to remember about the categories is that a new cost center will absorb the control indicator settings as they were configured at the moment of creation. Any future changes to a category will not have a retroactive impact on previously created cost centers. To affect an existing cost center, you must make desired changes manually. For example, a change to disallow secondary cost element planning on all production cost centers is made. Any future cost centers created from that time forward will be subject to this restriction. Any existing cost centers in the environment will not be affected. Each of the production cost centers will need to have its control indicators adjusted manually.

Time-Based Fields

With the use of the time dependency table, shown in Figure 9.10, SAP has regulated how often a field on the cost center master record can be changed. In addition to the dependency settings, the table provides for the ability to configure whether SAP should retain all historical settings.

FIGURE 9.10 The time dependency table

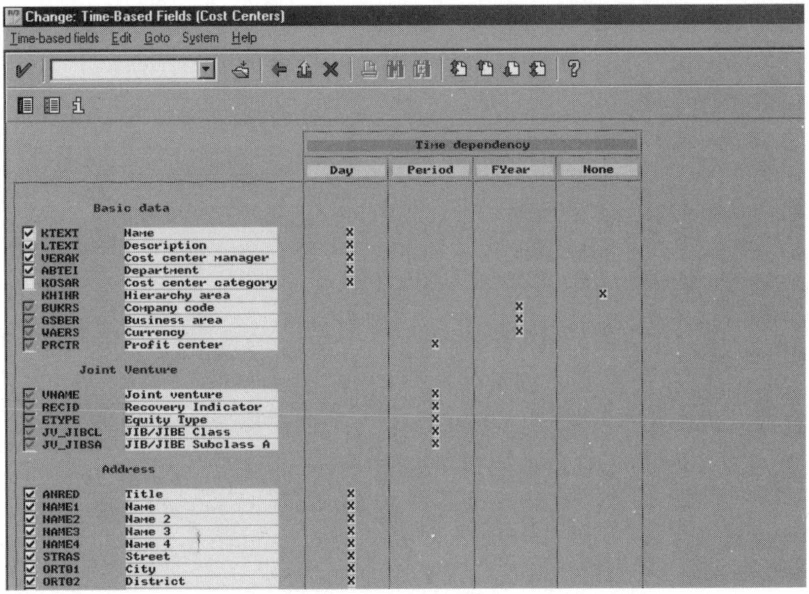

To access the screen with the time dependency table, follow the IMG menu path Controlling ➢ Overhead Cost Controlling ➢ Cost Center Accounting ➢ Master Data ➢ Cost Centers ➢ Define Time-Based Fields for Cost Centers.

MAINTENANCE OF THE TIME-BASED FIELDS

You can use the following methods to access the time dependency table:

Menu Path: **Controlling** ➢ **Overhead Cost Controlling** ➢ **Cost Center Accounting** ➢ **Master Data** ➢ **Cost Centers** ➢ **Define Time-Based Fields for Cost Centers**

Transaction Code: **OKEG**

As you can see in Figure 9.10, the historical tracking flag is set by entering an *X* in the box to the left of the field name.

There are four related areas of time dependency:

Day   A field with this setting can be changed daily without any warning.

Period   A field with this setting can be changed at any time. If the change occurs within a period, a warning may be given. The change can still be made, but caution should be used if the field is marked as historical.

FYear   A field with this setting can be changed only at the beginning of a new fiscal year. Any attempt to change the setting for the current validity interval will result in an error being returned by SAP.

None   Only the Hierarchy Area field is set with this dependency. There are no restrictions to making changes to the field.

SAP has hard-coded the time dependency settings for all cost center master record fields. There is no standard way of altering these settings. You can, however, through the activation of the historical flag, adjust whether changes to the record are tracked.

If it is important to track changes to the master record, each change will need to correspond to a new analysis period. The default analysis period on the master record is the original validity period given to the cost center. New periods can be configured directly on the same master record. (See "Establishing a New Analysis Period" later in this chapter for details.)

Creating/Changing Cost Centers

The cost center master record can be created from either the IMG or the user menu path. The IMG path is Controlling ➢ Overhead Cost Controlling ➢ Cost Center Accounting ➢ Master Data ➢ Cost Centers ➢ Create Cost Centers. Remember, when you create a piece of CO master data, it cannot easily be deleted, so plan your steps appropriately.

CREATING/MAINTAINING THE COST CENTER MASTER RECORD

You can get to the screen to create the cost center master record by using one of the following methods:

Menu Path: **Controlling** ➢ **Overhead Cost Controlling** ➢ **Cost Center Accounting** ➢ **Master Data** ➢ **Cost Centers** ➢ **Create Cost Centers**

Transaction Code: **KS01**

The create cost center request screen will appear, prompting you for input of a cost center number and validity period (see Figure 9.11).

FIGURE 9.11   The create cost center request screen

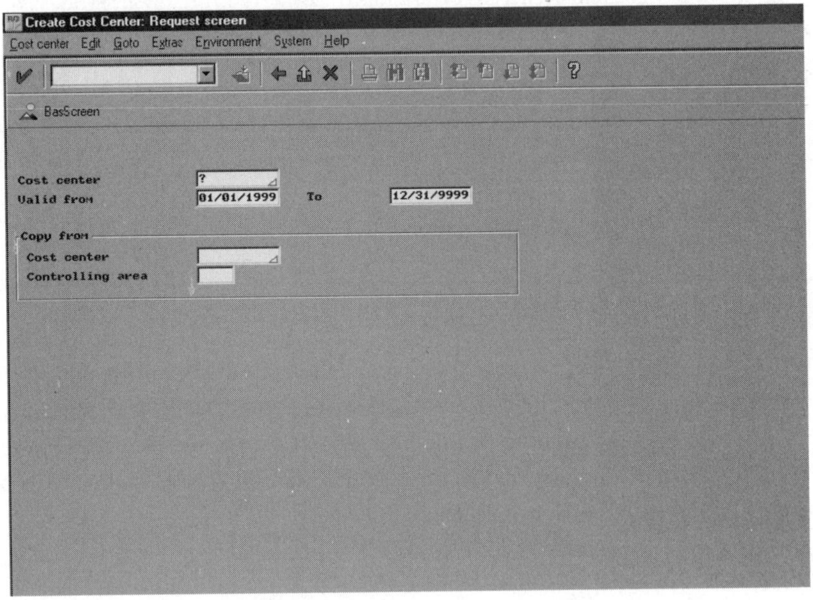

The fields you need to configure on this screen are as follows:

Cost Center   Enter an alphanumeric identifier for the cost center. The ID can be up to 10 characters in length.

Valid From/To   The validity period of the master record is the time frame within which postings may occur. Be certain that the period is significant enough in length to not interrupt activity within a given fiscal period. Additionally, be certain that the range is sufficient to support any history loads.

TIP   To save yourself potential rework, have in mind the numbering methodology you will be using before you begin.

When configuration is complete, press Enter. The create cost center basic screen appears (see Figure 9.12). Notice the number of fields that are required. You can see that the information from the request screen has carried forward into the basic screen and is now grayed out. To make a change to the ID or validity period now, you must exit the update prior to saving and restart.

FIGURE 9.12   The create cost center basic screen

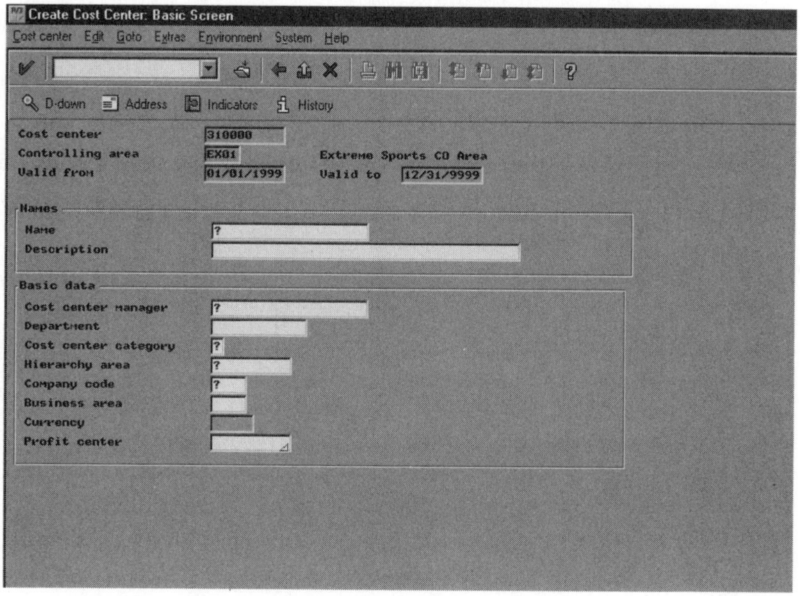

Let's take a look at the fields on the basic screen:

Name   Enter a name for the cost center. This field is required.

Description   Enter a description for the cost center.

Cost Center Manager   Enter the ID of the person in charge of the cost center. This field is required.

Department   Enter the name or ID of the department to which the cost center belongs.

Cost Center Category   Enter the category ID (see "Cost Center Categories" earlier in this chapter for details). This field is required.

Hierarchy Area   Enter the CCA standard hierarchy node to which the cost center will belong. This field is required.

N O T E   Remember that the cost center, or profit center in PCA, can be assigned only to the lowest node on the standard hierarchy. If you attempt to enter a master record at the summary level, SAP will stop the assignment with an error.

Company Code   Assign the cost center to a specific company code. This is necessary for proper FI integration of operating costs. This field is required.

Business Area   Enter a business area if you are utilizing the areas and expect to report with them.

Currency   In this case, Currency is grayed out. Controlling area currency, USD, was identified as the currency type for the controlling area. When you press Enter now, USD will populate the field automatically.

Profit Center   If PCA is active, enter a profit center to which the cost center is assigned.

When you have completed the entry, you can save the cost center (see Figure 9.13). It is wise, however, to review the control indicators before saving. Select the Indicators button. A box will appear with a list of activities that can be blocked (see Figure 9.14).

FIGURE 9.13   The create cost center basic screen configured for Extreme Sports

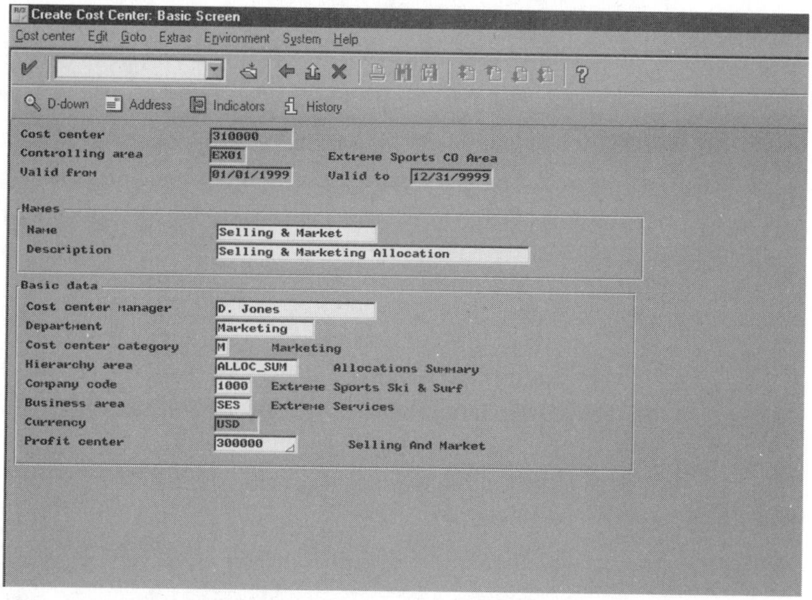

FIGURE 9.14   The Indicators pop-up box

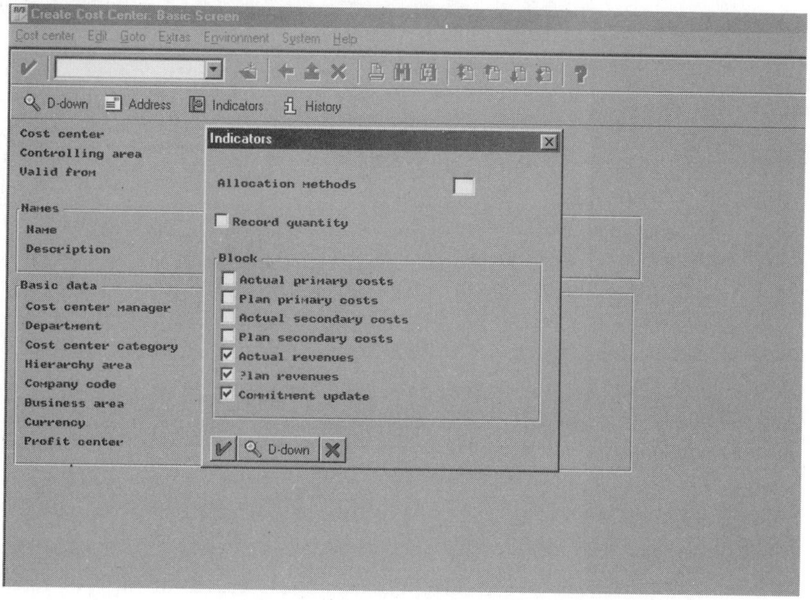

If you refer back to the section on cost center categories, you will remember that the reason for configuring the category settings first was to have the information automatically flow to the cost center upon creation. However, if you should decide to, you can make control changes to specific cost centers on the master record.

With the exception of Allocation Methods, the same categories appear on the master record and in the category table. The Allocation Methods field is not used by SAP at this time. Make any necessary changes to the indicators and press Enter to return to the basic screen.

To enter a name, street address, and tax jurisdiction code for the cost center, select the Address button and an input box will appear (see Figure 9.15). All fields are optional and can be changed at any time. Each can be set as time dependent, and changes can thus be tracked. When you have completed the address, press Enter and save the cost center.

FIGURE 9.15   The Address pop-up box

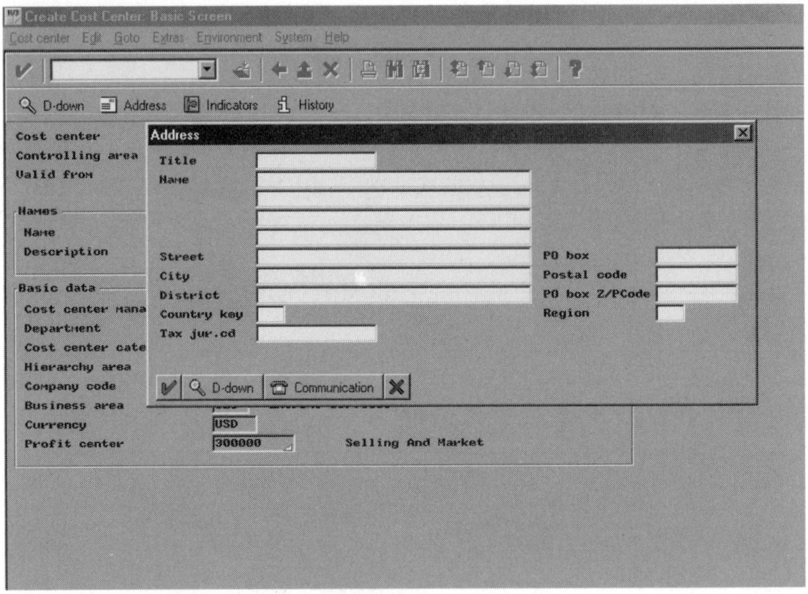

Establishing a New Analysis Period

If you flagged certain master data fields as historically relevant when you were maintaining the time dependency table, a new analysis period may be appropriate. The default analysis period for any CO master record is the original validity period established when the object was created (see "Creating/Changing Cost Centers"). As was mentioned in earlier sections, if you change a time-relevant field on the master record and do not create a new analysis period, the change will overwrite the previous setting. If a second analysis period is created, the change is maintained uniquely.

For example, Cost Center 310000 has an original validity period of 01/01/1999 to 12/31/9999 and carries cost center type M. If you were to change the type to H and not define a new analysis period, the cost center will be represented as always being H. A change document is generated, but you cannot analyze what activity may have occurred on the cost center when the center was type M versus when it was H. Conversely, if you establish a new analysis period, 07/01/1999 to 12/31/9999, then you can analyze activity for both the current and prior period range.

To create a new analysis period, you must be in the cost center master record that is to be changed. Once in the master record, use the following path to bring up the Analysis Period screen: Edit ➢ Analysis Period. The Analysis Period: Choose screen appears, as shown in Figure 9.16.

FIGURE 9.16   The Analysis Period: Choose screen

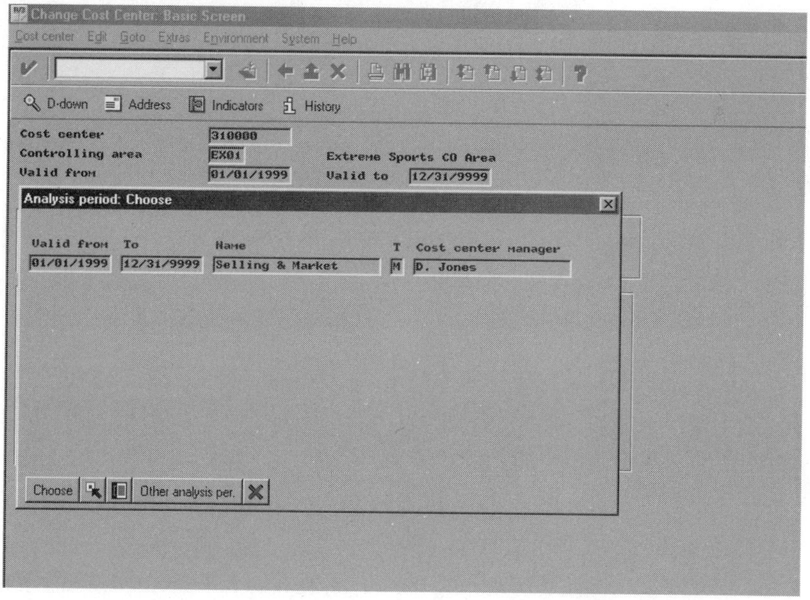

If you have not previously entered an analysis period, only the default settings will appear. If other periods have been established, they will be visible. To enter a new period, select the button labeled Other Analysis Per. A new analysis period box appears, providing the opportunity to enter a date range (see Figure 9.17). Prior to entering a range, be aware of the time dependency of the field you are changing.

FIGURE 9.17   The Other Analysis Period pop-up box

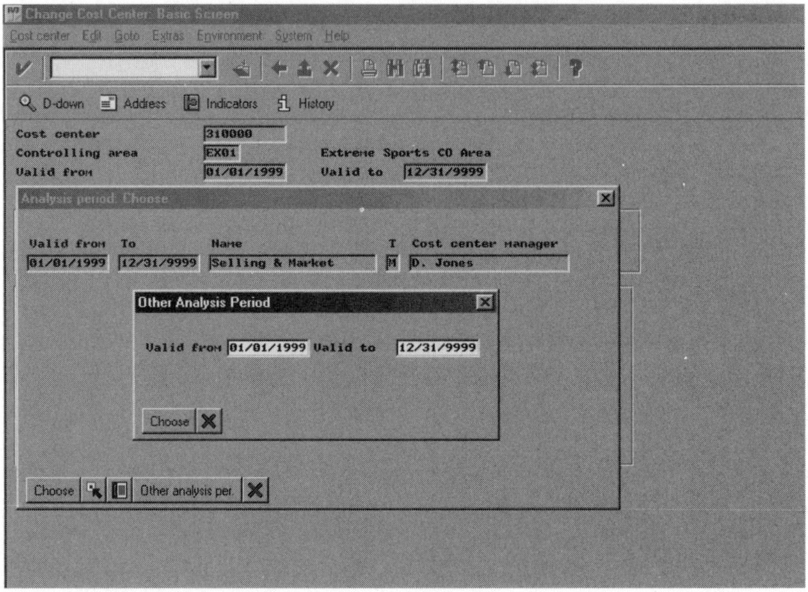

Referring back to the section on time-based fields, the following time dependencies have been established within SAP:

Day   A field with this setting can be changed daily without any warning.

Period   A field with this setting can be changed at any time. If the change occurs within a period, a warning may be given.

FYear   A field with this setting can be changed only at the beginning of a new fiscal year. The only fields with this setting are Company Code, Business Area, and Currency.

None   Only the Hierarchy Area field is set with this dependency. There are no restrictions to making changes to the field.

When establishing the range, be sure to keep these items in mind. After entering the new range, click Choose. The analysis period has replaced the default validity period in the basic screen.

If, for example, you want to change the company code assignment, which carries a time dependency of fiscal year, the new range must begin on the first day of the next fiscal year.

With the new analysis period active, make the changes to the master record and save. The changes will become effective on the first day of the new period range.

Additional Changes after New Analysis Period

Because you have two or more potential validity periods on that cost center, when you go to change the record again, a box will appear asking you to select an analysis period (see Figure 9.18). If you are currently in the master record, use the path Edit ➢ Analysis Period to switch between period ranges.

FIGURE 9.18   Changing the analysis period

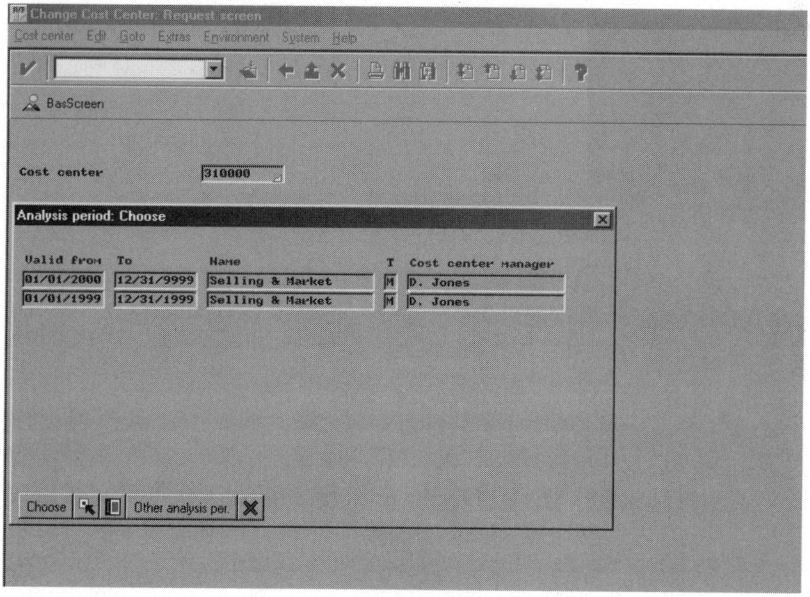

EXTREME SPORTS COST CENTER BASICS CONFIGURATION ANALYSIS

The majority of information provided in the cost center basics section was for the benefit of the accounting department and master data team. Extreme Sports controls both activities through its Shared Services organization.

Activity Types and Statistical Key Figures

Activity types and statistical key figures are the last two types of master data maintained within Cost Center Accounting. Each type is important to tracing and allocating internal activity within the Controlling module environment. Activity types are used by SAP to allocate, both directly and indirectly, expenses based upon an amount of output for a given cost center. The activity type becomes the vehicle through which the quantities are tracked. Examples of activity quantities include the following:

▶ Production hours

▶ Lbs. produced

▶ Energy consumed in kWh

Statistical key figures help the user track activity in another manner. Key figures are designed to be used in reporting and analysis and assist in the assessment or distribution of costs throughout the CCA environment. Key figures are statistical in nature and thus are invisible to the FI environment. Postings to a key figure do not integrate with PCA either. They are, however, powerful when utilized properly. Examples of key figures include the following:

▶ Units sold

▶ Number of employees

▶ Production hours

This section will outline key figures first, followed by activity types.

Statistical Key Figure Creation and Maintenance

Key figure creation and maintenance is far simpler than creation and maintenance of activity types, but then key figures have less functionality. However, with the proper development, a key figure can become invaluable to you from a reporting and allocation viewpoint. Key figures are exclusive to Cost Center Accounting (CCA) within CO, but they can be picked up and utilized by Profit Center Accounting. You will see later that much of the SAP master data is transferable to PCA (see Chapter 12). As with all CCA master data, you can create the record from either the IMG or the user menu. The IMG path is Controlling ➤ Overhead Cost Controlling ➤ Cost Center Accounting ➤ Master Data ➤ Statistical Key Figures ➤ Maintain Statistical Key Figures.

CREATION/MAINTENANCE OF STATISTICAL KEY FIGURES

You can create a key figure record by using the following methods:

Menu Path: **Controlling** ➤ **Overhead Cost Controlling** ➤ **Cost Center Accounting** ➤ **Master Data** ➤ **Statistical Key Figures** ➤ **Maintain Statistical Key Figures**

Transaction Code: **KK01**

Use one of the transaction configurations to access the initial create statistical key figure screen, shown in Figure 9.19.

FIGURE 9.19   The initial create statistical key figure screen

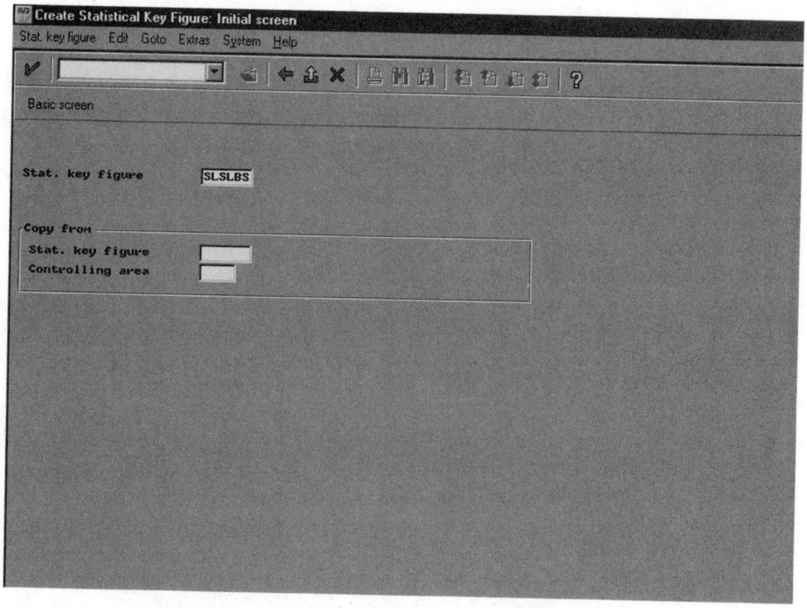

TIP   Before continuing, be sure that the controlling area is set properly. You can set the controlling area through the path Extras ➤ Set Controlling Area.

The fields on this screen are as follows:

Stat. Key Figure   Enter the name of the key figure that you will be creating. The name can be up to six alphanumeric characters in length.

Copy From   Fill in the following fields in the Copy From section:

Stat. Key Figure   If you choose to copy from a key figure in your controlling area or another, enter the name of the source key figure here.

Controlling Area   Enter the ID of the controlling area where the source key figure can be found.

Press Enter and the create statistical key figure basic configuration screen appears (shown in Figure 9.20 configured for Extreme Sports). Notice that the name of the key figure and the assigned controlling area were brought over from the initial screen and grayed out. You can no longer change these assignments on the master record. Your only recourse at this point, if you want to change the name or controlling area, is to not save the figure and start over.

FIGURE 9.20   The create statistical key figure basic configuration screen configured for Extreme Sports

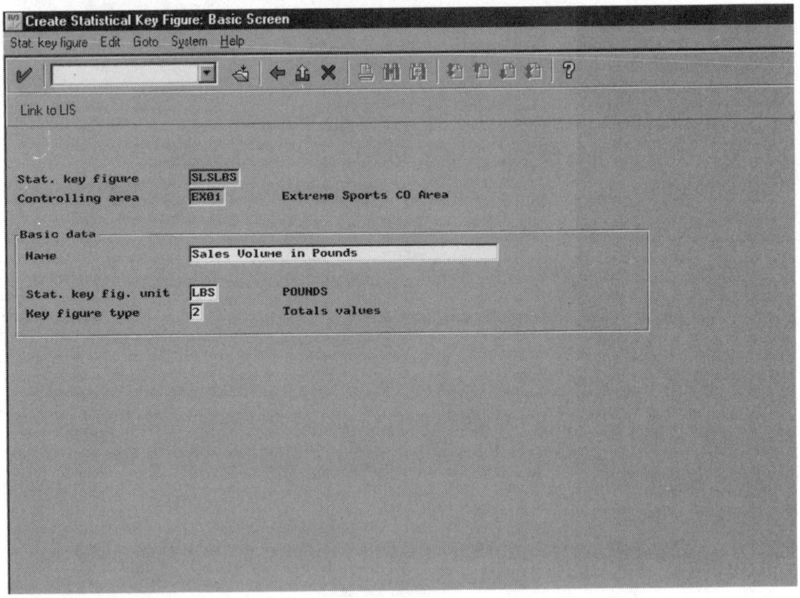

When you are happy with the information, begin completing the master record:

Name   Enter the descriptive name of the key figure. The name can be up to 40 characters in length.

Stat. Key Fig. Unit   Enter the unit of measure by which entries will be measured. Use the pull-down list for a view of possible entries. If you do not find the unit of measure you like, they are configurable. Examples include the following:

LBS   Pounds

EA   Each

H   Hours

Key Figure Type   With this setting, you can determine how the key figure will be utilized. You have two choices:

Type 1 (Fixed)   Fixed indicates that the amount entered will be consistent over all periods within a fiscal year and should be carried forward to each period. Examples of a fixed value might include the square footage of a building or the number of employees in a department. The amount does not change period to period.

Type 2 (Totals)   Totals indicates that the amount could change from period to period and therefore should not be carried forward into any future periods. Examples include the amount of kilowatt hours of electricity used or the number of units sold within a period.

N O T E   Corrections to Type 1 and Type 2 key figures are handled differently. To correct an entry in a Type 1 key figure, simply enter a new fixed value and the correction will be carried forward into all subsequent periods. Corrections to an entry in a Type 2 key figure require you to first erase the original entry with one of the same value but reversed +/– sign. Then simply enter the correct value for the period.

When complete, save the statistical key figure. If you desire to attach the key figure to an LIS structure, the next section will cover the details to establish the link.

Linking to LIS

An additional feature of statistical key figures is their ability to be linked to an LIS structure for automatic update. The Logistics Information System, or LIS, is made up of multiple information systems, including the Sales Information System (SIS), Inventory Controlling, Shop Floor Information System, and others. A structure within LIS is similar to a table in reporting, within which you can control what and how activity updates. A structure can combine three types of information: characteristics, time reference or period units (weeks, days, months), and key figures (currency or quantities).

When it's linked to an LIS structure, the statistical key figure gains the ability to update automatically rather than require manually entered values. Updates occur by running a special transaction within Cost Center Accounting:

KVA5   Activity Independent Key Figures

KVD5   Activity Dependent Key Figures

To establish the link, select the Link to LIS button. The first box to appear will ask how you want to search for the LIS key figure to link with (see Figure 9.21).

FIGURE 9.21   Selecting the search strategy for key figures

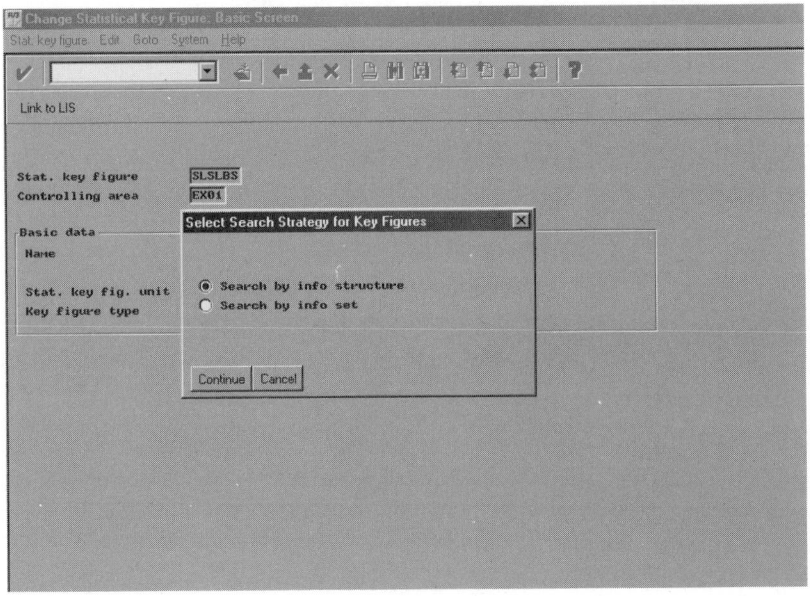

The two choices offered are similar, but distinctions are made:

Search by Info Structure   To search by information structures, you must have some knowledge of which module generates the data. Information structures will transfer both currency amounts and quantities.

Search by Info Set   Similar to information structures, info sets provide greater depth in the information by which they can search. However, as of version 3.1, only currency amounts can be automatically transferred.

The following examples will follow the path of searching by information structures.

The next screen to appear, shown in Figure 9.22, will ask you to select an application from which the information structure will update. It is vital that you select the proper application if you are to find the necessary structure and key figure. Select the desired application and continue. In the case of the Extreme Sports example, application 01 Sales and Distribution was selected.

FIGURE 9.22 Selecting an application

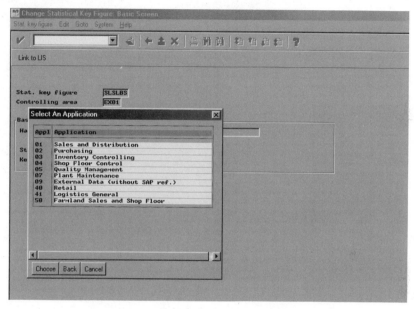

A list of available information structures will appear. The list will include both SAP-delivered and client-defined structures used for standard analysis. Review the list to determine the structure to which you want to attach your statistical key figure. The link is actually at the key figure level on the information structure. When an information structure is selected, a list of potential key figures will appear, as shown in Figure 9.23. The key figure is the object that contains the data and is the lowest level of the assignment.

FIGURE 9.23   A list of potential key figures

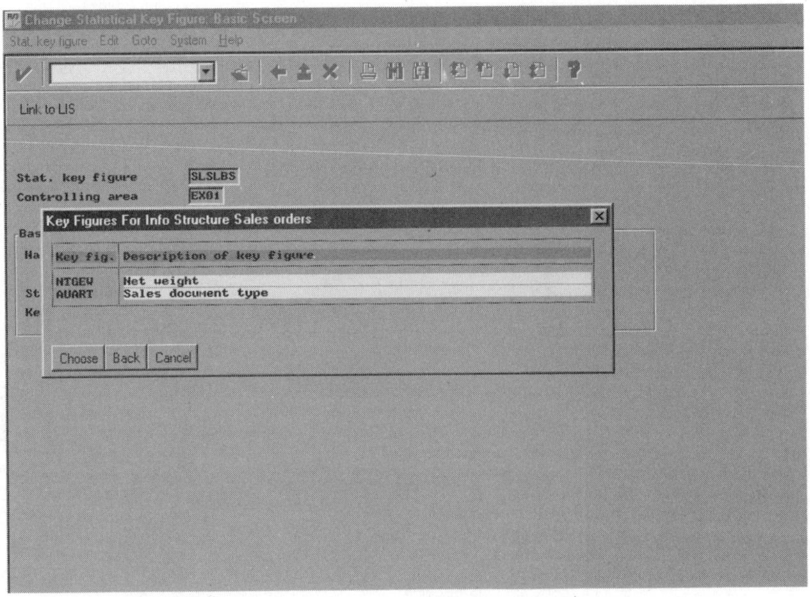

If you see the key figure you need in the list, select the object and SAP will establish the link automatically. If the key figure is not present, click Back and the information structure list will reappear. When the key figure has been selected, the basic screen will appear with the LIS link information established at the bottom of the master record, as shown in Figure 9.24. The information is grayed out because the link was established automatically by SAP and cannot be changed.

Here is a list of the fields on this screen:

Value Origin   The *A* in the field indicates that the statistical key figure will be determined automatically. SAP establishes the setting automatically.

Info Structure   This field contains the ID of the information structures you just selected. It may be helpful later if someone else needs to quickly identify how the statistical key figure is updated.

LIS Key Figure   This field contains the key figure on the information structure that updates the statistical key figure. Remember that the key figure is the object that holds the data within the information structure.

When configuration is complete, save the statistical key figure.

FIGURE 9.24 The LIS link information

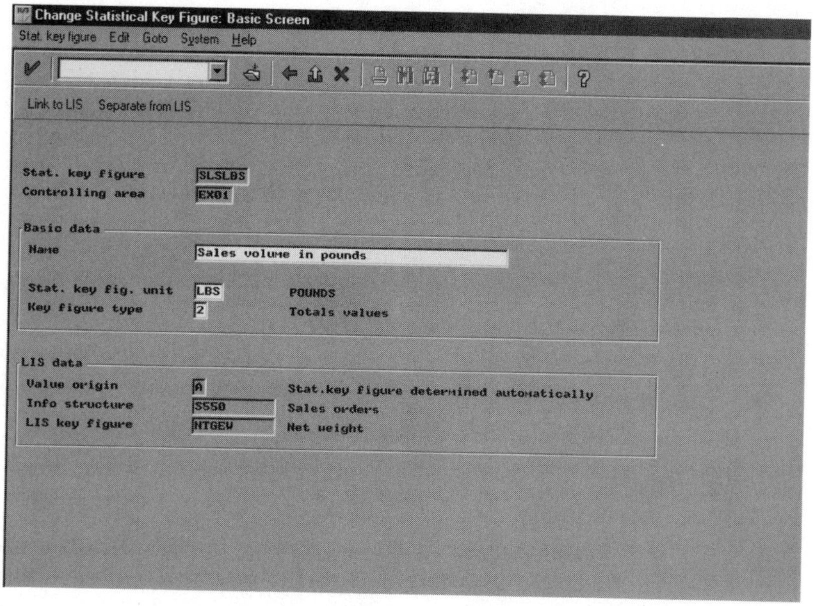

Changing the LIS Link

If changes are desired as a result of either a need to assign a new information structure or to no longer have the statistical key figure automatically update, the link can be broken. Enter the statistical key figure master record and select the button Separate from LIS. The link will disappear from the bottom of the master record, and you can begin again.

Activity Type Creation and Maintenance

Activity types are used within the SAP system to track activity, or output, within a cost center. Other objects within the controlling area will pull from a given cost center's resources and use them as their own. To ensure that proper credit is given at the proper rate and for the proper output type, activity types should be built at the proper level of detail. Examples of activity types include the following:

▶ Labor hours

▶ Overhead rate

▶ Electricity used

The function of activity types is to provide credit to the resource cost center at a specific rate times an amount of activity. To achieve this goal, activity types are assigned and planned on the sending resource cost center. As output is confirmed, the formula (rate * output type (hours)) is used to calculate a dollar credit/debit. A simple example follows.

Cost Center 1000 contains all the resources, or employees, that are used to support the plant maintenance functions. Cost Center 2000 requires service to a piece of its machinery; the service utilizes 40 hours of labor at a rate of $10/hr. At the end of the period, Cost Center 1000 is credited for $400 of labor, whereas Cost Center 2000 is debited for $400. The posting occurred as a result of the assignment of an activity type called Labor, which was planned with a rate of $10, to Cost Center 1000. The maintenance activity was allocated internally within Controlling. No Financial Accounting updates occurred.

The next section will provide you with the steps to set up an activity type within Cost Center Accounting. Because activity types are used throughout production execution and plant maintenance execution as well as by other modules, some comments may step outside the CCA boundary.

Additionally, the ideas of internal activity allocation and activity type planning will be touched upon. Prior to creating the first activity type, you will need to create an allocation account within the controlling area.

Creating the Allocation Cost Element

The allocation account is a secondary cost element and exists only in CO. The cost element is assigned on the activity type master record and is the cost element that will be posted to during the credit/debit confirmation process. The cost element can be created from either the IMG or the user menu. Keep in mind the number of unique activities you will need to track and be sure to create an accommodating number of cost elements.

Included here will be the IMG path and some simple guidelines for creating the allocation cost element. Refer to Chapter 8, "Cost Element Accounting," for detailed steps.

A transaction selection screen will appear if you use the menu path as opposed to the transaction code. Select Create Allocation Cost Element. The create secondary cost element screen will appear. Here are some key points to creating the cost element:

▶ The cost element category should be 43, Internal Activity Allocation.

▶ Use an account number outside of your primary account range. It will make the account more easily recognizable.

▶ Use a name and description that clearly defines the activity (Maintenance Labor versus Production Labor). Reporting and analysis will be made easier.

When you have completed the allocation cost element creation process, move on to maintaining the time-based fields on the activity types.

CREATION OF AN ALLOCATION COST ELEMENT

You can use the following methods to create an allocation cost element:

Menu Path: **Controlling** ➢ **Overhead Cost Controlling** ➢ **Cost Center Accounting** ➢ **Master Data** ➢ **Activity Types** ➢ **Maintain Allocation Cost Elements**

Transaction Code: **KA06**

Maintaining the Time-Based Fields

The concepts of time-based field settings are the same for activity types as they are for cost centers. As you make changes to fields on the activity type master record, keep in mind the time-based settings. Additional analysis periods may be required. Use the following IMG menu path: Controlling ➢ Overhead Cost Controlling ➢ Cost Center Accounting ➢ Master Data ➢ Activity Types ➢ Define Time Based Fields for Activity Types to maintain the fields.

TIME–BASED FIELD MAINTENANCE FOR ACTIVITY TYPES

You can use the following methods to maintain time-based fields for activity types:

Menu Path: **Controlling** ➢ **Overhead Cost Controlling** ➢ **Cost Center Accounting** ➢ **Master Data** ➢ **Activity Types** ➢ **Define Time Based Fields for Activity Types**

Transaction Code: **OKEI**

The change time-based fields screen will appear (see Figure 9.25).

FIGURE 9.25   The change time-based fields screen

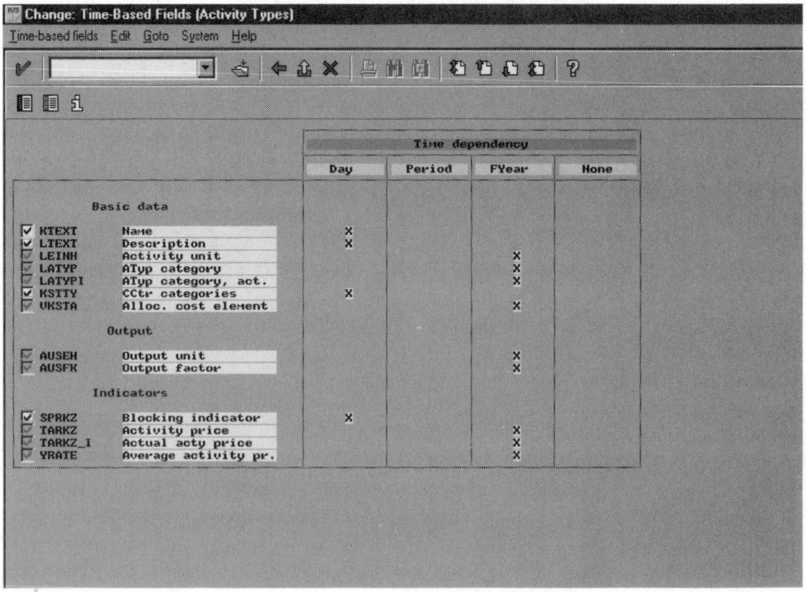

You will notice that the majority of the fields are flagged for historical tracking. The four not automatically set are described here:

Name   Enter the name of the activity type.

Description   Enter a description of the activity type.

CCtr Categories   On the master record, you can limit the type of cost center the activity type can be assigned to by establishing a cost center category.

Blocking Indicator   Use this field to determine if the activity type is blocked from planning.

Make the historical flag settings as needed and save. You will, however, want to review the time dependency of each of the fields before creating or changing an activity type master record. Once completed, you can move on to create the activity type master record.

Creating/Maintaining the Activity Type

The activity type, being master data, can be created through either the IMG or user menu. The IMG path is Controlling ➤ Overhead Cost Controlling ➤ Cost Center Accounting ➤ Master Data ➤ Activity Types ➤ Create Activity Types.

CREATION/MAINTENANCE OF ACTIVITY TYPES

You can use the following methods to get to the screen for creating activity types:

Menu Path: **Controlling** ➤ **Overhead Cost Controlling** ➤ **Cost Center Accounting** ➤ **Master Data** ➤ **Activity Types** ➤ **Create Activity Types**

Transaction Code: **KL01**

The initial create activity type screen will appear (see Figure 9.26).

FIGURE 9.26   The initial create activity type screen

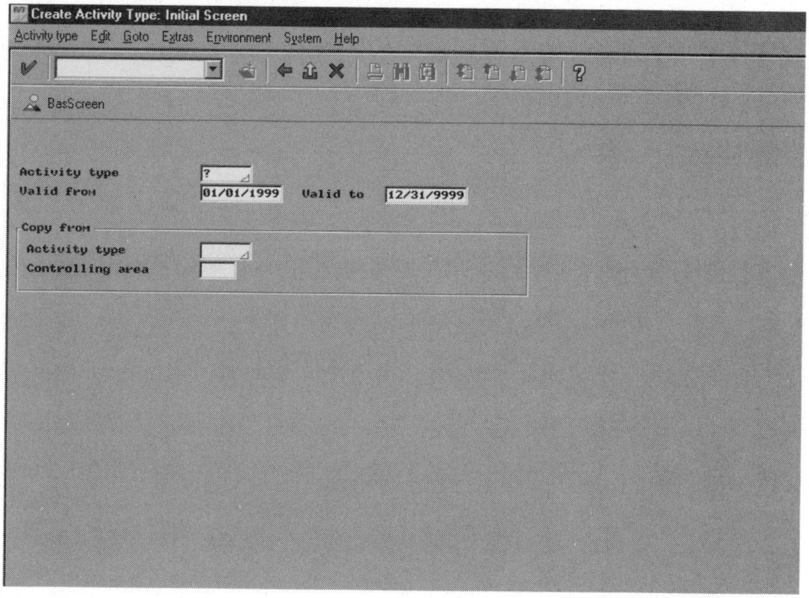

Here are the fields on this screen:

Activity Type   Enter the ID of the activity type you are creating. The ID can be up to six characters long.

Valid From/To   Enter the validity period of the activity type.

> **TIP** When maintaining the validity period, pay attention to the beginning date. If you are implementing midyear but want to plan for the entire year including prior months, the activity type must be made valid for all prior periods.

Press Enter when the ID and validity period has been created. The basic create activity type screen appears (see Figure 9.27).

FIGURE 9.27   The basic create activity type screen

![Create Activity Type: Basic Screen showing fields for Activity type MTLBR, Controlling area EX01 Extreme Sports CO Area, Valid from 01/01/1999 Valid to 12/31/9999, Names section with Name and Description, Basic data section with Activity unit and CCtr categories, Allocation section with Allocation possible/No allocation options and Default values including ATyp category, Cost element, Activity price, Average activity pr., and Variant values for actual allocation]

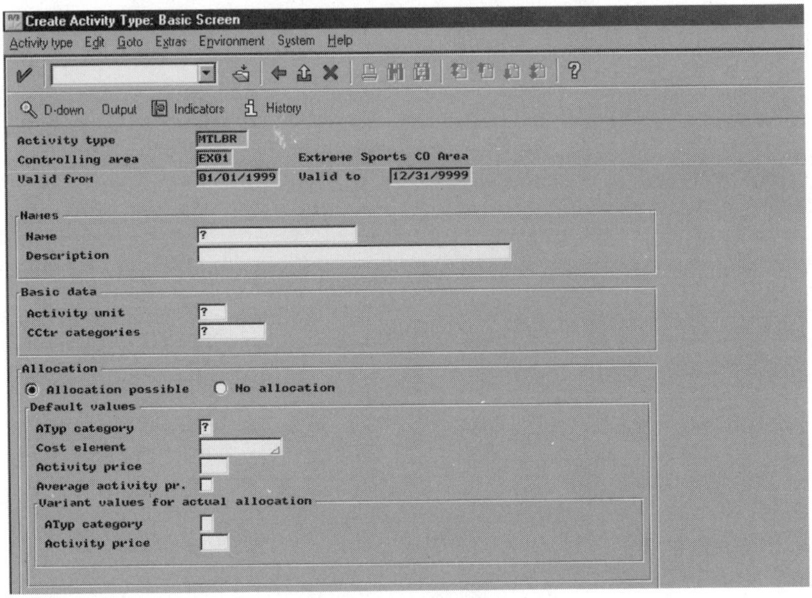

The first thing to notice is that the proper controlling area has been set and defined on the record. Next, review the record for which fields are required. These will be the minimal settings necessary to make the record available for use:

Name   Enter the name of the activity type. This field is required.

Description   Describe the activity in greater detail.

Activity Unit   Enter the unit of measure in which the activity type is measured (hours, minutes, and gallons per minute). Use the drop-down list to display possible entries. This field is required.

CCtr Categories   Enter the cost center type for which the activity type is valid for planning and internal activity allocations. If you enter an *, the activity type is valid for all cost center types. It is recommended that changes to this category not be made within a fiscal period. The potential for inconsistencies is too great. This field is required.

Allocation Possible/No Allocation   This setting will default to Allocation Possible.

N O T E   The setting for No Allocation works in conjunction with Activity Type Category 4 only.

The Default Values section will establish the default settings for plan and actual allocation activity:

ATyp Category   There are two separate sections to complete for the activity type category for plan and actual allocation. The first, seen in the Default Values section of the screen, is used to denote the default method for both plan and actual activity allocations. The category determines how the activity may be planned and how actual activity may be allocated. There are four potential categories to choose from:

Category 1 (Manual Entry, Manual Allocation)   Use this category if you desire to measure actual activity against a planned activity rate. For example, to process a credit for overhead activity OHLBS, you enter at the end of a period the actual production quantity in pounds. During the internal allocation process, SAP will take the actual amount entered and multiply it by the planned activity price.

Category 2 (Indirect Calculation, Indirect Allocation)   Categories 2 and 3 are both related to indirect allocation of activity. Category 2 should be used if, within your business, you deem it too difficult to accurately calculate the actual quantity of activity on a given cost center. In these cases, tracing and weighting factors on the receiver are used to determine the amount of credit to the sender. For example, Cost Center 100 is the central maintenance center for a production facility. Cost Centers 101, 201, and 301 all have had standard work provided for their respective cost centers by Cost Center 100. Activity MTLBR is planned on Cost Center 100 with a rate of $25/HR. One thousand hours of activity has occurred over the last period. So the total amount of credit coming to Cost Center 100 is $25,000, or $25 * 1000 hours. In this example, it is impossible to know the exact amount of hours that were applied to Cost Center 101, 201, and 301. In addition, there was activity from three other cost centers that contributed to the cost. It is determined that only 70% of the cost should be applied to 101, 201, and 301.

To facilitate the internal allocation, a tracing factor of # of Jobs Started is used to track activity. The number of jobs begun for each of the three cost centers is 10, 15, and 20 respectively. A weighting factor of 70% will ensure that only the appropriate percentage of costs will be allocated during the processing. Based upon the tracing factors, the following postings will occur:

Cctr 101: (($25,000/50 jobs) * 10 Jobs) * .70 = $3,500

Cctr 101: (($25,000/50 jobs) * 15 Jobs) * .70 = $5,250

Cctr 101: (($25,000/50 jobs) * 25 Jobs) * .70 = $8,750

Category 3 (Manual Entry, Indirect Allocation)   When you can accurately determine the amount of activity on the sender, the use of Category 3 becomes important. Similar to Category 1, the formula, (actual activity * a planned rate) is used to determine the amount of sender credit. Tracing factors are used during the allocation process to determine that amount of cost each receiving center is to be posted with. For example, Cost Center 100 has a planned labor rate of $25. At the end of the period, the center is posted with 1000 hours of actual maintenance hours. A tracing factor, # of Jobs Completed, is used to determine the amount of cost that is to be allocated to each of the three maintenance cost centers: 101, 201, and 301. Cost Center 101 completed 10 jobs, Cost Center 201 completed 15 jobs, and Cost Center 301 completed 25, for a total 50 jobs completed.

During processing, the following calculations occur to provide for the proper allocation amounts:

Cost Center 101: (10 Jobs/50 Jobs) * $25,000 = $5,000

Cost Center 201: (15 Jobs/50 Jobs) * $25,000 = $7,500

Cost Center 301: (25 Jobs/50 Jobs) * $25,000 = $12,500

TIP The sender rule must use the setting Posted Quantities. Any of the receiver rules can be used, except Fixed Quantities.

Category 4 (Manual Entry, No Allocation)   All planned and actual activity is entered manually. It is not possible to allocate activity with this category. Values are entered in Cost Center Accounting using the following menu path: Actual Postings ➤ Non-Allocatable Activities. The category is used when a cost center accrues costs that cannot be allocated to other CO objects using internal activity allocation. For example, a shipping cost center accrues activity costs for all marketing cost centers based upon the amount of daily shipments. These costs cannot be allocated internally.

Cost Element   Enter the allocation cost element that both the sender and receiver will be posted with (see "Creating the Allocation Cost Element" earlier in this chapter for details).

WARNING Be certain that the validity period of the cost element is equal to, or greater than, the validity period of the activity type to which it is being assigned. If there is discrepancy, SAP will not allow the cost element to be used.

Activity Price   As with the ATyp Category field, there are also two locations to enter an activity price indicator. The first setting, found in the Default Values section, is used to determine how the plan and actual activity price is calculated. There are three choices:

Option 01   The activity price is calculated automatically based upon plan activity and costs of the cost center in question. Both the fixed and variable portions of the variable price are calculated in the same manner. The combination of the fixed and variable prices adds to the total activity price.

Option 02   The activity price is calculated automatically based upon planned costs and capacity. The main difference between option 02 and 01 is in the calculation of the fixed portion of the price. Planned capacity on the cost center, in conjunction with planned costs, are used to determine the fixed activity price.

NOTE If you determine that option 01 or 02 is necessary for your solution, then you will be required to calculate the planned activity price (transaction code KSPI). Refer to the Version/Fiscal Year settings on the controlling area version to determine the activity price calculation setting.

Option 03   The activity price is determined manually.

Average Activity Pr.   If this field is activated, activity prices will have a constant value for the entire fiscal year. Because of the field's time dependency, it can be changed only at the beginning of a fiscal year.

The Variant Values for Actual Allocation section allows you to differentiate actual allocations from the actual/plan settings established in the Default section.

ATyp Category   In addition to the four categories available in the Default Values section, two additional categories are found here:

Null   Same category as the plan default.

Category 5 (Target-to-Actual Allocation)   Target-to-actual activity allocation uses the receiving cost center's operating rates to determine the actual activity quantities. No manual entry is allowed.

Activity Price   There are two different methods available for calculating the actual activity price; they are different from the plan method established in the Default Values:

Option 5   The actual price is calculated automatically based upon actual activity. To utilize the option, you must run the actual activity price calculation.

Option 6   The actual price is calculated automatically based upon capacity. The variable portion of the price will be determined based upon actual activity, whereas the fixed portion will be based upon capacity.

When configuration is complete, save the activity type (see Figure 9.28). The activity type can now be planned on the appropriate cost center. Because activity-based costing (ABC) is not covered, much of the extensive activity type functionality is not demonstrated. If ABC is in scope for your project, it is recommended that you attend one of the SAP courses on the subject matter prior to beginning.

The next section will cover the development of the following periodic allocations: assessments, distributions, and periodic repostings.

FIGURE 9.28   The basic create activity type screen configured for Extreme Sports

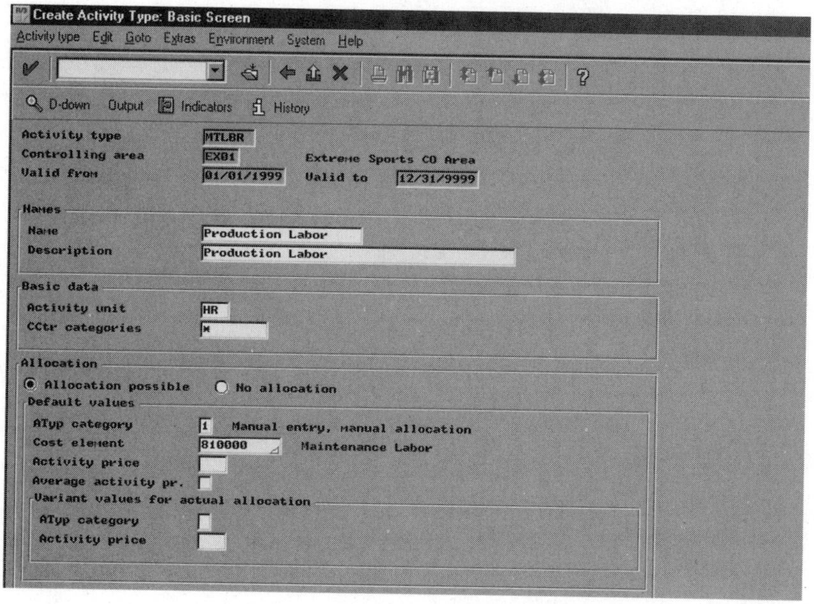

Assessments, Distributions, and Repostings

In the past, accounting departments spent numerous hours manually allocating operating activities among their Strategic Business Units (SBUs) to get a more accurate profitability picture. Although the worth of such allocations will not be debated, SAP's capabilities in this area will be discussed. Imputed cost calculations and indirect activity allocations have already been covered in prior sections. The three remaining allocation methods to be described are assessments, distributions, and periodic repostings.

All CO allocations, or periodic allocations as SAP refers to them, act in a similar manner. Costs posted to an original object, called a sender, are allocated via a set of rules to another object called a receiver. With respect to assessments and distributions in cost center accounting, the sender will always be a cost center. But the receiver can be any other CO object, like an order, a cost object, or a cost center. Periodic repostings allow for any CO object to be a sender or receiver.

Another differentiating feature among the three is how each posts within CO. Due to the method in which they post, both periodic repostings and distributions will allocate primary costs only. Assessments have the capability to allocate both primary and secondary costs. Keep this in mind when determining which method is appropriate.

This section will discuss the configuration elements necessary to create the assessment, distribution, and periodic reposting cycles and segments. The creation of an allocation cycle and segment will also be covered. There are numerous options when making your settings, with many unique ways of grouping tracing factors, sender values, and receiver weighting. Experimentation will be important when building your solution.

The first allocation type to be discussed is assessments. However, the concepts covered, like cycle/segment creation and allocation rules, will be universally applicable to all three types. Where differentiation occurs, it will be noted.

Periodic Allocations: Overview

When it is unimportant, or not possible, for the user to know the breakdown of costs that a cost center will receive in an allocation, assessments are a good, functional solution. Allocating general and administrative costs to an SBU is a good example of when assessments would work. In this scenario, it is probably unimportant for the SBU manager to know the specific detail behind the allocation; they need to know only the amount of G&A costs they have received. Further analysis is available through CCA reporting. If it is important that original cost elements be posted on both sender and receiver, distributions or periodic repostings are the solution.

Allocation configuration at the smallest level is defined as a segment. Segments are the individual rules through which an allocation determines what and how to assess. Primary and secondary costs are combined at the cost center level and assigned in some way to receiver cost centers. Related segments are grouped together in what is called a cycle.

The cycle is the object that is run during the month-end processing. It is possible to have just one cycle for a given controlling area, with all allocation segments assigned. This would be impractical, however, due to the performance issues that would inevitably occur. Rather, multiple cycles should be created and run sequentially.

A key feature to all periodic allocations is the ability to reuse the settings repeatedly over many periods or years. The first step in defining an allocation is establishing the allowed receiver types, followed closely by developing the assessment cost element, if applicable, and then, creation of the segments and cycles. Begin by looking at the SAP-delivered allocation receiver types.

Allocation Receiver Types

SAP allows you to determine the receiver settings for each of the three types of allocations. Allowing differentiation between the two allocation types, actual and plan, provides additional flexibility. The allocation type determines how the allocation is used. These settings act in the same manner as field status variants in how they control what fields are made available for entry and what data may be included. All of the settings in this table are controlling area dependent, so feel comfortable in experimenting with what works well for your solution.

We will review the cost center settings for the allocation type Actual. Remember that receiver type settings can be made only for repostings, distributions, and assessments. To eliminate needless redundancy, only the receiver type settings for an assessment will be detailed. The concepts are transferable to both distributions and periodic repostings.

 TIP   The contents of this section are FYI only. It is quite possible that the SAP-delivered settings will never have to be augmented.

To maintain the receiver type settings, follow the IMG menu path Controlling ➤ Overhead Cost Controlling ➤ Cost Center Accounting ➤ Actual Postings ➤ Period End Closings ➤ Assessment ➤ Determine Assessment Receiver Type.

MAINTENANCE OF THE ALLOCATION CHARACTERISTICS FOR THE SENDER/RECEIVER

You can use the following methods to maintain receiver type settings:

Menu Path: **Controlling ➤ Overhead Cost Controlling ➤ Cost Center Accounting ➤ Actual Postings ➤ Period End Closings ➤ Assessment ➤ Determine Assessment Receiver Type**

Transaction Code: **KCAU**

The customizing allocation field characteristics overview screen appears (see Figure 9.29).

FIGURE 9.29 The customizing allocation field characteristics overview screen

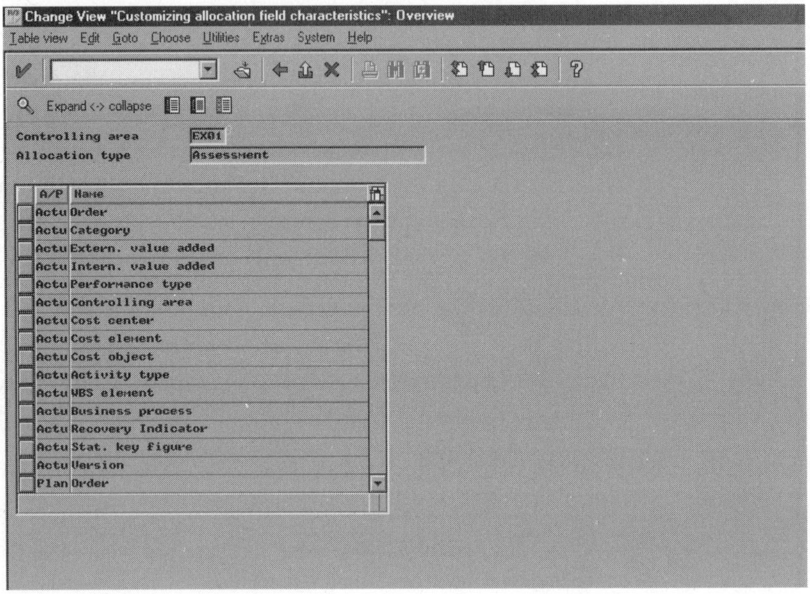

Scroll down the screen and select the Actual allocation type with Cost Center as the field. The customizing allocation field characteristics details screen for cost center appears (see Figure 9.30).

FIGURE 9.30 The customizing allocation field characteristics details screen

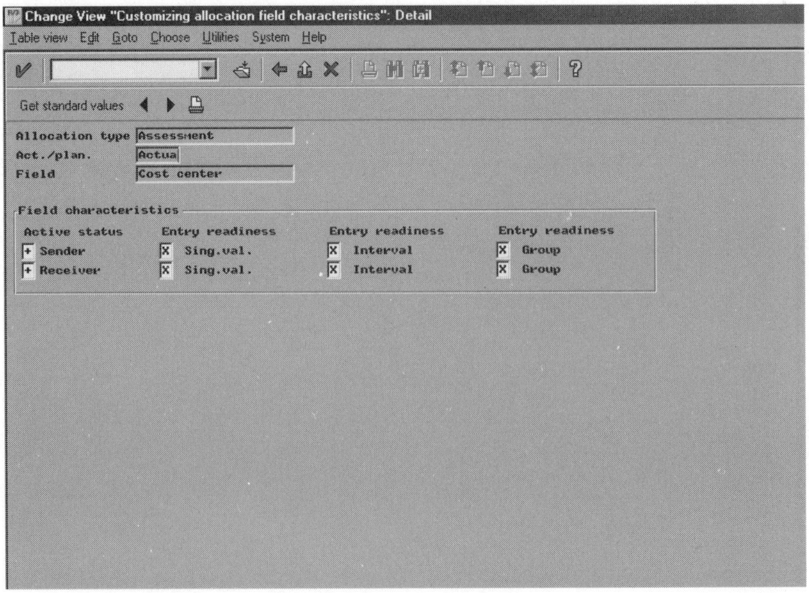

The characteristics detail screen will provide different options depending on the field you are maintaining. Some fields can be used as a sender object, a receiver object, or a tracing factor object. In our example, cost center can be utilized as both a sender and a receiver. The concepts will be easier to understand if an example of an allocation is provided. In this case, an assessment is used.

See Figure 9.31 for an example of an assessment segment. As settings are changed in the allocation field characteristics screen, you will see the segment fields for cost center appear or disappear. In the example, the SAP-delivered settings are being used.

FIGURE 9.31 An example of an assessment segment

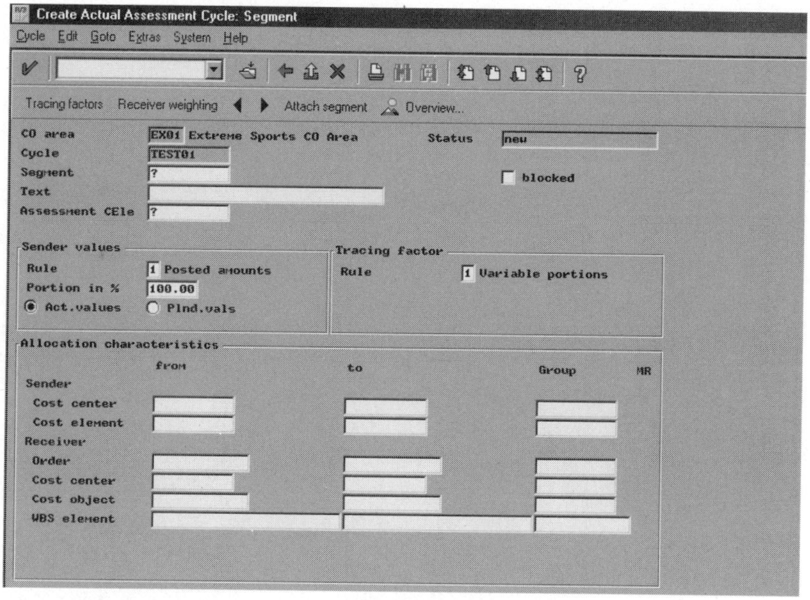

Referring back to Figure 9.30, a brief description of each column and its impact is listed here:

Active Status   Determines if the field is required, optional, or hidden during allocation maintenance.

Entry Readiness (Sing. Val.)   Determines whether you can enter a value in the From column on the allocation segment screen.

Entry Readiness (Interval)   Determines whether you can enter a value in the To column on the allocation segment screen.

Entry Readiness (Group) Determines whether you can enter a value in the Group column on the allocation segment screen.

TIP In this example cost center, it is possible to remove a field from the assessment screen entirely. To accomplish this, remove all the settings from each of the Entry Readiness columns.

Returning to Figure 9.31 and our assessment segment screen example, see what happens when the Entry Readiness Sing. Val. and Interval fields for the sender are set to not allow entry. Figure 9.32 is an example of the allocation field characteristics screen, and Figure 9.33 shows the results of the settings on the assessment segment screen.

FIGURE 9.32 The allocation field characteristics screen with the Entry Readiness Sing. Val. and Interval fields for the sender set to not allow entry

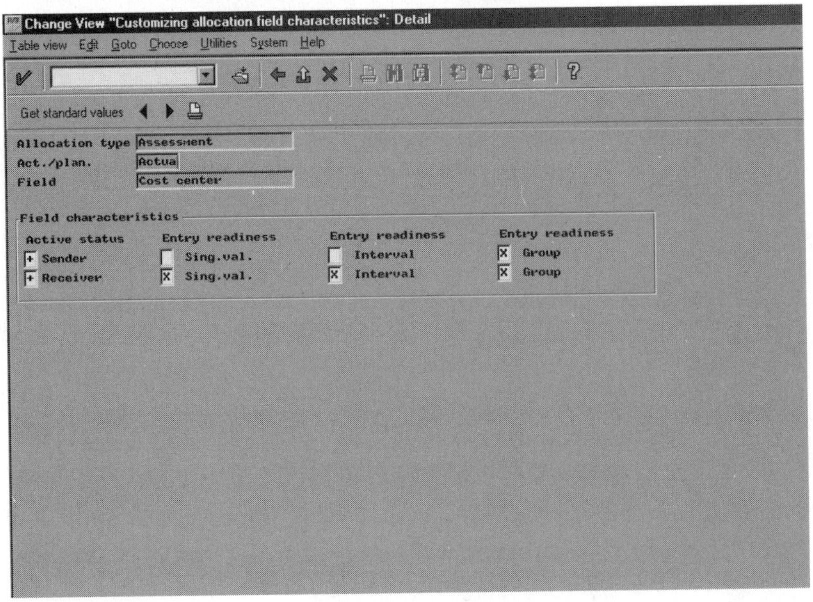

FIGURE 9.33   The results of the settings on the assessment segment screen

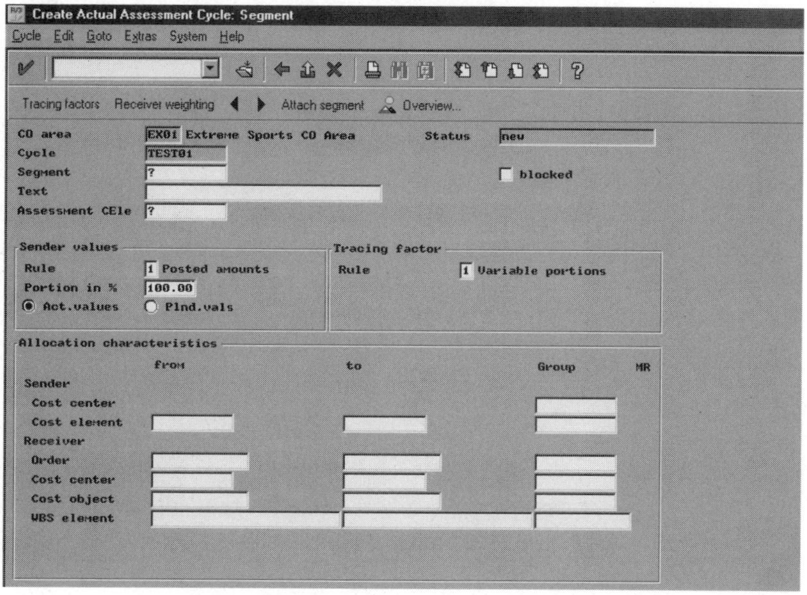

![Create Actual Assessment Cycle: Segment screen]

Notice in Figure 9.33 that the From and To fields disappear from the segment screen for the sender cost center. If you determine at a later date that you want the columns returned, simply reset them for entry.

NOTE   Any changes made to the allocation field characteristics screen will be active for all allocations, both new and previously created. For the previously created allocations, the fields will be removed from sight, but the settings, if any, will remain valid. Therefore, if the field had entries before it was removed, the entries are still good. Keep this in mind if you have any allocations that require constant maintenance.

The next step in allocation development is creation of the assessment cost element.

Assessment Cost Element

Because assessments allow you to settle both primary and secondary costs, a new type of cost element called an assessment element must be created. The assessment element is a secondary cost element used to post to both the sender and receiver during processing. Similar to the allocation cost element created in "Activity Types and Statistical Key Figures" earlier in this chapter, the assessment cost element can be created from either the IMG or user menu. The user menu path is Accounting ➢ Controlling ➢ Cost Elements ➢ Master Data ➢ Cost Element ➢ Create Secondary.

CREATION/MAINTENANCE OF THE ASSESSMENT COST ELEMENT

You can create an assessment cost element by using the following methods:

Application Menu Path: **Accounting ➢ Controlling ➢ Cost Elements ➢ Master Data ➢ Cost Element ➢ Create Secondary**

Transaction Code: **KA06**

The create secondary cost element screen appears. Because the details have been covered in previous chapters, only some key points to creating the cost element are provided:

▶ The cost element category should be 42, Assessment Cost Element.

▶ Use an account number outside your primary account range. It will make the account more easily recognizable.

▶ Use a name and description that clearly define the activity (Advertising Assessment, Selling & Marketing Assessment). Reporting and analysis will be made easier.

Save the assessment cost element. The next section will cover the development of an actual allocation.

Allocation Creation

The allocation can be created from either the IMG or the user menu. For demonstration purposes, a cost center assessment will be built. Where a unique field setting for a specific type of allocation may occur, it will be noted. The IMG paths for all three types are listed in the shortcut boxes.

CREATION OF THE COST CENTER REPOSTING

You can get to the screen to create cost center reposting by using the following methods:

Menu Path: **Controlling** ➤ **Overhead Cost Controlling** ➤ **Cost Center Accounting** ➤ **Actual Postings** ➤ **Period End Closings** ➤ **Assessment** ➤ **Define Periodic Repostings**

Transaction Code: **KSW1**

CREATION OF THE COST CENTER DISTRIBUTION

You can use the following methods to create cost center distributions:

Menu Path: **Controlling** ➤ **Overhead Cost Controlling** ➤ **Cost Center Accounting** ➤ **Actual Postings** ➤ **Period End Closings** ➤ **Assessment** ➤ **Define Distribution**

Transaction Code: **KSV1**

CREATION OF THE COST CENTER ASSESSMENT

You can use the following methods to create cost center assessments:

Menu Path: **Controlling** ➤ **Overhead Cost Controlling** ➤ **Cost Center Accounting** ➤ **Actual Postings** ➤ **Period End Closings** ➤ **Assessment** ➤ **Define Assessment**

Transaction Code: **KSU1**

The initial create actual assessment cycle screen appears. Give the cycle a name and a valid start date. When entering the start date, it is best to provide the first day of a fiscal period. That way, all postings within the period will be selected. Press Enter and the create actual assessment cycle header screen appears (see Figure 9.34).

FIGURE 9.34   The create actual assessment cycle header screen

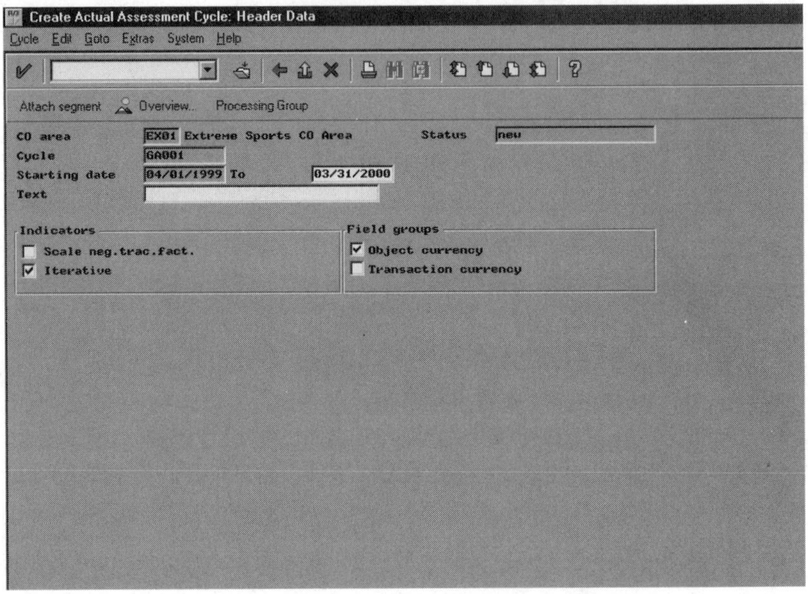

The allocation, or assessment, cycle header provides settings that are valid for all attached segments. Areas like controlling area, validity periods, indicators, and currency types are found in the header. Here, you will find a listing of the pertinent fields on the header and definitions of how they should be utilized:

Starting Date   You provided the starting date of the cycle on the initial screen. Within the header, you have the ability to provide the ending date for the validity period range.

Text   Enter a high-level description of what the cycle will accomplish.

The fields in the Indicators section are as follows:

Scale Neg. Trac. Fact.   Negative tracing factor may come into play if you determine that a segment will use actual posted values rather than fixed amounts or rates. Within the allocation, tracing factors are used to determine the amount to be posted to the receiver. The factors can include amounts from key figures, activity types, or actual/plan costs. Negative tracing factors are important when the tracing factor selected involves variable portions. Below is an example of the impact of negative tracing factors on an allocation.

Example: Sender cost center 1000 wants to allocate $10,000 to three receiving cost centers: 2000, 3000, and 4000. The tracing factor is set to Variable Portions and uses actual postings to statistical key figure PROD, net production activity.

The actual key figure values for each cost center are shown in Table 9.1. Table 9.2 shows the calculations without negative tracing factors active.

TABLE 9.1   **Key Figure Values for Each Cost Center**

Cost Center 2000 = 100

Cost Center 3000 = 50

Cost Center 4000 = −50

Net Tracing Factor = 100

TABLE 9.2   **Calculations without Negative Tracing Factors Active**

Cost Center 2000: $10,000 * 100/100 = $10,000

Cost Center 3000: $10,000 * 50/100 = $ 5,000

Cost Center 4000: $10,000 * −50/100 = $ −5,000

Net Allocation = $10,000

The net allocation value is accurate at $10,000, but on an individual cost center basis, the amounts are wrong. In Tables 9.3 and 9.4, you will see the impact of adjusting for negative tracing factors. The largest negative factor is set to zero, and the absolute value is added to each of the other factors.

TABLE 9.3   **Key Figure Values for Each Cost Center**

Cost Center 2000 = 150

Cost Center 3000 = 100

Cost Center 4000 =   0

Net Tracing Factor = 250

TABLE 9.4   Calculations with Negative Tracing Factors Active

Cost Center 2000: $10,000 * 150/250 = $6,000

Cost Center 3000: $10,000 * 100/250 = $4,000

Cost Center 4000: $10,000 *   0/250 = $ 0

Net Allocation = $10,000

Cost center 4000, with the negative tracing factor of −50, does not receive any value. Be certain to activate the setting if you feel there is any opportunity to have a negative tracing factor.

Iterative   If this setting is active, the segments within the cycle will be processed iteratively. The iteration occurs during segment processing.

Example: In Segment 1, cost center 1000 wants to allocate $1000 to cost center 2000 and 3000, 50% to each. In turn, in Segment 2, cost center 2000 wants to allocate 100 % of its posted amount to cost center 1000 and 3000, also 50% each. Table 9.5 shows the steps taken during an iterative cycle.

TABLE 9.5   Calculation Base for Iterative Cycle

Step	Ctr 1000	Ctr 2000	Ctr 3000
1. $1000 from Ctr 1000	$0	$500	$500
2. $500 from Ctr 2000	$250	$0	$250
3. $250 from Ctr 1000	$0	$125	$125
4. $125 from Ctr 2000	$62.50	$0	$62.50
5. $62.50 from Ctr 1000	$0	$31.25	$31.25
Net Allocation Amount	$0	$0	$1000

In the example given, the iteration would continue until the entire $1000 was allocated to cost center 3000. If there is no similar link between the segments in a cycle, do not activate iteration. The processing time for this type of cycle is considerably more than one in which iteration is not required.

The fields in the Field Groups section are as follows:

Consumption   This field is used by distributions and periodic repostings only. If it's selected, consumption quantities will be allocated along with the dollars. A precondition to using this setting is that all senders must have quantities posted on them. If the condition is not met, SAP will deliver a warning and the allocation will be stopped.

Object Currency   Controlling area currency is the default currency for CO allocations. By activating this setting, you are requesting that the object currency be taken into account during the calculation and posting. SAP will calculate and post the object currency results and controlling area results separately. A precondition to using object currency is that all sender and receiver objects must use the same currency type. If a discrepancy arises, SAP ignores the setting and posts using only the controlling area currency.

Transaction Currency   If this setting activated, the allocation values are calculated in the transaction currencies on the sender and then posted to the receivers. If the setting is not activated, all postings occur in controlling area currency only.

Example: Cost center 1000 has activity in two currencies: $1000 in DEM and $1500 in MXP. You want to allocate 75% of the activity to cost center 2000 and 25% to cost center 3000. If Transaction Currency is activated, the allocation postings will produce the following line items, as shown in Table 9.6.

TABLE 9.6   Transaction Currency Postings

Ctr 1000	Ctr 2000	Ctr 3000
$1000 MXP		
$1500 DEM		
($1000) DEM	$750	$250
($1500) MXP	$1,125	$375

The results of the allocation include six line item postings with Transaction Currency active rather than three if it were not active. Keep it in mind that having Transaction Currency active will increase the number of line items posted.

TIP   Use the path Cycle ➤ Check to have SAP review the master data validation.

When you have completed the header detail, begin to add the segments to the cycle. Select the Attach Segment button. The segment detail configuration screen appears (see Figure 9.35).

FIGURE 9.35   The segment detail configuration screen

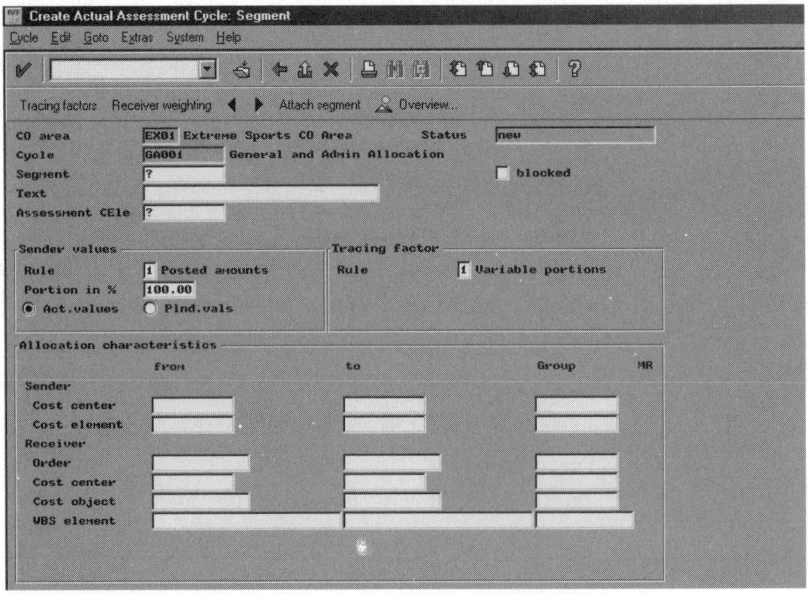

Begin the segment definition by filling in the following fields:

Segment   Enter a unique 10-character ID defining the segment.

Text   Describe the function of the segment.

Assessment Cost Element   (Used by Assessments only.) Enter the assessment cost element that will be used to post to the sender and receiver. See the section on assessment cost element creation.

Blocked   If this box is checked, the segment will be excluded from cycle processing.

Rule (Sender Values)   Select how the sender values will be calculated. Here are the options:

1 Posted Amounts   If this option is selected, SAP will use the amounts posted to the sender object through whatever transactions have occurred.

2 Fixed Amounts   If this option is selected, SAP will ask you to maintain the fixed amounts with which the sender objects (cost center) will be posted. Each receiver's portion will be determined by the tracing factors. A button called Sender Values will appear in the icon bar. Select it and a screen will appear for you to enter the amounts per object.

3 Fixed Rates   This option is similar to Fixed Amounts, but you enter fixed activity prices rather than amounts.

Portion in %   Enter the percentage of sender activity you want to allocate. Anything less than 100% will result in a portion of the sender value remaining on the sender object.

Act. Values/Pland. Val   Select which type of sender values you wish to allocate.

Rule (Tracing Factor)   Select the method by which the amount receiving objects will be posted with is calculated. There are four options:

1 Variable Portions   When using variable portions, SAP determines the allocation amount automatically, based upon the tracing factor selected. (See the setting for Scale negative tracing factors for details on the impact of this selection.) The use of variable portions is appropriate if you want to always derive the posting from the actual or planned activity on a cost center. For example, suppose you allocate your actual G&A expense based on the planned ratios. Additionally, you have the opportunity to add a receiver weighting to the receiving objects by selecting the Receiver Weighting button. The default setting is 1. Select the Tracing Factors button and enter the appropriate information. See Figure 9.36 for a view of the screen.

FIGURE 9.36   The tracing factors screen with the Variable Portions option chosen

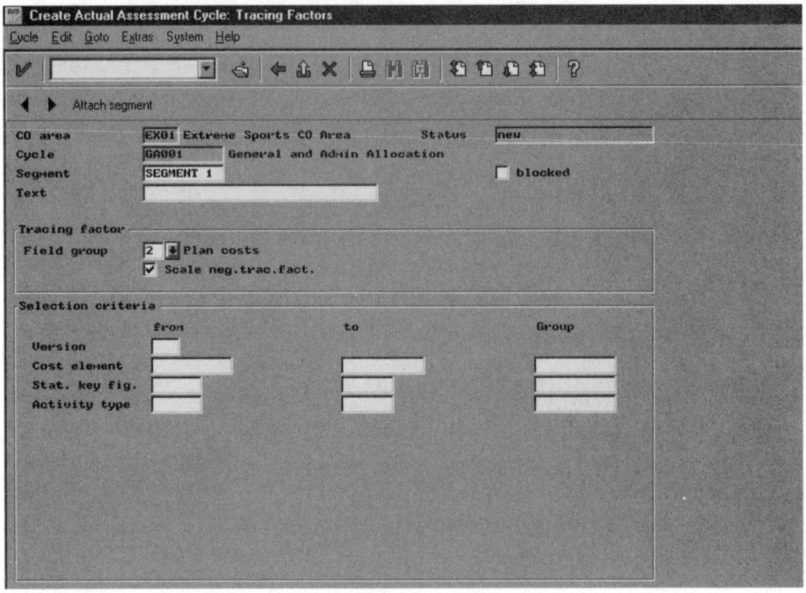

2 Fixed Amounts   If you choose Fixed Amounts in the Rule field, select the Tracing Factors button, and within the tracing factors screen, enter the amounts that should be posted to each receiver. The amount of the sender credit will be the sum of the fixed amounts posted to the receivers. See Figure 9.37 for a view of the screen.

FIGURE 9.37   The tracing factors screen with the Fixed Amounts option chosen

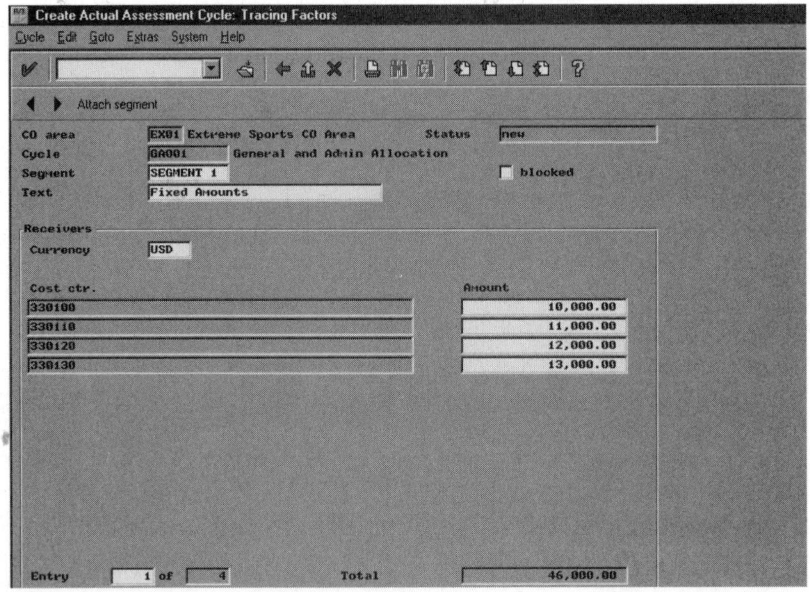

3 Fixed Percentages   If you choose Fixed Percentages in the Rule field, select the Tracing Factors button, and within the tracing factors screen, enter the percentage of cost allocation to be posted to each receiver. The total percentage is not to exceed 100%. If the tracing factor percentage is less than 100%, the percentage of cost less than 100 will be left on the sender. See Figure 9.38 for a view of a completed percentage screen.

FIGURE 9.38   The tracing factors screen with the Fixed Percentages option chosen

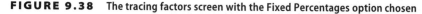

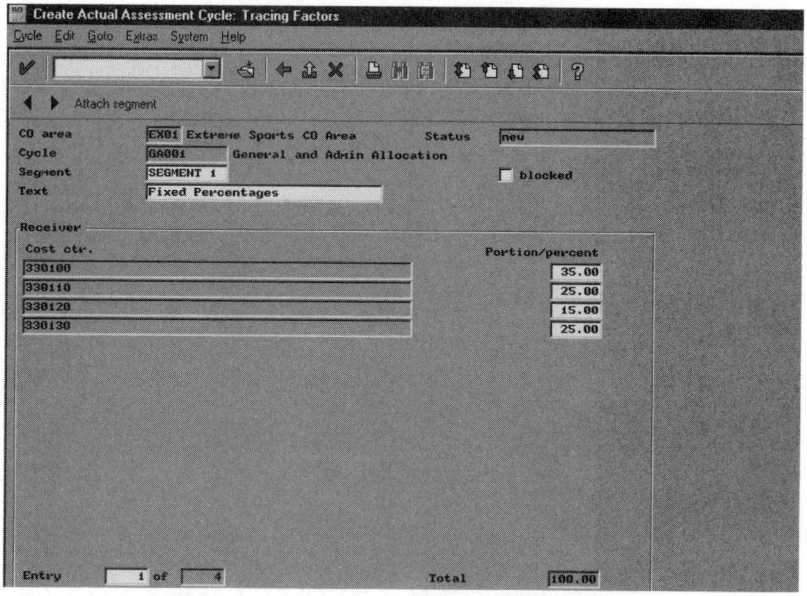

4 Fixed Portions   If you choose Fixed Portions in the Rule field, select the Tracing Factors button, and within the tracing factors screen, enter the portion of allocation with which each receiver is to posted. This option is similar to Fixed Percentages except you can exceed 100 in the portion allocated to the receivers. Review the following portions and the accompanying formula for explanation: Cost center 1000 wants to allocate $10,000 to cost center 2000 with a portion of 75, to cost center 3000 with a portion of 75, and to cost center 4000 with a portion of 100. The total portion amount is 250 (75 + 75 + 100). The amount each cost center is to receive is calculated in Table 9.7. See Figure 9.39 for a view of the completed tracing factor screen with the Fixed Portions option chosen.

TABLE 9.7 Calculations with Use of Portion Tracing Factors

Cost Center 2000: $10,000/250 * 75 = $ 3,000

Cost Center 3000: $10,000/250 * 75 = $ 3,000

Cost Center 4000: $10,000/250 * 100 = $ 4,000

Net Allocation = $10,000

FIGURE 9.39 The tracing factors screen with the Fixed Portions option chosen

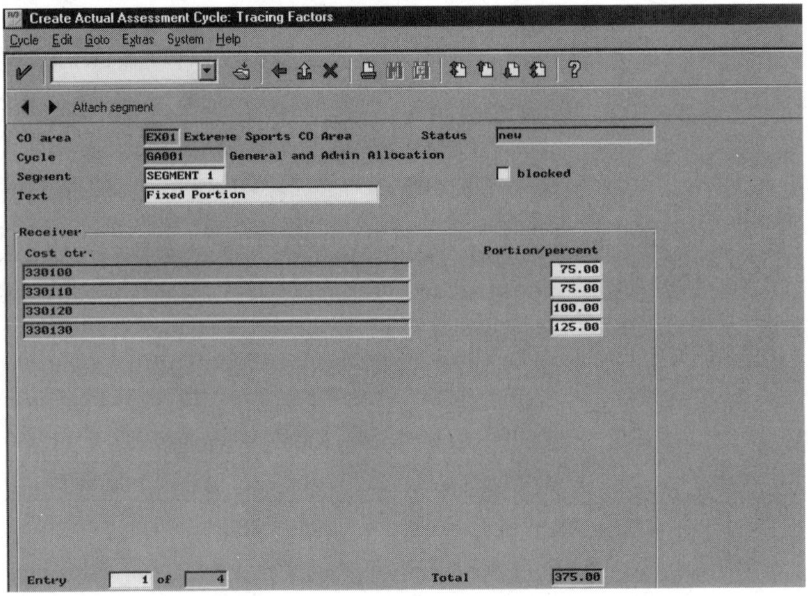

The final section to configure in the segment detail configuration screen (see Figure 9.35) is the Allocation Characteristics section. There are two subsections, Sender and Receiver:

1. Enter within this section the ranges of valid sender/receiver objects. The objects can vary from cost centers to WBS elements, depending on the type of allocation you are creating. The key is to include only those objects that are required. Object groups, like cost center groups, are a good exclusionary tool.

2. If you want to allocate all costs assigned to your sender objects, do not limit the cost elements included within the allocation. Leaving the Cost Element

range blank is the easiest way to include all cost element postings in an allocation calculation.

3. Once the senders and receivers have been identified, you can maintain all tracing factors and receiver weights.

Once you have completed the segment, additional segments can be quickly added by selecting the Attach Segment button. As you add the segments, keep in mind processing speed and cycle integration. See the next section, "Allocation Development Issues."

When you have completed the allocation, run a quick master data check. Use the menu path Cycle ➢ Check and SAP will validate the master data included within the allocation. When configuration is complete, save the allocation.

Allocation Development Issues

The preceding section took you through the creation of a single cycle and segment. It is probable that your solution will require multiple cycles containing multiple segments. This is not unusual. Before building a cycle, however, identify any dependencies that may need to exist at either the segment or cycle level.

Dependencies will determine the order with which a cycle/segment will process. A dependent cycle is one that requires the results of a another previously run cycle or cycles before it can successfully process its allocation. The same meaning covers any dependent segments. Selecting the Iterative indicator on the cycle header will ensure that the attached segments are processed as dependent. Cycles do not have the advantage of an iterative indicator.

You must force the execution of each cycle in the proper order by either entering them properly on the allocation execution screen (see Figure 9.40) or running them individually in order.

FIGURE 9.40   The allocation execution screen

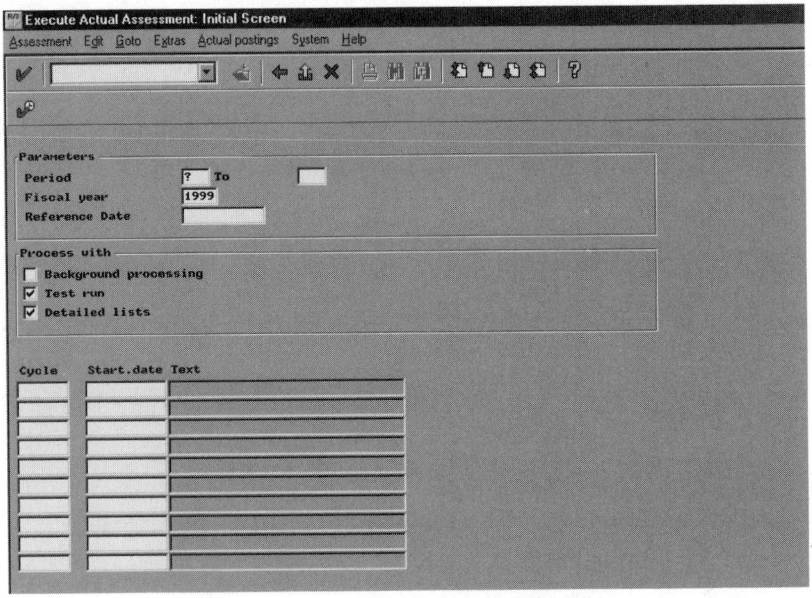

A second development issue deals with the proper number of cycles and segments to build. As stated earlier, SAP will support a one-cycle, one-hundred-segment allocation, but it is completely impractical. There are two things to keep in mind when deciding how many cycles and segments to build:

▶ You have no ability to correct a single segment's posting within an allocation cycle. If an error occurs within a segment posting, the entire cycle must be reversed, the segment must be corrected, and then the cycle can be rerun. For a large cumbersome cycle that takes several hours to run, a reversal could become very costly.

▶ Consider the timing of your closing cycle. If too many segments are tied together, you may negatively influence the closing and reporting schedule. An example would be a cycle with all SBU-specific allocations contained within. If one SBU is not ready to process, no SBU allocations can occur. You should always consider breaking apart unrelated cycles and segments.

Remember that it will be important to experiment with allocations to find the proper mix. Expect to make changes periodically throughout the year to tweak for performance and timing.

The next section will take you through some of the relevant planning topics for Cost Center Accounting.

EXTREME SPORTS PERIODIC ALLOCATIONS CONFIGURATION ANALYSIS

Extreme Sports will utilize cost center assessments to allocate its general and administration costs from its Shared Services organization to each of its operating divisions. Distributions will be utilized for the purpose of reorganizing actual postings. As the cost center structure is modified, actual activity to date may need to be moved to the new area. Distributions will be the tool of choice.

Cost Center Accounting: Planning

Much of the theory for planning and budgeting within Cost Center Accounting will not be discussed in this section. Rather, the topics covered will enhance some basic functionality. Some general theory will inevitably come out, but it is impossible to cover every industry's planning methodology. Additionally, the goal of the section is not to provide detailed analysis of SAP planning integration.

Instead, the section will describe the configuration necessary to ensure that integration occurs if desired. Development of manual planning layouts and how allocations can be utilized will also be covered. Much of what SAP offers as preconfigured tools will be used to meet your planning needs. The first section relates to version control and the necessary controlling area settings.

Controlling Area Settings/Version Control

Settings on the controlling area will determine to what level planning integration will occur within Cost Center Accounting. Figure 9.41 is a view of the fiscal year parameters of the controlling area for version 0. The details behind the settings are covered at length in Chapter 7 in the section "Maintain CO Versions." Review the section so that you can be aware of the impact that each of the fields has in the planning process.

FIGURE 9.41   The fiscal year parameters of the controlling area for version 0

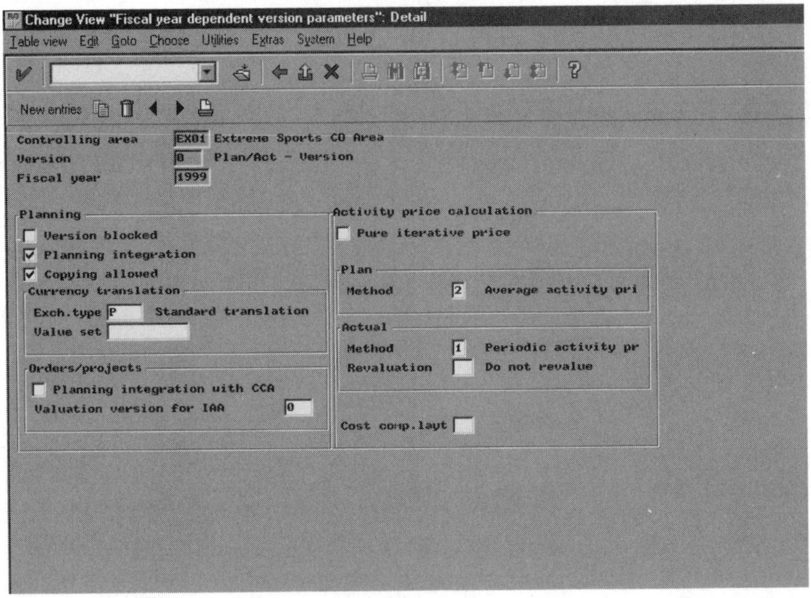

For a quick reference, however, here are two fields that should be considered when you're deciding on the level of planning integration:

Planning Integration   This field should be activated if you want any planned activity on the cost center to integrate with other modules.

Planning Integration with CCA   Activate this setting if you want to have internal order/WBS element plans integrate with Cost Center Accounting. The integration is a two-way door; cost center plans can affect orders, and order planning can affect cost centers.

These settings are controlling area/version/fiscal year specific. If you desire, you can have multiple versions, each with unique settings. Version control and the concept of multiple versions are discussed in the next section.

Planning Versions

Utilization of version control, or maintaining multiple planning versions, can enhance a company's ability to build complex planning scenarios. To make better use of SAP's flexibility, it is recommended that you have more than one planning version. The de facto version from which you will draw your actual/plan comparisons is version 0, because only version 0 is updated in real time with actual transactional data. Prior to creating a controlling area-specific version in Cost Center Accounting, you must define the general version ID. The creation of the general version ID is covered in Chapter 7, in the section "Maintain CO Versions" (review the section for more detailed analysis).

By creating a general CO version, you have made the ID available for use by all controlling areas. The assignment to controlling is not automatic, meaning that all versions are not available to all controlling areas upon creation. However, when you are defining the controlling area settings, SAP will ask you if you want to copy the new version to the controlling area that is set at that time. If you answer yes, the version—along with its controlling area, fiscal year, and delta version settings—is copied to your controlling area. The necessary steps and transaction code for defining a new planning version are listed in order here:

1. Create general version ID for CO (transaction code OKEQ).

2. Define settings for controlling area. (Version 0 setting is automatic for all controlling areas and is available during controlling area creation.)

3. Define settings for fiscal year.

4. Define settings for delta version (if applicable).

Once a plan version is created, plan data can be entered. SAP provides you with a tool that allows you to copy plan data from one version to another. The next section will elaborate on this feature.

Copying Plan Data   One key feature of version control is the ability to copy one version to another, as long as the configuration is set to support the activity (see Figure 9.41). To use the copy planning functionality, follow the user menu path Accounting ➢ Controlling ➢ Cost Center ➢ Planning ➢ Planning Aids ➢ Copy Planning.

COPY PLANNING FOR COST CENTER ACCOUNTING

You can use the following methods to use SAP's copy planning functionality:

Application Menu Path: **Accounting ➢ Controlling ➢ Cost Center ➢ Planning ➢ Planning Aids ➢ Copy Planning**

Transaction Code: **KP97**

The initial copy planning screen will appear (see Figure 9.42). Any of these settings can be changed at any time between copies.

FIGURE 9.42   The initial copy planning screen

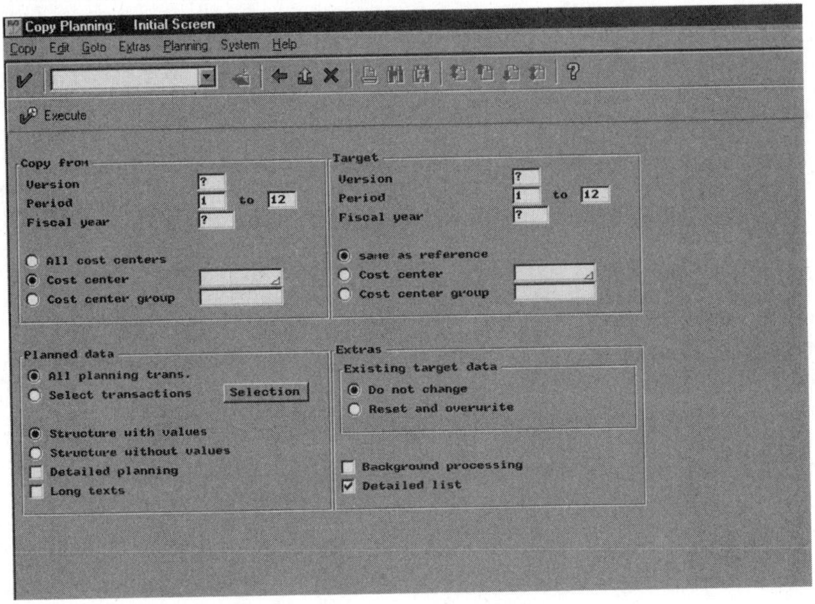

The key fields in the Copy From section are as follows:

Version   Enter the version you want to copy.

Period/Fiscal Year   Enter the period range and year of the data to be copied. There is no limitation to copying across fiscal years.

Cost center selection   You have a choice of including all cost centers within a controlling area in the copy or including a smaller subset.

Here are the key fields in the Target section:

Version   Enter the version you want to receive the copy.

Period/Fiscal Year   The period range must equal the range entered in the Copy From section. Also, if you're copying to a future fiscal year, be sure to have the year defined for the controlling area.

Cost center selection   You can select to copy to the cost centers that were identified in the Copy From section or augment the range of centers. There are certain copy relationships SAP will not support in the copy process. Sending data from all cost centers to a single cost center is one of these relationships.

Here are the key fields in the Planned Data section:

Planning transactions/selections   Use these fields to determine whether postings from all planning transactions can be copied. It is usually best to accept all transactions.

Structure With/Without Values   Select With Values if you want to copy the planned postings to the target version. If you want the copy to erase plan data in the target version and replace it with all *$0s*, select Without Values.

Detailed Planning   Select this field if you want to copy detailed planning. There are limitations, however. If this field is activated, both the sender and target settings must have the same fiscal year settings and must be copying to more than one period and the value dates must be equivalent.

Long Texts   If this field is selected, SAP will copy any long text entered for the plan.

The key fields in the Extras section are listed here:

Existing Target Data   If you have existing plan data in your target version and you do not want the entry erased with the copy, select Do Not Change in the Existing Target Data box. If data is to be replaced with the copy regardless of any existing data, select Reset and Overwrite.

Background Processing/Detailed List   If the plan data records coming from the sender cost centers are significant, run the transactions in the background. If not, the choice is yours. Select the Detailed List check box to receive detail about the copy.

When you've completed your settings, execute the transaction. You cannot save the settings as a variant, so each time you want to copy, the entries will have to be remade. When completed, a detailed report will appear offering statistics specific to the copy.

N O T E   Cost Center Accounting is limited to copying only plan data across versions. The same limitation is not present in Profit Center Accounting (PCA). You will see PCA's ability to copy across record types in Chapter 11.

Planning Revaluation

Another nice feature of cost center planning is the ability to revalue existing plan data without rekeying. SAP allows the user to adjust, by percentage, any existing plan data within any version. Revaluation will come in handy during "what-if" analysis and when making broad but general plan adjustments. An example for revaluation use might be to increase salaries, taxes, and benefits in all shared services cost centers by 5%. For 150 cost centers, the change may take hours. But with the proper cost center and cost element sets, revaluation could handle the change in seconds.

Be aware that, as with most of the planning configuration, the revaluation can be created from both the user menu and IMG. The IMG menu path is Controlling ➢ Overhead Cost Controlling ➢ Cost Center Accounting ➢ Planning ➢ Planning Aids ➢ Define Revaluation ➢ Create Plan Revaluation.

CREATION OF A PLAN REVALUATION

You can use the following methods to get to the screen to create a plan revaluation:

Menu Path: **Controlling** ➢ **Overhead Cost Controlling** ➢ **Cost Center Accounting** ➢ **Planning** ➢ **Planning Aids** ➢ **Define Revaluation** ➢ **Create Plan Revaluation**

Transaction Code: **KPU1**

The create plan revaluation request screen will appear (see Figure 9.43).

FIGURE 9.43   The create plan revaluation request screen

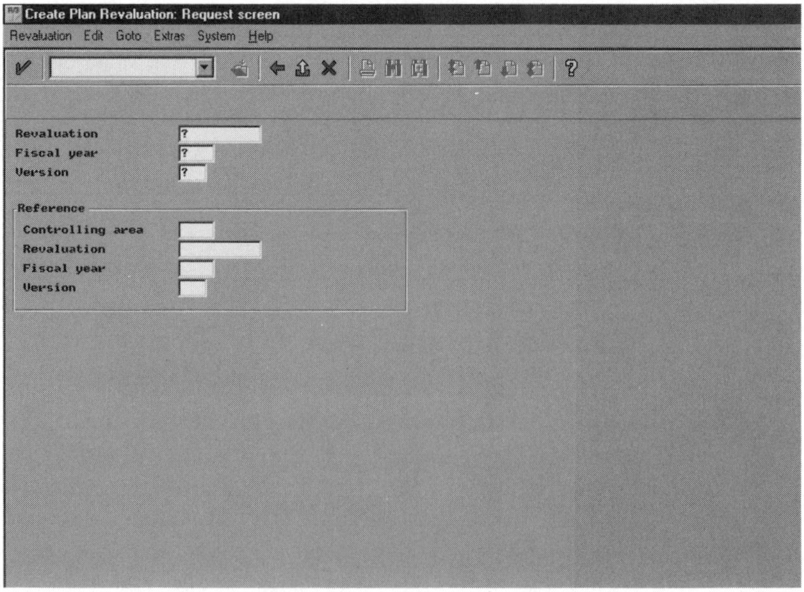

Begin defining the revaluation by establishing the ID/fiscal year/version relationship:

Revaluation   Enter a 10-character ID for your revaluation. This field is required.

Fiscal Year   Enter the fiscal year for which the revaluation is valid. The validity period is limited to a single fiscal year. This field is required.

Version   Enter the version that you want the revaluation to affect. This field is required.

When you've filled out these fields, press Enter. The create plan revaluation select screen will appear (see Figure 9.44). Within the screen, you define which cost centers and cost elements the revaluation will impact.

FIGURE 9.44   **The create plan revaluation select screen**

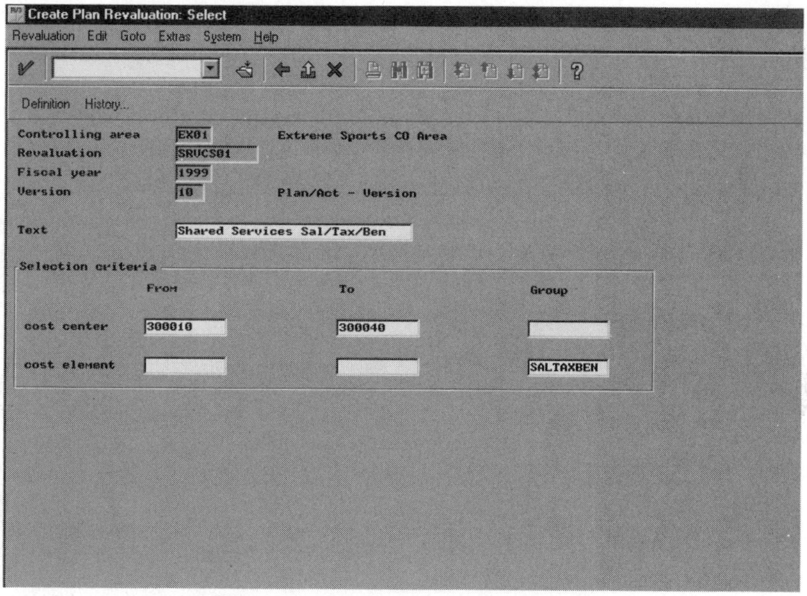

WARNING   All cost centers included in the revaluation will be augmented, so be careful when entering the object ranges.

Begin by providing the revaluation with a text description:

Text   Enter a description for the revaluation. It is likely that you will have more than one revaluation, so be clear in your description.

Cost center selection Enter a single cost center or a range/group of cost centers that should be augmented by the revaluation.

Cost element selection Enter a single cost element or a range/group of cost elements that should be augmented by the revaluation. Only primary cost elements can be revalued. Secondary and assessment cost elements are excluded.

TIP A properly developed cost element group can provide flexibility in your ability to define revaluation percentages.

In the example provided (see Figure 9.44), a range of Extreme Sports' shared services cost centers was entered, as well as a cost element group comprising salary, tax, and benefit accounts.

Click the Definition button to establish the percentage changes for the cost element range/group by period. The create plan revaluation definition screen will appear (see Figure 9.45).

FIGURE 9.45 The create plan revaluation definition screen

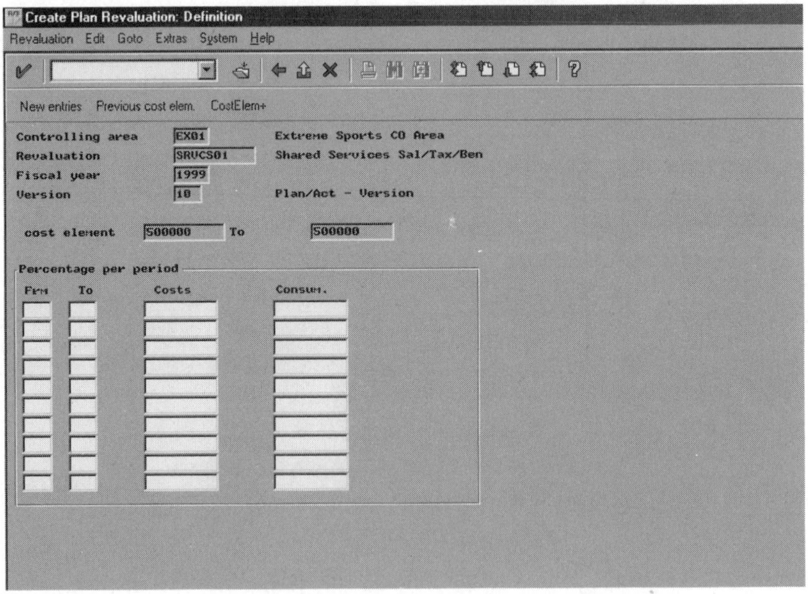

The definition screen allows you to enter percentage changes, either up or down, for the cost elements selected in the prior screen. Notice the range of cost elements that appears in the middle of the screen. In the example provided, a cost element group

was defined to encompass a range of salary, tax, and benefit accounts. The cost element group can be seen in Figure 9.46. The same group of accounts could have easily been added as one From/To range of 500000 to 540000 in the selection screen, but the impact would have been different on the definition screen.

FIGURE 9.46   The cost element group used in planning revaluation

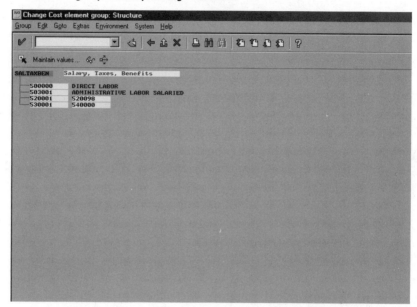

If a single range of accounts is included, there can be no differentiation between cost elements when assigning percentages, meaning that a 5% increase to cost element 500000 and a 10% increase to cost element 503001 would not be possible. Although across-the-board increases are acceptable in many cases, in the example provided, the increases required a different percentage adjustment for administrative labor and direct labor. The only way to achieve this differentiation is through a cost element group.

By building a cost element group that applies both cost elements on separate lines, and not in a range like cost elements 520001–520098, you gain the ability to enter percentages uniquely. Referring back to the create plan revaluation definition screen (see Figure 9.45), begin completing the revaluation by deciding which period range you want the percentage increase to affect and entering it into the From/To columns:

From/To   Enter the range of periods the percentage change is to affect. You can have a unique percentage change for each fiscal period.

Costs   Enter a percentage change, positive or negative, for the specific cost element(s) in question. The change will affect dollars only, not quantities.

Consumption   Enter a percentage change, positive or negative, for the specific cost element(s) in question. The change will affect consumption quantity planned for the cost center(s)/cost element(s).

When you have completed the screen but other cost element(s) exist within the range, select the Cost Element + button to move to the next element or range of elements. When all percentages have been applied, save the revaluation. The plan revaluation can now be executed through the CCA user menu.

Maintaining/Deleting Plan Revaluation

The plan revaluation can be maintained for all cost centers, cost elements, and percentage changes entered. Be careful, however, that you do not delete or make a change to a revaluation without first reversing any prior runs. Once a revaluation is deleted, the postings cannot be reversed for that same definition. A new revaluation would have to be designed to mask the effects of the prior one. The same principle applies to any revaluation changes. Always reverse the effects from the prior run. Otherwise, you are augmenting the revalued plan amounts rather than the original postings.

Planning Allocations

The development of periodic allocations like assessments and distributions was covered earlier in the chapter. These same tools can be developed for use during cost center planning. The concepts that are applied to allocate actual expenses can be used to develop planning allocations. Tools like plan distributions and plan imputed costs are used for primary cost element planning, and plan assessments are used in secondary cost planning.

Because of the nature of planning allocations, they should not occur until after the manual planning and revaluations have occurred. Review "Activity Types and Statistical Key Figures" earlier in this chapter for development detail.

Planning Layouts: Overview

During the process of cost planning, users enter information into SAP through the use of planning layouts. The layouts represent the options the user has on the screen when entering the data. Choices may include, among others, whether they can enter activities, cost elements, key figures or some combination of all three. Additionally, layouts may limit the version or period a user can plan. Layouts provide you with a tool to tailor the planning environment to meet your exact business requirements.

SAP delivers a number of planning layouts with the software that will meet the majority of your planning needs. However, your solution may require that a unique new layout be created. The following section will take you through the necessary development steps.

> **TIP**   Review the SAP-delivered planning layouts before building your own. It will be helpful to copy an existing layout rather than develop one from scratch. You will find it easier to delete unnecessary data than build new data.

Planning layouts use the same design platform that accompanies the report development tool Report Painter. Concepts like General Data Selection, Columns, Rows and Variables are all as relevant with planning layouts as they are with reports. Because of the variety of solutions available, a simple example of a cost element-planning layout will be provided. Review the following screen shots of a SAP cost element-planning layout, Cost Element Standard 1-101.

Figure 9.47 is the basic layout view. It comprises columns and rows that make up the enter screen. Rows may be made up of various characteristics, like cost elements, that will hold the data when planned. These are represented by the two characteristics ActTyp and Cost Elem, located in the far-left column. The columns may be made up of key figures, or key figures and characteristics, and can determine the form in which the data is held. Examples include fixed versus variable costs, CO currency versus Object Currency, and dollars versus quantity units. In this example, an attribute, Distribution Key (DK), was added. The attribute provides additional flexibility to planning.

FIGURE 9.47 The basic layout view for the SAP cost element-planning layout

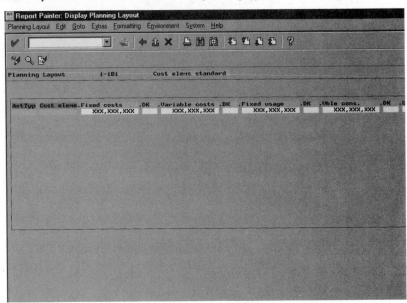

Figure 9.48 is a view of the General Data Selection screen for this planning layout. The General Data Selection screen provides characteristic settings available for the entire layout. The four characteristics chosen here—Version, Period, Fiscal Year, and Cost Center—have been assigned variables, meaning the user will be prompted for entry during planning. It is just as easy to hard-code the values for these characteristics. An example of this would be entering the value of 2000 directly into the Fiscal Year field in place of the variable. The fiscal year value for this layout would then always be 2000. When you provide for user entry through the use of variables, the layout becomes more flexible.

TIP All planning layouts are controlling area independent.

FIGURE 9.48   The General Data Selection screen for the SAP cost element-planning layout

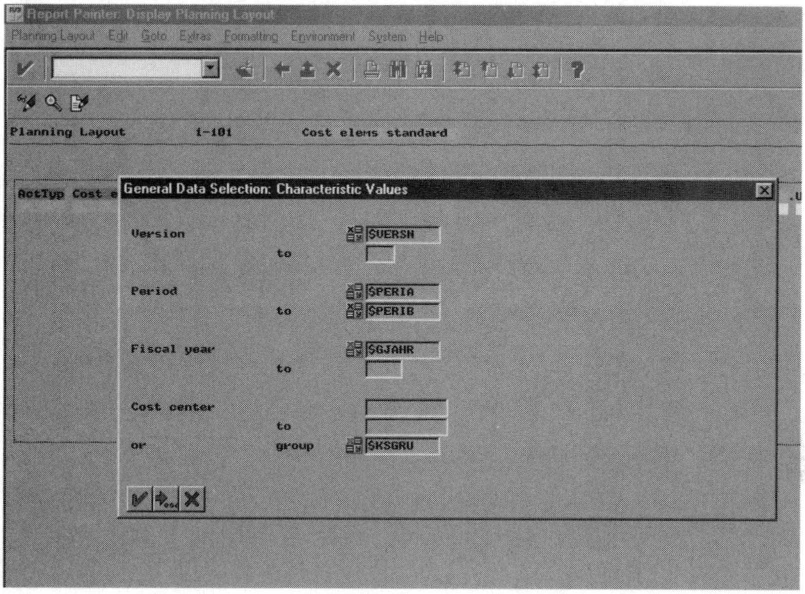

Planning Layouts: Creation

Similar to creating a new report, it is often more expedient to build a new planning layout if it is created from a copy. If, however, your layout is too unique and would require extensive rework, then it is recommended that you start from scratch. The example provided here is rather simple but will be built from scratch. For the sake of the demonstration, the parameters in the sidebar "Extreme Sports Cost Element Planning Layout Configuration Analysis" will apply to the layout.

EXTREME SPORTS COST ELEMENT PLANNING LAYOUT CONFIGURATION ANALYSIS

Extreme Sports has a need to develop a quarterly cost element-planning layout called EX01QTRPLAN. Although entered on a quarterly basis, the cost should spread evenly to each of the periods within the quarter. To add flexibility, the users should be allowed to enter such variables as cost center, cost element, plan version, and fiscal year. The layout of the data entry screen should have each of the four quarters represented by columns and the cost elements represented in rows. As stated earlier, Extreme Sports has decided to track its activity only at the object class level. Capitalized cost transfers between companies are now easily segregated from the production cost transfers.

The IMG menu path Controlling ➤ Overhead Cost Controlling ➤ Cost Center Accounting ➤ Planning ➤ Manual Planning ➤ User Defined Planning Layouts ➤ Create Cost Planning Layouts for Cost Element Planning ➤ Create Cost Planning Layout will take you to the cost element-planning layout screen.

CREATION OF THE COST PLANNING LAYOUT

You can use the following methods to create the cost planning layout:

Menu Path: **Controlling ➤ Overhead Cost Controlling ➤ Cost Center Accounting ➤ Planning ➤ Manual Planning ➤ User Defined Planning Layouts ➤ Create Cost Planning Layouts for Cost Element Planning ➤ Create Cost Planning Layout**

Transaction Code: **KP65**

The Report Painter Create Planning Layout screen will appear. At the Create Planning Layout Screen, provide the layout with an ID, a description, and the ID of the planning layout to be copied. Click Continue and the Report Painter form screen will appear (see Figure 9.49).

FIGURE 9.49   The Report Painter form screen

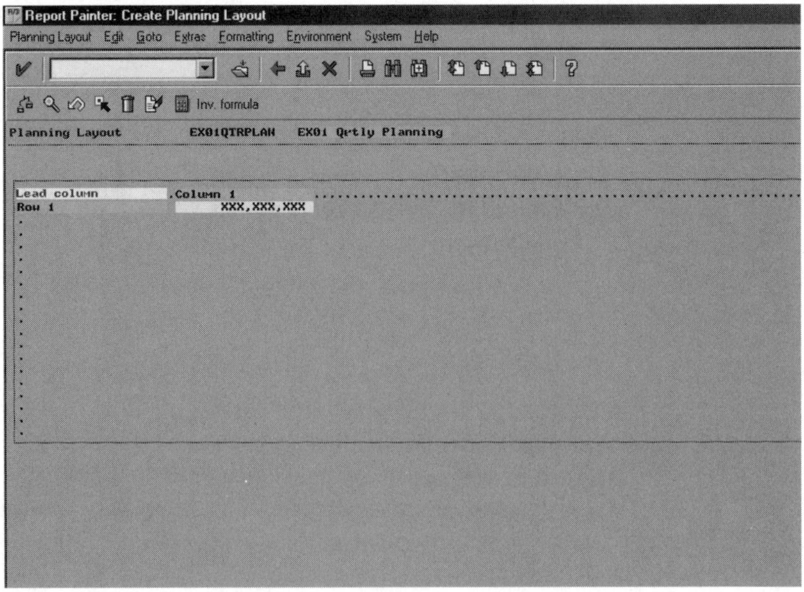

Begin development by establishing the characteristics you wish to plan. In the example description, cost element is the only characteristic the user is to enter. Additionally, it is defined that the cost elements should be entered in the rows. This is an important piece of information because it determines which area of the report (columns or rows) will hold the characteristic value. The first step in the example will be to define the general data selections.

NOTE   The order of the steps taken is not important, only that all is accomplished before saving.

General Data Selection   Settings defined in the General Data Selection (GDS) screen become default values for the entire planning layout. Keep this in mind when creating your columns and rows. By first establishing a variable in the GDS, you will eliminate the need for definition elsewhere, which can save you development time (case in point, the fiscal year definition for Extreme Sports' planning layout).

The development decision to define a single fiscal year, version, and cost center range for the entire layout has been made. When defined centrally, each of these characteristics will be maintained only once and will have just one value.

TIP   Utilizing the general data selection to define your characteristic values ensures consistency in the value definition. If, however, you want a unique value defined per column or row, do not use the general data selection as your definition point.

Begin the process by using the following menu path from the planning screen: Edit ➢ General Data Selection ➢ Display/Change. The General Data Selection Characteristics screen will appear (see Figure 9.50). It is in this selection window that you decide which characteristics will be defined within the GDS. Based upon the Extreme Sports planning example, Fiscal Year, Version, and Cost Center will all be selected. When complete, hit Enter and the GDS Characteristics Values screen will appear (see Figure 9.51).

FIGURE 9.50   The General Data Selection Characteristics screen

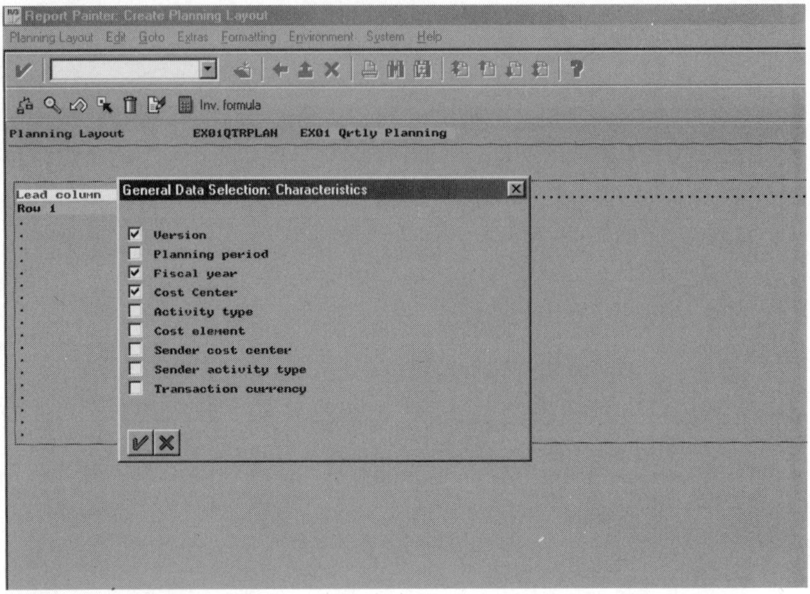

FIGURE 9.51   The GDS Characteristics Values screen

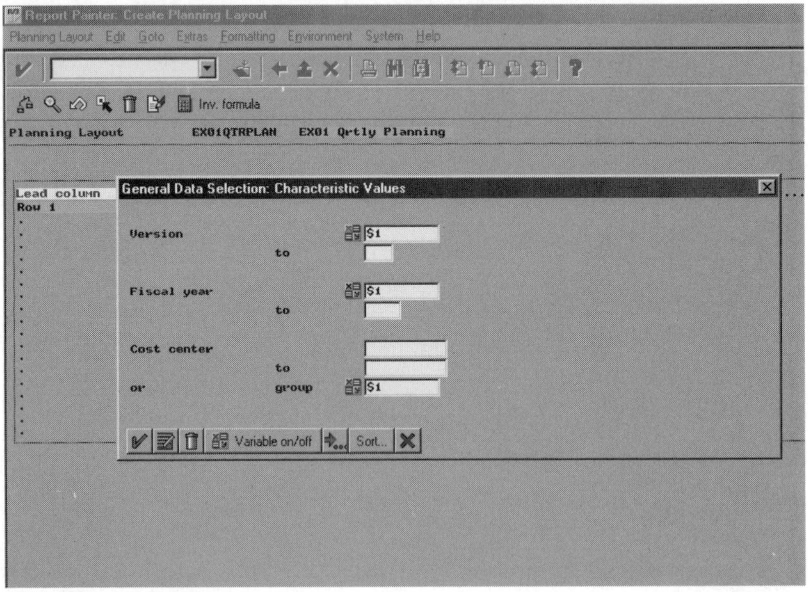

The values window is asking you to define the parameters for what can be planned when using this layout. To provide maximum flexibility, the layout should allow each user to enter the value ranges significant for plan entry each time they plan. This is accomplished by assigning variables to the value fields.

Place the cursor in the From field for both Version and Fiscal Year and in the Group field for Cost Center and click the Variable On/Off button. SAP delivers default global variables that will populate the field automatically, as shown in Figure 9.51. Press Enter and the general data selection is complete. The next phase in the layout development will be the creation of the layout rows.

Defining the Rows   Layout development requires you to run through a number of different windows before you are finished. To narrow the characteristic selection to only cost element, double-click the column block titled Lead Column. A Choose Characteristics window appears (see Figure 9.52). The window holds a number of available characteristics that can be planned. Select the Cost Element radio button and press Enter.

FIGURE 9.52   The Choose Characteristics window

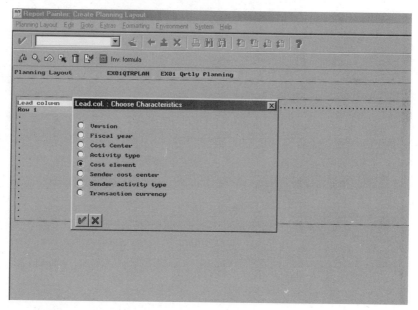

The second window (see Figure 9.53), Characteristic Values, asks you to define what values of the cost element can be planned. Notice that the default setting for cost element is an asterisk. If left alone, the planning layout will automatically allow all cost elements defined within the controlling area to be planned. Referring to the layout description, it was stated that Extreme Sports wants to allow the users to determine which cost elements and cost centers are to be planned. A variable will have to be established for the Cost Element Group field. Place the cursor in the field and select the Variable On/Off button. SAP delivers a default global variable for cost element group, $1, that will populate the field automatically. Press Enter when you're finished with this screen.

FIGURE 9.53   The Characteristic Values window

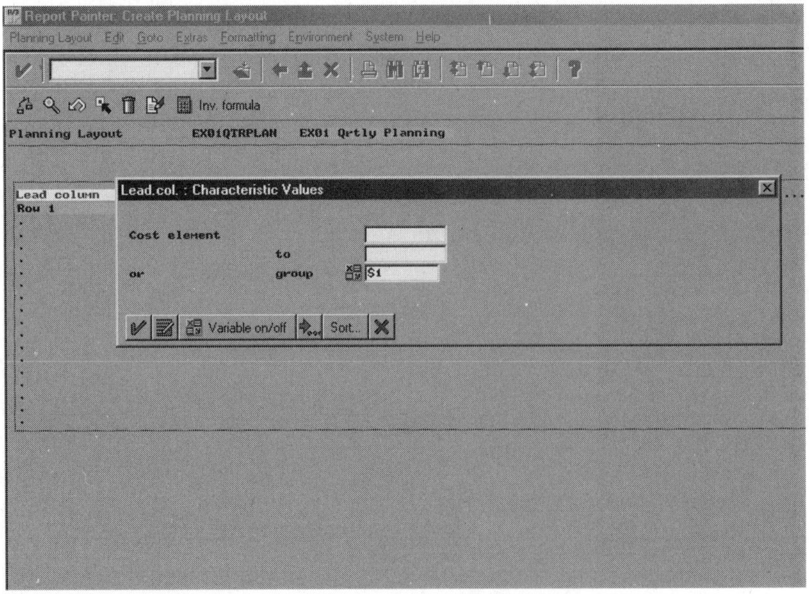

The third window to appear is used to define the column text. Either leave the default value, Cost Element, or enter a description of your own. The text entered here will be viewed as the row description during planning. Press Enter when you are finished. A fourth window will appear, asking you to define how the values will be displayed during planning entry (see Figure 9.54).

FIGURE 9.54   The Structure of Lead Column window

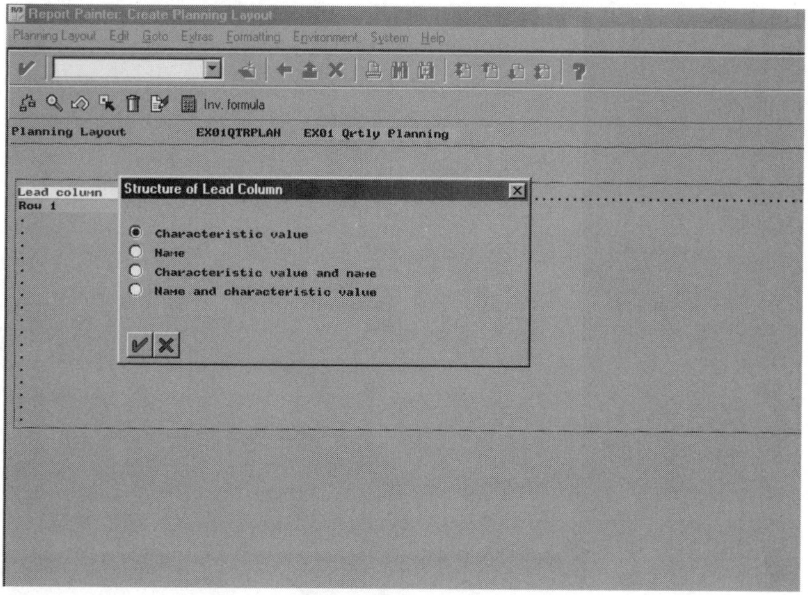

The selection definitions are simple:

Characteristic Value   If this button is selected, only the value of the characteristic will be displayed during planning. In the example provided, a cost element value would be 500000.

Name   If this button is selected, the name of the characteristic selected will be displayed. Again using the example provided, instead of the cost element number 500000, the description of the cost element, Labor/Salaries, would appear.

Characteristic Value and Name   Both the value and name are displayed during planning (the value first).

Name and Characteristic Value   Both the name and value are displayed during planning (the name first).

Select whichever meets your requirements. For the demonstration, only Characteristic Value will be selected. Press Enter and the fifth window will appear, asking you to enter the text length of the lead column. Your decision will be based on your selection in the preceding screen. The maximum length you can define is 30. Press Enter and you have completed the definition of the lead column.

Defining the Columns   The third phase within the layout development will be the addition of the Key Figure columns. Based upon the example description, Extreme Sports has asked that the layout allow for quarterly planning. Therefore, a column that represents each of the four quarters must be created. Begin the process by double-clicking the Column 1 field. A window will appear, asking you to select a key figure definition (see Figure 9.55). The list of standard key figures is extensive, but because you are planning on only cost element, only the key figures capturing plan costs are valid. Based upon Extreme Sports' requirements, the key figure Total Planned Costs in CO Area Currency will be selected. In some circumstances, planning fixed and variable costs separately may be appropriate. You must evaluate the unique needs of each instance. Press Enter when your selection is complete.

FIGURE 9.55   **The Key Figures window**

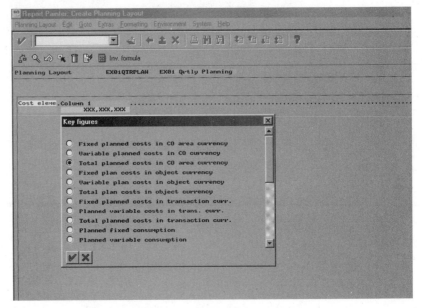

The second window in the column definition will ask you to define a characteristic to be associated with the key figure (see Figure 9.56). The characteristic assignment is used to ensure that only necessary information is available in the layout during planning. In the example, it is stated that only quarterly amounts are to be entered by the user and that the Fiscal Year field is to be flexible. Based on the requirements, only Planning Period will be selected as a characteristic. When the selection is complete, press Enter and the Characteristic Values window appears (see Figure 9.57).

FIGURE 9.56   The Choose Characteristics window

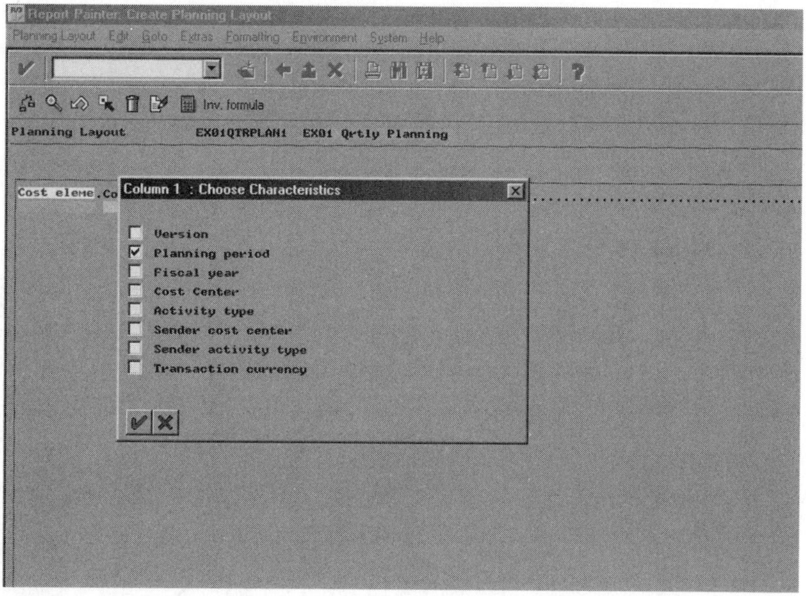

FIGURE 9.57   The Characteristic Values window

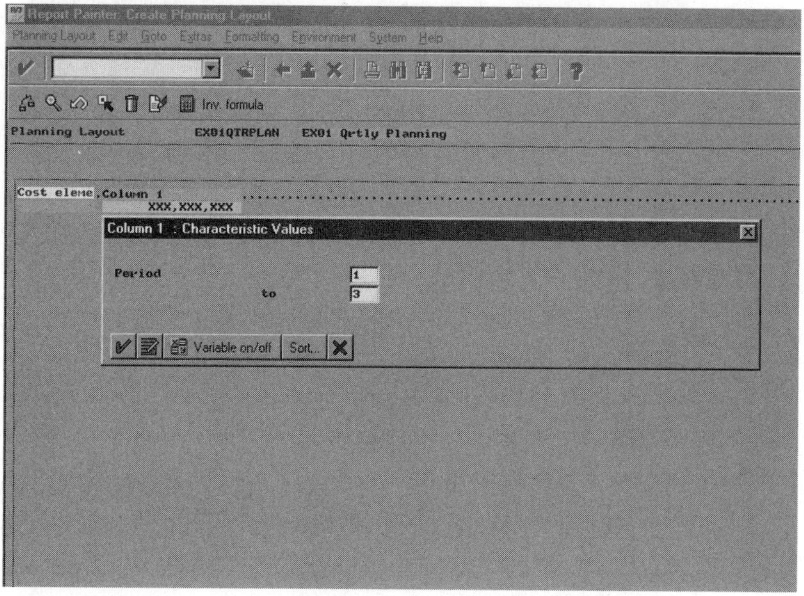

The value window gives you an opportunity to either define for the user the values of the characteristics selected or allow the user to decide by using a variable. Before completing the screen, think about the required uses for the layout. In the case of the planning period values, the first quarter of each fiscal year will always be represented by the fiscal periods 1 through 3. Nothing will change this fact. Thus, hard-coding the first quarter planning period values into the fields is appropriate. When the selection is complete, press Enter. A window will appear asking you to define the column text heading (Figure 9.58).

FIGURE 9.58   The Enter Texts window

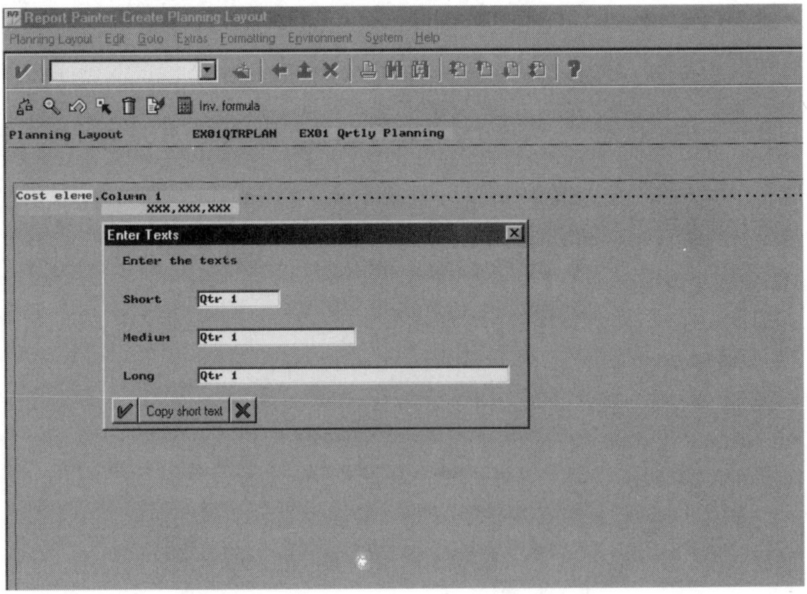

The column text window operates in the same manner as any text window. Enter the description of the column you are defining. For the example layout, the column has been defined as Qtr 1 (see Figure 9.58). Press Enter and the column definition is finished. The column will appear on the layout definition screen. It will be necessary to repeat these steps for each of the four quarters within a fiscal year, changing the planning period values accordingly. A quick way of adding columns is to copy.

Copying Columns   To copy a column, simply place the cursor on the column you wish to copy and click the select icon. You will notice that the column will change color and a new set of buttons will appear in the header. Next, either click the copy icon or select the F7 key on your keyboard to copy the column. You will notice that an exact duplicate of the column has appeared on the screen. To make the necessary changes to the copied column, double-click on the column header and cycle through the windows. In the case of the Extreme Sports example, only the planning period values and the text window will need to change. When you're finished, you can save the layout and begin utilizing it during cost center planning. However, in some cases, additional detail is required. Attributes are designed for this purpose and are covered in the next section.

Defining Attributes Attributes provide additional flexibility to the planning screens by defining in greater detail the quantity or dollar amount being planned. Attribute values include, among others, unit, exchange rate type, action, and distribution key. By adding the attribute action to the planning screen, the user would have the ability to determine if the amounts being planned should replace, be added to, or be subtracted from any existing amounts. If the attribute were not present, the system would default with the replace option.

In support of the Extreme Sports planning layout, the attribute Distribution Key is required. Because the planning periods are covering a range, a distribution key will be necessary to determine the exact amount that should post to each period within the range. By adding the distribution key, the user can select how the amounts will post. To place the attribute before the first column, place the cursor just to the right of the column and select the Define Element button. The Select Element Type window will appear (see Figure 9.59), asking you to define the new column. Select the Attribute radio button and press Enter.

FIGURE 9.59 The Select Element Type window

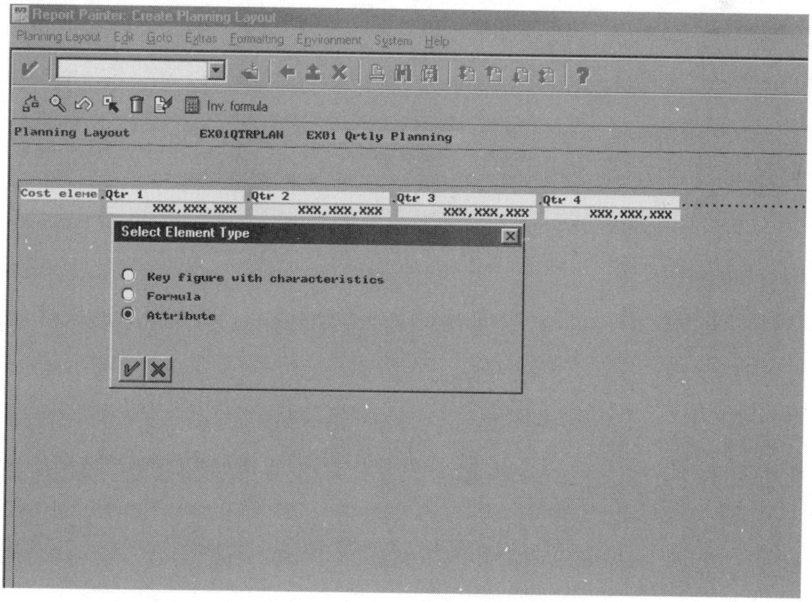

The second window to appear will ask for the attribute definition (see Figure 9.60). In the example, Distribution Key will be selected. Review the other attributes available for future reference. Once the selection is made, press Enter again. The third window will ask for the key figure definition.

FIGURE 9.60   The Choose Attribute window

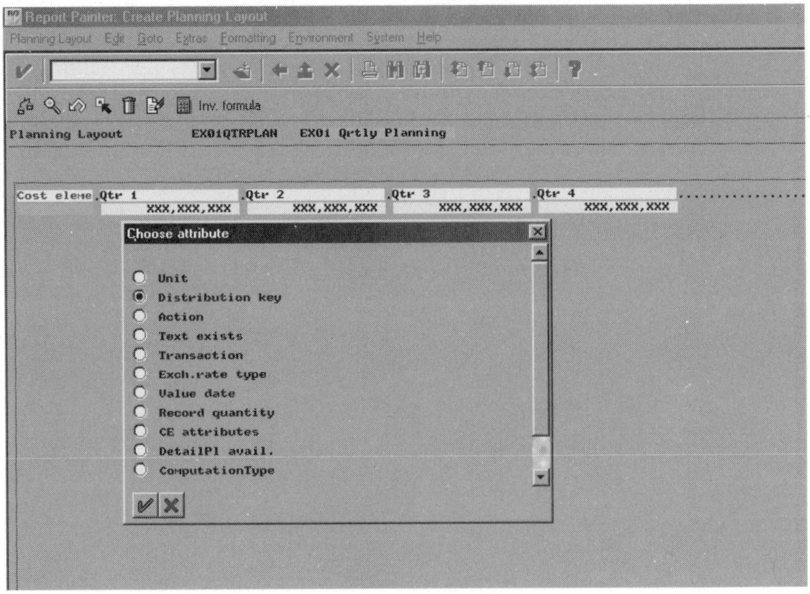

Remember, the key figure defines what type of data is to be utilized in, or acted upon by, the column. In this case, the distribution key will be affecting the planning columns defined earlier. Because these columns were defined as Total Planned Costs in CO Area Currency, consistency demands that the distribution key be defined the same. Once it's selected, press Enter and a window requesting the attribute characteristics will appear (see Figure 9.61).

FIGURE 9.61   The Choose Characteristic for Attribute window

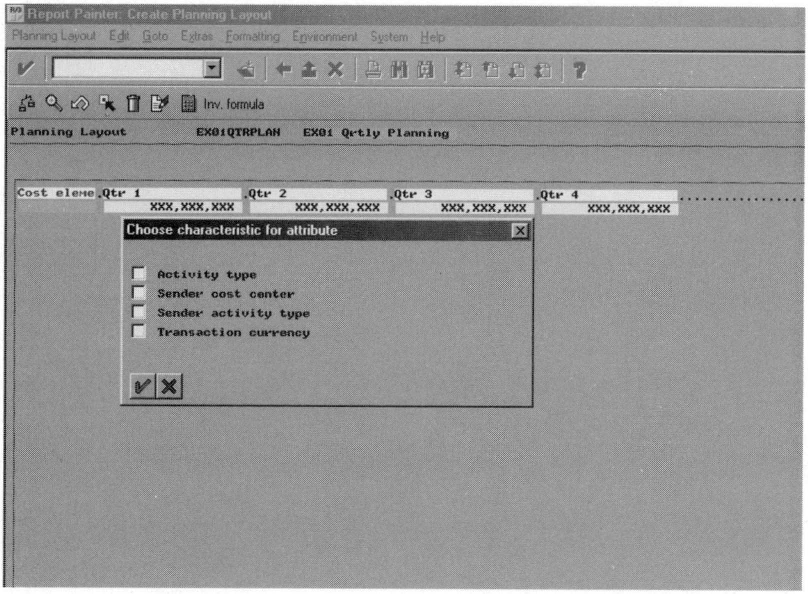

For the distribution key, only the fiscal year field must be maintained. Recall that the fiscal year was defined in the general data selection and so is not visible in this window. If, in your solution, you need further differentiation, please apply accordingly. After selecting the field, move to the next window and maintain the characteristic value. In the manner in which the columns and rows were maintained, set a variable for any necessary field's value. Because no characteristics were selected in the example, the Characteristic Values window was bypassed. The final window to process is again the text window. Keep the text window requirements in mind when maintaining the value (see "Defining the Columns" for detail). The attribute has now been created.

Because the same key figure, Total Planned Costs in CO Area Currency, was defined for each column and the attribute, only one has to be defined for the layout. The distribution key value will be good for all columns. If each column had been defined differently, multiple distribution keys would have been necessary. Once the layout is complete, check it for errors by selecting the Check button. When it's error free, save the planning layout. For a view of the completed layout, see Figure 9.62. It is now available for use in cost center planning.

FIGURE 9.62   The completed cost element-planning layout

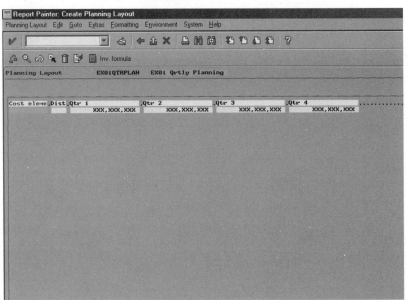

Planning Profiles

Planning profiles within SAP marry a planning layout with an appropriate area of planning (for example, cost centers, orders, profitability analysis). SAP delivers four standard profiles with the software:

SAP101   Primary Costs/Activity Types/Stat. Key Figures

SAP102   Activity Inputs/Activity Types/ Stat. Key Figures

SAP103   Costs, Revenues/Activity Types/Activity Price/Stat. Key Figures

SAP104   Secondary Order Costs/Activity Types for Component Splitting/ Activity-Dependent Key Figures

The majority of CO planning requirements can be covered with profiles SAP101 and 102. In the preceding section, the development of the planning layout EX01QTRPLAN was provided. To use the layout, it must be assigned to a planning profile. During the planning process, the profile is set prior to data entry.

The menu path Controlling ➢ Overhead Cost Controlling ➢ Cost Center Accounting ➢ Planning ➢ Manual Planning ➢ Create User Defined Planning Profiles will take you to the planning profile development section of SAP.

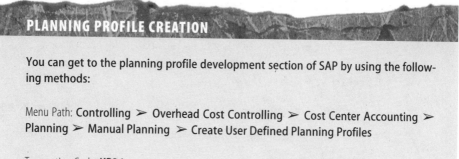

PLANNING PROFILE CREATION

You can get to the planning profile development section of SAP by using the following methods:

Menu Path: **Controlling** ➤ **Overhead Cost Controlling** ➤ **Cost Center Accounting** ➤ **Planning** ➤ **Manual Planning** ➤ **Create User Defined Planning Profiles**

Transaction Code: **KP34**

The CO planner profile overview screen will appear (see Figure 9.63).

FIGURE 9.63   The CO planner profile overview screen

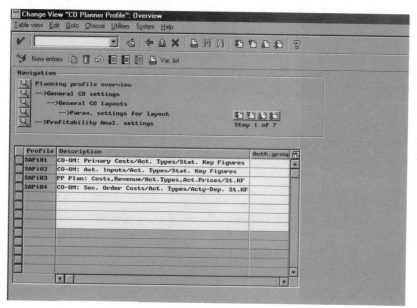

There are (up to) four possible sections that must be defined during profile creation:

Section 1 (Profile Overview)   Define the profile ID.

Section 2 (General CO Settings)   Determine planning area settings.

Section 3 (General CO Layouts)   Assign the CO planning layout to a specific planning area.

Section 4 (Parameter Settings for Layout; optional)   If desired, you can preset values for the variables assigned in the planning layout.

During profile creation, sections 1–4 are developed in order.

Section 1: Profile Overview

To add a new profile, select the New Entries button and fill in the following fields:

Profile   Enter an alphanumeric ID for the new planning profile.

Description   Enter the profile description.

Authorization Group   If your company is using authorization groups to control system access, this field may be relevant. There are five activities that can be controlled with an authorization group:

▶ Create (01)

▶ Change (02)

▶ Display (03)

▶ Delete (06)

▶ Execute (16)

Profile ZEXQTR—EX01 CCTR QTR Planning Profile was created for the example. Press Enter and the new profile ID will become grayed out. Select the new layout ID and move to the General CO Settings section.

Section 2: General CO Settings

SAP will automatically assign three planning areas with your new profile (see Figure 9.64). You have the ability to add other planning areas by selecting the New Entries button. When the new entry screen appears, use the drop-down box to select the additional areas.

FIGURE 9.64   The CO planning profile planning areas assignment screen

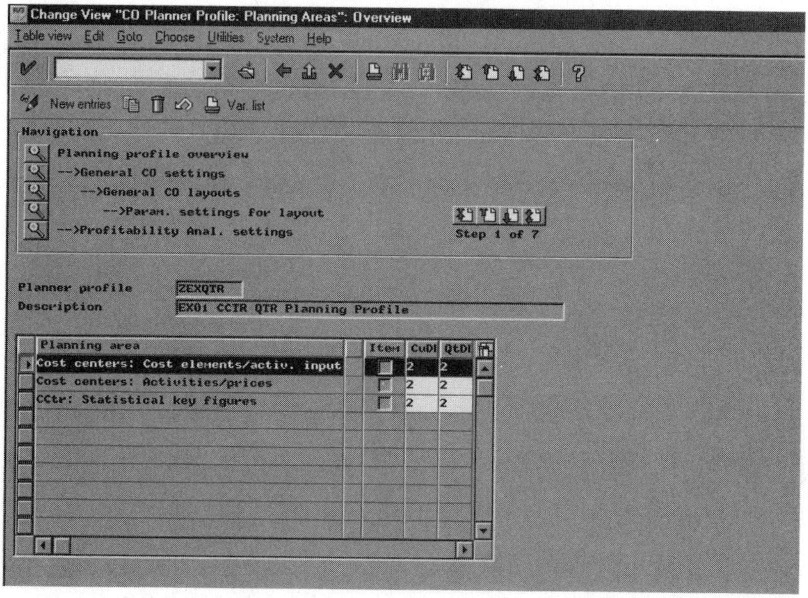

Once all areas have been defined for the profile, you must assign a layout to each. The example layout EX01QTRPLAN is to be used in the planning of primary costs in Cost Center Accounting only. Additional areas will not be necessary for the example profile. Review the delivered planning areas to find one that may be appropriate for your solution. Select the planning area that is to receive your profile and move to the General CO Layout section.

Section 3: General CO Layout

Assigning the layout is done by simply using the drop-down box in the Layout field to pull in the desired ID. You are allowed one and only one layout per planning area, as denoted by the single layout field. In Figure 9.65, you will see the assignment of the example layout EX01QTRPLAN.

FIGURE 9.65   The New Entries screen for the planning layout assignment

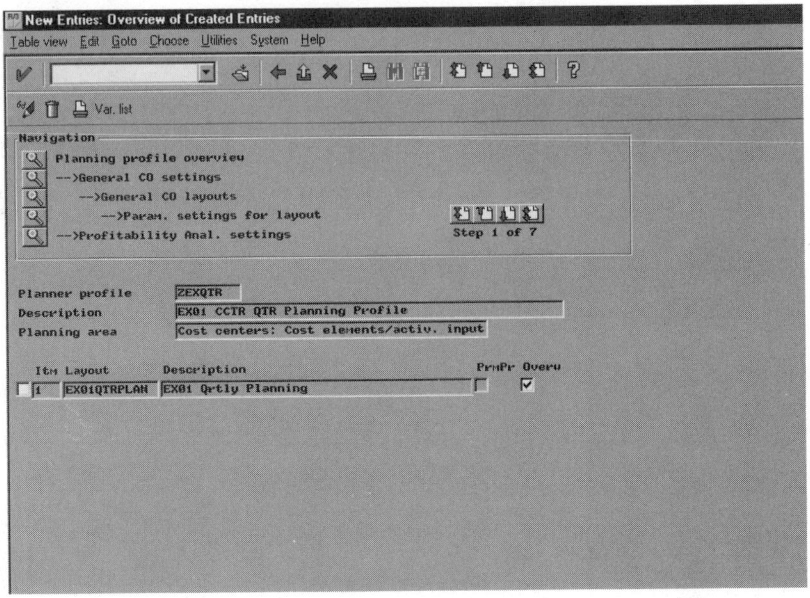

At the end of the layout line, you will notice two check boxes. Here are the definitions of both fields:

PrmPR (Pre-Parameterization)   This indicator denotes whether parameter settings have been made for the layout variables. The field will activate automatically if the optional section 4 (Parameter Settings for Layout) is maintained.

Overw (Overwritten)   This indicator denotes whether the user can overwrite the default parameter settings, maintained in step 4, during the time of planning.

Once the assignment has been made, the profile can be saved and used during planning. However, if you want to establish some default values for the assigned layout's variables, select the layout and move to section 4.

Section 4: Parameter Settings for Layout

The screen that will appear is a view of the planning screen the user will see when the profile is utilized. Figure 9.66 is a view of the planning screen for the layout EX01QTRPLAN. As stated earlier, the fields provided for input on this screen were designated in the layout by the use of variables (see "Planning Layout: Creation" for details). You may enter any valid default data within the field and save. When the user brings up the planning screen, the new parameter settings will default.

FIGURE 9.66   The pre-parameterization screen for the planning layout.

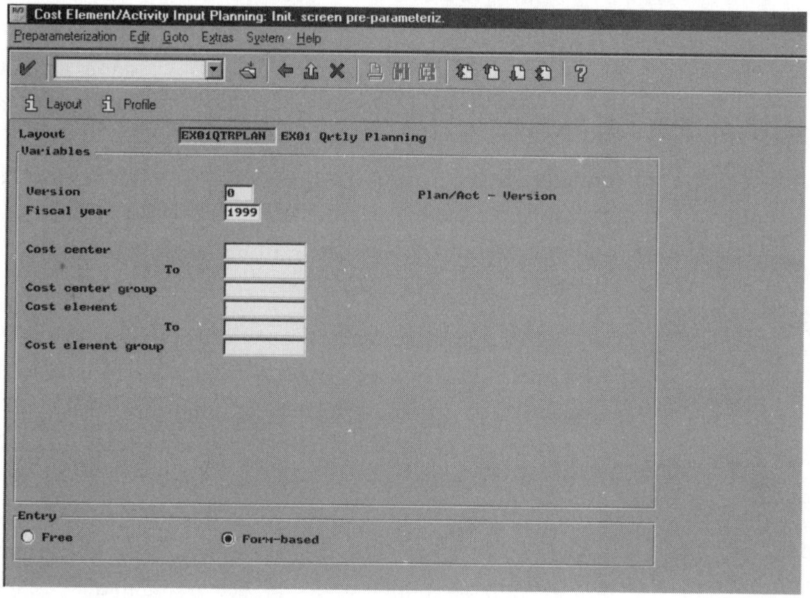

Planning Profile Misc.

When you return to the General CO Layouts section, you will notice that both the PrmPR and Overw buttons have been selected. Return to the General CO Settings section and repeat steps 2 through 4 as needed. Remember that each planning area must have a layout assignment if it is to be utilized for said area. However, the profile will work for the single planning area that has been completed.

With the completion of the planning profile, the cost center planning is finished. The next section will provide insight into CO's two methods of automatically combining cost elements and cost objects.

Automatic Account Assignment in CO

At a high level, the logic applied to automatic account assignment in CO is similar to that in FI. During posting activity, SAP automatically determines coding block items based upon certain rules. In Chapter 3, you learned that these rules are defined for FI through activity processing keys like BSX (Inventory Postings). In the case of BSX, the company code/material valuation class involved in the material movement determines the account to be posted. For the CO account assignment, accounts are not determined, but rather CO objects.

CO account assignment will automatically determine the cost center, profit center, order, and/or business area based on a company code/cost element relationship. The company code will determine the controlling area affected. When updates affecting a mapped cost element occur in SAP, if no other real CO object has been identified in the coding block, the default defined on the account assignment table, TKA3A, will be used. If, however, a real CO object has been previously defined, it will not be overwritten by the account assignment configuration. The specifics to the account assignment table configuration will be covered in detail. There is a second level of automatic assignment available on the cost element/controlling area level.

In some cases, a general controlling area assignment may be more appropriate than one specific to a company code. The cost element master record offers an opportunity to directly define a default account assignment for either a cost center or an order. Because there are only two possible object assignments, there is less flexibility. Additionally, the cost element level account assignment will be overwritten if a matching cost element mapping exists in the account assignment table for a company code assigned to the same controlling area. The details behind the master record maintenance will also be covered in detail.

Automatic Account Assignment Table: TKA3A

Maintenance of the automatic account assignment table can be accessed from numerous locations within overhead cost controlling. The IMG menu path Controlling ➢ Overhead Cost Controlling ➢ Cost Center Accounting ➢ Actual Postings ➢ Manual Actual Postings ➢ Maintain Automatic Account Assignment will take you through Cost Center Accounting.

The automatic account assignment default assignments screen will appear (see Figure 9.67).

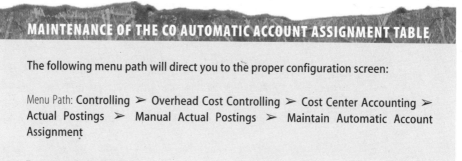

MAINTENANCE OF THE CO AUTOMATIC ACCOUNT ASSIGNMENT TABLE

The following menu path will direct you to the proper configuration screen:

Menu Path: **Controlling** ➤ **Overhead Cost Controlling** ➤ **Cost Center Accounting** ➤ **Actual Postings** ➤ **Manual Actual Postings** ➤ **Maintain Automatic Account Assignment**

Transaction Code: **OKB9**

FIGURE 9.67   The automatic account assignment default assignments screen

To better understand the example configuration settings, review the sidebar "Extreme Sports Automatic Account Assignment Configuration Analysis" before proceeding.

EXTREME SPORTS AUTOMATIC ACCOUNT ASSIGNMENT CONFIGURATION ANALYSIS

Extreme Sports has two immediate account assignment requirements: The first is to assign all miscellaneous sales postings to the Misc. Sales profit center 140000. Misc. Sales generates most of its revenue from selling returned or traded-in equipment and should not affect the profitability of the other brands or divisions. One exception to the rule covers miscellaneous sales generated from contract services. These revenue dollars should route to the services Misc. Sales profit center 150000. The second assignment Extreme Sports requires is the routing of all maintenance activity to a central maintenance cost center for all company codes.

Overview Screen

At the initial screen, select the New Entries button to begin defining your account assignments. The automatic account assignment default assignments overview screen appears (Figure 9.68).

FIGURE 9.68   The automatic account assignment default assignments overview screen

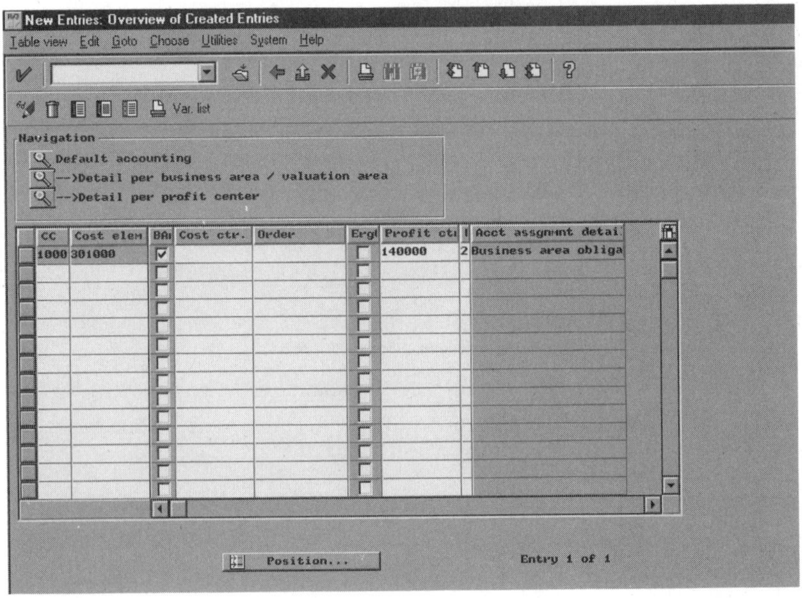

The fields are as follows:

Company Code (CC)   Enter the company code ID that is to be affected by the account assignment activity.

Cost Element   Enter the cost element used to derive the object assignment.

Business Area Indicator (BArIn)   If this field is active, the business area assignment will override another business area defined in the posting. The priority assignment is important if costs must be forced into a single business area regardless of cost centers assigned elsewhere. If you are not using business area(s) in your solution, the setting is not functional.

TIP   Remember that you can have only one real CO account assignment in any posting.

Cost Ctr.   If applicable, enter the cost center ID that is to be defaulted into the coding block. Remember that there must be a relationship between the company code and cost center for the entry to be valid.

Order   If applicable, enter the order ID that is to be defaulted into the coding block. Remember that there must be a relationship between the company code and order for the entry to be valid.

Profit Center   If applicable, enter the profit center ID that is to be defaulted into the coding block. Only revenue elements can have a profit center default assignment. Unlike the cost center and order assignments, there is no relationship between profit center and company code. Instead, the validity check is at the controlling area level. Both the company code and the profit center must belong to the same controlling area for a valid assignment.

Detailed Account Assignment (D)   SAP allows for account assignment by valuation area and/or business in addition to company code. For example, the cost center to be assigned is 1000 unless the business area is AAA; then the cost center assignment is changed to 2000. There are four possible entries:

0 (Default setting)   Leave the field empty if you do not require additional assignment.

1 (Valuation Area Obligatory)   Select this option if you want to use the valuation area in the account assignment determination rule.

2 (Business Area Obligatory)   Select this option if you want to use the business area in the account assignment determination rule.

3 (Valuation Area/Business Area Obligatory)   Select this option if you want to use both in the account assignment determination.

If you have assigned a business area to the cost center or order master record, it will be difficult to differentiate account assignment by business area. The Extreme Sports solution will utilize this setting to differentiate its Misc. Sales postings.

Account Assignment Detail   Enter a text description describing the selection in the Detailed Account Assignment field.

If your solution does not require the use of Detailed Account Assignment, you can save the settings at this time. The account assignment is complete. In the Extreme Sports example, however, Detailed Account Assignment is going to be used to route the miscellaneous sales from contract services to the proper profit center. Review Figure 9.68 for a view of the overview screen settings necessary to route the general Misc. Sales to profit center 140000.

Detail per Business Area/Valuation Area

At the automatic account assignment default assignments overview screen, select the row to which you want to add detail assignments to and click the Detail per Business Area/Valuation button in the Navigation box. The specific assignments overview window appears (see Figure 9.69).

FIGURE 9.69   The specific assignments overview window

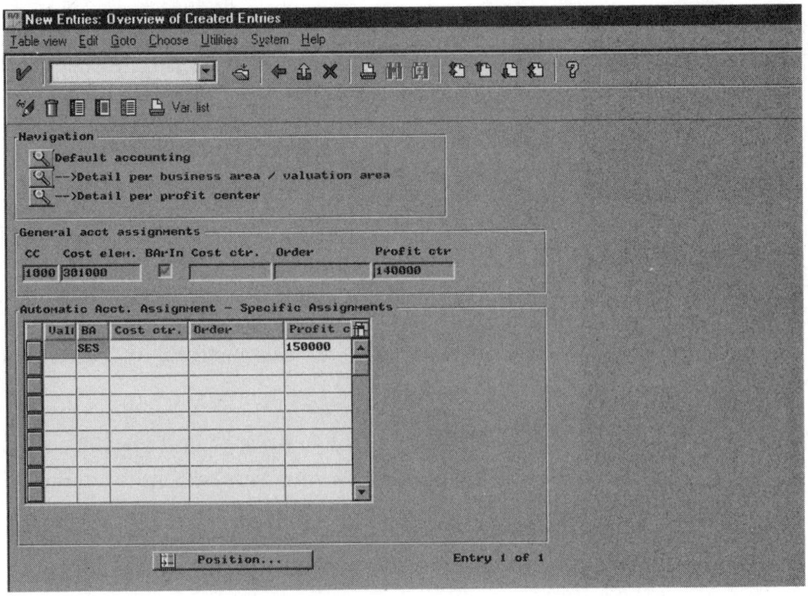

The fields in this window are as follows:

Valuation Area (ValA)   If applicable, enter the valuation area to be used to route the posting to the proper CO object.

Business Area (BA)   If applicable, enter the business area to be used to route the posting to the proper CO object.

Cost Center/Order/Profit Center   Enter the valid object ID to be used in the coding.

For the Extreme Sports solution, business area SES, Extreme Services, will be used to identify those miscellaneous sales postings that are to reroute to profit center 150000. Once the business area assignments are set, when the user processes the invoice and enters the business area SES 150000 rather than 140000 will default into the profit center field. See Figure 9.69 for a view of the Extreme Sports account assignment settings.

Default Account Assignment—Cost Element Master Record Maintenance

The second method of CO account assignment is to maintain the cost element master record for a default object assignment. Referring to the second of the two Extreme Sports account assignment requirements, all maintenance costs in the controlling area are to be routed to a single cost center. Rather than set a rule in the account assignment table for each company code in the controlling area, it would be quicker and easier to maintain the assignment on the cost element.

Navigate to the Change View of the cost element master record (see Chapter 8 for details). Once at the master record, select the Default Acct. Assgn. button (see Figure 9.70). A box will appear asking for a CO object entry. Enter either a cost center or internal order ID and press Enter (see Figure 9.71). Save the cost element and the assignment is complete. When the user processes any activity for the cost element and does not enter a real account assignment object, the default will post automatically.

FIGURE 9.70   The change view screen for cost element master record maintenance

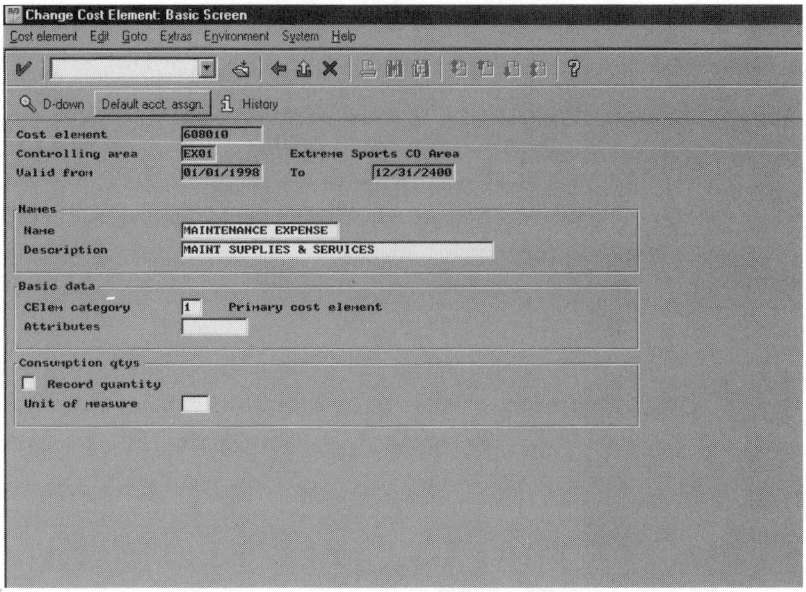

FIGURE 9.71   The Default Account Assignment window on the cost element master record

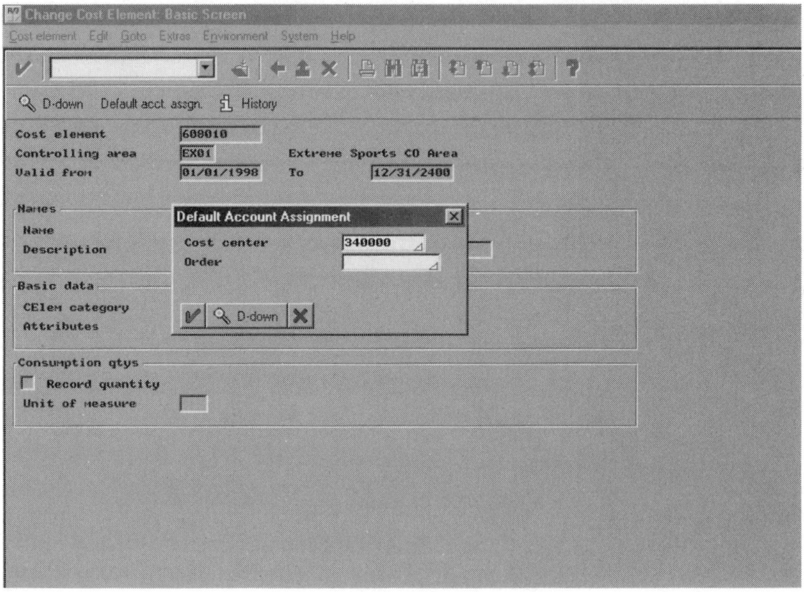

Account Assignment Summary

CO automatic account assignment is complete. It is recommended that you experiment with each solution to find which will provide the proper fit for your company. One important thing to remember about CO automatic account assignment is that the default will not override an existing account assignment entry. Unlike the FI account determination activity, CO account assignment is only effective if the user is not manually overriding the activity. If your intention is to allow SAP to derive the CO object, be certain that you have identified the step in your procedure so that the user community is aware.

Summary

As seen by the amount of time spent discussing master data development, Cost Center Accounting is only partially maintained through table configuration. Although most of the menu paths provided routed you through the IMG, that was more for consistency than it was a requirement. A lot of the work involved can be accessed through the user menus.

This chapter provided good breakdowns of which items were master data and which were configuration data. The sections dealing with controlling area maintenance, version control, and planning mostly involved traditional configuration activity. Periodic allocation development, standard hierarchy creation, and activity type/statistical key figure creation were more master data related. The combination of the two produced a fully functioning Cost Center Accounting module.

There are several key areas to remember:

▶ Get the standard hierarchies right. They are key to reporting and allocations.

▶ Organize your allocation cost elements in a unique number range sequence.

▶ Be aware of dependencies when building your periodic allocations.

Know the differences between the impacts of the CO account assignment table TKA3A and the Default account assignment on the cost element master record. Here is a detailed list of the topics covered in this chapter:

Introduction to Cost Center Accounting Configuration

Cost Center Accounting Standard Hierarchy

Adding New Hierarchy Nodes

Changing/Moving/Deleting Hierarchy Nodes

Internal Order Accounting

FEATURING:

▶ **INTERNAL ORDER ACCOUNTING CONFIGURATION**

▶ **CONTROLLING AREA MAINTENANCE**

▶ **SETTLEMENT CONFIGURATION**

▶ **PLANNING/BUDGETING/AVAILABILITY CONTROL**

▶ **STATUS MANAGEMENT**

▶ **ORDER TYPE CONFIGURATION**

To many developers and users, Internal Order Accounting is one of the most difficult areas within CO to understand. Unlike cost centers and profit centers, which have been in mainstream accounting for some time, internal orders and their unique properties will be a new concept to most people.

Some references will be made to settlement objects like maintenance orders, production orders, and capital investment orders, but the majority of this chapter will be spent defining the configuration steps for internal orders only. However, the basic concepts supporting order type development—in particular, planning, budgeting, and settlement—are similar across all order types.

Internal Order Configuration

There are some areas within SAP, such as Cost Center Accounting, in which configuration can be done in any sequence. But in other areas, the type of information required for a certain step must first be completed in a prior step. Internal order development is one of those areas in which a specific order of configuration must be followed for the object to be properly configured.

From the developer's viewpoint, the order type is the central figure in Internal Order Accounting. The order type determines what information can be held, how it will be settled, planning and budgeting parameters, authorizations, what order master data is required, and how it will be displayed on the screen. Figure 10.1 provides a view of the detail screen in order type configuration. Note the number of field options available. When developing the order type, it is important to begin the process with the end in mind.

FIGURE 10.1   The maintain order types detail screen

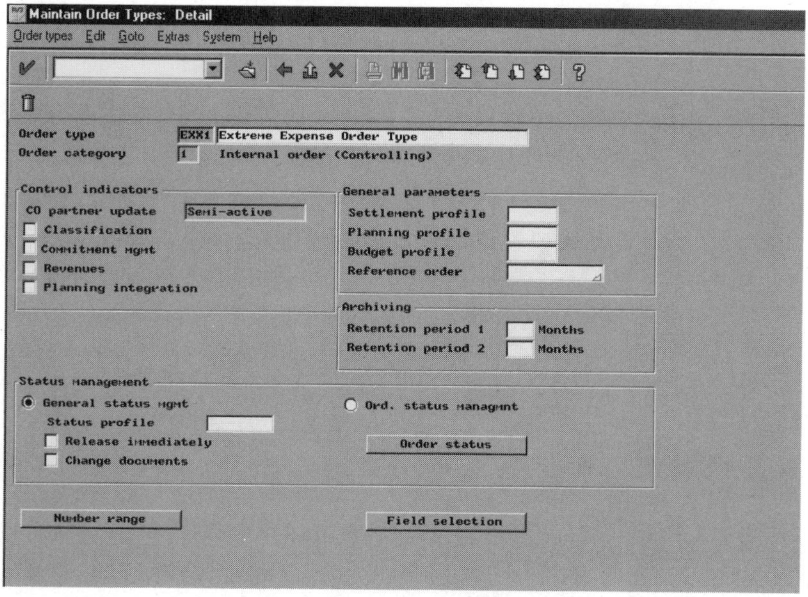

Looking at the General Parameters section of the order, you can see fields for the settlement profile, planning profile, and budgeting profile. Each of these would have to be configured and assigned prior to successfully completing the order type. Additionally, the Status Management section offers two options, one of which (General Status Mgmt) would also have to be completed prior to being utilized by the order type. The importance of mentioning them here is to give further explanation to the iterative nature of the order development cycle.

Much of the configuration within Internal Order Accounting is controlling area independent and thus can be used universally within the client. Additional controlling area–specific development is almost always required, but the item itself is accessible to all controlling areas. The next section will begin the process of Internal Order Accounting development with the maintenance of the controlling area.

Controlling Area Maintenance for Internal Order Accounting

Like each module in Controlling, Internal Order Accounting must be activated for the controlling area prior to beginning development. Activating the proper indicators was covered in Chapter 7, but review Figure 10.2 for a refresher. As you can see, both order management and commitment management are active for the controlling area. The benefits of commitment management will become evident later in the chapter.

FIGURE 10.2   Activating the proper indicators for Internal Order Accounting

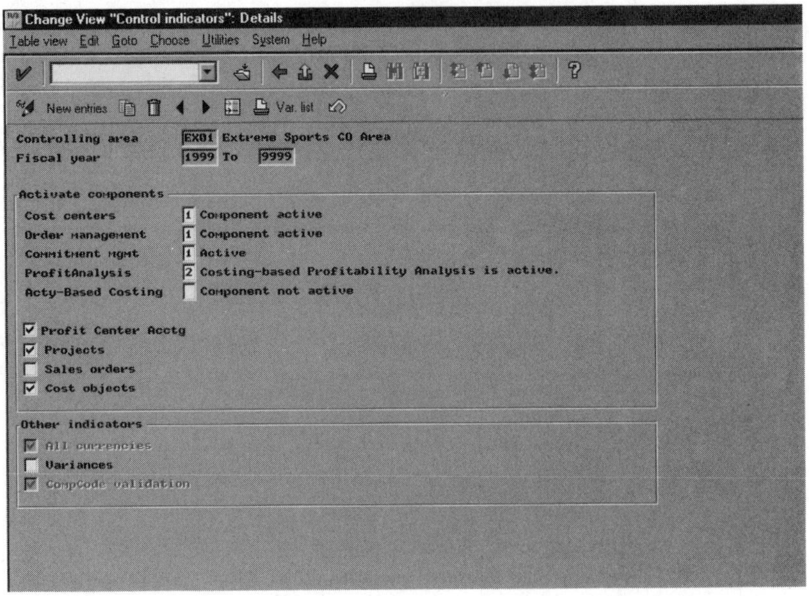

After you are satisfied with your controlling area settings, move to the next section.

Order Settlement Configuration

Settlement can be described as the process of moving costs incurred on a sender object to one or more receiving objects. In the case of an internal order, costs are incurred on the order through goods issues or receipts, journal entries, internal activity allocations, or other settlements and settled to a cost center, order, fixed asset, or account, just to name a few. All offsetting postings on the sender are posted automatically, and the receiver will retain the history of the posting even if it in turn makes another settlement. The account(s) utilized in the posting activity is dependent upon the settlement structure configuration and what type of account activity is maintained. This section will begin by looking at the settlement cost element.

Settlement Cost Element

Settlement cost elements are used in a specific case to act as the sender and receiving account during settlement. If Settlement Element is activated within the settlement assignment (see "Settlement Structure" later in this chapter), either a primary or secondary cost element will be needed to facilitate the posting. The receiving object will determine whether you use a primary or secondary element. The section on settlement structure development will cover the question in detail, but a brief description is appropriate. If the receiver is external to CO, like a G/L account or fixed asset, a primary cost element must be used because of the necessary FI impact. If the receiver is internal within CO, like a cost center, a secondary cost element is required.

As for the settlement cost element, refer to Chapter 8 for detailed analysis on establishing a cost element. Use the menu path Controlling ➢ Overhead Cost Controlling ➢ Overhead Cost Orders ➢ Actual Postings ➢ Settlement ➢ Maintain Settlement Cost Elements and the simple guidelines provided to create the settlement cost element.

SETTLEMENT COST ELEMENT

You can get to the settlement cost element configuration screen by using these methods:

Menu Path: **Controlling** ➢ **Overhead Cost Controlling** ➢ **Overhead Cost Orders** ➢ **Actual Postings** ➢ **Settlement** ➢ **Maintain Settlement Cost Elements**

Transaction Code: **KA01 (Primary Cost Element), KA06 (Secondary Cost Element)**

A transaction selection screen will appear if you use the menu path as opposed to the transaction code. Select either Create Primary Cost Element or Create Secondary Cost Element. The cost element creation screen will appear. Keep in mind these key points when creating the cost element:

▶ Cost Element Category should be either 21, for internal (secondary) settlement, or 22, for external (primary) settlement.

▶ Use an account number outside your primary account range. It will make the account more easily recognizable.

▶ Use a name and description that clearly defines the activity (Capital Costs or Maintenance Expense). Reporting and analysis will be made easier.

N O T E Remember that secondary cost elements are relevant only for CO postings and do not require a corresponding G/L account in FI.

When creating a primary settlement cost element, be certain to create the G/L account in the chart of accounts first. Depending on your settlement and reporting strategy, it may be necessary to create more than one settlement cost element. Many companies prefer to see some level of segregation among material costs, overhead, and labor. The next section will provide more details on how this segregation can be accomplished.

Settlement Structure

The settlement structure defines the what and how of the settlement process. It is the main component of the settlement profile, which will be discussed later in this chapter. Its purpose is twofold:

▶ To define which cost elements on the order can be settled. This group of cost elements is called the *origin*.

▶ To determine which cost element, called the *settlement cost element*, will be used to debit and credit the sending order and receiving object.

Each area, the origin and settlement cost element, is combined and uniquely defined within a *settlement assignment*. SAP offers the flexibility to differentiate how you want costs settled through the use of multiple settlement assignments on a single settlement structure.

You can begin the settlement structure development process with the menu path Controlling ➤ Overhead Cost Controlling ➤ Overhead Cost Orders ➤ Actual Postings ➤ Settlement ➤ Maintain Settlement Structure.

The settlement structure overview screen will appear, providing you with a look at the many settlement structures defined in your client to date. Remember that each new settlement structure is available for all controlling areas in the client.

Select the New Entries button. An entry screen will appear, asking you to provide the new settlement structure with a two-character ID and description. Press Enter and green arrow back to the settlement structure overview window. You are now ready to define the settlement assignment(s).

SETTLEMENT STRUCTURE

You can get to the settlement structure configuration screen by using these methods:

Menu Path: **Controlling** ➤ **Overhead Cost Controlling** ➤ **Overhead Cost Orders** ➤ **Actual Postings** ➤ **Settlement** ➤ **Maintain Settlement Structure**

Transaction Code: **OKO6**

Settlement Assignment

The settlement assignment, as stated earlier, is used to uniquely define the combination of the origin and the settlement cost element. It is important at this juncture to have your settlement strategy defined for the order type that will be using this settlement structure. The strategy will have direct impact on the depth of the assignment development. A simple strategy may be implemented, resulting in all order costs being grouped under one origin and settled to one account. Or it may be complex, with each unique cost type—like labor, materials, and consulting, for example—being settled to separate settlement accounts. In either case, segregation is created with the number of settlement assignments defined and configured.

N O T E   Remember that the settlement structure is controlling area independent and that other controlling areas may use the settlement assignment IDs you define. However, the origin and settlement cost element portions of the settlement assignment are controlling area *dependent* and thus require configuration specific to your solution and area.

From the settlement structure overview screen, begin defining the settlement assignment by double-clicking your newly created settlement structure ID. The change view settlement assignment screen will appear. From here, select the New Entries button from the header and the screen will transfer to change mode and allow new entries to be made (see Figure 10.3).

FIGURE 10.3   The settlement assignment overview screen in change mode

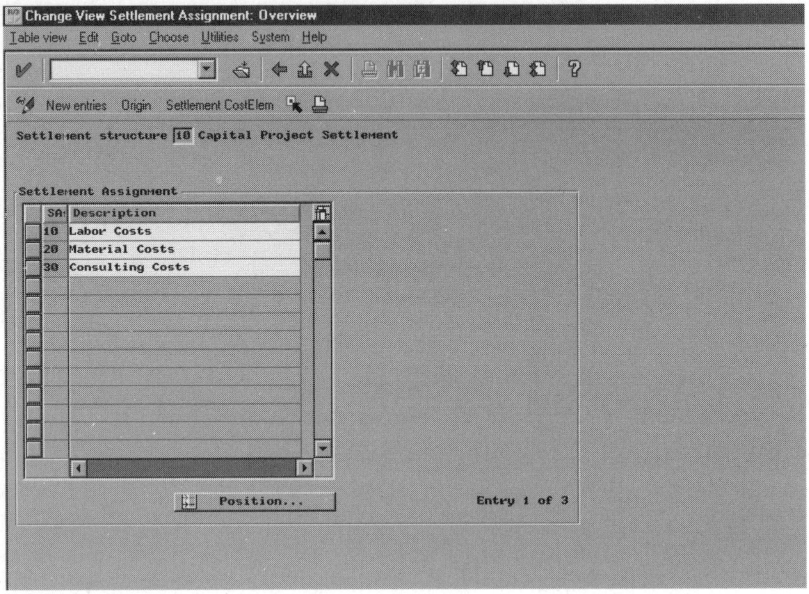

Fill in the following fields:

SAs (Settlement Assignment)   This field is used by SAP to define the settlement activity. Enter an ID up to three characters long for the settlement assignment.

Description   Enter the settlement assignment description.

When each assignment has been defined, save the configuration and green arrow back to the overview screen.

Origin

Within the origin, you can define through a cost element group which costs can be settled by the settlement assignment. Both primary and secondary cost elements can be contained within the group. To establish the origin, place the cursor on the settlement assignment being maintained and select the Origin button. The origin overview screen will appear (see Figure 10.4).

FIGURE 10.4   The origin overview screen in change mode

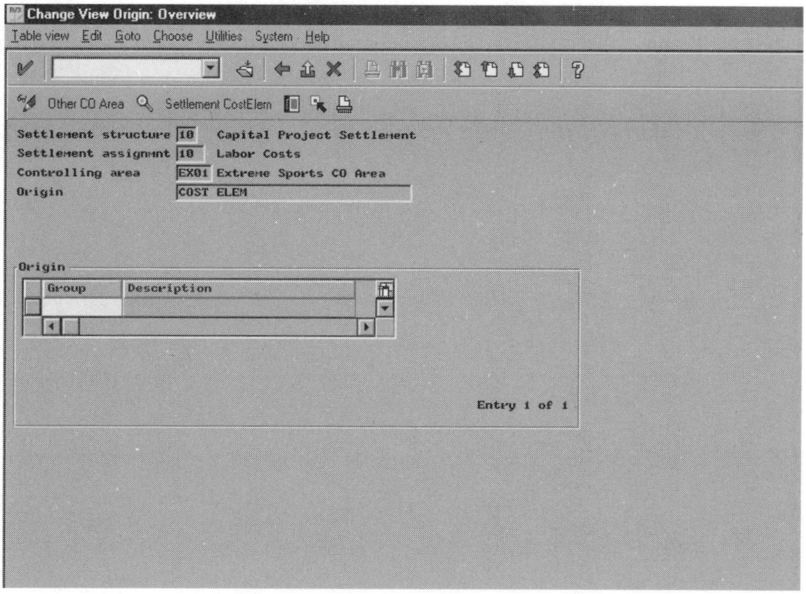

As you review the screen, take time to notice the assignment information. Look to see that you are in the proper settlement assignment and that the correct controlling area is active. As you migrated to the origin screen, a new button labeled Other CO Area appeared in the icon bar. The button allows you to set and maintain another controlling area for that settlement assignment. Remember that the origin and settlement cost element sections of the settlement assignment are the only controlling area–dependent sections of the settlement structure.

If the origin has not been maintained to date for your controlling area, the Origin field will be empty. To add a group, select the New Entries button. The Origin Group entry field will convert to change mode (Figure 10.4 is a view of the screen in change mode). At this point, it is possible to enter a preexisting cost element group that you may have configured earlier. If you haven't configured one, SAP allows you to define the group from the entry screen. Simply enter the name you would like to give your origin cost element group and press Enter. A box will appear asking if you would like to create the cost element group. Select Yes and continue. The Create Cost Element Group screen will appear (see Figure 10.5).

FIGURE 10.5   The Create Cost Element Group screen

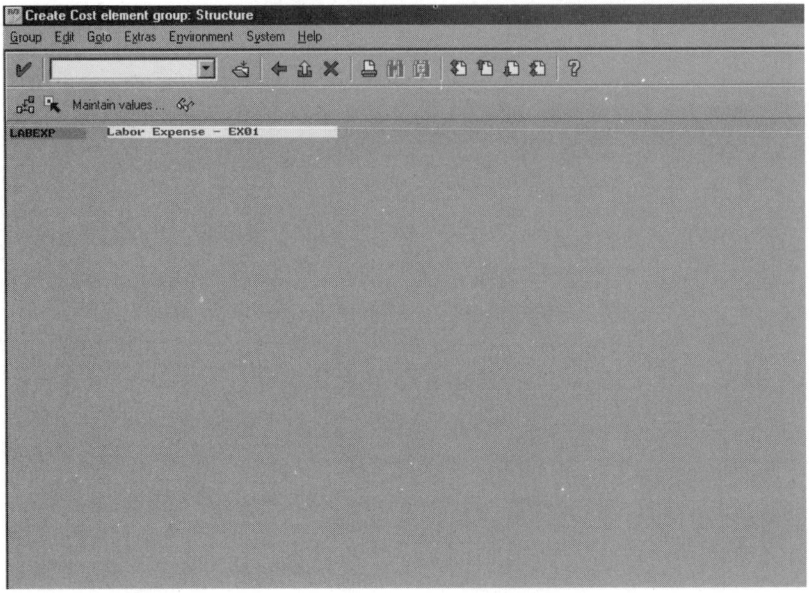

There are two choices when creating cost element groups: build a hierarchy with other defined groups or define individual cost elements and/or ranges of cost elements. In this example, we'll maintain ranges of cost elements. Select the Maintain Values button and the Edit Single Values pop-up screen appears (see Figure 10.6).

FIGURE 10.6   The Edit Single Values pop-up screen

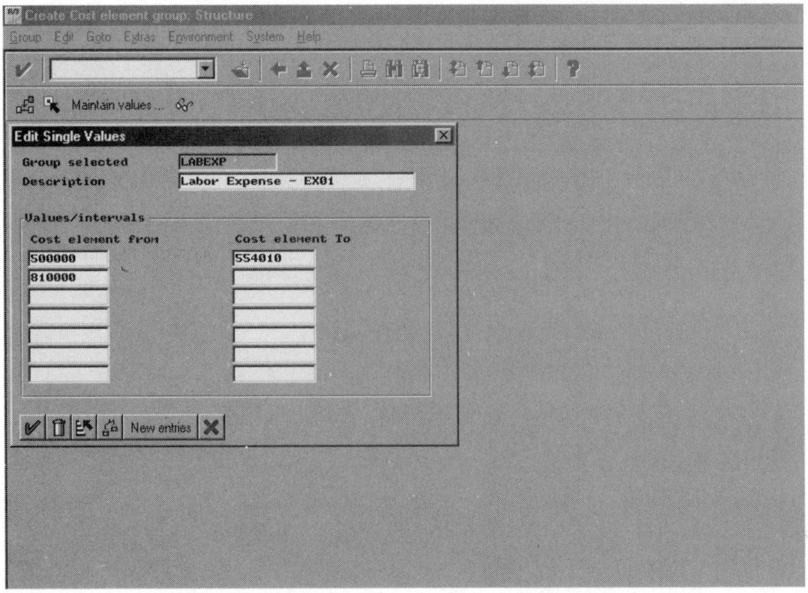

Fill in the following fields:

Description   Enter a description of the cost element group.

Cost Element From/To   Enter a cost element or a range of cost elements to be included in the group. Be certain to include any secondary cost elements that may be relevant (assessment elements, internal activity allocation elements, and other settlement cost elements, for example).

Press Enter and the cost element group structure will appear. Save the group when you are satisfied and the screen will automatically return to the origin overview. Notice that the new cost element group has been defined for the assignment (see Figure 10.7). Save the changes and green arrow back to the settlement assignment screen to maintain the remaining assignments. When origin has been completed, move to the second step in settlement assignment development and maintain the settlement cost element.

FIGURE 10.7   The origin overview screen with a new cost element group

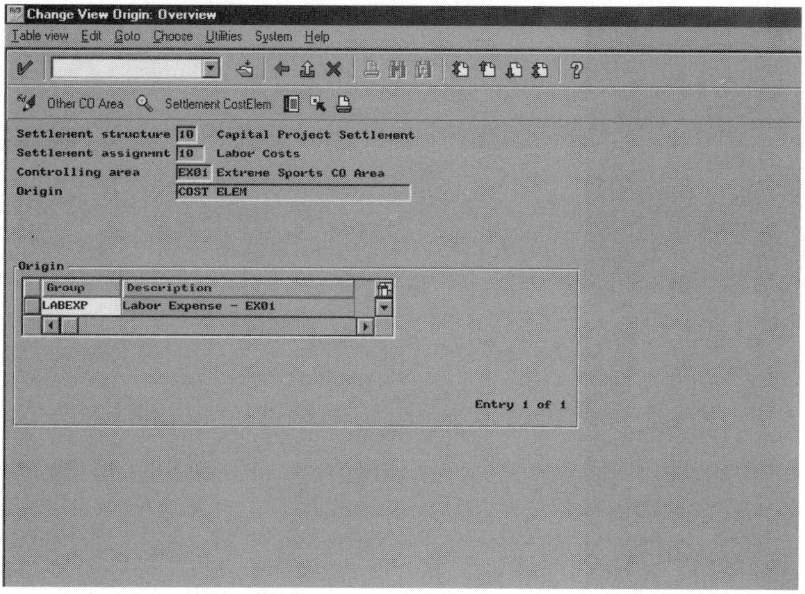

TIP   When transporting the settlement structure, be certain that the cost element groups the structure uses exist in the receiving client. You can easily determine if the group is valid for the controlling area and the settlement assignment if the description appears in its designated field. If the group does not exist in the client, the name will appear in the ID field, but the Description field will be empty. Once the cost element group is created in the controlling area, the Description field will populate automatically.

Settlement Cost Element

The settlement cost element is the section of the settlement assignment that determines which cost element(s) is posted to both the sender and receiver during settlement. It is recommended that you become familiar with the two types of settlement, internal and external, prior to continuing. Here are quick definitions of each:

Internal settlement   Refers to the type of settlement in which postings are internal to CO. An example would be any order settlement in which the receiver is another CO object, such as a cost center, cost object, CO-PA segment, or another order, to name a few. Because the postings never cross into FI, a secondary cost element must be used to facilitate the postings. The original account posting on the order, such as a goods receipt posting, is maintained and is the bridge between CO and FI.

External settlement   Refers to the type of settlement in which postings are external to CO. An example of an external order settlement would be one in which the receiver was a G/L account or fixed asset. Because the settlement would result in a cross into FI, a real or primary cost element would be needed. The original account posting is also maintained in this example, but a second posting would be added.

Take your time when educating yourself about order settlement. It is one of the more difficult concepts to grasp within SAP because of the uniqueness of the CO environment. Continue with the settlement cost element assignment by selecting one of the settlement assignments and clicking the Settlement CostElem button. The receiver type configuration screen will appear. Select the New Entries button. The grayed-out portion of the screen will turn white, and you can maintain the assignment by filling in the following fields:

Account Assignment Category (AAC)   Here, you define which object is a valid receiver for the settlement assignment. Use the pull-down button for a complete listing of choices. If you forget to maintain the assignment category for a necessary object (cost center, G/L account) and then attempt to settle to that type of object, SAP will return an error.

Original Cost Element (OCE)   If OCE is selected and the cost element is a primary element, SAP will always use the original cost element that is posted to the order as the settlement cost element. The rules change when the cost element posted to the order is a secondary element.

If, for example, an order is posted with a type 42 (internal activity cost element), used during labor confirmations, then OCE will be applicable only for CO objects like cost centers. If settlement is required to a G/L account or Fixed Asset, a settlement cost element must be used.

If, however, an order is posted with a type 21 (settlement cost element), OCE cannot be used with any object, CO or not. A settlement cost element must be used every time.

Proper use of the origin is necessary when a broad range of cost elements can be posted to an order. You will have to segregate the posting activity using multiple settlement assignments, with each assignment representing a unique cost element group. For example, you might have your labor confirmations in one group, all of your settlement activities that might be received on an order in a second group, and all of your primary account activity in a third.

An example of the accounting impacts of OCE using only primary cost elements is defined in Table 10.1.

TABLE 10.1   Impacts of Original Cost Element Settlement: Order 1000 Settles to Cost Center 2000

Original Account Debits—Order 1000

Cost Element 600000 $250

Cost Element 610000 $150

Total $400

Settlement Account Credits—Order 1000

Cost Element 600000 – ($250)

Cost Element 610000 – ($150)

Total   ($400)

Settlement Account Debits—Cost Center 2000

Cost Element 600000 $250

Cost Element 610000 $150

Total $400

Settlement Cost Element   If applicable, enter a settlement cost element. Refer to the section on settlement cost element creation for details. OCE must not be active if a settlement cost element is to be defined. See Table 10.2 for a breakout of the accounting impacts when settlement cost element is used.

TABLE 10.2   Impacts of Settlement Cost Element Settlement: Order 1000 Settles to Cost Center 2000

Original Account Debits—Order 1000

Cost Element 600000 $250

Cost Element 610000 $150

Total $400

Settlement Account Credits—Order 1000

Cost Element 900000 – ($400)

Settlement Account Debits—Cost Center 2000

Cost Element 900000 $400

NOTE   Remember, if you are settling to an object that will result in an FI posting, such as a fixed asset, an external settlement cost element is required.

When you've completed the settlement cost element assignment, save the settings (see Figure 10.8). Green arrow back to the settlement assignment screen to maintain the other assignments if necessary. When you've done so, save the settlement structure. The next section will speak briefly to the pros and cons associated with using either OCE or settlement cost element.

Original Cost Element vs. Settlement Cost Element

It should be understood that there are no significant technical reasons for selecting original cost element over settlement cost element, although SAP does recommend using settlement cost element to cut down on the number of line items posted during order settlement. Probably the best reason that one solution is chosen over another is the likelihood of the user group to easily grasp the concepts surrounding settlement.

FIGURE 10.8   The saved settings for the settlement cost element assignment

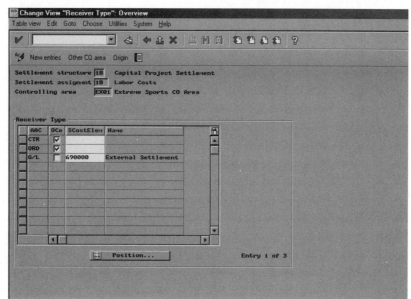

EXTREME SPORTS SETTLEMENT STRUCTURE CONFIGURATION ANALYSIS

For its projects, Extreme Sports wants to see the costs segregated into labor, materials, and consulting on its cost center statements. One way to ensure that this occurs is to define settlement assignments for each cost group. In Extreme Sports' case, three settlement assignments were defined: 10 (Labor Costs), 20 (Material Cost), and 30 (Consulting Costs). Additionally, Extreme Sports has chosen to use Original Cost Element instead of Settlement Cost Element. The decision was based on management's view that each cost center manager would like to see an account breakdown of any project settlement that hit their cost center. Because each origin group contained at least one secondary cost element, the settlement to G/L account required a settlement cost element because it is an external object.

Origin Structure

The origin structure—or as it's sometimes referred to, the source structure—is another component of the settlement profile. It is used by SAP during settlement rule creation to quickly segregate order activity. If the user wants the flexibility to uniquely define settlement rules per cost element group, the origin structure is the tool to use. Like the settlement structure, it must be created and maintained prior to its assignment in the settlement profile. Unlike the settlement structure, though, prior creation and maintenance is not a requirement in most cases.

The origin structure functions as follows: A user determines that all consulting fees should be settled to cost center 1000, all labor costs should be routed to cost center 2000, and finally, all material costs should be capitalized to an asset. Now the user could research the order postings and manually calculate that $1,150.73 of the total order costs is for consulting, $2,235.08 is for labor, and $4,893.45 is for material costs. Then, individual rules could be maintained for each dollar amount. However, the process could get complicated if this example was a large project, or if, instead of applying to one project, the rules applied to many similar projects. Origin structures can manage this separation automatically.

By establishing cost element groups that represent each of the major expense groups—consulting, labor, and materials—and assigning them to an origin structure, the user can use the structure to reduce the settlement rule count to three. The settlement rules would state that all costs that fall in the consulting cost element group settle to cost center 1000, all costs that fall in the labor element group settle to cost center 2000, and all material costs identified by the material cost element group settle to the asset.

Figure 10.9 illustrates how origin structures can be used in settlement rule creation. The user has determined that all order costs that are labor related will settle to cost center 1000 by virtue of the origin structure LAB. All nonlabor costs will settle to cost center 2000 because of the origin structure assignment NLB. The following configuration detail will step you through the process of origin structure creation.

FIGURE 10.9   Settlement rule creation with origin structures

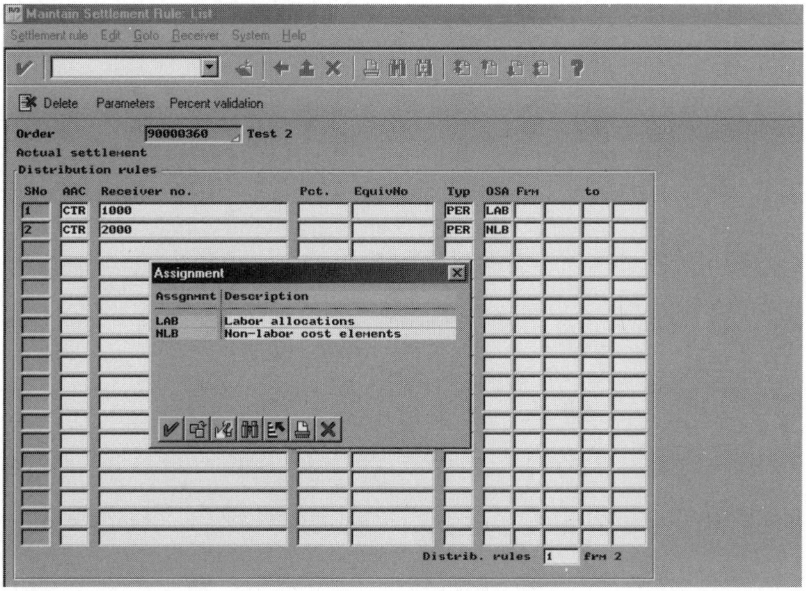

There are three steps to maintaining the origin structure:

1. Create the origin structure ID.

2. Create the origin assignments.

3. Assign the origin cost element groups to each origin assignment.

Begin the process by using the menu path Controlling ➢ Overhead Cost Controlling ➢ Overhead Cost Orders ➢ Actual Postings ➢ Settlement ➢ Maintain Source Structure.

ORIGIN (SOURCE) STRUCTURE

You can get to the origin (source) structure configuration screen by using these methods:

Menu Path: **Controlling** ➢ **Overhead Cost Controlling** ➢ **Overhead Cost Orders** ➢ **Actual Postings** ➢ **Settlement** ➢ **Maintain Source Structure**

Transaction Code: **OKEU**

The origin allocation layout overview screen appears. Select the New Entries button and the origin structure ID creation screen appears (see Figure 10.10).

FIGURE 10.10 The origin structure ID creation screen

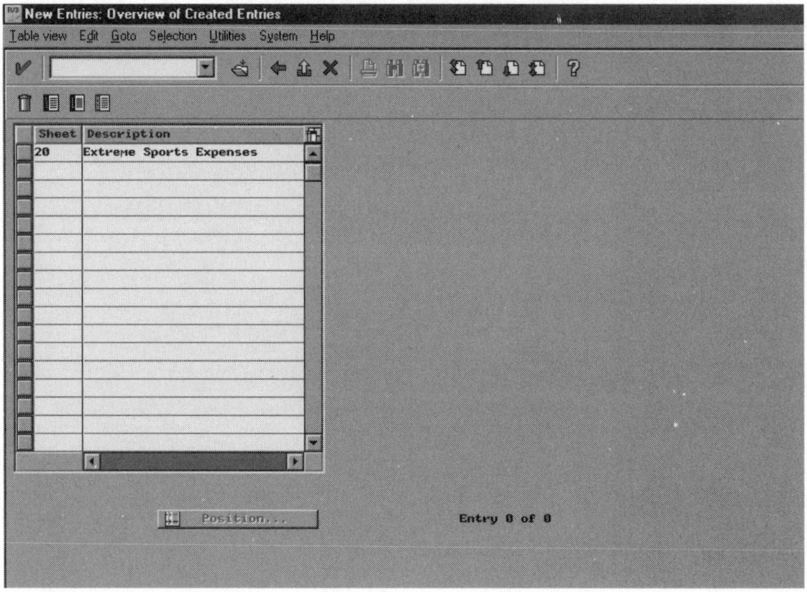

Fill in the following fields:

Sheet Enter a two-character ID representing your origin structure. It is this ID that will be assigned to the settlement structure.

Description Enter a description of the origin structure.

Save the origin structure ID. SAP will not allow you to continue development until you have saved. The origin structure development continues with the creation of the origin assignments. Referring to the earlier example, the assignments would be LAB (representing labor) and NLB (representing nonlabor activities).

Select the origin ID you wish to maintain and select the Details button from the icon bar. The Assignments to Original Layout screen appears. Select the New Entries button from the icon bar to create the assignment IDs. The origin assignment creation screen appears (see Figure 10.11).

FIGURE 10.11 The origin assignment creation screen

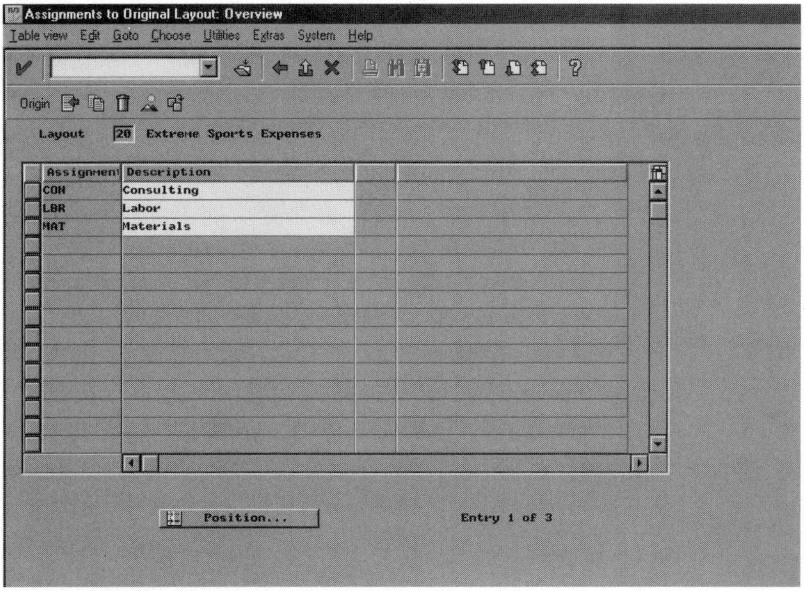

The fields on this screen are as follows:

Assignment Enter a three-character ID representing the origin assignment.

Description Enter the description of the assignment ID.

Save the settings when complete. The next step is to create and assign the origin assignment. This is accomplished by selecting one of the assignments you just created and selecting the Origin button found in the icon bar. The Origin Data for Assignment box appears (see Figure 10.12).

FIGURE 10.12   The Origin Data for Assignment pop-up box

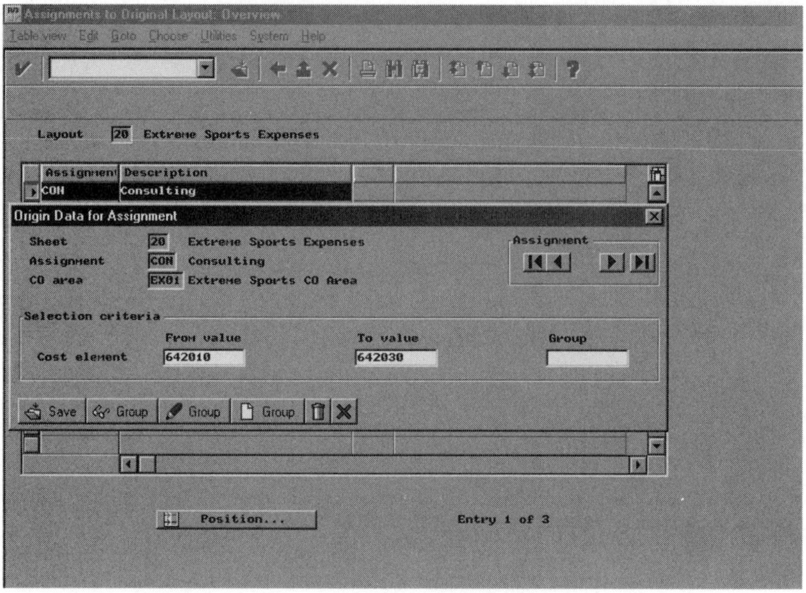

Notice that the assignment box outlines which origin layout sheet you are maintaining, as well as which assignment and for what controlling area. Here are the fields you'll need to complete:

Assignment box   The Assignment box in the upper right corner allows you to toggle between assignments. However, each new assignment must be saved before you can maintain another. If you rotate to another assignment prior to saving the settings on the current assignment, the detail will be erased.

Cost Element From Value/To Value   Enter a range of cost elements that relate to the assignment being maintained. In the example, a range of consulting cost elements is assigned.

Cost Element Group   If an unbroken range of cost elements is not available, a cost element group can be assigned. You have the option of using an existing group or creating a new group from this window. If a new group is desired, simply enter the name of the cost element group in the field and select the create group icon at the bottom of the box. A familiar cost element group creation screen will appear. Complete, save the group, and green arrow back to the assignment box. It is also possible to display and change cost element groups that have been assigned by using buttons found at the bottom of the box.

When you have maintained all the assignments in your origin layout, save the screen. The origin assignments can now be used during settlement rule creation. The next section continues the discussion of settlement structures by touching briefly on the PA settlement structure.

EXTREME SPORTS ORIGIN STRUCTURE CONFIGURATION ANALYSIS

To ease the burden on its project managers, Extreme Sports chose to configure an origin structure containing the breakout of its three main cost components: labor costs, material costs, and consulting costs. Because an order will contain numerous postings throughout a period, a large burden would have been placed on the managers to detail the cost breakdown. With the origin structure, anyone can easily establish the settlement rules necessary to break down the costs.

PA Settlement Structure

The Profitability Analysis (PA) settlement structure is the link between costing-based PA and the FI module. It is similar in function to the order settlement structure, which links order activity to both FI and CO objects. It comes into play, in this example, only when you are settling to a profitability segment. The PA settlement structure will be discussed in greater detail in Chapter 12. The areas in which it is relevant for internal order settlement, like in the settlement profile assignment, will be touched on here.

Costing-based Profitability Analysis, or CO-PA, is defined by two main components: characteristics and value fields. An example of a characteristic would be a Material, Distribution Channel, Profit Center, or Customer. Combinations of specific characteristic values, like Distribution Channel Southeast and Customer 101000-Acme Shoes, make up what are called profitability segments. Characteristics are used by both costing-based and account-based CO-PA.

A value field is the quantity or value associated with any CO-PA transaction. Value field examples include Sales, Cost of Sales, Quantities, and Expenses. Account-based CO-PA has no need for value fields because all postings are maintained by account. Therefore, sales activity is maintained and posted to the sales account in CO-PA. But costing-based CO-PA requires specific mapping to a value field to facilitate posting activity from SD, MM, and FI. The vehicle through which FI postings are mapped to value fields is the PA settlement structure.

Simply stated, the PA settlement structure matches account-related postings resulting from FI activity (like a goods receipt on an internal order) to a value field in Profitability Analysis. In this example, an order type is configured to support original cost element settlement. Account 60000-Materials is posted to an order through a goods receipt transaction. You now wish to settle the order activity to a profitability segment in CO-PA. In our example, the operating concern contains a value field for material expense called MATEXP. For the settlement to process, the account 60000 must be mapped to the CO-PA value field MATEXP. All potential account postings must be mapped in some fashion to facilitate all settlement transactions.

Order accounting is unique in its relationship with CO-PA in that there can be more than one settlement structure used. For FI and SD, there can be only one PA structure developed. The system will not recognize a second. What this means for you is that each order type you develop can settle its costs uniquely to CO-PA. In order type 1000, all material expenses would settle to value field MATEXP. However, by virtue of having a different PA settlement structure assigned to it, all material expenses posted to an order of type 2000 would settle to a value field called PROJECT.

The details surrounding PA settlement structure development are covered in Chapter 11. It is a good idea to review it if CO-PA is active within the controlling area. Now that all preliminary settlement configurations are complete, you are ready to configure the settlement profile.

Settlement Profile

The settlement profile is the piece of order configuration that provides the order type with the details of how it can settle its costs. It accomplishes this by controlling how a settlement rule can be defined for a given order. The settlement profile stands as an accumulation of the other areas of settlement previously configured within this chapter, as well as the addition of new pieces of customization not yet seen. Each order type can have a different settlement profile, but each must have one assigned. Use the following menu path to begin configuration of the settlement profile: Controlling ➤ Overhead Cost Controlling ➤ Overhead Cost Orders ➤ Actual Postings ➤ Settlement ➤ Maintain Settlement Profile.

If you use the menu path, a box will appear asking whether you want to maintain the settlement profile or assign a profile to an order type. Select Maintain Settlement Profiles and the settlement profile configuration screen will appear. To create a new settlement profile, select the New Entries button. The new entries detail screen will appear. Figure 10.13 is a view of the completed settlement profile 90 that Extreme Sports will be using to track its expense-related project costs.

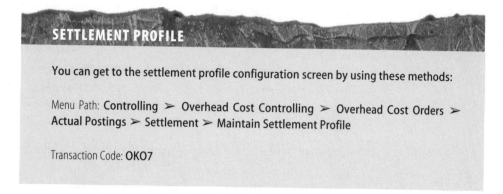

SETTLEMENT PROFILE

You can get to the settlement profile configuration screen by using these methods:

Menu Path: **Controlling ➤ Overhead Cost Controlling ➤ Overhead Cost Orders ➤ Actual Postings ➤ Settlement ➤ Maintain Settlement Profile**

Transaction Code: **OKO7**

FIGURE 10.13   The settlement profile configuration screen

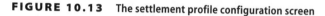

As with other configuration screens you have seen, this one will be described in terms of its field groupings.

The fields in the Actual Costs/Cost of Sales section relate to overall control of the order in relation to when it may be closed and archived:

Must Be Settled in Full   This setting forces the value of the order to be $0 before it can be closed. SAP will return a hard error if an attempt is made to close the order with a balance. Because most companies prefer to see their operating expenses in CCA, the majority of internal orders will fall into this category. Also, when integrating with Investment Management, it will be important to activate this measure so that balance sheet calculations are accurate.

Can Be Settled   If this setting activated, costs can be settled from the order, but it is not mandatory. If you attempt to close an order with a balance and with this setting, SAP will return a warning. It is more rare that you would want to leave balances on the order when closing. Again, most companies prefer to have their operating expenses reported consistently through one location, like CCA.

Must Not Be Settled   Actual costs cannot be settled if this setting is active. When the order is closed and has a balance, SAP will return a message communicating the balance. This might be used in conjunction with a sales-related order.

The fields in the Default Values section relate to how the order will determine what cost elements are valid for settlement and how the postings will occur:

Settlement Structure   This field was described in detail earlier. It is the only value that must be configured on the profile. Remember that the structure is controlling area independent and must be maintained accordingly.

PA Settlement Str.   This field was described earlier. It is mandatory if you will be settling order-related costs to CO-PA.

Default Object Type   This field provides the order with a defaulting receiver object type during settlement rule creation. The defaulting receiver object can be changed on the order settlement rule in production. Examples include the following:

CTR   Cost Center

ORD   Order

PSG   Profitability Segment

For certain order types (such as sales-related orders, repetitive collectors, and investment orders), specific default objects will be required. Examples of default objects include the following:

Sales-related order types   PSG is the default object.

Repetitive collectors (orders)   MAT or material is defaulted.

Investment orders   FXA is the default object.

Origin Structure   This field was described in detail earlier. It is not a mandatory setting, but it can be of assistance to the user during settlement rule creation.

Settings in the Indicators section relate to how the user can define the dollar values to be settled:

100%-Validation   If this field is activated, SAP will check to make sure all costs will be settled by the rules the user has established on the order. If less than or greater than 100% of the costs is not covered by the rules, SAP will return a warning when the order is saved. You can still save the order, but SAP will return an error when attempting to settle. The setting is relevant for periodic settlements only. Overall settlements must always equal 100%.

%-Settlement   If this field is activated, the user can maintain settlement rules on the order that determines the dollar value by percentage (see Table 10.3 for an example).

TABLE 10.3   Percentage (%) Settlement Example

Order Cost Total:	$10,000	
Rule 1: Cost Center	1000	60%
Rule 2: Cost Center	2000	40%
Total		100%
Settlement Breakdown		
Cost Center	1000	$6,000
Cost Center	2000	$4,000
Total		$10,000

Equivalence Numbers   If this field is activated, equivalence numbers can be used as an alternative to percentages. If it is easier for the user to set up a proportion as opposed to calculating percentages, then equivalence numbers are appropriate. In the example in Table 10.4, the settlement rule apportion cost is based on the number of employees in each cost center.

TABLE 10.4   Equivalence Number Settlement Example

Order Cost Total: $10,000

Rule 1: Cost Center 1000—6 employees

Rule 2: Cost Center 2000—13 employees

Rule 3: Cost Center 3000—18 employees

Total: 37 employees

Settlement Breakdown

Cost Center 1000   (6/37) $1,621.62

Cost Center 2000 (13/37) $3,513.51

Cost Center 3000 (18/37) $4,864.87

Total: $10,000

Amount Settlement   If this field is activated, the user can establish settlement rules with dollar value amounts. One thing you will notice during settlement rule creation is that, in version 3.*x*, SAP does not provide a field on the settlement rule list screen. You have to go directly to the distribution rules screen for the receiver to enter the amounts.

Variances   Activate this field only if you want to settle production-related costs to CO-PA. The setting should be used in conjunction with order-related and repetitive production order types. The system will automatically create a settlement rule for the profitability segment linked to the material being produced. For costing-based CO-PA, refer to the section on PA settlement structure for an explanation of the relationship between cost elements and value fields.

The fields in the Valid Receivers section relate to what type of object(s) the user can create settlement rules for. The fields are specific SAP objects for which a settlement rule can be maintained (see Figure 10.13 for a complete listing). There are three potential settings for each receiver:

Null   If the box is left blank, a receiver cannot be used to create settlement rules. If the user attempts to create a settlement rule for a receiver that hasn't been maintained, an error will be returned.

1   This setting allows a settlement rule to be created for the specific receiver.

2 This setting makes a settlement rule mandatory for a specific receiver. If a settlement rule has not been maintained for a receiver marked as mandatory, SAP will return an error when the order is saved.

You can see the power of maintaining a proper receiver list. Use these settings carefully, as a controlling influence over how the users are supposed to use the order type.

The fields in the Misc. Parameters section relate to order posting and archiving:

Document Type You must provide the order with a document type with which the settlement documents will be labeled. A recommendation is to use a separate document type for settlements. It will be easier to analyze and segregate the activity. This is a mandatory setting.

Max. No. Dist. Rls This setting provides the order with the maximum number of settlement rules the user can maintain. The maximum number is 999. Although 999 may not always be practical, you can do harm to your productivity if you do not maintain a high enough number.

Retention This field determines how long, in months, the settlement document must be retained in the system before it can be archived. Consult the company policy for the proper setting. SAP will default the setting to three months.

TIP As you make changes to the settlement profile settings, they become valid retroactively on all existing orders. That means that all orders currently outstanding will become subject to the changes. Keep this in mind before proceeding.

Save the profile when you're finished. The next section will cover pertinent number range configuration.

EXTREME SPORTS SETTLEMENT PROFILE CONFIGURATION ANALYSIS

For its expense-related projects, Extreme Sports created Settlement Profile 90-EX01 Expense Orders. Because all costs must be maintained on a cost center for reporting, it was important that the profile ensure complete settlement before closing the order. To inhibit the users from settling to unwanted objects, the settlement structure and valid receivers would allow rules only for cost centers, orders, and G/L accounts. To provide a measure of flexibility, Extreme Sports wanted the profile to allow settlement rules to be created for both percentages and dollars. Finally, Extreme Sports decided to segregate its settlement activities with a unique document type, ST. This will make analyzing posting activity easier once all its plants are up and running.

Maintain Number Ranges for Settlement

As you have assigned number ranges to activities in other areas of SAP configuration, so also must a number range assignment be made for settlement documents. In the case of settlement documents, the number range assignment is at the controlling area level. You will notice that there are similarities in the assignment steps for settlement documents and the assignment for CO activities covered in Chapter 7. Because the steps are a little different, though, they will be documented in detail. The number range assignment location can be accessed by using the menu path Controlling ➢ Overhead Cost Controlling ➢ Overhead Cost Orders ➢ Actual Postings ➢ Settlement ➢ Maintain Number Ranges for Settlement Documents.

MAINTAIN NUMBER RANGE ASSIGNMENT

You can get to the settlement document number range configuration screen by using these methods:

Menu Path: **Controlling** ➢ **Overhead Cost Controlling** ➢ **Overhead Cost Orders** ➢ **Actual Postings** ➢ **Settlement** ➢ **Maintain Number Ranges for Settlement Documents**

Transaction Code: **SNUM**

The number range for settlement documents CO objects screen will appear. The first step in the process to assign a number range is to create a group number range to which your controlling area can be assigned. Select the Maintain Groups button and the Maintain Number Range Groups screen will appear. SAP will deliver a default group for standard accounting documents that can be used for your controlling area. For performance reasons, SAP recommends that, in environments with multiple controlling areas, each area receive its own number range. For the sake of demonstration, we'll create a new interval.

Use the menu path Group ➢ Insert to bring up the Insert Group box, shown in Figure 10.14.

FIGURE 10.14   The Insert Group box

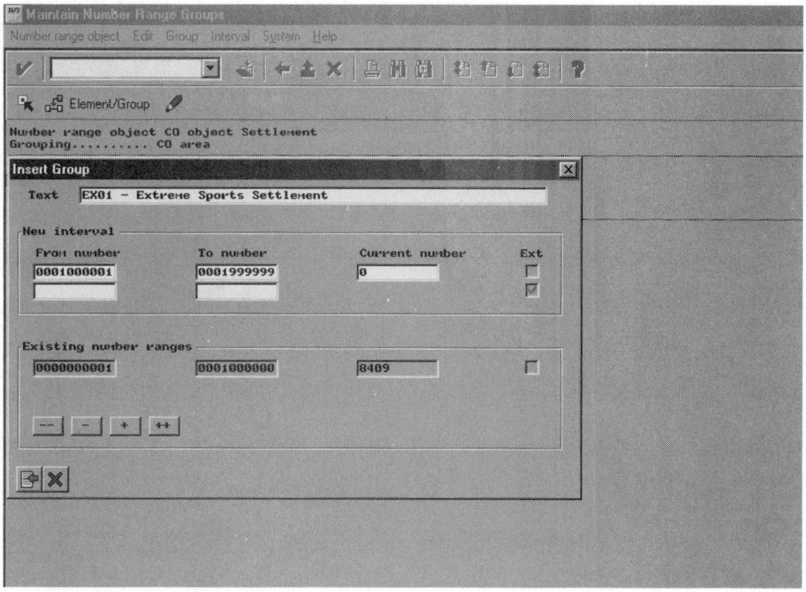

Here are the fields in the Insert Group box:

Text   Enter a description for the number range you are adding. Be certain to describe it uniquely and clearly.

From/To Number   Enter the number range you want for your settlements. If you anticipate multiple controlling areas, leave enough room in the range to accommodate the other areas. You will see any existing ranges noted at the bottom of the Insert Group box. Do not overlap the range or SAP will return an error.

Select the insert icon at the bottom of the box. You will notice that the new interval appears on the Maintain Number Range Groups screen.

The second step is to assign your controlling area to the new range. You will find a listing of all unassigned controlling areas below the number range intervals in a section labeled Not Assigned. Place the cursor on the controlling area in question and click the select element icon. Notice that the controlling area becomes highlighted. This is SAP's signal that the item has been selected.

To assign the selected controlling area to the number range, place a checkmark in the box next to the number range group and click the Element/Group button. The selected controlling area will move from the Not Assigned section to the new number range group (see Figure 10.15). Save the number range assignment.

FIGURE 10.15   The maintained number range group assignment for EX01, Extreme Sports

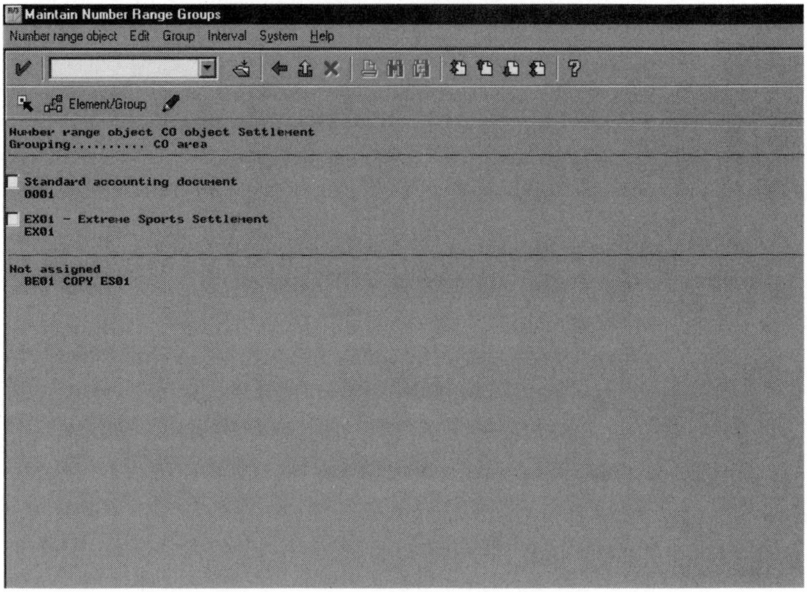

Maintain Number Range Groups

Number range object   Edit   Group   Interval   System   Help

Element/Group

Number range object CO object Settlement
Grouping.......... CO area

☐ Standard accounting document
   0001

☐ EX01 — Extreme Sports Settlement
   EX01

Not assigned
   BE01 COPY ES01

WARNING   Always remember to never transport your number ranges. Manually assign the ranges in each client to ensure the integrity of your document numbering.

EXTREME SPORTS SETTLEMENT NUMBER RANGES CONFIGURATION ANALYSIS

Currently, only one controlling area will exist for Extreme Sports, so the need to segregate the document number ranges is not an issue. But if further expansion were to force a second controlling area, Extreme Sports would establish a second settlement document number range per SAP's recommendation.

Order Settlement Configuration Overview

All necessary order settlement configurations have now been covered. It is important that you experiment with various settings before determining what works for your project. Be certain to engage the users as much as possible during the development process. The concepts surrounding settlement will be completely foreign to many and, because of this, could result in a lot of rework on your part.

The next section will cover order-planning and budgeting configuration. Depending on your company's intended use for Internal Order Accounting, planning can be very simple or extremely complex. Topics to be covered include unit costing, plan/budget profiles, and availability control.

Order Planning and Budgeting

Internal order planning is another area in which one solution or type of planning will not fit all scenarios. For simple projects with a short life span, overall order planning may be the perfect solution, and a more complex project spanning an entire year or more may require a detailed unit cost planning approach. Further functionality provides the ability to fully integrate order planning with Cost Center Accounting, Profit Center Accounting, and special ledgers.

In the CO module, SAP makes a distinction between planning and budgeting. Planning implies that an iterative process may occur in which many different versions of the plan may be developed until one is decided upon. The budget, which can be defined as a detailed work plan describing how the approved amount will be allocated, is developed once the overall plan has been confirmed. The budget is the tool through which project management will approve and allocate costs within the internal order. Linked with the internal order budget is SAP's budget management system, known as availability control.

Availability control, its concepts surrounding commitment and cost management, and its relationship to the budget are important to proper internal order development. Through proper configuration, availability control can assist your project manager by monitoring ongoing project variances and initiating specific actions when tolerances are reached. It is important to note here that not all configuration scenarios surrounding internal order planning and budgeting can be covered in this chapter.

This section is meant to raise awareness of functionality and to explain specific configuration settings. You should focus on the concepts covered first and the explanation of the table views configured second. Both are important, and by the end of the section, you will be able to apply these concepts in developing your own planning strategy. The development section will begin with a brief description of the three available degrees of internal order planning.

Internal Order Planning/Budgeting: Basics

SAP provides you with three levels of internal order planning, with each level more detailed than the preceding:

Overall Planning   The simplest form of internal order cost planning available. Plan costs are maintained at the order level and can be detailed on an overall and/ or annual view. If the purpose of planning is to compare total actual project costs to plan, overall planning is a good solution. Another use may be to temporarily plan at an overall level and, when better information is available, plan at a more detailed level.

Cost Element/Activity Planning   Similar to the planning found in CCA. Used for more detailed project tracking because it offers the user a cost structure view. Both costs and revenues can be planned for an internal order. Note that to plan revenues on an order, specific order type settings must be made (see the section on order type development).

With cost element/activity planning, you have the ability to integrate your planning efforts with CCA. A fully integrated order plan will receive its activity prices from an assigned cost center plan. As activity rates change on the cost center, they are updated on the order. Activity planning on the order is available whether integration is active or not. In either case, there are implications for the controlling area maintenance screen in how SAP will determine the activity prices.

Unit Costing   Related to cost element/activity planning. Predominantly used in circumstances in which you have access to more information, like quantities and rates of consumption. Expenses specific to the cost element level are broken down to greater detail through the use of costing sheets and valuation variants. Integrated planning is not available at the unit-costing level.

Here is an example of how unit costing is used: You have a project for which you want to track labor and material costs at a detailed level. The project work will be covered by three separate shifts of people, all working in the same cost center and using the same cost elements for salary and material consumption. Using unit costing, you can differentiate the plan allocation by each shift without using additional cost elements.

It is important to remember that you are not limited to one level of planning. It is entirely possible that you could have a project that begins at an overall planning level, moves to a cost element level of detail once more information is available, and finally moves to unit costing level if even a greater level of detail is necessary. The first step in internal order planning is the maintenance of the CO versions within the controlling area.

Controlling Area Version Maintenance

Because versions are used in all areas of CO, it is important to always revisit them when configuring a new section like order accounting. Figure 10.16 is a view of the fiscal year parameters of the controlling area for version 0. The details behind the settings are covered at length in Chapter 7 in the section "Maintain CO Versions." Review the section so that you can be aware of the impact each field has in the planning process. You can get to the CO version control screen using the menu path Controlling ➢ Controlling General ➢ Organization ➢ Maintain Versions.

FIGURE 10.16   Fiscal year–dependent view for version 0

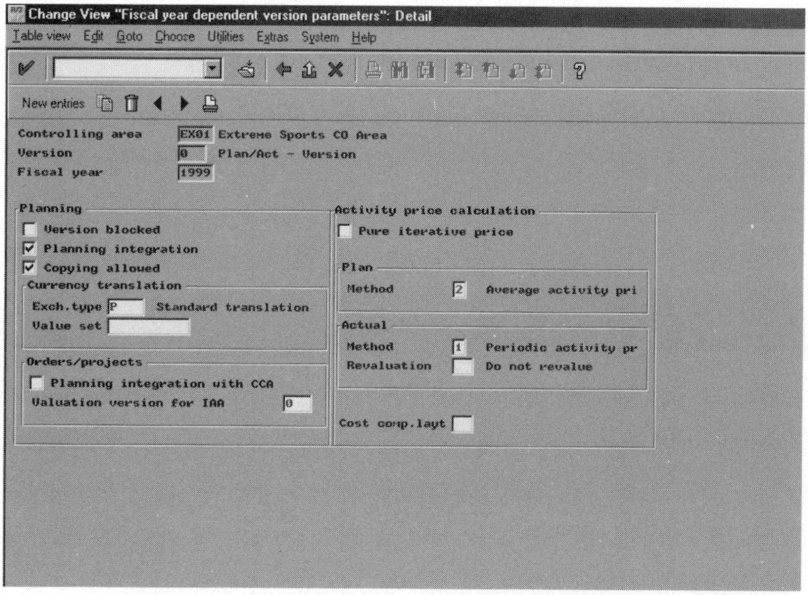

MAINTAIN CO VERSIONS

You can use either of the following methods to get to the CO version control screen:

Menu Path: **Controlling** ➢ **Controlling General** ➢ **Organization** ➢ **Maintain Versions**

Transaction Code: **OKEQ**

Because of their importance to order planning, pay close attention to the following two fields when reviewing the field definitions in Chapter 7:

Planning Integration with CCA   Activate the setting if you want to have internal order/WBS element plans integrate with Cost Center Accounting. The integration is a two-way door; cost center plans can affect orders and order planning can affect cost centers.

Valuation Version for IAA   This setting is relevant only when Planning Integration with CCA is not active. Enter the version from which you want SAP to extract the activity price information for the activity types used as inputs to the orders/WBS elements.

Planning Version Control

Although only one version is necessary to utilize CO planning, SAP provides the flexibility to use multiple versions during any planning cycle. Because order planning is different from Cost Center Accounting planning in that all orders may not always be developed at the time of planning, multiple versions may not always be necessary. If, however, you decide to use multiple versions, know that you have the same copy functionality found in Cost Center Accounting. The merits of multiple versions and configuration settings are covered in both Chapter 7 and Chapter 9.

The next section will provide you with the necessary steps to completing internal order planning and budgeting.

Internal Order Planning/Budgeting: Profile Development

Overall plan and budget profiles are used by SAP to control such things as planning views, formats, and detail planning sets. Additionally, unique to a budget profile is the ability to determine availability control activation. Although not required during order type development, profile assignments are necessary prior to any internal order planning or budgeting that is occurring. Both plan and budget profiles are maintained in a similar manner and can be configured and applied quickly.

WARNING   Remember that all budget and plan profiles are controlling area independent. Any changes made to a profile will affect all orders that are assigned to said profile, regardless of the controlling area in which the orders reside.

Areas of concern when configuring the planning profile include how many years out will be planned and visible, whether cost element planning or unit costing will be used, and whether planning will occur for overall values, annual values, or both. Remember that circumstances will not always be the same for each order type you develop, so try not to attempt to build one "universal solution." It will be far easier to build unique plan profiles for the more unusual internal order uses. Budget profile configuration is similar in the ease of development, but some of the questions or concerns when developing are unique.

Budgeting within SAP is limited to just order accounting and project systems because of their unique project management properties. And not all internal order solutions include the use of budgeting as an option. Budgeting and budget profiles offer the developer an opportunity to control procurement by linking the profile with both a capital investment profile and availability control. From a version perspective, budgeting defaults to version 0 and cannot be rerouted. Like planning profiles, knowing the users' requirements relative to the time horizon and entry screen views is relevant. The next section will begin covering the configuration processes for both budget and plan profiles, with plan profiles covered first.

Plan Profile Development

Begin plan profile configuration by defining the profile ID. Follow the menu path Controlling ➤ Overhead Cost Controlling ➤ Overhead Cost Orders ➤ Planning ➤ Manual Planning ➤ Define Planning Profile for Overall Value Planning.

DEFINE PLANNING PROFILE FOR OVERALL VALUE PLANNING

You can get to the internal order planning profile configuration screen with either of the following methods:

Menu Path: **Controlling** ➤ **Overhead Cost Controlling** ➤ **Overhead Cost Orders** ➤ **Planning** ➤ **Manual Planning** ➤ **Define Planning Profile for Overall Value Planning**

Transaction Code: **OKOS**

If you use the menu path, a decision box will appear asking whether you want to define the planning profile or assign a profile to an order type. Select the "Define planning profile for overall cost planning" line. The COST planning for CO orders screen will appear. Two profiles—000001 (general budget/plan profile) and 000002 (CO production order profile)—are delivered with the system. You have the authority to change each of these profiles, but it is recommended that you create your own.

Select the New Entries button and the details of created entries screen will appear (Figure 10.17 shows the screen configured for Extreme Sports). Notice that only the Profile ID box is a required entry. It is possible to create a shell and fill in the other fields later. This may be a good idea when you're creating a new order type and you want a placeholder for the planning profile.

FIGURE 10.17   The completed Extreme Sports planning profile

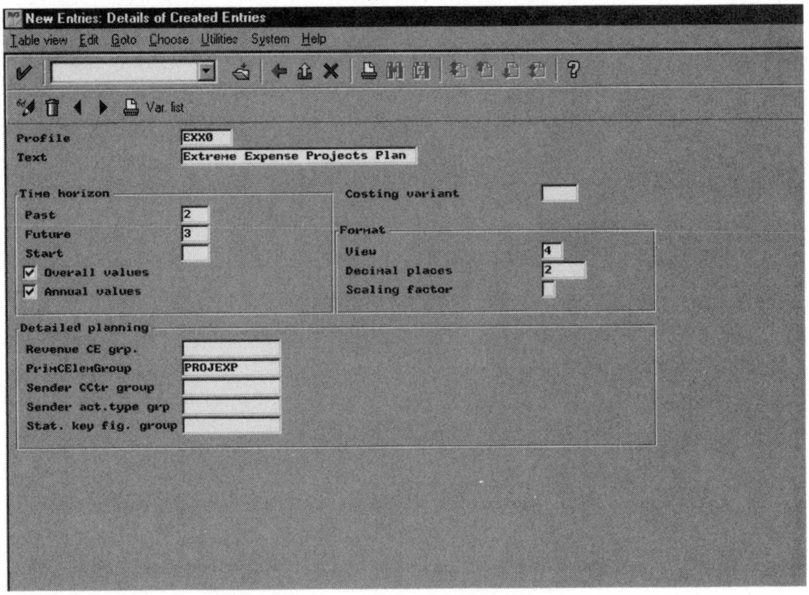

Begin the configuration by defining the profile's ID:

Profile   Enter an alphanumeric ID (up to seven characters) describing the planning profile.

Text   Enter a description of the planning profile. Be sure to be clear because the profile is controlling area independent and you do not want its use to be misinterpreted.

The fields found in the Time Horizon section relate to the planning years available for user input and review:

Past   This field refers to the number of years before the start year the user will be able to plan/budget.

For example, if 2 is entered in the field and the current or start year is 2000, the user will be able to view or change the plan or budget back to 1998.

Future   This setting is similar to the Past setting. It refers to the number of years beyond the start year the user will be able to plan.

For example, if 3 is entered and the current or start year is 2000, planning will be allowed through 2003.

Start   This field refers to the first year that planning/budgeting will be accessible to the user. The number entered here will be added to the current fiscal year to determine the start year.

For example, suppose the current fiscal year is 2000. If you enter 2 in this field, the first year allowed for planning is 2002. Caution should be used when making the entry because this value becomes the basis for all future planning settings. If you want to default the current fiscal year as the start year, leave this field empty.

Overall Values   Check this field if you want to allow the user to plan for overall values on the order. At the highest level, an order or project can be planned for total cost regardless of the year it is consumed.

For example, suppose an order has a total planned cost of $500,000. This would be considered its overall value. For capital investment orders, it is recommended that this setting be active.

Annual Values   Check this field if you want to allow the user to plan annual expenditures for an order.

For example, suppose an order has a total planned cost of $500,000. This setting would allow the user to plan the cost expenditures across years. In the example, $200,000 would be planned for 2000, $200,000 for 2001, and $100,000 for 2002.

N O T E   Activating the Overall and Annual Values fields does not make them required. If your project has no preference, it is recommended that you activate both.

Costing Variant   If detailed planning is required, enter a costing variant. The costing variant ID is linked to the valuation variant that determines activity and material prices. The costing variant assigned here becomes the default for the user to enter the activity cost estimate.

If you are unsure whether unit cost planning will be used, leave the field empty. You have the ability to enter a variant later if it becomes necessary.

Fields in the Format section relate to the view the user will have on the planning entry screen:

View   Enter the number of the default view you want displayed next to the Plan Entry column. The user may change these views at the plan entry screen. The following choices are available:

03 (Accumulated)   Displays the total plan accumulated over the allowed planning years.

04 (Remainder)   Derived by the formula (Planned total – Accumulated).

05 (Planned Total)   The sum value of the total plan entered for the order.

06 (Previous Year)   Displays the values planned for the previous year.

08 (Costing)   Displays any values entered using unit costing.

09 (Cost Element Planning)   Displays any amounts entered at a cost element planning level. These values will be denoted with a lowercase *c*.

Decimal Places   Enter the desired number of decimal places in which you want to plan.

Scaling Factor   If scaling is important when planning, enter the scaling factor here.

For example, if you want to plan in thousands, enter 3 in the Scaling Factor field. As you enter the plan, only the scaled amount will appear. The total amount is entered in the planning table.

With a scale of 3, a plan of $1,000,000 is entered as $1,000 on the planning screen.

If cost element–level detail or planning integration is desired, you can save time by entering the default master data sets in the Detailed Planning section:

Revenue CE Grp.   If desired, enter the revenue element group to be defaulted during revenue element–level planning on the order. For revenues to be planned on an order, the order type must allow revenue postings. Planning entries must be entered as a negative, that is, with a preceding minus (–) sign.

PrimCElemGroup   If desired, enter the primary cost element group to be defaulted during cost element–level planning on the order. Entering a defined group of cost elements is a good way to limit the user's ability to plan.

Sender CCtr Group   If desired, enter the cost center group that you want to be the default for activity input planning. Planned activity is relayed from the cost center group, and as activity is recorded, the group is credited accordingly.

Sender Act. Type Grp   If desired, enter the activity type group that you want to be the default for activity planning on the order. If maintained, when the user selects the Activity Input button on the order-planning screen, this activity type group will appear as the only option.

Stat. Key Fig. Group   If desired, enter the statistical key figure group to be defaulted during key figure planning on the order. Entering a defined group of key figures is a good way to limit the user's ability to plan.

When the settings are complete, save the profile. An example of profile EXX0 (Extreme Expense Projects Plan) is seen in Figure 10.17. Remember that these profiles can be changed on the fly, meaning that any setting changes resulting in some functionality addition or deletion will be immediately visible on all relevant orders. Relevant in this case is any orders with the planning profile in question. In the next section, the subtle differences provided by budget profiles will be covered.

EXTREME SPORTS ORDER PLANNING PROFILE CONFIGURATION ANALYSIS

Due to the diversity of Extreme Sports' internal order needs, multiple profiles will be developed to support various expense and capital project types. In the case of profile EXX0, it will be used to support cost element–level planning on all basic expense projects. All expense projects will be created at the beginning of the fiscal year at just an overall project level. As the projects are activated, a cost element–level plan will be developed for each project for just the accounts found in the cost element group PROJEXP. Unit costing will not be necessary for these project types. Though they are expense projects, they may still span multiple years, thus the need for the three-year visibility.

Budget Profile Development

Budgeting within SAP provides the user with enhanced project management capabilities not provided by internal order planning. Where an internal order plan is an estimate of expenditures made at the beginning of a fiscal year, a budget represents the actual approved amount of funding for a given order. Because the budgeted amount is maintained separately, you have the opportunity to do plan-versus-budget comparisons. Additionally, you are afforded the ability to control spending through the use of availability control.

Because many of the same fields are described in the plan profile configuration section, only the unique budget profile fields will be described in detail. Begin by reviewing a blank profile template seen in Figure 10.18. To access the configuration screen, use the menu path Controlling ➢ Overhead Cost Controlling ➢ Overhead Cost Orders ➢ Budgeting and Availability Control ➢ Maintain Budget Profile.

FIGURE 10.18   The completed Extreme Sports budget profile BUDGT1

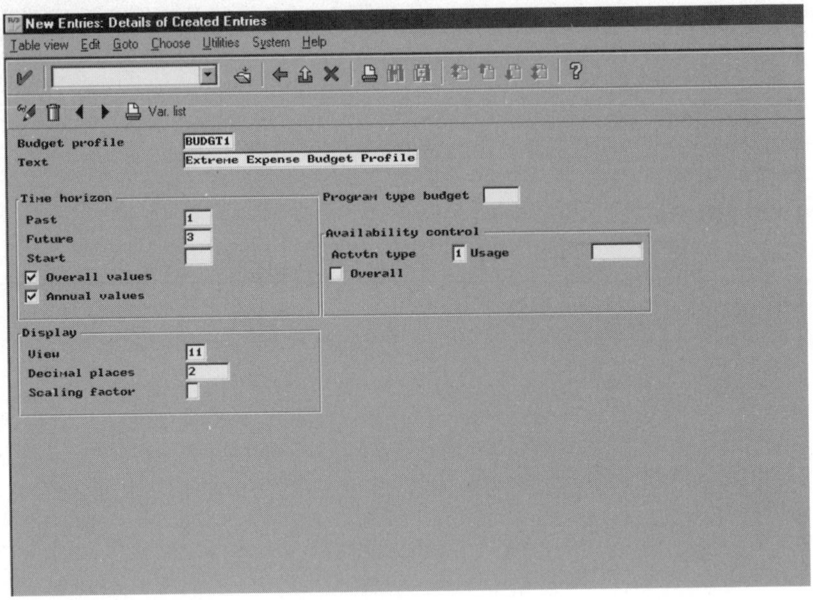

DEFINE BUDGET PROFILE

You can get to the internal order budget profile configuration screen with either of the methods listed here:

Menu Path: **Controlling** ➢ **Overhead Cost Controlling** ➢ **Overhead Cost Orders** ➢ **Budgeting and Availability Control** ➢ **Maintain Budget Profile**

Transaction Code: **OKOB**

The budget profile for CO orders screen will appear. Select the New Entries button to bring up a new profile entry screen. Immediately, you will notice the similarities between the budget profile and plan profile configuration screens. The Time Horizon and Display fields all have the same definitions, but three new self-explanatory views are available in the View field:

07 Assigned The total amount of funds, commitments plus actual postings, that have been posted to an internal order.

11 Current Budget The total budget currently available, including any supplements, transfers, and returns.

12 Release Related to functionality in Funds Management and Project Systems only.

Also notice that the Detailed Planning section is not present. Internal order budgeting is maintained at only the highest order level. Cost element budgeting is not available. There are two new sections of the profile that you should pay attention to:

▶ Program Type Budget

▶ Availability Control

After reviewing the plan profile field definitions for the related configuration fields, proceed to the two new sections.

The Program Type Budget section is related to Investment Management (IM). Enter the ID for a valid IM program type only if the orders using the profile will be assigned to a capital investment program. With this assignment, the only way these capital orders can receive budget allotments is through a direct distribution from the capital investment program. See Chapter 13 for more details.

The fields in the Availability Control section are as follows:

Actvtn Type   This setting determines how availability control will be activated for a given internal order. There are three options:

0   Availability Control cannot be activated.

1   Availability Control will automatically activate upon assignment of the budget to an internal order.

2   Availability Control will be activated in the background.

Usage   This field is used in conjunction with background activation and funds commitments and is maintained as a percentage. When the percentage of funds entered in this field is achieved or exceeded, availability control is automatically activated.

Overall   Select this box if you choose to have the availability check occur against the overall budget of the project. If this field is left unchecked, availability checks will occur against the annual budget values.

N O T E   Keep in mind that, if availability control is to check against annual budget values, the next year's budget will have to be established before postings can occur. If you attempt to post a document without a budget in the future, SAP will return whatever failing action you have configured in Availability Control.

When you have completed the budget profile configuration, save the settings. The next section will continue the budget management development cycle by covering the steps necessary to configure availability control.

EXTREME SPORTS ORDER BUDGET PROFILE CONFIGURATION ANALYSIS

Budget profile BUDGT1 will be used to support expense-related projects for Extreme Sports. Availability control will be activated as soon as an order has been budgeted, which is Extreme Sports' signal that a project has been approved. This process fits in with its project management procedure of not allowing any procurement until the funds have been assigned.

Availability Control Configuration

The idea behind availability control is that SAP should alert you when you are about to exceed some predefined percentage of project spending. This is accomplished through the establishment of spending tolerance levels associated with each budget profile/controlling area relationship. Availability control must be set up for each profile individually. There is no opportunity to create a "universal" setting for all profiles.

There is much flexibility available in establishing the tolerance levels, as well as actions that result when the levels are exceeded. Once active, each setting can be changed without causing harm to previously budgeted orders. It may seem counterintuitive, but the more complex the solution, the easier it is for you to understand how and when the budget was exceeded. The only step in configuring availability control is the creation of tolerance levels. You can reach the necessary table with the menu path Controlling ➤ Overhead Cost Controlling ➤ Overhead Cost Orders ➤ Budgeting and Availability Control ➤ Define Tolerance Limits for Availability Control.

DEFINE AVAILABILITY CONTROL

You can get to the availability control configuration screen with the following method:

Menu Path: **Controlling** ➤ **Overhead Cost Controlling** ➤ **Overhead Cost Orders** ➤ **Budgeting and Availability Control** ➤ **Define Tolerance Limits for Availability Control**

The availability control tolerance limits entry screen will appear (see Figure 10.19). This is the only table entry screen necessary to complete availability control configuration. Take time to notice the two entries in Figure 10.19. The same budget profile, BUDGET, is defined twice in the table, with some differences in the Actn (Activation) and Usage columns. SAP establishes a relationship, called a key, between the profile, controlling area, activity group, and action. You are allowed only one unique value entry per this relationship. SAP will return an error otherwise.

FIGURE 10.19   The availability control tolerance limits entry screen

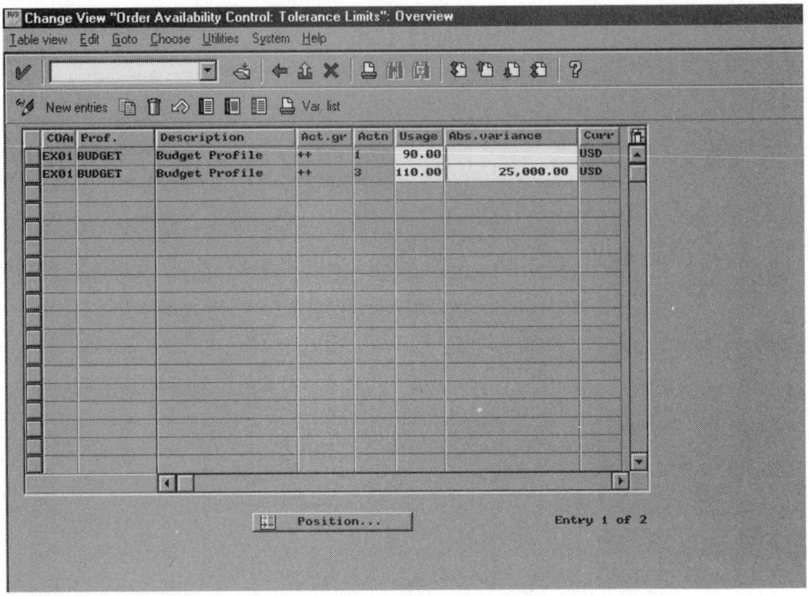

Of the existing entries, you are allowed to make changes to only the Usage and Abs. Variance columns. To modify any of the key fields on an existing entry, you need to delete the entry and start anew. The process for creating a new entry is begun by selecting the New Entries button. The created entries overview screen appears, allowing you to define your new tolerance limits (see Figure 10.20).

FIGURE 10.20   The availability control settings for budget profile BUDGT1

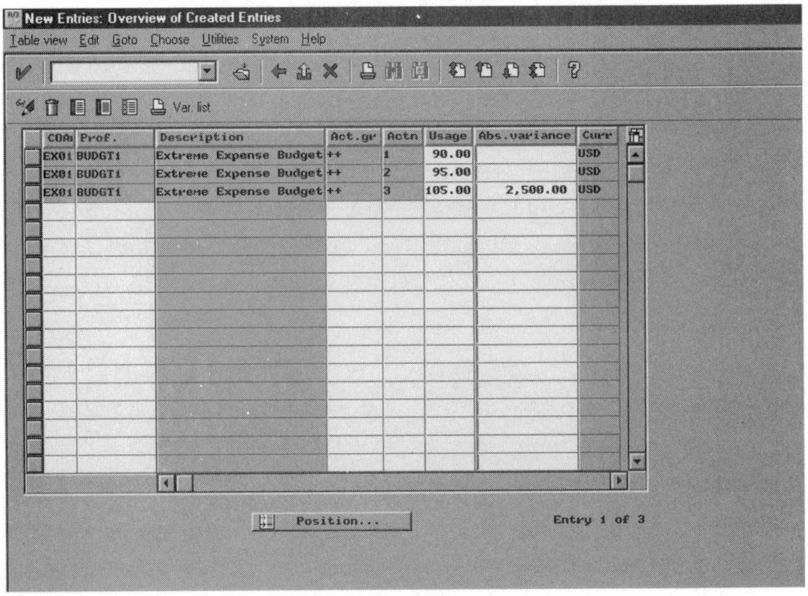

The key fields for availability control settings are as follows:

COAr (Controlling Area)   Enter the ID of the controlling area on which these settings will have an impact.

Prof. (Budget)   Enter the ID of the budget profile for which availability control is being set up.

Description   Manual entry is not allowed in this field. The description will be taken from the assigned budget profile ID.

Act.Gr (Activity Group)   Based on the setting in this field, SAP will determine whether an activity against an order is relevant for availability check. There are 10 potential activity group settings:

++ (All Activity Groups)   All relevant activity against an assigned order is checked against the tolerance limit. The tolerance limits associated with the All Activity Groups setting are ignored if another activity group, like 01 (Purchase Requisition), is defined.

00 (Purchase Requisition)   Only purchase requisition activity against an order is checked against the tolerance limit.

01 (Purchase Order)   Only purchase order activity against an order is checked against the tolerance limit.

02 (Orders for Project)   Related to Project Systems. If this setting is selected, tolerance limit checks will occur during the planning process to ensure that the order plan does not exceed the stated limits.

03 (Goods Issue)   Only goods issues to the order will be subject to the tolerance limit checks.

04 (Financial Accounting Document)   Only postings to an order that results in a financial accounting document will be subject to the tolerance limit checks. Internal CO activity, like order settlement, will not be picked up.

05 (CO Document)   Similar in concept to 04. Only postings to an order that result in a CO document, like settlement, will be subject to the tolerance limit check.

06 (Budgeting)   Similar in concept to 02. During budget updates, SAP will check to see if the stated tolerance limits have not been exceeded.

For example, suppose the original budget on a project was $1,000. Current actual postings and stated commitments total $945 on the order. A tolerance limit has been set to return an error if 100% of the budget is exceeded. If someone attempts to reduce the budget on the order to $900, SAP will return an error because the current actuals + commitments will be 105% of the overall budget.

07 (Funds Reservation) Only postings resulting from a manual funds reservation will be subject to the tolerance limit checks. Funds reservations are manual commitments you place on the order for costs that you expect to incur in the future.

08 (Fixed Prices in the Project) Related to Project Systems. Only fixed-price costs will be subjected to tolerance limit checks.

Actn (Action) The setting in this field denotes the action SAP will take if a defined tolerance limit is exceeded. There are three potential actions that can be taken:

1 (Warning) SAP will return a warning at the time of system update. However, the user will be able to continue with the transaction, and the update will occur.

2 (Warning with Mail) SAP will return a warning and send a SAPMail message to the assigned budget manager. Additional configuration is necessary for this action to work (see "Budget Manager Maintenance"). However, the user will be able to continue with the transaction, and the update will occur.

3 (Error) SAP will return an error at the time of update, and the transaction will not be able to post.

Usage Expressed as a percentage, this amount represents the threshold for total funds committed to an order. If the threshold percentage is exceeded, the assigned action is triggered.

For example, if the budget for an order is $1000 and the usage percentage is set to 95%, when 95.1% of the budget is used, the appropriate action will be triggered.

Abs. Variance (Absolute Variance) Expressed as a dollar amount, this setting represents the total permitted amount of budgeted overrun.

For example, if the budget for an order is again $1000 and Abs. Variance is set at $150, SAP will trigger the appropriate action once the total commitment on the order exceeds $1,150.

When you are establishing the tolerance limits, SAP recommends an either/or scenario. However, maintaining both fields does no harm, and in some cases, it may be vital for proper control (see the Extreme Sports scenario). If both are maintained, the assigned action is triggered when one of the two limits is exceeded.

Once the tolerance limits have been assigned, configuration is complete and you can save the settings. Remember, if you want to change any of the key fields after pressing Enter, you will have to delete the entry and start again. Figure 10.20 provides you with a view of the Extreme Sports availability control settings for budget profile BUDGT1. Notice that action 2 (Warning with Mail) was maintained for the profile. The next section will cover the necessary configuration to ensure that the SAPMail can be sent.

EXTREME SPORTS AVAILABILITY CONTROL SETTINGS CONFIGURATION ANALYSIS

For the expense projects using this profile, Extreme Sports sought to use a three-tiered control system set at 90%, 95%, and 100%. A warning would be returned at the 90% level. Any new purchase requisitions or orders would trigger the warning and let the purchasing agent know that the budget ceiling was close. The budget manager, in this case the project manager, wanted to be made aware of any budgets exceeding 95%. The SAPMail system is a good communication tool and would be developed to send mail messages. Because projects are allowed 5% (or $2,500) overrun, no errors would occur until these levels had been exceeded. If the budget is high enough, it is possible for a project to have an overrun greater than $2,500 and not yet be at 105% of the budget, hence the need for both tolerance limit settings. For simplicity, Extreme Sports chose the All Activity Group indicator, ++. This way, it is assured that all actions taken on an order will be subject to tolerance limit checks.

Budget Manager Maintenance

When you're maintaining the Action settings for availability control, SAP offers you a decision of whether to return a warning with or without a mail message (see the preceding section, "Availability Control Configuration"). If you chose setting 2 (Warning with Mail), you must establish the proper budget manager settings before the mail process will work.

N O T E   It is assumed within this section that SAP Office has been properly developed in the system. You will want to clear this with your Basis group before proceeding.

Simply stated, you have to assign a manager ID to an order type and/or object class for the mail to be routed properly. One shortcoming to note is that the assignment is maintained at a high level within the system. There is no opportunity to assign a manager at an order or project level. However, if your solution provides you with unique order types for which responsibility can be properly segregated, the setting is appropriate. Use the menu path Controlling ➢ Overhead Cost Controlling ➢ Overhead Cost Orders ➢ Budgeting and Availability Control ➢ Maintain Budget Manager to get to the budget manager configuration screen.

MAINTAIN BUDGET MANAGER

You can get to the budget manager configuration screen with either of the following methods:

Menu Path: **Controlling ➢ Overhead Cost Controlling ➢ Overhead Cost Orders ➢ Budgeting and Availability Control ➢ Maintain Budget Manager**

Transaction Code: **OK14**

Notice that the entries are controlling area specific. Select the New Entries button to get to the overview entry screen (see Figure 10.21 for the Extreme Sports budget manager settings).

FIGURE 10.21   The budget manager settings for Extreme Sports

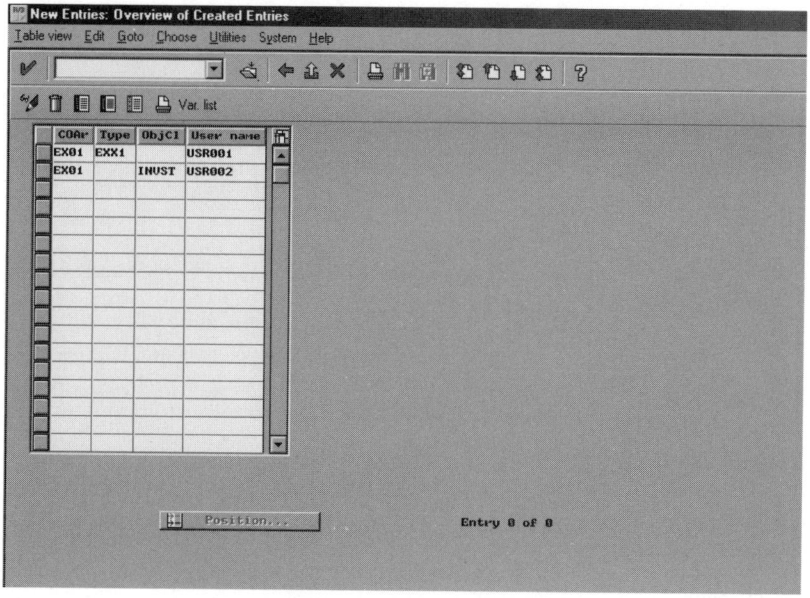

Here are explanations of the fields on this screen:

COAr (Controlling Area)   Enter the ID of the controlling area on which these settings will have an impact.

Type (Order)   If applicable, enter the order type over which the budget manager should be made aware of budget overruns. This field is optional if you will be maintaining the ObjCl field. It is recommended, if possible, that you consider only this setting. See "Order Type Development" later in this chapter for development details.

ObjCl (Object Class)   If applicable, enter the object class over which the budget manager should be made aware of budget overruns. A detailed explanation of object classes is provided in Chapter 8. As with order type, this field is optional if the Order Type field is maintained.

User Name   Enter the SAP ID of the assigned budget manager. Check with your Basis group if you have system ID questions.

When you're finished, save the settings.

There is no limit to the number of persons who can be assigned to a given object class or order type. Once users are assigned, every time a properly maintained order has exceeded its budget, a SAPMail message will be sent to the manager's Office Inbox with the following information:

- ▶ Internal order number

- ▶ Relevant document number, such as an accounting or settlement document

- ▶ A detailed value description of the amount of budget remaining

- ▶ The name and ID of the individual who processed the transaction

- ▶ The name(s) of all other recipients of the message

Additionally, the manager will have the ability to run some reporting directly from the message, affording them the chance to quickly analyze the situation.

When you are making the decision whether to maintain the order type and/or object class, keep in mind these two points:

- ▶ There are only four object classes available. If assignments are made at this level only, the manager could become deluged with a number of messages daily. The exception to this rule could be the use of the object class INVST (Investments). If your organization has but a few capital managers, it might prove useful to have the assignment at this level.

- ▶ By maintaining both the order type and the object class, you are stating that you intend to use the same order type with multiple object classes. This should be discouraged from a reporting and analysis view.

The recommended approach is to assign at the order type level first, analyze if you are receiving the proper level of notification, and then determine if further maintenance is required.

Because there may be opportunities to exclude specific types of costs from the availability control checks, SAP offers the chance to make specified cost elements exempt. The configuration settings are found in the next section.

EXTREME SPORTS BUDGET MANAGER ASSIGNMENT CONFIGURATION ANALYSIS

Within the Extreme Sports order type solution, EXX1 will be used for expense-related corporate projects only. Separate order types will maintain capital only and capital/ expense mixed projects. Because of this segregation, a single manager could be assigned to track budget overruns. Extreme Sports likes the flexibility of the SAPMail system and feels it is a good tool for maintaining awareness. The company centralizes capital management with a few persons, one of which is USR002. The object class INVST will be used strictly for capital projects and capital investment orders. Both of these will be covered in detail in Chapter 13.

Exempting Cost Elements from Availability Control

SAP offers the chance to exclude certain types of costs from the tolerance limit checks of availability control by specifying exempt cost elements. The menu path used to get to the configuration table is Controlling ➢ Overhead Cost Controlling ➢ Overhead Cost Orders ➢ Budgeting and Availability Control ➢ Define Exempt Cost Elements for Availability Control.

DEFINE EXEMPT COST ELEMENTS FOR AVAILABILITY CONTROL

You can use the following methods to get to the necessary configuration screen:

Menu Path: **Controlling** ➢ **Overhead Cost Controlling** ➢ **Overhead Cost Orders** ➢ Budgeting and Availability Control ➢ Define Exempt Cost Elements for Availability Control

Transaction Code: **OPTK**

The cost elements exempted from availability control screen appears. Figure 10.22 shows the screen configured for Extreme Sports. Select the New Entries button to get a fresh view.

FIGURE 10.22   Exempt cost elements for Extreme Sports

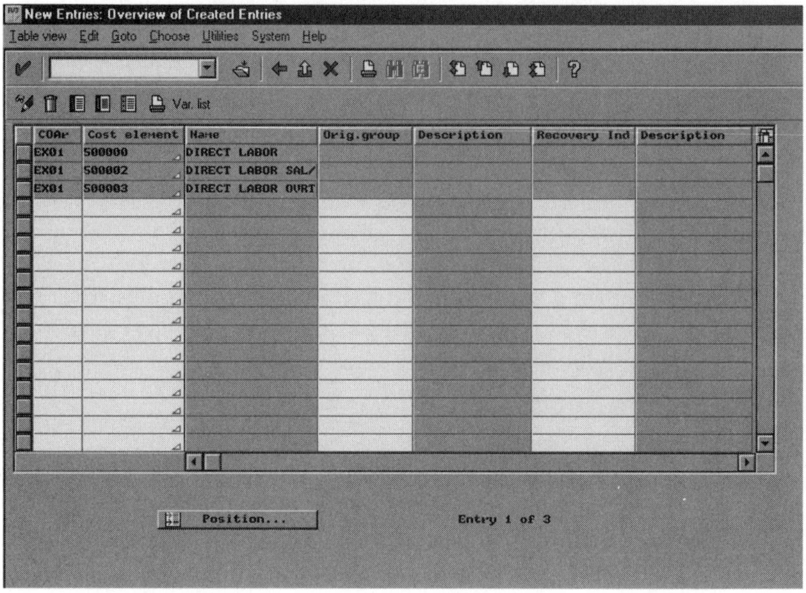

Here are the relevant fields with brief descriptions:

COAr (Controlling Area)   Enter the ID of the controlling area on which these settings will have an impact.

Cost Element   Enter the ID of the cost element to be excluded from availability control checks. Once the ID is entered, any postings with the cost element will be ignored.

Name   This field is automatically populated with the name of the cost element entered in the previous field.

Origin Group   This field is related to product costing. Origin groups allow the system to segregate further material costs. You must create an origin group and costing view maintenance on the material master before you can maintain this field.

Description   This field is automatically populated with the description of the origin group.

Recovery Ind (Indicator)   This field is related to Joint Venture Accounting. It helps to identify which partners are accountable for which costs. We recommend that you review the SAP notes on the Joint Venture Accounting system before utilizing this field.

Description   This field is automatically populated with the description of the recovery indicator.

When you're finished, save the settings. The table can be updated as often as necessary, but changes are not effective in a retroactive manner. The next section will provide a composite of the various number range assignments required for order planning and budgeting.

Internal Order Planning and Budgeting Number Range Maintenance

This section will briefly cover the two areas necessary for completing the number range assignments for planning and budgeting:

▶ Activity assignments at the controlling area level

▶ Number range interval assignments for planning/budgeting

Activity assignments were covered in detail in Chapter 7. This will be just a review.

Maintain Number Range Assignment for Planning/Budgeting Transactions

Always remember to review previously established transaction number range assignments when beginning configuration of a new submodule. It is not uncommon to miss needed transactions, and the planning functionality will not work until the assignments are made. The menu path to maintain number range assignments is Controlling ➣ Overhead Cost Controlling ➣ Overhead Cost Orders ➣ Planning ➣ Basic Settings ➣ Assign Planning Transactions to Number Ranges.

MAINTAIN NUMBER RANGE ASSIGNMENTS

You can get to the number range assignment control screen with either of the following methods:

Menu Path: **Controlling** ➣ **Overhead Cost Controlling** ➣ **Overhead Cost Orders** ➣ **Planning** ➣ **Basic Settings** ➣ **Assign Planning Transactions to Number Ranges**

Transaction Code: **KANK**

Number range assignments are covered in detail in Chapter 7 in the section "Assign Number Ranges to Controlling Area." Figure 10.23 provides a view of the planning transaction assignments for Extreme Sports' controlling area EX01.

FIGURE 10.23   Planning transaction assignments for controlling area EX01

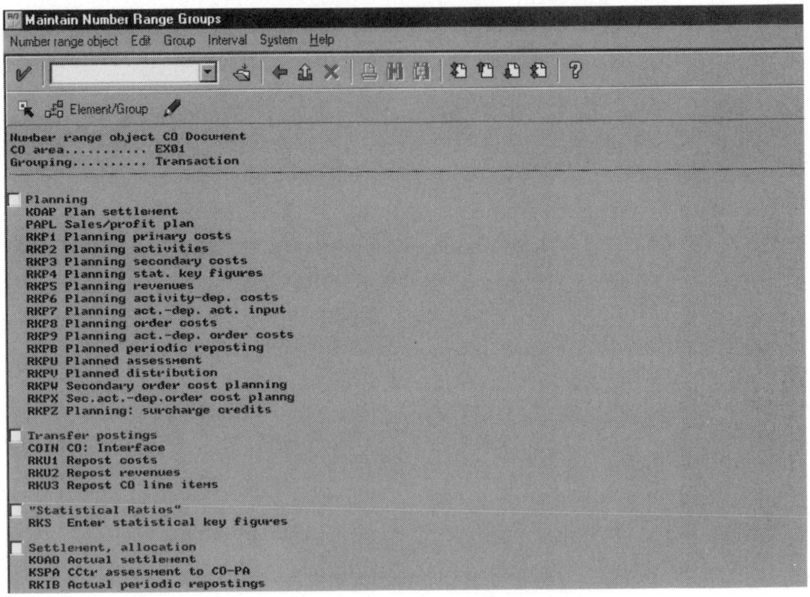

TIP   When you are in the number range assignment table, it is always prudent to check all transaction assignments.

Maintain Number Ranges for Planning and Budgeting

SAP links the objects for planning and budgeting under one number range, so maintenance is easy. Use the menu path Controlling ➢ Overhead Cost Controlling ➢ Overhead Cost Orders ➢ Budgeting and Availability Control ➢ Maintain Number Ranges for Budgeting to get to the number range maintenance screen.

The number ranges cost planning and budgeting screen appears. This screen is similar to the number range screen for CO document assignment. Number range intervals are used to differentiate between types of postings. The default intervals for planning and budgeting include the following:

03   Overall Order Planning

04   Order Budgeting

MAINTAIN NUMBER RANGES FOR PLANNING/BUDGETING OBJECTS

You can get to the necessary configuration screen with either of the methods listed here:

Menu Path: **Controlling** ➤ **Overhead Cost Controlling** ➤ **Overhead Cost Orders** ➤ **Budgeting and Availability Control** ➤ **Maintain Number Ranges for Budgeting**

Transaction Code: **OK11**

The number range intervals are predefined by SAP and are not subject to change. You do have the ability to determine the range value, so be sure that the ranges are wide enough and that they do not overlap. To maintain the range interval, select the Maintain Interval button in the body of the screen. From here, you have the ability to create and maintain the planning intervals. Figure 10.24 provides you with a view of the number range intervals for Extreme Sports.

FIGURE 10.24   The number range intervals for planning and budgeting

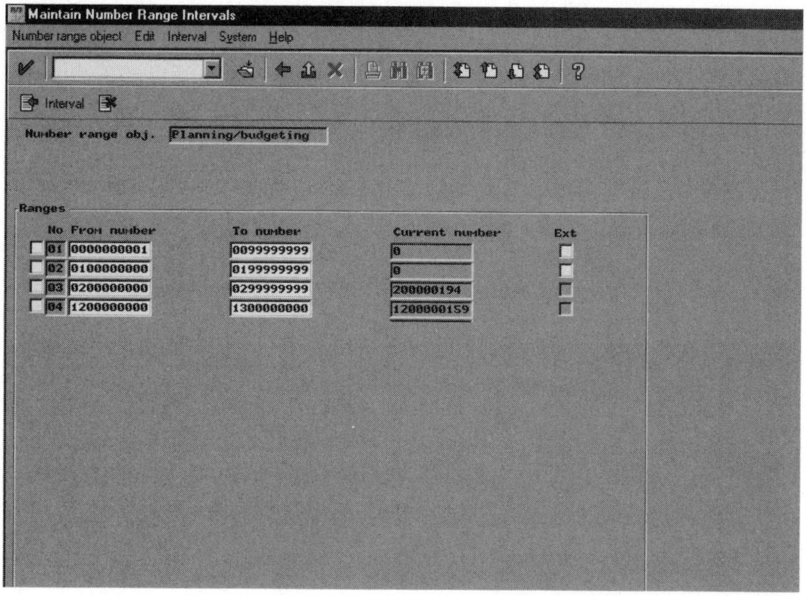

NOTE   Be aware that the documents for planning and budgeting do not allow for external numbering. And, as with all number ranges, do not transport them into your production system. Rather, manually create the number range wherever necessary.

When the number range assignments are complete, planning and budgeting configuration is finished. You are now ready to apply both the planning and budgeting profiles to any order type. The next section is the last in the iterative process of internal order type development. Once it's completed, you will be ready to fully develop an internal order type.

Internal Order Status Management

Status management is the act of determining and managing what transactions are valid for an order at any given time within its life cycle. The term *life cycle* was coined by SAP to refer to an order's fluid existence, moving from one phase to another until it is closed. The complexity of order accounting is no more visible than the complexity involved with the development of status management.

As with anything in SAP, there are two options to choose from when determining a status management type. Each of these solutions, along with any additional configuration, will be covered in detail:

General status management   The most flexible of the two statuses. Recommended because of its ability to be easily applied to multiple order types.

Order status management   Less flexible then general status management in its selection and grouping of transactions. Also, must be coded directly on the order type.

The indicator for using either general status management or order status management is found on the order type master record. Although the configuration method of each varies, there are common threads between them called phases or system statuses. A phase can be described as the status of an order during its lifecycle. There are four phases available for an order to exist within:

▶ Created

▶ Released

▶ Technically Complete

▶ Closed

As an order moves from one phase to another, the group of allowed business transactions changes. For example, when an order has the status of Created, FI postings are not allowed, but all planning functionality may be available. The concepts that will be covered here may seem complicated or confusing, so please take your time when moving through the material. The first status management type to be covered will be order status management.

Order Status Management

Order status management is defined for each order type directly on the order type master record. There are several key concepts to understand about order status management:

▶ Transaction groups are used to determine what business transactions are allowed for each of the four phases. SAP delivers five groups as defaults. User-defined transaction groups must be developed outside of order status management configuration.

▶ Order status is used to sequence the movement between phases. Transaction groups are maintained at this level. The majority of your up-front strategy time should be spent around this topic. How an order will move between phases is at the core of Internal Order Accounting.

▶ The system status is maintained by SAP as a way of alerting the user that a specific action has been applied to the order. Examples of system statuses include CRTD (Created), REL (Released), and SETC (Settlement Rule Created). In order status management, you have less influence over how the system status updates.

▶ Authorizations can be set at each order status level, meaning that you will have the ability to assign authority to move between statuses.

Begin the development process by entering the order type master record with the menu path Controlling ➢ Overhead Cost Controlling ➢ Overhead Cost Orders ➢ Order Master Data ➢ Define Order Type.

DEFINE ORDER STATUS MANAGEMENT

You can get to the necessary configuration screen with either of the following methods:

Menu Path: **Controlling** ➢ **Overhead Cost Controlling** ➢ **Overhead Cost Orders** ➢ **Order Master Data** ➢ **Define Order Type**

Transaction Code: **KOT2**

The maintain order types overview screen appears, offering you many choices. Remember that all order types are controlling area independent, so changes made here will be felt everywhere. If you have previously created an order type, double-click the type to enter the master record. If not, select the New Entries button. New order type development is covered in a later section and will not be covered here. For the examples given, order type EXX1, which can be seen in Figure 10.25, will be maintained.

FIGURE 10.25 The order type master screen for EXX1, Extreme Expense Order Type

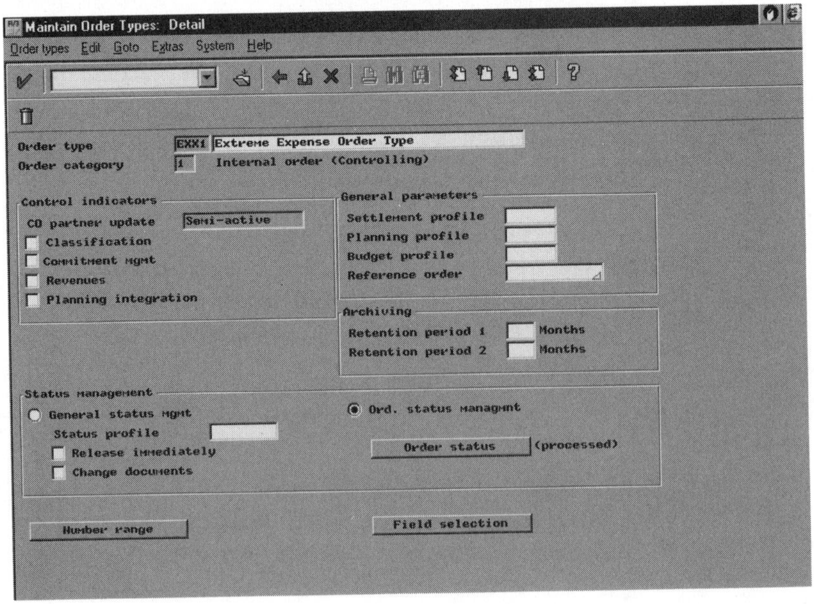

At the maintain order types detail screen, select the radio button next to the Ord. Status Management field. Select the Order Status button and the maintain order types status overview screen appears. The screen will be blank except for the Order Type field. It is here that you will begin configuring the order statuses. From the icon bar, select the New Entries button. A new status screen appears (Figure 10.26 shows the completed maintain order types status detail screen). Descriptions of the fields found here are listed below and broken into three sections: the header, the Phase section, and the Indicator section.

FIGURE 10.26   The completed maintain order types status detail screen

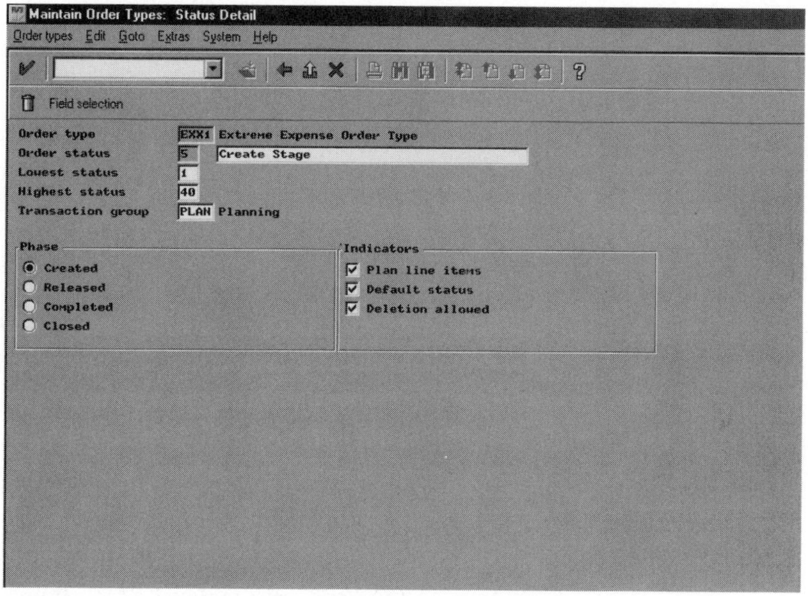

The fields in the header are as follows:

Order Type   This field is carried over from the overview screen. It is the ID of the order being maintained.

Order Status   Enter a numeric ID and description of the order status in question. If this is your first status, it is recommended that you do not start at 1. You may realize later in the order type development that another status is needed below this initial point. Begin at either 5 or 10 to allow for this further development.

An order status strategy might look like the following:

05   Create

10   Plan

20   Approved & Released

30   Technically Complete

40   Closed

Each of these order statuses would have separate transaction groups assigned, providing a clean differentiation.

Lowest Status   This field represents the lowest order status to which an order can move when it has the order status defined in the Order Status field as its current status. The order status ID does not have to exist in the system to be entered here. If your current lowest order status is 05 but you want to cover potential order statuses below 05, you can enter a 01.

Highest Status   This field represents the highest order status to which an order can move when it has the order status defined in the Order Status field as its current status. The order status ID does not have to exist in the system to be entered here. If you know that your highest status will be 40 but it has not been entered yet, it can be assigned at this time.

For example, assume that order status 10 (Plan) is maintained with a Lowest Status value of 05 and a Highest Status value of 30. When an order of this type has an order status of 0, the order status can go back only as far as 05 and forward only as far as 30. The order status cannot be changed to 40. For the order to be closed, the order status would first have to be changed to a status with a Highest Status setting of at least 40.

Transaction Group   Enter the transaction group ID you want to associate with the order status. A transaction group will provide the order with the allowed business transactions that may be initiated. SAP delivers five default groups that may be used at any time:

ALL   Contains all transactions an order may initiate.

ABSL   Contains all transactions necessary to complete a monthly close for orders.

NOPL   Contains all transactions for an order except planning transactions.

PLAN   Contains only the order planning transactions.

RECH   Contains only transactions that allow primary cost and overhead postings.

You may use any of these groups or create your own (see the section called "Transaction Group"). A transaction group must be assigned for you to process any transactions on the order.

There is a predefined set of business transactions that are allowed at each phase. Only these transactions will ever be allowed, regardless of what is contained in the assigned transaction group. To reiterate an earlier example, you will never be able to initiate FI postings to an order if the system status is Create. A complete listing of available business transactions by phase can be found on the order itself. As you change the order status, select the Status button and then the Business Transaction button. This will provide you with a list of allowed and disallowed transactions for that phase.

TIP It is recommended that you not change the delivered transaction groups by adding or deleting business transactions. Rather, create a new group by copying one of those groups that were delivered with the system.

Each order status must declare one of the phases in the Phase section. SAP tracks the phases on the order record through a system status. There is a system status with the same name for each of the defined order phases. The phase selected will have an impact on the allowed transactions, so choose carefully. The phases are as follows:

Created   The initial phase for most order types. Generally, all planning business transaction will be allowed with this phase.

Released   The most widely used phase. All business transactions are available for use in this phase.

Completed or Technically Complete   Generally, all business transactions except planning and budgeting are available for use in this phase.

Closed   No business transactions are available for use in this phase.

Finally, here are the fields in the Indicators section:

Plan Line Items   Select this field if you would like to document plan line items in this order status.

Default Status   Select this field if you want this order status to default upon order creation.

Deletion Allowed   Select this field if you want to be able to set the deletion flag on the order when it is in this status.

Repeat the steps as necessary until your entire order status management strategy has been implemented. The next section will take you through the steps of creating the transaction group.

Transaction Group

To get to the transaction group configuration screen, use the menu path Controlling ➢ Overhead Cost Controlling ➢ Overhead Cost Orders ➢ Order Master Data ➢ Define Transaction Groups for Status Management.

DEFINE TRANSACTION GROUPS

You can get to the transaction group configuration screen with either of these methods:

Menu Path: **Controlling ➢ Overhead Cost Controlling ➢ Overhead Cost Orders ➢ Order Master Data ➢ Define Transaction Groups for Status Management**

Transaction Code: **KOV2**

The maintain transaction group overview screen appears, showing you the five default groups mentioned earlier. Double-click any one of the delivered groups for an idea of how a maintained transaction group looks. Figure 10.27 provides you with a view of the transaction group ALL.

To create your own transaction group, select the New Entries button. The Maintain Transaction Groups New Entry screen will appear. Let's examine the fields.

Transaction Group   Enter the ID and description for the new group. The ID can be up to four characters in length.

Trans (Transactions)   There are 67 business transactions available for selection. To place one in the group, select the box next to the transaction ID.

When you have finished assigning transaction codes, save the group. You can make changes to these groups at any time, with immediate impact to your order status. Remember the SAP-defined relationship between the phases and allowed business transactions. No harm will come from assigning a transaction group with a disallowed transaction to an order status. The transaction will just not work when the order is in that phase.

FIGURE 10.27   A detailed view of the transaction group ALL

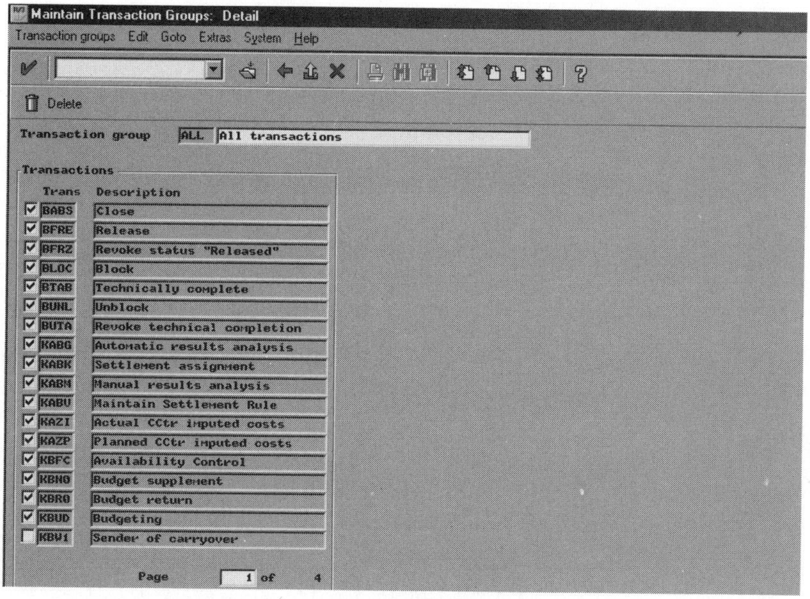

For example, suppose you have created a new group called Post that includes the transaction RFBU (FI: Postings). The transaction group is then assigned to an order status with phase Create. The order status will remain valid, with other transactions still functioning. However, when you attempt to make an FI posting to the order with this status active, it will error out.

Transaction groups can be used across controlling areas and order types. Keep this in mind when making any changes to existing groups.

EXTREME SPORTS ORDER STATUS MANAGEMENT CONFIGURATION ANALYSIS

Extreme Sports has chosen to not use order status management as its tool for controlling its order types. It prefers the flexibility and benefits provided by general status management. These include not having to manually configure the status solution on each of its order types and having greater ability to configure its own status control functions.

General Status Management

General status management is defined on the order type by assigning a status profile to it. It is this profile that will be configured here. Many of the concepts introduced in order status management, such as order phases and system status, are relevant here. Some items that are not carried over include transaction groups and order statuses. Here are some new key concepts that should be introduced up front:

► User statuses can be used to provide differentiation from the predefined system statuses. If needed, a user can update the user status on an internal order without affecting the system status, thus giving greater control to the user.

► The order status has been replaced with a new field called Status or Sequence Number. The meanings are similar in that the status number is used to align or sequence the various statuses.

► Allowed transactions are coded directly to each status number. New functionality allows a system status to update automatically when a certain transaction is run. An example would be having the system status automatically set to REL (Released) when the budgeting transaction KBUD is run.

► An Authorization Key field is provided for easy security profile development.

There are three major steps to completing the status profile. They can be completed at the same instance in stages. The steps, in order, are as follows:

1. Define the user status strategy.

2. Assign allowed object types.

3. Define allowed/disallowed transactions per status.

Define User Statuses

To access the status profile creation screen, use the menu path Controlling ➢ Overhead Cost Controlling ➢ Overhead Cost Orders ➢ Order Master Data ➢ Define Status Profile.

The change status profile overview screen appears. There are a number of profiles delivered with your system that you will probably never use. It is our recommendation that you start from scratch when building your new profile because many of the delivered profiles have not been completely maintained. If you have previously created another profile, you can use the copy function during creation. If not, select the New Entry button to bring up a status profile definition box (see Figure 10.28).

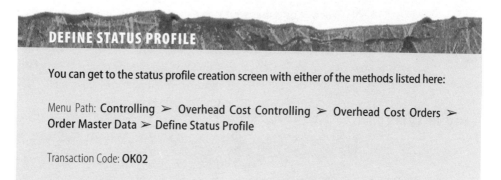

DEFINE STATUS PROFILE

You can get to the status profile creation screen with either of the methods listed here:

Menu Path: **Controlling** ➢ **Overhead Cost Controlling** ➢ **Overhead Cost Orders** ➢ **Order Master Data** ➢ **Define Status Profile**

Transaction Code: **OK02**

FIGURE 10.28   The status profile definition box

There are three fields to fill out:

Status Profile   Enter the status profile ID. The ID can be up to eight alphanumeric characters in length.

Description   Enter the status profile description. Make the definition clear because these can be used across controlling areas.

MaintLanguage   Enter the indicator for the language in which you wish the profile to be maintained. An *E* represents English.

Select Enter. Notice that your new status profile ID has been placed among the other profiles. You now have a placeholder for your profile. You can save the table and maintain the ID later, or you can continue with the maintenance now. To continue now, select the profile by either double-clicking the profile ID or choosing it through the icon bar. The User Status window will appear (see Figure 10.29).

FIGURE 10.29   The User Status screen

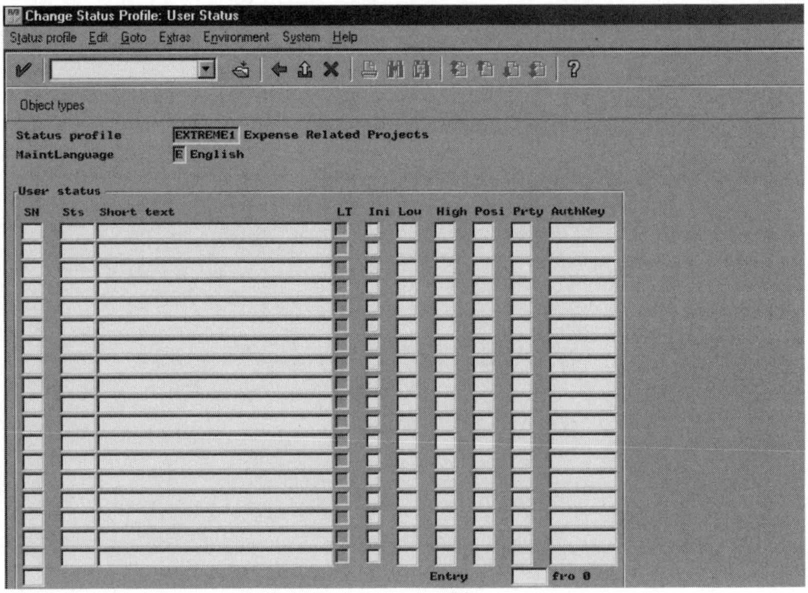

Here are descriptions of the fields found on the screen:

SN (Sequence or Status Number)   Enter a two-digit numeric ID. This field defines the order in which the statuses should be processed. It is similar to the Order Status field found in order status management. It is recommended that you start the status numbering at 10 or higher. This will allow for new, lower-level statuses to be input later. Also, use consistent gaps between all assigned statuses for the same reason.

Sts (User Status)   Enter an ID of up to four alphanumeric characters in length that is representative of the current user status. This status will be visible in the User Status section of the order record.

Short Text   Enter a description of the user status. Be clear on what the status represents to make control analysis easier.

LT (Long Text)   If this field is active, it is a signal to let you know that there is long text available for the status. To enter long text, you first have to be at the default User Status screen. Place the cursor on the status you want to update and use the menu path Goto ➤ Long Text. A text editor window will open for you to enter the information. Save the text and green arrow back to the User Status screen. The LT box will not have a check in it.

Ini (Initial)   Select this field if the status is to be active upon order creation.

Low (Lowest Status)   This field represents the lowest status to which an order can move when it has this user status defined as its current status. The user status ID does not have to exist in the system to be entered here. If your current lowest order status is 05 but you want to cover potential order statuses below 05, you can enter 01. See the example provided in "Order Status Management" for additional details.

High (Highest Status)   This field represents the highest status to which an order can move when it has this user status defined as its current status. The order status ID does not have to exist in the system to be entered here. If you know that your highest status will be 40 but it has not been entered yet, it can be assigned at this time. See the example provided in "Order Status Management" for additional details.

Posi (Position)   On the order record, user and system statuses can be displayed from the Control Data screen by selecting the Status button. The numeric entry in the Position field will determine its location in the status view. SAP will display up to eight statuses at a time. The statuses will default in the order by sequence number.

Prty (Priority)   This field works in conjunction with the Posi field setting. If two or more statuses have the same position setting, the priority field is used to determine order. A priority 1 takes precedence over a priority 2 and so on.

AuthKey (Authority Key)   This field is used by your security group to define a user's authorization profile. If this field is maintained properly, only users with this authorization key in their security profile will be able to update an order to the defined status. The authorization object used by SAP is B_USERSTAT.

The authorization keys must be defined prior to being added to the status profile. See the section on authorization key configuration for details.

It is helpful to have a control strategy mapped out before beginning the development, but it's not required. You will have the opportunity to change the settings on everything except the position and priority. When you have completed the status definition, save the profile before continuing. Figure 10.30 is an example of a defined user status strategy used by Extreme Sports. The next step will be to define the object types for the status profile.

FIGURE 10.30   User status definitions for status profile EXTREME1

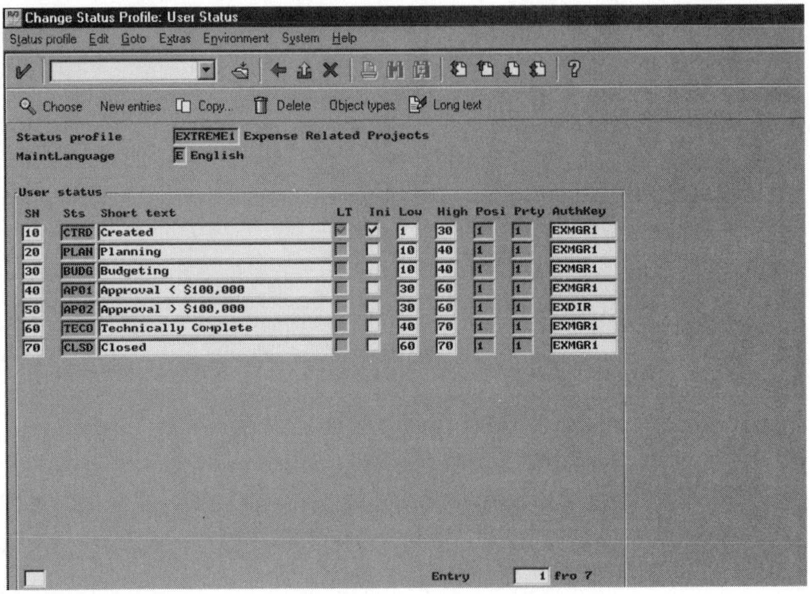

Define Object Types

Object types were first introduced in Chapter 8 during reconciliation ledger configuration. As stated then, there are only eight object types available for reconciliation ledger use. However, there are significantly more that exist in other areas of the system, each with its own responsibility. They range from development objects used in ABAP development to production objects used in PP/PC. In status profile configuration, you acknowledge through object type assignment which objects are authorized to use the profile.

When you configured order status management, you developed directly on the order type. The object type was known immediately. However, in general status management, the object type is not recognized until the status profile is assigned. Status profile configuration is being shown as a part of Internal Order Accounting. But objects outside of the module use status profiles as well, thus the need to determine on the profile itself which objects type are authorized

To assign valid object types, you must be at the User Status screen. In most instances, you will move immediately to this step after completing the status definitions. If not, use the menu path Controlling ➤ Overhead Cost Controlling ➤ Overhead Cost Orders ➤ Order Master Data ➤ Define Status Profile and select the proper profile.

At the User Status screen, select the Object Types button (see Figure 10.30). The Permitted Object Types window appears, shown in Figure 10.31.

FIGURE 10.31   The Permitted Object Types assignment screen

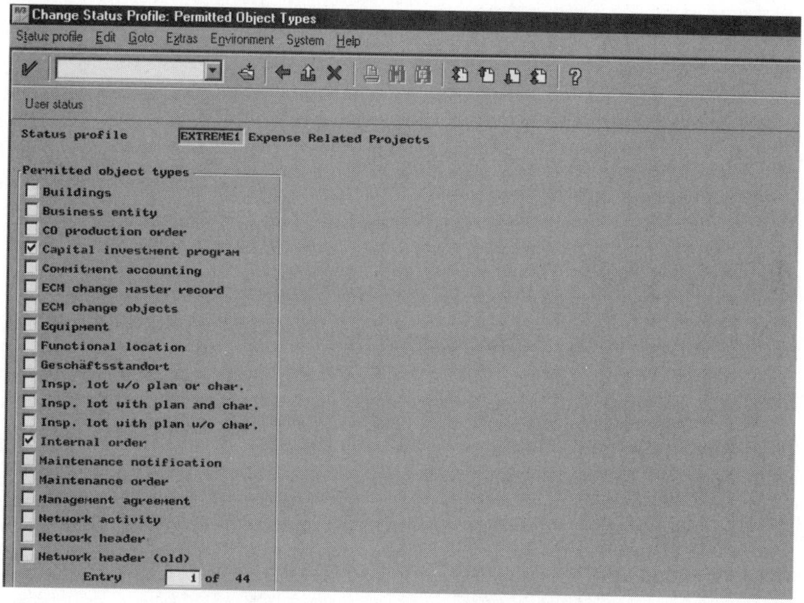

There are too many object types to provide definitions for all. Here is a short list of potential objects that may be used in conjunction with Internal Order Accounting:

► Internal Order

► Capital Investment Program

► Maintenance Orders

► WBS Element

To authorize an object type, select the box next to the object type name found in the Permitted Object Types section. When you're finished, save the settings. You can update these settings at any time. The last step in status profile development is the definition of allowed business transactions.

Define Business Transactions

To access the transaction control section of the status profile, you must be at the User Status screen. In most instances, you will move immediately to this step after completing the status definitions. If not, use the menu path Controlling ➢ Overhead Cost Controlling ➢ Overhead Cost Orders ➢ Order Master Data ➢ Define Status Profile and select the proper profile.

To move to the transaction control section, select a status by either double-clicking the status ID or choosing it through the icon bar. A Transaction Control window will appear. When you enter the control window for the first time, the control screen will be empty. To make the first assignments, or to make additional assignments to a previously maintained status, select the New Entries button. A complete listing of potential business transactions will appear (see Figure 10.32).

FIGURE 10.32   **The New Entry screen during transaction control maintenance**

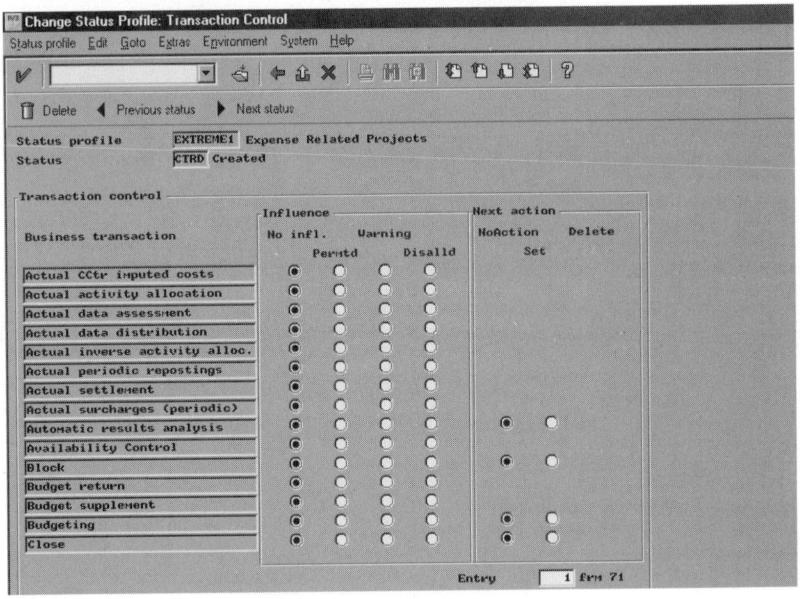

At this point, you begin determining which transactions you want to allow for the status. The window is broken into three main sections: Business Transactions, Influence, and Next Action.

The Business Transactions section contains a listing of the transactions available for selection in the status:

Transactions   There are 71 transactions to choose from. Many of the definitions can be found in the SAP Help text.

The Influence section will determine whether or not the business transaction will be allowed. The fields are as follows:

No Infl. (No Influence)   This is the default setting. If it's left alone, the business transaction will not appear in the available set viewed here. For the business trans–action to receive any reaction, the setting must be changed. The setting does not prohibit the order from using the transaction.

Permtd (Permitted)   If this field is set, the business transaction will be allowed for the status being maintained.

Warning   If this field is set, the business transaction will be allowed, but a warning will be produced during execution. The user will have the ability to post the transaction.

Disalld (Disallowed)   If this field is set, the transaction will be disallowed for the status being maintained. This is the opposite of no influence because you are purposefully eliminating the transaction from the user's authority.

Settings in the Next Action section influence the automatic activation or deletion of a user status:

NoAction   This is the default setting. If this setting is left on, the execution of the business transaction will have no effect on status activation.

Set   If this is set, execution of the related business transaction will automatically activate the status. For example, your internal order solution calls for an order to be automatically released when the order is budgeted. To accomplish this, the Set status indicator should be set for the Budgeting transaction on the Released user status. The next time an order using this profile is budgeted, the user status will automatically change to REL (Released).

N O T E   The Lowest/Highest status settings must work in conjunction with any of the Action settings. If they are not in sync, the action will not take place.

Delete   If this is set, execution of the related business transaction will automatically delete the status. This setting is not widely used.

Figure 10.33 offers a view of the transaction control settings employed by Extreme Sports for its expense-related projects. The view shows settings that will automatically set the status to AP01 upon release. Based on the user status settings, the order will have to have moved to a PLAN status before the action will have any effect (see Figure 10.30).

see Figure 10.30

FIGURE 10.33   The maintained Transaction Control screen for Status Profile EXTREME1

	Change Status Profile: Transaction Control

Status profile Edit Goto Extras Environment System Help

New entries   Delete   ◀ Previous status   ▶ Next status

Status profile   EXTREME1 Expense Related Projects
Status   AP01 Approval < $100,000

Transaction control

Business transaction	Influence				Next action		
	No infl.	Permtd	Warning	Disalld	NoAction	Set	Delete
Inventory difference	○	●	○	○			
Lock budgeting	○	●	○	○	●	○	
Lock planning	○	●	○	○	●	○	
Maintain Settlement Rule	○	●	○	○	●	○	
Manual funds reservation	○	●	○	○			
Manual results analysis	○	●	○	○	●	○	
Material purchase order	○	●	○	○			
Material purchase requisition	○	●	○	○			
Planning primary costs	○	●	○	○			
Planning revenues	○	●	○	○			
Planning secondary costs	○	●	○	○			
Post goods issue	○	●	○	○			
Release	○	●	○	○	○		●
Remove deletion flag	○	●	○	○	●	○	
Repost CO line items	○	●	○	○			

Entry   31 frm 61

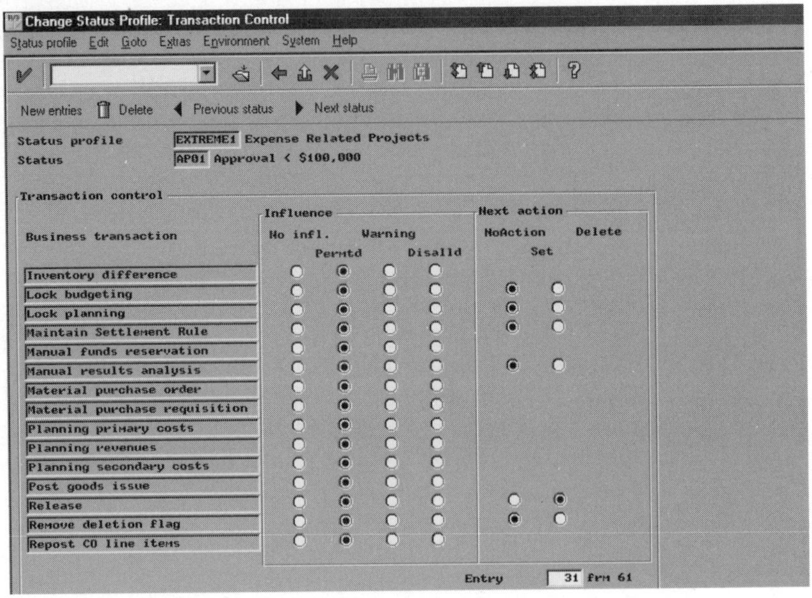

Be certain to properly maintain each user status within the profile. It will be trial and error for a while during the development phase. You will undoubtedly find that certain settings have been misapplied during your configuration. Just be diligent and cover all the bases.

TIP   Keep good documentation of the settings as you are developing. This will help immensely when you are ready to configure the solution in the transport client.

The next section is relevant if you are using the authorization keys in the status profile. In it, we will cover the necessary configuration steps for creating a new authorization key.

Maintain Authorization Keys

Authorization key creation is a simple one-step process. There is little configuration involved here because all you're doing is setting up an ID. The security group will use this ID and a few authorization objects to establish the proper authorization profile. To access the authorization key window, use the menu path Controlling ➢ Overhead Cost Controlling ➢ Overhead Cost Orders ➢ Order Master Data ➢ Define Authorization Keys for Status Management.

EXTREME SPORTS GENERAL STATUS MANAGEMENT CONFIGURATION ANALYSIS

Extreme Sports has chosen to use general status management as its tool for controlling its order types. It plans on using the same status profile on two types of internal orders and a maintenance order type. Updates are easier in this case because a single profile can be maintained as opposed to maintaining three order types separately. Also, the ability to more tightly control the control settings is another plus. In the example provided, status profile EXTREME1 will be used with order type EXX1, which will be configured in the next section.

DEFINE AUTHORIZATION KEYS

You can get to the authorization key window with either of these methods:

Menu Path: **Controlling** ➢ **Overhead Cost Controlling** ➢ **Overhead Cost Orders** ➢ **Order Master Data** ➢ **Define Authorization Keys for Status Management**

Transaction Code: **BS52**

The authorization key overview screen will appear. To define a new key, select the New Entries button. The table will now allow for new authorization keys. Maintain the following two fields:

Authkey (Authorization Key)   Enter the ID of the authorization key. It can be up to eight alphanumeric characters. Be sure to make it unique because the ID can be used across controlling areas.

Description   Enter the description of the authorization key.

When you're finished, save the settings. You can enter as many as needed, and the table can be updated at any time.

Status management is now complete. The groundwork has been laid, and you can now begin order type development. The next section will cover the configuration steps necessary to building a new order type from scratch.

Order Type Development

You have now completed the necessary steps to fully develop an order type. At the beginning of this chapter, order type EXX1-Extreme Expense Order Type was shown in its beginning stages (see Figure 10.1). An order type ID can be created and saved as a placeholder with no additional configuration done. As stated earlier, and as shown throughout the chapter, order type configuration is an iterative process. Plan, budget, and status profiles must all be created prior to assignment to the order type. Each step has some iterative development as well.

Define Order Types

Begin the order type configuration process by accessing the order type definition window with the menu path Controlling ➢ Overhead Cost Controlling ➢ Overhead Cost Orders ➢ Order Master Data ➢ Define Order Types.

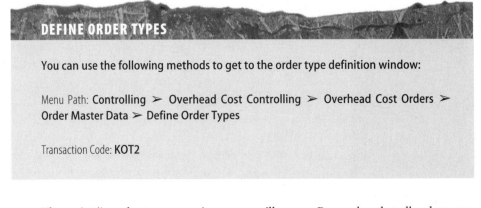

DEFINE ORDER TYPES

You can use the following methods to get to the order type definition window:

Menu Path: **Controlling** ➢ **Overhead Cost Controlling** ➢ **Overhead Cost Orders** ➢ **Order Master Data** ➢ **Define Order Types**

Transaction Code: **KOT2**

The maintain order types overview screen will appear. Remember that all order types are controlling area independent, so changes made here will be felt everywhere. If you have previously created an order type, like EXX1, double-click the type to enter the master record. If not, select the New Entries button. An order type entry box appears (see Figure 10.34).

FIGURE 10.34   The order type definition entry screen

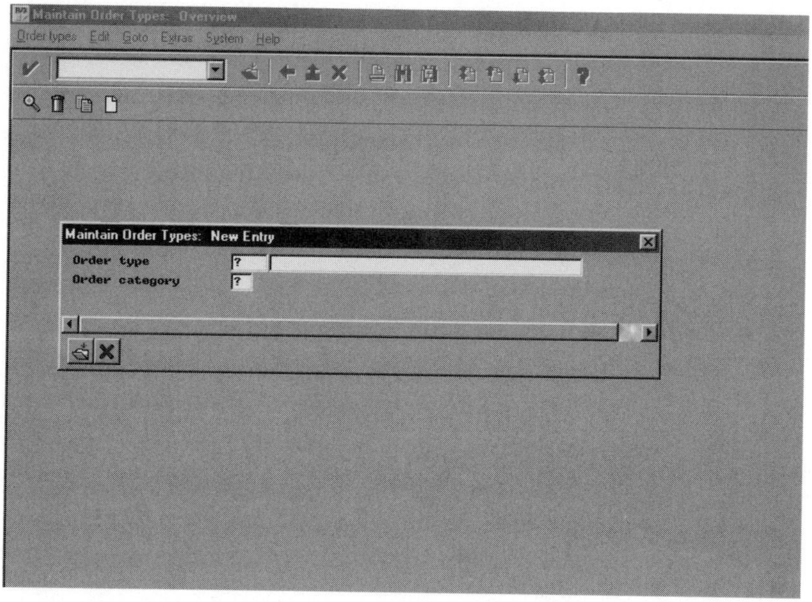

Maintain both of the following entry fields:

Order Type   Enter the ID for the new order type. The ID can be up to four alphanumeric characters in length. In the text box next to the field, enter a description for the order type.

Order Category   Enter the category of the order type being developed. There are 13 potential choices. Select 1 for internal orders.

Select save when you've filled in the fields. The maintain order types detail screen will appear (refer back to Figure 10.1). This screen may look familiar because it was accessed during order status management configuration. Notice that the order type ID and category were carried over from the entry box and are now not configurable. At this point, if you want to change the order type ID or category, you will have to delete the order type and start again. Only the description field is configurable. Begin the process by maintaining the necessary fields as they are listed and defined below.

The Control Indicators section determines what areas are active for the order type:

CO Partner Update   This field determines how an order will post during CO allocations. This setting will influence the number of data records maintained in order accounting. There are three choices available (Semi-Active is the default setting):

Active   In ranking from highest to lowest with regard to the number of records maintained during allocations, Active ranks number one. A totals record will be maintained for all parties involved.

Semi-Active   This is second highest in the number of records posted. During order-to-order allocations, such as settlements, a totals record for both objects will be maintained. For allocations between an order and a cost center, such as repostings, a totals record will not be maintained for the order on the cost center.

Not Active   No totals record is maintained on the receiving object regardless of whether it is an order or not.

Classification   If you want to utilize classifications to organize the order type, this field must be activated. Prior to using classifications, it is recommended that you review the literature provided by SAP.

Commitment Mgmt   Select this field to activate commitment management for the order type. If it's active, commitments such as purchase requisitions and purchase orders can be tracked on the order type. It is recommended that the setting always be selected for project-related order types in which procurement is a predominant activity.

Revenues   If you plan on tracking revenues on the order type, this flag must be set. If it's not, SAP will return an error when an attempt is made to post a revenue element.

Planning Integration   This setting relates to the Planning Integration with Cost Center Accounting setting found on the CO version screen. If planning integration is active here, plan data can be automatically passed to Profit Center Accounting. To activate this setting, the CO Partner Update setting must read Active. You don't need to set this if you do not intend to completely integrate with Profit Center Accounting.

Settings in the General Parameters section determine your settlement, budgeting, and planning controls (these files were all developed in earlier sections):

Settlement Profile   Enter the ID of the settlement profile to be used by the order type. The settlement profile controls such things as the settlement and origin structures. The profile development was covered in an earlier section. For EXX1, settlement profile 90 will be used.

Planning Profile   Enter the ID of the planning profile to be used by the order type. The planning profile will determine the levels of planning available on an order type and help define some default planning groups. Complete planning profile development was covered in an earlier section. For EXX1, planning profile EXX0 will be used.

Budget Profile   Enter the ID of the budget profile to be used. The profile will control, among other things, budgeting views and availability control activation. Complete budget profile and availability control configuration was covered in previous sections. For EXX1, budget profile BUDGT1 will be used.

Reference Order   If, during internal order creation, you wish to always copy a specific order, enter the order number here. Then, during order creation, the active fields from this reference order will automatically be copied into the new order's active fields. There is another opportunity to enter a reference order during order creation. An alternative to this field setting is the use of model orders.

The Archiving section is responsible for deleting and/or archiving the internal order master records. The archiving or deleting of order master records from your database should be a part of your overall archiving strategy. The fields are as follows:

Retention Period 1   Enter the number of months that must pass between when the deletion flag was set and when the deletion indicator can be activated on the master record.

Retention Period 2   Enter the number of months that must pass between when the deletion indicator was set and when the master record can be archived or deleted.

The combination of the retention periods is the minimal amount of time that the order master record must reside in your database before it can be removed. Keep this in mind when making the setting.

The fields in the Status Management section determine the type of transaction control the order type will use:

General Status Mgmt   Activate this radio button if general status management is to be used. See the section on general status management configuration for details. For EXX1, general status management will be activated. There are several settings available, each of which is described here:

Status Profile   If general status management is activated, you must enter a status profile.

Release Immediately   If this setting is selected, a new order created with this order type will be released immediately. The setting is effective only when used in conjunction with general status management.

Change Documents   If this setting is selected, all status changes for an order will be documented.

T I P   Enter a profile only if general status management is going to be used. Otherwise, the profile setting will be ignored.

Ord. Status Management   Activate this radio button if order status management is to be used. See the section on order status management configuration for details.

You have gotten as far as you can without saving the order type. There are two sections left: Number Range and Field Selection. Before either of these areas can be configured, the order type must be saved. SAP will provide you with an error message if you forget. If you are happy with the configuration settings so far and wish to continue, save the order type. You will remain in the maintain order types detail screen. Continue development with the assignment of the number ranges.

Number Range Assignment

Select the Number Range button at the bottom of the maintain order types detail screen. The Maintain Number Range Groups screen appears. The screen looks similar to the activity assignment screen you maintained earlier in the chapter. Each order type within SAP must be assigned to a defined number range group. It is this group assignment from which the new order type will determine its order number.

Scroll the screen and review the default number range groups. If these will not suffice, you have the ability to create your own groups. To accomplish this, use the menu path Group ≻ Insert. An Insert Group box will appear asking for you to provide a name and number range (see Figure 10.35). For complete interval creation details, see Chapter 7. Save the group when you're finished. The next step is to assign the order type to your new group interval.

You will find the new order type ID in the Not Assigned section at the bottom of the Maintain Number Range Groups screen. To assign the order type, select the ID by double-clicking it or by using the select element icon. Next, place a checkmark in the box next to the group to which you want to assign the order type and click the Element/Group button in the header. The order type will move from the Not Assigned category to the proper group interval (see Figure 10.36). Be sure to save the settings when you're finished. Green arrow back to the order type definition screen to continue with the last section of order type configuration.

FIGURE 10.35   The Insert Group box completed for expense projects

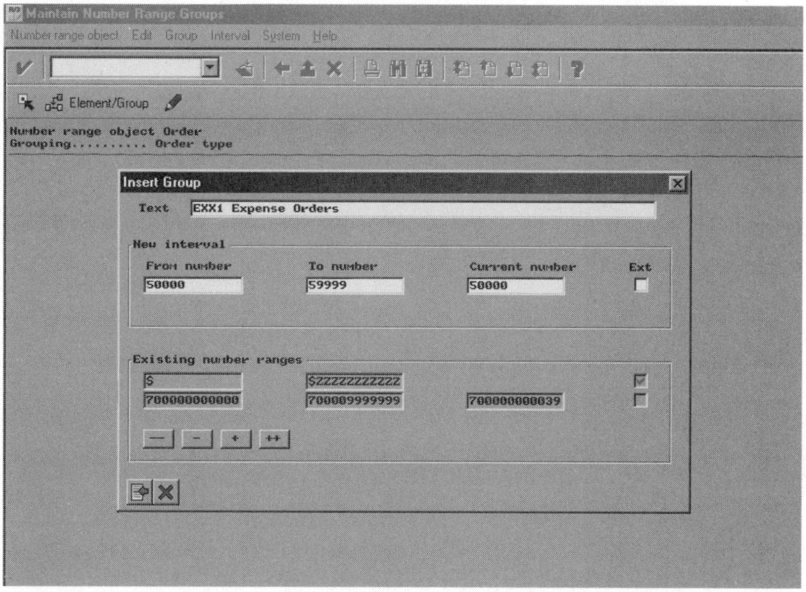

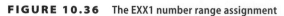

FIGURE 10.36   The EXX1 number range assignment

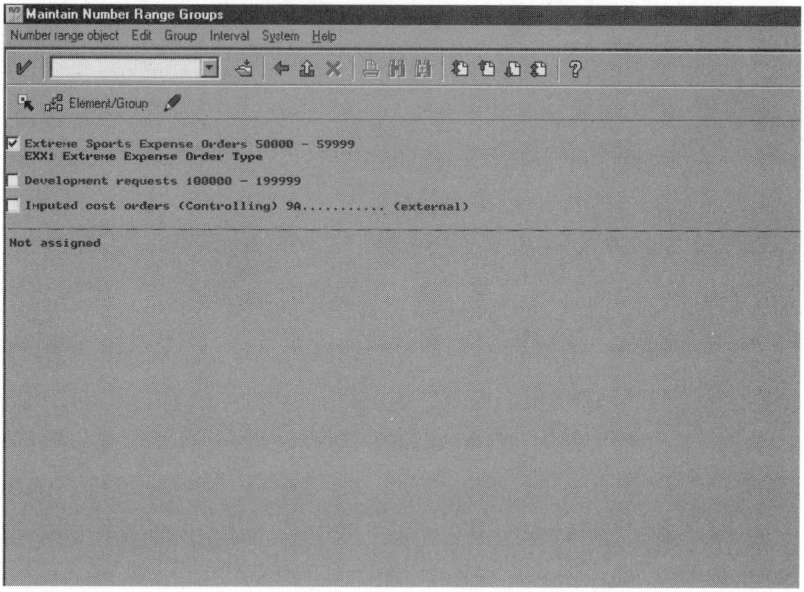

TIP   You will know if the Number Range, Order Status, or Field Selection areas have been maintained if the word *processed* appears next to the button on the order type.

EXTREME SPORTS NUMBER RANGES CONFIGURATION ANALYSIS

Extreme Sports wanted clean segregation for its expense-related projects, so a new number range interval was created. The order number range of 50000–59999 was created and the order type EXX1-Extreme Expense Order Type was assigned. For most internal orders, internal number range assignments, like the EXX1 assignment, is the best solution. In those special circumstances in which the order number must tie to another non-SAP ID, external order numbering may be acceptable.

Field Selection Configuration

For each order type, you must maintain the field selection view before it can be used. The field selection settings offer you control over the order view the user will have during order creation and maintenance. By activating, hiding, or requiring certain fields on the order master record, you can control what information the user maintains. All orders have the same set of fields available to them. To update the field selection, you must be at the maintain order types detail screen.

Select the Field Selection button at the bottom of the maintain order types detail screen. The Change Field Selection screen will appear. Spend some time familiarizing yourself with all the potential fields before continuing. When you're comfortable, begin the field selection process. Here is an overview of the potential settings:

Modifiable Fields   This is a complete listing of each field on the order master record.

Hide   If this radio button is selected, the field will not appear on the order master record.

Display   If this radio button is selected, the field will appear on the order record, but it will be grayed out, so no changes will be allowed. If you are using a model or reference order to create your order, the Displayed fields will not update with any settings.

Input   This is the default setting. If it's left alone, the field will be available for input on the order master record.

Req. (Required) Entry   If this is selected, the field will contain a question mark (?) signaling to the user that it is required.

HiLi (Highlighted)   If this is checked, the field setting will be highlighted on the order master record.

It is always a good idea to minimize the number of fields from which the user has to choose on the order master record. And it is a great idea to make required those fields that you absolutely want completed. The settings can be updated at any time, with a retroactive impact to previously created orders. Figure 10.37 gives you a partial view of the field selection maintenance for order type EXX1. Save the settings when you're finished.

FIGURE 10.37   Field selection settings for order type EXX1

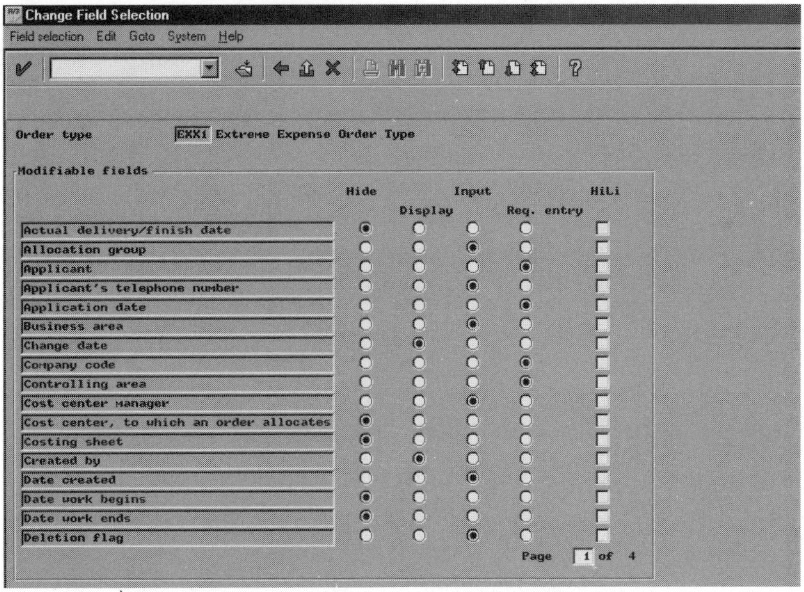

The settings are universally accepted for the order type. But if your solution calls for the use of order status management, you have one more option available to you. This is covered in the next section.

Field Selection for Order Status Management

For those solutions using order status management, a second level of field selection, at the status level, is possible. In addition to the Field Selection button on the maintain order types detail screen, a Field Selection button exists on the status overview screen. If you choose to maintain the order status field selection, it is recommended that you do so cautiously.

The settings on the status field selection screen will supercede the settings on the maintain order types detail screen when it comes to making a field required that was previously not required. It will not, however, remove a requirement established by the details field selection view. Also, with the status field selection settings, you have the authority to hide a field that is required by the details field selection views.

Because this is all very confusing, you should proceed with caution. If used properly, it can be a nice feature to make certain fields required at the different order statuses. But if not watched, it can also shut your order processing down.

EXTREME SPORTS FIELD SELECTION CONFIGURATION ANALYSIS

Because order type EXX1 has chosen to use general status management as its control object, all field selection settings will be made from the maintain order types detail screen. Only the fields necessary for entry will be made available to the user during order creation and maintenance.

Summary

The concepts presented in Internal Order Accounting are new and may be somewhat difficult to grasp. Topics like settlement structures, settlement cost elements, and order types have not been used in many packaged systems prior to SAP. And because of the depth of many of these topics, only one or two examples could be shown. Our hope is that, as with all the chapters, enough detail is provided to lead you to your own conclusions. If you had to pick one area on which to focus the majority of your attention, spend that time with the concepts surrounding settlement. Among all the areas of order configuration, these are the trickiest to master.

For your review, the topics covered in this chapter included the following:

Internal Order Configuration

Controlling Area Maintenance for Internal Order Accounting

Order Settlement Configuration

> Settlement Cost Element
>
> Settlement Structure
>
> Origin Structure
>
> PA Settlement Structure
>
> Settlement Profile
>
> Maintain Number Ranges for Settlement
>
> Order Settlement Configuration Overview

Order Planning and Budgeting

> Internal Order Planning/Budgeting: Basics
>
> Internal Order Planning/Budgeting: Profile Development
>
> Internal Order Planning and Budgeting Number Range Maintenance

Internal Order Status Management

> Order Status Management
>
> General Status Management

Order Type Development

> Define Order Types

CHAPTER 11

Profitability Analysis

FEATURING:

▶ **COSTING-BASED VS. ACCOUNT-BASED CO-PA**

▶ **OPERATING CONCERN DEVELOPMENT**

▶ **CHARACTERISTIC DERIVATION**

▶ **ASSIGNING VALUES TO VALUE FIELDS**

▶ **CO-PA PLANNING**

▶ **ACTIVATING CO-PA**

▶ **CO-PA REPORTING**

▶ **CO-PA TRANSPORTS**

The Profitability Analysis submodule within SAP is also known as CO-PA, COPA, and P.A. In this chapter, we will refer to it as CO-PA. CO-PA gives you the ability to analyze your profitability on many different segments and characteristics. It acts like an information receptacle that can be analyzed from many different angles and viewpoints. CO-PA combines the elements of gross margin reporting found in the SD module with other relevant expenses that you decide to bring over to CO-PA to give you a better view of profitability below gross margin for products, customers, sale organizations, or any other of the many characteristics by which you can report in CO-PA.

Costing-Based vs. Account-Based CO-PA

There are two different ways in which CO-PA can capture and hold data—costing based and account based. The operating concern is the central tenet of CO-PA. The operating concern is the structure that you define to hold data for CO-PA and to use as the basis for reports. An operating concern can use costing-based, account-based, or both forms of CO-PA simultaneously. Both forms use characteristics to store data about the information that is updated in CO-PA. Characteristics comprise such things as customer, sales office, sales group, material number, strategic business unit, company code, profit center, sales employee, controlling area, product hierarchy, and so on. Characteristics will be covered in more detail in the section on operating concern development. The main difference in how the two methods store data involves quantities and values. In costing-based CO-PA, values and quantities are stored in value fields. Value fields group together similar values and quantities—a good way to think of value fields is as large groupings of accounts or cost elements. Value fields will also be covered in more detail in the section on operating concern development. Account-based CO-PA updates values in accounts—the same accounts (cost elements) that are used in FI and the rest of CO.

Costing based is the original method that was created for CO-PA updates and groupings. Costing-based CO-PA is designed to allow you to manage sales based on when sales documents update and when data is transferred from FI and other modules. Normally, the largest amount of data transferred into CO-PA is from SD billing documents. It is important to understand the document flow in SD; the normal document flow is as follows:

1. Sales Order

2. Delivery (the delivery creates the goods issue, which debits COGS, or Cost of Goods Sold, and credits Inventory)

3. Billing document (the billing document updates A/R, Sales Revenue, Discounts, Freight, etc.)

When costing-based CO-PA is used, CO-PA is not updated until the billing document is created—at which time COGS, Revenue, Discounts, Freight, and so on are updated all at once. COGS is updated when the billing document is created because the SD condition type VPRS copies in the COGS from the goods issue. Always remember that costing-based CO-PA follows the final updating document, not necessarily when the account was posted.

Account-based CO-PA was created to allow users to reconcile CO-PA data to FI data. It captures values according to the account posted to instead of value fields. Account-based CO-PA is updated at the time the account is posted to. As with costing-based CO-PA, the largest amount of data transferred to CO-PA is normally from billing documents. Using account-based CO-PA, CO-PA is updated during the delivery (goods issue) and the creation of the billing document. The normal SD document flow is as follows:

1. Sales Order

2. Delivery (the delivery creates the goods issue, which debits COGS and credits Inventory—COGS is updated in CO-PA at this time)

3. Billing Document (the billing document updates A/R, Sales Revenue, Discounts, Freight, etc.)

As you can see, the difference between this scenario and the costing-based scenario is that in costing based, COGS is not updated at the time of delivery (goods issue); it is updated at the same time revenue, discounts, freight, and so on are updated—at the time of billing. In account-based CO-PA, COGS is updated in CO-PA at the time of delivery (goods issue); revenue, discounts, and freight are not updated until the time the billing document is created. This can lead to timing differences when analyzing profitability of certain products. COGS can be overstated at any point in time because it is updated before the revenue that is associated with it is updated, which creates time of delivery (goods issue) versus time of billing differences. This also allows for account-based CO-PA to be out of balance with costing-based CO-PA because of update timing differences.

So which method should you use? It depends on your requirements and uses of CO-PA data. Most companies use costing-based CO-PA because it is more aligned with the true purpose of CO-PA—managing sales profitability information. However, some companies use account-based CO-PA in conjunction with costing-based CO-PA because of the needs of the accounting department that uses SAP to reconcile CO-PA to the general ledger. Because costing-based CO-PA updates based on documents instead of when the currency posts to the G/L, it is a hard battle to fight in terms of making accountants understand that it is not important to reconcile CO-PA to the G/L. Reconciling is not the purpose of CO-PA. Nonetheless, if your users feel compelled to try, it is much easier to do via account-based CO-PA. You can also help mitigate reconciliation fears by making the revenue and sales discount accounts that come off of the billing document post automatically only (see Chapter 3 to find out how to set up your G/L accounts to accomplish this task). If you use both methods of CO-PA in your operating concern, the characteristics that you define are valid for both methods. The difference in the two methods is that costing based uses value fields to update currency values and account based stores currency values in their related cost element. The focus of this chapter will be on costing-based CO-PA. Table 11.1 summarizes when different elements are updated in the different types of CO-PA.

TABLE 11.1   Timing Updates in CO-PA

Element	Costing Based	Account Based
Revenue	Billing Document	Billing Document
Sales Discount	Billing Document	Billing Document
Freight	Billing Document	Billing Document
COGS	Billing Document	Delivery (Goods Issue)
FI Expenses	FI Posting	FI Posting
Internal/Sales Orders	Settlement	Settlement
MM Variances	FI Posting	FI Posting
PP Variances	Settlement	Settlement

Operating Concern Development

As was stated earlier, the operating concern is the central tenet of CO-PA. It decides how the data you capture is stored in CO-PA as well as what characteristics are captured for each piece of data. Before you begin development of your operating concern, it is important to map out what type of data you want to capture in addition to the characteristics that are important to your company for CO-PA reporting purposes. It is easy to add characteristics to your operating concern, but it is very, very difficult to remove them from your operating concern once they have been posted to. CO-PA is also somewhat of a system hog in that it stores redundant data, so it is important to store only the information you really need for profitability reporting more than once. In CO-PA, you also have a fixed number of characteristics you can use in each operating concern. It is a good idea to not use all of your characteristics in your initial rollout of CO-PA. It is always a good idea to leave room for your company to grow and to capture new characteristic requirements as your business grows and changes. It is important to remember that we are demonstrating the configuration of costing-based CO-PA in this chapter.

WARNING   In all versions of SAP, several fixed characteristics are delivered with each operating concern. In version 3.1, you can define up to an additional 30 delivered or user-defined characteristics in your operating concern. In version 4.*x*, you can define up to an additional 50 delivered or user-defined characteristics. Don't use up all of your characteristics at once.

Once you have your CO-PA design completed, you are ready to define the structure of your operating concern. You will recall that the operating concern name (ESOC) was created in Chapter 7 without any of the related structures. To define the structure of your operating concern, follow the menu path Controlling ➤ Profitability Analysis ➤ Basic Settings ➤ Maintain Operating Concern.

You are taken to the Maintain Operating Concern overview screen, shown in Figure 11.1. Extreme Sports' operating concern (ESOC) was selected from the pull-down menu.

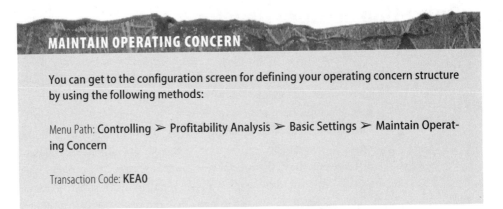

MAINTAIN OPERATING CONCERN

You can get to the configuration screen for defining your operating concern structure by using the following methods:

Menu Path: **Controlling** ➤ **Profitability Analysis** ➤ **Basic Settings** ➤ **Maintain Operating Concern**

Transaction Code: **KEA0**

FIGURE 11.1   The Maintain Operating Concern overview screen

Operating Concern Attributes

The first step in defining your operating concern structure is to define the attributes of the operating concern. The operating concern attributes control the time frame "buckets" in which CO-PA is updated. To create the attributes for your operating concern, click the Attributes radio button and then click the Create button. You are taken to the Create Attributes configuration screen, shown in Figure 11.2.

FIGURE 11.2 The Create Attributes configuration screen

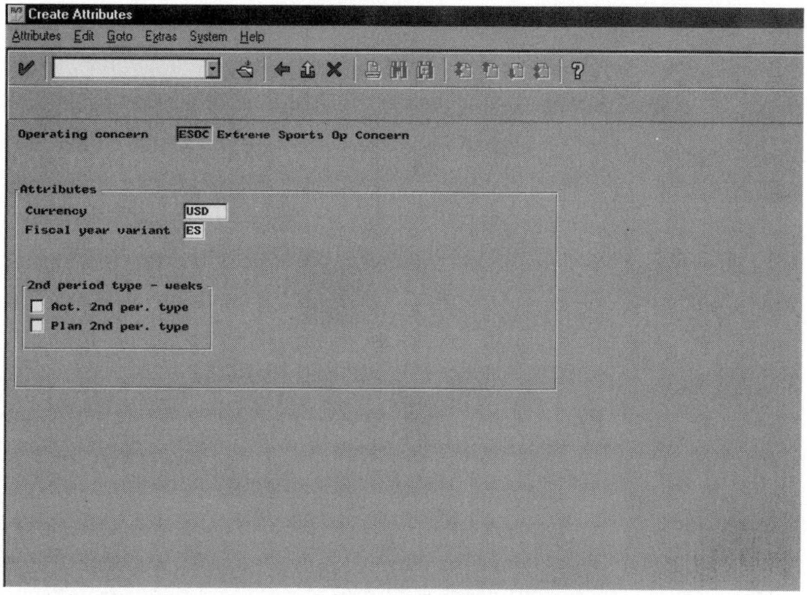

Here are explanations of the fields shown in Figure 11.2:

Currency Enter the identifier of the currency you want to use as the CO-PA currency. When you use costing-based CO-PA, values are posted in the CO-PA currency only; any incoming foreign currencies are automatically translated into the CO-PA currency before CO-PA is updated. CO-PA stores values in only one currency, which is another reason it is hard to tie out costing-based CO-PA to FI. Every time you post a document into CO-PA, a foreign currency translation occurs, whereas in FI and PCA, you can store up to three currencies and can report off of the company code currency.

Fiscal Year Variant Enter the identifier of the fiscal year variant you want to use for CO-PA. Your CO-PA fiscal year variant should match your controlling area fiscal year variant. Once you set the fiscal year variant, it cannot be changed unless it is changed to a fiscal year variant that has more posting periods than the original fiscal year variant that was assigned.

Act. 2nd Per. Type Select this indicator if you want actual data that is posted into CO-PA to be stored in weekly values as well as in the normal period values (defined from the fiscal year variant). Be very careful when deciding whether or not to use this option and the next. Capturing data in weekly buckets can be a real system drag when it comes to reporting, and you'll need additional database storage for the increased data volume.

Plan 2nd Per. Type   Select this indicator if you want plan data that is posted into CO-PA to be stored in weekly values as well as in the normal period values (defined from the fiscal year variant). Again, be very careful when deciding whether or not to use this option.

Once you have configured your options, click the save icon. Green arrow back a screen to the Maintain Operating Concern overview screen (Figure 11.1).

EXTREME SPORTS OPERATING CONCERN ATTRIBUTES CONFIGURATION ANALYSIS

The operating concern of Extreme Sports (ESOC) was assigned attributes in this section. The operating concern currency was set to USD, which is the same as the controlling area currency for Extreme Sports' controlling area EX01. The operating concern fiscal year variant was set to ES. ES is the fiscal year variant utilized by all of Extreme Sports' company codes. It is also the fiscal year variant for controlling area EX01. Extreme Sports does not have any requirements to store profitability data by week. Therefore, both the plan and actual indicators for second period type posting periods were left blank (null).

Creating Characteristics for Your Operating Concern

Now that you have created and saved the attributes of your operating concern, you are ready to create its data structures. The data structure definition controls which characteristics and value fields you will use in your operating concern. Remember, once a characteristic is included in your operating concern and is posted to, it is next to impossible to delete the characteristic. To create the data structures for your operating concern, click the Data Structures radio button and then click the Create button (refer back to Figure 11.1). You are presented with an informational message telling you that the changes you are about to make are valid for all clients. This means that changes are client independent. The operating concern structure is client independent, but it must be generated and activated individually in each client in order to receive updates. CO-PA changes are an eclectic mix of client-independent and client-dependent changes. The nature of CO-PA changes will be explained in more detail in "CO-PA Transports" later in this chapter. After closing the informational message, you are presented with a pop-up box asking you if you want to copy the structure of another operating concern. Select the Do Not Copy radio button and click Continue. You are then presented with yet another pop-up box, which contains the textual name of the operating concern and allows you to select whether you are creating the costing-based or account-based operating concern structure. Select the Costing Based radio button and then click Continue. You are taken to the create characteristics configuration screen, shown in Figure 11.3.

FIGURE 11.3   The create characteristics configuration screen

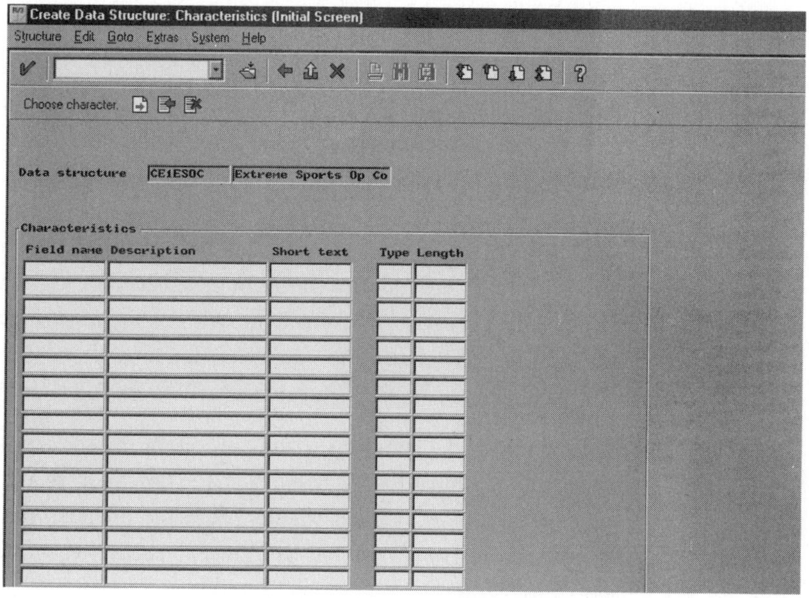

CO-PA comes with several *fixed* characteristics. Fixed characteristics are part of the operating concern and cannot be changed or deleted. To view the fixed characteristics that come with every operating concern, follow the menu path Extras ➢ Display Fixed Fields (from the screen shown in Figure 11.3). You are presented with a screen listing various characteristics. Characteristics of type F are fixed characteristics; they are generally available for your use in drill-down reporting. Characteristics of type T are technical characteristics; these characteristics are stored in line items but generally are not available for reporting. Fixed characteristics come delivered with hard-coded *derivations* that determine how the characteristic value is updated and with what. For user-defined and other delivered characteristics, a derivation needs to be created for the characteristic so the characteristic can be updated with values. Derivations will be covered in detail in a later section in this chapter.

Additional characteristics can be added from already existing characteristics in the field catalogue and from reference tables that can be read by CO-PA, or user-defined characteristics can be added. We will add some characteristics of each type to operating concern ESOC. According to SAP online documentation, you should be able to get all of your profitability reporting needs from an additional 10–20 characteristics. Be careful not to use up all of your characteristics in one shot.

The field catalogue contains all fixed characteristics and value fields, other delivered characteristics and value fields that can optionally be used in CO-PA, and user-defined characteristics (after they are created in an operating concern). In technical terms, the field catalogue is table TKEF. To add a characteristic from the field catalogue, click the Choose Character. button shown in Figure 11.3. Alternatively, you can follow the menu path Edit ➢ Field Catalogue ➢ Choose Charact. You are presented with a list of characteristics included in the field catalogue. If you want to add more than one characteristic at a time, you can select the check box next to each characteristic you want to add and then click the Confirm button, or you can choose just a single characteristic. Once you have selected the characteristics, click the Confirm button and they are added to the list in the create characteristics configuration screen. The delivered characteristics from the field catalogue—Country, Product Hierarchy, Sales Office, and Sales Group—were selected for Extreme Sports' operating concern. The derivation for these characteristics will be created later in the chapter.

You can also add characteristics to your operating concern from reference tables that can be read by CO-PA. To add a characteristic from a reference table, follow the menu path Edit ➢ Reference Table ➢ Choose Field from the screen shown in Figure 11.3. You are presented with the Choose Reference Table pop-up screen, shown in Figure 11.4.

As you can see, you can choose from tables in the customer master record, material master record, SD partner functions, and SD document type fields. Extreme Sports would like to make customer planning group a characteristic in its operating concern. You will recall the configuration and uses of customer group from Chapters 5 and 6. To add Customer Planning Group as a characteristic in the operating concern, we will use reference table KNB1 of the customer master table (company code data). Double-click the table name KNB1 in the Choose Reference Table pop-up screen, and a listing of the fields that are available for use as characteristics in CO-PA appears. We will select field FDGRV (customer planning group). Adding a field from a table to the characteristic list is the same as adding a field from the field catalogue. Once the reference field is added to the characteristic list, you have the option of changing the characteristic field name. You cannot change the data-element name, field type, or length. We will leave the field name (FDGRV) the same.

FIGURE 11.4 The Choose Reference Table pop-up screen

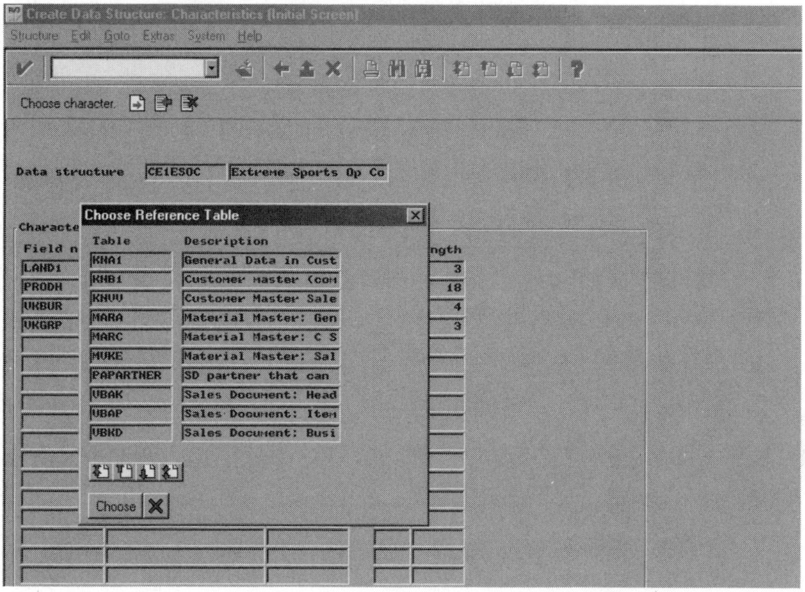

Four user-defined characteristics were also added to the operating concern. To add user-defined characteristics, you need to type in a field name, a long description, a short description, the type of field (numeric or character), and the field length. The user-defined characteristics that were added to ESOC are Product Group, Product Line, Product Category, and Trade Organization. A naming convention should be used for user-defined characteristics to differentiate them from delivered characteristics. The most common industry practice for naming conventions for user-defined characteristics is to begin the name with *WW*. We have followed this convention in the book. The listing of Extreme Sports' additional characteristics is shown in Figure 11.5.

FIGURE 11.5   **Extreme Sports' additional characteristics**

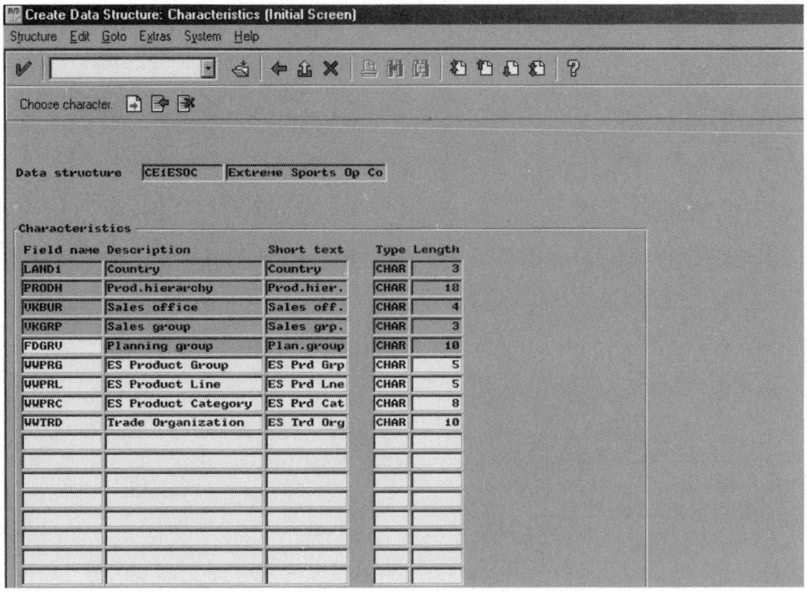

For user-defined characteristics, there are two additional fields that you can configure, which are not shown in Figure 11.5. Click the double right arrow icon on the bottom of the screen (the button is not shown in the screen shot), and you are presented with two additional check boxes: Time and CR. Select the time check box if your characteristics deal with some dimension of time, such as day, week, hour, and so on. Select the CR check box if there is a conversion routine stored in the domain of your characteristic. A good example of the use of this field is to mask leading zeros and display the remaining characters as right justified.

EXTREME SPORTS CHARACTERISTIC CREATION CONFIGURATION ANALYSIS

In this section, you learned that every operating concern comes with fixed characteristics that cannot be deleted or changed. They contain such fields as Company Code, Customer, Controlling Area, and so on. In addition to the fixed characteristics that were delivered with operating concern ESOC, several other characteristics were selected for inclusion. The characteristics Country, Product Hierarchy, Sales Office, and Sales Group were selected from the field catalogue. These characteristics will help Extreme Sports meet its needs for reporting profitability by sales country and

EXTREME SPORTS CHARACTERISTIC CREATION CONFIGURATION ANALYSIS (CONTINUED)

product hierarchy and also provide a reporting structure for its sales department by reporting on sales office and sales group. The characteristic Customer Planning Group was selected from the reference table KNB1. (Customer planning group configuration was covered in Chapters 5 and 6.) Reporting profitability by customer planning group will help Extreme Sports analyze sales by its own customer segmentation strategy and allow it to refine and change customer planning groups as time goes on. The user-defined characteristics Product Group, Product Line, Product Category, and Trade Organization were also added to operating concern ESOC. The Product Group, Product Line, and Product Category characteristics will further help Extreme Sports analyze profitability by its product hierarchy. The characteristic Trade Organization will help Extreme Sports report on sales for different trade organizations, such as NAFTA and the European Union. The population of these user-defined characteristics will be covered later in this chapter.

Creating Value Fields for Your Operating Concern

The next step is to create value fields for your operating concern. As was explained earlier, value fields are what actually store the values (relating to both currency and quantity) in your operating concern. Value fields take the place of G/L accounts for storing currency data. However, creating a 1:1 relationship between G/L account and value fields is not their purpose. A value field should group similar types of currency transactions (such as Revenues, Sales Discounts, COGS, etc.) into one *bucket*. You can also use value fields to store quantities such as sales quantities so you can determine profitability per unit. To create value fields for your operating concern, click the right arrow icon on the top button bar (see Figure 11.5). You are taken to the define value fields screen, shown in Figure 11.6.

FIGURE 11.6   The define value fields screen

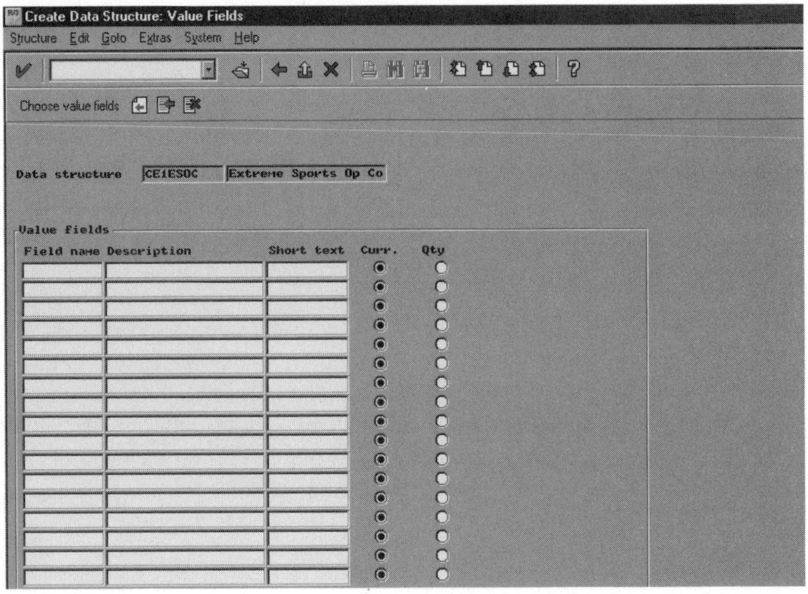

Unlike characteristics, there are no fixed value fields. You must choose each value field you would like to use. But similar to characteristics, there are delivered value fields, which are also stored in the field catalogue. To choose a value field from the field catalogue, click the Choose Value Fields button. The Field Catalogue screen, shown in Figure 11.7, is displayed.

Figure 11.8 displays the value fields that will be included in operating concern ESOC. The value fields Sales Quantity, Revenue, Stock Value, and Outgoing Freight were selected for use from the field catalogue. In addition to the value fields selected from the field catalogue, some user-defined value fields were also created. Those include Sales Discounts, Salesmen Salaries, and Promotional Expenses. As with user-defined characteristics, a naming strategy should be used for user-defined value fields. Normally, user-defined value field names begin with *VV*. This naming convention has been used in this book. In addition to naming the value field, you must add a long description and a short description and select either Qty (quantity) or Curr. (currency).

FIGURE 11.7   The Field Catalogue screen

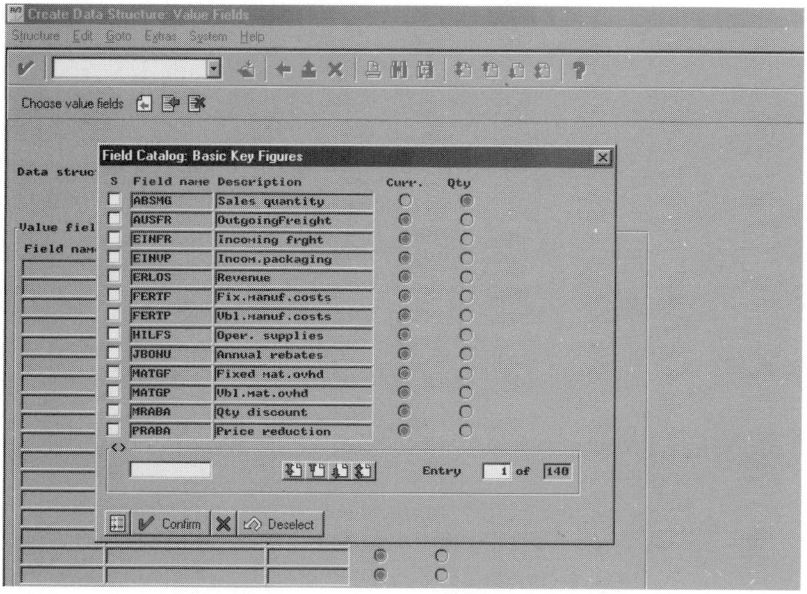

FIGURE 11.8   ESOC value fields

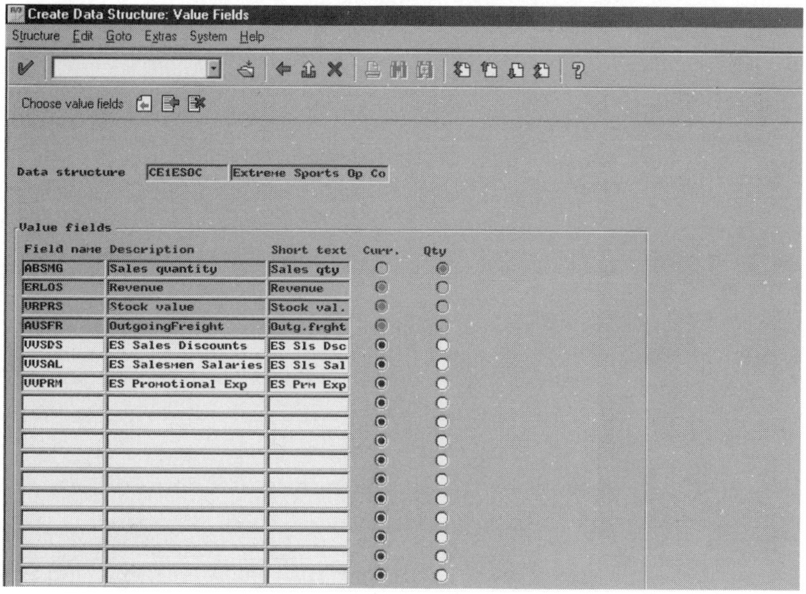

We will show you how to assign values to value fields in "Mapping SD Condition Types to Value Fields (the SD Interface)" and "PA Settlement Structure" later in this chapter.

EXTREME SPORTS VALUE FIELD CREATION CONFIGURATION ANALYSIS

In this section, value fields were created for operating concern ESOC. Value fields store the quantity and currency values of numbers posted into CO-PA. They take the place of G/L accounts and are meant to group similar values together—there should not be a 1:1 relationship between a value field and a G/L account. The following value fields were selected from the field catalogue for inclusion in Extreme Sports' operating concern: Sales Quantity, Revenue, Stock Value, and Outgoing Freight. The Sales Quantity value field will capture the quantity (number) of items that are sold and posted into CO-PA. Extreme Sports utilizes several different revenue accounts for FI purposes. All revenue postings (regardless of account) will be stored in the Revenue value field. The Stock Value value field will store the COGS amount for Extreme Sports' products. The freight that is incurred to ship the product to the customer location will be stored in the Outgoing Freight value field. The following user-defined value fields were included in operating concern ESOC: Sales Discounts, Salesmen Salaries, Promotional Expenses. All sales discounts granted on the billing document (regardless of account) will be stored in the Sales Discounts value field. The salaries of Extreme Sports' salespeople will be captured in the Salesmen Salaries value field via a CO-PA cost center assessment. Any promotional expenses, whether incurred on the billing document or FI, will be stored in the Promotional Expenses value field. This value field will be updated via a PA settlement structure from FI or from a condition type in SD.

Save, Activate, and Generate

Once the characteristics and value fields for the operating concern have been decided upon, the next step is to save, activate, and generate it. We have added characteristics and value fields to Extreme Sports' operating concern, but they are not saved as part of the operating concern structure yet. Before saving the operating concern structure, however, it is a good idea to check it for errors.

To check the structure for errors, follow the menu path Structure ➤ Check from the screen shown in Figure 11.8. You can follow this menu path from the characteristic definition screen as well. If the check program finds no errors, the data structure can be saved. To do so, follow the menu path Structure ➤ Save. Saving the structure saves the definition of the selected characteristics and value fields with your operating concern. Execute the menu path Structure ➢ Save from one of the operating concern structure screens (characteristic definition or value field definition), and a pop-up box appears. The Generate New Check Tables pop-up box, shown in Figure 11.9, informs you that new check tables must be created for some of the characteristics.

FIGURE 11.9   The Generate New Check Tables pop-up box

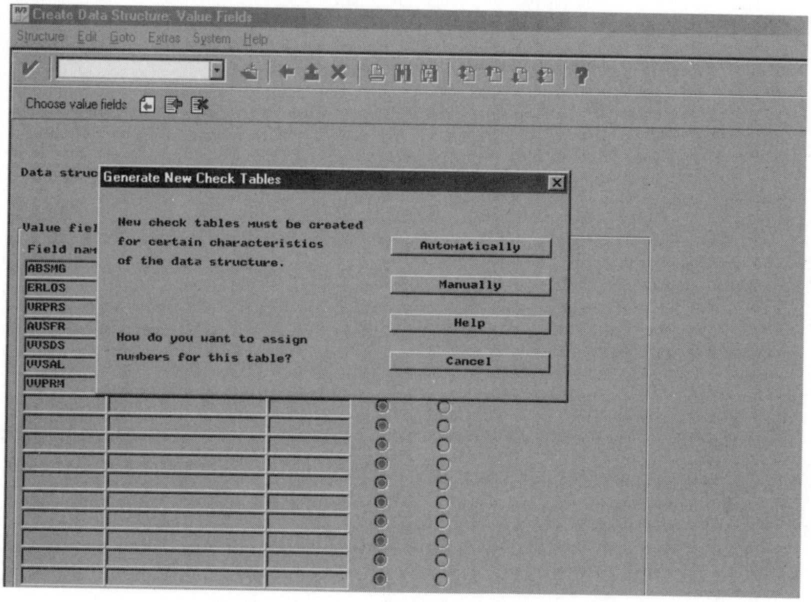

Check tables store the key values for user-defined characteristics that were created in the operating concern. You manually enter the available values for user-defined characteristics in these tables. You can have the system automatically determine the names of the check tables, or you can manually determine them yourself. The names of the check tables are T*xx*, where *xx* is a number. Unless you are using ALE, it is normally a good idea to let the system name your check tables automatically. If you use more than one production system that shares information (ALE), you'll probably want to name the check tables yourself to avoid naming conflicts with the other distributed system. Extreme Sports will allow the system to automatically determine the names of check tables. Click the Automatically button to save the operating concern structure. Once the save operation is complete, the action log for saving and activating the operating concern is displayed. The save log is shown in Figure 11.10.

FIGURE 11.10 The save and activate operating concern action log

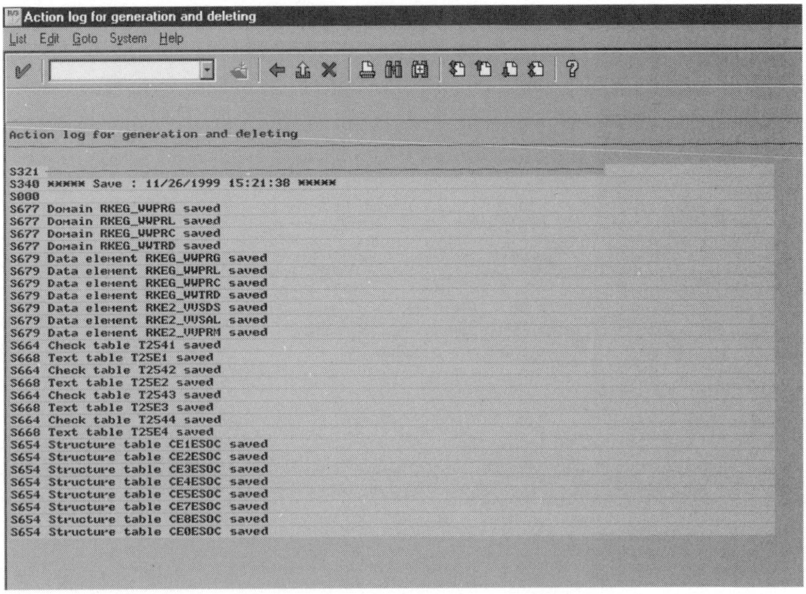

As you can see, domains and data elements were created for the user-defined characteristics and value fields that were included in operating concern ESOC. In addition, check tables and text tables were generated for the user-defined characteristics. Population of the check and text tables will be covered later in the chapter. You will also notice that several tables beginning with CE*ESOC were created and saved in the database. All CO-PA tables begin with *CE* followed by a number and then the name of the operating concern (ESOC in our example). The CO-PA tables that were saved will be explained in more detail in the next section.

Now that the data structure for operating concern ESOC has been saved, it must be activated. Saving the data structure only creates the tables, domains, and date elements in the database. In order for the tables and other elements to be used, they must be activated. Activation lets the database know that the objects are ready to be used in postings. To activate the data structures, you need to follow the menu path Structure ➢ Activate. When this menu path is activated, SAP will generate the appropriate structures in the database and provide you with status information. Once all of the structures have been created and activated in the database, the action log is once again displayed, but this time with new messages telling you that each structure was activated in the data dictionary. Once you have reviewed the logs and determined that no additional action is needed, you can green arrow back out of the log and out of the create value fields or create characteristics screen.

After you exit out of the Maintain Operating Concern overview screen, the Generate Environment pop-up screen, shown in Figure 11.11, is displayed. Select the Yes button to generate the data structures of your operating concern. The generation process may take a few minutes. Once your operating concern has been correctly generated, you should receive the message "Environment of Operating Concern ESOC (your operating concern ID) Has Been Generated Completely." Generating the operating concern creates the internal ABAP programs that are used by CO-PA. Generation is necessary because the table names and structure of the tables are different for each operating concern. After an operating concern is transported, it must generated in the target client. This will be covered in more detail in "CO-PA Transports" later in this chapter.

FIGURE 11.11   **The Generate Environment pop-up screen**

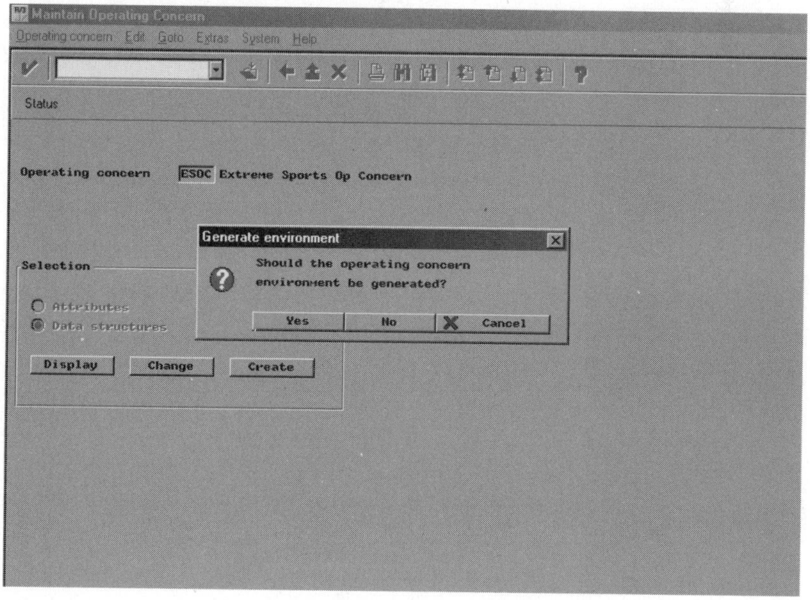

CO-PA Tables

As you saw in the action log in Figure 11.10, several tables were created from the definition of our operating concern data structure. The most important tables in terms of understanding CO-PA will be explained in this section. You should also consult SAP online documentation for further detail.

The core tables that form an operating concern are CE1*xxxx*, CE2*xxxx*, CE3*xxxx*, and CE4*xxxx*, where *xxxx* is the ID of your operating concern. We will begin with an explanation of CE4*xxxx* and work our way back to CE1*xxxx*. As you review online SAP documentation and attend SAP training courses, you will notice that CO-PA is often described as a data cube with a picture of a multidimensional cube. This is a good analogy because that is precisely what CO-PA is—a large data cube. You can slice and dice the data cube every which way to use it for reports and to analyze profitability data. Data is stored in the data cube in profitability segments. Profitability segments are unique combinations of characteristics in your operating concern. Not all characteristics are defined at the segment level (such as the technical T-type characteristics in the field catalogue). You also have the option to include and exclude some characteristics from the segment level. Table CE4*xxxx* is the profitability segment level table. CE4*xxxx* stores each possible combination of characteristic values (as they are posted) and assigns each combination a profitability segment number. Profitability segment numbers greatly enhance performance on drill-down reporting. CE4*xxxx* comes with a standard index and a secondary index. SAP will determine which index provides the best performance.

Table CE3*xxxx* stores data in its first summarized form. Where table CE4*xxxx* stores only combinations of characteristics and creates a profitability segment number, CE3*xxxx* stores the values of value fields along with the profitability segment number. CE3*xxxx* does not store any actual characteristic values (there are no characteristic fields in the database structure of CE3*xxxx*), only the profitability segment number. CE3*xxxx* is also utilized by drill-down reporting to enhance performance.

Table CE2*xxxx* stores plan line item data. This table stores all values—characteristic values, value field values, and the profitability segment for all plan postings in CO-PA. All characteristics, including technical T-type characteristics, are included and posted to in CE2*xxxx*.

Table CE1*xxxx* stores actual line item data. This table stores all values—characteristic values, value field values, and the profitability segment for all actual postings in CO-PA. As with the actual line items table, all characteristics, including technical T-type characteristics, are included and posted to in CE1*xxxx*. You can create drill-down reports from the line item tables (CO-PA drill-down reporting will be covered later in this chapter). You can display line items in CO-PA, but it is a very performance-exhaustive and lengthy process. You should access line items only when you absolutely need to view characteristics that are not part of the segment level.

Besides the core tables (CE*xxxx*) that were described earlier, you will notice that some additional tables were created. These tables all begin T25*xx*, where *xx* equals a number or a letter followed by a number. These tables are user-defined characteristic check tables and text tables, respectively. You will recall from "Save, Activate, Generate" earlier in this chapter that we were given the choice of allowing the system to automatically determine check table numbers or manually assigning them. We chose the automatically create option. The system therefore created tables T2541, T2542, T2543, and T2544. These tables store the valid characteristic values for user-defined characteristics. The tables T25E1, T25E2, T25E3, and T25E4 store the text descriptions of the characteristic values that are defined in check tables T2541, T2542, T2543, and T2544, respectively. The population of these tables will be covered in the next section.

Characteristic Derivation

All characteristics are populated via derivation. All fixed characteristics that come delivered with your operating concern have a set derivation that is used in ABAP code behind the scenes. Derivation of fixed characteristics cannot be changed. For the other characteristics that are added to an operating concern—from the field catalogue, from reference tables, and user-defined—characteristic derivation must be defined. There are three ways to create characteristic derivation: the derivation table, derivation structures and rules, and derivation user-exits.

The Derivation Table

Typically, characteristics added to an operating concern from the field catalogue and reference tables automatically generate a derivation in the derivation table. However, the derivations that are created can be changed. To view, create, and change derivations in the derivation table, follow the menu path Profitability Analysis ➢ Master Data ➢ Characteristics ➢ Characteristic Derivation ➢ Maintain Derivation Table.

MAINTAIN DERIVATION TABLE

You can get to the configuration screen for the derivation table by using the following methods:

Menu Path: **Profitability Analysis** ➢ **Master Data** ➢ **Characteristics** ➢ **Characteristic Derivation** ➢ **Maintain Derivation Table**

Transaction Code: **KE4K**

The derivation table configuration screen, which is displayed after following one of the configuration methods, is shown in Figure 11.12.

FIGURE 11.12   The derivation table configuration screen

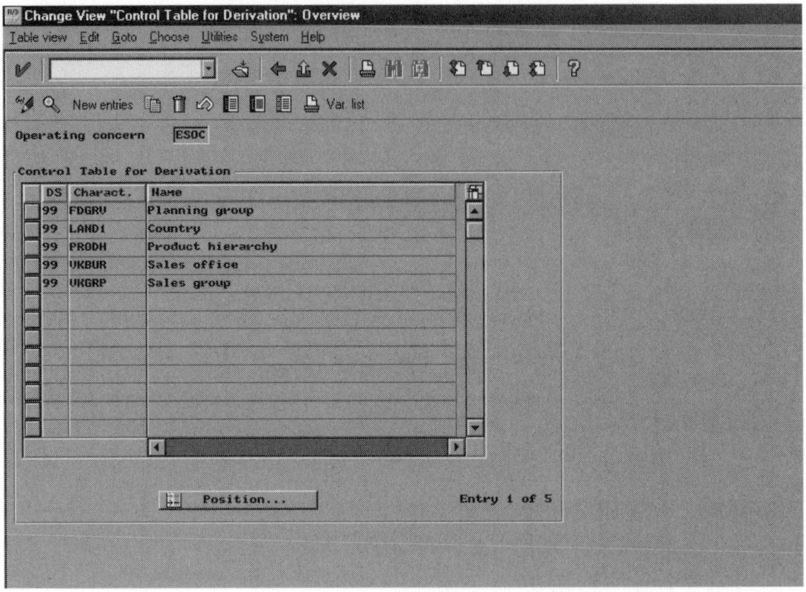

As you can see, the system has already generated entries in the derivation table for the additional characteristics added from the field catalogue and from reference tables. Derivation sequence 99 is generated by the system. If you alter any of the delivered derivations in sequence 99, you could cause posting problems because the system expects to use the derivation that it created. To better understand these entries, let's take a look under the hood of one of them. By double-clicking the PRODH (Product Hierarchy) characteristic, we are taken to the control table for derivation entry screen, shown in Figure 11.13.

You can see that the characteristic Product Hierarchy is derived from the Material Master: Sales Data table (MVKE). The field that is used to supply data from MVKE is PRODH. For SAP to use the master data table for derivation, the table's primary key must be able to be formed from characteristics in the CO-PA line item table. The primary key of the table must be entered in the key fields on the bottom of the screen. In this case, the key field for MVKE is a concatenated key of ARTNR, VKORG, and VTWEG. After reviewing the derivation entry, green arrow back a screen to the derivation table configuration screen (Figure 11.12).

FIGURE 11.13   The control table for derivation entry screen

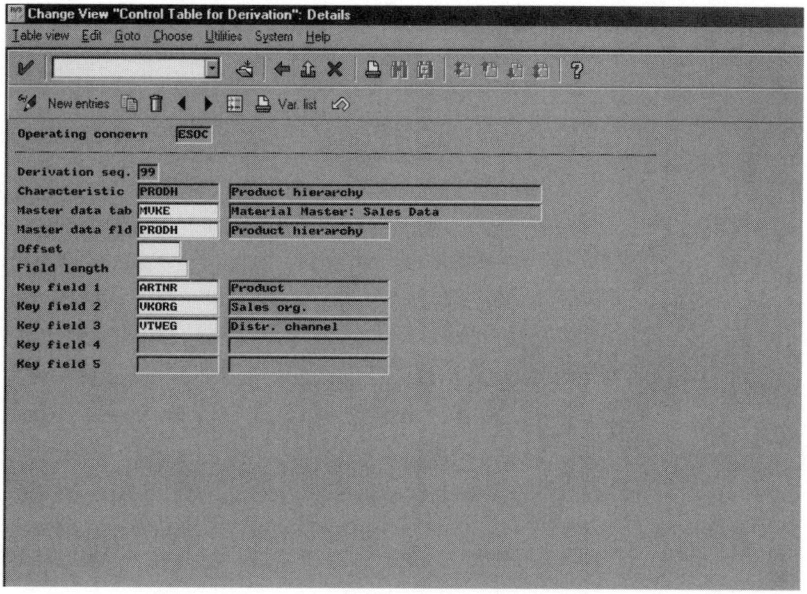

You will recall from the creation of the operating concern data structure that four user-defined characteristics were created: WWPRG (Product Group), WWPRL (Product Line), WWPRC (Product Category), and WWTRD (Trade Organization). We will now create derivation table entries for characteristics WWPRG, WWPRL, and WWPRC. These three characteristics can all be derived from the single characteristic PRODH (Product Hierarchy). We have already looked at the how the derivation for PRODH is performed. Extreme Sports has defined its product hierarchy so that the first five characters of its product hierarchy represent the product group, the next five characters represent the product line, and the last eight characters represent the product category. To create a derivation table entry, click the New Entries button in the derivation table configuration screen (Figure 11.12). You are taken to the create new derivation table entry screen, shown in Figure 11.14.

FIGURE 11.14   The create new derivation table entry screen

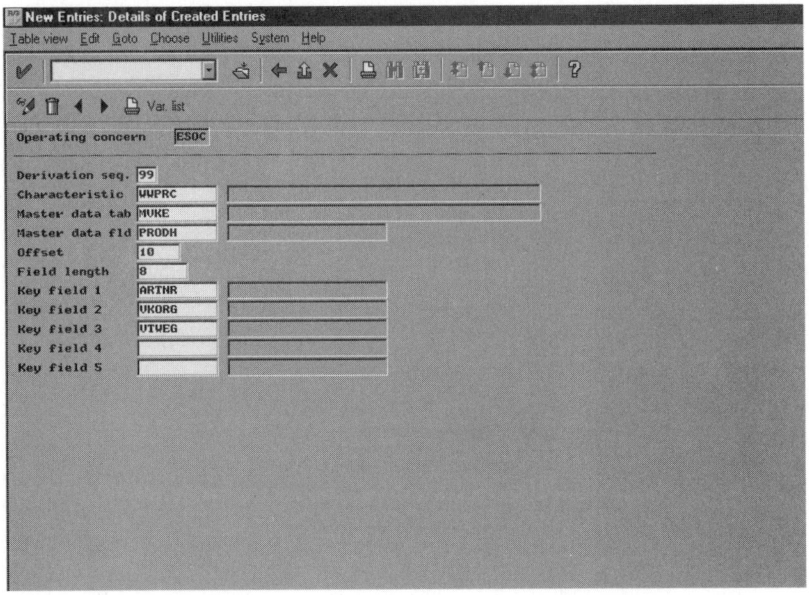

The derivation table entry for Product Category (WWPRC) is shown in Figure 11.14. The existing derivation sequence (99) was used for this derivation. Characteristic WWPRC uses the same master data table, master data field, and key fields as the characteristic PRODH. The difference is that an offset of 10 characters and a length of 8 characters is assigned to this derivation for WWPRC. The offset is given because Product Category consists of only the last 8 characters of the product hierarchy. The offset ensures that we are picking up the correct characters. The derivation table entries for Product Group (WWPRG) and Product Line (WWPRL) are exactly the same as the derivation for Product Category, with the exception of the offset and field length fields. For Product Group, the offset field is set to 0 and the field length field is 5. For the Product Line characteristic, the offset field is set to 5 and the field length field is also set to 5.

EXTREME SPORTS DERIVATION TABLE CONFIGURATION ANALYSIS

In this section, you learned that the system automatically creates entries in the derivation table during operating concern generation for characteristics that were added to the operating concern from the field catalogue or from reference tables. We used the derivation table to create a derivation from three of our user-defined characteristics: Product Group, Product Line, and Product Category. The derivation for these characteristics is very similar to the derivation for Product Hierarchy because each one of these characteristics is a part of the overall product hierarchy defined for Extreme Sports. The derivation table can be used for characteristics that can be defined by one of the master data tables in the pull-down list inside of the table entry and for characteristics in which the primary key of the master data table can be defined by characteristics that occur in the line item table for the operating concern. In addition to these requirements, you can also specify an offset in order to indent the entry and the field length that should be populated for the characteristic. In Extreme Sports' case, Product Group is the first five characters of the product hierarchy, Product Line is the next five characters, and Product Category is the last eight characters. Entries in the derivation table were made for these characteristics.

Derivation Structures and Rules

Another form of derivation is achieved via derivation structures and rules. Generally, user-defined characteristics are derived this way. Derivation structures and rules use values of characteristics that have already been derived in order to derive the value of characteristics that haven't. In configuration, you define the derivation structure that is to be used by the derivation rule. The derivation structure defines the characteristic that is being derived as well as the characteristic(s) from which it is being derived. The derivation rule is maintained by the user and contains the values of the characteristics that combine to derive the value of the characteristic that is being derived. The best way to understand derivation structures and rules is to just jump in... here we go.

To get to the configuration screen for derivation structures, follow the menu path Profitability Analysis ➤ Master Data ➤ Characteristics ➤ Characteristic Derivation ➤ Define Derivation Structures.

DEFINE DERIVATION STRUCTURES

You can get to the configuration for derivation structures by using the following methods:

Menu Path: **Profitability Analysis** ➢ **Master Data** ➢ **Characteristics** ➢ **Characteristic Derivation** ➢ **Define Derivation Structures**

Transaction Code: **KE04 (Create), KE05 (Change), and KE06 (Display)**

You are presented with a pop-up box asking you whether you want to create, change, or display a derivation structure. In this example, we want to create a derivation structure (transaction code KE04). Click the create icon or enter the transaction code KE04 and you are taken to the create derivation structure identifier configuration screen, shown in Figure 11.15.

FIGURE 11.15   The create derivation structure identifier configuration screen

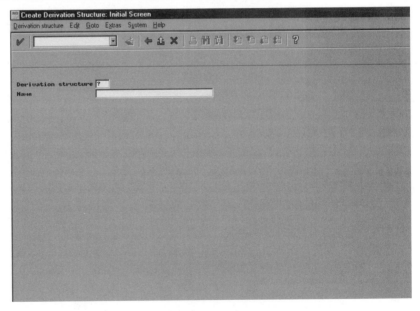

In this screen, you need to define a three-character identifier for the derivation structure and a textual description (ES1 and ES Trade Organization in our case). Press

Enter and you are taken to the create derivation structure detail configuration screen, shown in Figure 11.16.

FIGURE 11.16   The create derivation structure detail configuration screen

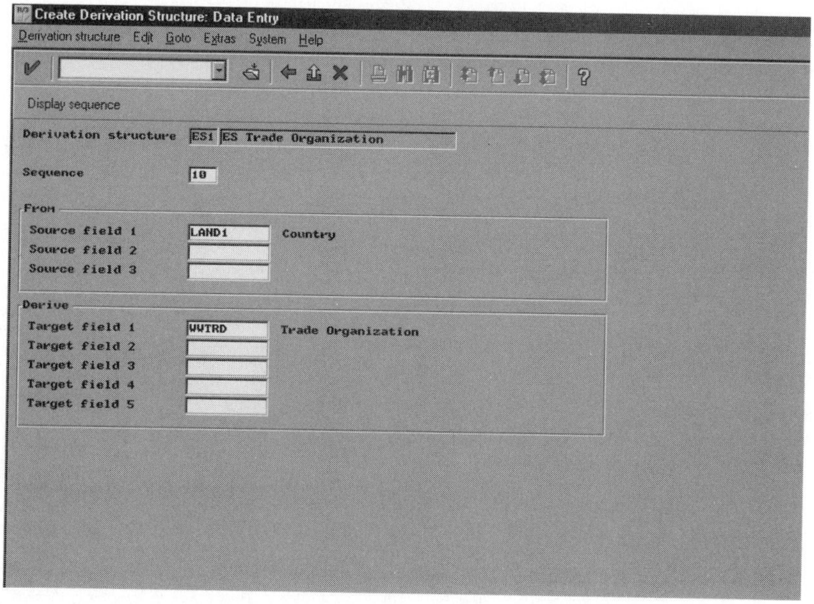

The fields in Figure 11.16 are explained here:

Derivation Structure   The derivation structure identifier and description are defaulted in from the previous screen (the create derivation structure identifier screen).

Sequence   You can have more than one derivation structure in an operating concern. You should have a separate derivation structure for each unique characteristic that you wish to derive from the value of another characteristic. The derivations are executed in sequence from the lowest sequence number to the highest. For example, if you need to derive characteristic Y from characteristic X, and if characteristic X is being derived in another structure, the derivation structure for characteristic X should have a lower sequence number than the derivation structure for characteristic Y. It is a good idea to give sequence numbers in increments of 10. That way, you can move structures around and create new structures later on in the order in which they need to be run.

Source Field X   The source fields contain the characteristics that you want to use to derive the value of the characteristic in question. You can define up to three source characteristics per derivation structure.

Target Field X   The target fields contain the characteristics that you are deriving. You can derive values for up to five characteristics in one derivation structure. Normally, you will have only one target field.

When the information is entered, the structure needs to be saved. To do so, click the save icon. You are then presented with the Table for Derivation Rules pop-up box, shown in Figure 11.17.

FIGURE 11.17   The Table for Derivation Rules pop-up box

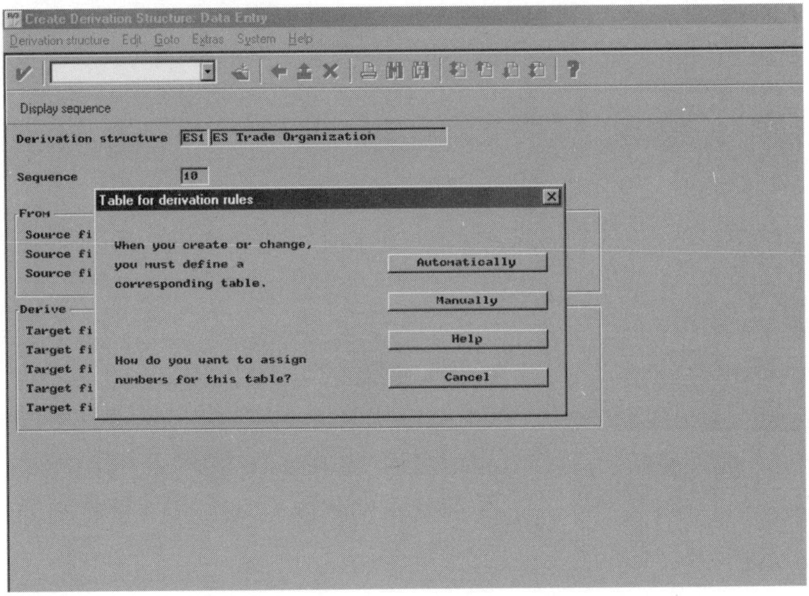

For each derivation structure that is created, a corresponding table is created in the database. The table name is K9*xxx*, where *xxx* is a sequential number that is used for naming the tables. You have the option of having the system automatically assign a table name, or you can manually assign it (the *xxx* numbers only). If you are using ALE, it is a good idea to assign the table numbers manually; otherwise, select the Automatically option. Extreme Sports will allow the system to assign table names automatically.

Before we populate our derivation rule (which is created via our derivation structure), we must maintain characteristic values for the user-defined characteristics that are involved in the derivation structure. You will remember from our discussion on CO-PA tables that the system generated check tables and text tables for each user-defined characteristic in operating concern ESOC. To populate the user-defined characteristic check and text tables, follow the SAP application menu path Accounting ➤ Controlling ➤ Profit. Analysis ➤ Master Data ➤ Charact. Values ➤ Change.

MAINTAIN CO-PA MASTER DATA

You can get to the populate characteristics selection screen by using the following methods:

Application Menu Path: **Accounting ➤ Controlling ➤ Profit. Analysis ➤ Master Data ➤ Charact. Values ➤ Change**

Transaction Code: **KES1**

The populate characteristics selection screen (Figure 11.18) is displayed after following one of the configuration transactions.

FIGURE 11.18   The populate characteristics selection screen

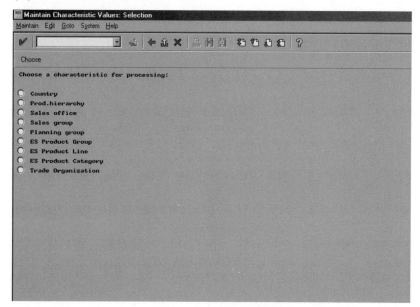

All characteristics, not just user-defined characteristics, are available for selection. You have to be very careful when maintaining characteristics that were created from

the field catalogue and reference tables. These characteristics are generated via a check table by the CO-PA system, but they are maintained by the key SAP table. When you create new entries for these characteristics, you are creating entries in the underlying configuration tables. Because these characteristics often deal with data from other parts of the system (not necessarily FI/CO), it is a good idea to not maintain characteristic values for these characteristics in CO-PA; because you create them here, they are available for use in the rest of the system. You should work in conjunction with the developers in charge of the part of the system from which the characteristic is generated to create the entry in the underlying configuration menu. All values currently in the underlying system table are available to CO-PA. In this example, we will maintain characteristic values for our user-defined characteristic Trade Organization. In order to maintain values for this characteristic, we will check the radio button next the characteristic name and press the Enter key. After selecting the appropriate characteristic (Trade Organization) and pressing Enter, you are taken the characteristic values screen (Figure 11.19).

FIGURE 11.19 The characteristic values screen

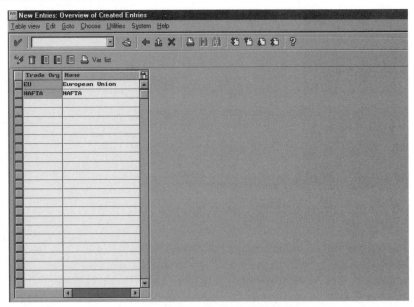

As you can see, we have maintained two values for the user-defined characteristic Trade Organization: NAFTA and EU. These values will be used in our derivation rule. By displaying the technical information on this screen, we see that we are actually maintaining check table T2544 and text table T25E4, which were created when we activated our operating concern.

We are now ready to populate our derivation rule. The derivation rule is the front end of the derivation structure that we created earlier. The derivation rule contains the values that make up the logic of the derivation. The derivation rule is typically maintained by the users and is accessed via the SAP application menu path Accounting ≻ Controlling ≻ Profit. Analysis ≻ Master Data ≻ Derivation Rules ≻ Create.

CREATE DERIVATION RULES

You can get to the screen for creating derivation rules by using the following methods:

Application Menu Path: **Accounting** ≻ **Controlling** ≻ **Profit. Analysis** ≻ **Master Data** ≻ **Derivation Rules** ≻ **Create** (*or Change*)

Transaction Code: **KE07 (Create), and KE08 (Change)**

After entering the menu path or transaction code for creating derivation rules, you are presented with the define derivation rule initial screen, shown in Figure 11.20.

FIGURE 11.20   The define derivation rule initial screen

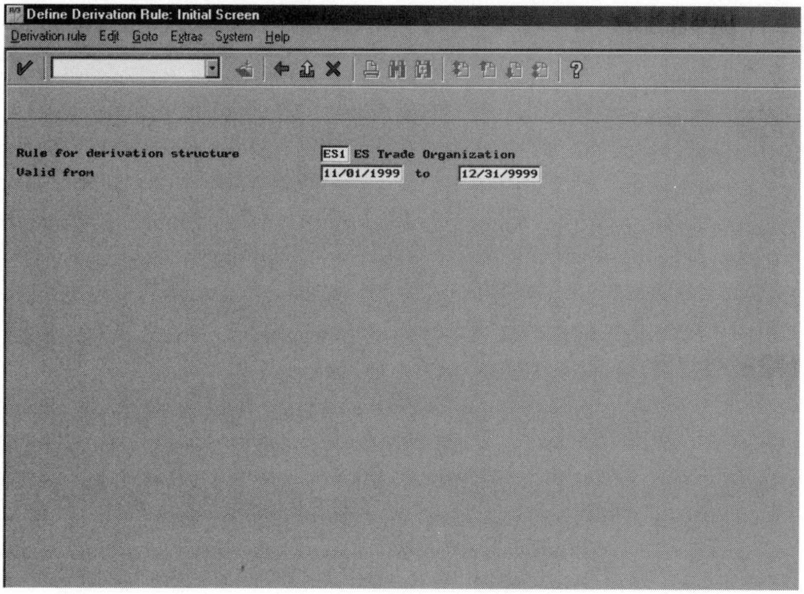

In the screen presented in Figure 11.20, you need to enter the identifier of the derivation structure that the derivation rule is to use, as well as the validity dates for the derivation rule. You can have several validity dates with different values for each derivation rule. After entering the derivation structure identifier and the validity date, click the green checkmark icon. You are presented with the derivation rule entry screen, shown in Figure 11.21.

FIGURE 11.21 The derivation rule entry screen

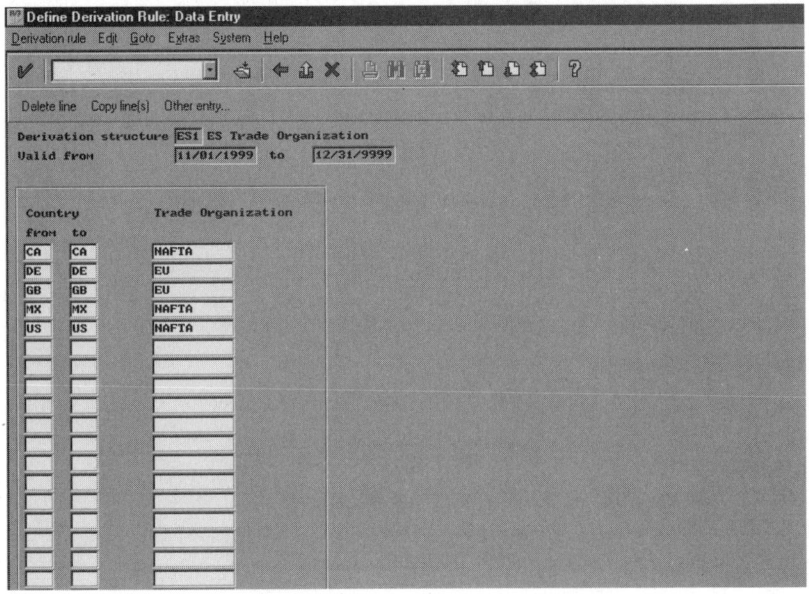

EXTREME SPORTS DERIVATION STRUCTURES AND RULES CONFIGURATION ANALYSIS

In this section, a second type of derivation was configured—derivation structure and rules. Derivation structures are simply the configuration behind derivation rules. They define what characteristics you will be using to derive the value of the target (derived) characteristic. Standard delivered (fixed) and additional characteristics from the field catalogue and reference tables already have characteristic values maintained for them. User-defined characteristics require that valid values are maintained for them

---

EXTREME SPORTS DERIVATION STRUCTURES AND RULES CONFIGURATION ANALYSIS (CONTINUED)

before they are used in derivation rules and before the proper value name will be displayed in drill-down reporting. The user-defined characteristic Trade Organization had values maintained for it in this section. These values will be used in the derivation rule. The derivation rule (which is based on of the derivation structure) was maintained so that different country values derive the trade organization (NAFTA or EU) from values entered in the Trade Organization characteristic value check table.

User-Exit Characteristic Derivation

If the derivation table or derivation structures do not provide you with enough flexibility to derive all the characteristics you need, there is a third option: user-exit characteristic derivation.

SAP comes delivered with two user-exits for characteristic derivation. The first exit is executed before other types of derivation take place (derivation table and derivation structures/rules). The second exit is executed after other types of derivation take place (derivation table and derivation structures/rules). You'll remember from Chapter 1 that user-exits are delivered programs that you are free to program with your own logic. The user-exit code is called from a main SAP program; once the user-exit has finished processing, control returns to the main SAP program. These user-exits provide you with a lot of flexibility to provide values for complex user-defined characteristics that you might otherwise not be able to use. You should consult with one of your ABAP team members if you decide to use one of the user-exits. You can find out more about the user-exits by following the menu path Controlling ➢ Profitability Analysis ➢ Tools ➢ SAP Enhancements.

CO-PA USER-EXITS

You can learn more about/select CO-PA user-exits by using the following method:

Menu Path: **Controlling** ➢ **Profitability Analysis** ➢ **Tools** ➢ **SAP Enhancements**

> **TIP**   Be sure to read the online IMG information about the CO-PA user-exits by double-clicking the task name in the IMG. You will learn that there are user-exits other than just the exits for characteristic derivation available to CO-PA.

Assigning Values to Value Fields

You might still be asking yourself, How do I get currency values into CO-PA if I don't use cost elements or G/L accounts? What's the deal with these "value fields"? In this section, we're going to explain in detail how you transfer currency and quantity values into value fields. There are several different methods: mapping SD condition types to value fields; the PA settlement structure, which maps cost element groups to value fields; and cost center to CO-PA assessments.

Mapping SD Condition Types to Value Fields (the SD Interface)

As you learned earlier in this chapter, the majority of data that is transferred into CO-PA comes from SD billing documents. SD uses conditions to represent different activities when creating a billing document (Revenue, Discounts, COGS, Freight, etc.). The conditions are given values based on the configuration of each condition type (e.g., Revenue condition type is set to $10/unit). You can also map quantity fields from SD documents to quantity value fields in CO-PA.

With a basic understanding of what condition types are, you are now ready to map condition types to value fields. This piece of configuration is the first step in configuring the SD interface. You can get to the configuration screen for mapping SD condition types to value fields using the menu path Controlling ➤ Profitability Analysis ➤ SD Interface ➤ Assign Value Fields.

After following one the configuration methods, you are prompted to enter the ID of the operating concern that you are configuring. You are then taken to the map condition types to value fields configuration screen, shown in Figure 11.22.

ASSIGN CONDITION TYPES TO VALUE FIELDS

You can get to the configuration screen for mapping condition types to value fields by using the following methods:

Menu Path: **Controlling** ➤ Profitability Analysis ➤ SD Interface ➤ Assign Value Fields

Transaction Code: **KE4I**

FIGURE 11.22   The map condition types to value fields configuration screen

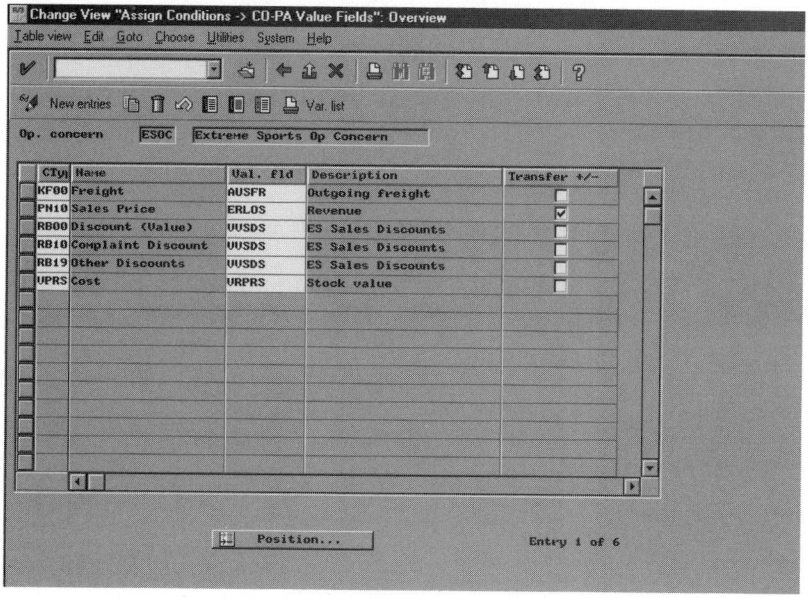

The project team at Extreme Sports has already mapped SD condition types to value fields for operating concern ESOC. To map condition types to value fields, you need to click the New Entries button. After doing so, you can select the correct condition type from the pull-down list (you will need to work in conjunction with your SD team to determine what condition types they are using). You then assign the condition type to a value field that you created earlier. The Transfer +/– field allows you to change the natural sign of the incoming value into CO-PA. For example, if a value normally has a credit balance, it will transfer into CO-PA with a minus sign (standard accounting notation). If you want to transfer the value of a credit balance item into CO-PA without the minus sign, you would activate the Transfer +/− field for that condition type. You have to map every condition type that you are using into CO-PA. If a condition type isn't mapped, you will get an error during billing document creation, and the accounting documents will not be created/posted.

EXTREME SPORTS MAPPING SD CONDITION TYPES TO VALUE FIELDS CONFIGURATION ANALYSIS

In this section, the SD condition types used by Extreme Sports were mapped to value fields in operating concern ESOC. As you can tell from the configuration, many different condition types can be mapped to one value field. Currently, Extreme Sports is using only standard-delivered condition types for the creation of billing documents. After discussions with the SD team at Extreme Sports, it was determined that the following conditions were being used for the reason specified below:

KF00   Outgoing Freight

PN10   Sales Price (Revenue)

RB00   Sales Discounts

RB10   Sales Discounts

RB19   Other Discounts

VPRS   Cost (COGS)

The condition types were mapped to their corresponding value fields in CO-PA. For condition type PN10, which was mapped to value field ERLOS (Revenue), the Transfer +/− field was activated so that the natural balance credit sign (−)would not be transferred into CO-PA.

The next step in configuring the SD interface is to map SD quantity fields to CO-PA quantity value fields. You can get to the configuration screen for mapping SD quantity fields to CO-PA quantity value fields by using the menu path Controlling ➢ Profitability Analysis ➢ SD Interface ➢ Assign Quantity Fields.

It is important to note that the configuration methods in the Assign SD Quantity Fields to Value Fields shortcut box affect a client-independent table. For more information on client-independent transports, refer to Chapter 1. The map SD quantity fields to CO-PA quantity fields configuration screen, shown in Figure 11.23, is displayed after following one of the configuration transactions.

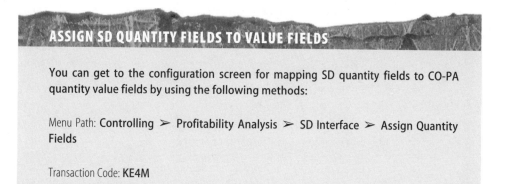

ASSIGN SD QUANTITY FIELDS TO VALUE FIELDS

You can get to the configuration screen for mapping SD quantity fields to CO-PA quantity value fields by using the following methods:

Menu Path: **Controlling** ➤ Profitability Analysis ➤ SD Interface ➤ Assign Quantity Fields

Transaction Code: **KE4M**

FIGURE 11.23   The map SD quantity fields to CO-PA quantity fields configuration screen

The configuration for this step is very similar to the configuration that just took place for mapping condition types to value fields. You have the option of assigning the following quantity fields to CO-PA quantity value fields:

BRGEW	Gross Weight
FKIMG	Invoiced Quantity
FKLMG	Billing Quantity in SKU (Stock Keeping Unit)

KBMENG	Cumulative Confirmed Quantity
KLMENG	Cumulative Confirmed Quantity
KWMENG	Order Quantity
LSMENG	Required Delivery Quantity
NTGEW	Net Weight
VOLUM	Volume

The quantity fields that you use depend on your business requirements. The quantity value fields are used in calculations to determine profitability by sales quantity.

EXTREME SPORTS MAPPING SD QUANTITY FIELDS TO CO-PA QUANTITY VALUE FIELDS

In this configuration step, SD quantity fields were mapped to CO-PA quantity value fields. Currently, Extreme Sports is using only one quantity value field: (ABSMG) sales quantity. Additional quantity fields may be added at a later time. You do not need to be as judicious with creating value fields as you are in creating characteristics. It was determined that the SD quantity field FKIMG (Invoiced Quantity) best matched the quantity needs of Extreme Sports' profitability reporting requirements. FKIMB was mapped to value field ABSMG.

The third and final step in configuring the SD interface is to reset value fields. This activity is optional. This piece of functionality is useful if you have certain types of billing documents that you do not want to transfer into CO-PA. A good example of this might be intercompany sales—you may not want intercompany data skewing your profitability on normal sales. You can get to the configuration screen for resetting value fields by following the menu path Controlling ➤ Profitability Analysis ➤ SD Interface ➤ Reset Value Fields.

After following one of the configuration transactions and clicking the New Entries button, you are taken to the reset value fields configuration screen, shown in Figure 11.24.

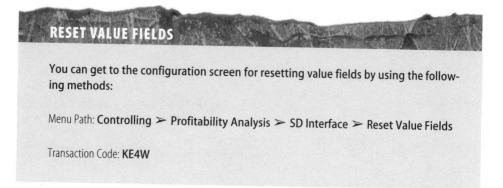

RESET VALUE FIELDS

You can get to the configuration screen for resetting value fields by using the following methods:

Menu Path: **Controlling** ➤ Profitability Analysis ➤ SD Interface ➤ Reset Value Fields

Transaction Code: **KE4W**

FIGURE 11.24   The reset value fields configuration screen

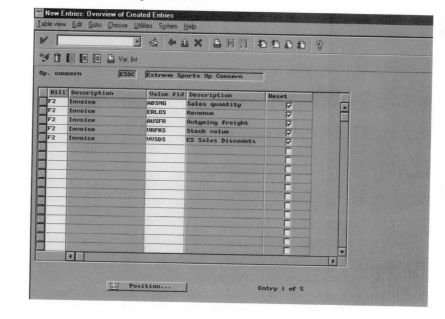

The configuration for resetting value fields is fairly straightforward. You need to select the value fields that are to be reset by billing document type and then activate the Reset field. It is important to note that resetting a value field will not stop a CO-PA document from being created. The CO-PA document that is created will contain characteristic values but will not have any values updated in the value fields that are reset. This can be a little confusing when reviewing accounting document updates from billing documents because, when you look at the reconciliation ledger, it will look like a CO-PA entry has been created and you'll see that a CO-PA document was created.

EXTREME SPORTS RESET VALUE FIELDS CONFIGURATION ANALYSIS

Billing document type F2 is used by Extreme Sports to record intercompany sales. It is not used for any other purpose. The management of Extreme Sports does not want to view intercompany sales information in CO-PA. They want the data in CO-PA to reflect profitability to external customers only. Because of this requirement, every value field was reset to 0 for billing document type F2.

PA Settlement Structure

The concept of CO settlement was covered extensively in Chapter 10. In this section, we will focus on the configuration needed for the PA settlement structure. The PA settlement structure can be used to transfer costs from FI and order-related accounting (internal, SD, SM, and PP).

SAP comes with two shell PA settlement structures: FI and SD. The FI settlement structure is the structure that is always used to transfer costs from FI postings to CO-PA. You can use the SD settlement structure or create your own. For order settlement, you assign the PA settlement structure to use in the settlement profile for a specific order type. The configuration of the FI PA settlement structure and other PA settlement structures is exactly the same. We will focus on the configuration of the FI PA settlement structure in this section. To get to the configuration screen for PA settlement structures, follow the menu path Controlling ➢ Profitability Analysis ➢ Actual Postings ➢ Direct Postings from FI/Internal Activity Allocation from CO.

DEFINE PA SETTLEMENT STRUCTURES

You can get to the initial configuration screen for PA settlement structures by using the following methods:

Menu Path: **Controlling** ➢ **Profitability Analysis** ➢ **Actual Postings** ➢ **Direct Postings from FI/Internal Activity Allocation from CO**

Transaction Code: **KEI1**

After following one of the configuration methods, you are taken to the PA settlement structure listing screen (see Figure 11.25). Despite the menu path alluding to the FI PA settlement structure, as you can see, all PA settlement structures are listed in the PA settlement structure listing screen.

FIGURE 11.25   The PA settlement structure listing screen

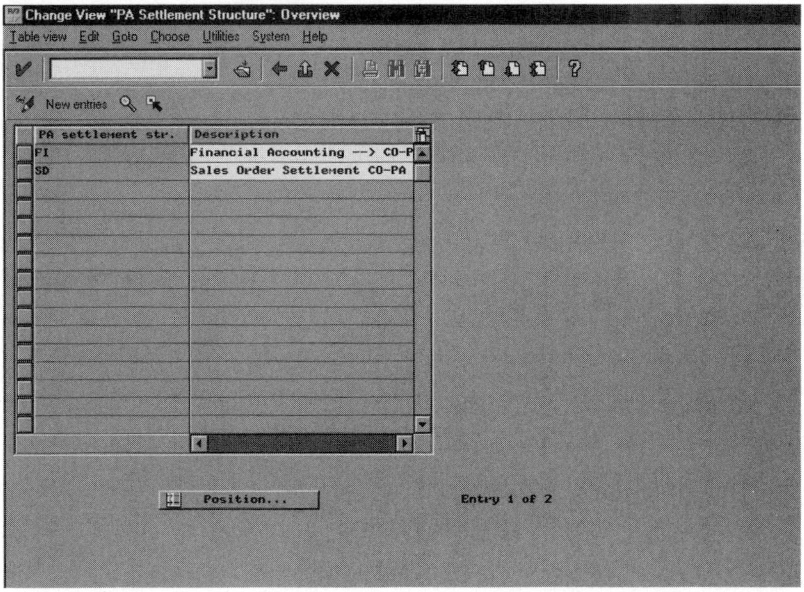

Configure the FI PA settlement structure by double-clicking the FI entry. You are taken to the PA settlement structure assignment configuration screen, shown in Figure 11.26.

FIGURE 11.26 The PA settlement structure assignment configuration screen

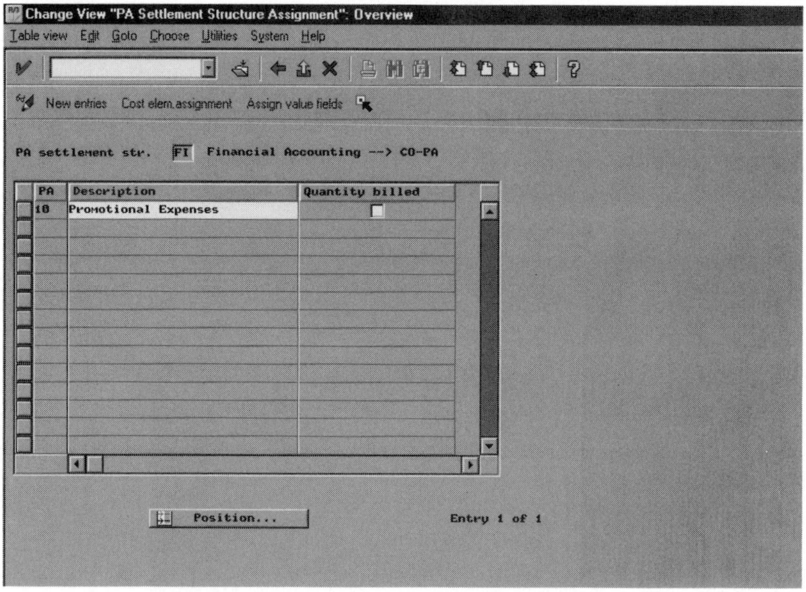

The PA field is for the PA assignment. You should place a numerical entry in this field to distinguish this assignment from other PA assignments. Each PA assignment is allocated a cost element group, which is in turn assigned to a CO-PA value field. After deciding on a PA assignment field name, you should enter a textual description of the type of values that are being transferred in the cost element group for this assignment. By activating the Quantity Billed field, you can transfer quantity values from sales orders. After making the required entries in the PA, Description, and Quantity Billed fields, you are ready to assign a cost element group to the entry. To do so, select the PA assignment field by clicking the gray box next to the entry. Then click the Cost Elem. Assignment button. You are taken to the PA settlement structure origin configuration screen, shown in Figure 11.27.

FIGURE 11.27   The PA settlement structure origin configuration screen

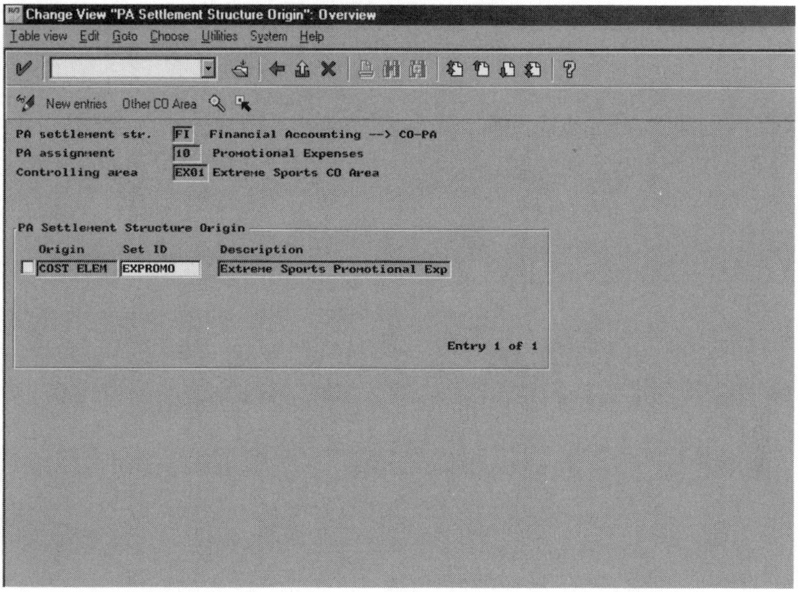

In the Origin field, use the pull-down box to select the Cost Elem entry. This tells the system that a cost element group is being used for the origin (costs to settle). In the Set ID field, enter the name of the cost element group that contains the cost elements you want to map in the PA assignment field. A cost element/cost element group can be assigned to only one value field. A value field, however, can have more than one cost element/cost element group assigned to it. The Description field defaults in from the description of the cost element group. After entering this information, click the save icon and then green arrow back to the PA settlement structure assignment configuration screen (Figure 11.26).

You are now ready to assign the cost element group that was assigned to the PA assignment field entry to a CO-PA value field. To assign the cost element group to a value field, click the Assign Value Fields button shown in Figure 11.26. You are taken to the assign settlement structure line to value fields configuration screen, shown in Figure 11.28.

FIGURE 11.28   The assign settlement structure line to value fields configuration screen

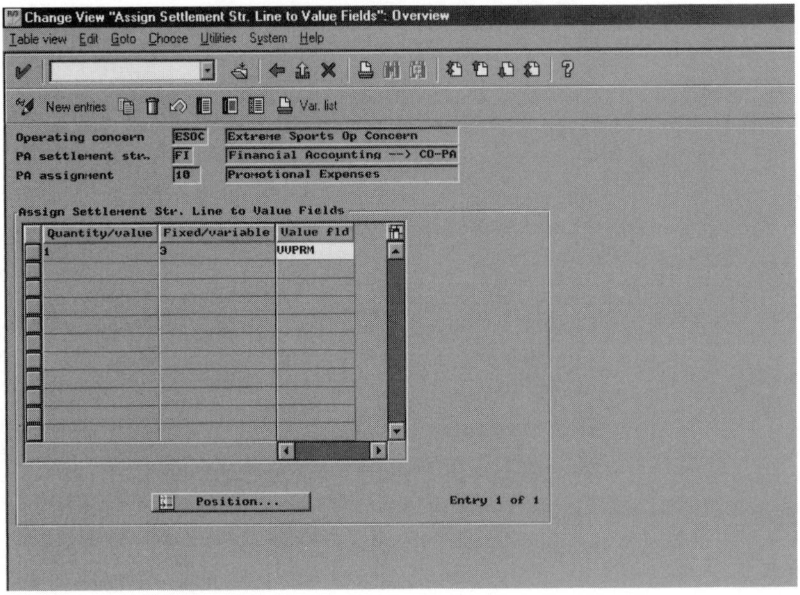

The fields shown in Figure 11.28 are explained here:

Quantity/Value   You have the option of selecting either a quantity or a value indicator (a single PA assignment field can be assigned to both a value field and a quantity field [for SD orders] by activating the Quantity Billed field in the PA settlement structure assignment configuration screen and having a separate line item in this screen for both values and quantities):

1   Value Field

2   Quantity Field

Fixed/Variable   In SAP, you have the option of assigning fixed amounts, variable amounts, or the sum of fixed and variable amounts. If you want to be sure to pick up all values, select the Sum of Fixed and Variable Amounts option. The available entries are as follows:

1   Fixed Amounts

2   Variable Amounts

3   Sum of Fixed and Variable Amounts

Value Fld   Select the identifier of the value field in your operating concern to which you want to assign the cost element group. A listing of value fields is available by clicking the pull-down menu on the field.

Once you have entered all of the fields, click the save icon to record all of your value assignments. Once you have done this, the configuration for the PA settlement structure is complete. Of course, you can always go back and add more entries to the structure if needed.

EXTREME SPORTS PA SETTLEMENT STRUCTURE CONFIGURATION ANALYSIS

In this section, the FI PA settlement structure was configured for Extreme Sports. The only accounts that may receive a direct posting into CO-PA from FI are for promotional expenses. Because of this, PA assignment field 10 was created for promotional expenses. Because these are FI expenses and not revenues from SD orders, the Quantity Billed field was not activated. The cost element EXPROMO, which contains all of the promotional expense accounts for Extreme Sports, was mapped to PA assignment field 10 for promotional expenses. The cost element group EXPROMO was assigned to value field VVPRM (ES Promotional Expenses). These expenses are values, so the option 1 was selected in the Quantity/Value field in the assign settlement structure line to value fields configuration screen. Extreme Sports wants all promotional expenses, regardless of whether they are classified as fixed or variable, mapped to CO-PA. Because of this requirement, option 3 was selected for the Fixed/Variable field. As Extreme Sports' business grows over the years, the FI PA settlement structure will be maintained to mapped additional types of expenses into CO-PA.

Cost Center to CO-PA Assessments

The concepts and configuration of cost center assessments were covered in great length in Chapter 9. In addition to these cost center assessments, you can run cost center assessments into CO-PA. This is a good way to transfer CO expenses that are part of your profitability reporting into CO-PA. Instead of having a receiving cost center, internal order, or cost object, you have a receiving profitability segment (and value field). Some companies choose to transfer all of their P&L (income statement) reporting out of the CO-PA module. The cost center to CO-PA assessment functionality is a necessary tool to allow this to occur. We recommend that all costs have a cost center or internal order as the real account assignment object. You should then settle the costs from the internal order or assess the costs from the cost centers into CO-PA. Making CO-PA the real account assignment object for costs and making the cost center or internal order the statistical posting is a very messy proposition that has a profound impact on the ability to correct erroneous postings.

The concept of cost center assessments has already been covered, so we will focus on the differences between a normal cost center assessment and a cost center to CO-PA assessment. As with most things in SAP, you can get to the same screen in many different ways—thus is the case with defining cost center to CO-PA assessments. In this section, the IMG path is shown as the preferred navigation. However, you can also get there through the SAP application menu. To begin customizing cost center to CO-PA assessments, follow the menu path Controlling ➤ Profitability Analysis ➤ Actual Postings ➤ Define Structure of Cost Center Assessment.

DEFINE CO-PA COST CENTER ASSESSMENT

You can begin the cost center to CO-PA assessment configuration by using the following methods:

Menu Path: **Controlling ➤ Profitability Analysis ➤ Actual Postings ➤ Define Structure of Cost Center Assessment**

Transaction Code: **KEU1 (Create), KEU2 (Change)**

You are prompted with a dialog box asking if you want to create, change, or display an assessment. After choosing the create option (transaction code KEU1), you are presented with a screen asking you for the name of the cycle as well as its start date. This screen should be familiar to you from your work in Chapter 9. Enter the cycle name and start date. You are then presented with the create actual assessments header data configuration screen (Figure 11.29).

As you can see, the only two fields that are different than the fields on the normal cost center assessment header data screen are the CO (controlling area) field and the Tracing Factor field. In the CO field, enter the identifier of the controlling area to which the operating concern is assigned. In the Tracing Factor field, enter a 1 for costing-based CO-PA or a 2 for account-based CO-PA. After entering the required header information, clicking the save icon, and then clicking the Attach Segment button, you are taken to the create actual assessments segment configuration screen, shown in Figure 11.30.

FIGURE 11.29   The create actual assessments header data configuration screen

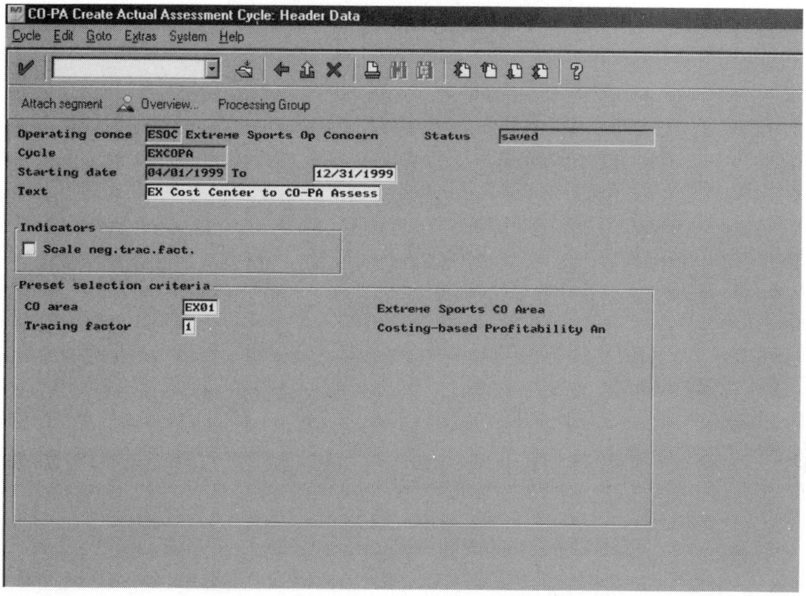

FIGURE 11.30   The create actual assessments segment configuration screen

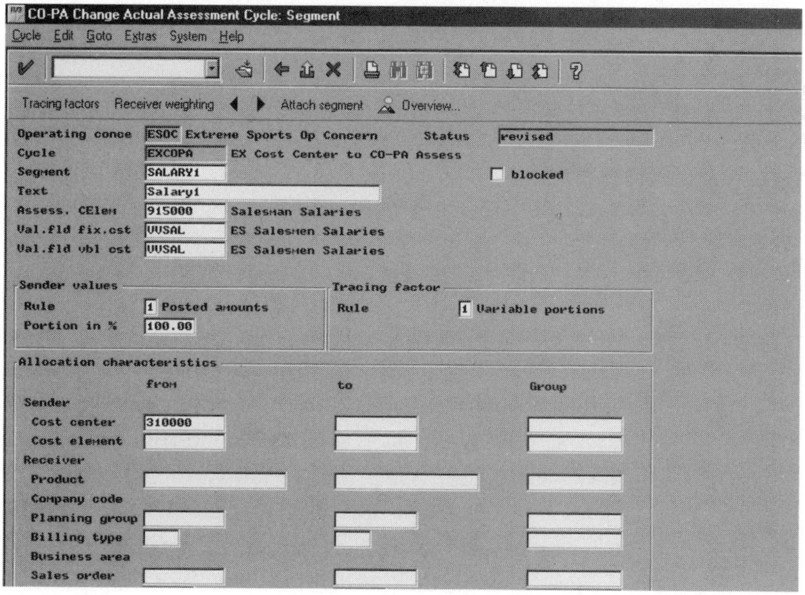

This screen should look somewhat familiar to you. It is the same as the segment configuration screen for normal cost center assessments, with a few exceptions. We will cover the exceptions here. For a detailed explanation of the rest of the fields, please

refer to Chapter 9. The Val. Fld Fix. Cst and Val. Fld Vbl Cst are required fields. In them, you specify the value field that fixed costs should be posted to and the value field that variable costs should be posted to, respectively. Normally, the value field is the same (but it does not have to be) for both fixed and variable costs. The other difference lies in the Receiver fields. The only valid receiver for this type of assessment is a profitability segment. You are able to maintain the exact profitability segment that you want to post to. The remaining characteristics for operating concern ESOC appear farther down on the screen. You are free to define virtually every characteristic except for some of the SAP-delivered characteristics, such as company code and business area. These characteristics are derived in the normal fashion (through standard delivered CO-PA core ABAP code).

EXTREME SPORTS COST CENTER TO CO-PA CONFIGURATION ANALYSIS

The configuration of cost center to CO-PA assessments is very similar to the configuration of normal cost center assessments. The differences lie mainly in assigning a value field(s) and a profitability segment as your receiver values. Some companies use the cost center to CO-PA assessment functionality to bring overall costs into CO-PA for full P&L reporting. Extreme Sports will use cost center to CO-PA assessments for a limited number of expenses from specific cost centers.

CO-PA Planning

CO-PA planning provides lots of functionality to allow you to produce the type of planning needed by your company. Some of the standard features of CO-PA planning include the ability to copy actual values to a plan version, the ability to copy values from one plan version to another plan version, top-down distribution to spread a plan to lower characteristic levels based on past history, and the ability to transfer plan data to Sales and Operation Planning (SOP). The standard functionality just described is by and large end-user functionality that requires to zero to very little configuration. Most of the configuration steps for planning were shown in Chapter 9. In this section, we will address those essential areas that have already been covered, showing the CO-PA menu paths and transactions to achieve the same configuration, as well as some planning configuration unique to CO-PA.

Planning Versions

Planning versions were covered in detail in Chapter 9. You can have several different planning versions activated for a controlling area in a single fiscal year. How you use the planning versions is up to you and the functionality needed by your company (client). As with all CO postings, version 0 is where actual data is always posted. You can also post plan values in version 0. If you want to post plan data to anything other than version 0, you must create a new version. To create planning versions for CO-PA, follow the menu path Controlling ➤ Profitability Analysis ➤ Basic Settings ➤ Maintain Versions.

MAINTAIN PLAN VERSIONS

You can get to the configuration screen for creating/maintaining CO-PA planning versions by using the following methods:

Menu Path: **Controlling ➤ Profitability Analysis ➤ Basic Settings ➤ Maintain Versions**

Transaction Code: **OKEQ (Remember this transaction code from Chapter 9?)**

Planning Revaluation

As with cost center planning revaluation, CO-PA planning revaluation allows you to change plan data without manually rekeying the plan. The configuration for this functionality was also covered in Chapter 9. To configure CO-PA planning revaluation, follow the menu path Controlling ➤ Profitability Analysis ➤ Planning ➤ Planning Aids ➤ Define Revaluation.

DEFINE PLANNING REVALUATION

You can get to the configuration for planning revaluations by using the following methods:

Menu Path: **Controlling ➤ Profitability Analysis ➤ Planning ➤ Planning Aids ➤ Define Revaluation**

Transaction Code: **KEF1**

Planning Layouts

Planning layouts allow the user to enter plan data into the system. The planning layout formulates the screen in which the user enters data. The configuration of CO-PA planning layouts is exactly the same as the configuration for cost center planning layouts, with the exception of the menu path used to create them and the table from which they are built. One other thing you should know about CO-PA planning layouts is that whatever you define as the profitability segment to be planned becomes the selection screen for the planning layout. All pieces (characteristics) of the profitability segment defined by the planning layout must be entered on the selection screen. This means that you may need more than one planning layout if you want to plan at different levels within CO-PA. Some companies do not plan down to the most detailed level; instead, they keep it at a higher level. They then use CO-PA top-down planning functionality to "drive-down" and spread the plan to lower-level characteristics.

As we mentioned earlier, the only configuration differences between cost center planning layouts and CO-PA planning layouts is the menu path and table used to create them. To create CO-PA planning layouts, follow the menu path Controlling ➢ Profitability Analysis ➢ Planning ➢ Manual Planning ➢ Define Planning Layout.

DEFINE PLANNING LAYOUTS

To configure CO-PA planning layouts, use one of the following methods:

Menu Path: **Controlling ➢ Profitability Analysis ➢ Planning ➢ Manual Planning ➢ Define Planning Layout**

Transaction Code: **KE14 (Create), KE15 (Change), KE16 (Display)**

Planning Profiles

Planning profiles tie planning layouts together with the application area to which they relate. As with previous sections, the detail configuration of planning profiles is the same as the configuration covered in Chapter 9 for cost center accounting.

To configure CO-PA planning profiles, follow the menu path Controlling ➢ Profitability Analysis ➢ Planning ➢ Manual Planning ➢ Define Planner Profiles.

DEFINE PLANNER PROFILES

You can configure CO-PA planning profiles by using the following methods:

Menu Path: **Controlling** ➢ **Profitability Analysis** ➢ **Planning** ➢ **Manual Planning** ➢ **Define Planner Profiles**

Transaction Code: **KP34**

External Data Transfer

Finally, a piece of planning we haven't covered before! CO-PA allows you to use external data transfer functionality to transfer both plan and actual data into CO-PA from files created by external systems. The focus of this section will on the external transfer of plan data. The configuration of actual external data transfer is exactly the same. Only the SAP-delivered upload programs differ.

The first piece of configuration needed for external data transfer is your external data transfer structure. The external data transfer structure is actually a table that you (or your Basis team) create. The table is used during the upload program to store data and map fields to profitability segments and value fields. You are free to choose what you put into the table—you definitely need all of the characteristics and value fields that you want to plan with. It doesn't hurt to include more, and it probably isn't a bad idea to include all characteristics and value fields while you are creating the table. In addition to the characteristics and value fields that you are planning on, you must include the version field for planning external data transfer. You are required to enter the proper version on the upload program screen. To create the table, you must have a developer's key. Depending on your project, you may or may not have a developer's key, and your Basis team may or may not want you to create tables. Instead of describing how to create tables, we will focus on looking at the SAP standard delivered external data transfer structure. You probably can't use this structure because the characteristics and value fields in your operating concern will more than likely differ from the example table. To create an external data transfer structure, follow the menu path Controlling ➢ Profitability Analysis ➢ Tools ➢ CO-PA Data Transfer ➢ Define Structure of External Data.

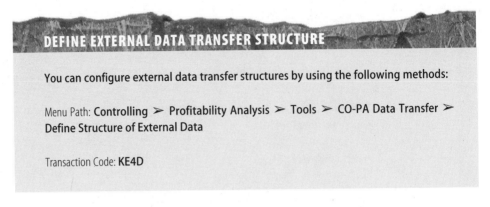

DEFINE EXTERNAL DATA TRANSFER STRUCTURE

You can configure external data transfer structures by using the following methods:

Menu Path: **Controlling** ➤ **Profitability Analysis** ➤ **Tools** ➤ **CO-PA Data Transfer** ➤ **Define Structure of External Data**

Transaction Code: **KE4D**

You are taken to the create external data transfer structure screen (Figure 11.31).

FIGURE 11.31   The create external data transfer structure screen

As you can see, the sample external data transfer structure COPA999 defaults on the screen. As stated before, instead of creating our own external data transfer structure, we will view the sample external data transfer structure. Click the Display button and you are taken the display table/structure data dictionary screen, shown in Figure 11.32.

FIGURE 11.32   The display table/structure data dictionary screen

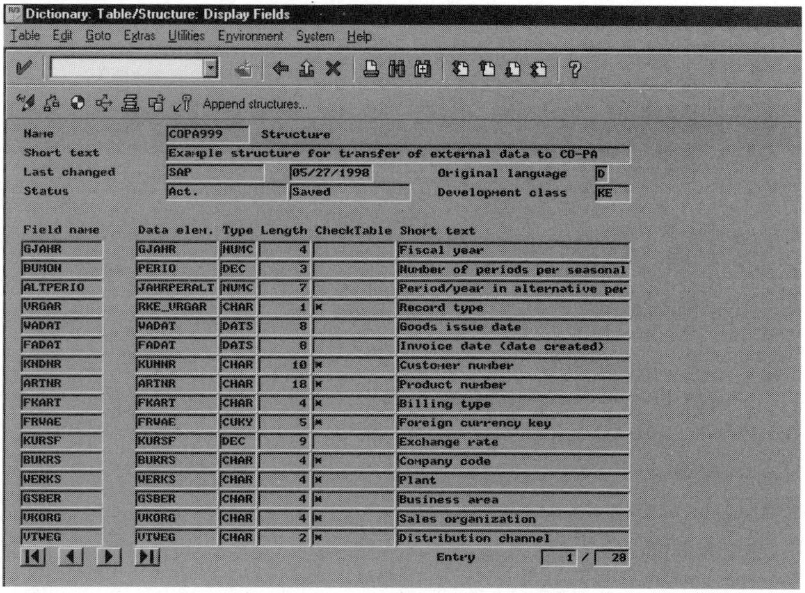

This screen is the same display that was discussed in Chapter 1 (data Dictionary Display). The needed characteristic and value fields are included in the table. Be sure to map all of your needed characteristics and value fields (including the version characteristic) in your table.

The second configuration step for external data transfer structure is to create an assignment group. The assignment group maps the external data transfer structure that you just created with your operating concern. When running the upload program, you will specify the assignment group instead of the table to be used. To create an assignment group, follow the menu path Controlling ➤ Profitability Analysis ➤ Tools ➤ CO-PA Data Transfer ➤ Define Assignment Group.

DEFINE ASSIGNMENT GROUPS

You can configure assignment groups by using the following methods:

Menu Path: **Controlling** ➤ **Profitability Analysis** ➤ **Tools** ➤ **CO-PA Data Transfer** ➤ **Define Assignment Group**

Transaction Code: **KE4Z**

It is important to note that the configuration of assignment groups is client independent. After entering one of the configuration methods and clicking the New Entries
button, you are taken to the create new assignment group configuration screen,
shown in Figure 11.33.

FIGURE 11.33   The create new assignment group configuration screen

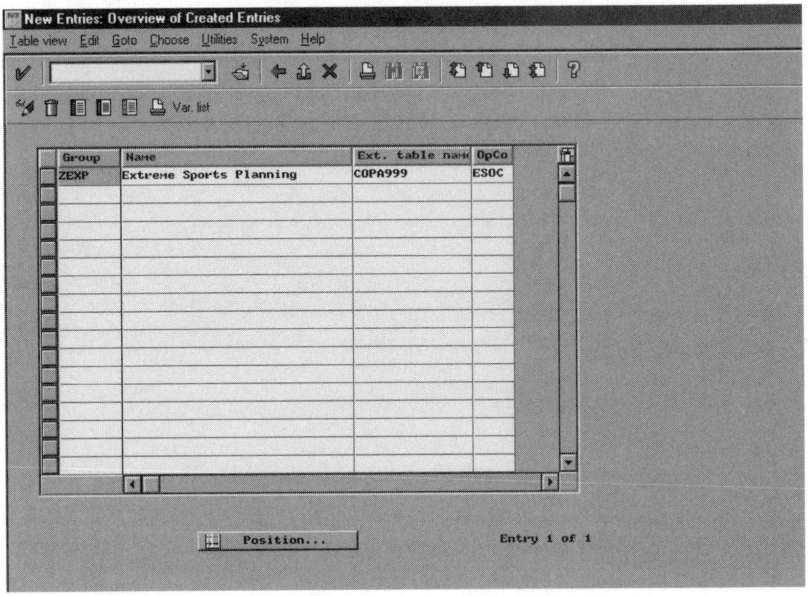

In this screen, you need to create a four-character identifier for your assignment
group. You then define a descriptive name for the assignment group and tie the
group to the external data transfer structure you just created, as well as to your operating concern.

The third and final configuration step for external data transfer is to define your field
assignment. Defining your field assignments is simply mapping fields from the
external data transfer structure (table) to corresponding characteristic and value
fields in your operating concern. This allows the upload programs to post data to the
correct places in your operating concern. To map the external data transfer structure
fields to characteristics and value fields in your operating concern, follow the menu
path Controlling ➤ Profitability Analysis ➤ Tools ➤ CO-PA Data Transfer ➤
Define Field Assignments.

DEFINE FIELD ASSIGNMENTS

You can configure the mapping of external data transfer structure fields to the corresponding characteristics and value fields in your operating concern by using the following methods:

Menu Path: **Controlling** ➤ **Profitability Analysis** ➤ **Tools** ➤ **CO-PA Data Transfer** ➤ **Define Field Assignments**

Transaction Code: **KE4E**

You are prompted for the assignment group that you would like to configure. Enter the assignment group (ZEXP in our example) and you are taken to the maintain field assignments configuration screen, shown in Figure 11.34.

FIGURE 11.34   The maintain field assignments configuration screen

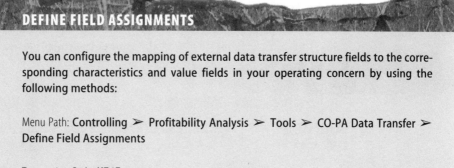

The configuration for this step is fairly simple. You simply need to choose the corresponding CO-PA field name (characteristic or value field) for each field in the

external data transfer structure. Standard delivered characteristics and characteristics added from the field catalogue and reference tables are automatically mapped by SAP. You need to map only your user-defined characteristics and user-defined value fields. This holds true only if you use the same data elements in your external data transfer structure that SAP uses in the CO-PA tables.

EXTREME SPORTS EXTERNAL DATA TRANSFER CONFIGURATION ANALYSIS

Extreme Sports will use external data transfer functionality to load plan data into CO-PA. The plan data will be created in other systems and then exported to a sequential file. The sequential file will then be uploaded into CO-PA via the upload program, which will use the external data transfer structure that is created. The necessary pieces of configuration for this functionality are an external data transfer structure, an assignment group, and mapping fields of the external data transfer structure to CO-PA fields (characteristics and value fields).

Planning Number Ranges

As is always the case, don't forget to assign number ranges. The configuration for number ranges has been covered several times in this book. The unique feature of CO-PA planning number ranges is that you must assign each record type—F (Billing), D (Cost Center Costs), and so on—to an interval. To configure number ranges for CO-PA planning, follow the menu path Controlling ➤ Profitability Analysis ➤ Planning ➤ Define Number Ranges for Plan Data.

DEFINE PLAN NUMBER RANGES

You can configure number ranges for CO-PA plan data by using the following methods:

Menu Path: **Controlling** ➤ **Profitability Analysis** ➤ **Planning** ➤ **Define Number Ranges for Plan Data**

Transaction Code: **KEN2**

Activating CO-PA

Costing-based CO-PA was activated for controlling area EX01 in Chapter 7. CO-PA must be activated in the controlling area before it will work. You can also activate CO-PA in the controlling area by using the menu path Controlling ➢ Profitability Analysis ➢ Actual Postings ➢ Activate Profitability Analysis (transaction code KEKE).

In addition to activating CO-PA in the controlling area, you must assign the controlling area to an operating concern. A controlling area can be assigned to only one operating concern, but one operating concern can be assigned to several controlling areas. To assign your controlling area to an operating concern, follow the menu path Enterprise Structure ➢ Maintain Structure ➢ Assignment ➢ Controlling ➢ Assign Controlling Area to Operating Concern.

ASSIGN CONTROLLING AREAS TO OPERATING CONCERNS

You can use the following methods to assign your controlling area to an operating concern:

Menu Path: **Enterprise Structure ➢ Maintain Structure ➢ Assignment ➢ Controlling ➢ Assign Controlling Area to Operating Concern**

Transaction Code: **KEKK**

The assign controlling area to operating concern configuration screen appears (Figure 11.35).

FIGURE 11.35 The assign controlling area to operating concern configuration screen

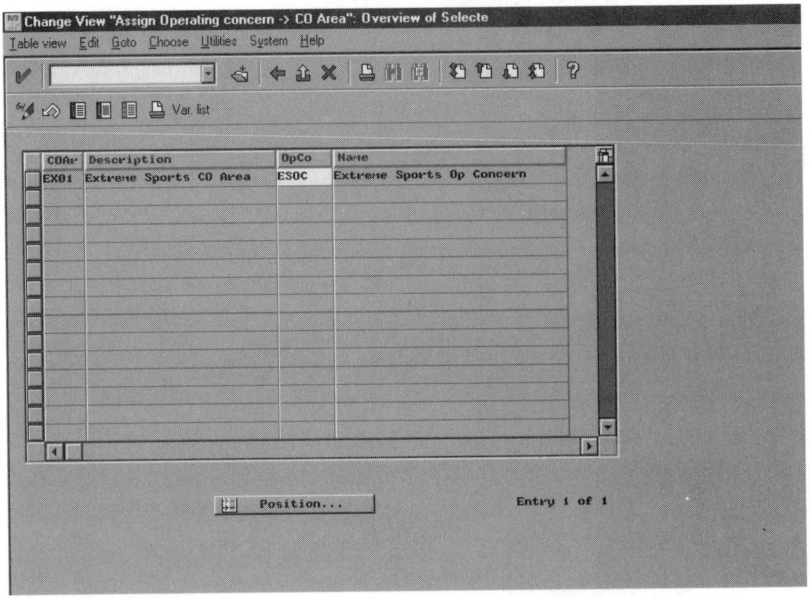

Again, don't forget to assign number ranges. You need to assign number ranges for actual CO-PA postings. To do so, follow the menu path Controlling ➢ Profitability Analysis ➢ Actual Postings ➢ Define Number Ranges for Actual Postings.

DEFINE NUMBER RANGES FOR ACTUAL POSTINGS

You can configure number ranges for CO-PA actual data by using the following methods:

Menu Path: **Controlling** ➢ **Profitability Analysis** ➢ **Actual Postings** ➢ **Define Number Ranges for Actual Postings**

Transaction Code: **KEN1**

CO-PA Reporting

So what do we do with all of the profitability data that we're capturing in our CO-PA structures? How can you report off of CO-PA data? Very simply, with one of the neatest tools in all of SAP: drill-down reporting. Drill-down reporting affords you the flexibility to "slice and dice" your CO-PA data any which way you want, based on your defined profitability segments, of course. Drill-down reporting can also be used in a few other of the submodules, such as Investment Management and Treasury (of course, CO-PA data and profitability segments are not used in these submodules). Drill-down reporting lets you choose the characteristics and value fields that you want to report off of. With CO-PA reporting, you can also drill-down on a characteristic to see other characteristic values associated with it (for example, all materials sold to a specific customer). The focus in this section will be on the creation of drill-down reporting, not how to use the report. Once you build your sample report, be sure to play around with it by running it and trying different drill-downs and features that are delivered within the report.

Generally, there are two different types of CO-PA drill-down reports: basic reports and form reports. Basic reports allow you to select a limited number of variables, the characteristics you want, and the value fields you want. The display of the basic report is generally simpler than that of the form report, and you are more limited in what you can do. Form reports allow you to arrange the data and perform calculations in ways that basic reporting does not allow. In this section, we will create a form report. Once you learn how to create a form report, creating a basic report will be a piece of cake!

Report Line Structures

The use of report line structures is optional. However, we recommend using them. Before we begin, it is important to note that in Release 4.x, report line structures are referred to as key figure schemes. Report line structures allow you to create different "buckets" for your value fields. That is, they allow you to combine and perform calculations on different value fields to come up with a report line structure element to use in a report. When creating a report/form, you are allowed to use either value fields or a report line structure. Report line structures allow for consistency in reporting. For example, suppose you define an element such as Net Revenue. Whenever you choose to use Net Revenue in a report, you know that the report is performing the same Net Revenue calculation as all other reports that use Net Revenue. It can be very frustrating when it appears that you are reporting the same information in more than one report and you get different results. By using report line structures, you can avoid this situation.

Now that you have a basic understanding of what a report line structure is, you are ready to create one. To do so, follow the menu path Controlling ➤ Profitability Analysis ➤ Information System ➤ Report Components ➤ Define Report Line Structures.

DEFINE REPORT LINE STRUCTURES

You can configure report line structures by using the following methods:

Menu Path: **Controlling** ➤ **Profitability Analysis** ➤ **Information System** ➤ **Report Components** ➤ **Define Report Line Structures**

Transaction Code: **KER1**

In the screen that appears, click the New Entries button and you are taken to the report line structure overview screen, shown in Figure 11.36.

FIGURE 11.36   **The report line structure overview screen**

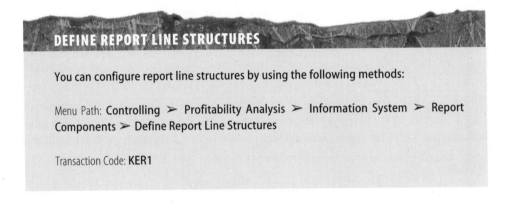

Give your report line structure a two-character identifier in the LS field and a description in the Medium Text field, then click the save icon. Double-click the entry that you just created (EX in our example). The report line structure configuration screen appears (Figure 11.37).

FIGURE 11.37   The report line structure configuration screen

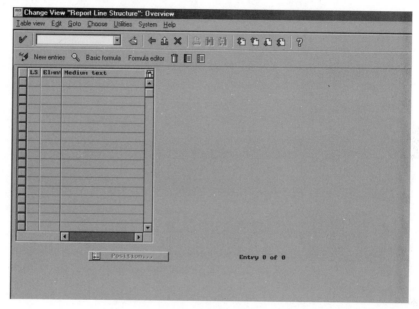

Report line structures contain elements, which are formulas that combine value fields. As you can see in Figure 11.37, the key field for each line is report line structure (LS) and element (Elmnt). To create a new element, click the New Entries button to access the new line element overview screen, shown in Figure 11.38.

FIGURE 11.38   The new line element overview screen

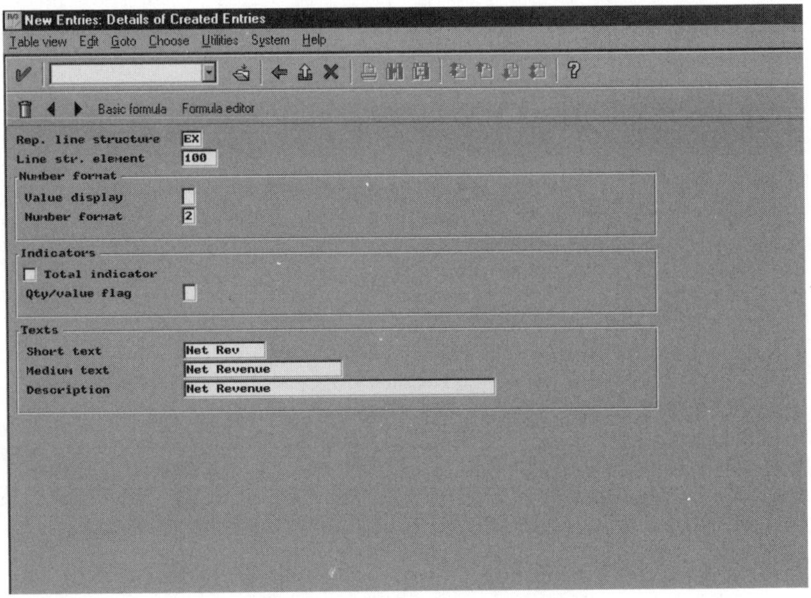

Here are explanations of the fields shown in Figure 11.38:

Rep. Line Structure   The report line structure identifier defaults in based on the report line structure you selected for processing.

Line Str. Element   This is the identifier that makes the formula unique. CO-PA values are automatically numbered by the system in the number range 9001 through 9999. This means that you have the number range 1 through 8999 available to you for naming your structure elements.

Value Display   Using this field, you can force the values displayed by this structure element to default a display factor for this element. If you leave the field null, the actual value will display. Using the pull-down arrow on this field you can make the values display in 10s, 100s, 1000s, and so on.

Number Format   This field controls the number of decimal places displayed for this element. You can choose from 0 through 5. The entry 2 in our example specifies that two decimal places be displayed.

Indicators   The fields in the Indicators section—Total Indicator and Qty/Value Flag—can be chosen if you are using a user-defined ABAP program to perform formula calculations. You do not need to maintain these fields if you aren't. If you are, you already know what these fields are for.

Texts   In the Texts fields, enter descriptions of what the element is used for.

Once you have maintained these fields, you are ready to define the formula that makes your report line structure element. To create your formula, click the Basic Formula button. The line structure element basic formula overview screen appears (Figure 11.39).

FIGURE 11.39   The line structure element basic formula overview screen

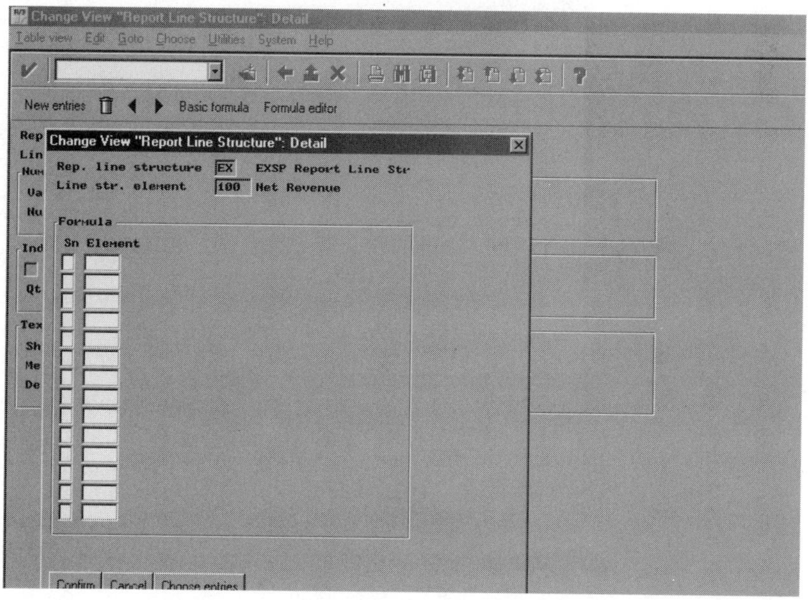

From the screen, click the Choose Entries button. You are taken to the element selection screen, shown in Figure 11.40.

FIGURE 11.40   The element selection screen

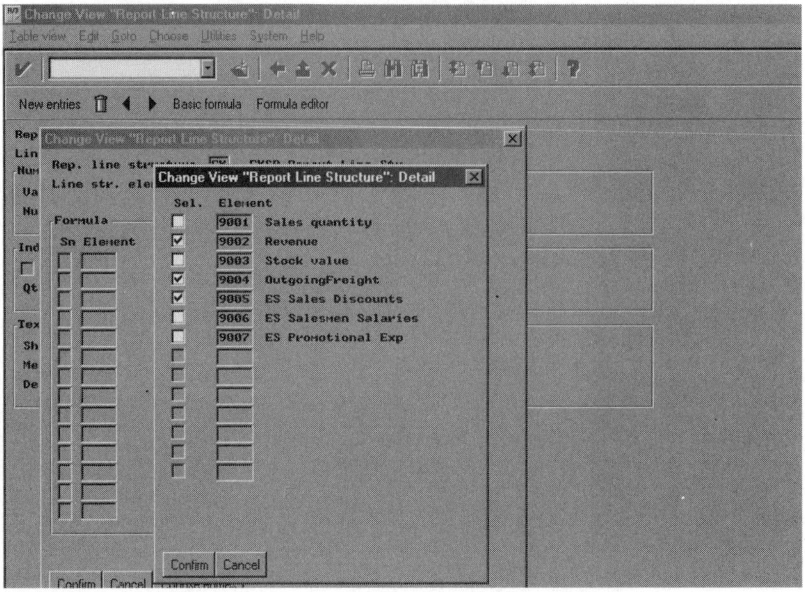

As you can see, all of the value fields in operating concern ESOC have been given an element value between 9001 and 9999. Select the check box next to each value field that you want to use in your formula and then click the Confirm button. When you do so, the values are added to the line structure element basic formula overview screen (Figure 11.39). The updated screen is shown in Figure 11.41.

As you can see, all of the selected value fields are returned to the overview screen. Each value field is defaulted with the + sign, meaning that they are all added together. You can, however, change the sign in this screen to a – sign to subtract values. Multiplication and division can be performed using the formula editor option, which will be explained later in this section. The net revenue element basic formula screen for Extreme Sports is displayed in Figure 11.42.

FIGURE 11.41 The updated line structure element basic formula overview screen

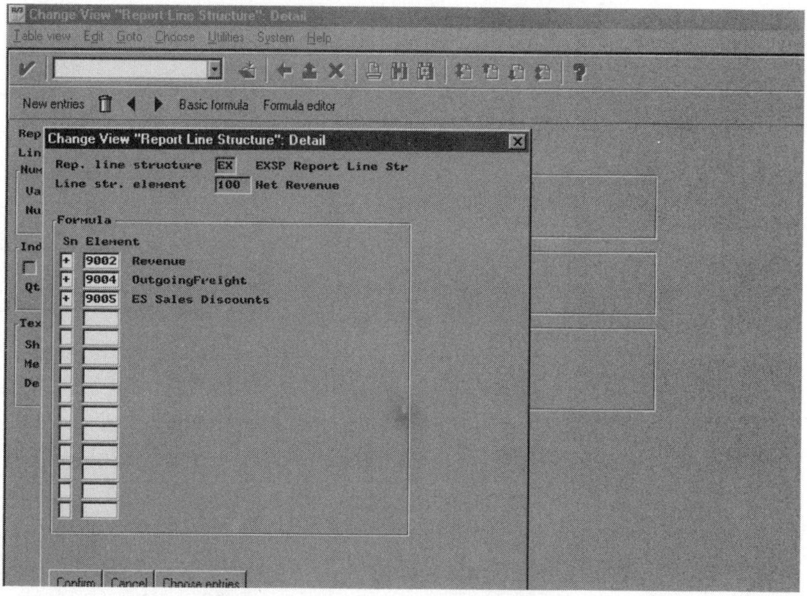

FIGURE 11.42 The net revenue element basic formula screen for Extreme Sports

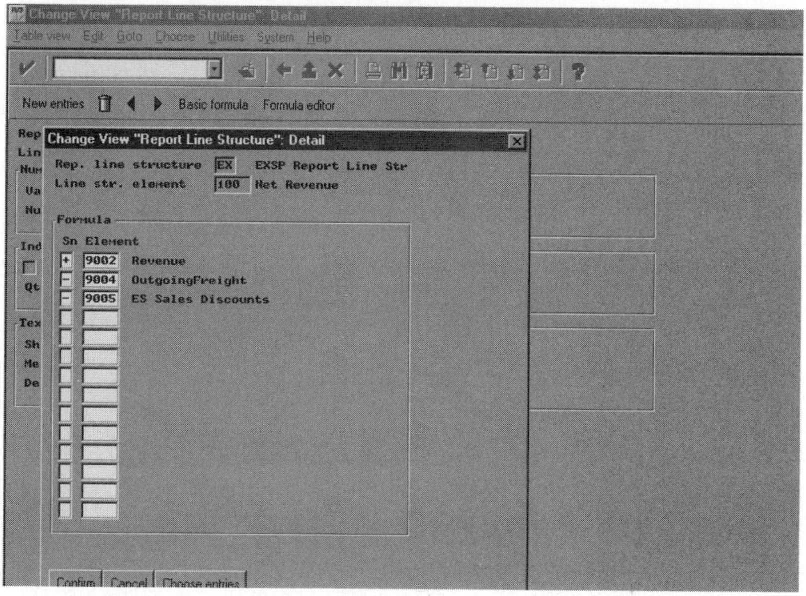

After entering in your formula, click the Confirm button. You are returned to the new line element overview screen (Figure 11.38). From this screen, click the save

icon. Once you do, your element is available for use in the report line structure. It is now possible to select the element that you just created (in addition to value fields) when you create formulas for new elements.

In the preceding example, we created the formula element by using the basic formula option. You can also use the formula editor option to create more complex formulas that use multiplication and division as well as addition and subtraction (which is used in basic formulas). The basic configuration for another element (101, Net Revenue/ Unit) has already been created. As its name implies, we need to perform division to create this element. This can be accomplished by using the formula editor. The simplest way to do this is to select the elements you want to use via the Basic Formula button. Do not be concerned with the + and – signs at this point. After you use the Basic Formula button to select the proper elements and you return to the new line element overview screen, click the Formula Editor button. You are presented with the line element formula editor configuration screen, shown in Figure 11.43.

FIGURE 11.43   The line element formula editor configuration screen

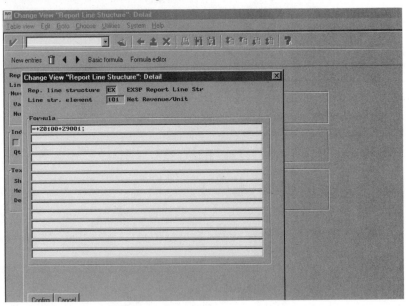

The elements selected—100 (Net Revenue) and 9001 (Sales Quantity)—are already in our formula and are being added together. Because it is a formula, a *Z* is added before each element identifier. From the formula editor screen, you can change the + sign to a / sign to divide Net Revenue by Sales Quantity. Do not forget that each formula ends in a semicolon (;). The system defaults in the semicolon, but if you're not careful, it's pretty easy to overwrite it. The edited formula for Net Revenue/Unit is shown in Figure 11.44.

FIGURE 11.44 The edited formula for Extreme Sports

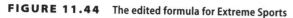

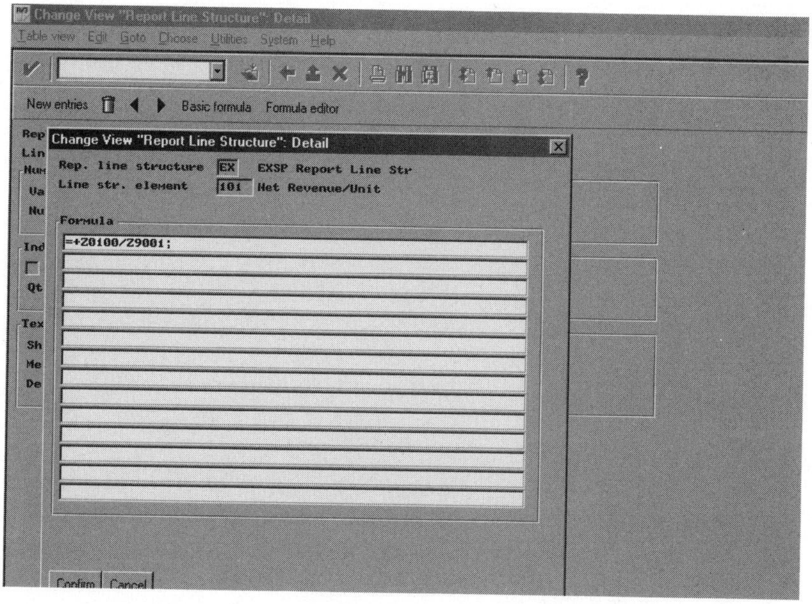

EXTREME SPORTS REPORT LINE STRUCTURE CONFIGURATION ANALYSIS

Report line structures will be in all profitability reports created for Extreme Sports. This will allow for consistency in reporting. You learned that you can use both basic formulas and the formula editor to combine and perform calculations on different values to create report line structure elements. Once you create an element, it can be used in the formula for other elements. Two of the elements of Extreme Sports' report line structure EX were configured in this section. Additional elements that were not shown were also created to be used later in reporting.

Forms

Forms allow you to group data and perform calculations in the way that you want on a report. They also define the variables that are used to select data, as well as whether you are bringing plan values, actual values, or both. When you create a report, you reference a form (in our example). Each report can use only one form, but a form can be used by many reports.

Let's jump in. To create a form, follow the menu path Controlling ➤ Profitability Analysis ➤ Information System ➤ Report Components ➤ Define Forms.

DEFINE FORMS

You can configure forms by using the following methods:

Menu Path: **Controlling** ➤ **Profitability Analysis** ➤ **Information System** ➤ **Report Components** ➤ **Define Forms**

Transaction Code: **KE34 (Create), KE35 (Change), KE36 (Display)**

After following the menu path and clicking the create icon or executing transaction code KE34, you are taken to the CO-PA create form configuration screen, shown in Figure 11.45.

FIGURE 11.45   The CO-PA create form configuration screen

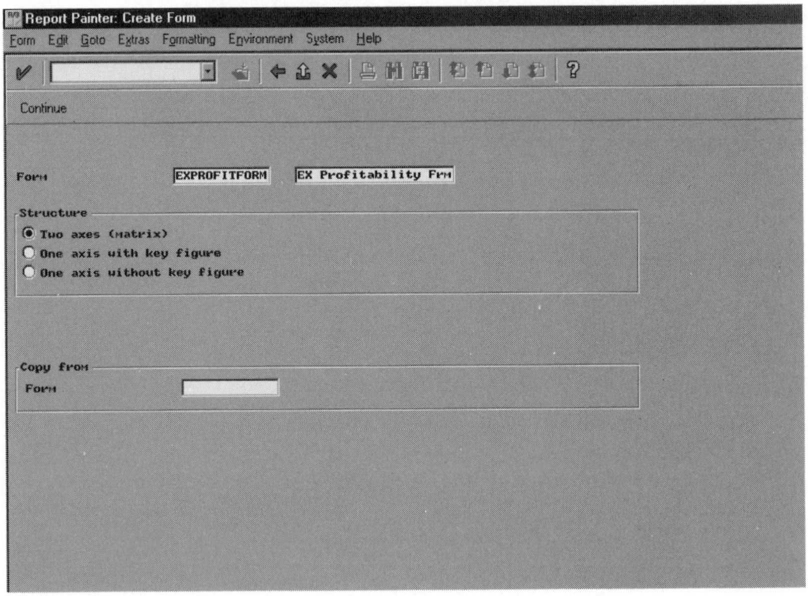

In this screen, you need to define a form identifier (EXPROFITFORM in our example) and enter a description for the form (EX Profitability Frm in our example). You will also notice that you have the option of creating one of three types of forms:

► Two axes (matrix)

► One axis with key figure

► One axis without key figure

The two axes form is by far the most flexible of the three types. Using the matrix form (two axes), you are able to define both the row and column structure of your report. In this type of form, you can choose characteristics, value fields, elements of a report line structure, predefined elements, or a formula. As always, you choose the characteristics to be used by the drill-down structure in the report creation itself. We will use a matrix form in our example.

The one axis with key figure form allows you to define either the row structure or the column structure. The default screen is to define rows, but you can define columns instead by following the menu path Goto ➢ Column Display from within the form. In this type of form, you can choose value fields, elements of a report line structure, predefined elements, or a formula.

The one axis without key figure form allows you to define either the row structure or the column structure. The default screen is to define columns, but you can define rows instead by following the menu path Goto ➢ Row Display from within the form. In this type of form, you cannot choose value fields or elements of a report line structure; you can only choose characteristics.

Now let's continue with our example and create our matrix form. From the CO-PA create form configuration screen (Figure 11.45), press Enter and you are presented with the create CO-PA form definition configuration screen, which is shown in Figure 11.46.

FIGURE 11.46   The create CO-PA form definition configuration screen

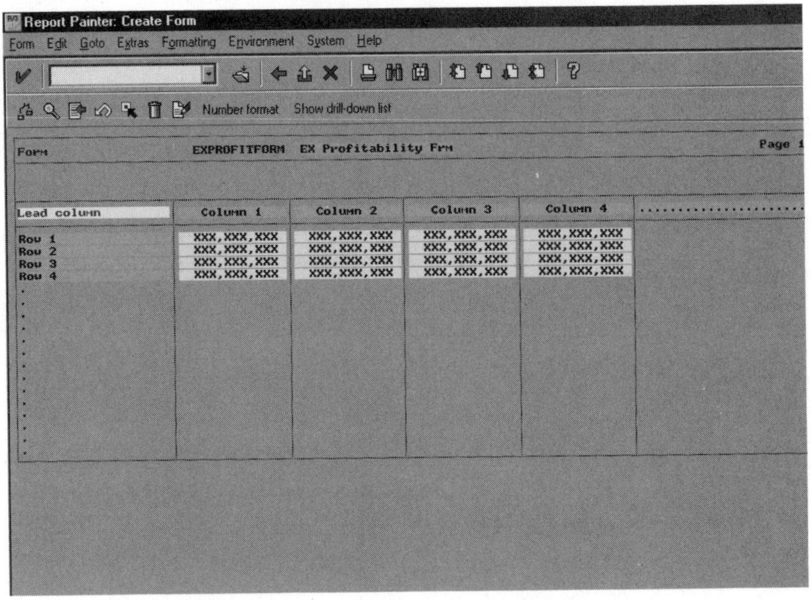

You are free to create both the row and column structure of the report because this is a matrix (two axes) report. When you create your row and column structure, you are creating your detail list. For this form, Extreme Sports would like the detail list to resemble a normal financial statement with different values listed as the rows and Actual, Plan, and Variance Amounts as the columns. Let's begin by defining our rows. Double-click the field that says Row 1. The Select Element Type pop-up screen appears, as shown in Figure 11.47.

We will select the Element of Line Str. option to keep in accordance with Extreme Sports' requirement of ensuring data integrity across reports. Press Enter and you are presented with a list of report line structures that have been created for your operating concern. After selecting the appropriate report line structure (EX in our case) and pressing Enter, you are presented with the listing of elements in the Value Fields pop-up screen, shown in Figure 11.48.

FIGURE 11.47   The Select Element Type pop-up screen

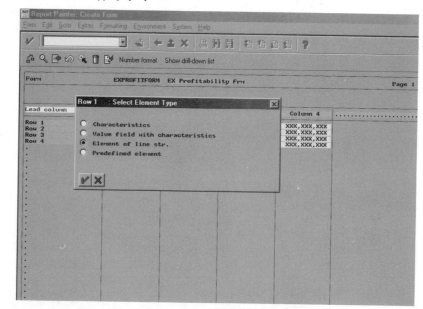

FIGURE 11.48   The listing of elements in the Value Fields pop-up screen

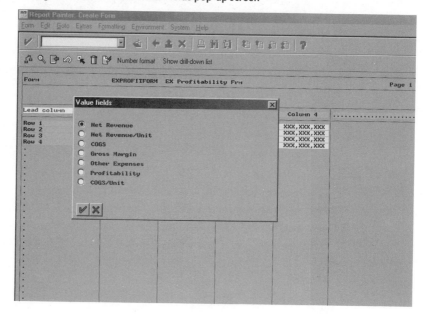

The screen presented in Figure 11.48 should look familiar because it lists the elements (plus a few) that we created for our report line structure. In this example, we will select the Net Revenue element radio button. After selecting the radio button and pressing Enter, you are presented with a listing of characteristics that you can choose to be processed with the report line structure element. You only need to select characteristics that are unique to the report line structure element. Characteristics will also be selected in the column structure (for plan and actual values in this example), and characteristics that relate to the entire form are defined in the general data selection of the form (the general data selection will be explained later in this section). The characteristic selection screen is shown in Figure 11.49.

FIGURE 11.49   The characteristic selection screen

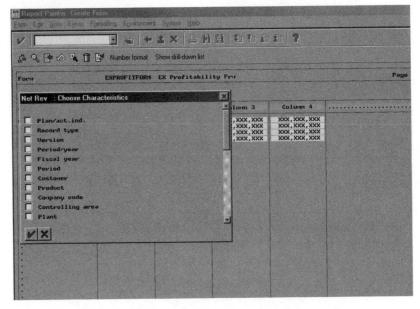

For the purposes of this form, you do not need to select any characteristics with the report line structure elements that are being selected for the row structure. Just click the green checkmark icon in the characteristic selection screen and you are presented with the Enter Texts pop-up screen, as shown in Figure 11.50.

FIGURE 11.50   The Enter Texts pop-up screen

FIGURE 11.50   The Enter Texts pop-up screen

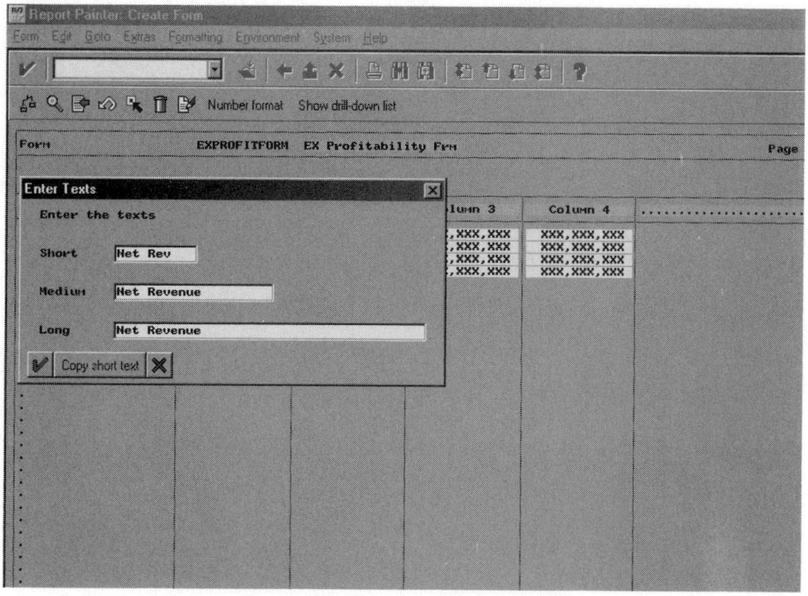

You are free to define the short, medium, and long textual descriptions for your row. After you enter the text values and press Enter, the row is fully defined for your form. We will continue creating the rows that are needed by our form.

We are now ready to define the column structure for our form. To begin creating the column structure, double-click the Column 1 field in the create CO-PA form definition configuration screen (Figure 11.46). The Select Element Type pop-up screen (Figure 11.47) appears, except this time you can choose only between characteristics and predefined elements because we used key figure (value fields or elements of a report line structure) in our row definition. You cannot mix and match the two within a single row or column structure; it must be one or the other. We will choose the Characteristics radio button and press Enter. The characteristic selection screen (Figure 11.49) appears. This time, however, we will choose the Plan/Act. Ind. option. Press Enter and the Characteristic Values pop-up screen (Figure 11.51) appears.

FIGURE 11.51   The Characteristic Values pop-up screen

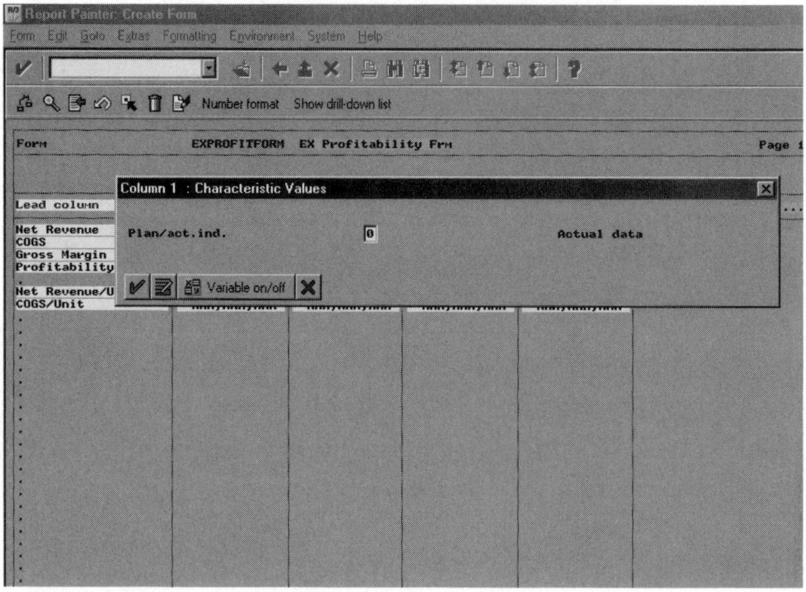

You are allowed to assign a single value to the characteristic value or define the characteristics as a variable. In this specific example, we have entered a single value of 0 for actual data. The value of 1 could also be specified for plan values. However, if you specify plan values, you must also select the characteristic Version so you can specify the plan version from which the values should be selected (remember that actual values are selected from version 0, so the Version characteristic is not needed for actual values). Variables will be covered when we discuss general data selections later in this section. After entering your characteristic values and pressing Enter, you are presented with the Enter Texts pop-up screen (Figure 11.50). Enter the text for the column and press Enter. The column is defined for your report, and you are returned to the create CO-PA form definition configuration screen (Figure 11.46). The Plan Data column was created in exactly the same way the Actual Data column was created, except the Version characteristic was selected in addition to the Plan/Act. Ind. characteristic, and in the Characteristic Values screen, we selected 1 for plan data in the Plan/Act. Ind. characteristic and 0 for plan version 0 in the Version characteristic. You are now ready to create the Variance column, which will utilize a formula.

To create the Variance column, double-click the Column 3 field (we already used column 1 for actual data and column 2 for plan data). You are presented with the Select Element Type pop-up screen, except this time the choices are characteristics, predefined elements, or formulas. Select the Formula radio button and press Enter. The Enter Formula pop-up screen appears (Figure 11.52).

FIGURE 11.52   The Enter Formula pop-up screen

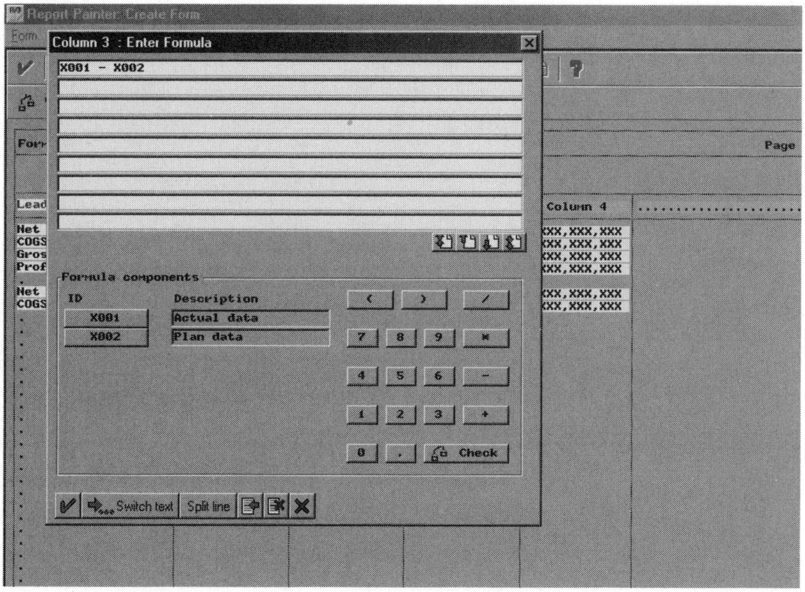

The columns that have been previously defined are available for use in the formula, and we can perform addition, subtraction, multiplication, and division in our formulas. In this example, we'll subtract the plan data value from the actual data value to produce the result for our Variance column, which we are currently defining. After entering your formula and pressing Enter, you are presented with the now very familiar Enter Texts pop-up screen. Enter your text and press Enter, and you are returned to the create CO-PA form definition configuration screen.

The entire row and column structure for the form is now complete and is presented in Figure 11.53.

FIGURE 11.53   The complete row and column structure for form EXPROFITFORM

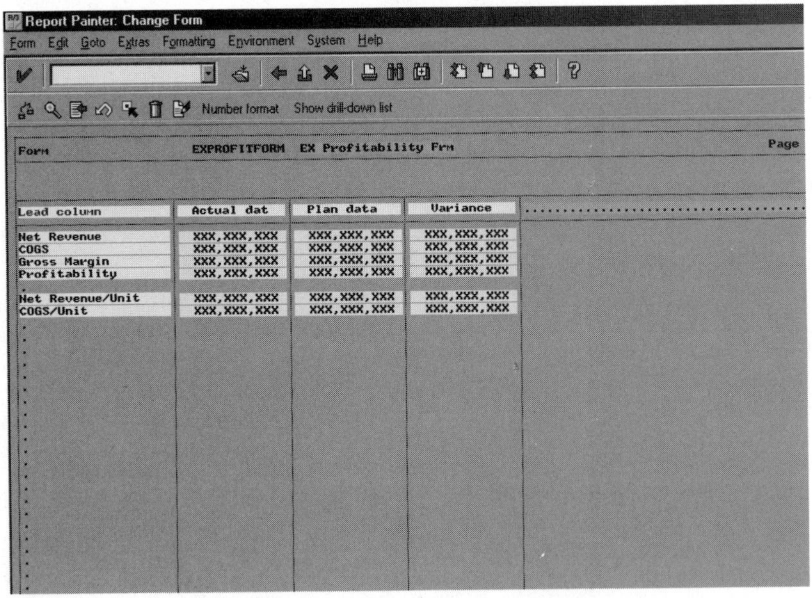

The next piece of configuration that is needed to complete our form is the general data selection. The general data selection defines the information that is needed by the entire form. In the general data selection of the form, you are able to choose different characteristics your form will use. To define your general data selection, follow the menu path Edit ➤ General Data Selection ➤ Display/Change from inside the form creation screen. You are presented with the familiar characteristic selection screen (Figure 11.49). The only difference is that the characteristics that were selected for the row or column structure are not available for selection in general data selection. The characteristic values for general data selection screen is shown in Figure 11.54.

You will notice that the configuration in the characteristic values for general data selection screen is somewhat different than the configuration in the characteristic values screen that was maintained earlier. We have used variables for some characteristic values in this situation. There are two types of variables: local variables and global variables.

FIGURE 11.54   The characteristic values for general data selection screen

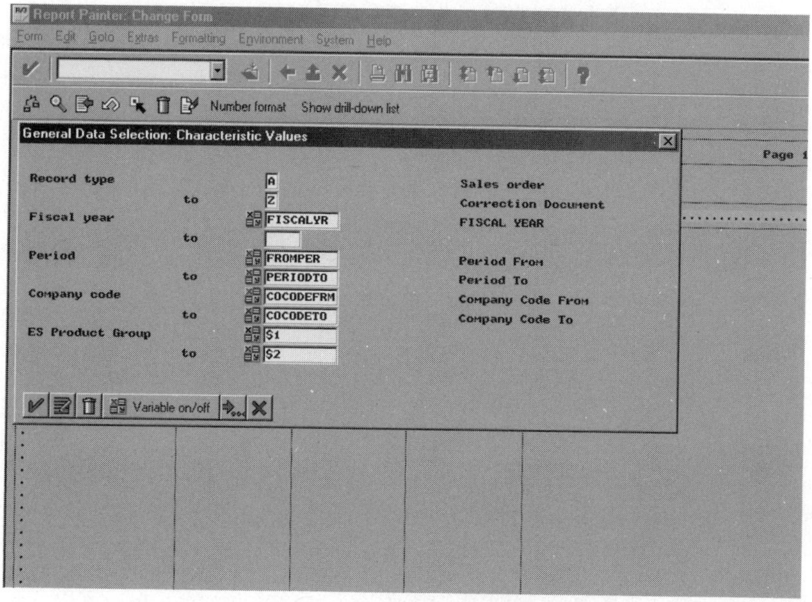

Once global variables are defined, they can be used by reporting forms in all operating concerns. Global variables are created for a specific field in a table and can be marked as mandatory, optional, and so on. You can also create global variables for text values, formulas, and many other things. To create global variables, follow the menu path Controlling ➤ Profitability Analysis ➤ Information System ➤ Report Components ➤ Define Variables for Reports or enter transaction code KE3E. All global variables begin with &. We will not show the configuration of global variables in the book—if you gotten this far, you can handle it on your own!

Local variables are defined within a form. They can be used only by the form in which they are created. You do not have all of the options you have with global variables when you use local variables. The user must always enter global variables. Whether you use global variables or local variables is up to you. Just know that you have a lot more flexibility to control processing when you use global variables. Local variables begin with $.

To use a variable instead of a fixed value for a characteristic, you need to select the characteristic value field by single-clicking in it. Next, click the Variable On/Off button (see the bottom of the screen shown in Figure 11.54). The characteristic is now a variable. If you want to use a global variable, select it from the pull-down box in the Characteristic Value field. If you want to use a local variable, enter a local variable name beginning with $ in the characteristic value field.

You can also define the drill-down list your report will use. The drill-down list, as explained earlier, includes such things as all materials sold to a certain customer. From within the form, you can define what value columns are displayed in the drill-down list. Using our form as an example, you might want columns to display actual net revenue, plan net revenue, actual profitability, and plan profitability. To define the columns to be displayed in the drill-down list, follow the menu path Extras ➢ Drill-Down Display ➢ Select Row/Columns from within the form creation screen. You can then select row/column combinations from the form detail to be combined and used as singular columns in the drill-down display. If you do not define your own drill-down structure, the system defaults the drill-down display to groupings of all rows and columns. In this example, the default would be a grouping of net revenue with three columns underneath it for actual data, plan data, and variance, then a grouping of COGS with three columns underneath it for actual data, plan data, and variance—the pattern continues for all of the rows that have been defined in the form. You can view the current structure of your drill-down list by clicking Show Drill-Down List in the create CO-PA form definition configuration screen (Figure 11.46).

The final piece of configuration to complete the form is to check the form for errors. To do so, click the check icon (the button, which is on the far left, looks like a hanging scale made out of monitors) in the create CO-PA form definition configuration screen. After you run the check successfully without errors, you can save the form.

EXTREME SPORTS CO-PA FORM CREATION CONFIGURATION ANALYSIS

Extreme Sports wants to provide maximum flexibility in its reporting solution. Therefore, it was determined that form reports and two axes (matrix) forms would be used for this report. Using the matrix form, we were able to define both the row and column structure of the report. In this example, the rows were defined as elements from the report line structure EX—you can also assign characteristics to each element of a report line structure or value field, but it was not needed in this case. The column structure of the form used characteristics and formulas to report on actual values, plan values, and the variance between the two. The general data selection of the form allowed us to choose additional characteristics that are used by every piece of the form. We used both global and local variables in defining the general data selection characteristics. There are many more advanced features that can be implemented for specific requirements within the form. The knowledge gained in this section can be applied and will give you a good base to pick up on additional tools you can use as you get more complex reporting requirements.

Creating the Report

We have now defined all of the reporting components that are needed by our report. The final step is to create the actual report itself. This is the also the simplest step because most of the hard work was done in the other components. At this point, it is important to remember that drill-down reports, like all other reports (with the exception of some ABAP reports), pull data from summarized information—this means that you do not have available to you all of the data that is available in the line items that make up the data. CO-PA drill-down reports actually pull data from the CE3*xxxx* table in conjunction with CE4*xxxx*.

As you learned earlier, you can create two types of reports: basic reports and form reports. We will continue with our example of creating a form report. To create a CO-PA report, follow the menu path Controlling ➢ Profitability Analysis ➢ Information System ➢ Report ➢ Create Profitability Report.

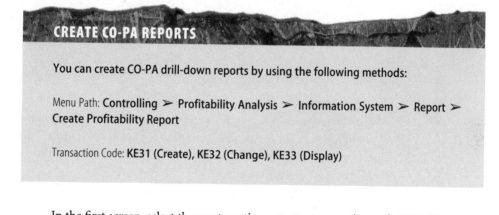

CREATE CO-PA REPORTS

You can create CO-PA drill-down reports by using the following methods:

Menu Path: **Controlling ➢ Profitability Analysis ➢ Information System ➢ Report ➢ Create Profitability Report**

Transaction Code: **KE31 (Create), KE32 (Change), KE33 (Display)**

In the first screen, select the create option or enter transaction code KE31. You are taken to the create profitability report initial screen, shown in Figure 11.55.

FIGURE 11.55   The create profitability report initial screen

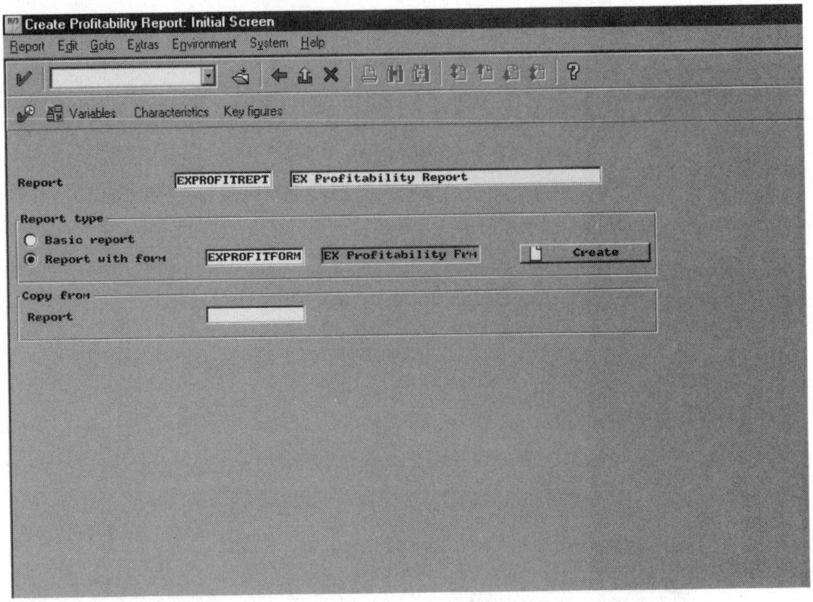

As you can see, you have the option to create basic reports or to create form reports. In this example, we will create a form report using the form we created in the preceding section. Be sure to click the Report with Form radio button and to indicate the form name in the text box. You also need to give the report an identifier as well as a description in the top two fields on the screen. After entering all of the required information, click the Variables button. You are presented with the create profitability report variables screen, shown in Figure 11.56.

All of the variables that we defined in the general data selection part of our form appear in the variables screen. Here, we can enter default values for the variables (like company code 1000 to 1400) that can be overridden at the time the report is run. However, you are not required to enter default values. If at this point you decide that you do not want a variable to be used for the report, you can enter a default value and deselect the Enter at Execution check box. In effect, this hard-codes the values you want to use for the variable so users can no longer enter their own values. Once you have made all of your configuration settings for variables, you are ready to define the report's characteristics. Click the Characteristics button and you are taken to the create profitability report characteristics screen, shown in Figure 11.57.

FIGURE 11.56   The create profitability report variables screen

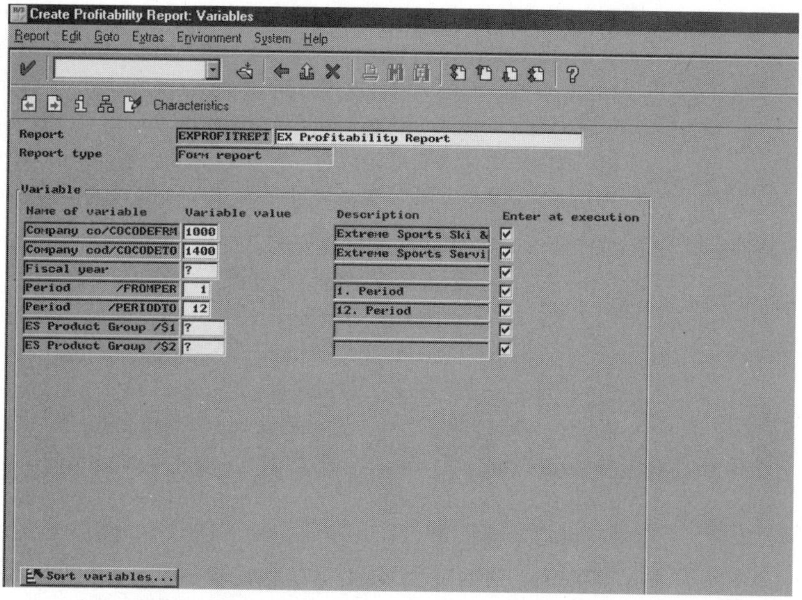

FIGURE 11.57   The create profitability report characteristics screen

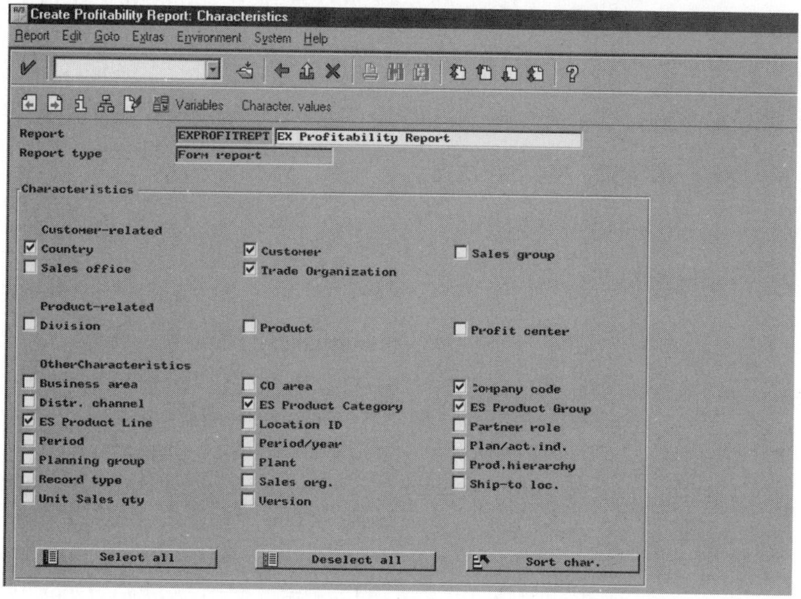

In this screen, you define the characteristics you want to use in the drill-down screen. To drill down (slice and dice) on a characteristic, you must select it in this screen (even if you chose the characteristic in the form definition). If you so desire, you also have the option of entering characteristic values to further limit the data is pulled for the report. Because we are using a two axes (matrix) form with key figures, we are not able to define key figures (value fields or elements of a report line structure) within the report. However, when you use basic reports or a one axis form without key figure, you choose from within the report the key figures to be used.

As you get more and more data in the system, and use more characteristics and variables in your report, your reporting performance becomes slower. One way to increase performance is to define from within the report the structure from which the data is pulled. You can choose between current data and summarization levels. Current data is by far the slowest method that can be used. Summarization levels are special summary tables that are filled with only specific characteristics that are needed by your report(s). This makes reporting performance much faster. Each report can pull off of only one summarization level, but each summarization level may be used by more than one report. You can have more than one summarization level in your operating concern, but make sure that you don't define very many (or more than you need), because summarization merely stores redundant data. You must also take up processing capability within the system to "fill" your summarization levels. The configuration of summarization levels is fairly straightforward (once you understand CO-PA and its data structures, which you know now!). You can configure summarization levels from within the Tools level under CO-PA in the IMG. You can define whether your report is to use summarization levels or not, as well as the reaction of the system if a summarization level is not found, by executing the menu path Extras ➢ Summarization Level from within the create profitability report characteristics screen. After entering the menu path, you are presented with the Read Summarization Level pop-up box, as shown in Figure 11.58.

You have a choice of running the report off of current data or off of a summarization level. If you choose to run the report off of a summarization level, you can define whether you get an error, a warning, or no message at all if a summarization level does not exist. If you choose the Error Message option, the report cannot be run until a summarization level has been created (and filled) for it. If you choose the Warning option, the user is presented with a warning informing them that a summarization level does not exist for the report. The user then has the option of either canceling the running of the report or running the report of off current data. If you choose the No Message option, the report will try to pull data from a summarization level. If no summarization level exists, it will automatically pull the information from current data without any interaction from the user of the report.

FIGURE 11.58   The Read Summarization Level pop-up box

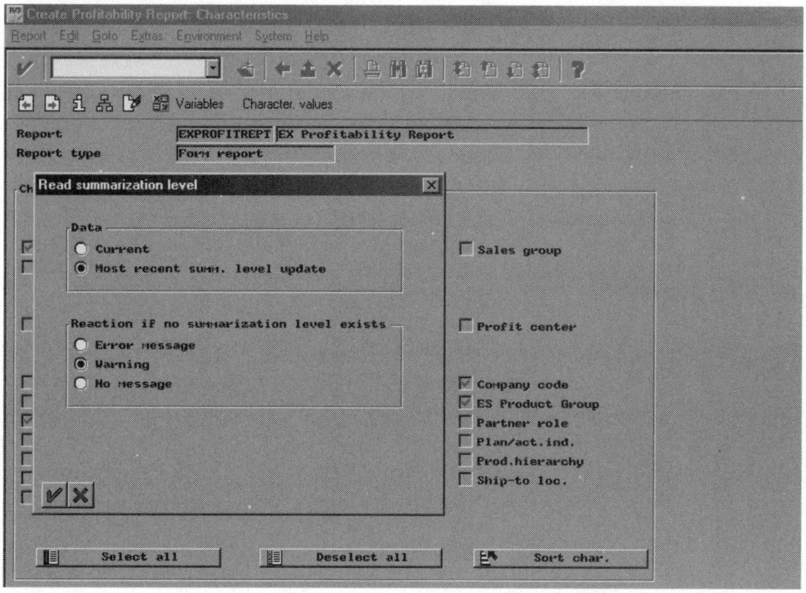

After you have defined all of your characteristic information and how data should be read, click the save icon. The report is now saved, you are done configuring it, and you can actually run it.

EXTREME SPORTS CREATE REPORT CONFIGURATION ANALYSIS

In this section, Extreme Sports completed its reporting configuration by creating the report itself. The report was created as a form report, using the form EXPROFITFORM that was created earlier. From within the report, we configured some of the variables that were defined in the form default values. The report user will be presented with a selection of all the variables and the default values that we entered here. The user has the option to overwrite the default values. We also chose several characteristics to be used in the drill down functionality of the report. We will be able to group data by each characteristic and drill down to additional data about the characteristic, such as which product groups were sold to customer X. We also set the

EXTREME SPORTS CREATE REPORT CONFIGURATION ANALYSIS (CONTINUED)

form to read data from summarization levels instead of current data. If a summarization level is not available for the report, users will receive a warning message that will allow them to cancel the report or to pull the data from current data (the base CO-PA data structures). We were not able to define key figures (value fields or elements from a report line structure) inside of the report because we defined the report as a form report using a matrix form that already includes the key figures. We are able to define key figures within the report for the basic report type and the single axis without key figures form report type.

CO-PA Transports

Creating and executing CO-PA transports can be tricky. With a few exceptions, CO-PA transports are not automatically recorded, even when they occur in a client with automatic recording of changes turned on. Because of the technical nature of CO-PA, SAP wants to group together specific objects in a transport in the correct order. The transport created by SAP is a combination of both client-independent and client-dependent objects. You learned in Chapter 1 that you should not group client-dependent and client-independent changes in the same transport request. CO-PA is the exception to the rule because SAP creates the transport. To create a CO-PA transport, follow the menu path Controlling ➢ Profitability Analysis ➢ Tools ➢ Transport. Be sure to read the IMG documentation that is provided with this step in order to more fully understand the transport creation process that happens in this activity.

CREATE CO-PA TRANSPORT

You can create CO-PA transports by using the following configuration methods:

Menu Path: **Controlling** ➢ **Profitability Analysis** ➢ **Tools** ➢ **Transport**

Transaction Code: **KE3I**

You are presented with the choose transport objects screen, shown in Figure 11.59.

You have several choices of what you can include in your transport. When you select each option, you will be prompted with a list of dependent objects that can be included or excluded. To be safe, it is usually a good idea to include all dependent objects. When you choose the Operating Concern option, you *must* choose all dependent objects that are presented. If you do not, you are at risk of corrupting or incompletely defining your operating concern in the source client. After you transport your operating concern, you *must* generate the environment of the operating concern in the source client before the operating concern can be used. You generate the operating concern from the same configuration screens you used to define your data structures and generate the operating concern the first time. Just go into the operating concern configuration screen and click the Generate Environment button that should appear on the button bar. If it is not displayed, click the Status button and then the Generate Environment button will appear. As was explained earlier, you only need to generate the operating concern environment in a single client within a system environment (development, QA, or production). Once you generate the environment in one client, it is generated in all clients within the system environment.

FIGURE 11.59   The choose transport objects screen

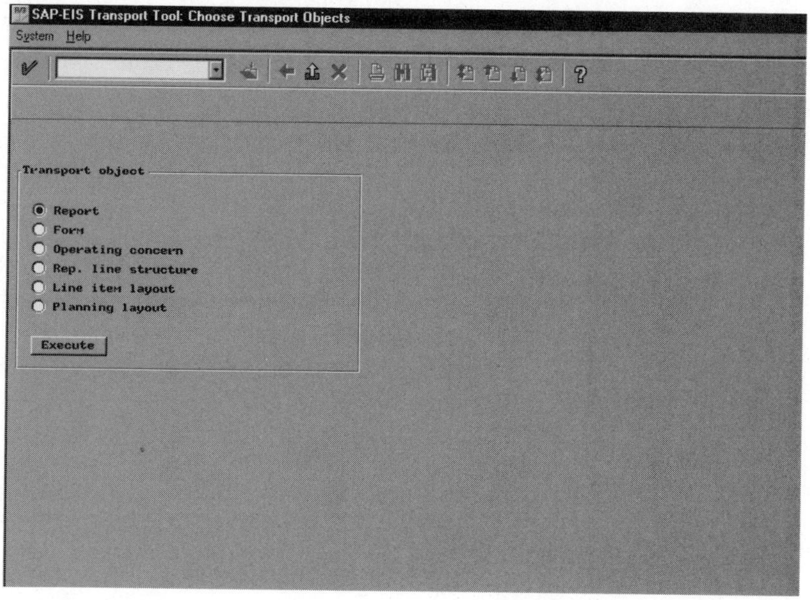

When you run your operating concern transport into a new system environment, it is a good idea to have minimal or (if possible) no activity on the system. You definitely cannot be processing billing transactions or order settlement to CO-PA transactions while the transport is running, and you will get errors in these transactions until the operating concern environment is generated. To minimize this risk, it is a good idea to deactivate CO-PA within your controlling area immediately before the transport is run into the environment and then reactivate CO-PA immediately after the operating concern environment has been successfully generated.

You can transport reports, forms, and planning layouts if you wish. Most companies, however, allow these types of reporting transactions to be created directly in production. This is a safe procedure because creating these types of objects is not configuration that affects how the system processes data—they are only structures to pull data to report off of.

Summary

In this chapter, you learned the concepts and configuration behind the Profitability Analysis (CO-PA) submodule. We discussed the purposes of CO-PA and the different types of CO-PA that can be used: account based and costing based. We then created and activated our operating concern data structure and generated the operating concern environment. Building on the operating concern that was created, we configured the rest of the CO-PA functionality needed by Extreme Sports. It is important to keep in mind that CO-PA is a mix of standard configuration and technical table and data structure creation.

If you remember one thing from this chapter, remember to use characteristics sparingly. Characteristics are limited resources within your operating concern, and as your business changes over the years, you may want to add additional characteristics. You cannot add additional characteristics later if you use them all up in the first shot. The fewer characteristics you use, the better your performance will be when reporting in CO-PA. CO-PA is a powerful tool, and with power comes complexity. Be careful out there.

Specifically, the following topics were covered in this chapter:

Costing-Based vs. Account-Based CO-PA

Operating Concern Development

Operating Concern Attributes

Profit Center Accounting

FEATURING:

▶ INTRODUCTION TO PCA CONFIGURATION

▶ BASIC SETTINGS AND MASTER DATA REVIEW

▶ ASSIGNMENTS IN PCA

▶ ACTUAL POSTING MAINTENANCE

▶ PLANNING

Profit Center Accounting, or PCA as it is often called, is not an "official" Controlling module component. Instead, it rests in an area of SAP called Enterprise Controlling (EC). EC also contains the applications Executive Information Systems (EC-EIS) and Consolidations. The purpose of PCA is to provide a client with the opportunity to analyze and report internal profitability for its organization. Although PCA resides outside of the CO module, it remains integrated with CO through its controlling area/company code relationships. By its very nature, PCA is a tool that can be manipulated to meet most of your demands.

The chapter will focus on the high-level development needs of most projects. From activating the module within the controlling area to establishing proper planning parameters, the emphasis will be on quickly getting you up and running. Refinements can occur after. To begin the process, an overview of the necessary configuration areas will be covered.

Introduction to PCA Configuration

Portions of Profit Center Accounting (PCA) configuration were covered in Chapters 7 and 9 during the setup of the CO Enterprise Structure and Cost Center Accounting. In Chapter 7, "Controlling (CO) Enterprise Structure," PCA was activated within the controlling area and the PCA portion of version 0 was maintained. In Chapter 9, "Cost Center Accounting," the PCA standard hierarchy was defined and the dummy profit center was created and assigned to the controlling area. This chapter will build upon that configuration.

NOTE Review Chapters 7 and 9 before proceeding. Each chapter will provide you with some necessary PCA configuration steps.

In reality, there is not much to the configuration of PCA. You have the opportunity to maintain version settings and create planning parameters. You will be required to maintain document types, and you can influence the updates during internal goods movements. But the majority of your development time will be spent designing the standard hierarchy and determining profit center assignments. This will be key to fulfilling all reporting and planning requirements.

It can be assumed that the reason you are developing PCA is to meet some profitability reporting requirements that do not align with your company code structure. At times, areas of responsibility within an organization span existing legal structures.

A more prevalent scenario is one where the areas of responsibility subdivide a single legal entity, as in a company whose areas of responsibility are geographically based. Each region—potentially North, South, East, and West—are held accountable for profitability targets. The sum of these regions would be equal to a single legal company code. Profit Center Accounting allows an organization to route all profitability- and most balance sheet–related information to a profit center. Much of this routing is accomplished through the aforementioned PCA assignments.

Another module similar in function to Profit Center Accounting is Special Purpose Ledger, or FI-SL. In fact, PCA itself was developed as a preconfigured special ledger solution. FI-SL is SAP's version of the ultimate reporting tool. It allows you to gather, consolidate, and report on information from all other SAP modules and any external source through development of personalized database tables. These tables form what is called a table group and are the backbone to FI-SL development. Because PCA is a delivered FI-SL solution, its table group, ledger, and activity assignments are predetermined and not directly configurable without the use of user-exits. However, this in no way limits the functionality or flexibility of PCA's reporting capabilities. Table 12.1 provides you with a breakdown of the PCA table group.

TABLE 12.1 EC-PCA Table Group Contents

Table	Description
GLPCO	Object Table for Account Assignment Objects
GLPCC	Additional Object Table
GLPCA	Actual Line Items Table
GLPCP	Plan Line Items Table
GLPCT	Summary (Totals) Table, used to facilitate reporting

The concept of a "ledger," which was mentioned earlier, is worth elaboration. In the FI-SL environment, the ledger is an object related to the table group. It is through the ledger that all fiscal year variant, company code, and activity assignments are made. The ledger is also key in many of the controls FI-SL establishes to manage transactional updates. With PCA, you get a predefined ledger, called 8A-Profit Center Accounting, that contains all activity assignments necessary for startup. The activity assignments cannot be augmented, but you do have the ability to control SAP's decision-making process during data transfer through a number of user-exits.

As you activate PCA for each of your controlling areas, all assigned company codes are automatically associated with the ledger, thus there is no manual maintenance needed. All controlling areas that exist within any instance use the same table group and ledger.

Because PCA is external to both FI and CO, there is not the limitation of ensuring that FI and CO are in balance at all times within PCA. This can be advantageous to you when you want to include externally generated data through PCA postings. It can also become a problem if not carefully monitored. Through the configuration of specific document types, you will have the ability to control whether unbalanced entries are acceptable or not.

In the next section, you will begin PCA configuration with a review of the basic controlling area and master data settings. As needed, refer back to Chapters 7 and 9 for insight into previously configured sections of SAP.

Basic Settings and Master Data Review

Prior to jumping into the heart of PCA configuration, it is important to spend some time ensuring that the proper basic configuration settings have been made. For PCA, that means reviewing the controlling area for the proper PCA activation, analyzing the specific PCA settings and assignments, and finally, maintaining the PCA standard hierarchy. The next section will once again take you through the steps necessary to review the controlling area maintenance screens.

Controlling Area Maintenance

When beginning Profit Center Accounting configuration, the first thing you will want to do is check to see that PCA is activated within the controlling area you are working in and that all the settings are appropriate. The PCA-related controlling area and standard hierarchy settings were maintained in Chapter 9 and are still relevant here. As a refresher, the menu path for getting to the maintenance window and some helpful hints are provided in this section. After setting the controlling area, use the menu path Enterprise Controlling ➤ Profit Center Accounting ➤ Basic Settings ➤ Maintain Controlling Area Settings.

Figure 12.1 is a view of the PCA-relevant controlling area settings. You will recall from Chapter 9 that certain aspects of PCA configuration were completed to maintain the cost center master record. To this end, the PCA-related controlling area settings and

MAINTAIN CONTROLLING AREA SETTINGS

You can get to the configuration screen to maintain controlling area settings by using either of the following methods:

Menu Path: **Enterprise Controlling** ➢ **Profit Center Accounting** ➢ **Basic Settings** ➢ **Maintain Controlling Area Settings**

Transaction Code: **OKE5**

FIGURE 12.1   Controlling area settings related to PCA

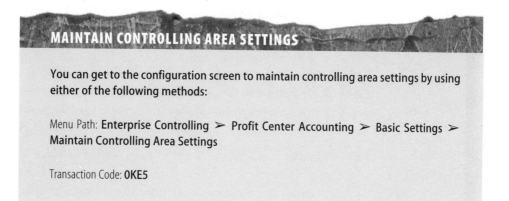

dummy profit center were created. Additionally, the PCA standard hierarchy was defined and profit centers were created to house the newly created cost centers (there will be more on this topic in "Assignments in Profit Center Accounting" later in this chapter).

Listed here are some key fields with comments:

Dummy Profit Center   The dummy profit center is the default profit center for the entire controlling area. There can be only one dummy profit center per controlling area. EX01_Dummy was configured in Chapter 9.

Standard Hierarchy   EX01_PCA was created in Chapter 9. Once you have created and assigned profit centers to the hierarchy, the name cannot be changed.

Elim. of Internal Business   Activate this field if you want to eliminate internal activity between two or more account assignment objects that are assigned to the same profit center. This setting can be activated or deactivated even after postings have occurred in the controlling area. However, the effects will not be felt in a retroactive manner. Previous posted amounts will not be picked up or eliminated.

Store Transaction Currency   If you want the transaction currency stored in PCA, flag this field. Data volumes will increase, but if the transaction currency is different from the controlling area or profit center currency, it may be important for reporting. Like the Elim. of Internal Business setting, this can be activated or deactivated even after postings have occurred.

Control Indicator   The system will default the current year as the From fiscal year. All settings are good from this year forward. If you make changes, SAP will identify a new From range. Be certain that Active Indicator is set to Active (checked).

When you have reviewed the settings and are satisfied, save the controlling area and continue to the next section, "Analyze/Update PCA Settings."

Analyze/Update PCA Settings

Either during the development period or when in production, you have the ability to immediately check the settings for PCA. Because PCA uses the tools of FI-SL to update itself with plan and actual data, it must follow the rules that govern that system. These rules and concepts take the form of utilizing customizing-specific and internal control tables to monitor and control transaction data updates. At times, such as when customizing transports have an impact on PCA configuration, it is possible that these internal control tables may need regeneration. Through the Analyze Settings transaction, you will be able to review these control tables to find any resulting inconsistencies. The following is a breakdown of the major sections of the Analyze Settings report:

▶ Fiscal Year Active indicator

▶ PCA settings for the controlling area, which let you know, among other things, the name or the PCA standard hierarchy and dummy profit center

▶ Control parameters for company code assignments attached to the controlling area

▶ Control parameters for both plan and actual postings

▶ General Parameter settings, which provide you with relative currency information

▶ Activity assignments in PCA

▶ Various master data and standard hierarchy checks for profit centers assigned in PCA

The program is helpful in that it provides a concise overview of the PCA environment and can quickly lead you to potential problems.

NOTE Prior to running the program, be sure that you have properly set the controlling area. You are not afforded an opportunity during the execution step, and SAP will analyze the settings of the controlling area at that time.

To run the Analyze Settings program, use the menu path Enterprise Controlling ➢ Profit Center Accounting ➢ Basic Settings ➢ Analyze Settings.

ANALYZE SETTINGS

You can get to the Display Settings for Profit Center Accounting screen with either of the following methods:

Menu Path: **Enterprise Controlling** ➢ **Profit Center Accounting** ➢ **Basic Settings** ➢ **Analyze Settings**

Transaction Code: **1KE1**

The Display Settings for Profit Center Accounting screen appears, offering an option to run the program with a master data check. If you have any concerns related to PCA in this area, select the box and then execute the program. Figure 12.2 is a partial view of the output from the program. There are several pages you will have to sort through when reviewing the settings. Unfortunately, if errors or inconsistencies are found or changes need to be made, they cannot be made from this screen. You will have to go to each of the affected areas individually to change the settings.

FIGURE 12.2   A view of the results of the Analyze Settings program

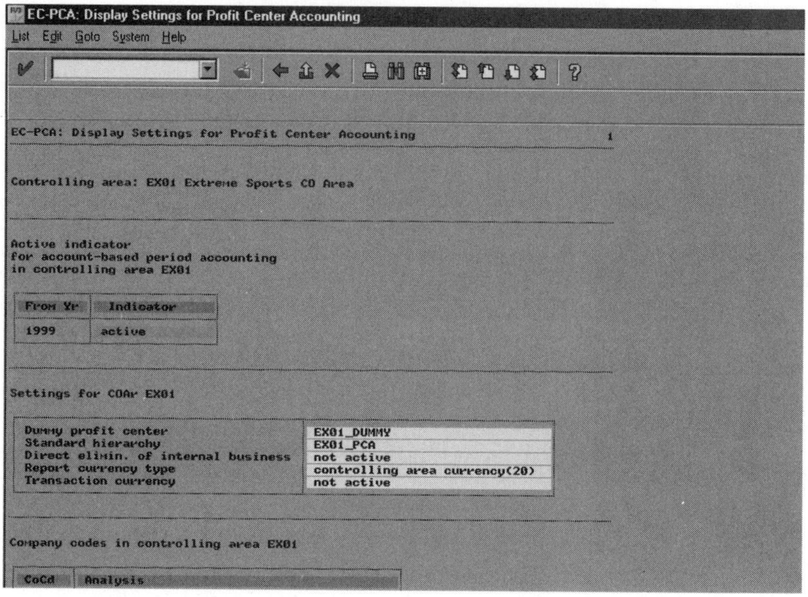

TIP   Because the Analyze Settings program consolidates a lot of control information for PCA, it is a great configuration reference guide.

As a result of your analysis, you may realize that inconsistencies exist in one or more of the internal control tables of PCA. These tables control things like company code assignment and plan/actual updates. If errors exist, it is probable that a quick regeneration of the environment will solve the problem. The regeneration program is contained in the IMG and can be found using the menu path Enterprise Controlling ➤ Profit Center Accounting ➤ Basic Settings ➤ Update Settings.

UPDATE SETTINGS

You can get to the Update Settings regeneration screen by using the following methods:

Menu Path: **Enterprise Controlling** ➤ **Profit Center Accounting** ➤ **Basic Settings** ➤ **Update Settings**

Transaction Code: **OKE4**

You are not afforded an execution screen because the program is executed immediately. Once it's completed, a results document that segregates the update analysis by controlling area will appear on the screen. Figure 12.3 provides you with a view of the results document. Notice that all control information is maintained at the company code level. At this time, you can rerun the Analyze Settings program to ensure that the problem has been resolved. The next section will take you through some of the master data requirements of Profit Center Accounting.

FIGURE 12.3   The Update Settings results for EX01

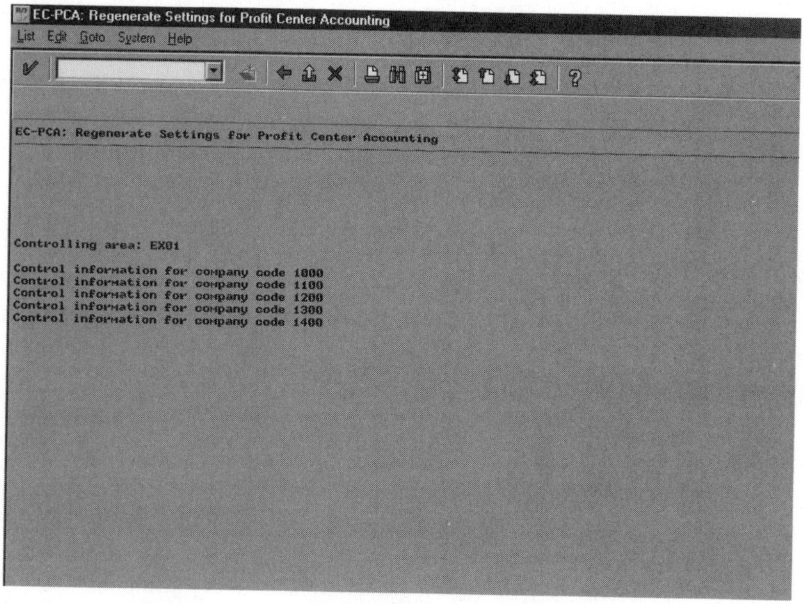

Master Data Settings

Much of the master data development for PCA, like the standard hierarchy and dummy profit center creation, was covered in Chapter 9 and should be reviewed before continuing. An outline of some of the master data items that should be reviewed is provided here:

Maintain the standard hierarchy   If you anticipate that the PCA standard hierarchy will resemble the CCA hierarchy created earlier, you have the option of copying the CCA hierarchy and then augmenting it as you see fit. This must be done prior to any manual creation in PCA. Be sure to create a special node that will contain the dummy profit center.

TIP   If a lot of maintenance will be necessary, we do not recommend the CCA copy procedure. It will be less confusing to build the hierarchy from scratch.

Create the dummy profit center   In many cases, the dummy should be created prior to cost center creation. If it was not, you will need to create the dummy here. Remember that there is only one dummy profit center per controlling area.

Create profit center master records   After the hierarchy is built, you will need to begin creating the profit centers. As with the standard hierarchy creation process, you have the option of copying the existing cost centers to create your new profit centers. One limitation to the copy process is that each new profit center is created with the same cost center number. Prior to running the copy program, you must create a cost center group containing the set of cost centers to be copied. This set will be entered on the copy execution screen.

One area that is new is the maintenance of the time-based fields found on the profit center master record. In CCA, you were limited to what you could influence in this area. In PCA, however, SAP allows you to identify which fields will be time sensitive. To access this window, you need to use the menu path Enterprise Controlling ➢ Profit Center Accounting ➢ Master Data ➢ Specify Time-Based Fields.

MAINTAIN TIME-BASED FIELDS

You can use the following methods to get to the time-based master field maintenance screen:

Menu Path: **Enterprise Controlling** ➢ **Profit Center Accounting** ➢ **Master Data** ➢ **Specify Time-Based Fields**

Transaction Code: **OKE7**

The EC-PCA Time-Based Master Data Fields maintenance screen will appear (see Figure 12.4). If it is important to track changes to the master record, each change will need to correspond with a new analysis period. The default analysis period on the master record is the original validity period given to the profit center. New periods can be configured directly on the profit center master record in the manner in which it is configured for the cost center (see Chapter 9 for details). To define a field as time based, check the box next to the field name. When you're finished, save the settings. These can be updated as often as you like.

FIGURE 12.4   The EC-PCA Time-Based Master Data Fields screen

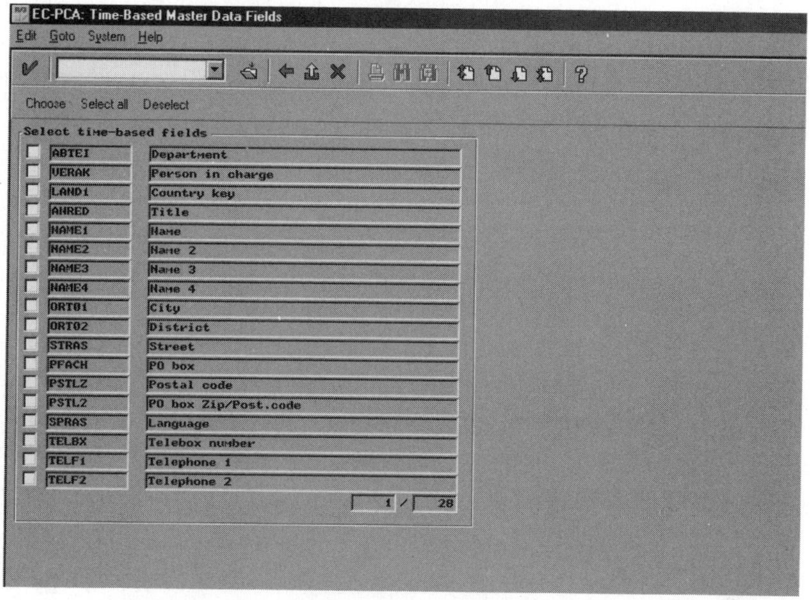

Now that the basic structure of PCA has been established, it is time to begin the assignment process. This procedure will be covered in the next section.

EXTREME SPORTS TIME-BASED FIELD MAINTENANCE CONFIGURATION ANALYSIS

Extreme Sports does not have an immediate need to maintain any of the fields at this time. This, of course, may change at a future date.

Assignments in Profit Center Accounting

Profit Center Accounting is in some sense a parasite. It generates very few transactional postings itself, relying instead on the data being generated by other sources, such as goods movements through production and receiving and billing documents through sales. These external transactions update PCA through object assignments. The assignments are an important facet to configuring PCA because, without them, a properly established environment will never include all the data necessary for reporting.

It has already been established in earlier chapters that cost centers and internal orders all require a profit center assignment at creation time when PCA is active. Through this assignment, all updates are passed to PCA and the link to the original object, namely the internal order or cost center, is maintained. You will always know that the PCA posting originated from that object. These types of assignments will not be covered in this section because they are hereditary to the creation process of those master records. Similar to the assignment process of the internal order and cost center is the creation process of the master records of cost objects, projects, maintenance orders, and fixed assets. These are all manually controlled and assigned during creation.

Where it is important to spend your assignment time is in one key area: the material master. Through this assignment, the majority of the PCA postings will occur. This section will cover the material assignment concepts and then move into sales order substitutions, which may become necessary based on your material assignment solution.

Material Master Assignment

With a single assignment on the material master record, you will have identified for SAP the default profit center for all sales orders, production orders, goods movements, material transfers, and physical inventory adjustments. The view to be maintained on the material master record is the Sales: General/Plant Data view. A display of the material master view can be seen in Figure 12.5.

FIGURE 12.5   The Sales: General/Plant Data material master view

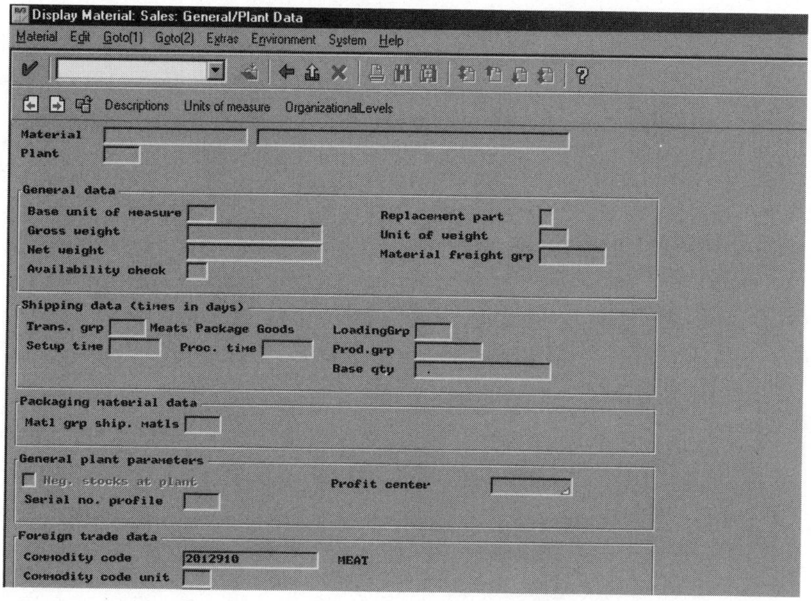

As with all material master maintenance, the setting will have to be maintained for each plant to which the material will be assigned. The Profit Center setting is in the General Plan Parameters field group found in the middle of the view. Each unique material/plant can have a different profit center assignment. The choice of profit center on this master record is one that should be given a lot of thought. The decision will be partly determined by your company's inventory management philosophy. By this we mean that the decision will be made by the area within your organization that owns the inventory. It could be manufacturing or sales and marketing.

If manufacturing owns the inventory and all the cost responsibility that comes with it, it makes sense to assign the material to a manufacturing profit center. This profit center would then be responsible for all inventory balances and would incur any inventory adjustment charges. If, however, the sales organization is responsible for the inventory, a sales and marketing profit center is appropriate. Your choice here will influence whether the section of this chapter that cover sales order substitution is relevant for your solution.

SAP will route, by default, all revenue and cost of sales data related to the selling of a material to the profit center assigned on the General Plant/Data view of the material master record. Changing the profit center assignment directly on the sales order can supercede the material master assignment. However, this may turn out to be impractical if you have a number of different materials assigned to each sales order. A second method of controlling the profit center assignment is through the maintenance of the sales order substitution, which can be used to route not only the revenue and cost of sales of a sales order but also the accompanying A/R customer balance. In either case, just know that you can reroute this assignment with some careful planning.

For a new project, the profit center assignment on the material master is best done during the material master conversion process. Be sure to add the Profit Center field to whatever CATT you have built to support the conversion loads. If you are in a maintenance and support mode, it is more likely that you will be adding or changing the profit center assignment on a handful of materials at a time. To assist with these changes, SAP provides you with a tool called fast assignment that will allow you to have an impact on a few materials, an entire product hierarchy, or anywhere in between in a single transaction.

Fast Assignment

To access the fast assignment screen, use the menu path Enterprise Controlling ➢ Profit Center Accounting ➢ Assignments to Profit Centers ➢ Material ➢ Perform Fast Assignment.

PERFORM FAST ASSIGNMENT

You can get to the assign material number fast assignment screen by using the following methods:

Menu Path: **Enterprise Controlling ➢ Profit Center Accounting ➢ Assignments to Profit Centers ➢ Material ➢ Perform Fast Assignment**

Transaction Code: **1KEB**

The Assign Material Numbers to a Profit Center screen will appear (see Figure 12.6). Notice that both Profit Center and Plant are required fields. This is because the fast assignment program will update the Sales: General/Plant Data view on each material master record, which, as you'll remember, is unique for each plant/material combination.

FIGURE 12.6 The Assign Material Numbers to a Profit Center data entry screen

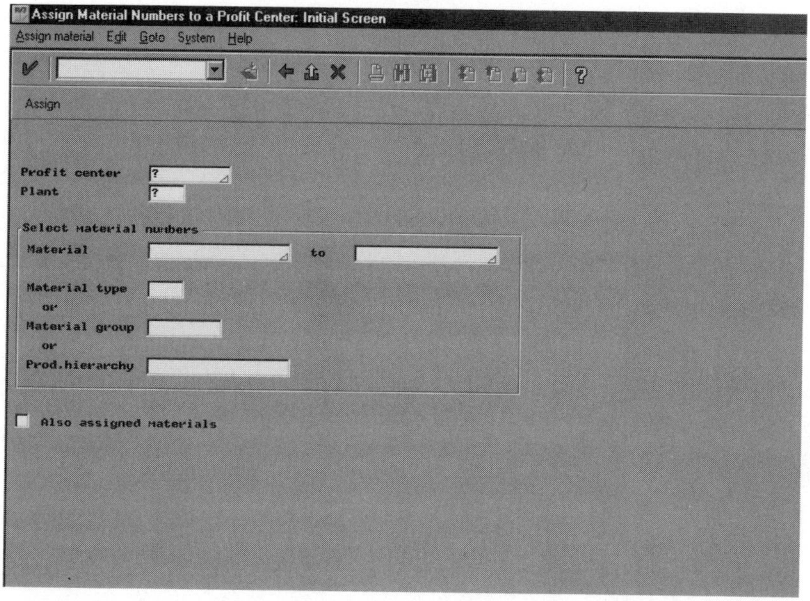

Begin the process by maintaining each of the relevant fields. A short description of each field is supplied here:

Profit Center Enter the number of the profit center that should be assigned to the material(s).

Plant Enter the ID of the plant to which the material is assigned. If the material is assigned to more than one plant, you will have to run the fast assignment for each plant.

In the Select Material Numbers section, you define the range of materials to be updated with the profit center assignment:

Material From/To Enter a material number or a range of material numbers to be updated.

Material Type If applicable, enter the ID for the material type that is to receive the profit center assignment. The material type is maintained at a higher level within the material hierarchy, so the breadth of the change will be great. Examples of a material type include FERT (Finished Goods) and HALB (Semi-Finished Goods). See the SAP Help text for details.

Material Group   If applicable, enter the ID for the material group to receive the profit center assignment. The material group is maintained one level down from the material type. See the SAP Help text for details.

Prod. Hierarchy   If applicable, enter the ID of the product hierarchy that is to receive the profit center assignment. You may select the hierarchy at any level, product group, product line, or product category. See the SAP Help text for details.

Also Assigned Materials   If this field is selected, SAP will maintain all material numbers that reside in the range, regardless of whether they have previously received a profit center assignment. If this field is not selected, the system will update only those materials that were previously unassigned.

When you have completed the selection, click the Assign button to execute the program. A screen will appear providing you with a list of those material numbers selected. You now have the opportunity to specifically define which materials are to be maintained. If all are appropriate, use the Select All button and click Save. The material master records will be updated immediately.

Sales Order Substitution: Creation

If your solution requires you to assign the material master to a profit center that is different than the one responsible for P&L reporting, you will probably have to maintain the PCA sales order substitution. Like the substitutions that were covered in Chapter 2, the sales order substitution uses information from the coding block and reroutes the profit center assignment based on rules that you define. To access the substitution creation screen, use the menu path Enterprise Controlling ➢ Profit Center Accounting ➢ Assignments to Profit Centers ➢ Sales Order Substitution ➢ Define Substitutions.

SALES ORDER SUBSTITUTION CREATION

You can get to the substitution creation screen with either of the methods listed here:

Menu Path: Enterprise Controlling ➢ Profit Center Accounting ➢ Assignments to Profit Centers ➢ Sales Order Substitution ➢ Define Substitutions

Transaction Code: **OKEM**

The substitution creation screen will appear (see Figure 12.7). To create a new substitution, use the path Substitution ➤ Create. Because substitutions were covered in such detail in Chapter 2, only the high-level requirements will be provided.

FIGURE 12.7   The substitution creation screen

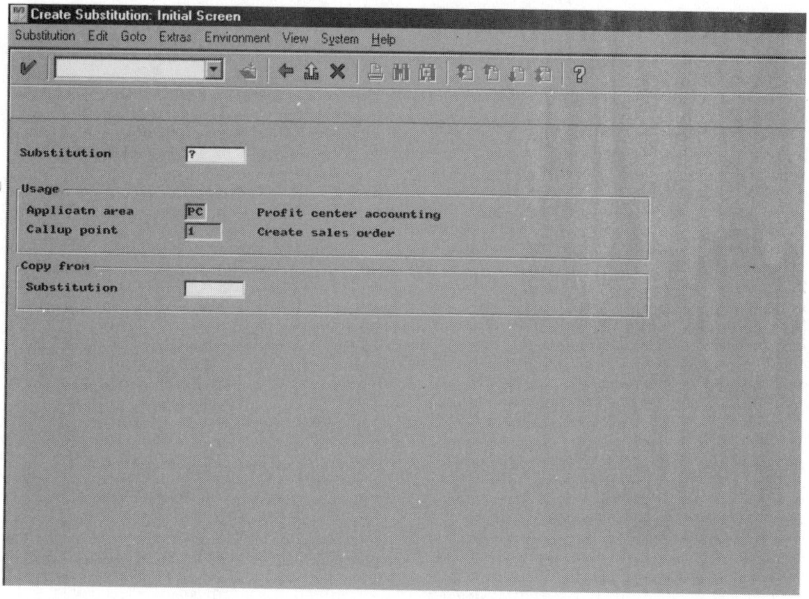

The following fields are on the substitution creation screen:

Application Area   The application area is the module or submodule for which you wish to create the substitution. It should always be PC (Profit Center Accounting) for the sales order substitution.

Callup Point   The callup point determines when the substitution is run. The callup points that are available are dependent upon the application area that is selected. For PC (Profit Center Accounting), the only callup point available is 0001 (Create Sales Order).

From the create substitution screen, the Fields for Substitutions dialog box appears when you want to insert a substitution rule (see Figure 12.8).

FIGURE 12.8 The Fields for Substitutions dialog box

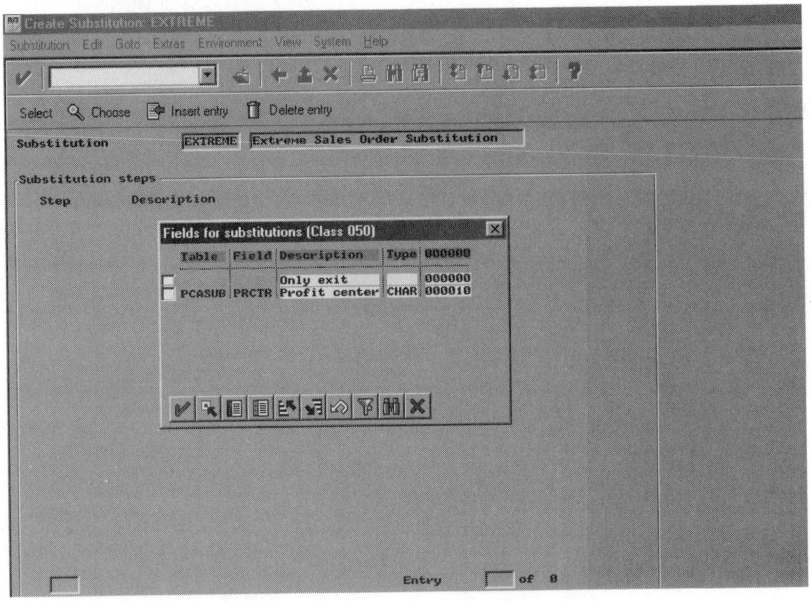

You will be provided with two choices:

Only Exit If this field is chosen, a constant value selection will not be available for maintenance. The only update path will be through the use of the substitution user-exit explained in Chapter 2.

Profit Center This field gives you the flexibility to substitute through either a constant profit center value assignment or the substitution user-exit. This field setting is recommended because it does not limit your choices. Figure 12.9 provides you with a view of the sales order substitution EXTREME, used by Extreme Sports.

Review Chapter 2 for a quick update on the concepts of Boolean logic and syntax, which you'll use when you create substitution rules. After the sales order substitution creation is complete, the next step is to determine the activation setting.

FIGURE 12.9   The substitution rule window for sales order substitution EXTREME

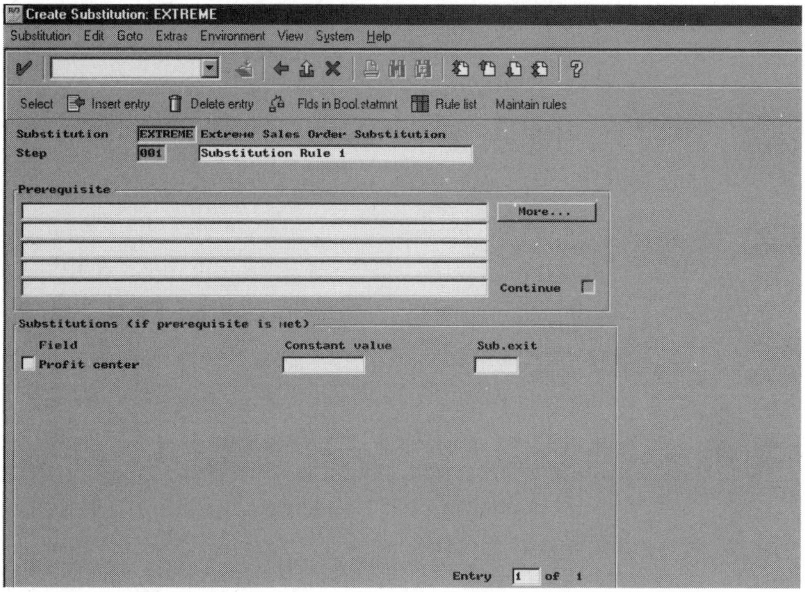

Sales Order Substitution: Activation

When the substitution is complete, you must provide an appropriate activation setting. This setting differs from the one you used in Chapter 2 to activate your functional area substitution. To access the sales order substitution activation screen, use the menu path Enterprise Controlling ➢ Profit Center Accounting ➢ Assignments to Profit Centers ➢ Sales Order Substitution ➢ Assign Substitution Rules.

SALES ORDER SUBSTITUTION ACTIVATION

You can get to the Substitution for Profit Center in SD activation screen by using either of the methods listed here:

Menu Path: **Enterprise Controlling** ➢ **Profit Center Accounting** ➢ **Assignments to Profit Centers** ➢ **Sales Order Substitution** ➢ **Assign Substitution Rules**

Transaction Code: **OKEL**

At the EC-PCA: Substitution for Profit Center in SD screen, select the New Entries button. In the appropriate fields, enter the controlling area and name of the substitution you previously created. In the Active Status column, you are given three activation choices for the substitution:

Blank   Leave the column blank if you do not want substitution activated.

1   If this option is selected, the substitution is activated and all profit center values will be derived through the substitution rules. This is the most common setting.

2   If this option is selected, the substitution will be used only during sales order transactions related to cross-company codes.

When you're finished, save the activation settings. Figure 12.10 is a view of the activation status for Extreme Sports' sales order substitution EXTREME. This completes the process of material master assignments. It is vital that this integration point is communicated to all appropriate development parties and monitored by you. To help you monitor all PCA assignments, SAP provides you with a tool called the assignment monitor.

FIGURE 12.10   The activation status for sales order substitution EXTREME

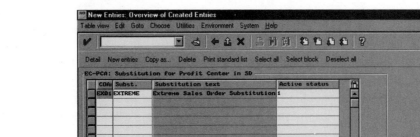

EXTREME SPORTS SALES ORDER SUBSTITUTION CONFIGURATION ANALYSIS

In the current and future Extreme Sports organization, the sales and marketing departments are responsible for all finished goods inventory balances as well as all revenue production. Based on this allocation of responsibility, only the responsible marketing profit centers will be placed on the material master record, negating the use of the sales order substitution functionality.

PCA Assignment Monitor

The PCA assignment monitor is a tool that allows you to quickly assign many objects to a profit center or a group of profit centers. Through the monitor you will be able to view the following items:

- ▶ Materials
- ▶ Cost centers
- ▶ Orders
- ▶ Work Breakdown Structures
- ▶ Cost objects

To access the assignment monitor window, use the menu path Enterprise Controlling ➢ Profit Center Accounting ➢ Assignments to Profit Centers ➢ Check Assignments.

PCA ASSIGNMENT MONITOR

You can use the following methods to get to the assignment monitor window:

Menu Path: **Enterprise Controlling ➢ Profit Center Accounting ➢ Assignments to Profit Centers ➢ Check Assignments**

Transaction Code: **1KE4**

The assignment monitor window looks much like those you find when accessing the various submodules from the user menu (see Figure 12.11). To review any of the previously mentioned assignment objects, you simply navigate through the user menu and follow the simple selection instructions. And remember that the tool can be as helpful in identifying those things that do not have an assignment as it is for those that do.

FIGURE 12.11   **The EC-PCA assignment monitor main window**

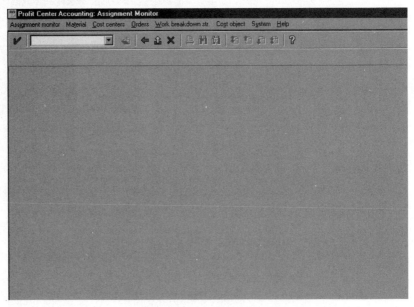

In the next section, we'll begin the process of preparing PCA to accept actual postings.

Actual Posting Maintenance

Preparing Profit Center Accounting to accept actual postings can be very simple or very complex, depending on the needs of your company. On the simple side, all that is required is to activate the fiscal year control parameters, create the proper document types, and define the necessary number ranges. For more complex solutions, additional account assignments may be maintained, and internal goods movements can be defined and segregated to enhance the profitability picture for each profit center. A review of the two PCA profitability-reporting philosophies, Period Accounting and Cost of Sales Accounting, should be touched upon prior to continuing.

Because both Cost of Sales and Period Accounting are supported in the FI, PCA also must allow for either. Period Accounting tracks profitability through use of revenue and cost elements. The principle behind Period Accounting states that all costs and revenues incurred within a given period—including sales, deductions, cost of sales, costs of production, and all overhead expenses—summed together net the total operating profit. As a delivered system, PCA is set up to support the Period Accounting approach with the standard reports found in its information system. Cost of Sales Accounting takes a different approach.

Cost of Sales Accounting also tracks revenue, but the revenue is compared to only the cost of sales associated with the quantity sold during the period. Manufacturing costs incurred in the period are held in inventory and not recognized until the time the inventory is sold. Additional selling and marketing and overhead expenses are also recognized in the period, with the net result being the profitability for that period. To facilitate the Cost of Sales Accounting approach, you must first develop and maintain the functional areas and functional area substitution in FI. Both of these were covered in detail in Chapter 2.

The first step in the configuration process is to maintain the control parameters for actual postings.

EXTREME SPORTS PROFITABILITY ACCOUNTING APPROACH CONFIGURATION ANALYSIS

Extreme Sports uses the Period Accounting approach to tracking and reporting profitability. Thus, all configuration demonstrated will support this method of accounting.

Set Control Parameters

With the control parameters settings, you are defining how postings will update in the PCA environment. Prior to accessing the window, be certain that the proper controlling area is set. You will not be afforded an opportunity later. Use the menu path Enterprise Controlling ➢ Profit Center Accounting ➢ Actual Postings ➢ Set Control Parameters for Actual Data to access the proper screen.

SET CONTROL PARAMETERS FOR ACTUAL POSTINGS

You can get to the necessary configuration screen to set control parameters for actual postings by using the following methods:

Menu Path: **Enterprise Controlling** ➤ **Profit Center Accounting** ➤ **Actual Postings** ➤ **Set Control Parameters for Actual Data**

Transaction Code: **1KEF**

The overview screen will appear. Make sure the set controlling area is the proper one. Select the New Entries button from the header to bring up a fresh screen. The settings are maintained by fiscal year. You do not need to make new settings each year; they are good from the year defined forward. Figure 12.12 is a view of the control settings for Extreme Sports' controlling area EX01.

FIGURE 12.12   The control parameter settings for controlling area EX01

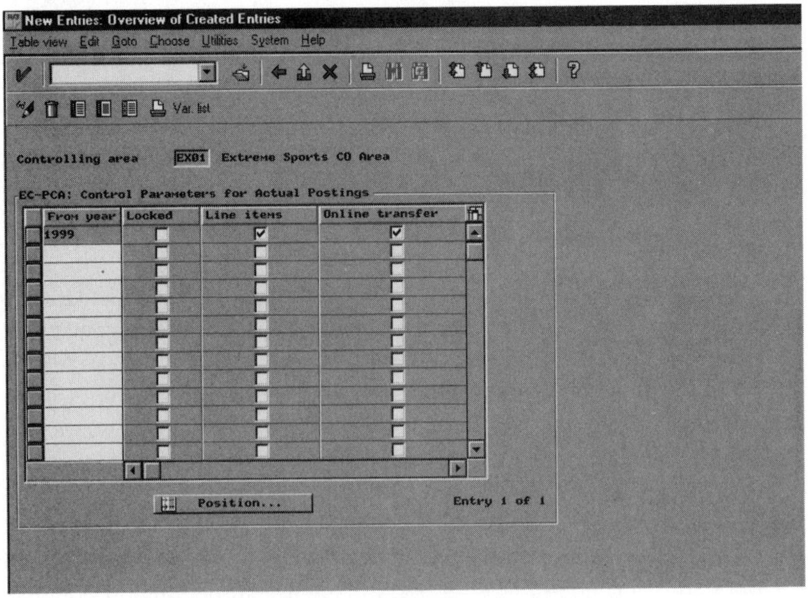

The column names and descriptions are provided for your convenience (the control parameters determine how actual postings update in PCA):

Controlling Area The value pulls in automatically and represents the currently set controlling area.

From Year Enter the fiscal year from which the parameter settings should be activated. The settings are good from this fiscal year forward.

Locked Set this indicator if you wish to lock the controlling area from any actual postings for that fiscal year setting. Set this indicator only if you have configured a new group of fiscal year settings that begin after the most recent fiscal year identified on the table. For example, fiscal year 1995 is locked only when new settings are available for fiscal year 1997.

Line Items Activate this setting if you want line items transferred to PCA. This will increase the number of documents posted in your system, but in many cases, it is a must if you are required to do any detailed analysis.

Online Transfer Activate this setting if you wish SAP to update the PCA ledger automatically during any transaction activity. If this setting is left inactivated, you will be required to transfer the postings manually. This is not recommended due to the number of programs that must be run and the fact that some postings could get double-counted if you are not careful.

When you're finished, save your settings. The next section will take you through the necessary document type configuration steps.

EXTREME SPORTS CONTROL PARAMETERS FOR ACTUAL POSTINGS CONFIGURATION ANALYSIS

Extreme Sports wants as much online transfer activity as possible from its SAP solution. Additionally, line item analysis will be vital, at least initially, to the success of the project.

Define Document Types: Actual

By this time, you have been exposed to the document principle and are familiar with what a document type does in SAP. In FI, the document type lets SAP know, among other things, which transactions are to be posted. In PCA, the document type controls things like what currencies the posting can be maintained in, the document number range, and whether the transaction must be balanced. Remember, earlier in the chapter it was stated that PCA exists outside the environments of FI and CO and thus can allow an unbalanced entry to occur. It is through the document type configuration that this is controlled.

Begin the process by using the menu path Enterprise Controlling ➤ Profit Center Accounting ➤ Actual Postings ➤ Define Document Types to access the proper screen.

DEFINE DOCUMENT TYPES FOR ACTUAL POSTINGS

You can get to the valid document types configuration screen with either of the following methods:

Menu Path: **Enterprise Controlling** ➤ **Profit Center Accounting** ➤ **Actual Postings** ➤ **Define Document Types**

Transaction Code: **GCBX**

The valid document types window will appear displaying the default document type A0. You can use this delivered document type or create your own. As with all SAP-delivered objects, it is recommended that you create your own rather than augment the standard. To create the document type, select the New Entries button and a fresh screen will appear. To assist you with the configuration, the column names and descriptions are provided here:

Doc. (Document) Type   Enter a two-character ID that represents the document type.

TC (Transaction Currency)   Activate this setting if you want the transaction currency stored at the time of posting. Recommended.

C2 (Second Currency)   Activate this setting if you wish to also capture the posting in a second currency (local/company code). Recommended.

C3 (Third Currency)   Activate this setting if you wish to also capture the posting in a third currency. Recommended.

TIP   It is easiest to select all three currency settings. Updates will occur only for those that exist in the controlling area.

Bal. (Balance) Check   Here you are offered the option of allowing unbalanced entries in PCA. There are three options:

0   An error is returned if the balance is not zero. This will force all PCA entries to be balanced.

1   A warning is returned if the balance is not zero. If you wish to offer the flexibility of unbalanced entries, this is a good setting.

2   No balance check is conducted.

Local/Global   These columns are grayed out. The settings here represent the number range assignment given to each document type. This will be maintained in the actual number range assignment section.

Description   Enter a text description for your document type. Be certain the description is clear because these document types are controlling area independent.

Figure 12.13 shows the settings for document type AX, which will be used by Extreme Sports to post actuals into PCA. You are free to create as many document types as you see fit, without any repercussions. During document entry, the user will be required to enter a document type. If you wish to offer different controls for different types of entries, you have that capability.

FIGURE 12.13   Extreme Sports' document type AX

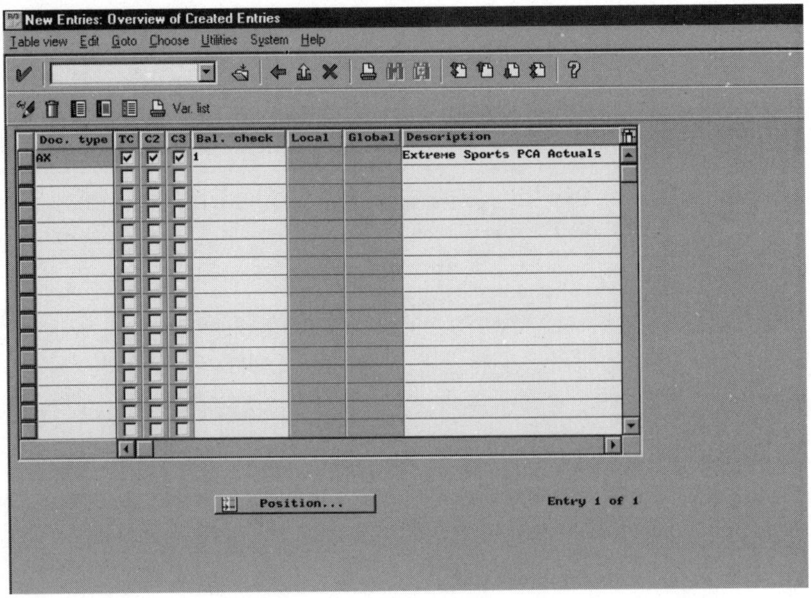

The next section supporting actual posting configuration covers the number range assignment for the new document type. You will not be able to make a PCA entry without one.

EXTREME SPORTS DOCUMENT TYPE FOR ACTUAL POSTINGS CONFIGURATION ANALYSIS

Extreme Sports chose to create its own document type because it wanted to make changes to the settings that were delivered with A0. All three PCA-related currencies will be allowed for actual transactions. The flexibility offered here does not make them required, but rather gives the user the option. As to the balance checking, here Extreme Sports votes for the flexibility provided by SAP with the assignment of a warning on any unbalanced entries. Although they won't be encouraged, an unbalanced entry is an easy way of clearing up an error. Remember, the PCA books are meant for internal reporting only.

Number Range Assignment: Actual

Like the many number range assignments you have maintained so far, the PCA actuals number range is very similar in its configuration steps. As noted earlier, the document type is used as the number range assignment object and thus must be completed first. To access the number range assignment screen, use the menu path Enterprise Controlling ➤ Profit Center Accounting ➤ Actual Postings ➤ Maintain Number Ranges.

MAINTAIN NUMBER RANGES FOR ACTUAL POSTINGS

You can get to the number ranges for local G/L documents screen by using either of the methods listed here:

Menu Path: **Enterprise Controlling** ➤ **Profit Center Accounting** ➤ **Actual Postings** ➤ **Maintain Number Ranges**

Transaction Code: **GB02**

At the number ranges for local GL documents window, select the Maintain Groups button from the icon bar. This will lead you to the Maintain Number Range Groups screen (see Figure 12.14). Notice that the Extreme Sports document type AX appears in the Not Assigned area. At this time, you need to check that all relative company code number range intervals have been properly maintained.

FIGURE 12.14   The Maintain Number Range Groups screen

Maintain Number Range Groups

Number range object   Edit   Group   Interval   System   Help

Element/Group

Number range object Local GL document
Grouping......... Document type

☐ Act. document from direct posting with GB01
   AB
☐ Planned doc. from direct posting with GB01
   PB
☐ Group without text

☐ Group without text

☐ Gruppe ohne Text

☐ New group with a new number range for Company 0001

Not assigned
  AX

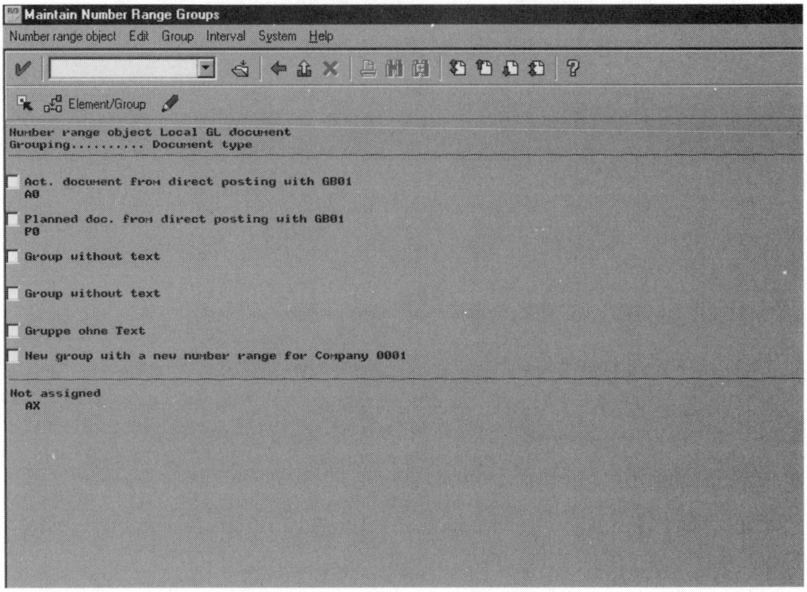

To accomplish this, select the maintain icon found on the icon bar. A dialog box appears, asking you to enter a company code. Enter your respective company code ID and press Enter. If the company code number range interval has been properly maintained, a screen similar to the one in Figure 12.15 should appear. If not, select the insert interval icon and define the number range interval for your company code.

TIP   Be sure to extend the fiscal year associated with the number range interval far enough into the future. It can be a maintenance nightmare to create new number range intervals for each fiscal year.

When you're finished, save the settings and green arrow back to the Maintain Number Range Groups screen.

To assign the new document type to a range, select the document type by double-clicking the ID directly. Then select the range Act. Document from Direct Posting with GB01 and click the Element/Group button. The selected document type will move to its new assigned range. Save the number range settings.

If you return to the valid document types screen, you should see that the new document type AX now has a number range defined for it under the Local column (see Figure 12.16). You will have to repeat these steps for each new document type created.

FIGURE 12.15   The number range interval screen for Extreme Sports' company code 1000

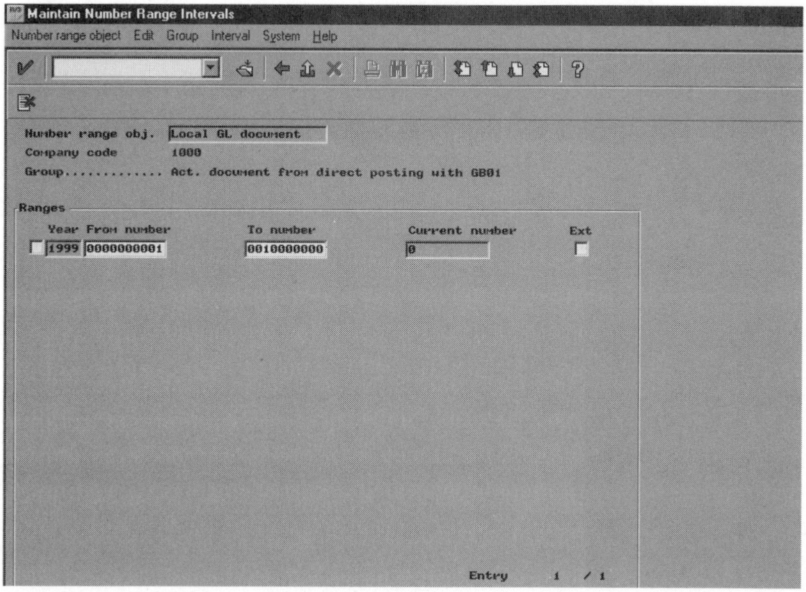

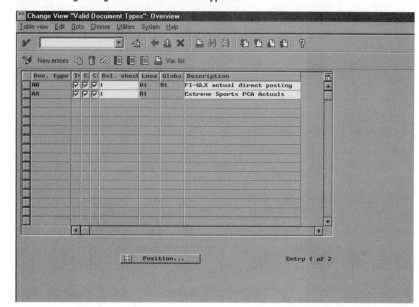

FIGURE 12.16   The number range assignment for document type AX

This completes the basic settings necessary for PCA actual postings to occur. The next few sections will begin to take you through the more complex settings you may require to complete your PCA solution.

Assign Revenue Elements to Profit Centers

The default account assignment table TKA3A was covered in detail in Chapter 9. It is recommended that you review the section prior to maintaining any additional settings here. In that chapter, settings were established to route contract services revenue, revenue element 301000, to the Misc. Sales profit center 140000. The menu path to reach the account assignment table is Enterprise Controlling ➤ Profit Center Accounting ➤ Actual Postings ➤ Assign Revenue Elements to Profit Centers.

MAINTAIN DEFAULT ACCOUNT ASSIGNMENTS

You can get to the screen to configure the account assignment table with either of the methods listed here:

Menu Path: **Enterprise Controlling** ➤ **Profit Center Accounting** ➤ **Actual Postings** ➤ **Assign Revenue Elements to Profit Centers**

Transaction Code: **OKB9**

These settings can be maintained at any time, but the effects are not retroactive. There is an additional account assignment tool that is available to PCA only. This assignment relates a cost/revenue element posting to a single profit. Unique to this table is the ability to assign balance sheet accounts. Remember that balance sheet accounts exist in FI only, meaning you do not have the ability to create cost or revenue elements. PCA allows the assignment of these accounts through this table only.

Choose Additional Balance Sheet and P&L Accounts

In addition to the default account assignment screen covered earlier, you have the choice of assigning additional cost elements or balance sheet accounts to a given profit center. Standard SAP functionality allows you to transfer at period's end the primary balance sheet accounts, including A/P, A/R, assets, material stocks (raw and finished goods), and work-in-process. The balances for the payables, receivables, assets, and material stocks will default to the profit center that is assigned to the relative master record involved: material master for A/P, A/R, and material stock balances; fixed assets for the asset balances. For the work-in-process balance, the profit center assignment on the order or project will be used. To avoid double counting, these accounts should not be maintained in this table.

> **WARNING**   SAP will not warn you that you are adding one of these default transfer accounts in the table at the time of entry. The first time you will notice is during your review of the PCA balance sheet.

Use the menu path Enterprise Controlling ➤ Profit Center Accounting ➤ Actual Postings ➤ Choose Additional Balance and P&L Accounts to access the additional account assignments screen. The settings are controlling area dependent, so be certain that the proper controlling area is set.

MAINTAIN ADDITIONAL BALANCE SHEET AND P&L ACCOUNTS

You can use the following methods to get to the additional balance sheet and P&L account configuration screen:

Menu Path: **Enterprise Controlling ➤ Profit Center Accounting ➤ Actual Postings ➤ Choose Additional Balance and P&L Accounts**

Transaction Code: **3KEH**

At the additional balance sheet and P&L account screen, select the New Entries button to make the new assignments. The configuration settings are simple and require little explanation:

Acct From/To   Enter the range of accounts you want to default to a profit center.

Def. PrCtr (Default Profit Center)   Enter the ID of the profit center to which the accounts are to be assigned.

When you're finished, save the settings (see Figure 12.17). Remember to not overlap any of the defined transfer balance sheet accounts during maintenance.

FIGURE 12.17   EX01 additional assignment table

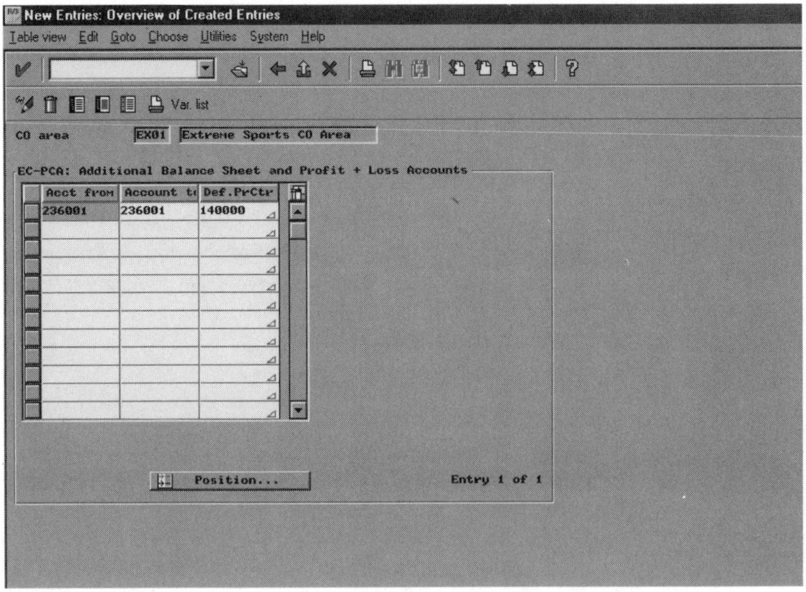

Balance Carry Forward Indicator Maintenance

If you have maintained any settings on the additional balance sheet and P&L account assignment table, it is necessary to set the balance carry forward indicator for the PCA environment. You will want to properly roll all transferred accounts to the proper retained earnings account. To access the carry forward window, use the menu path Enterprise Controlling ➢ Profit Center Accounting ➢ Actual Postings ➢ Balance Carried Forward ➢ Allow Balances to Be Carried Forward.

ACTIVATE BALANCE CARRY FORWARD FOR PCA

You can get to the allow balance carried forward screen by using the following the methods:

Menu Path: Enterprise Controlling ➢ Profit Center Accounting ➢ Actual Postings ➢ Balance Carried Forward ➢ Allow Balances to Be Carried Forward

Transaction Code: **2KET**

The overview screen is very simple to navigate. Simply select the Balance Carry Forward (Bal. CF) box found in the window (see Figure 12.18). Save the settings when you're finished. The second step in the balance carry forward configuration process is the assignment of the retained earnings account to the chart of accounts. Because this step was completed in the section "Configuring G/L Account Master Records" in Chapter 3, it will not have to be configured here.

FIGURE 12.18   The balance carried forward activation screen

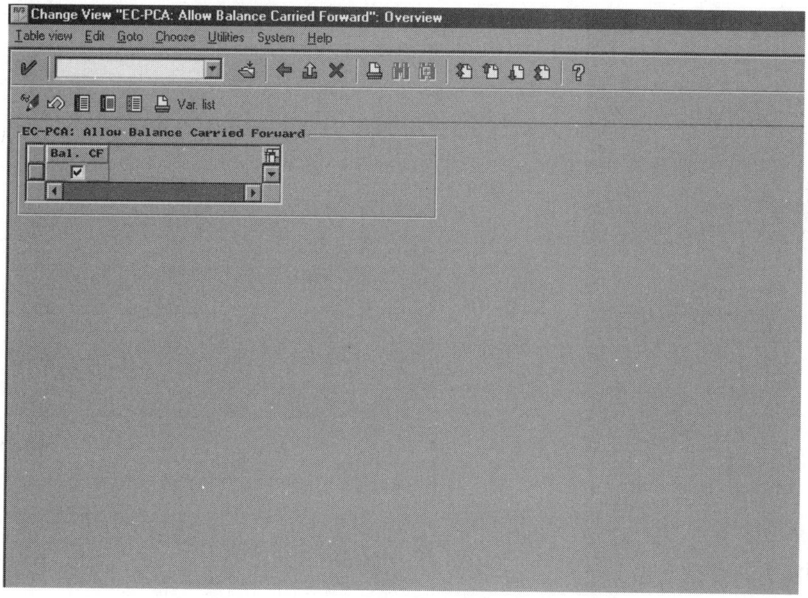

This completes the section on actual posting configuration. You have now completed enough PCA configuration to ensure that all transactional data flows will update properly and that all direct postings are possible. The next section of the chapter will take you through the necessary steps to configure basic PCA planning functionality.

EXTREME SPORTS ADDITIONAL BALANCE SHEET ENTRIES CONFIGURATION ANALYSIS

Extreme Sports will not be producing full balance sheets out of PCA, so there is no immediate need to maintain this table. The entry shown in configuration was for demonstration purposes only.

Profit Center Accounting: Planning

There are two approaches to Profit Center Accounting planning that are standard within SAP: manual profit center planning and transferring plan data from other CO applications. In many instances, PCA planning is a combination of both types. From a configuration viewpoint, the preparation to use manual planning is a more involved process. The development involved in transferring plan data is centered around CO version maintenance, with some order type configuration sprinkled in. Because the manual approach requires the majority of the configuration effort, most of this section will be dedicated to this approach.

To begin, an overview of plan version maintenance, document type creation, and number range assignment will be provided for your review. From there, an explanation of PCA's use of planning parameters and the associated configuration will be covered. And finally, a brief explanation of the copy plan data transaction will round out the section.

Plan Version Maintenance

PCA uses and is controlled by the same CO versions, as with all CO applications. Within the version you have the ability to control whether plan data from other applications is updated automatically in PCA or if you have to manually transfer the postings. For automatic updates into PCA, you should expect interaction to come from only Cost Center Accounting and Internal Order Accounting. All other plan data will have to be transferred manually. The valid CO objects available for manual data transfer include the following:

- ▶ Cost centers
- ▶ Internal orders
- ▶ Projects
- ▶ Networks
- ▶ Account-based profitability segments
- ▶ SOP orders (sales/operations-related orders)
- ▶ MRP orders

N O T E   Only account-based CO-PA can transfer plan data to PCA due to the cost element requirement in PCA plan postings. You must have defined both the profit center and controlling area in the CO-PA plan entry.

Plan version maintenance was covered in detail in Chapters 7, 9, and 10, so only a review of some key topics is necessary here. To access the CO version table, use the menu path Enterprise Controlling ➢ Profit Center Accounting ➢ Planning ➢ Maintain Versions.

MAINTAIN CO VERSIONS

You can get to the CO version table with either of the following methods:

Menu Path: **Enterprise Controlling** ➢ **Profit Center Accounting** ➢ **Planning** ➢ **Maintain Versions**

Transaction Code: **OKEQ**

As you have seen in past maintenance, the CO versions screen will appear. As always, SAP allows you to use as many planning versions as you like. There are two key screens related to automating the transfer of plan data:

▶ The screen with settings for Profit Center Accounting

▶ The screen with fiscal year settings

Settings for PCA

Move to the PCA settings window by selecting the version to be maintained and selecting the Settings for Profit Center Accounting button found in the Navigation section of the window. The PCA fiscal year dependent version parameters overview screen appears (Figure 12.19).

FIGURE 12.19   The PCA fiscal year dependent version parameters settings

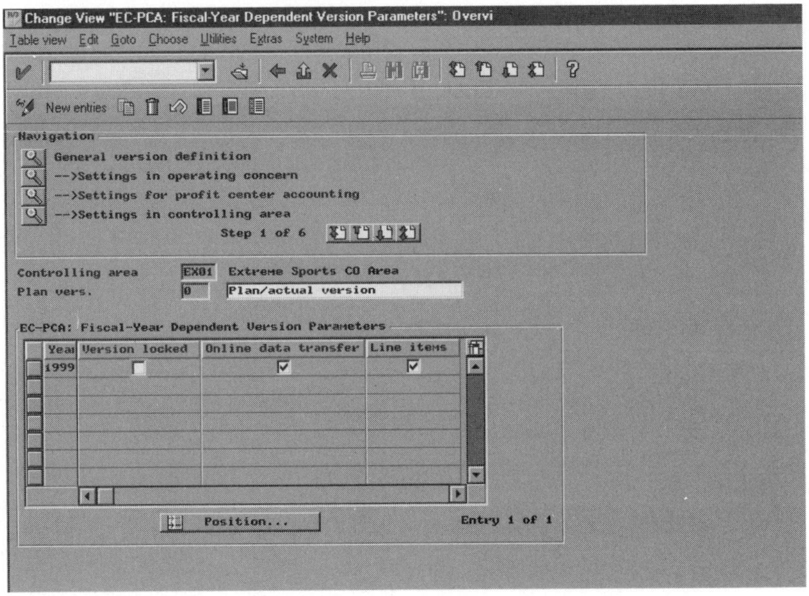

On the PCA fiscal year dependent version parameters screen, the effects of the following fields are important:

Online Data Transfer   The setting must be activated if you wish to transfer plan postings from CCA and order accounting online. This will almost always be activated because of the need to transfer actuals real time.

Line Items   This setting must be activated if you want line item changes to be documented. Also, activating this setting will make manual plan transfers easier because you will have to ability to retransfer plan activity. When it's activated, you have the opportunity to retransfer plan items at an individual object (order, cost center) level. If it's not activated, you will have no recourse but to retransfer all the object values for the given type. See Figure 12.20 for a view of the manual transfer screen for PCA plan data.

Maintain or review these settings and move to the fiscal year parameters screen.

Settings for Fiscal Year

Scroll through the navigation section of the CO versions maintenance screen to find the Settings for Fiscal Year button and select it. The fiscal year dependent version parameters detail window will appear (see Figure 12.21). Of the many fields found on this screen, there is only one you want to be most concerned with from a PCA perspective: Planning Integration.

FIGURE 12.20   The PCA manual transfer screen for plan data

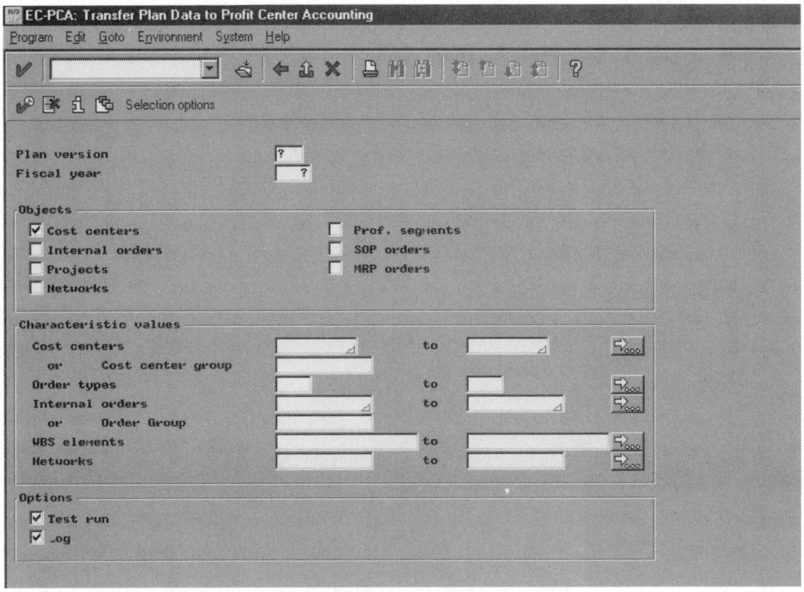

FIGURE 12.21   The fiscal year dependent version parameters detail screen

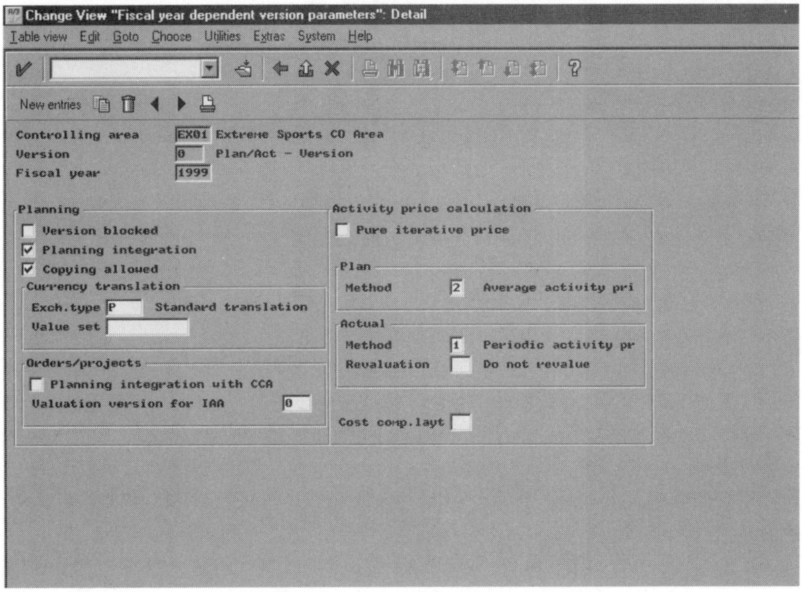

Activate Planning Integration if you want to transfer plan data from cost centers to Profit Center Accounting automatically online. Although no plan data exists in the

version, you can change this setting. If plan data has been posted, the integration indicator can be activated through transaction KP96 (Activate line items and planning integration). Once it's activated, SAP posts previously planned line items.

To fully automate plan postings into PCA, you have to also maintain each order type to allow planning integration.

Order Type Maintenance

In "Order Type Development" in Chapter 10, you learned that you must maintain the planning integration field to allow plan updates into PCA. Figure 12.22 is a view of the order type EXX1 used by Extreme Sports for expense-related project tracking.

If Planning Integration is active here, plan data can be automatically passed to Profit Center Accounting. To activate this setting, the CO Partner Update setting must read "Active" (see Figure 12.22). This setting does not need to be activated if you do not intend to completely integrate with Profit Center Accounting.

When maintenance of these three areas is complete, your version is ready to accept automated plan updates from CCA and Order Accounting into PCA. The second task in PCA planning configuration is the development of the planning document type. Similar to the one established to support actual postings, it must be established before any postings can occur.

FIGURE 12.22   The order type master screen for EXX1

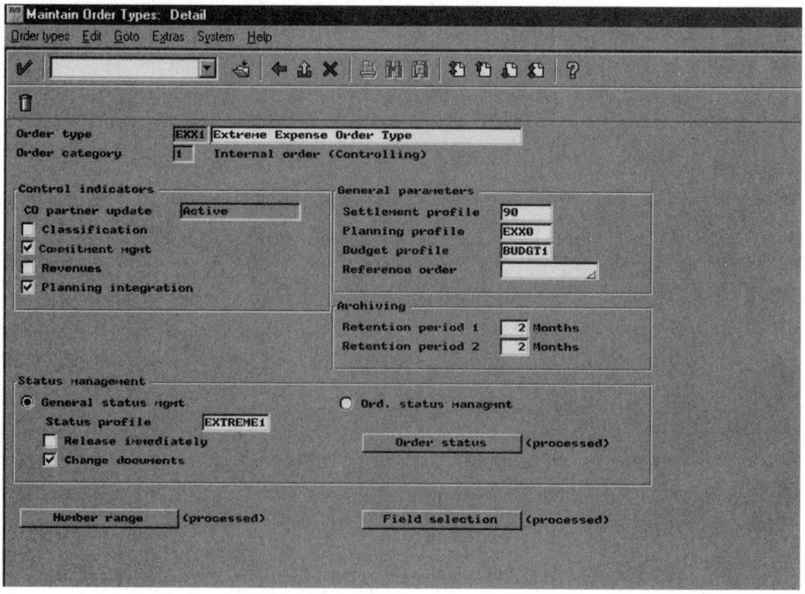

Define Document Types: Plan

The plan document type is simple to create. The process is identical to the process for establishing a document type to support actual postings. SAP delivers plan document type P0 as the default. You are welcome to use this one or create your own. It is recommended that you create your own if you anticipate making any changes to the default settings. To access the plan document type screen, use the menu path Enterprise Controlling ➢ Profit Center Accounting ➢ Planning ➢ Define Document Types.

DEFINE DOCUMENT TYPES FOR PLAN POSTINGS

You can get to the plan document type screen with either of the following methods:

Menu Path: **Enterprise Controlling** ➢ **Profit Center Accounting** ➢ **Planning** ➢ **Define Document Types**

Transaction Code: **GCBA**

The plan document type screen will look similar to the one used to create actual types. As a matter of fact, the process is identical, so the steps won't be re-created here. Review the section on actual document type creation for detailed descriptions of each of the fields. Figure 12.23 is a view of the plan document type PX, which will be used by Extreme Sports for PCA planning.

FIGURE 12.23   Extreme Sports' document type PX

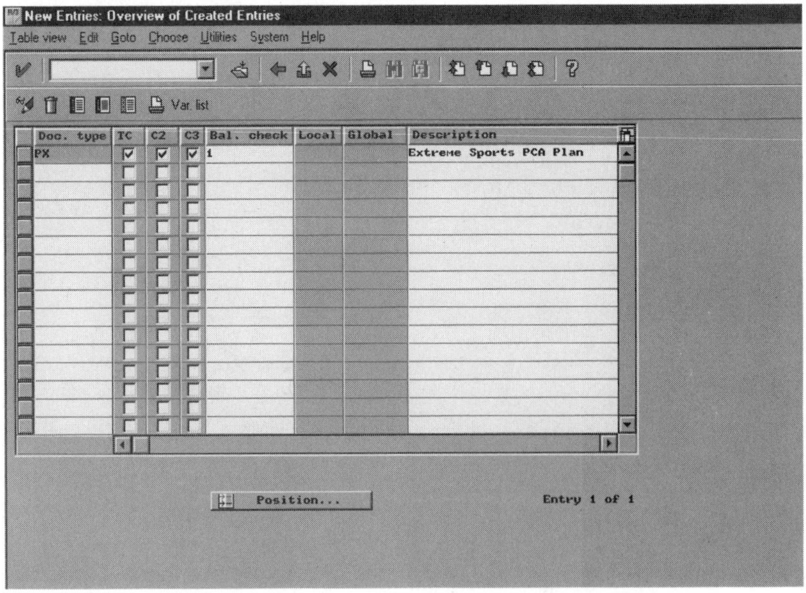

Like actual postings, all plan updates can be maintained in three currencies:

▶ Transaction currency (TC), held as the primary currency

▶ Local currency or company code currency (C2)

▶ Reporting currency (C3)

You will also have to maintain these same settings on the planning parameters screen if you want to manually plan in each currency type. There is more on this in "PCA Planning Parameters" later in this chapter. You have the opportunity to create as many planning document types as necessary. When you are finished, the last step in the process will be to assign them to a number range.

Number Range Assignment: Plan

The configuration steps to assign number ranges to a plan are identical to the steps to assign number ranges to the PCA actuals. As noted earlier, the document type is used as the number range assignment object and thus must be completed first. To access the number range assignment screen, use the menu path Enterprise Controlling ➤ Profit Center Accounting ➤ Planning ➤ Maintain Number Ranges.

EXTREME SPORTS DOCUMENT TYPE FOR PLAN POSTINGS CONFIGURATION ANALYSIS

Again, Extreme Sports chose to create its own document type because it wanted to make changes to the settings that were delivered with P0. All three PCA-related currencies will be allowed for plan postings. For balance checking, here again Extreme Sports chose the flexibility SAP offers with the assignment of a warning on any unbalanced entries.

MAINTAIN NUMBER RANGES FOR PLAN POSTINGS

You can get to the number range assignment screen by using the following methods:

Menu Path: **Enterprise Controlling** ➢ **Profit Center Accounting** ➢ **Planning** ➢ **Maintain Number Ranges**

Transaction Code: **GB02**

For the exact steps necessary to assign the plan document type and a number range interval, review the section on number range assignment for actual document types. The only difference is that you are maintaining the screen for the plan type. Once you're finished, plan document type creation is complete. The next section will take you through the concept of the PCA planning parameters and the accompanying set maintenance.

PCA Planning Parameters

Planning parameters are used by PCA as the control utility for manual plan entry on a profit center. Through the parameter, you can determine such things as what periods, profit centers, cost elements, and currencies can be planned. During the planning parameter creation steps, you will be asked to provide the parameter with a planning set ID. This set is really a multidimensional set containing both profit centers and cost elements used in the planning process. To properly maintain the parameter, this set must be created up front.

Planning Set Creation

SAP delivers with the system three planning sets you can use:

8A-PLANSET-1   Used as the basic profit center/cost and revenue element planning set.

8A-PLANSET-2   In addition to the objects allowed in 8A-PLANSET-1, you will be allowed to plan the partner profit center. The partner profit center is the offset profit center on a two-sided transaction.

8A-PLANSET-3   Used when you want to plan the functional area. This planning set is useful only for those companies using the cost of sales approach to report profitability.

Each of these sets contain variables that require the user to enter a profit center group, a cost element group, a partner profit center group, or a functional area during plan data entry. This is fine in most cases because the responsibility is on the user to determine the proper profit center/cost element mix. If, however, you wish to control the situation more, it is recommended that you create your own planning set to be used with your new planning parameter. There is a one-to-one relationship between the planning parameter and the planning set, so choose carefully. It may actually turn out that multiple sets and parameters will be needed for your solution.

Set creation is table specific; that is, all sets must be assigned to a planning table to be used properly by SAP. For PCA, the table to use is GLU1. You may be thinking that you should be using GLPCT, the PCA plan line items table, but GLPCT is used for reporting sets only. If GLU1 is not used, your sets will not be visible in the planning parameter screen.

In addition to the table assignment, there are four different types of sets that can be created to support PCA planning:

Basic   A set that is used to hold the values, whether individual or within a range of values, of a single type of object like a profit center or cost element. This is used as the building block for more complex single-dimension and multi-dimension sets. The basic set can also contain formulas and formula and value variables.

Single-Dimension   Similar to the basic set, a single-dimension set can hold the values of only a single type of object also. However, you can assign a number of basic sets of the same type to easily build a hierarchy or other complex groups.

Data   Used mainly in reporting, the data set is used to derive or narrow the values and quantities selected.

Multi-Dimension   Allows for a complex grouping of two or more objects in a single set using any combination of basic, single-dimension, and data sets. The one stipulation is that the object type must not be defined more than once within the set. This type of set will be the one you will use predominantly during planning parameter creation.

Detailed set creation was covered in Chapter 2, so the steps won't be retraced here. However, a menu path to use to access the set creation screen is provided. It is Enterprise Controlling ➤ Profit Center Accounting ➤ Sets and Variables ➤ Maintain Sets.

SET MAINTENANCE FOR PLAN PARAMETER CREATION

You can get to the set creation screen with either of the following methods:

Menu Path: **Enterprise Controlling ➤ Profit Center Accounting ➤ Sets and Variables ➤ Maintain Sets**

Transaction Code: **GS01**

Figure 12.24 is shown as a reference for what the screen should look like. You have the ability to copy from an existing set or you can create your own. Spend some time up front planning your set usage. It will be critical that you have all the right objects in place when the user wants to begin plan entry.

WARNING   Remember to select GLU1 as the table in which to create the planning set.

FIGURE 12.24   The initial set creation screen

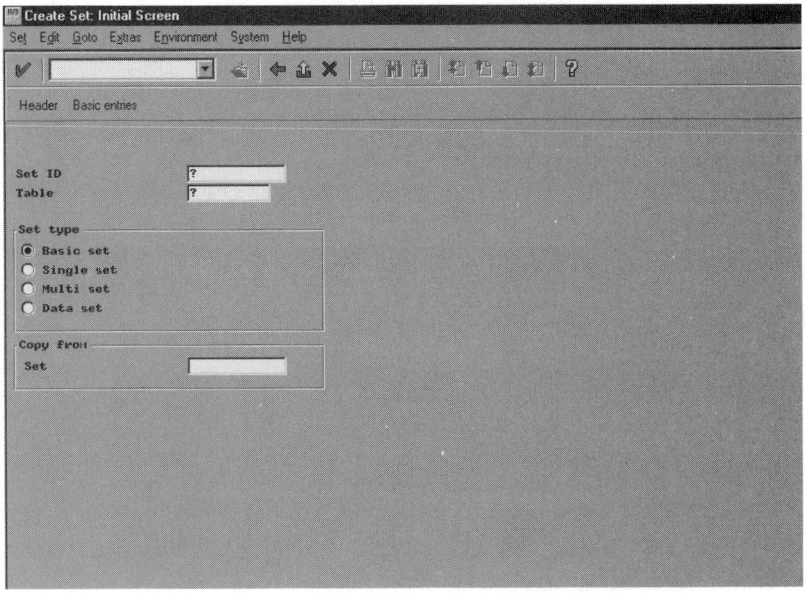

Figure 12.25 is a view of the planning set EXTREME-PCA, which will be used by Extreme Sports for PCA plan entry.

FIGURE 12.25   A view of a multi-dimension set, EXTREME-PCA

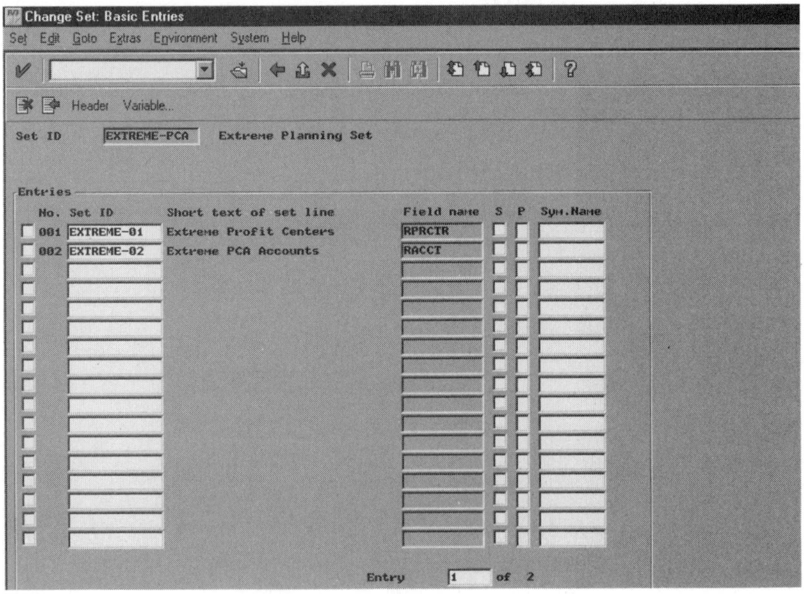

Once you have completed the set creation, you are ready to create the planning parameter.

Planning Parameter Creation

To access the planning parameter creation screen, use the menu path Enterprise Controlling ➢ Profit Center Accounting ➢ Planning ➢ Maintain Planning Parameters.

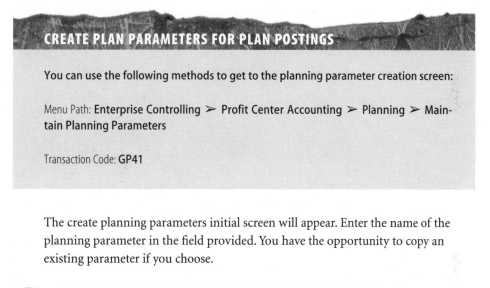

CREATE PLAN PARAMETERS FOR PLAN POSTINGS

You can use the following methods to get to the planning parameter creation screen:

Menu Path: **Enterprise Controlling ➢ Profit Center Accounting ➢ Planning ➢ Maintain Planning Parameters**

Transaction Code: **GP41**

The create planning parameters initial screen will appear. Enter the name of the planning parameter in the field provided. You have the opportunity to copy an existing parameter if you choose.

TIP The parameter will be controlling area independent, so be sure the name you choose is clear and descriptive.

Select the General button or press Enter. The general part screen appears. There are two parts to a planning parameter: the general part and the FI-SL part. On the general part screen, some of the field settings will default in, others you will have to maintain manually. Figure 12.26 shows the planning parameter EX-PCA01, which will be used by Extreme Sports to enter its plan data.

FIGURE 12.26   The general part settings planning parameter EX-PCA01

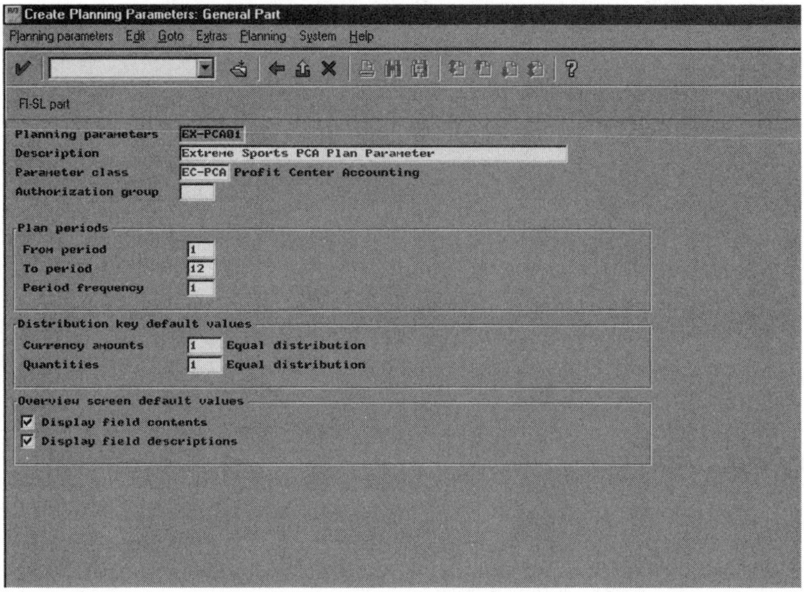

All field settings can be changed except the parameter ID. Review the following fields and their descriptions as you complete your ID:

Planning Parameters   The value in this field defaults from the initial screen. The only way to change the ID now is to delete the parameter and start again.

Description   Enter enough of a description for your parameter to make it easily recognizable from a selection menu.

Parameter Class   Enter **EC-PCA** or **FI-GLX** as the parameter class. This will ensure that the planning parameter is used only in PCA or Special Ledger (FI-SL) planning.

Authorization Group   This field is not required. If you are using authorization groups in your security maintenance, this field may be relevant. See your SAP authorizations group for maintenance details.

The fields in the Plan Periods section determine the range of frequency for valid plan periods:

From/To Period   Enter the range of periods for which this parameter is valid.

Period Frequency   This field relates to the periodicity of plan entry. If you wish to enter plan data on a quarterly basis, the frequency would be 3, or once every three months.

The fields in the Distribution Key Default Values section determine the default distribution for both the currency and quantity amounts:

Currency Amounts/Quantities   Enter the default distribution key for both types of data. A distribution key is a tool SAP provides that allows you to determine the spread of data across a given period range. With a properly defined distribution key, you could spread annual plan amounts across a 4-4-5 fiscal year or make an even spread by month.

The fields in the Overview Screen Default Values section control the view on the planning screen. They determine whether the objects being planned (profit center/ cost element) will be displayed by their ID and/or their description:

Display Field Contents   Select this field if you want the ID of the field contents to be displayed. For example, if you want the profit center number to be displayed on the planning screen, select this field.

Display Field Description   Select this field if you want the description of the field to be displayed. For example, if you want the profit center description to be displayed on the planning screen, select the field.

It is possible to have both settings on at the same time, and it is often the recommended approach.

This completes the general part of the planning parameter. You must now maintain the FI-SL portion of the parameter to complete the configuration. To migrate to the window, select the FI-SL Part button. As with the general part fields, the FI-SL fields will be described. Figure 12.27 shows the FI-SL portion for planning parameter EX-PCA01.

FIGURE 12.27 The FI-SL settings for planning parameter EX-PCA01

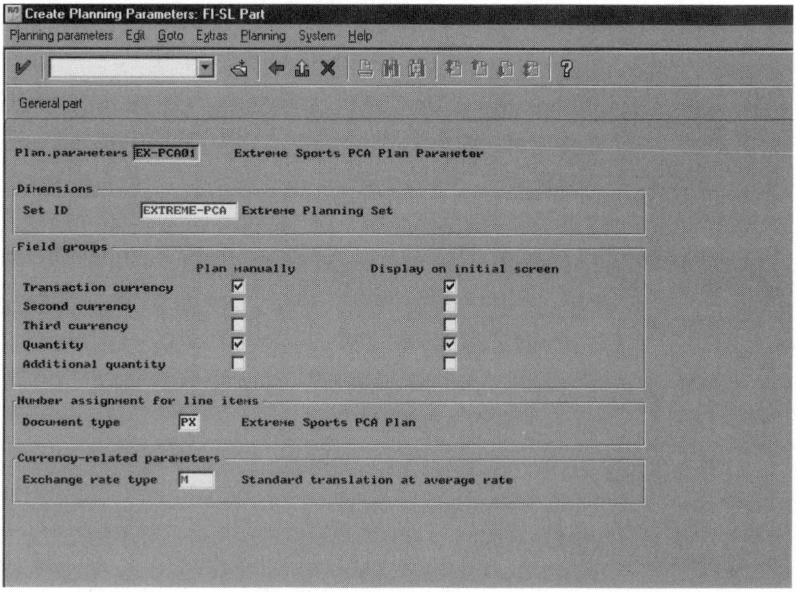

The Dimensions section defines the parameter planning set:

Set ID Enter the ID of the planning set you created earlier. The planning set entry is required. With this setting, you are determining what object values the user will have access to during the planning process. This is a good control mechanism if you want to limit the ability to enter or view plan entries.

The fields in the Field Groups section determine which currency and quantity fields are allowed and/or required during plan entry. The fields are divided into two settings: Plan Manually and Display on Initial Screen. If you want to allow planning in any of these areas, it must be checked in the Plan Manually column. All the Initial Screen setting accomplishes is determining which fields default on the first plan entry screen. The user will have the authority to scroll to the other allowed currencies and quantities. The fields are as follows:

Transaction/Second/Third Currency By activating a currency, you are allowing the user to plan in that currency. Leave these inactive to block any postings.

Quantity/Additional Quantity PCA allows you to maintain two quantity fields. Select either one, both, or none.

The Number Assignment for Line Items section assigns a plan document type to your parameters:

Document Type   Enter the document type if you are maintaining plan postings at the line item level. If you are, a PCA plan doc will need to be created for each plan entry. If not, leave this field blank.

The Currency-Related Parameters setting is necessary when planning in multiple currencies:

Exchange Rate Type   Enter the ID of the exchange method relevant to your company's needs. Rate type M, standard translation at an average rate, will default.

When you are finished, be sure to save the planning parameter. This completes the steps necessary for planning parameter creation. You are now at a point in your PCA planning development where you can manually enter plan data. The last section in PCA planning will show you the subtle differences between the copy plan data transaction for PCA and the one found in CCA.

EXTREME SPORTS PLANNING PARAMETER CREATION CONFIGURATION ANALYSIS

Extreme Sports will be creating a number of planning parameters to support its manual plan entry. It found that the delivered planning sets offered too much breadth. Because each profit center manager will be entering their own plan, Extreme Sports would like to narrow the scope of profit centers and accounts to choose from. Additionally, it anticipates one day creating new distribution keys to support quarterly plan entries. And the planning parameter is the perfect place to make sure the distribution keys default properly.

Copy Plan Data

As with Cost Center Accounting, with PCA you have the ability to copy data to various plan versions. The main difference between the two systems is PCA's ability to copy actuals into a plan version. SAP accomplishes this by extending the source data selections on the PCA side to include the record type. The record type is used to classify the type of data being held in the database and includes four values:

0 Actuals

1 Plan

2 Actual Assessments/Distributions

3 Plan Assessments/Distributions

To get a better feel for the concepts, follow the user menu path Accounting ➢ Enterprise Controlling ➢ Profit Center Accounting ➢ Planning ➢ Copy Data to Plan to view the PCA plan copy window.

COPY DATA TO PLAN

You can get to the PCA plan copy configuration screen with either of the methods listed here:

Application Menu Path: **Accounting** ➢ **Enterprise Controlling** ➢ **Profit Center Accounting** ➢ **Planning** ➢ **Copy Data to Plan**

Transaction Code: **KE62**

The PCA Copy Data to Plan window appears (Figure 12.28). In the Source Data section, you will see the field setting for Record Type. By selecting 0 (Actuals), you will be able to copy actual data to a plan version. Additionally, an entry in the field labeled Plan. Parameters is required. This is SAP's way of limiting the amount of transactional data that will be copied across versions. Everything else should look familiar because it is similar to the CCA copy screen described in Chapter 9.

This brings to an end the necessary PCA planning configuration. You are now ready to begin manually planning and/or transferring your plan data into PCA. It is important that you experiment with the transfer postings to be certain that all the bugs are rung out and that all the users' needs are met.

Summary

Profit Center Accounting development is very straightforward in a traditional configuration sense. There is not an infinite number of settings that can be tested to see which ones fit your scenario. Instead, there is a heavy reliance on making the proper object assignments and building an accurate standard hierarchy. Spend some time researching the reporting needs of your client prior to beginning the configuration. The changes become more cumbersome once you begin to have real postings in your environment. And finally, communication with all related modules is key to success. So be certain to include the persons from the MM, PP, and SD teams during the design and development phases.

The following topics were covered in this chapter:

Introduction to PCA Configuration

Basic Settings and Master Data Review

Controlling Area Maintenance

Analyze/Update PCA Settings

Master Data Settings

Assignments in Profit Center Accounting

Material Master Assignment

PCA Assignment Monitor

Actual Posting Maintenance

Set Control Parameters

Define Document Types: Actual

Number Range Assignment: Actual

Assign Revenue Elements to Profit Centers

Choose Additional Balance Sheet and P&L Accounts

Profit Center Accounting: Planning

Plan Version Maintenance

Define Document Types: Plan

Number Range Assignment: Plan

PCA Planning Parameters

Planning Parameter Creation

Copy Plan Data

CHAPTER 13

Investment Management

FEATURING:

▶ INVESTMENT MANAGEMENT CONFIGURATION

▶ INVESTMENT PROGRAMS, MEASURES, AND PROFILES

▶ INVESTMENT MANAGEMENT PLANNING AND BUDGETING

nvestment Management (IM) is an example of a SAP module that crosses both FI and CO. Because of the function it provides—namely, capital acquisition management—it purposefully resides in neither. The key integration points involved with either FI or CO are Asset Accounting, General Ledger Accounting, and Internal Order Accounting. Both General Ledger and Internal Order Accounting were covered in detail in prior chapters, so the concepts will only be mentioned here. Asset Accounting is not covered in any of the chapters, but its role as it relates to IM will be developed within this chapter.

Another integration point with IM is the SAP module called Project Systems (PS). Through the assignment of Work Breakdown Structures, or WBS elements, spending on PS-related capital projects can be monitored and controlled. Because Project Systems is beyond the scope of this book, WBS development will be mentioned but not shown. The focus of configuration will be on the IM module and its relationship to Internal Order Accounting. The chapter will begin with a brief explanation of IM configuration concepts.

Investment Management Configuration

Configuration for the Investment Management (IM) module is rather simple in that there are not too many working parts to manage. Of the areas necessary to configure to support internal order integration, only the program type and investment profile have not been covered in prior chapters. Concepts like order type, user status, and plan and budget profiles have been covered previously. How they are relative to IM configuration will be exposed.

The configuration itself that will be flushed out in the chapter will be simple and straightforward. Only those parts necessary to get IM up and running will be shown in any detail. To this end, asset accounting configuration will be mentioned but not shown. Before beginning the project, it is advisable to partner with whomever your asset expert is and let them know what your needs will be regarding asset class development. For demonstration purposes, a preconfigured asset class, AuC1 (Asset under Construction), will be shown.

Investment Management can be a good analysis tool for monitoring and reporting projects at a high level. Plan/Actual or Budget/Actual comparisons are examples of how IM can be useful. It is not a replacement for Project Systems and its task-oriented planning approach.

Before beginning, it is important to understand some of the terminology that will be used in the chapter:

Investment program   The user-defined capital budget hierarchy used to plan, budget, and monitor all capital spending. The investment program is developed in a hierarchical format.

Program position or investment node   Refers to a position found on the investment program hierarchy. At the lowest level of a hierarchy, a program position may relate to a capital project or project component.

Measure   Either an internal order or a WBS element. The measure, as SAP refers to it, is the cost collector through which spending will be controlled and monitored. It is the key integration object with Investment Management. WBS elements are the collectors associated with Project Systems, whereas internal orders are cost collectors found in the CO module. The measure is always assigned to the lowest program position within the investment program.

Begin IM development with the creation of master data items such as program types, investment profiles, and investment measures.

Program Types, Investment Measures, and the Investment Profile

Begin your Investment Management configuration with the creation of the program type, which could be described as the backbone of the investment program. The investment program provides an enterprise-wide view of capital spending and budgeting through a hierarchical representation. There are two steps associated with program type development:

1. Create the program type.

2. Assign approved objects for use with the program type.

Within the hierarchy, you would find the projects that make up your capital investment plan for one or multiple fiscal years, depending on your management style. Figure 13.1 provides you with a basic example of an investment program hierarchy. In this example, the program position PROJECT_001 (New Plant Roof) represents a single capital project. The program type is the control mechanism for the investment program; it regulates how planning and budgeting are accomplished through various profile assignments. Additional maintenance, although not required, will allow general status management to be activated through the order type.

FIGURE 13.1   Example of an investment program hierarchy

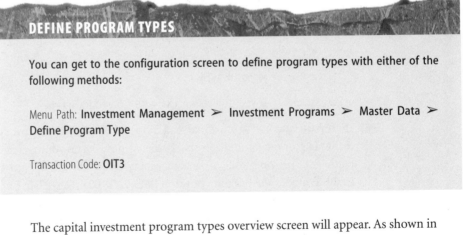

Create the Program Type

You can access the program type configuration screen by following the menu path Investment Management ➣ Investment Programs ➣ Master Data ➣ Define Program Type.

DEFINE PROGRAM TYPES

You can get to the configuration screen to define program types with either of the following methods:

Menu Path: **Investment Management** ➣ **Investment Programs** ➣ **Master Data** ➣ **Define Program Type**

Transaction Code: **OIT3**

The capital investment program types overview screen will appear. As shown in Figure 13.2, SAP will deliver with the system program type 0001.

FIGURE 13.2   The capital investment program types overview screen

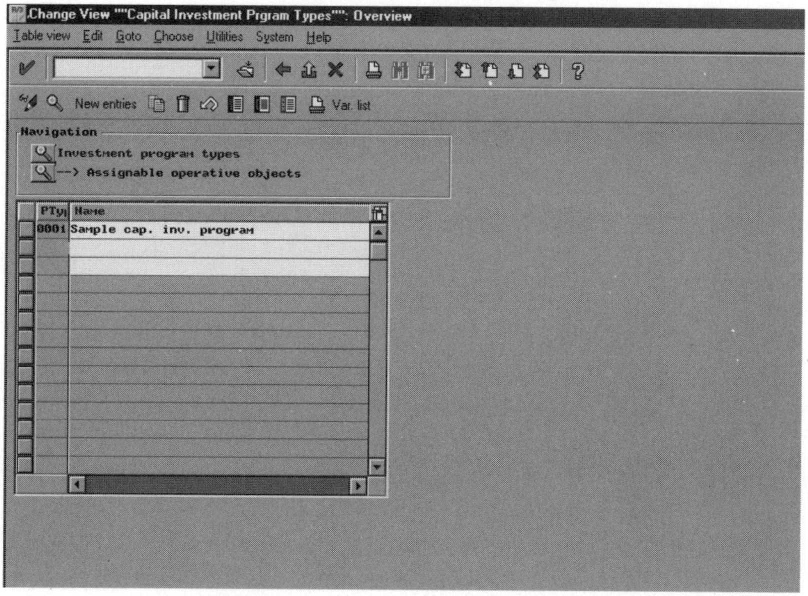

Begin step 1 by selecting the New Entries button to retrieve a detail entry screen. The process for developing a program type is similar to the process for creating an order type because there is an iterative approach required. Looking at the screen, you will see fields for a plan profile and a budget profile. Both of these files will have to be created and assigned prior to attempting any planning or budgeting with the program. The same principle applies with the Status Profile field. Status profile development was covered in Chapter 10, and the same concepts are at play here.

It is possible to create and save a program type without these profiles being assigned. They must, however, be assigned prior to creating an investment program. Once that occurs, the profiles on the program type cannot be altered without first deleting the investment program. This will prove more difficult to do once you have begun creating and assigning investment measures (orders and WBS elements). Review the following field definitions for the program type:

Program Type   Enter the ID and description of your program type. The ID can be up to four alphanumeric characters in length.

Budget Profile   The budget profile controls the view for Investment Management budgeting. A budget profile is not required during initial program type creation. It is recommended that you create it prior to capital investment program development. The profile is IM specific and thus is different than the one configured for Internal Order Accounting. See the section on Investment Management planning and budgeting profiles for details.

Plan. Profile   Similar to the budget profile, it is not required during the initial program type configuration. The plan profile controls the view for Investment Management planning. The profile is also IM specific and thus is different than the one configured for Internal Order Accounting. See the section on Investment Management planning and budgeting profiles for details.

Status Profile   This field is not required. Depending on your capital investment planning strategy, you may wish to control investment activity at the program-position level. A program position can be described as a project in the investment program hierarchy (see Figure 13.1). If assigned, the status profile will control the hierarchy node in the same way it controls an order type, by managing business transaction activity. For example, if the status profile is properly configured, you can control when budgeting may occur by determining what the user status on the program position must be to allow the business transaction. Review the section on status management in Chapter 10 before assigning the profile. The same profile you develop for Internal Order Accounting can be used here in Investment Management.

Repr. (Representative) Form   The entry here will control how the program position and the assigned measure are viewed during planning and budgeting. The program position and measure can each be displayed by either its ID, like an internal order number, or its text description. You have four values to choose from:

1   ID of the capital program position/ID of the measure (internal order or WBS element)

2   Text for the capital program position/text for the measure (internal order or WBS element)

3   ID of the capital program position/text for the measure (internal order or WBS element)

4   Text for the capital program position/ID of the measure (internal order or WBS element)

The setting can be changed whenever necessary. Because many text descriptions are lengthy, option 1 is a good all-around choice. Many people will easily identify with the order and project ID.

Object Class   Enter the object class of the measures that are to be maintained by this program type. With this option, SAP offers the ability to manage investment programs by object class. INVST (Investment) is a proper entry. However, SAP will not force you to use objects of this class type. For example, if INVST is selected here, you will still have the option of using orders with the object class value of OCOST (Overhead Cost).

Budget Dist. (Distribution)   This setting will determine the budget method for an assigned measure:

▶ If this setting is activated, the assigned measure must receive its budget from the node to which it is assigned. In effect, the budget is distributed from the program position.

▶ If this setting is not activated, the assigned measure can be budgeted directly.

For the greatest level of control, it is recommended that you activate budget distribution for the program type. Otherwise, there is no restriction to exceeding the budget of the program position. If budget distribution is activated, the program type will require a budget profile be assigned.

Figure 13.3 is a view of the program type ECAP, which will be used by Extreme Sports. When you are finished, save the program type. The next step will be to assign the approved objects to the new program.

FIGURE 13.3   A view of ECAP-Extreme Capital Investment Program Type

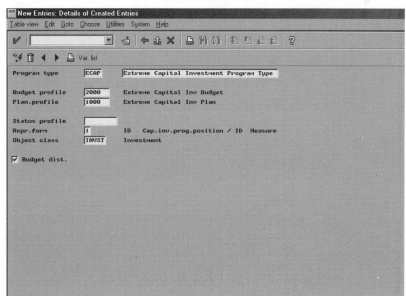

> **T I P**   You cannot delete an investment program from the user menu. The path is found in the IMG and is Investment Management ➤ Investment Programs ➤ Master Data ➤ Delete Programs. From this window, you will be able to delete any or all investment programs in the system.

Assign the Operative Objects or Measures

During the creation of the investment program, the user has to make a determination involving which types of measures are allowed for assignment for each position. Remember, measure assignment is the key integration point for Investment Management. If you assign the approved measures to the program type, all investment program positions will default with the settings. The user will not have to manually maintain the Allowed Measures section of the program position.

From the capital investment program types overview screen (Figure 13.2), place the cursor on the new program type and select the navigation button Assignable Operative Objects. An assignment screen will appear. Select the New Entries button to make the necessary assignment. You will have only two choices:

- ▶ OR-Orders
- ▶ PR-WBS Elements

For our example, Orders is selected (see Figure 13.4), but if you are unsure of whether Project Systems is in scope, select both. There are no detrimental effects from selecting them both. Save the settings when you are finished. Program type configuration is complete, and it can now be used for investment program creation. The next section will cover the concept of the investment measure and the development of the investment profile.

EXTREME SPORTS PROGRAM TYPE CONFIGURATION ANALYSIS

Extreme Sports will be using Investment Management to help manage its capital-related projects. Because Project Systems is beyond the scope of its project, the configuration is tailored for internal orders rather than WBS elements. Extreme Sports management has no interest in using status management for its investment programs. It feels the control provided by status management on the internal order is sufficient. Budget distribution was activated for the program type. Because it wants the investment program to accurately display and track all capital spending, each order must take its approved budget from the program position.

FIGURE 13.4   Order assignment to program type ECAP

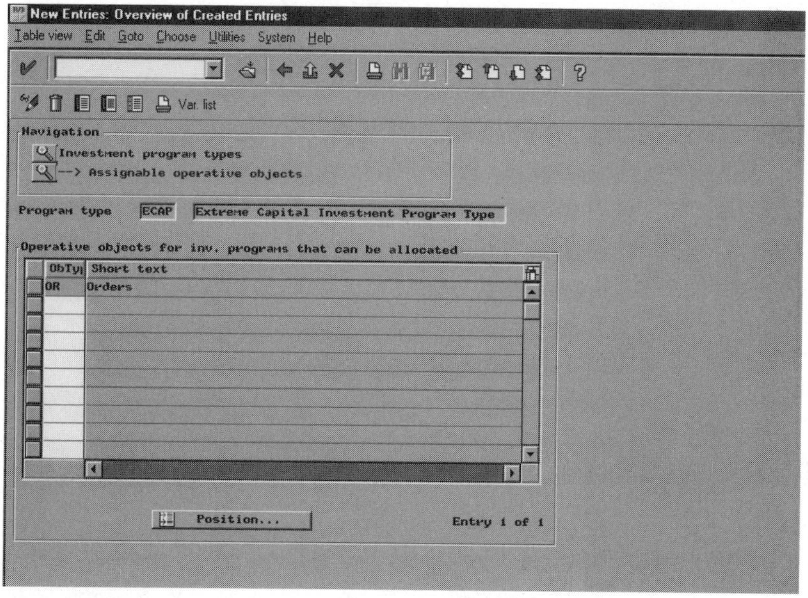

Investment Measures

As discussed earlier, there are two investment measures available for use with Investment Management: internal orders and WBS elements. With our focus on internal orders, WBS elements will not be discussed. To support Investment Management, you should consider creating a new order type. The IM order type, as it will be referred to in this section, will have to allow for different ways of budgeting and settling costs. This means order budget profiles different than those created to support expense project tracking need to be created.

The concepts for internal order creation covered in Chapter 10 are still relevant here. To help with your development, a checklist is provided that will outline the key areas when creating the IM order type. The majority of the differences with the order type relate to the integration with Fixed Asset Accounting and the Asset under Construction in particular:

Settlement structure   When creating the settlement structure for the IM order type, be certain to make FXA-Asset a valid receiver. Also, keep in mind that you will probably be doing some order-to-order settlements. And for certain amortization projects, it may become necessary to settle to a G/L account.

Settlement profile   Again, with the profile, be certain to make a fixed asset a valid receiver. In the Default Object Type field, enter FXA-Fixed Asset as the object type. This setting will force the asset as the default receiver on the settlement rule creation screen.

Origin structures   Depending on how the AuC class, Asset under Construction, will be determined, you may have to create additional structures. More on this will be covered in "Investment Profile" later in this chapter.

Object class   Be certain that the IM order has the object class designation of INVST (Investment). This will make it easier to track within the CO information environment.

Plan/budget profiles   You may be able to reuse a plan profile developed for an overhead cost order, but you will almost certainly have to build a new capital-specific budget profile. The main reason for this is related to availability control. Your company probably has different tolerance limits for capital spending than it does for operating expenditures. To build a new capital-specific budget profile, you will have to return to the Overhead Cost Controlling section of the IMG. An additional benefit to creating capital order–specific profiles is the chance to lock your capital order type with a specific investment program type. See Chapter 10 for details.

T I P   Using model orders is a good way to ensure that the proper fields are defaulting during order creation.

Your solution may require more than one IM order type, and this is not an issue with Investment Management. Any number of order types can be used in conjunction with a single investment program. It is recommended that you review Chapter 10 in detail before proceeding.

Investment Profile

The investment profile is the link between the internal order and the Asset under Construction. It will determine for the user which asset class is to be used for the Asset under Construction and execute the creation of the asset. The profile, once created, is assigned directly to the order master record during IM order creation.

EXTREME SPORTS INVESTMENT ORDER TYPE CONFIGURATION ANALYSIS

Because Extreme Sports segregates its capital spending by real and personal property, it has decided to create two investment order types, one for each property type. The orders will be planned and budgeted; the budget will be distributed from the assigned program position. Settlement configuration will allow for costs to be settled to only fixed assets and other orders. This is to ensure that no operating expenses will be routed through the order and moved to a cost center. Any expenses related to a project will be posted to an expense-related order type.

WARNING   You must first create the necessary special Asset under Construction classes to support Investment Management. Consult with your fixed asset consultant before proceeding.

Begin the profile definition by following the menu path Investment Management ➢ Investment Orders ➢ Master Data ➢ Define Investment Profiles.

DEFINE INVESTMENT PROFILE

You can get to the investment profile configuration screen by using the following methods:

Menu Path: **Investment Management** ➢ **Investment Orders** ➢ **Master Data** ➢ **Define Investment Profiles**

Transaction Code: **OITA**

The investment profile overview screen appears. SAP delivers investment profile 000001 with the system. To create a new profile, select the New Entries button. There is really no need to copy the delivered profile because it is simply maintained with a default asset class that you are probably not using. From the new investment profile entries screen, begin building your new profile (see Figure 13.5).

FIGURE 13.5 An empty new investment profile entries screen

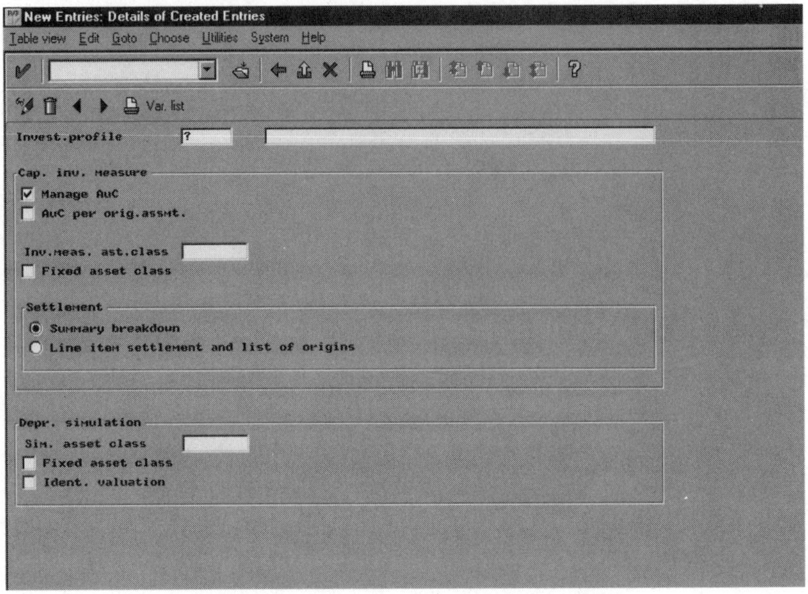

Here is a list of the available fields along with brief descriptions:

Invest. Profile Enter the ID and description for the new investment profile. The ID can be up to six alphanumeric characters in length.

The settings in the Cap. Inv. Measure section will determine how the Asset under Construction (AuC) is created and which asset class will be used:

Manage AuC If this field is selected, the system will determine one and only one AuC for each assigned measure. For example, when an investment order is created, the system will automatically create an asset master record that is linked to that order. A settlement rule will be automatically created during the first settlement to the AuC. This setting is recommended for most solutions seeking simplicity in asset management.

AuC per Orig. Assignment If this field is selected, the system will determine which AuC to settle to based upon the cost element origin assignment. This solution could potentially involve multiple AuCs per measure. For example, you could create an investment order that segregates real and personal property costs by origin assignment.

After selecting the AuC per Orig. Assignment field, press Enter and a button called Allocate Asset U. Cons. Classes will appear in the body of the window. With the

AuC per Orig. Assignment field, you have to manually match each origin group with an asset class. This button is a path to getting to the necessary allocation configuration window. Before selecting the button, save the investment profile. By saving the investment profile first, you will be able to maintain the assignments for the profile you are creating. For details, see the section "Define Assignment of AuC Classes per Origin Assignment."

Inv. Meas. Ast. Class (Investment Measure Asset Class)   Enter here the asset class of the AuC you want automatically created. This option is effective only if used in conjunction the Manage AuC setting.

N O T E   The AuC class must be maintained properly for use with Investment Management. An indicator that is found on the asset class master record and identifies that class for use with IM must be activated. Once it's set, assets of this special class can be posted to only through an investment order settlement.

Fixed Asset Class   If this field is selected, the user will not have the ability to change the asset class during AuC creation. The investment order will use the asset class defined in the preceding field to build the AuC. If the field is not set, the user will have the capability to choose their own asset class. The one limitation with not setting the field is that the order cannot be automatically released during creation; for the investment order, the AuC has to be created prior to the order's release. In most cases, you will want to activate this field in conjunction with the Manage AuC field setting.

SAP allows for two types of settlement for investment orders. Of these, Summary Breakdown is the easiest to manage:

Summary Breakdown   If this is selected, the order balance is treated as a whole number that can be settled against a single or many receivers. Increased system performance is a key reason for selecting this field, but there is a potential drawback. With summary settlement, there is no audit trail from the asset back to the measure. The costs are settled as a part of the total balance.

Line Item Settlement and List of Origins   If this option is selected, each line item on an investment order will be available for separate settlement rule maintenance; that is, each line item can be directed at a different receiver. This solution may provide more control over how costs are allocated, but at the price of a potential reduction in productivity. A positive characteristic of line item settlement is the opportunity it provides the user to drill back from the asset to the measure line item. This provides you with a good audit trail. Table 13.1 provides examples of both Summary and Line Item settlement.

TABLE 13.1 Comparison of Summary and Line Item Settlement

Summary Settlement: Order 1000	Actual Posting Settlement Amount
Line item 1: Cost Element 600000	$2500
Line item 2: Cost Element 610000	$1500
Line item 3: Cost Element 620000	$1000
Settlement Rule 1 to AuC	$5000
Line Item Settlement: Order 1000	**Actual Posting Settlement Amount**
Line item 1: Cost Element 600000	$2500
Line item 2: Cost Element 610000	$1500
Line item 3: Cost Element 620000	$1000
Settlement Rule 1 to AuC1	$2500
Settlement Rule 2 to AuC2	$1500
Settlement Rule 3 to Order	$1000

SAP gives you the ability to simulate depreciation costs for not only existing assets, but also planned capital expenditures through IM. The settings in the Depr. (Depreciation) Simulation section provide information relating to whether a default asset class should be used for all measures or whether the user should determine the simulation class during measure creation:

Sim. (Simulated) Asset Class   Enter the default asset class the system should use during the simulation.

Fixed Asset Class   If this field is selected, the user will not have the ability to change the asset class investment measure creation. The asset class selection will be taken from the entry in the Sim. Asset Class field. If this field is not set, the user will have the opportunity to enter a depreciation simulation asset class during the investment measure creation.

Indent. (Indicator for Uniform) Valuation   SAP allows you to allocate planned depreciation costs derived from the depreciation simulation to the following:

▶ Cost centers

▶ Asset classes

▶ Start-up dates

The costs can be distributed by percentages identified on either the investment order master record or the program position. Figure 13.6 provides you with a view of the distribution rules screen for the program position. The screen is identical to the one found on the order master record. To get to the simulation distribution screen, from the program position, use the menu path Extras ➢ Dep. Simulation Data.

FIGURE 13.6   Depreciation simulation fields found on the investment program position

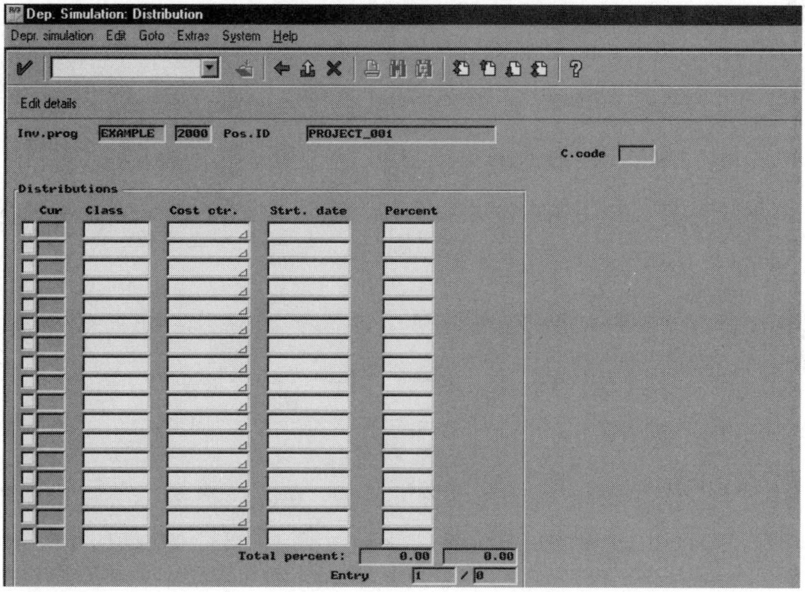

If this field is activated, SAP will keep the distribution start date and the depreciation terms constant for all similar asset classes. This will reduce the amount of effort you will have to undergo to maintain all the fields on the screen shown in Figure 13.6. Any changes to the depreciation terms or start date for one program position's asset class will automatically update all similar asset classes in the other program positions.

If this field is not activated, the system will allow you to manually determine depreciation rules and start dates for each of the asset classes. Any changes made to the depreciation rules on one program position for one asset class will not flow through to all program positions with similar asset classes.

For the simulation to work properly, each program position and/or measure must be maintained with accurate depreciation simulation data.

When you're finished, save the capital investment profile. Figure 13.7 provides you with a view of a completed profile. If you selected AuC per Orig. Assignment in the Cap. Inv. Measure section, then the next section will be important because it provides the next step in that area of configuration.

FIGURE 13.7   Investment profile EXCAP

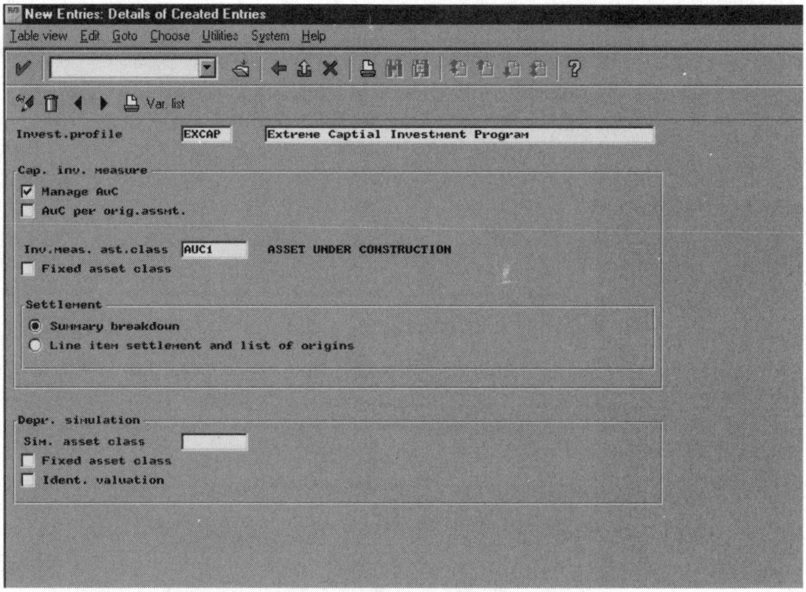

Define Assignment of AuC Classes per Origin Assignment

If you selected the AuC per Orig. Assignment field during the investment profile configuration, your profile will look similar to the one seen in Figure 13.8.

EXTREME SPORTS INVESTMENT PROFILE CONFIGURATION ANALYSIS

Extreme Sports' investment profile EXCAP is basic in its development. The company's desire to keep order management simple has led it to manage only one AuC per order and to maintain only summary settlements. Because it does not want to allow the user to select another asset class during AuC creation, the Fixed Asset Class indicator has been activated. Extreme Sports' capital management group will be running depreciation simulations from time to time. To ensure some integrity and make the maintenance easier, the indicator for uniform valuation was activated.

FIGURE 13.8   Investment profile EXAMPL using AuC per Origin Assignment

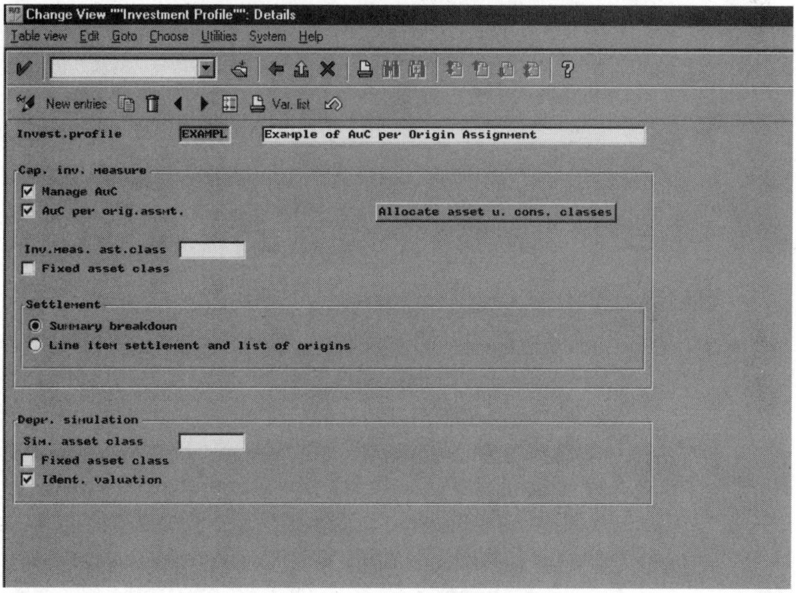

The next step in the process is to assign an AuC class to the origin structure. From the Change View screen on the investment profile, select the Allocate Asset U. Cons. Classes button. The origin assignment screen will appear. Figure 13.9 shows a view of a previously maintained investment profile called EXAMPL; you can see that origin assignments already exist.

FIGURE 13.9   A previously maintained origin assignments for investment profile EXAMPL

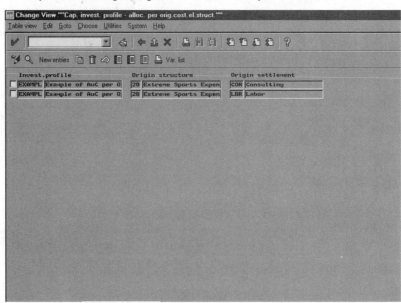

To add new origin assignments, select the New Entries button to bring up a detailed entries screen. Figure 13.10 is a view of a maintained origin assignment.

FIGURE 13.10   Origin assignment for investment profile EXAMPL

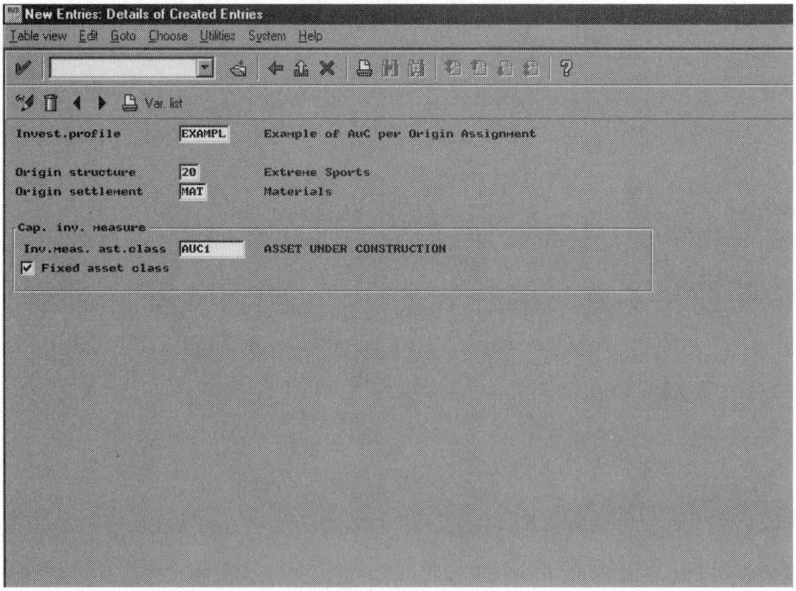

There are only a few fields to maintain, so it should go quickly. Review the list of field definitions here before continuing:

Invest. Profile   The profile ID will carry over from the preceding screen, so you don't have to enter it here.

Origin Structure   This field is used to provide differentiation of costs by cost element group. The structure will contain a number of origin assignments that define this segregation. Origin structure development was covered in Chapter 10.

Origin Settlement   Enter an origin assignment found in the origin structure defined in the preceding description. In the example provided, there are three origin assignments present within the origin structure: CON (Consulting Costs), LAB (Labor Costs), and MAT (Material Costs).

Inv. Meas. Ast. Class   Enter the default asset class that should be used to create the AuC.

Fixed Asset Class   If this field is activated, the user will not be able to manually determine the asset class to be used for creation of the AuC.

Save the origin assignment when you have finished. Repeat the origin assignment step as often as you need to completely cover the entire range of account activity. If an account is posted to an order that is outside of the ranges established here, you won't be able to settle the order.

In the next section, development of the necessary planning and budgeting profiles for IM will be introduced. These profiles are different than those covered in Internal Order Accounting and are necessary to complete the IM program type.

Investment Management Planning and Budgeting Profiles

Investment management provides numerous solutions for capital planning. You can plan the investment hierarchy directly, entering plan amounts on the lowest investment nodes and allowing the system to roll to a total. The concept is called *bottom-up planning*. Another option is to create as many of your investment measures as you can up front and then plan and assign them to the necessary investment node. You can then run a program that will take the plan from each of the measures and assign it to the investment node. The plan can then be rolled up. In both examples, the plan has to get onto the investment program hierarchy. This is key to the budgeting function and necessary for Plan-versus-Actual reporting.

Budgeting provides even more options. The process for budgeting is called *top-down*, and as its name implies, budget is distributed from the highest node down until it reaches all the lowest nodes in the hierarchy. If you have activated budget distribution within your program type, the last step for the budget is to distribute it to the assigned measure. Another feature to budgeting is the potential use of budget categories.

Budget categories allow the user to maintain multiple budget types within a single investment program. The most common use of categories is to segregate capital and expense portions of capital-related projects. In this case, both cost components can be planned/budgeted for the investment node and segregated during reporting and analysis. Earlier in this chapter, program type ECAP-Extreme Capital Investment Program Type was created with a plan profile 1000 and budget profile 2000 assigned to it. Each of these profiles will be covered in its respective section. Plan profile configuration will be shown first.

Investment Management Plan Profile

The plan profile creation process will seem similar to the one you used to create the order profile. To get to the proper configuration screen, use the menu path Investment Management ➢ Investment Programs ➢ Planning in Program ➢ Define Plan Profile.

DEFINE INVESTMENT MANAGEMENT PLAN PROFILES

You can get to the configuration screen to create plan profiles by using the following methods:

Menu Path: **Investment Management** ➢ **Investment Programs** ➢ **Planning in Program** ➢ **Define Plan Profile**

Transaction Code: **OIP1**

The capital investment planning profile screen appears. Figure 13.11 shows the completed investment plan profile 1000, which is used in the investment program ECAP. Select the New Entries button to bring up an empty profile template.

FIGURE 13.11 IM plan profile 1000

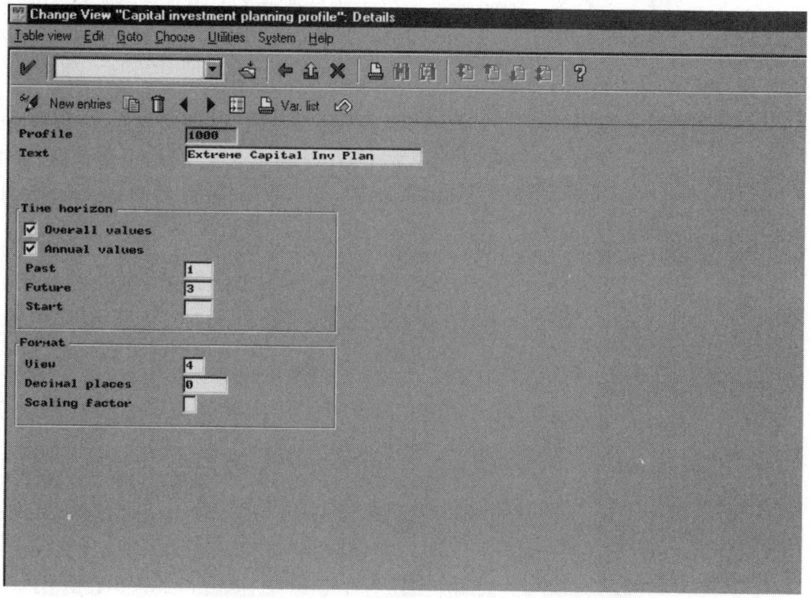

The maintenance is simple, and the necessary fields are described here:

Profile Enter an alphanumeric ID, up to six characters in length, that describes the planning profile.

Text Enter a description for the planning profile. Be sure to be clear because the profile is controlling area independent and you do not want its use to be misinterpreted.

The fields in the Time Horizon section relate to the planning years available for user input and review:

Overall Values Check this field if you want to allow the user to plan for overall values on the investment node. At the highest level, an order or project can be planned for total cost regardless of the year it is consumed. For example, if a project has a total planned cost of $500,000, $500,000 would be considered its overall value.

Annual Values Check this field if you want to allow the user to plan annual expenditures for an investment node. For example, suppose a project has a total planned cost of $500,000. This setting would allow the user to plan the cost expenditures across years: $200,000 would be planned for 2000, $200,000 for 2001, and $100,000 for 2002.

TIP   Activating the Overall and Annual Values fields does not make them required. If your project has no preference, it is recommended that you activate both.

Past   This setting refers to the number of years before the start year the user will be able to plan/budget. For example, if 2 is entered in the field and the current or start year is 2000, the user will be able to view or change the plan or budget back to 1998.

Future   This setting is similar to the Past setting. It refers to the number of years after the start year the user will be able to plan. For example, if 3 is entered and the current or start year is 2000, planning will be allowed through 2003.

Start   This setting refers to the first year that planning/budgeting will be accessible to the user. The number entered here will be added to the current fiscal year to determine the start year. For example, if the current fiscal year is 2000 and you enter 2 in the field, the first year allowed for planning is 2002. Caution should be used when making this entry because this value becomes the basis for all future planning settings. If you want to default the current fiscal year as the start year, leave this field empty.

Fields in the Format section relate to the view the user will have on the planning entry screen:

View   Enter the number of the default view you want to be displayed next to the plan entry column. The user may change these views at the plan entry screen. The choices are as follows:

01 (Distributed)   Displays the amount of plan that has been distributed to the lower nodes

02 (Distributable)   Displays the amount of plan remaining to be distributed

03 (Accumulated)   Displays the total plan accumulated over the allowed planning years

04 (Remainder)   Derived by the formula (Planned total – Accumulated)

06 (Previous Year)   Displays the values planned for the previous year

Decimal Places   Enter the desired number of decimal places in which you want to plan.

Scaling Factor   If scaling is important when planning, enter the scaling factor here. For example, if you want to plan in thousands, enter 3 in the Scaling Factor field. As you enter the plan, only the scaled amount will appear. The total amount is entered in the planning table. With a scale of 3, a plan of $1,000,000 is entered as $1,000 on the planning screen.

When you have completed the profile, be sure to save it. You can now assign the plan profile to your program type as it was described earlier in "Create the Program Type."

Investment Management Budget Profile

To create the IM budget profile, you will follow steps similar to those used to create the IM plan profile. To get to the necessary window, use the menu path Investment Management ➤ Investment Programs ➤ Budgeting in Program ➤ Define Budget Profile.

DEFINE INVESTMENT MANAGEMENT BUDGET PROFILES

You can get to the configuration screen to define Investment Management budget profiles with either of the methods listed here:

Menu Path: **Investment Management** ➤ **Investment Programs** ➤ **Budgeting in Program** ➤ **Define Budget Profile**

Transaction Code: **OIB1**

The capital investment budget profile screen will appear. To create a new profile, select the New Entries button and a budget profile details screen will appear. The field names and descriptions are almost identical to those found on the planning profile screen and described in the preceding section. The one area where the settings differ is with the number of view format choices you have.

When the profile settings are complete, save the profile. Figure 13.12 gives you a look at the IM budget profile 2000-Extreme Capital Inv Budget. As you did with the plan profile, you should also assign the budget profile to your program type when it is complete.

FIGURE 13.12   IM budget profile 2000-Extreme Capital Inv Budget

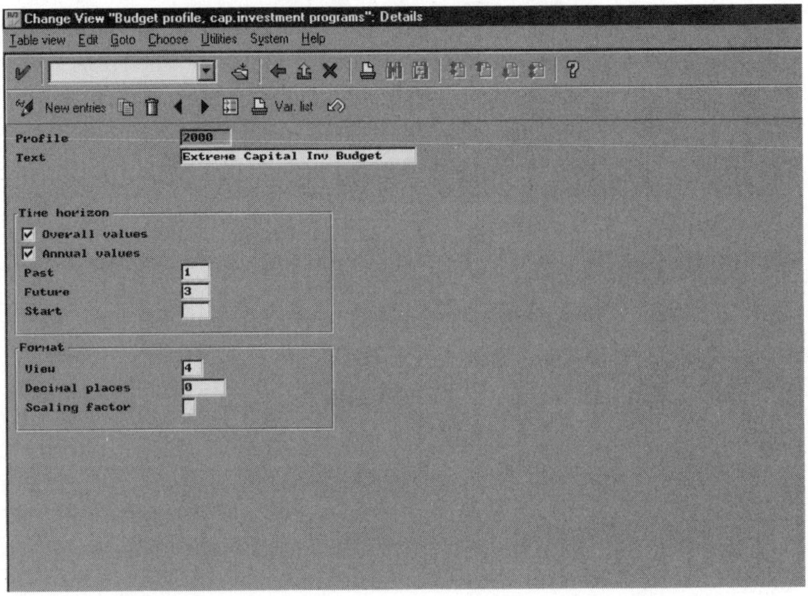

Budget Distribution

Though it has been covered in previous sections, we wanted to take a moment to talk about budget distribution. There are two main steps to developing budget distribution for use within IM:

1. Activate budget distribution within the program type.

2. Assign the program type to the internal order budget profile.

If you had been following along from the beginning of the chapter, you would have accomplished both of these steps by now. If not, you will want to revisit the sections on program type creation and investment measures.

Budget categories and their impact on IM budgeting will be covered next.

Budget Categories

If within your solution the company desires to plan and report on total project costs, including both capital and expense, then budget categories may be right for you. Through the use of categories, both budget and actual costs can be segregated so that they may be analyzed separately from the same investment node. For example, with two budget categories, one called CAPITAL and one called EXPENSE, you will be able to report budgeted capital and expense from the same investment node on your investment program hierarchy.

There are three steps to configuring budget categories:

1. Activate budget categories within the investment program.

2. Create the budget categories.

3. Assign an actual value percentage to each category.

Before proceeding, you need to know about a few of the drawbacks with using budget categories:

▶ You cannot use availability control. SAP does not allow you to distribute budget to the investment measure by category. Each measure must be budgeted manually.

▶ Exact actual costs cannot be sent to each category as they occur. Instead, they are recognized by each category during order settlement through the assignment of a usage indicator. Unfortunately, until the orders are settled, you will not know how much of the on-hand balance represents each category.

▶ Budget categories cannot be planned or budgeted individually. Instead, percentage rates are assigned to each category; the percentage rates correspond to the amount of budget each should receive. As you assign an investment measure to a program position, you will have the opportunity to enter the percentage of the budget each category should receive.

Step 1: Activate Budget Categories in Investment Program

To activate budget categories, select the Budg. Catg. field on the investment program master data screen. Figure 13.13 is a view of an investment program for Extreme Sports. Notice the field setting for budget categories. Investment program creation is accomplished by the user through the user menu path Accounting ➢ Capital Investment Mgmt ➢ Programs ➢ Master Data ➢ Investment Program Definition ➢ Create. However, because it is not related to configuration, the creation process will not be covered here.

FIGURE 13.13   The master data view of investment program EXTREME

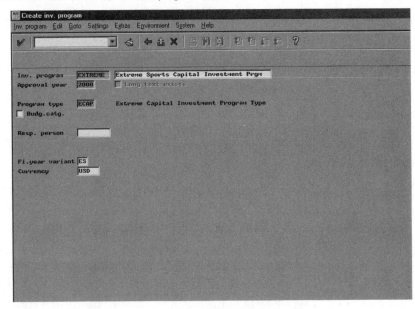

NOTE   Review the SAP-provided documentation on investment program creation for details.

Step 2: Create Budget Categories   To create your budget categories, use the menu path Investment Management ➢ Investment Programs ➢ Budgeting in Program ➢ Budget Categories ➢ Define Budget Categories.

DEFINE BUDGET CATEGORIES

You can use the following methods to get to the configuration screen to define budget categories:

Menu Path: **Investment Management** ➢ **Investment Programs** ➢ **Budgeting in Program** ➢ **Budget Categories** ➢ **Define Budget Categories**

Transaction Code: **OIT8**

The budget categories per program type screen will appear. Select the New Entries button to route to a creation screen. Figure 13.14 is a snapshot of the categories defined for program type ECAP.

FIGURE 13.14 The budget category definition for program type ECAP

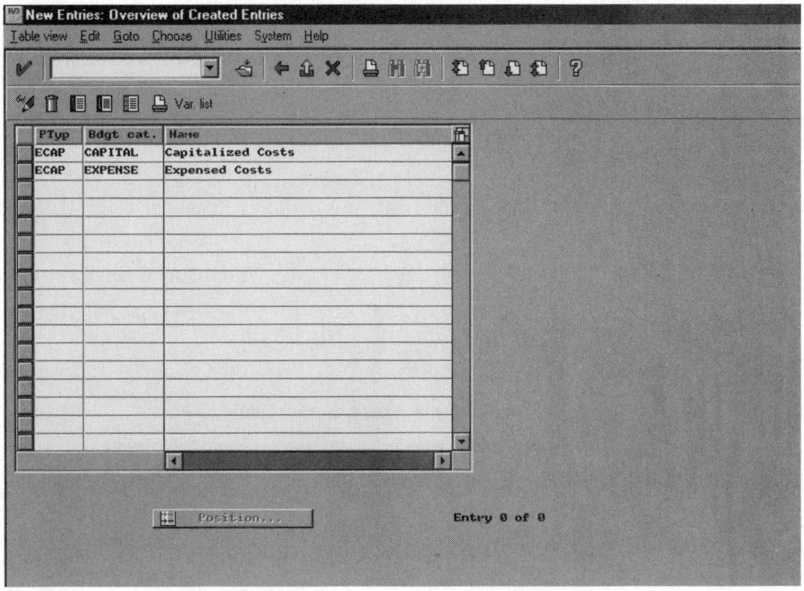

The necessary fields are defined here:

PTyp   Enter the program type to which the budget categories belong.

Bdgt Cat.   Enter the ID for each budget category. The ID can be up to 10 alphanumeric characters in length.

Name   Provide each category with a clear description.

When you're finished, save the categories.

Step 3: Assign Actual Values by Category   In this last step, you will define how actual costs will be routed to each of the budget categories. The menu path to use is Investment Management ➤ Investment Programs ➤ Budgeting in Program ➤ Budget Categories ➤ Assign Actual Values.

ASSIGN ACTUAL VALUES TO BUDGET CATEGORIES

You can get to the configuration screen to assign actual values to budget categories by using the following methods:

Menu Path: **Investment Management** ➤ **Investment Programs** ➤ **Budgeting in Program** ➤ **Budget Categories** ➤ **Assign Actual Values**

Transaction Code: **OIT5**

At the overview window, select the New Entries button to assign your categories. Figure 13.15 shows the settings for program type ECAP. In this step, you'll assign a usage indicator to each budget type.

FIGURE 13.15   Actual values assignment for program type ECAP

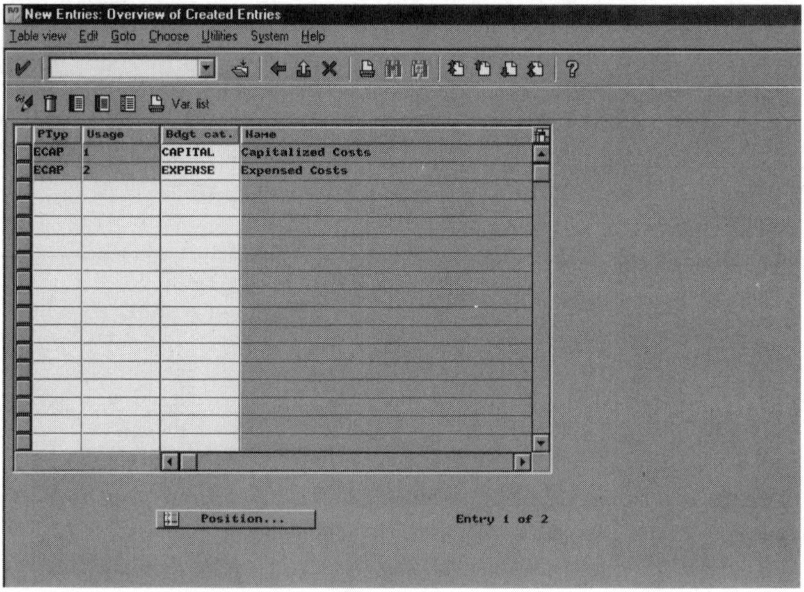

The key fields on this screen are as follows:

PTyp   Enter the program type to which the budget categories belong.

Usage   This indicator offers three settings (unfortunately, you are offered only three as standard with the system):

01   Capitalized to asset. For those costs that should be tracked as they are settled to an asset.

02   Noncapitalized incidental expenses. For those costs that are settled to an object other than an asset.

00   Not assigned. For those costs that cannot be classified as either.

Bdgt Cat.   Enter the ID of each budget category for which you wish to assign actuals. These must be created prior to their assignment here.

> **TIP**   SAP offers you the option of creating your own assignments through the maintenance of a user-exit, AAIP0001. Through this exit, you will get the added functionality of assigning actuals by cost element or cost element group.

When you're finished, save the assignments. Budget category development is complete. Because of the limitations placed on you, budget categories may not be a viable solution. If it sounds plausible for your situation, we recommend experimenting with the various settings.

The last section within Investment Management planning and budgeting has to do with number range assignments.

EXTREME SPORTS INVESTMENT PLANNING AND BUDGETING CONFIGURATION ANALYSIS

Budget categories are beyond the scope of the Extreme Sports solution. We provided this example for demonstration only. It is Extreme Sports' intention to fully utilize availability control with all its projects, so it cannot use categories. The company will use bottom-up planning and will enter the plan data directly on the investment program hierarchy. It felt it was too burdensome on its project managers to create a number of capital orders during the iterative planning process. This provides an opportunity to quickly make changes and reassign capital when necessary. Only when a project is going up for review will an order be created and planned. When approved, the order will have the amount of approved capital budget distributed to it.

Number Ranges for IM Planning/Budgeting Line Items

Investment Management uses the same planning number range assignment table as the one used for internal order planning and budgeting. If the number ranges were previously maintained, you do not have to repeat any steps here. If not, you can use the following menu path to define the necessary number range: Investment Management ➤ Investment Programs ➤ Planning in Program ➤ Define Number Ranges for Planning Line Items.

DEFINE INVESTMENT MANAGEMENT PLAN PROFILES

You can get to the configuration screen to define investment management plan profiles by using the following methods:

Menu Path: **Investment Management** ➤ **Investment Programs** ➤ **Planning in Program** ➤ **Define Number Ranges for Planning Line Items**

Transaction Code: **OK11**

The number ranges cost planning and budgeting screen appears. The screen is similar to the number range screen for CO document assignment. Number range intervals are used to differentiate between types of postings. The default intervals for Investment Management planning and budgeting are as follows:

10   Capital investment budgeting

11   Capital investment planning

The number range intervals are predefined by SAP and are not subject to change. You do have the ability to determine the range value, so be sure that the ranges are wide enough and that they do not overlap. To maintain the range interval, select the Maintain Interval button in the body of the screen. From here, you have the ability to create and maintain the planning intervals. Investment Management plan and budget profile development is complete. You can now safely plan your investment program hierarchy.

Summary

The information in this chapter came hard and fast and focused on getting IM up and running quickly. To write this chapter, we relied on the foundation built in many of the preceding chapters. Concepts such as order type, settlement structure, settlement profile, and user status are as relevant here as they are in Internal Order Accounting. The fact that the majority of IM development here is tied to orders rather than WBS elements is more an issue of scope than of functionality. IM integrates just as well with Project Systems as it does with order accounting. Take your time with the chapter and experiment with as many of the settings as possible before settling in on your decision. For your reference, here are the major sections in this chapter:

Investment Management Configuration

Program Types, Investment Measures, and the Investment Profile

Create the Program Type

Investment Measures

Investment Profile

Investment Management Planning and Budgeting Profiles

Investment Management Plan Profile

Investment Management Budget Profile

Useful Transaction Codes, Tables and Programs

n this appendix, we will recap the configuration transaction codes presented in the book. We'll also list transaction codes not covered as well as useful programs and tables. The tables are arranged via subject content that, in most cases, corresponds to the chapters of the book.

TABLE A.1 General and Cross-Module Configuration Transaction Codes

Transaction Code	Description
SB09	Process Flow View of the Business Navigator
SB10	Component View of the Business Navigator
SE10	Customizing Organizer
SPRO	Enter the IMG
SM30	Table Maintenance
SM31	Extended Table Maintenance
SE12	Data Dictionary Change and Display
SE11	Data Dictionary Display
SE16	The Databrowser
OSS1	Log On to OSS
SU53	Authorization Object Request
SE38	Run/Change/Display a Program
SA38	Run a Program
SM35	Batch Input Session Overview
SE01	View Transport Logs
GGB0	Create/Change Validation
GGB1	Create/Change Substitutions
GGB4	Activate Validations and Substitutions
SNR0	Maintain Number Range Objects

TABLE A.2 General and Cross-Module Configuration Tables

Table(s)	Description
E071 and E071K	Transport tables; displays all transports affecting a given object
V_GB01C	Customizing table for Boolean fields in substitutions and validations
GB01	SAP-delivered table that lists all fields that can be used in substitutions and validations
SADR	Address data (which doesn't transport well)

TABLE A.3 General and Cross-Module Configuration Program

Program	Description
RGUGBR00	Program to regenerate sets, validations, and substitutions

TABLE A.4 FI Enterprise Structure Transaction Codes

Transaction Code	Description
OBY7	Copy Chart of Accounts
OB29	Fiscal Year Variant
OBBO	Posting Period Variant
OX02	Company Codes—Create, Check, and Delete
OBY6	Company Code Global Parameters
EC01	Copy Company Code
OY01	Country Definitions
OB22	Parallel Currencies
OX03	Business Areas
OKBD	Functional Areas

TABLE A.4   FI Enterprise Structure Transaction Codes (Continued)

Transaction Code	Description
OBBG	Assign Country to Tax Calculation Procedure
OBCO	Specify Structure for Tax Jurisdiction Codes
OBCP	Define Tax Jurisdiction Codes
FTXP	Maintain Tax Rates
OBCL	Set Tax Codes for Non-Taxable Transactions

TABLE A.5   General Ledger/Chart of Accounts Transaction Codes

Transaction Code	Description
OBD4	Account Groups
OB53	Retained Earnings Variant
OB15	Sample Account Rule Types
FSK2	Sample Account Data Transfer Rules
OB67	Allocate a Company Code to a Sample Account Rule Type
OBY9	Transport Chart of Accounts
OBY2	Copy G/L Accounts from the Chart to the Company Code
OBC4	Field Status Variants
OB41	Posting Keys
FBKP	Automatic Account Assignments
OB40	Define Tax Accounts
OBYA	Cross-Company Code Automatic Account Assignment
OBYC	MM Automatic Account Assignment

TABLE A.5 General Ledger/Chart of Accounts Transaction Codes (Continued)

Transaction Code	Description
OB58	Financial Statement Versions
O7Z3	Line Item Layouts
OBVU	Special Fields
O7S7	Sort Variants
O7R1	Totals Variants
OBA4	Tolerance Groups
OB57	Allocate Users to Tolerance Groups
FBN1	G/L Number Ranges
OBA7	Document Types
OBU1	Assign Default Posting Keys to Document Types
O7E6	Fast Entry Screens
ORFB	Financial Accounting Configuration Menu (Before the IMG, there were configuration menus; there won't be any in later releases.)
OBL1	Automatic Postings Documentation
OB32	Maintain Document Change Rules

TABLE A.6 General Ledger/Chart of Accounts Programs

Program	Description
RFBISA10	Copy multiple G/L Accounts from Company to Company or from Client to Client
RFBISA20	Import G/L Accounts Created by RFBISA10 (copying from client to client)
RFTAXIMP	Import Tax Codes/Tax Jurisdiction Codes

TABLE A.7   General Ledger/Chart of Accounts Tables

Table	Description
BSEG	G/L Document Line Item Table
TTXD	Tax Jurisdiction Code Structure Table
T030	Automatic Account Assignments Table
TZUN	G/L Account Sort Key (Allocation Field) Table

TABLE A.8   Table A.8: Accounts Payable Transaction Codes

Transaction Code	Description
FI12	House Banks
FCHI	Check Lots
FCHV	Void Reason Codes
FBZP	Payment Program
OBD3	Vendor Groups
XKN1	Create Number Ranges for Vendor Groups
OBAS	Assign Number Ranges to Vendor Account Groups
FK15	Copy Vendor Master Records Creation Program
FK16	Copy Vendor Master Records Upload Program

TABLE A.9   Accounts Receivable and Credit Management Transaction Codes

Transaction Code	Description
OBB8	Terms of Payment A/R and A/P
OB46	Interest Indicator

TABLE A.9 Accounts Receivable and Credit Management Transaction Codes (Continued)

Transaction Code	Description
OB82	Make Interest Indicator Available to the Interest Calculation Program (Arrears)
OBAC	Reference Interest Rates
OB81	Assign Reference Interest Rates to Interest Indicators
OBV1	Interest Calculation Automatic Account Assignment
OBBE	Reason Codes
OBCR	Reason Code Conversion Version
OBCS	Map External Reason Codes to Internal Reason Codes
OBXL	Assign G/L Accounts to Reason Codes
OBXI	Cash Discount Amount
OBA3	Customer Tolerance Groups
OB45	Credit Control Areas
OB01	Credit Risk Categories
OB02	Credit Representative Groups
OB51	Assign Employees to Credit Representative Groups
OB39	Days in Arrears Calculation
OBD2	Customer Groups

TABLE A.10 Treasury Transaction Codes

Transaction Code	Description
OB10	Create Lockbox Accounts
OBAY	Define Lockbox Control Parameters

TABLE A.10   Treasury Transaction Codes (Continued)

Transaction Code	Description
OBAX	Lockbox Posting Data
OT05	Source Symbols
OT14	Planning Levels
OT13	Planning Groups
OT47	Assign Logistics Transactions to Planning Levels
OT17	Treasury Groupings
OT18	Treasury Grouping Headers
OT16	Cash Management Account Names
OT29	Activate Company Code Treasury Updates
OBBY	Electronic Bank Statement Transaction Types
OT55	Assign Transaction Types to House Banks
OT57	Electronic Bank Statement Posting Rules
OT51	Map External Transactions to Posting Rules
OT59	Posting Rules Automatic Account Assignment
GCRF	Currency Translation Ratios

TABLE A.11   CO Enterprise Structure Transaction Codes

Transaction Code	Description
OX06	Controlling Areas
OKKP	Activate CO Components for Controlling Areas
KANK	CO Document Number Ranges

TABLE A.11 CO Enterprise Structure Transaction Codes (Continued)

Transaction Code	Description
KEP8	Operating Concern Definition
OKEQ	Planning Versions

TABLE A.12 Cost Element Accounting Transaction Codes

Transaction Code	Description
OKB2	Automatic Cost Element Creation
OKB3	Create Batch Input Session for Automatic Cost Element Creation
KA06	Create Secondary Cost Elements
KA01	Create Primary Cost Elements
KSAZ	Overhead Costing Sheet
KALA	Activate Reconciliation Ledger
OBYB	Maintain Automatic Account Assignments for the Reconciliation Ledger
OK13	Number Ranges for Reconciliation Ledger Activity

TABLE A.13 Cost Center Accounting Transaction Codes

Transaction Code	Description
KSH2	Cost Center Standard Hierarchy
OKE5	Profit Center Accounting Settings for the Controlling Area
KCH2	Profit Center Standard Hierarchy
KE59	Create Dummy Profit Center
OKA2	Cost Center Categories

TABLE A.13   Cost Center Accounting Transaction Codes (Continued)

Transaction Code	Description
OKEG	Cost Center Time Dependency Fields
KS01	Create Cost Center
KK01	Statistical Key Figures
OKE1	Activity Types Time Dependency Fields
KL01	Activity Types
KCAU	Assessment Receiver Types
KSW1	Periodic Repostings
KSV1	Distributions
KSU1	Assessments
KP97	Copy Plan Data
KPU1	Planning Revaluation
KP65	Cost Planning Layout
KP34	Planning Profiles
OKB9	Cost Element Automatic Account Assignment

TABLE A.14   Internal Orders Transaction Codes

Transaction Code	Description
OKO6	Settlement Structure
OKEU	Origin (Source) Structure
OKO7	Settlement Profile
SNUM	Settlement Document Number Ranges
OKOS	Internal Order Planning Profile

TABLE A.14   Internal Orders Transaction Codes (Continued)

Transaction Code	Description
OKOB	Budget Profile
OKOC	Availability Control
OK14	Budget Manager Maintenance
OPTK	Exempt Cost Elements for Availability Control
KANK	Planning Number Ranges
OK11	Maintain Number Ranges for Planning and Budgeting Objects
KOT2	Order Status Management
KOV2	Transaction Groups
OK02	Status Profile
BS52	Authorization Keys for Status Management
KOT2	Order Types

TABLE A.15   Profitability Analysis Transaction Codes

Transaction Code	Description
KEA0	Operating Concern Maintenance
KE4K	Derivation Table
KE04	Create Derivation Structures
KE05	Change Derivation Structures
KE07	Create Derivation Rules
KE08	Change Derivation Rules
KE4I	Assign Condition Types to Value Fields
KE4M	Map SD Quantity Fields to CO-PA Quantity Value Fields

TABLE A.15   Profitability Analysis Transaction Codes (Continued)

Transaction Code	Description
KE4W	Reset (zero out) Value Fields
KEI1	CO-PA Settlement Structure
KEU1	Create Cost Center to CO-PA Assessment
KEF1	Planning Revaluations
KE14	Create Planning Layouts
KP34	Planning Profiles
KE4D	External Data Transfer Data Structures
KE4Z	External Data Transfer Assignment Groups
KE4E	Map External Data Transfer Fields to Characteristic and Value Fields
KEN2	CO-PA Planning Number Ranges
KEKK	Assign Controlling Area to Operating Concern
KEN1	CO-PA Actual Data Number Ranges
KER1	Report Line Structures
KE34	Create Forms
KE31	Create Report
KE3I	Create Transports

TABLE A.16   Profit Center Accounting Transaction Codes

Transaction Code	Description
1KE1	Analyze Basic Settings
0KE4	Update Settings

TABLE A.16 Profit Center Accounting Transaction Codes (Continued)

Transaction Code	Description
ORK1	Profit Center Time-Based Fields
1KEB	Fast Assignment
0KEM	Sales Order Substitution
0KEL	Activate Sales Order Substitution
1KE4	Assignment Monitor
1KEF	Control Parameters for Actual Data Transfer
GCBX	Actual Document Types
GB02	Number Range Assignments
OKB9	Assign Revenue Elements
3KEH	Assign Additional Balance Sheet and P&L Accounts to PCA
2KET	Activate Balance Carry Forward for PCA
OKEQ	Maintain Versions
GCBA	Plan Document Types
GP41	Plan Parameters

TABLE A.17 Investment Management Transaction Codes

Transaction Code	Description
OITA	Investment Profile
OIP1	IM Plan Profile
OIB1	Budget Profile
OIT8	Budget Categories

TABLE A.17   Investment Management Transaction Codes (Continued)

Transaction Code	Description
OIT5	Assign Actual Values to Budget Categories
OK11	Number Ranges

INDEX

Note to Reader: In this index, **boldfaced** page numbers refer to primary discussions of the topic; *italics* page numbers refer to figures.

B

C

G

P

U

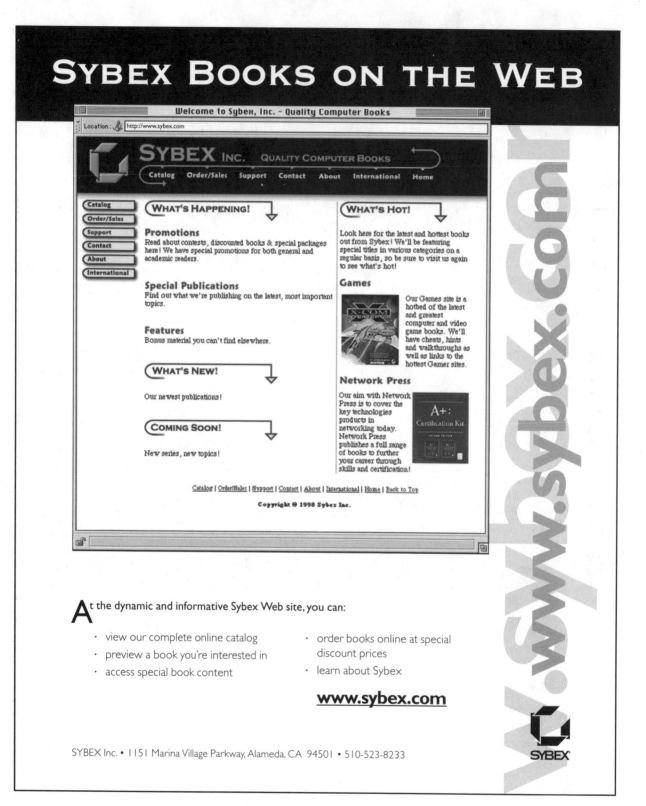

SYBEX BOOKS ON THE WEB